Understanding and Teaching Emotionally Disturbed Children and Adolescents

Understanding and Teaching Emotionally Disturbed Children and Adolescents

THIRD EDITION

Phyllis L. Newcomer

pro·ed
An International Publisher

8700 Shoal Creek Boulevard
Austin, Texas 78757-6897
800/897-3202   Fax 800/397-7633
www.proedinc.com

An International Publisher

© 1980, 1993, 2003 by PRO-ED, Inc.
8700 Shoal Creek Boulevard
Austin, Texas 78757-6897
800/897-3202   Fax 800/397-7633
www.proedinc.com

Library of Congress Cataloging-in-Publication Data

Newcomer, Phyllis L.
    Understanding and teaching emotionally disturbed children and adolescents / Phyllis L.
Newcomer—3rd ed.
        p. cm.
    Includes bibliographical references and index.
    1. Mentally ill children—Education.   2. Mentally ill children—Treatment.   I. Title.

LC4165 .N48 2002
371.94—dc21

                                                                                    2001048733

This book is designed in Goudy.

Printed in the United States of America

1 2 3 4 5 6 7 8 9 10   06 05 04 03 02

48098446

CONTENTS

PART III ◆ Therapy and Interventions

PREFACE

This book is intended for both general and special education teachers, as well as for other professionals, such as counselors, social workers, and psychologists, who are interested in helping children and adolescents make healthy emotional adjustments. It contains extensive information on the types of emotional and social disorders that are experienced by school-age individuals. It also presents a broad spectrum of therapeutic approaches that may be used with children and adolescents in educational settings.

Although certain treatment procedures described in this text are used solely by members of the mental health professions, the focus is on illustrating methods of modifying approaches to therapy so that they may be used by classroom teachers. The underlying philosophy is that teachers are therapists (persons who promote health in others). Successful teaching involves much more than presenting academic content to students. It requires knowledge of individual development and learning styles, awareness of personality characteristics, appreciation of situational stresses that affect students, and, most critically, the personal flexibility to meet students' needs as they arise. In today's society, teachers must respond to a multitude of problems affecting their students if they are to promote learning. I hope that this book will help them to do so.

In organizing this text, I have attempted to provide readers with a thorough theoretical background for each approach to treatment that is discussed. I think that practitioners who need practical tools, for example, methodologies, models, strategies, or techniques, that are potentially helpful to children also need to understand how those tools evolved and the assumptions about human behavior that are fundamental to their evolution. In other words, for us to teach others effectively, our methods must be the products of our own informed thought and must reflect our own belief systems. Thus, I have sought to provide the reader with choices rather than answers and hope you feel that the effort is worthwhile.

PART

I

HISTORY AND THEORY

CHAPTER

OVERVIEW OF EMOTIONAL AND BEHAVIORAL DISORDERS

Historical Background

A variety of terms have been used to describe abnormal or maladaptive thoughts and behavior in people. Many of them, such as *mental illness* and *psychopathology*, were originally coined to describe adult conditions and for the most part have been regarded as too stigmatizing to apply to children. Another, less stigmatizing term, *emotional disturbance*, seen as more appropriate for use with children, appeared in the late 1900s (Reinert, 1972) and was used in the first two editions of this book. During the same period, the label *behaviorally disordered* became popular, particularly with professionals in the field of special education. It was seen as the least stigmatizing label by some (Smith, Wood, & Grimes, 1988), but as misleading by others because it ignored children's emotional conditions. Although these two terms were relatively prominent, they were by no means exclusive, as various states selected their own terminology, such as *emotionally handicapped, behaviorally impaired*, and so forth. In an effort to bring uniform standards to the field, in 1988 the National Mental Health and Special Education Coalition adopted the term *emotional and behavioral disorders* (EBDs; Forness & Knitzer, 1992). This term has been accepted by a wide variety of professional organizations and, for the most part, is used in this text.

Although the terminology has varied, the history of this field records attempts to understand the conditions, thoughts, and behaviors that may currently be subsumed under the labels *mental illness* for adults and *emotional and behavioral disorders* for children and youth. Among the earliest explanations was the notion that individuals whose behavior marked them as strange, odd, or simply different from their brethren were possessed either by evil or divine spirits. Archaeological evidence suggests that primitive man might have used *trephining*, a surgical technique involving chipping a hole in the skull, to release the evil spirits believed to have invaded individuals and robbed them of control over their behavior. (Surprisingly, signs of healing on some of the skulls of these primitive people indicate that they actually survived the treatment; however, we are left to wonder about their mental health.) The march of time and the development of humans from cave dwellers to members of relatively sophisticated civilizations such as those established in ancient China, Egypt, and Greece did little to modify the notion of possession by spirits. However, possession by good spirits, as well as by evil or demonic spirits, was considered a possibility. Bad spirits or demons were cast out by exorcism through use of prayers, magic, or, occasionally, purgatives, usually by a shaman or priest. (The continued use of this practice in current times underscores the ongoing belief in demonology among certain groups.) If a person's behavior signified possession by good spirits, the person was regarded as being chosen or touched by God and was revered as a seer or prophet or as one marked for greatness.

Such ideas prevailed until Hippocrates (ca. 460–377 B.C.), the Greek physician known as the father of medicine, recorded detailed descriptions of abnormal states that he designated as *melancholia, mania* (hysteria), and *phrentis* (brain fever). He defined them as forms of physical illness rather than states of demonic possession and attributed them to brain pathology, emphasizing the importance of heredity as well as actual injury to the head as causal factors. His classification system was based on clinical observation, a remarkable precursor of modern medical practice. His knowledge of physiology was somewhat lacking, however, and his explanation of illness as due to imbalances among the four bodily humors that he deemed responsible for physical health—yellow bile from the earth, black bile from water, red blood from fire, and mucus from the air—although colorful, was inaccurate. Regardless of these inaccuracies, Hippocrates inaugurated a medical approach to understanding maladaptive behavior and made the study of mental, emotional, and behavioral disorders the concern of physicians. This approach continued to some degree in later Greek and Roman societies, only to give way slowly but surely to the reaffirmation of superstitious belief in demonology that dominated in the dark ages of medieval times.

During the Dark (or Middle) Ages (A.D. 500–1500), the medical or physical approach to mental illness was largely lost in Western societies. Although an outstanding Islamic physician, Avicenna (A.D. 980–1037), produced cogent and humanistic writings regarding illnesses that he referred to as melancholia, epilepsy, mania, and hysteria, his work did not influence Western thinking. In Europe, clinical observation and scientific inquiry into abnormal behavior were forgotten, and, as in earlier eras, symptoms of mental illness were thought to be the result of the influence of the devil on the person's spirit or soul. Monks and priests kept voluminous records of the characteristics of various devils that possessed the weak or impious and caused strange or irrational behavior. They were responsible for treating such "possessions" by exorcising the evil spirits. The most benevolent form of treatment involved incantations and pleas for divine forgiveness. Less fortunate sufferers were whipped, stoned, or dunked in ponds, and the hard-core unrepentant were burned at the stake. The latter treatment was the only known "sure cure," although many miraculous recoveries were attributed to the other approaches.

The dominance of the belief in demonic possession was such that it continued to prevail into the 15th and 16th centuries. In addition to the idea that corporal possession by evil spirits caused madness, the belief grew that the spirits of certain individuals were possessed by Satan and that these persons, called witches, had evil, supernatural powers. These individuals were punished and frequently killed, sometimes in mass exterminations such as the Inquisition. Although the designation *witch* was applied to the politically rebellious and those rejecting Christianity, it also was attached to the mentally ill, much to their detriment. Although the clergy continued to bear the primary responsibility for dealing with the problem, the records of several prominent members of the medical profession of the period reveal that their attitudes were similar to those of the clergy. According to Coleman (1972), one physician, Fernel (1497–1558), reported cases of lycanthropy, the transformation of a human into a werewolf, and another, Plater (1536–1614), described the devil as the source of all mental illness.

All was not black, however, as toward the latter part of the Middle Ages and the beginning of the Renaissance, voices attributing bizarre or maladaptive behaviors to mental disorder of some type began to be raised once again. In the mid–16th century Johann Weyer (1515–1588), a German physician, published *The Deception of Demons*, in which he argued that many so-called witches were mentally sick. Similarly, an Englishman, Reginald Scott (1538–1599), wrote *The Discouerie of Witchcraft* (1584) to deny that spirits cause mental disorder. Neither of these individuals was honored in his lifetime, but the ideas of both eventually prevailed. As time passed, the "radical" ideas of these physicians coincided to some degree with certain aspects of the theories generated by several philosophers depicting the existence of "mind" as distinct from "soul," thereby directing attention away from the notions of spiritual causation or possession. Thomas Hobbes (1588–1679), John Locke (1632–1704), and George Berkeley (1685–1753) were influential in developing the concept of mental functions. Unfortunately, these emerging and reemerging ideas were of little immediate benefit to the "possessed" members of the population, who continued to be purged of their sins or, in a more "enlightened" vein, confined to institutions whose names evoke images of horror.

Early asylums or "madhouses" were similar to jails in that patients were often shackled or chained to walls or confined to crowded cells. One of the earliest of these institutions was Bedlam, established by Henry VIII in London in 1547. Even today the name denotes wild, chaotic conditions. Other "bedlams" were established in other countries throughout the 17th and 18th centuries. Patients lived in their own excrement, eating slop. Often for small fees paid to wardens, members of the public were permitted to view the "animals." Although conditions improved in the 19th century, the use of physical restraints, straitjackets, electrical shocks, and so forth did not argue for the humaneness of treatment.

However, even though the path to humane treatment of mentally disordered persons was not smooth, as the domination of the clergy began to wane in the 17th century and the notion of possession weakened, the stage was set for dramatic reforms that began to alter these conditions and eventually returned the study of disturbed behavior to the purview of the physician. Philippe Pinel (1745–1826), a French physician who became director of Bicêtre hospital after the French Revolution, is famous for unchaining the mental patients and advocating more humane forms of treatment. His approach, known later as moral treatment, influenced the work of his associates and students, the most important of whom was Jean Itard (1775–1838). Itard's classic book, *The Wild Boy of Aveyron* (1801), reported his efforts to educate Victor, a boy who had been abandoned in a forest and whose behaviors were indicative of mental illness and mental retardation. In turn, Itard's work influenced educators such as Edward Seguin and Maria Montessori and helped establish teaching as an important component of treatment.

In America the famous physician Benjamin Rush (1745–1813), recognized as the father of American psychiatry, argued for more humane treatment of the mentally ill. He deplored the use of corporal punishment and stressed the importance of education. Owing in part to his influence, troubled individuals were seen increasingly as sick and not solely responsible for their behavior, and their treatment improved.

In the 19th century the view of emotional and behavioral disorders (EBDs) as illnesses of the mind became firmly entrenched. Humanists such as Dorothea Dix (1802–1887) campaigned for appropriate services. Dix is credited with establishing the mental hygiene movement in America by garnering public support and funding for the establishment of mental hospitals throughout the country. Simultaneously, physicians began to pay increased attention to conscientious observation of their patients' behavior. They looked for common symptoms as clues to the origins of mental illness and formed schools of psychiatric treatment. Ambroise-Auguste Liebault (1823–1904), a French physician, founded the Nancy School and with his colleagues, particularly Hippolyte Bernheim (1837–1919), developed psychotherapy as a form of treatment. This school emphasized the relationship between patients' symptomology and their suggestibility, a premise that provided the foundation for the concept of functional illness, which is described later. A rival point of view flourished at the Salpêtrière School, operated by Jean-Martin Charcot (1825–1893). These physicians believed that disturbed symptoms were attributable to organic malfunctions or physical disease.

In addition, a more enlightened approach toward the use of education in the treatment of emotionally troubled persons continued to spread, with schooling provided within asylums for the "insane." Many of the teaching strategies employed during this period have remained as cornerstones of special education. These strategies include individualized assessment and instruction, sequenced learning, structured activities, and multisensory approaches.

In Germany, Emil Kraepelin (1856–1926) solidified the mental illness concept by developing a classification system of mental diseases according to distinct clusters of symptoms. He identified two major psychoses, *manic-depressive* and *dementia praecox* (in current terminology, *schizophrenia*). He also created two categories of disease, *endogenous* and *exogenous*. Endogenous maladies are of internal origin and are caused by some type of biological malfunction, such as brain damage or genetic defects. Exogenous illnesses are of external origin and are unrelated to biological factors.

◇   ◇   ◇

During this period the scientific method was being applied to the study of behavior. In 1879 Wilhelm Wundt (1832–1920) established the first experimental psychology laboratory at the University of Leipzig and developed experimental methodology that was later used to investigate behavior throughout the world. In the United States and England, empirical research involving hypothesis formation, observation, quantitative measurement, and controlled experimentation was undertaken by men like Gustav Fechner (1801–1887) and Sir Francis Galton (1822–1911). The significance of this movement is that it introduced an alternative to medical studies of pathological behavior by investigating normal behavior. It also placed importance on proof through measurement, an idea that was not part of the largely intuitive approach to the study of behavior undertaken in clinical or medical settings at that time.

Finally, the 20th century saw the study of disturbed conditions revolutionized by the impact of many diverse theoretical perspectives and social movements. Attention turned to helping children who engaged in antisocial or criminal behavior. Beginning in 1909 with the establishment of the Juvenile Psychopathic Institute, Dr. William Healy, Augusta Bronner, Grace Fernald, and Julia Lathrop pioneered the study of juvenile delinquents. Alfred Binet furthered the idea of using standardized laboratory methods to measure behavior with the development of his intelligence test. Arnold Gesell opened the Clinic for Child Development at Yale University, and the idea of mental health programs in public schools was advanced. Lauretta Bender helped organize an education program for the children with schizophrenia she treated at Bellevue Psychiatric Hospital in New York. In the 1940s Bruno Bettelheim, Fritz Redl, and their associates developed and expanded the principles of the "therapeutic milieu" for working with seriously disturbed and aggressive children, which provided the foundation for milieu or ecological therapy. Alfred Strauss and Laura Lehtinen published *Psychopathology and Education of the Brain-Injured Child* (1947), a seminal work that delineated the characteristics that interfere with children's ability to learn (inattentiveness, hyperactivity, distractibility, volatility) and provided the basis for the structured classroom model.

In a more global vein, throughout the 20th century the work of Sigmund Freud and his disciples in the psychoanalytic movement, the growth of the humanistic movement, the emergence of cognitive psychology, the contributions of Harry Stack Sullivan (1953) and the interpersonal theorists, the information gleaned from sociology and social psychology emphasizing cultural influences on behavior, the impact of behavioral theory, and the continued research into genetic and biochemical causes influenced our understanding of EBDs and provided approaches to their treatment. The major part of this book is devoted to presenting this information, that is, to discussing varied theoretical perspectives and the clinical or educational interventions they have spawned.

The sheer quantity of information available suggests that over the centuries, and particularly in the 20th century, we have made progress both in understanding and treating children's EBDs. At the most basic level, idealized images of trouble-free childhood have crumbled and sadder but more realistic pictures have taken their place. As for more specific accomplishments, the U.S. Congress addressed this issue in the Individuals with Disabilities Education Act of 1990 (IDEA). Also, a variety of professional organizations designed to serve the interests of children with EBD have evolved. Among the most influential are the Council for Children with Behavioral Disorders, a division of the Council for Exceptional Children formed in 1964; the Autism Society of America, formed in 1965; the National Mental Health and Special Education Coalition, created in 1987 by a jointure of the National Mental Health Association and the Council for Exceptional Children; and the Federation of Families for Children's Mental Health, established in 1989.

As interest in the field of children's emotional and behavioral disorders has increased, numerous journals have appeared to present increasingly sophisticated position papers and research results. Included in their number are the *Journal of Emotional and Behavioral Disorders, Behavior Disorders, The Journal of Special Education, Remedial and Special Education, Journal of Autism and Developmental Disorders, Journal of Applied Behavioral Analysis, Intervention in School and Clinic, Journal of Abnormal Child Psychology, Journal of Child and Family Studies,* and *Exceptional Children,* to name but a few.

Of course, the availability of information does not always translate readily into practice, and those professionals working most closely with troubled children deplore the seemingly slow progress—at-risk children not identified or identified only after their problems have become so severe that they cannot be overlooked, inadequate services, and shortsighted or haphazard school-based planning. Indeed, as we begin the 21st century, practitioners in the field are faced with the challenge of addressing several clearly delineated issues, notably prevention, placement, instruction, and outcomes.

Issues for the 21st Century

Prevention

Special educators have long espoused the value of early intervention, that is, identifying and trying to solve a problem before it becomes worse, or, in the words of Deputy Sheriff Barney Fife, resolving to "nip it in the bud." The word *early* in this context does not refer to the age of the child, but to the age of the problem. As educators learn more about children's EBDs, it becomes increasingly obvious that, unlike fine wine, children's disorders usually do not improve with age. Whelan (1998) pointed out that identifying problems before they mushroom into serious disorders not only makes good sense from a humanistic perspective but also is cost-effective. It is far less costly to spend a relatively small amount of money on preventive activities such as screening children for problems, observing potentially problematic behaviors, or conferencing with parents than it is to fund children's placements in private residential schools or psychiatric facilities.

Whelan (1998) calls school- or curriculum-based preventive interventions "secondary" approaches. They help children learn to use more effective problem-solving and coping skills and to become more successful in interpersonal relationships. More essential or "primary" approaches to the prevention of emotional and behavioral disorders involve resources not usually controlled by schools, such as prenatal care, adequate nutrition, medical care, safe living conditions, and protection from parental abuse. Citing the inadequacy of community resources that provide these primary services to children, Whelan echoes the opinions of many other educators when he calls for the extension of the school's responsibility to include programs that address many of these social issues.

Although it appears that the tools and techniques required for secondary-level prevention of emotional and behavioral disorders are readily available to educators, they frequently are not used. Kauffman (1997) offers a variety of reasons for this frustrating state of affairs. Many people still believe that children outgrow stages of life when their behavior suggests emotional difficulties. Educators also are troubled by the issue of labeling, which carries a social stigma; the fact that even the best identification tools result in false-positives; and the possibility that early identification may discriminate against minority groups. Finally, the ever-present concern about cost is an issue. Added to Kauffman's list are the belief that identifying children at risk to develop emotional and behavioral disorders is not within the purview of school personnel and the rationale that this type of screening would upset parents. For any number of reasons, children identified for special education services tend to have severe, long-existing problems (Duncan, Forness, & Hartsough, 1995).

Given the reluctance of school authorities to undertake secondary-level prevention programs, it is not difficult to understand why the suggestion that school responsibility for prevention be extended to the primary level has been met with resistance. It is true that the concept of "wraparound" services is discussed and that some "wraparound" services, usually in the form of aides who devote themselves exclusively to one child throughout the day, are provided. However, the idea of using the schools to integrate the activities of many diverse social organizations so that comprehensive wraparound service is provided to families is seen as impractical and inappropriate by many Americans who believe that the proper function of schools is to teach academic subject matter. Certainly there has been no groundswell of popular support for the idea.

Placements

The availability of appropriate placements for children with EBDs emerges as a surprising problem for the 21st century. Many special educators thought this issue was settled with the passage of IDEA and the regulations that mandated a continuum of alternative placements for children with various types of disabilities. Children would be served in the least restrictive environment, that is, the placement closest to the general education classroom that best met each child's needs. The least restrictive environment might be general education class-rooms with supporting services, resource rooms in general education schools, self-contained special classes with mainstreaming in general education classes, special day schools, day programs at residential schools or hospitals, residential schools or inpatient hospitals, homebound instruction, or schools in juvenile detention centers and prisons (Kauffman & Smucker, 1995). Also, any child's placement or least restrictive environment might change as the child's needs changed.

The availability of appropriate placements for children with EBDs has be-come an important issue because of the emergence of what is best described as the "full inclusion" movement. The term *inclusion* refers to placing children with special needs in general education classrooms and is an outgrowth of the "regular education initiative," which holds that this type of arrangement is ben-eficial for all children with disabilities (Stainback & Stainback, 1991). Unlike the concept of least restrictive environment, inclusion ignores the issue of the child's specific educational needs. The assumption is made that the value of socializing with and learning from students in general education classes tran-scends any benefits that might be gained from more restrictive placements, re-gardless of those special needs. Also, unlike mainstreaming, which provides students with combinations of special placements and placements in the gen-eral education classroom, "full inclusion" provides only the general education placement.

Ironically, the notion of full inclusion has gained wide acceptance in the schools. Costs associated with the education of children with disabilities may have influenced this wide acceptance. Having general classroom educators bear the primary responsibility for educating children who might otherwise require the services of special educators in alternate placements certainly reduces costs. However, it is also true that many parents have been persuaded by the advo-cates of this movement that efforts to deny a child full inclusion violate basic rights to equal education. Also, many well-meaning educators are committed to the idea that all children can be educated by good instruction in a well-run general education classroom.

The controversy over this issue is extensive. Opponents of the idea of full inclusion for all children are particularly concerned about the welfare of chil-dren with EBDs (Diamond, 1993; Kauffman & Lloyd, 1995; Morse, 1994). *The Illusion of Full Inclusion*, edited by Kauffman and Hallahan (1995), explores this issue fully and offers particularly cogent arguments against the premise that all students with disabilities should be included in general education classrooms. Other professionals (e.g., Bateman & Chard, 1995) are concerned with the illegality involved in ignoring the mandate from IDEA to provide a continuum of placements.

The issue of appropriate placements for students with disabilities is further complicated by the school's responsibility to provide educational environments for secondary-level students that will help them make successful transitions from school to work or to higher level educational placements. Some school districts have attempted to fulfill this obligation by providing extra help to students with disabilities who are enrolled in college preparatory courses. Often, however, the students do not perform at a level that makes them viable candidates for success in higher education settings. Other school districts offer children with disabilities a less demanding curriculum, a solution that makes them vulnerable to charges of discrimination. In still other cases, a curriculum that integrates academic study with specific vocational training is used. This type of arrangement is most attractive to students who are interested in employment rather than additional education after graduation from high school.

Unfortunately, the literature suggests that existing transitional programs for students with disabilities often are not successful. Myles and Simpson (1998) reported that the school dropout rate for young people with EBDs ranges from 39% to 47%. Also, the National Organization on Disability/Harris Survey of Americans with Disabilities (Harris & Associates, 1994) found that these individuals tend to be unemployed or underemployed. Those who find jobs often are underpaid. Employment opportunities are limited by inadequate interpersonal skills, academic skills, and specific vocational training (Clark, Carlson, Fisher, Cook, & D'Alonzo, 1991). Similar problems reduce the probability of success at postsecondary education, even when supportive or remedial services are provided.

In reporting the results of the National Longitudinal Transition Study, funded by the federal government, the U.S. Department of Education (1995) noted that regardless of type, transition programs are effective only when students succeed in them. This conclusion suggests that secondary schools need to have a variety of placement options for students with disabilities and that individual students should be encouraged to select the option that best meets his or her specific needs. Halpern (1994) believes that transitional programming should begin no later than age 14.

Outcomes

In the latter part of the 20th century, interest in children's mental health increased substantially. According to Epstein, Kutash, and Duchnowski (1998), 1984 was a banner year. Funds provided by the National Institutes of Mental Health (NIMH) established the Child and Adolescent Service System Program, which instigated the development of service systems for children with EBDs. The NIMH and the National Institute for Disability and Rehabilitation Research cofunded two research and training centers directed toward the EBD population, and the Office of Special Education Programs sponsored research in that field. A decade later, Congress funded the Comprehensive Children's Mental Health Services Program, which administers services demonstration projects in 22 sites. This outpouring of funding and interest suggests that people in positions of power finally have recognized the importance of trying to bring about positive outcomes for children and youth with EBDs.

After culling the literature, Kauffman (1997) reported seven outcome goals targeted for action by the U.S. government:

1. Expand positive learning opportunities and results
2. Strengthen school and community capacity
3. Value and address diversity
4. Collaborate with families
5. Promote appropriate assessment
6. Provide ongoing skill development and support
7. Create comprehensive and collaborative service systems

These goals clearly delineate the comprehensive nature of this relatively new focus on outcomes. Community-based systems of care have been implemented in many states to pursue these goals. Most but not all of these programs tend to show improved outcomes in clinical status, functional status, satisfaction, safety, and cost (Rosenblatt, 1998). However, Burns, Hoagwood, and Maultsby (1998) have pointed out that consistent results are difficult to obtain in the absence of a "full-fledged" national strategy to achieve and evaluate outcomes. It remains to be seen if the results of current efforts will encourage the development and implementation of such a national strategy.

Definition

As noted previously, the term *emotional and behavioral disorders* is one of many labels used to classify certain abnormal, atypical, or deviant behaviors. Alternative terms include *emotional disturbance, behavioral disorder, emotional maladjustment, mental disorder, psychosocial disorder,* and *mental illness,* among others. Many individuals use *emotional and behavioral disorder* to refer to children's psychological problems in the same manner that *mental illness* is applied to adults. The federal government prefers the term *serious emotional disturbance* for use with children. Both terms are generally viewed as more encompassing than *behaviorial disorder*, which implies problems stemming from faulty learning and which is also often applied to children and youth. The terms *serious emotional disturbance* and *socially maladjusted* frequently are associated because the maladaptive behavior patterns associated with emotional disturbance affect social interactions. Currently, however, federal law as specified originally in the Education for All Handicapped Children Act of 1975 (P.L. 94-142) defines these as separate conditions, denying special education services to "socially maladjusted" persons who are not diagnosed as seriously emotionally disturbed.

Although the term *emotional and behavioral disorders* appears to be gaining acceptance among professionals in the field, there still is no complete agreement as to what it represents. Unlike a classification that refers to a specific condition (e.g., measles), it is a superordinate label that can be applied to any of a vast number of different behaviors and attitudes. Furthermore, the meaning of the term varies with the philosophies or paradigms of those who use it. Thus, the perspective of a consulting psychiatrist may vary greatly from that of a classroom teacher. The importance of theoretical perspective on the definition of any label in this area was recognized years ago by Wyne and O'Connor (1979, p. 31), who presented three definitions associated with three distinct points of view: psychodynamic, behavioral, and developmental–ecological. The psychodynamic perspective emphasizes inadequate ego development, the behavioral approach focuses on inappropriate learned behaviors, and the developmental–ecological point of view concentrates on behavioral deviance irrespective of etiology. In addition to these theoretical approaches, a perspective that emphasizes cognitive processes, as well as a biochemical perspective that focuses exclusively on etiology, that is, the effects of the physical–chemical environment prenatally, during labor and birth, or at any subsequent time (Rimland, 1969), might be added. (These perspectives are discussed in Chapter 2.)

In educational circles, for many years the most frequently used definition appeared to reflect a developmental–ecological point of view (Bower, 1981). This definition, which ignores etiology and described characteristics, was accepted by the U.S. Department of Education and included in IDEA. It specified that serious emotional disturbance is indicated by problematic behavior in one or more of five characteristic areas (*Federal Register*, 1977, 1985, 1991, Section 300.5 [b] [8]):

1. An inability to learn that cannot be explained by intellectual, sensory, or health factors

2. An inability to build or maintain satisfactory interpersonal relationships with peers or teachers

3. Inappropriate types of behavior or feelings under normal circum-
    stances

4. A general or pervasive mood of unhappiness or depression

5. A tendency to develop physical symptoms or fears associated with
    personal or school problems

The federal regulations departed from Bower by adding a sixth criterion—that
an observed behavior problem must adversely affect educational performance.
In addition, these maladaptive behaviors and attitudes must occur frequently,
over time, and be of sufficient intensity to evoke concern.

Although Bower's definition appears to be functional, individuals with
alternative perspectives, as well as some who share Bower's perspective
(e.g., Schulz & Turnbull, 1983; Wood, 1985), find it inadequate and have
criticized it for being ambiguous about serious emotional disturbance and for
excluding the socially maladjusted. Because of widespread discontent, professionals from a variety of associations and advocacy groups came together under
the auspices of the National Mental Health and Special Education Coalition in
the late 1980s to propose a new definition (Forness & Knitzer, 1992, p. 13):

I.   The term emotional or behavioral disorder means a disability charac-
     terized by behavioral or emotional responses in school programs so
     different from appropriate age, cultural, or ethnic norms that they ad-
     versely affect educational performance, including academic, social,
     vocational or personal skills, and which:

     a. is more than a temporary, expected response to stressful events in
         the environment;
     b. is consistently exhibited in two different settings, at least one of
         which is school-related; and
     c. persists despite individualized interventions within the education
         program, unless, in the judgment of the team, the child's or youth's
         history indicates that such interventions would not be effective.

     Emotional or behavioral disorders can co-exist with other disabilities.

II. This category may include children or youth with schizophrenic dis-
     orders, affective disorders, anxiety disorders, or other sustained distur-
     bances of conduct or adjustment when they adversely affect educa-
     tional performance in accordance with section I.

The foregoing definition appears to be more comprehensive and more detailed than Bower's effort. However, any attempt to define *emotional or behavioral*

disorder or *serious emotional disturbance* is a difficult task. The application of these behavioral labels is based on inferences about behavior and reflect the attitudes and opinions of the observers of that behavior, that is, the members of the society in which the behavior took place. Behaviors that violate cultural rules, laws, or mores (Peterson & Ishii-Jordan, 1994) and run counter to social values (Moynihan, 1993) are most likely to be perceived as indicative of "emotional or behavioral disorder."

Understanding what the term *emotional or behavioral disorder* means should be facilitated by knowledge of the major perspectives and schools of thought on the topic. To that end, this chapter concludes with a discussion of global perspectives of EBD, and the major schools of thought about the topic are presented in Chapter 2.

General Perspectives

General perspectives of EBD reflect three major emphases: disability, deviance, and alienation.

Disability Perspective

Viewing EBD as a disability reflects a medical point of view. It emphasizes the existence of internal pathological conditions that generate aberrant behaviors. As is the case with physical illness, where symptoms such as a stomachache may signify a disease such as an ulcer, certain inappropriate behaviors that are detrimental to self or others are symptomatic of underlying disorders. Such behaviors are signals that something is wrong with the person—that the person is sick. By implication, if the individual did not suffer from a particular disorder, then he or she would not behave inappropriately. Therefore, the individual is not directly responsible for his or her behavior but is being driven by forces that he or she may neither understand nor be able to control.

Because pathological conditions exist *before* an individual behaves inappropriately, and, in fact, cause the inappropriate behavior, overt behavior per se does not necessarily mark an individual as disordered. Two boys may demonstrate the same set of behaviors, for example, steal cars regularly and drive them at high speeds until they run out of gas. One individual acts in such fashion because he has an emotional disorder and his reason is clouded by his condition. The other person seems emotionally healthy but simply enjoys taking cars for joy rides. On the surface at least, the latter individual is not driven to car theft by underlying pathology; he consciously decides to behave in a manner that he regards as advantageous. Although the behaviors are identical and are regarded as being outside the socially acceptable behavioral norms of any community, they alone do not establish the condition of disturbance.

Clearly, from the disability perspective the underlying factors that cause behavior are critical to the diagnosis of a pathological condition. These factors are the physical and psychological processes that constitute the "persona," the combination of biological, developmental, and learned events that characterize the individual and determine behavior. They involve physiological and neural operations as well as the psychological variables of needs, drives, and attitudes. When EBD exists, these factors are diseased or problematic in some manner. In the example cited above, the individual with EBD may be motivated by self-destructive urges that distort his perceptions of the world and cause irrational behavior.

Information about the causal factors that may underlie behavior cannot be gathered by mere observation of surface acts, even when observations are precise and carefully made. Generalizations about the pathological conditions influencing behavior can be formulated only through extensive psychiatric, psychological, and psychoneurological evaluation. This sort of examination is designed not only to establish the existence of EBD but also, through the measurement of psychological and neurological operations, to determine the specific cause of the condition. To return to our example, the emotionally disturbed car thief might be suffering from an organic lesion; his surface behaviors are merely symptoms of his underlying pathology. In this type of case a thorough neurological examination should reveal the cause of the problematic behaviors. In other cases where causal factors may be subtle or masked by the individual's lack of awareness or deliberate defensiveness, the importance of extensive, probing clinical evaluation by highly trained professionals is better illustrated. For example, our car thief who claimed to be joy riding may also have a serious emotional disorder and may be attempting to conceal the fact that the theft of the cars was done in obedience to "directives from God."

To aid in the diagnosis of EBD (or, in the terminology of those emphasizing the disability perspective, "mental disorders"), several prominent medical organizations have produced classification systems. The World Health Organization (1992) has developed the tenth revision of the *International Classification of Diseases*. The most widely used classification system in the United States, published by the American Psychiatric Association, is the *Diagnostic and Statistical Manual of Mental Disorders* (4th ed.; DSM–IV; 1994). This manual names and describes hundreds of specific pathological mental conditions. The sheer number of diagnostic categories included attests to the importance of applying the precise disability label to the afflicted individual. It also reflects the traditional medical belief that the specific diagnosis determines the choice of treatment, and that such treatment is based on knowledge of the underlying condition(s) causing the behavioral symptoms. These assumptions persist despite evidence that psychiatric categories of this type frequently do not influence treatment (Merrell, 1994).

Although the types of disorders presented in the DSM–IV that occur in children and youth are discussed later, the extreme popularity of this clinical tool makes a cursory discussion of its organization helpful. The DSM–IV presents a multiaxial diagnostic system. Abnormal behavior is divided into two axes. Axis I reports all mental disorders (e.g., Conduct Disorder, Attention Deficit/Hyperactivity Disorder, Anxiety Disorders, Mood Disorders) except personality disorders and mental retardation, which are included on Axis II. The separation ensures that the Axis II disorders will not be ignored when they coexist with a disorder listed on Axis I. Axis III codes medical conditions that might affect the disorders listed on Axes I and II (e.g., diabetes might cause depression). Axis IV codes the psychosocial and environmental problems that might influence the diagnosis and treatment of the disorders listed on Axes I and II. Axis V is the Global Assessment of Functioning, which deals with the individual's ability to cope with everyday life.

The diagnostic categories are listed under 18 broad headings, beginning with "Disorders Usually First Diagnosed in Infancy, Childhood, or Adolescence." Most of these disorders and those in other categories (e.g., mood disorders) that are applied to children and youth are discussed in Chapter 3.

The DSM–IV classification categories illustrate the extent to which, from the disability perspective, EBDs may be thought of as fixed rather than culturally relative conditions. In other words, although a disorder might have been induced by sociocultural conditions, once established it is a pathological state that for the most part transcends the mores of any specific culture; the symptomatic behaviors that lead to the diagnosis of the pathological condition would be viewed as problematic in a variety of cultural settings. In a similar vein, the existence of an emotional disorder at any specific time does not necessarily depend on displays of deviant behavior during that specific time. A psychotic individual might have been mentally ill for a long time even though the person's overt behaviors did not significantly deviate from established social norms. Such might be the case, for example, when an upstanding citizen suddenly, for no apparent reason, slaughters his friends or neighbors. The illness causing such bizarre behavior probably existed long before the behavior occurred.

From the disability perspective, diagnosis and much of the treatment of persons with EBD is conducted largely by medical personnel. Psychiatrists, physicians who specialize in mental disorders, bear primary responsibility for treatment, although they may be assisted by members of related professions, such as psychiatric social workers or clinical psychologists. A principal component of treatment is drug therapy, the use of tranquilizing or sedating drugs to control the symptoms of mental illness. Also, psychotherapy may be conducted.

Treatment facilities include mental hospitals, psychiatric facilities, and mental health clinics. Although treatment may vary, depending on the theoretical approach held by the practitioner, it often focuses on the source of the individual's emotional disorder and usually involves the use of drugs. If the problem is perceived as having a psychological or sociocultural basis, the individual's attitudes and ideas, both conscious and unconscious, must be altered.

To reiterate, the principal points associated with the disability perspective of EBD are as follows:

- EBD is viewed much as physical disease is regarded—as an internal pathological state.
- The disorder causes the individual to engage in sick behaviors symptomatic of the underlying problem.
- Overt behavior per se does not indicate EBD; the internal forces motivating overt behavior determine the existence of EBD.
- Diagnosis of EBD must involve more than observation of overt behavior; it must include measurements of psychological and possibly psychoneurological functioning.
- Diagnosis must be conducted by trained medical personnel and members of related professions.
- The focus of diagnosis must be on identifying the condition that is causing the problematic behavior.
- Emotionally disturbed states often transcend specific cultures; they are not culturally relative.
- Treatment is conducted primarily by psychiatric (medical) personnel in medical facilities.
- Treatment focuses on the individual's underlying pathology.

Deviance Perspective

From the deviance perspective, the existence of EBD is determined by the extent to which an individual's behavior deviates from the norm. One form of deviation involves breaking social rules. A society establishes rules or standards of appropriate behavior that reflect its values, beliefs, convictions, and traditions. Such rules may be formalized in laws or may be implicit, unspecified criteria for social interaction. For the most part, each member of the society is expected to conform to such rules or risk negative consequences because rule breaking is perceived as harmful or threatening to the general welfare. Technically, rules are enforced by the citizenry; the behavior of each citizen is subject to evaluation by every other citizen. When an individual's overt behavior falls outside the limits deemed appropriate by the majority of the community, he or she may be designated as mentally disturbed or, in the case of children or youth, emotionally or behaviorally disturbed. In effect, each of these designations is a label that may be applied to rule breakers and represents one of many categories of deviance.

Just as the DSM–IV psychiatric clinical classification system illustrates the disability perspective, empirical classification systems illustrate the deviance perspective. Empirical classification uses statistical analyses such as factor analysis or cluster analysis to measure patterns of behavior that are related or clustered (intercorrelated). Data about large samples of children's behaviors are gathered with questionnaires, checklists, or rating scales. The correlation of items show which behaviors tend to cluster together to form a syndrome or behavioral dimension. Research consistently identifies two broad behavioral dimensions (Achenbach, 1985; Quay, 1986). One encompasses acting-out behaviors such as fighting, temper tantrums, verbal and physical aggression, disobedience, and destructiveness. The best-known designations for this dimension are *externalizing* or *undercontrolled* (Achenbach, 1991; Achenbach & Edelbrock, 1989) and *conduct disordered* (Quay & Peterson, 1987).

The second dimension encompasses characteristics such as anxiety, shyness, and social withdrawal, and has been labeled *internalizing* or *overcontrolled* (Achenbach, 1991; Achenbach & Edelbrock, 1989) and *anxiety-withdrawal* or *personality* problem (Quay & Peterson, 1987). In addition to these two general dimensions, research has identified a number of more specific or narrow-band syndromes, including depressed, hyperactive, delinquent, aggressive, schizoid, socially immature, and somatic behaviors (Achenbach, 1991).

Two instruments commonly used to measure broad-band syndromes are the *Child Behavior Checklist* (CBCL; Achenbach, 1991) and the *Revised Behavior Problem Checklist* (RBPC; Quay & Peterson, 1987). Using the original *Behavior Problem Checklist*, Cullinan and Epstein (1985) found that children with EBD scored higher than other children, both handicapped and nonhandicapped, on every dimension but were particularly deviant on the conduct disorder dimension. Notably, from a deviance perspective, the emotional and behavioral characteristics measured by these statistically devised instruments are present to some degree in the general population of children and youth. The critical determinant of EBD is the extent or degree to which an individual who displays these characteristics deviates from the norm.

The issue is not as clear as it may seem, however, because norms in specific subcultures may vary. Therefore, although an individual's behavior may result in a designation of EBD, as with the disability perspective, behavior per se, no matter how extreme or unusual it may appear, does not necessarily indicate EBD. Behavior deemed deviant in one circumstance might be judged appropriate in another. To use an extreme example, a sniper who indiscriminately shoots 13 strangers appears to be demonstrating deviant behavior. However, if the sniper was a soldier shooting 13 enemy soldiers, the behavior would be appropriate to the situation; if the soldier failed to shoot, the behavior might be regarded as deviant by society. The environmental circumstances affecting an individual—the social milieu—help define the normalcy of behavior. Such variables are part of the criteria that community members use to judge the appropriateness of behavior.

A deviance perspective of emotional disturbance might best be seen as a "social" or "culturally relative" point of view. A society arbitrarily chooses to regard behaviors as acceptable or deviant. For example, hallucinations and delusions, symptoms of severe emotional disturbance from the disability perspective, are viewed as normal and appropriate occurrences in societies that encourage the use of mind-expanding drugs and regard such experiences as religious events. Also, homicide was sanctified in head-hunting societies but is regarded as extremely deviant (under most circumstances) in our culture. Ullmann and Krasner (1969) noted that behavior can never be viewed as pathological if it is normal for a particular society:

> A critical example is whether an obedient Nazi concentration camp commander would be considered normal or abnormal. To the extent that he was responding accurately and successfully to his environment and not breaking its rules, much less coming to the professional attention of psychiatrists, he would not be labeled abnormal. Repulsive as his behavior is to mid-twentieth-century Americans, such repulsion is based on a particular set of values. Although such a person may be made liable for his acts—as Nazi war criminals were—the concept of abnormality as a special entity does not seem necessary or justified. If it is, the problem arises as to who selects the values, and this, in turn, implies that one group may select values that are applied to others. This situation of one group's values being dominant over others' is the fascistic background from which the Nazi camp commander sprang. (p. 15)

From the deviance perspective, the term *emotional and behavioral disorder* is not synonymous with *mental disease*. The term does not imply that underlying pathological conditions cause atypical or bizarre behavior. The whole question of underlying causation is not critical to determining the existence of a problematic condition. The extent to which behavior is socially inappropriate determines the classification, not the forces motivating the inappropriate behavior. For example, two individuals might share intense feelings of hatred for their neighbor. One person violates community standards by physically assaulting the neighbor, whereas the other is content to engage in verbal abuse. The first individual's overt behavior exceeds acceptable social limits and thus is considered emotionally disordered. Although the other person maintains similar internal feelings of hatred, that individual's overt behavior does not violate community norms, and the person is not perceived as emotionally or behaviorally disordered.

The societal norms used to classify behavior are varied and complex. As noted, the critical variable is not specific behaviors. Many of the antisocial or self-destructive behaviors that characterize EBD are demonstrated by children and youth. They violate social rules by driving too fast, telling lies, drinking too much alcohol, fighting, cheating on tests, defying authority, and so on. Yet, relatively few individuals are assigned the EBD designation. Society establishes behavioral norms that encompass a range of acceptable deviant behavior. Deviant behaviors indicate a problem only when they fall outside this range. Generally, this happens when deviant behaviors occur (a) with excessive frequency, (b) with great consistency, and (c) in unusual abundance. Too many deviant acts displayed too often over too long a time mark an individual's behavior as different from the norm. In effect, deviant behaviors become typical or characteristic of the individual's personality. They alarm, concern, inconvenience, or irritate others, thereby inviting community intervention and the possible designation of EBD.

Some behaviors deviate so dramatically from societal norms that a single act may indicate that an individual has an EBD. The behavioral dimensions of frequency, consistency, and abundance are unimportant. Acts such as murder or attempted suicide are examples of such behavior. However, even these behaviors may occur in circumstances that mark them as normal rather than deviant. A murder may be regarded as justified, as when an enraged teenage boy acts to defend his mother or siblings from abuse. An individual who attempts suicide might be construed as engaging in a courageous act if death is chosen over suffering. Regardless of the apparent degree of deviance associated with certain acts, the judgment as to whether it reflects an EBD depends on circumstances and the particular attitudes and values of the community.

Because EBDs are established by socially deviant behaviors, they are not fixed conditions. An individual is not either afflicted or well; in fact, the same individual might be construed as disordered in one community and normal in another, because standards vary. Adolf Hitler provides a good example. In a society other than Nazi Germany, he probably would have been regarded as a madman.

The impermanence of the EBD label is emphasized further by the variance in normalcy criteria among subcommunities of a large community. Specific schools constitute subcommunities, and behaviors such as fighting or truancy that are regarded as deviant in one school may be regarded as typical in another. On a broader scale, states, cities, towns, boroughs, and neighborhoods form communities, and each establishes unique criteria for deviance. In some cases community values conflict. Behavior regarded as normal in a specific neighborhood may be viewed as deviant at the city or state level.

Further variation in the criteria of deviance exists within communities. Behaviors may be deemed appropriate or inappropriate depending on variables such as an individual's age, gender, race, social class, or education. An adolescent male who fights frequently, uses profanity in public, drives recklessly, and so forth may be regarded as less deviant than an adolescent female who behaves similarly. The latter's gender produces more stringent behavioral requirements. Even behavior as extreme as homicide may be evaluated differently depending on the prestige and power of the murderer. An individual without influence or status in the community who commits murder is likely to be viewed with less sympathy than a well-connected, "substantial" citizen who commits the same crime.

As a general rule, a designation of deviance tends to be applied more readily to the less mature, less influential, less economically independent members of the community. Thus, children, who obviously are controlled by others and are economically dependent, qualify as a population whose behaviors are frequently regarded as deviant. A child who fights, lies, and cheats in school may be considered to have EBD, whereas an adult who behaves similarly would be less likely to earn such a label.

Variation in what constitutes deviant behavior is demonstrated further by the fact that the type of behavior regarded as abnormal fluctuates as societal norms and community attitudes change. Today's deviant act is tomorrow's acceptable behavior. For example, women once prevented by social mores from drinking alcoholic beverages in public can now drink without fear of reprisal.

Obviously, when individuals have internalized the behavioral norms that prevail in one community, they may experience difficulty adjusting to the dominant norms of another community. A teenage boy from an inner-city ghetto who has learned to regard aggression as appropriate and necessary for survival can be expected to have difficulty in a school setting that regards such behavior as inappropriate.

Because socially inappropriate behavior is a critical variable in defining EBD from a deviance perspective, treatments of individuals identified as having

EBD are designed to teach socially appropriate behavior. Emphasis is on adjusting responses to typical interactions that occur in daily living. Therefore, treatment is not the sole purview of the psychiatric or medical community but can be conducted by a variety of different individuals, including parents and teachers.

From a deviance perspective, then, *EBD* is a label that may be applied to a vast number of diverse behaviors. The term has little specific meaning; it simply represents a particular category of deviance. Other, similar categories are criminality and delinquency.

To reiterate, the principal points associated with the deviance perspective are as follows:

- The term *EBD* is a label that may be assigned to those whose behavior deviates from social norms.

- The existence of an EBD is inferred.

- The designation of EBD is arbitrary because it depends on community judgments and communities vary in their views and tolerance of deviance.

- The etiology of EBDs is relatively unimportant; it does not determine who is labeled.

- The diagnostic label *EBD* is one of several that may be assigned to deviant persons.

- EBDs do not refer to fixed conditions, because their identification depends on environmental circumstances.

- Many behaviors indicative of EBD are commonly displayed by people. Often the frequency, constancy, and abundance of behaviors displayed mark an individual as deviant.

- Treatment involves teaching individuals socially appropriate behavior so that they can function effectively. It may take place in mental hospitals or in other facilities such as schools or prisons.

- Treatment is not limited to members of the medical profession but may be undertaken by teachers, clergymen, parents, or other individuals interested in the welfare of the individual.

Alienation Perspective

The alienation approach to understanding EBDs emerged as a major perspective during the mid–20th century. Unlike both the disability and deviance points of views, this perspective emphasizes the positive aspects of human nature. People are seen as inherently healthy, motivated to fulfill or actualize their potential by living constructive lives and behaving in a socially responsible manner. To maintain a state of positive mental health, each person seeks to engage in meaningful activities in a society that welcomes individual creativity and provides opportunities for self-actualization.

EBDs are perceived as developing when individuals are frustrated in their quest to fulfill their potential by a materialistic society that equates success in life with money and power, that denies opportunity to persons with different values who refuse to "play the game," that frustrates creativity by straining human ideas through the sieve of mindless bureaucracy, and that is dominated by its own self-interest. As individuals become increasingly aware of these circumstances, they feel futile, lonely, and alienated from society as a whole. They feel emotionally disturbed, although in reality they are neither mentally sick or disordered nor simply engaging in deviant behaviors because they have not learned any better. Their troubled feelings are an understandable response to a materialistic, mechanistic, inhumane society. Thus, the car theft behavior that was described previously might be viewed from this perspective as a series of poor choices about behavior made by an alienated, frustrated individual who perceives that the inequities in society act as a barrier to healthy self-actualization. Even the response of the society from alternative perspectives, that is, a designation of deviance with ensuing labeling of some type (*emotionally and behaviorally disordered* or *criminal*), or the diagnosis of a mental disorder (with the ensuing implications of sickness and wrongness), when viewed from the alienation perspective, serves the purpose of the inhumane society. There is an interesting twist of logic associated with the alienation perspective that suggests that persons who accept the values of a sick society and perpetuate its dedication to destructive, inhumane acts are themselves in grave emotional jeopardy, despite the fact that they engage in neither socially deviant nor psychiatrically disordered behaviors and may never regard themselves or be regarded by others as emotionally disturbed.

Another ramification of the alienation point of view is the relationship between minorities, including women in a patriarchal society, and barriers to self-actualization. As expected, greater frustration and fewer avenues for fulfillment result in higher incidence rates by the less dominant groups of "deviant" or "disordered" behaviors. A disproportionate percentage of racial minorities engage in antisocial behavior, and a significantly greater number of females than males undertake psychotherapy to solve emotional problems.

The issue of whether or not specific behaviors are sufficient to characterize an individual as having an EBD is not germane from this perspective, nor is the question of specific etiology. Efforts to teach a person to behave differently in specific situations (conform) or to attach a particular disability label that slots the individual into a specific category clearly miss the point. They will never seriously affect emotional and behavioral problems because they direct attention away from the societal barriers that hurt or wound individuals and cause them to feel emotionally distraught and to behave accordingly. A far more important issue pertains to recognizing the uniqueness and dignity of each individual and being aware of the extent to which individuals' perceptions are valuable.

Regarding the issue of cultural relativity, the problems affecting the individual and causing personal distress are caused by the forces of the culture that the individual is part of. Theoretically, problems would disappear in humane societies. However, in the real world, problems transcend specific cultures because the dominant values in most existing societies are similarly inhumane.

To reiterate, the principal points associated with the alienation perspective are the following:

- Human beings are basically healthy and inherently motivated toward actualizing their potential and leading constructive, socially responsible lives.

- EBD is neither a disease nor a series of deviant behaviors caused by inappropriate learning.

- Persons viewed as having EBD are reacting to a dehumanizing society that restricts their path to self-actualization.

- Individuals upset by the society deserve respect for responding to malignant social values.

- Persons who accept the values of the society may be in greater emotional jeopardy than those who react against them.

- Members of the underclasses are more likely to reject social values because they experience more barriers to self-actualization.

- Issues of etiology and cultural relativity are not important.

- Treatment is undertaken by professionals who adhere to the humanistic point of view. Extensive focus is on the environmental forces affecting an individual.

Comparative Analysis

Each of the three perspectives on EBD offers a unique answer to the question "What is an emotional and behavioral disorder?" From the disability perspective, it is a disease that exists within an individual regardless of cultural values. From the deviance perspective, it is a label assigned to those who break social rules and therefore is culturally relative. From the alienation perspective, it is a response to a materialistic, inhumane society that interferes with individual self-fulfillment.

In modern society the disability perspective is a powerful point of view. It has both strengths and weaknesses. One of its principal strengths is that it attempts to establish a culture-free classification system for EBDs. Thus, individuals may be recognized as manifesting a specific disorder if they display certain behaviors, regardless of who they are and where they are.

A second, related advantage is that the development of an elaborate classification system for pathological conditions provides a frame of reference for understanding unusual or inappropriate behaviors. It is a means of organizing what otherwise would be a mass of fragmented pieces of information. The importance of organizing such information is that it permits the systematic investigation of common conditions that is necessary for the generation and verification of scientific hypotheses. For example, if individuals demonstrate behaviors such as disorientation, bizarre speech, and confused ideation, they might be classified as schizophrenic. Once classified, they might be studied with other schizophrenics to isolate the common symptoms of that condition.

A third advantage of the disability perspective lies in the emphasis it places on determining the etiology of disturbed conditions. The isolation of the causes of these conditions paves the way for early intervention and more meaningful treatment. For example, if it were to be proved conclusively that the absence of certain enzymes is responsible for schizophrenia, specific treatment to replace the enzymes might prevent the onset of the disease.

One final advantage is that the disability model is basically a therapeutic approach to the problem of emotional disturbance. It is based on the assumption that kind, compassionate treatment will restore normalcy, and that individuals should not be punished because they are afflicted.

Unfortunately, several of the elements of this approach listed as strengths are double-edged swords. First, the disability classification system is often misused. Disability classification categories are primarily descriptive; they describe rather than explain behavior. For instance, *schizophrenia* is simply a label attached to a category of behaviors. A person who exhibits such behaviors is described as schizophrenic. The term does not explain why such behaviors occur, and it cannot be construed as representing the cause of those behaviors. To conclude that an individual's bizarre behavior is caused by schizophrenia is similar to concluding that the bizarre behavior is caused by bizarre behavior, because those specific acts resulted in the application of the descriptive label *schizophrenia*.

Second, the emphasis placed on causality is often misleading. It is a relatively easy matter to accurately observe and record samples of an individual's overt behavior. It is far more difficult to measure the internal psychological or neurological operations that cause those overt behaviors. It is even more difficult to discern whether or not such internal operations are diseased. Currently, the instrumentation used to diagnose disturbed conditions is relatively crude. Many tests and other assessment devices lack the levels of reliability and validity necessary to engender confidence in their results. As a result, the conclusions drawn regarding states of internal mental pathology are often unverifiable speculations. As diagnosis moves away from inferences that refer directly to overt, observable behavior, toward inferences about the inner workings of the psyche or brain, the possibility of errors in judgment increases. This situation is typified all too frequently when mental health experts testifying in criminal cases form diametrically opposite conclusions about the mental state (sanity or insanity) of a particular individual.

Third, the establishment of an elaborate classification system often only results in disability labeling. Unfortunately, any indication that an individual is disordered is stigmatizing. The mere application of a disability label conveys negative characteristics to others. Therefore, particularly when disability labeling does not result in specific treatment but is done primarily for purposes of classification, the benefits to the labeled individual are questionable. The literature in education is replete with studies of the negative effects of disability labeling on children's self-concepts, teachers' attitudes, parents' opinions, and so forth.

A final disadvantage of the disability approach is that it may perpetuate a superior–subordinate doctor–patient relationship that implies that the physician will solve the patient's problems. The doctor–patient model also may minimize the importance of the social milieu and the effectiveness of other key people in the environment, such as parents and teachers, in producing attitudinal and behavioral changes in children with emotional and behavioral problems.

Unlike the medical orientation of the disability perspective, the deviance perspective springs from the disciplines of sociology and cultural anthropology. It too has strengths and weaknesses. Its advantages are inversely related to the disadvantages associated with the disability perspective.

One advantage of the deviance perspective is that it emphasizes the importance of circumstances *outside* the individual to the study of disturbance. If emotional disturbance is a culturally relative condition, it cannot be studied in a vacuum. The forces or social milieu that surround the individual must be considered.

Second, the deviance perspective emphasizes the arbitrary nature of disability labeling. Because such labels are assigned in response to deviations from community norms, individuals may be designated as having an EBD on the basis of chance. They may engage in particular behaviors in an intolerant rather than a tolerant community. An example of such chance categorization occurs when a child is viewed as emotionally and behaviorally disordered in one classroom but as normal in another.

Third, the deviance perspective directs attention to overt behaviors in the diagnosis and treatment of EBD. The advantage of this focus is that it provides direct information about the behaviors that must be altered if the individual's problems are to be lessened.

The principal disadvantage of the deviance perspective is that it equates EBD with nonconformity. It does not provide for the existence of abnormal conditions unless society labels behavior as abnormal. The validity of this assumption is questionable. Socially accepted behavior may be pathological. For example, the activities of Hitler's storm troopers in Nazi Germany can be construed as pathological, although they did not violate the norms of that particular society.

A second disadvantage is that normality is not synonymous with conformity. Deviant behaviors do not always signify abnormality. Nonconforming members of society frequently revitalize social customs and engender new growth. Unless there are standards within a society that transcend social acceptability, many creative, unorthodox people who engage in deviant behavior would be labeled as disordered. Obviously, the nonconforming behavior of Thomas Jefferson, George Washington, Benjamin Franklin, and many other revolutionaries, as well as inventors such as the Wright brothers and Thomas Edison, and artists such as da Vinci, Rembrandt, and Michelangelo cannot be viewed as indicative of emotional disorder.

A third and related problem concerns treatment. If EBDs are synonymous with socially inappropriate behaviors, the therapist is placed in the position of teaching the deviant individual socially acceptable behaviors. To do so, the therapist must make a value judgment as to the goodness or badness of behaviors, that is, what is to be taught or extinguished. Under these circumstances the Wright brothers might have been punished for working on their airplane and rewarded for building better bicycles.

The last of the general perspectives, the alienation point of view, is extremely different from both other perspectives. A principal advantage is that it presents a far more global view of the problem, directing attention not to the individual but to the society. Few individuals would disagree that the values of modern societies, with emphasis on wealth, power, and the use of force to obtain them, are distorted. Additionally, many people recognize that technological advances have far outstripped the development of humanistic attitudes and that individuals are increasingly becoming faceless cogs in a mechanistic wheel. Thus, a perspective that relates these social forces directly to EBD fills an important void.

The second advantage of the alienation approach is that it accentuates the positive in people, assuming that they are capable of reorganizing their lives by making choices for more constructive activities. This philosophy directly affects treatment, by emphasizing the importance of both treating emotionally disordered persons with respect and encouraging them to take responsibility for their own growth and development.

An advantage related to the previous point is the emphasis on individual differences advocated by the alienation perspective. Effective strategies for working with persons whose behavior indicates emotional distress must be geared to each individual's specific needs.

Finally, this approach has none of the problems associated with the other two perspectives, for example, disability labeling, doctor–patient relationships, minimizing forces in the social milieu, and associating disturbance with nonconformity.

The disadvantage of this approach is a problem of circular reasoning. Cultures do not exist independently of people. Citizens create the warped values that in turn are said to make them emotionally and behaviorally disordered.

Summary

For the sake of clarity, the three general perspectives on EBD discussed in this chapter have been presented as unique, competing points of view. However, it is more accurate to say that each perspective answers a different question about the topic. The deviance point of view attempts to delineate *how* an individual becomes identified as emotionally disturbed. It depicts the labeling process that operates in a particular society. The disability perspective attempts to explain *what types* of emotional disturbance exist and *what causes them*. It provides culture-free criteria for the diagnosis of pathological conditions. The alienation perspective explores *why* individuals become emotionally disturbed. It is a global examination of cultural malaise.

In one sense the disability model can be subsumed under the deviance perspective. Professionals who determine which individuals are mentally disordered can be thought of as the social agents responsible for categorizing a deviant individual. In another sense the disability perspective is broader than the deviance perspective because it provides absolute standards for the diagnosis of EBD. However, those who adhere to an alienation perspective would argue that both other approaches are representative of a repressive, dehumanizing society.

Regardless of which philosophy appears appealing at this point, the stage is set to explore the implications of each position in greater detail. If one regards emotionally and behaviorally disordered persons as inherently different from the nondisordered population, then one must determine whether the individual's problem is a biological phenomenon due to faulty genes, neural functioning, or biochemistry, or whether the disorder was developed because of environmental stress that activated certain predispositions within the individual.

If one accepts the premise that environmental circumstances determine who will become emotionally and behaviorally disordered, then one must decide whether those circumstances are viewed most accurately as a sequence of specific interactions between an individual and varied environmental agents or as a total or global phenomenon involving a multitude of sociological variables.

STUDY QUESTIONS

1. Discuss why the term *emotional and behavioral disorder* is difficult to define. Then define it in your own words and use the information in Chapter 1 to determine how each general perspective influences your definition.

2. Compare and contrast the disability, deviance, and alienation perspectives on emotional disturbance. Then decide if Adolf Hitler could be regarded as having EBD. Justify your conclusions with references to any perspective.

3. A child in your class cries frequently, refuses to complete her assignments, and complains often of illness. From an alienation perspective, discuss how you might help the child.

4. Consider the case of "Son of Sam," the man from New York who shot and killed or injured several young women and their dates. He reported that God instructed him to kill. At his trial he was judged sane and sentenced to life imprisonment. From the information in Chapter 1, what perspective influenced that decision?

References

Achenbach, T. M. (1985). *Assessment and taxonomy of child and adolescent psychopathology*. Beverly Hills, CA: Sage.

Achenbach, T. M. (1991). *Manual for the Child Behavior Checklist/4–18 and 1991 profile*. Burlington: University of Vermont, Department of Psychiatry.

Achenbach, T. M., & Edelbrock, C. S. (1989). Diagnostic, taxonomic, and assessment issues. In T. H. Ollendick & M. Hersen (Eds.), *Handbook of child psychopathology* (2nd ed., pp. 53–69). New York: Plenum Press.

American Psychiatric Association. (1994). *Diagnostic and statistical manual of mental disorders* (4th ed.). Washington, DC: Author.

Bateman, B. D., & Chard, D. (1995). Legal demands and constraints on placement decisions. In J. M. Kauffman, J. W. Lloyd, D. P. Hallahan, & T. A. Astuto (Eds.), *Issues in educational placement: Students with emotional and behavioral disorders* (pp. 285–316). Hillsdale, NJ: Erlbaum.

Bower, E. (1981). *Early identification of emotionally handicapped children in school* (3rd ed.). Springfield, IL: Thomas.

Burns, B., Hoagwood, K., & Maultsby, L. (1998). Improving outcomes for children and adolescents with serious emotional and behavioral disorders: Current and future directions. In M. Epstein, K. Kutash, & A. Duchnowski (Eds.), *Outcomes for children and youth with emotional and behavioral disorders and their families* (pp. 685–708). Austin, TX: PRO-ED.

Clark, G. M., Carlson, B., Fisher, S., Cook, I., & D'Alonzo, B. (1991). Career development for students with disabilities in elementary schools: A position statement of the Division on Career Development. *Career Development for Exceptional Individuals, 14*(2), 110–120.

Coleman, J. (1972). *Abnormal psychology and modern life*. Glenview, IL: Scott, Foresman.

Cullinan, D., & Epstein, M. H. (1985). Adjustment problems of mildly handicapped and nonhandicapped students. *Remedial and Special Education, 6*(2), 5–11.

Diamond, S. C. (1993). Special education and the great god, inclusion. *Beyond Behavior, 4*(2), 3–6.

Duncan, B. B., Forness, S. R., & Hartsough, C. (1995). Students identified as seriously emotionally disturbed in day treatment: Cognitive, psychiatric, and special education characteristics. *Behavior Disorders, 20*, 238–252.

Education for All Handicapped Children Act of 1975, 20 U.S.C. § 1400 *et seq.*

Epstein, M. H., Kutash, K., & Duchnowski, A. (Eds.). (1998). *Outcomes for children and youth with emotional and behavioral disorders and their families*. Austin, TX: PRO-ED.

Forness, S. R., & Knitzer, J. (1992). A new proposed definition and terminology to replace "serious emotional disturbance" in Individuals with Disabilities Education Act, *School Psychology Review, 21*, 12–20.

Halpern, A. S. (1994). The transition of youth with disabilities to adult life: A position statement of the Division on Career Development and Transition, the Council for Exceptional Children. *Career Development for Exceptional Individuals, 17*(2), 115–124.

Harris & Associates. (1994). *National Organization on Disability/Harris Survey of Americans with Disabilities*. New York: Author.

Individuals with Disabilities Education Act of 1990, 20 U.S.C. § *et seq.*

Kauffman, J. M. (1997). *Characteristics of emotional and behavioral disorders of children and youth*. Upper Saddle River, NJ: Prentice Hall.

Kauffman, J. M., & Hallahan, D. P. (Eds.). (1995). *The illusion of full inclusion: A comprehensive critique of a current special educational bandwagon*. Austin, TX: PRO-ED.

Kauffman, J. M., & Lloyd, J. W. (1995). A sense of place: The importance of placement issues in contemporary special education. In J. M. Kauffman, J. W. Lloyd, D. P. Hallahan, & T. A. Astuto (Eds.), *Issues in educational placement: Students with emotional and behavioral disorders* (pp. 3–19). Hillsdale, NJ: Erlbaum.

Kauffman, J. M., & Smucker, K. (1995). The legacies of placement: A brief history of placement options and issues with commentary of their evolution. In J. M. Kauffman, J. W. Lloyd, D. P. Hallahan, & T. A. Astuto (Eds.), *Issues in educational placement: Students with emotional and behavioral disorders* (pp. 21–44). Hillsdale, NJ: Erlbaum.

Merrell, K. W. (1994). *Assessment of behavioral, social, and emotional problems: Direct, objective methods for use with children and adolescents*. New York: Longman.

Morse, W. C. (1994). Comments from a biased point of view. *The Journal of Special Education, 27*, 531–542.

Moynihan, D. P. (1993). Defining deviancy down. *American Scholar*, 62(1), 17–30.

Myles, B. S., & Simpson, R. L. (1998). *Aspergex Syndrome: A guide for educators and parents*. Austin, TX: PRO-ED.

Office of the Federal Register. (1977). *Code of federal regulations* (Tit. 34; pp. 300–399). Washington, DC: U.S. Government Printing Office.

Office of the Federal Register. (1985). *Code of federal regulations* (Tit. 34; pp. 300–399) Washington, DC: U.S. Government Printing Office.

Office of the Federal Register. (1991). *Code of federal regulations* (Tit. 34; pp. 300–399). Washington, DC: U.S. Government Printing Office.

Peterson, R., & Ishii-Jordan, S. (Eds.). (1994). *Multicultural issues in the education of students with behavioral disorders*. Cambridge, MA: Brookline.

Quay, H. C. (1986). Classification. In H. C. Quay & J. S. Werry (Eds.), *Psychopathological disorders of childhood* (3rd ed., pp. 1–34). New York: Wiley.

Quay, H. C., & Peterson, D. R. (1987). *Manual for the Revised Behavior Problem Checklist*. Coral Gables, FL: Author.

Reinert, H. (1972). The emotionally disturbed. In B. Gearheart (Ed.), *Education of the exceptional child*. San Francisco: Intext.

Rimland, B. (1969). Psychogenesis versus biogenesis: The issues and the evidence. In S. C. Plog and R. B. Edgerton (Eds.), *Changing perspectives in mental illness* (pp. 96–122). New York: Holt, Rinehart & Winston.

Rosenblatt, A. (1998). Assessing the child and family outcomes of systems of care for youth with serious emotional disturbance. In M. H. Epstein, K. Kutash, & A. Duchnowski (Eds.), *Outcomes for children and youth with emotional and behavioral disorders and their families* (pp. 329–362). Austin, TX: PRO-ED.

Schulz, J., & Turnbull, A. (1983). *Mainstreaming handicapped students: A guide for classroom teachers*. Boston: Allyn & Bacon.

Smith, C. R., Wood, F. H., & Grimes, J. (1988). Issues in the identification and placement of behaviorally disordered students. In M. C. Wang, M. C. Reynolds, & H. J. Walberg (Eds.), *Handbook of special education: Research and practice* (Vol. 2, pp. 95–124). New York: Pergamon Press.

Stainback, W., & Stainback, S. (1991). A rationale for integration and restructuring: A synopsis. In J. W. Lloyd, N. N. Singh, & A. C. Repp (Eds.), *The regular education initiative: Alternative perspectives on concepts, issues, and models* (pp. 226–239). Sycamore, IL: Sycamore.

Strauss, A., & Lentinen, L. (1947). *Psychopathology and education of the brain-injured child*. New York: Grune & Stratton.

Sullivan, H. (1953). *The interpersonal theory of psychiatry*. New York: Norton.

Ullmann, L., & Krasner, L. (1969). *Psychological approach to abnormal behavior*. Englewood Cliffs, NJ: Prentice Hall.

U.S. Department of Education. (1995). *Seventeenth annual report to Congress on implementation of the Individuals with Disabilities Education Act*. Washington, DC: Author.

Whelan, R. J. (1998). *Emotional and behavioral disorders: A 25 year focus*. Denver, CO: Love.

Wood, F. (1985). Issues in the identification and placement of behaviorally disordered students. *Behavioral Disorders*, 10, 219–228.

World Health Organization. (1992). Mental and behavioural disorders: Diagnostic criteria for research, Chap. 5 in *International classification of diseases* (10th rev.). Geneva: Author.

Wyne, M., & O'Connor, P. (1979). *Exceptional children: A developmental view*. Lexington, MA: D. C. Heath.

THEORETICAL MODELS
OF EMOTIONAL AND
BEHAVIORAL DISORDERS

Theoretical models of emotional and behavioral disorders (EBDs) vary greatly. Their diversity is partially reflected by the extent to which they represent disability, deviance, or alienation perspectives. Disability theories regard forces within the individual as important causal factors. The most extreme disability perspective is represented by theories with a biological orientation. To a large extent, biological theories focus attention exclusively on the human organism and ignore social or cultural forces. They attribute the development of EBDs to organic pathology, that is, actual physiological disorders such as brain lesions, endocrine imbalances, and so forth.

A disability perspective also is represented by certain psychological theories with a psychodynamic orientation. From their frame of reference, EBDs have a functional rather than an organic basis, that is, etiology is due to psychological rather than physical problems. Although causation usually involves an interaction of internal and external factors, many of these theories resemble the biologically oriented theories in viewing forces inside the individual as being of primary importance.

Other psychological theories reflect a deviance perspective. Primary among these are theories that emanate from behavioral psychology. The behavioral approach minimizes the importance of internal psychological or organic states as causal agents, focusing attention on external conditions. Fundamental behavioral theory stresses the relationships between specific environmental events called stimuli and learned behavioral responses.

Also reflecting a deviance frame of reference are theoretical positions emanating from cognitive psychology. These perspectives resemble behavioral approaches in that they also are relatively unconcerned with identifying or diagnosing pathological psychic or organic states. They relate deviant behaviors indicative of emotional disturbance to faulty or illogical thought processes.

The final group of theories adhering to a deviance perspective have their roots in social psychology and in the related discipline, sociology. These sociocultural perspectives examine the deviant behaviors that result from events that occur in a broad cultural or multicultural context.

The alienation perspective is reflected in theoretical positions associated with phenomenological (humanistic) and existential psychology. These theories minimize the importance of etiology, focusing instead on the external social forces or stresses that distort the emotional development of essentially healthy people.

The discussion that follows presents the principal tenets associated with seven theoretical models of emotional disturbance, beginning with the biological and psychodynamic positions, progressing through behavioral, cognitive, and sociocultural positions, and ending with phenomenological and existential points of view.

Biological Model

Theories reflecting a biological orientation maintain that EBDs are forms of mental disease, pathological conditions that exist because of deficiencies or abnormalities in the individual. The behaviors that characterize mental disorders are caused by organic malfunctions, that is, actual physical disorders of some type. Such malfunctions may be due to neural, biochemical, genetic, or developmental deficits. The most extreme representation of this position attributes a direct cause-and-effect relationship to physiological malfunctions and behavioral disorders (Rimland, 1969). More moderate positions hedge against the biological orientation slightly and postulate a biogenetic cause–environmental catalyst–behavioral disorder paradigm (Plomin, 1994, 1995; Plomin & Rutter, 1998; Rutter, 1995). The latter position holds to the necessity of biological malfunctions in mental disorders but grants the possibility that such inherent physiological deficits might lie dormant if not triggered by environmental factors. In both cases the relationship between cause and effect is linear in that a specific set of variables (causal) leads to a predictable effect. A further expansion of this paradigm introduces the concept of self-regulating systems (Carson & Butcher, 1992). A self-regulating system occurs when an effect operates as the cause of a new effect, thereby extending and seriously complicating the cause-and-effect relationships. Despite slight variations in these approaches, the precipitating agents—biological factors—are necessary for the development of all types of EBDs.

From the biological perspective, diagnosis and treatment are focused primarily on the afflicted individual. For the most part, diagnosis centers on identifying the etiology of the illness. Such efforts focus on organic functions, particularly on biochemical and neural operations. Less emphasis is placed on the social or psychological aspects of the problem. In some cases the in utero environment is regarded as more important than the environmental events that occur after birth. Treatment features the administration of drugs or chemicals to influence the functioning of the central nervous system. With increasing frequency, reeducation to assist the afflicted individuals in adapting to their disabilities is also included. Theorists adhering to this orientation often are interested in research, which they believe will eventually reveal the physical or organic basis for mental disorders.

Genetic Etiology

Research into the influence of genetics on human behavior is rapidly expanding and continuously revealing evidence supporting the influence of the genes (Plomin & Rutter, 1998). The impact of genetic structure on the individual may take a variety of forms.

In some cases individuals may receive a single dominant gene pair from one parent that causes a characteristic (brown eyes) or disorder or recessive gene pairs from both parents (blue eyes). Among pathological disorders, Huntington's chorea, a fatal neurological disease that onsets in adulthood, is transmitted by a single dominant gene, whereas Tay-Sachs disease, a fatal disorder of the nervous system that attacks very young children, usually of Ashkenazic Jewish descent, is transmitted by two pairs of receptive genes. Also, sex-linked conditions involve genes on the sex chromosomes, particularly recessive genes on the X chromosome contributed by the female. Daughters receive an X chromosome from each parent; therefore, a defective recessive gene is countered by a dominant normal gene and the disorder is not contracted. Sons receive from their father a Y chromosome that carries no normal gene; consequently, the recessive gene transmitted on the X chromosome prevails and the disease is manifested.

Genetic defects also may be due to chromosomal abnormalities. Examples are the extra chromosome (three instead of two) found in chromosome 21, which causes physical and cognitive abnormalities in most cases of Down syndrome, and the extra X chromosome found in biological males who have engaged in extraordinarily violent and aggressive behavior, a condition known as Klinefelter's syndrome. Other types of genetic defects occur in the positioning of the genes that are located on each chromosome. There is evidence that gene irregularities on chromosomes 5, 9, 10, 11, 18, and 19 may predispose individuals to schizophrenia (Bassett, 1992).

Recently, investigations into genetic causation of EBDs have been facilitated by the study of molecular genetics (Flint, 1996). Investigators look for a relationship between patterns of behavior and genetic markers in family members (linkage analysis) or relationships between specific genes and characteristics or behaviors among unrelated people (association analysis). They also have begun to study the far more complex relationships among multiple genes and behavior or characteristics. However, these investigations are still in relatively primitive stages, and many studies of genetic defects still are undertaken by identifying behavior patterns in persons who are related, such as identical twins, families, and adopted individuals (Plomin, 1994).

The probability of disordered characteristics being inherited is increased when they occur more frequently among related individuals than among members of the general population; the influence of environment also can be assessed (Plomin, 1994). Identical twins who share the same genetic inheritance would be expected to develop similar conditions if mental disorders are transmitted through the genes. Other family members, even fraternal twins, would be less vulnerable than identical twins but more likely to develop the illness than members of families with no incidence of the disease (Edelbrock, Rende, Plomin, & Thompson, 1995). The extent to which adopted children of disordered parents or nonpredisposed children adopted into disordered families manifest disorders yields more evidence of the relative impact of hereditary and environmental factors (Braungart-Rieker, Rende, Plomin, DeFries, & Fulker, 1995).

Attempts to investigate the inheritance of mental disorders usually have involved serious conditions such as schizophrenia and, to a lesser extent, manic-depressive disorders. The research designs used have frequently investigated concordance (agreement) rates between twins, or incidence figures among children of parents with mental disorders. Although a vast body of literature exists, much of it is confounded by methodological weaknesses, particularly the failure to control for the influence of environment. However, because some of the studies used participants who were not raised by their biological parents, the results of the literature as a whole permit the formation of qualified conclusions regarding genetic etiology.

Studies of Twins. In a review of early studies investigating the relationship between family history and the incidence of schizophrenia, Buss (1966) found that although incidence figures varied, and studies with better methodological controls reported lower concordance rates, the degree of concordance between identical twins (67%–86%) compared with that between fraternal twins (3%–17%) provided evidence of a genetic component, but not exclusive of environmental factors. Studies done later show lower concordance rates, 46% for identical twins compared to 14% for fraternal twins (Gottesman, 1991; Nicol & Gottesman, 1983), but still provide evidence of genetic causation.

Research involving discordant identical twins (Gottesman & Shields, 1982; Pollin, Stabenau, & Tupin, 1968) found that the schizophrenic twins had other types of biological problems not present in the nonschizophrenic twins. The authors concluded that these conditions, such as low birth weight and soft neurological signs, might be related to the manifestation of schizophrenia. A more recent study of discordant identical twins (Suddath, Christison, Torrey, Casanova, & Weinberger, 1990) used a technique called magnetic resonance imaging (MRI) to examine the subjects' brains. They found evidence of reduction in the size of the anterior hippocampus of the brains of the schizophrenic twins. This result also suggests that biological factors unrelated to the genes may be involved in schizophrenia and helps explain why the concordance rate among identical twins is not higher. However, because it is likely that the cluster of symptoms classified as schizophrenia may be caused by more than one factor, this research does not negate the conclusion that genetics factors also are involved as causal agents.

Additional investigations of the hypothesis of genetic causation of schizophrenia have involved the offspring of the discordant pairs of identical twins. If genetic factors play an important role in the manifestation of the disease, the rate of occurrence should be significantly high among both the children of healthy twins and the children of schizophrenic twins. If environment, that is, being reared by a schizophrenic parent, is of primary importance, there should be significant differences in rates of occurrence favoring the children of the schizophrenic twins. Gottesman and Bertelson (1989) found an incidence rate of 17% for children of nonschizophrenic twins, which was not significantly different from the incidence rate for the children of the schizophrenic twins, providing strong support for the genetic hypothesis.

Parent–Child Studies. A similar type of research involves the incidence of mental illness among the children of psychotic persons. Gottesman (1991) reported that 46% of offspring of two disordered parents and 13% of offspring of one disordered parent developed the disorder.

More germane to the biological position are studies of children who were separated at birth from their psychotic parents. Wender, Kety, Rosenthal, Schulsinger, and Ortmann (1986) compared adopted offspring of manic-depressive parents with adopted children of nondisordered parents. They found the rate of depression eight times greater for the offspring of manic-depressive parents. Also, suicide was 15 times more likely among members of this group. This evidence of a strong genetic component is supported by the results of studies involving the extended families of persons with manic-depressive and schizophrenic disorders; the incidence of the disease is significantly higher among the relatives of patients (Kendler, McGuire, Gruenberg, & Walsh, 1994; Parnas et al., 1993) than it is among the general population.

It is wise to interpret these data cautiously, for although there appears to be an inherited predisposition to develop certain mental disorders, the full implications of the interaction of genetic and environmental factors are far from clear. Also, even for identical twins, concordance rates are far below the 100% that would be expected if genetics were the sole factor in the manifestation of a pathological disorder. Also, researchers have been unable to find any characteristic genetic defects among the psychotic samples studied. Apparently, the genetic predispositions that exist do not follow Mendel's law of inheritability through a single, dominant gene. Rimland (1969) has noted that deviation from the Mendelian model is not unusual in genetic disorders, citing similar patterns in inherited physical disorders such as tuberculosis and diabetes. The fact remains, however, that future research must seek to establish the specific problems in genetic coding that are directly responsible for the manifestations of these serious disorders. Until that occurs, critics of the biological model cannot be refuted completely when they argue that environmental effects are of significance.

Biochemical Etiology

A second line of research pursued by those who adhere to a biological orientation features investigations into the biochemical causes of emotional disturbance. These studies focus on the chemical processes that influence interactions among neurons and the metabolic functions involved in energizing nerve cells. The majority of such investigations have been conducted with persons suffering from manic-depressive disorders, schizophrenia, and, to a lesser degree, autism. Those pursuing this type of research have attempted to identify an endogenous hallucinogen, that is, a body chemical that might cause symptoms such as the hallucinations and disorganization of thought and affect that characterize schizophrenia and other psychotic conditions or one that might cause the symptoms of autism. The strategies used in this process have included measuring levels of biochemicals involved in neurotransmission in the bloodstreams of disordered and nondisordered people; administering hallucinogenic precursor substances such as tryptophan that converts to serotonin, a biochemical involved in neurotransmission; administering serotonin along with additional biochemicals that inhibit its breakdown into other substances; and increasing levels of substances that act to reduce levels of serotonin (Kane, 1992). Although higher levels of serotonin have been found in the bloodstream of schizophrenic adults and autistic children, for the most part the results of research involving regulation of levels of serotonin have been disappointing (Anderson & Hoshino, 1997). The mental states produced by the chemicals bear only superficial relationship to those associated with the real psychotic state.

A similar line of research involves the assimilation of dopamine, a neurotransmitter for a variety of brain pathways (Comer, 1999). Schizophrenia is attributed to an excess of dopamine or to too many dopamine receptors. Administration of certain antipsychotic drugs, called neuroleptics, block dopamine action and reduce symptoms of the psychosis. However, these drugs also reduce symptoms associated with other conditions, suggesting that dopamine may not cause schizophrenia but may amplify the symptoms once they are caused by other factors.

Biochemical causation of manic-depressive psychoses has been related to the level of catecholamines, a biogenic amine in the blood. However, many researchers regard the catecholamine-level premise as too simplistic, and more current research interest is focused on neuroendocrine irregularities and abnormal receptor systems interfering with neurotransmission (Thase, Frank, & Kupfer, 1985).

Although investigators are encouraged about the relationship between biochemicals and psychosis, as yet they have not established reliable evidence that biochemical agents are responsible for pathological mental conditions. The relationship between faulty biochemistry and mental disorder is similar to that of the chicken and the egg; it is difficult to know which came first. It is possible that psychopathology causes alterations in brain biochemistry, rather than vice versa. This possibility is substantiated by the fact that no differences have been found in the brain waves and biochemistry of people who have recovered from manic-depression and control groups of nondisordered persons. In addition, there is no substantial evidence of a relationship between biochemical factors and less serious manifestations of EBDs such as simple phobia.

Neurological Etiology

A third approach to substantiating the biological basis of mental illness involves the investigation of neurological disorders. From this perspective, mentally disordered people have malfunctioning autonomic nervous systems that predispose them to develop these conditions. One vein of this research involves investigations of the relationship between malfunctioning neural excitatory and inhibitory processes and inappropriate autonomic arousal, a premise first suggested by the Russian physiologist Ivan Pavlov (1941). More recent research of this hypothesis investigates perceptual and cognitive operations. A large body of literature documents deficiencies in schizophrenic people in visual tracking (Neale & Oltmanns, 1980), processing sensory information (Woods, Kinney, & Yurgelun-Todd, 1986), maintaining attention (Silberman & Tassone, 1985), and reflex hyperactivity (Kinney, Woods, & Yurgelun-Todd, 1986). However, there is no hard evidence that these information-processing deficits cause schizophrenia.

A second avenue of neurological research investigates the structural properties of the brain in various clinical populations. Modern computer procedures such as computerized axial tomography (CAT), magnetic resonance imaging (MRI), and positron-emission tomography (PET) permit these investigations. A CAT scan integrates multiple X-ray views of the brain to produce a single reconstructed image that enables researchers to study slices or cross-sections of the brain. In an MRI scan the nuclear magnetic movements of ordinary hydrogen in the body's water and fat are analyzed. A PET scan permits direct measurement of information related to brain function by scanning receptors of gamma emissions from selected areas of the brain.

A large body of evidence attests to structural differences in the brains of individuals with schizophrenia (Bornstein, Schwarzkopf, Olson, & Nasrallah, 1992; Cannon & Marco, 1994; Klausner, Sweeney, Deck, & Haas, 1992). CAT scan research first identified cortical atrophy, a reduction in brain volume characteristic of persons with schizophrenia. PET studies have identified abnormally low activity in the frontal and temporal lobes of individuals with schizophrenia. Decreased brain volume has been related to the severity of hallucinations, disorganized speech (temporal region), blunted affect, and low motivation (frontal region) experienced by individuals with schizophrenia. MRI research has revealed an abnormal enlargement of the brain's ventricles, particularly on the left side of the brain. Ventricles are hollow areas filled with cerebrospinal fluid lying within the brain core (Andreasen, Nasrallah, Dunn, Olson, & Grove, 1996; Cannon & Marco, 1994; Pearlson et al., 1989). The degree of ventricle enlargement correlated positively with cognitive impairment, negative symptoms, poor social adjustment, and poor response to antipsychotic drugs (Bornstein et al., 1992; Klausner et al., 1992). Although there is a slight possibility that these phenomena may not be causal but may be produced by the drugs used to treat schizophrenia, the bulk of the evidence suggests otherwise. Extension of this avenue of research relates soft neurological signs in children at risk for schizophrenia and ventricular enlargement in adults with schizophrenia (Cannon, Mednick, & Parnas, 1989), suggesting a progressively debilitating neurological process as the cause of schizophrenia.

In investigations of conditions other than schizophrenia, PET scans of individuals suffering from anxiety disorders have revealed irregularities in the portion of the brain stem called the locus ceruleus. No concrete evidence of structural alterations in the brains of persons with manic-depressive disorders has been established. Instead, several studies have investigated the hypothesis that abnormal brain waves cause these conditions. Thase et al. (1985) showed a relationship between abnormal brain waves during sleep and mood disorder. Baxter, Phelps, Mazziotta, Schwartz, and Gerner (1985) found variation in brain metabolic rates from subnormal to supernormal for depressed and manic states.

A related avenue of investigation into the neurological basis of mental illness focuses on childhood disorders. Several studies have shown a high incidence of neurological abnormalities such as epilepsy and pathological reflexes in children and youth with psychoses or autism (Comer, 1999; Minshew, Sweeney, & Bauman, 1997). Autism, a childhood condition characterized by impaired social interaction, communication disorders, and ritualistic behaviors, has been shown to have a definite biological basis. In a longitudinal study, Hashimoto et al. (1995) used MRI technology to document irregularities in the growth of the brain stem and cerebellum of persons who developed autism. Also, a reduced number of cells and reduced cell density in the cerebellum and limbic system were found in the brains of children with autism (Minshew et al., 1997; Pennington & Welsh, 1997). There is some evidence that malformations may begin during the prenatal period.

Other investigations of emotionally and behaviorally disordered children focus on brain damage due to prenatal, perinatal, or postnatal influences. Prenatal damage to the fetus may be caused by the mother's abuse of alcohol or drugs such as cocaine or crack, or by diseases such as rubella and acquired immune deficiency syndrome (AIDS; Armistead, Forehand, Steele, & Kotchick, 1998; Hogan, 1998). Some researchers believe viruses enter the fetus's brain and remain latent until puberty or adulthood when they are reactivated to cause schizophrenic symptoms (Torrey, Bowler, Rawlins, & Terrazas, 1993). Damage may also occur at birth, primarily due to anoxia, an insufficient supply of oxygen during the birth process. Later in a child's life, any number of events, such as accidents, illness, physical abuse, lead poisoning, or malnutrition, can cause serious damage to the brain.

The concept of minimal brain injury that was popularized originally by Alfred Strauss, a neurologist, to explain the behavior of children experiencing serious learning and adjustment problems (Strauss & Lehtinen, 1947) remains relevant for research into biological causation. Strauss noted similarities between many of the children's behaviors and those of persons who had suffered obvious cerebral insult. Those common behaviors, called the Strauss syndrome, included hyperactivity, distractibility, lability, impulsiveness, and perseveration. Although the term *minimal brain damage* is no longer commonly used, many of these characteristics have become associated with the disability category *learning disabilities*, a condition that has been attributed to some type of unspecified brain damage or malfunction (Hallahan, Kauffman, & Lloyd, 1996).

In addition, considerable research has been conducted on persons classified in federal laws as suffering *traumatic brain injury* (TBI). This term represents a disability category that encompasses children and youth with significant, consciousness-altering brain damage that has been caused by an external event rather than by a degenerative disease or congenital condition (Snow & Hooper, 1994). This type of injury may be caused by accidents or by abuse, such as that which occurs when a child is beaten or shaken. The effects of TBI can be extremely far-reaching and include behaviors such as extreme aggression, hyperactivity, attention problems, mood swings, depression, low frustration tolerance, and poor social skills (Deaton & Waaland, 1994).

Developmental Etiology

The last of the biologically oriented investigations of EBDs focuses on children's development. As has been suggested previously, delays in development can be caused by genetic and neurological factors, and they can also occur as a result of early deprivation. For example, malnutrition of young children stunts brain growth, causing permanent brain damage because the greatest brain development occurs in very young children (Amcoff, 1980; Brown & Pollitt, 1996). Additionally, infants who are neglected and reared without stimulation are subject to alterations in the physical development of the brain. In both of these cases, although the initiating factors were environmentally based, the ensuing and permanent organic damage justifies including these conditions under the rubric of biological etiology. However, the most accurate representation of developmental deficits is to regard them as symptomatic rather than causal. Although research supports the fact that there are developmental differences between children with and without psychoses, the differences are a function of the psychosis. Clearly, the various avenues of research pertaining to biological causation are interrelated.

Impact on Education

Superficially it might appear that the biological perspective has little relevance for education. The biological model does not focus on school events. EBDs are caused by organic conditions. School experiences have relatively little to do with the development of these disorders. In addition, the physiological basis of an EBD suggests that the teacher's role in diagnosis and remediation is relatively unimportant. Problems of this type fall under the purview of medically trained personnel and their associates.

Interestingly, it is precisely because of the focus on internal, physical disabilities that the biological model may be said to have a significant influence on educators. The principal impact of this perspective is that it frees social agencies such as schools from accepting responsibility for creating conditions that contribute to the development of EBDs. In turn, some educators feel encouraged to regard many issues pertaining to these problems as outside their purview. Any attention that is directed to the issue is focused primarily on students who disrupt the classroom. Children whose EBDs cause them to withdraw, behave passively, or otherwise internalize their symptoms frequently are ignored because their behavior does not disturb classroom procedures.

Critique and Summary

The popularity of the biological model has reemerged in recent years. Research into biochemical functions and the startling evidence of damage to the structure of the brain as a cause of disorders such as schizophrenia have created a great deal of excitement and renewed interest in the study of biological etiology. Research has also begun to clarify the interaction of biological and environmental factors. Although the criticism that, despite intensive investigation, few definitive relationships have been established between biological functions and most types of mental disorders remains valid, those who adhere to this model remain convinced that they will eventually produce explanations for most, if not all, EBDs. Generally, their position can be summarized in the following statements:

- Emotional and behavioral problems are caused primarily by physiological disorders.

- Atypical or deviant behaviors are symptomatic of internal biogenic pathology.

- The etiology of the behavioral symptoms must be identified if effective treatments are to be developed.

- Diagnosis and treatment focus primarily on the human organism.

- Social or psychological forces may interact with biological factors to cause the development of EBDs.

- Research into genetic, neurological, biochemical, and developmental factors is the primary avenue for understanding the etiology of emotional disturbance.

- Treatment usually involves drug therapy; psychotherapy is less essential.

- Treatment facilities often are medical centers such as hospitals or clinics.

Psychodynamic Model

Theories associated with the psychodynamic school of thought retain the basic premise that EBDs are types of mental disabilities. The most significant variation from the biological perspective is the emphasis placed on psychological processes rather than physiological or organic factors as the primary determinants of the problematic behavior. The psychodynamic school opens the door to the study of human behavior as something other than a component of neural synapses or organic lesions. Pathology is due to the functioning of an individual's mind, or, more precisely, the psyche, the reservoir of all psychological functions. Psychological processes or functions involve all aspects of individuals' mental operations, their thoughts, emotions, perceptions, wishes, needs, desires, and so forth. An individual's psychological development is dependent to a certain extent on biological or organic functioning as well as on learned events. Inherited potentialities reach fruition in one way or another depending on the individual's environment. These biological (genetic or organic) factors constitute a predisposition in the individual that, given certain input from the environment, results in the development of particular psychic characteristics. For instance, an individual may display tendencies toward depression throughout life but become seriously depressed when the environmental stresses are untenable. Therefore, it is not the genes or actual neural operations that predicate behavior, but the manner in which an individual thinks, feels, reacts—that is, his psychological makeup. Mental disorders believed to be caused by malfunctioning psychological processes are termed *functional disabilities*, as opposed to physiologically based conditions, which are called *organic disabilities*.

Although the notion that many mental disorders are functional conditions has wide acceptance at present, it is a relatively novel point of view. Psychology was still in its infancy in the early 1900s, and clinical psychology, the study of pathological behavior, was not a viable field until much later. With the advent of clinical psychology, greater attention was directed to functional causation of

EBDs. Previously, disturbed emotional conditions were viewed as physical disorders having an organic basis.

Freudian Psychoanalytic Theory. To a large extent, the eventual recognition of the importance of psychological factors in mental disorders associated with the psychodynamic perspective can be attributed to Sigmund Freud (1856–1939), the father of psychoanalytic theory. Freud, a Viennese physician, began his career as a neurologist specializing in the diagnosis of organic diseases. In 1885 he studied in Paris with the eminent neurologist Jean-Martin Charcot (1825–1893) at the famous Salpêtrière school. During that period hysterical neuroses were prevalent and there was considerable dispute regarding their etiology. Although many physicians believed that hysterical symptoms such as paralysis must have an organic or physical basis, Freud began to doubt that premise. He was struck by the successful use of hypnosis to treat hysterical patients practiced at the rival Nancy School by the physicians Liebault and Bernheim. He became impressed by the notion that the symptoms of paralysis associated with hysteria were rooted in mental rather than organic malfunctions. On returning to Vienna, he collaborated with Josef Breuer (1824–1925), who was using hypnosis to encourage neurotic patients to speak openly about their feelings. Freud noted that such relaxed, uncensored speech frequently revealed the relationship between the patients' problems and their hysterical symptoms. He realized that his patients lacked conscious awareness of that relationship, and from this observation he hypothesized the existence of an "unconscious mind," that is, a body of thoughts and ideas that directly influence behavior despite the patient's ignorance of its existence. In 1893 he and Breuer authored *On the Psychical Mechanisms of Hysterical Phenomena* (Breuer & Freud, 1957), a landmark presentation of the constructs that were to serve as cornerstones of his psychoanalytic position and inspire the work of his followers that constitutes the psychodynamic model.

Freud's perspective of the causes of disturbed behavior can be understood only in the context of his theory of personality. Despite the fact that it is a psychological theory, Freud's concepts have a substantial biological basis and attribute great importance to hereditary factors. Human beings are viewed as the recipients of certain instinctual processes that constitute the primary driving forces in their lives. These provide the underlying bases for growth and development. Of equal importance to personality development is the extent to which our inherited predispositions are shaped by early childhood experiences. The occurrences during the first 5 years of life are critical to development. The inherited or biological components of personality, that is, our urges and instincts, form the portion of the psyche referred to as the *id*. The id consists of instincts toward life represented by constructive sexual energy called *libido* and by aggressive or destructive instincts toward death. Because the id is concerned with the immediate gratification of instinctual needs, it is pleasure oriented.

Parental controls and regulation, which are internalized during early development, form the psychic component termed the *superego*. The superego is similar to a conscience, in that it is concerned with right and wrong. The superego attempts to curb the uninhibited urges of the id. In so doing, it often operates through the third psychic component, the *ego*. The ego is the most pragmatic portion of the psyche, seeking to compromise between the pleasure-seeking urges of the id, the repressive forces of the superego, and the realities of the external world. Because the ego is oriented toward reality and adaptation, it is the force that ensures the survival of the individual through the use of reason.

Freud believed that behavior was determined by the interplay of id, ego, and superego and that the result of this interplay was intrapsychic conflicts that could, under certain conditions, lead to emotional disorders. Thus, he viewed personality as dynamic, not static. Because the sexual energy that activates psychic conflicts emanates from the id, gratification of sexual instincts is expressed in stages of development. The first, or oral, stage is marked by sucking and biting (first 2 years of life) and is followed by the anal stage (ages 2 to 3), in which the child is preoccupied with his or her bowel movements. The third, or phallic, stage (ages 3 to 6) sees the child's interest focus on its sex organs, whereas in the next stage, latency (ages 6 to 12), the child seems to lose all interest in sex. The culminating step in sexual development, the genital stage (after puberty), marks the advent of sexual maturity.

From Freud's viewpoint, healthy emotional development was dependent on the appropriate gratification of needs at each stage of development. Conflicts associated with each stage must be resolved without stifling or repressing the individual, or else problems with adult psychosexual development are assured. In other words, children frustrated by overcontrolling or repressive parents are stymied in growth and remain fixed at an early stage of development despite chronological maturation. For instance, a pathologically dependent and ineffectual adult is fixed at the oral stage and is still attempting to resolve the conflicts induced by the parental rejection that occurred during that period of development. Two variables, *fixation* at an early stage of development and *regression* to an infantile stage during periods of stress, mark disturbed behavior.

Freudian theory depicts conflict and turmoil as the natural course of events for human beings. The conflict-generating interaction among the intrapsychic subsystems of id, ego, and superego arouses anxiety, a critical component in the psychoanalytic model. Anxiety is a form of "psychic pain," an uncomfortable feeling akin to fear, but more pervasive. Freud described three types of anxiety: *reality anxiety*, which arises when a person is threatened by environmental events; *neurotic anxiety*, which occurs when a person's id impulses threaten to overwhelm ego controls, thereby causing socially unacceptable behavior; and *moral anxiety*, which occurs when the person considers engaging in behaviors that conflict with the superego or moral values. Anxiety forces the individual to act to resolve the precipitating conflict if possible and to establish a more tranquil state of psychic equilibrium. Thus, when children encounter predictable and inevitable conflicts with their parents, such as the oedipus situation (when a boy at the phallic stage of development competes with his father for his mother's affections), they must resolve them if mental health is to be retained. The ego either copes with the constant anxiety-evoking stresses of conflicting urges by rational measures or resorts to irrational protective measures termed *defense mechanisms*.

Defense mechanisms are the means by which an individual protects the ego by banishing threatening or anxiety-evoking thoughts from consciousness. *Repression* occurs when a disturbing thought or event is simply forgotten, as when a man forgets being beaten as a child by his father. *Projection* involves the attribution of unacceptable attitudes and anxiety-evoking feeling to others, as when an aggressive child attributes aggressive behavior to classmates. *Sublimation* occurs when an urge, such as the desire for forbidden sexual gratification, is channeled to socially acceptable activity, such as high academic achievement. *Displacement* involves altering the object of a feeling (usually hostile), for example, displacing anger at a parent to a teacher. *Reaction formation* refers to developing feelings that are directly opposite to those that are threatening, as when a mother is overprotective and oversolicitous of a child she dislikes. *Identification* involves assuming the attributes of another individual (or an institution) perceived as powerful or threatening, for example, identifying with the class bully and mimicking the bully's behavior. *Denial* refers to the refusal to face an unpleasant reality, as when a child denies failing a test. *Rationalization* occurs when one offers a good (socially acceptable) reason for the real reason for behavior, as when government spokespersons claim that policies that deny special services to students with handicaps are done to protect the children's self-image rather than to save money. *Regression* refers to behaving in an immature manner appropriate for an earlier stage of development, as when a U.S. senator has a temper tantrum. *Emotional insulation* is an attempt to protect the ego by passive behavior or withdrawal, as when a child who loses a parent becomes apathetic. *Intellectualization* is a means of limiting affective responses to a situation by developing incompatible, highly rational attitudes about it, as when a deserted husband insists that all relationships end in similar fashion regardless of individual behavior. *Overcompensation* occurs when a person who perceives himself as vulnerable strives mightily to give the opposite impression, as when a puny person becomes a highly successful marathon runner.

Defense mechanisms are unconscious psychic events. Individuals usually are not aware of using them. The child who projects aggressive urges onto classmates actually believes that he is inoffensive and that others respond aggressively, just as the child who displaces hostility toward a parent onto her teacher feels real anger at the teacher. Defense mechanisms are used by people to protect themselves from facing certain unpleasant truths. For example, children who have been taught that it is wrong to be angry at their parents are made anxious by this anger. They release the tension and reduce the anxiety that the conflict induces by using defense mechanisms. Defense mechanisms do not completely block disturbing thoughts, however. Urges that have been denied conscious expression emerge when ego controls are relaxed, as in dreaming or in slips of the tongue. All people use defense mechanisms. They become indicative of pathology when they prevent individuals from understanding and resolving debilitating problems.

By far the most important aspect of Freudian theory is the notion that human beings are only minimally aware of the causes of their behavior, that is, that they are propelled by unconscious forces that are too threatening to be part of consciousness. These forces cause serious emotional illnesses that are marked by such symptoms as hysterical conversion reactions (paralysis unrelated to physical injury), irrational fears or phobias, compulsive rituals, and so forth. Such pathological reactions may have no obvious relationship to an individual's current environmental circumstances. A child from a seemingly happy family situation suffers from school phobia. An apparently successful career man develops sudden blindness with no physical basis. These individuals are not consciously aware of the source of their problems, nor can they alleviate their symptoms by conscious will. Psychic relief and alleviation of symptoms can be gained only by psychotherapeutic techniques that free thoughts and emotions that have been trapped in the unconscious behind a wall of defense mechanisms. In other words, patients must be helped to understand the underlying feelings that control their behavior. Therefore, one aspect of treatment involves encouraging patients to speak in free, unstructured ways about themselves. They must say whatever they think, without the inhibitions that usually characterize social conversation. Termed *free association*, this technique unearths hidden feelings. Patients are helped to accept these feelings without guilt or shame. As patients accept and understand the feelings, anxiety is reduced and pathological symptoms disappear. Another means of uncovering unconscious information is *dream analysis*. When people sleep, their defenses are reduced and their feelings find an outlet in dreams. Some unconscious information is revealed directly, but other types are represented as symbols that require interpretation by a therapist. The therapist also is responsible for making the patient aware of any *resistance* (i.e., inability to pursue certain topics) that might develop and for recognizing *transference* (i.e., displacement of feelings onto the therapist).

Freud's theories are important because they led the way in directing attention to the psychic determinants of behavior. Those who followed him expanded and altered many of his tenets and branched into fields of study that currently have more popular acceptance than do the original Freudian theories. One group of psychoanalysts led by Anna Freud (1946) and Erik Erikson (1947) emphasized the role of the ego in determining behavior. Erickson's concepts also stressed the importance of social interactions, as did the theories of Karen Horney (1945) and Alfred Adler (1963). In fact, Adler's social emphasis led him to depict human beings as creative, active individuals who consciously select a "style of life" that brings self-fulfillment. Obviously, Adler's clearly humanistic position has small resemblance to the Freudian concepts of irrational man driven by socially unacceptable instincts, demonstrating the diversity within the psychodynamic perspective.

That diversity is further represented by contemporary approaches that adhere to this frame of reference, some of which are termed *object-relation theory*. These theories have a strong interpersonal focus, emphasizing the importance of child–parent interactions. Images and memories associated with an important object (parent) are *introjected*, or incorporated symbolically into the child's personality. Theoretically these internalized objects can exist independently of the ego and cause inner conflicts. Margaret Mahler (1952; 1897–1985) contributed greatly to this perspective, pointing out that young children do not differentiate self from others. The gradual development of a separate self is essential for mental health.

Impact on Education

Although the dominance of the psychodynamic approach waned in the second half of the 20th century, its major tenets, such as unconscious motivation, anxiety, early childhood experiences, and defense mechanisms, continue to influence thinking (Target & Fonagy, 1994). As a disability perspective, the psychodynamic approach to EBDs is like the biological model in its impact on education. It too tends to minimize the significance of school-related events. Problems are developed during early childhood years before children attend school. Although those individuals associated with the psychodynamic model may be more optimistic about the possibilities of curative treatment than are their biologically oriented brethren, such therapeutic intervention must result in the understanding of unconscious motivation for behavior if treatment is to be successful. Patients must develop insight into their behaviors; that is, they must be made consciously aware of the reasons for them. Superficial treatment of surface behavior does not solve problems and may worsen the situation by leading to symptom substitution, the substitution of another symptomatic behavior for the one that has been removed. Successful treatment from this point of view is beyond the skill of educators. Long and difficult, it can only be conducted by highly trained therapists. Actually, the psychodynamic emphasis on the seriousness and intractability of emotional dilemmas may be in itself enough to encourage educators to adopt a passive demeanor and to confine their efforts with emotionally and behaviorally disordered children to outside referrals and social segregation through special class placement.

Critique and Summary

The psychodynamic perspective, particularly the Freudian principles, has been strongly criticized on several bases. First, it presents a rather pessimistic view of human beings as programmed for strife and unhappiness, either by their biological drives or their early relationships. Second, many aspects of psychodynamic theory have not been investigated scientifically. Therefore, the major premises regarding human behavior remain unsubstantiated hypotheses. Third, it emphasizes the examination of unconscious, underlying motivation as the path to mental health, despite the fact that such awareness, even if it can be assumed to be accurate, has never been shown to alter behavior. Although the tenets of this school are less influential than they were in the past, they still affect treatments. They can be summarized as follows:

- Behaviors indicative of EBDs are caused primarily by internal psychic pathology.
- Both biological forces and early environmental influences contribute to the pathological condition.
- Unconscious beliefs and feelings must be identified if effective treatment is to be undertaken.
- The individual is not consciously aware of the source of the problem.
- Changing overt behavior is less important than dealing with the underlying conflicts that cause the behavior, because surface treatment merely results in symptom substitution.
- Treatment involves reducing anxiety by providing insight into past conflicts unearthed from the unconscious.
- Treatment facilities are usually medical centers.
- Treatment personnel are usually physicians.

Behavioral Model

Behavioral theories offer a pronounced contrast to both the biological and the psychodynamic models. Essentially, this approach represents an attempt to make psychology a science, that is, to evolve scientific principles of human behavior through empirical investigation. As in the physical sciences, ideas or tenets must be tested experimentally to determine their validity. Such experimental investigation cannot produce definitive results if the tenets in question are based on interpretations of subjective experiences such as feelings, attitudes, and so on. Therefore, the study of human behavior must be consigned to directly observable behavior, not to subjective experiences. The behavioral approach focuses on one particularly complex human activity, learning. One major aspect of behavioral theory provides a basis for formulating scientific principles regarding the stimuli and responses that constitute learning behavior and is often referred to as *S-R learning theory*.

Obviously, the basic assumption of the S-R position is that human behavior is learned. Children are not born speaking, walking, or, for that matter, punching classmates. They are exposed to certain stimuli in their environments that generate these responses. Thus, human behavior can be understood only as a function of direct interaction between individuals and their immediate environments.

Although the origins of the behavioral model can be found in the work of Ivan Pavlov, its development to a position of prominence was brought about by the contributions of three American psychologists, J. B. Watson (1878–1958), E. L. Thorndike (1874–1949), and B. F. Skinner (1904–1990). Pavlov's (1941) monumental contributions to the behavioral perspective centered on his discovery of the conditioned reflex. He found that a neutral stimulus such as a tone could elicit a response such as salivation if that stimulus had been previously associated with an unconditioned stimulus such as food. Termed *respondent* or *classical conditioning*, this type of learning depends on the close association of the conditioned and unconditioned stimuli. Thus, food, an unconditioned stimulus eliciting salivation, may be associated with a tone until the tone alone cues the response; then the tone may be associated with another conditioned stimulus such as a light until the latter stimulus elicits the response, and so on. Learning is dependent on the temporal or spatial proximity of the stimuli; they must be contiguous.

J. B. Watson extended Pavlov's principles and maintained that all behavior, including abnormal reactions, could be "conditioned" by external events. He presented his position, termed *behaviorism*, in his famous book *Psychology from the Standpoint of a Behaviorist* in 1919. The best known demonstration of his viewpoint was "the Albert experiment," in which Watson and Rayner

(1920), his associate, proved that they could condition fear in a child. They exposed Albert, an 11-month-old child who liked animals, to a loud noise every time he reached to play with a white rat. After a brief period of time, Albert cried at the sight of the animal even when the noise was discontinued. His fear generalized to all other furry animals and objects. Watson believed that all psychological responses were learned in like fashion.

Although Watson's concepts had a considerable impact on the psychological community, two other major S-R theorists, Thorndike and Skinner, broke and tilled the theoretical ground that makes behaviorism more than an interesting compilation of information about human learning. Thorndike (1913) formulated the *law of effect*, demonstrating that rewarded responses are learned, whereas those with negative results are weakened. With this elementary premise he placed the control of learning into human hands through reward and punishment. Skinner (1953, 1975) used that information to emphasize the importance of manipulating overt environmental events and the futility of speculating about functions occurring within the individual. Their combined conceptualizations form the bases of *operant conditioning*, the behavioristic model that has had such a penetrating impact on education.

Operant Conditioning

Simply stated, operant conditioning involves a situation in which an individual learns to make a response to achieve a particular end. The eliciting stimulus is of small importance, as the response is determined by its contingencies. For instance, a hungry monkey may learn to press a lever if that behavior produces food. Its response has not been directly elicited by a particular stimulus; it has learned to operate or manipulate the environment to gain a satisfying reward. It has undergone operant conditioning.

Both operant and classical conditioning are dependent on *reinforcement*, or the strengthening of the new response. In classical conditioning, reinforcement occurs by the repeated association of the stimulus and response, thus strengthening the learned response. In operant conditioning, reinforcement may be a positive contingency, such as a reward. Responses that are not reinforced either do not reoccur or are gradually extinguished, a process known as *extinction*.

Currently the behavioral position can be divided roughly into two camps. Skinner was an advocate of the most theoretically pure position. He insisted that only observable and measurable events are appropriate for scientific study. He rejected the idea that internal psychological functions are matters of importance, because their existence can never be confirmed empirically. Furthermore, he argued that because the manipulation of reinforcements is the only method of changing behavior, speculation regarding mental functioning serves no purpose. By the proper use of contingencies, learned acts that a person performs can be unlearned and new behavior taught. He believed that this is as much as anyone needs to know to alter human behavior.

Non-Skinnerian Theory

Other S-R theorists disagree with Skinner's aversion to the study of mental functions. They are interested in intervening variables, that is, the unobservable events occurring in the brain that account for such mental functions as memory, cognition, perception, and so forth. Included among these theorists are Albert Bandura, J. Dollard, W. K. Estes, E. R. Guthrie, Clark Hull, N. E. Miller, O. H. Mowrer, R. R. Sears, and D. W. Spence.

Bandura's (1965, 1977, 1986) theories have had particular significance in education. His ideas, described first as *social learning theory*, then as *social cognitive theory*, include two important concepts for understanding EBDs, *modeling* and *internal reinforcement*. Modeling is a means by which individuals acquire new behaviors through vicarious learning, without external reinforcement. They are exposed to behavior displayed by another person and they imitate it, as when a child learns aggressive behavior from an aggressive model. Internal reinforcement is the visualization of the consequences of behavior through cognitive operations. External reinforcement is not necessary to shape behavior, because the individual "knows" what will occur. For example, a person who avoids skating on thin ice does so because she understands the consequences of the behavior, not because her mother will reward her.

Despite various theoretical differences among the advocates of behaviorism, all look at behavior as modifiable through learning. Although they acknowledge the existence of hereditary and developmental components in learning, they regard them as relatively unimportant when compared to environmental influences. Therefore, the essence of their position is that behavior may be shaped, removed, or maintained by changing environmental events.

Treatment of Maladaptive Behavior

In the terminology of learning theory, EBDs are characterized by *maladaptive behavior* (Ullmann & Krasner, 1965). Individuals behave in a manner that is not advantageous to themselves or others because they (a) fail to learn behaviors that permit a healthy or beneficial adaptation to the environment and (b) learn maladaptive or nonbeneficial behaviors (Comer, 1999). Maladaptive behavior is amenable to treatment through environmental manipulation. The application of S-R learning principles to manipulate the environment and treat disturbed behavior is termed *behavior modification*. The following are typical behavior modification techniques:

- Use of aversive conditioning to eliminate maladaptive behaviors by withholding a reward when a particular behavior occurs (e.g., denying dessert to a child who refuses to eat dinner)

- Use of positive reinforcement with substitute adaptive behaviors (e.g., rewarding a child for stroking a dog rather than pulling its hair)

- Manipulating the environment to remove conditions that may be reinforcing undesirable behaviors (e.g., instructing classmates not to pay attention to a child's tantrums)

- Use of modeling to teach new responses (e.g., demonstrating appropriate social behavior on the playground and reinforcing the child for imitating the behaviors)

Because the behavioral model is a deviance perspective, the removal of the deviant or offending behavior is the basis for treatment. Behaviorists are not concerned with the premise that the behavior might be symptomatic of an underlying problem and that the extinction of one symptomatic behavior might result in symptom substitution. Each behavior is evaluated and treated as an independent activity.

Impact on Education

As might be expected, learning theory has made a significant impact on education. First, educators respond to it because it is in one sense an optimistic approach. Although it certainly depicts human beings as mechanistic (behavior determined by previous conditioning), instead of possessing free will and purposefulness, it emphasizes the possibilities of change and growth through environmental manipulation. A teacher can do little about children's genetic defects, biochemical malfunctions, or unconscious motivation other than to help the unlucky children accommodate to their conditions. In contrast, the learning theory approach emphasizes the role of the teacher, who, by using the correct strategies to promote new learning, can change behavior.

Second, because schools are devoted to learning, they are obvious natural settings for effecting behavioral change. Teachers are logical agents to promote learning in affective areas as well as in the academic realm. For example, the classroom is an ideal social environment to apply the notion of learning through modeling the behaviors of others (Bandura, 1965) because both teacher and class members can model constructive behaviors for children with EBDs.

Third, the clarity, specificity, and simplicity of behavioral principles make them very attractive to educators. Specific maladaptive behaviors can be targeted by any diligent observer, and the effectiveness of altering the contingency of target behaviors can be charted immediately. Thus, the educator may bring about a fast, efficient remedy to a problem that might otherwise disrupt the learning of the entire class.

Ironically, the simplicity and popularity of this approach in special education may be responsible for the negative aspects of its use. Behavioral interventions have been applied as a matter of routine, without sufficient planning. Also, these interventions have often been designed to control behavior rather than to help an individual change. Thus, the outcomes in applied situations have not always replicated the positive gains reported in research studies.

Critique and Summary

Insomuch as the behavioral frame of reference has always advocated the use of scientific research to demonstrate the validity of its basic premises, it has received well-deserved accolades. However, despite the popularity and utilitarian aspects of behaviorism, some individuals are quick to list what they construe to be serious disadvantages associated with this approach (Comer, 1999), including the following:

- Its focus on oversimplified aspects of behavior such as specific responses to specific stimuli and its avoidance of dealing with more elaborate dimensions of human experience such as hate, despair, and love.

- Its failure to incorporate subjective experiences into its explanations of behavior.

- Its use of conditioning techniques to alter the behavior of others. Such intervention involves decisions regarding the superiority of one person's values over another's.

Regardless of criticism, the behavioral approach has had considerable influence on the treatment of EBDs over the last 20 years and has been particularly useful to educators. Currently, many behavioral principles are being integrated with other perspectives, such as cognitive or social theory, with beneficial effects. The basic assumptions of the behavioral model may be summarized in the following statements:

1. The source of the problem is not specifically within the individual, but is a function of interaction between the person and the environment.

2. The problem is not caused by a pathological condition or illness, but by inappropriate learning.

3. The inappropriate behaviors can be corrected by manipulating the consequences of those behaviors.

4. Intervention must focus on altering overt behaviors. Speculation about nonbehavioral factors such as causation, feelings, and motivation is less important.

5. Intervention must include consideration of those environmental components that relate specifically to the maladaptive behavior in question. Other information pertaining to previous experiences is of less consequence.

6. Interventions can occur in homes and schools and can be conducted by any individual trained to apply behavior modification techniques.

Cognitive Model

The cognitive approach to understanding EBDs emphasizes the importance of *cognitive processes*—the thoughts, ideas, images, and so forth produced by the functioning of the brain or mind—as determinants of behavior. Theories focusing on cognitive operations as a critical determinant of behavior have gained steadily in influence during the past two decades. Many of the ideas associated with this approach that pertain to EBDs have evolved from theorists who, originally at least, defined themselves as behaviorists. Bandura (1995), previously discussed in the section on the behavioral model, placed great emphasis in his writing on the cognitive aspects of learning and evolved an integrated behavioral–cognitive–social learning theory. His perspective highlighted the individual's ability to learn vicariously, reflect on and evaluate behavior, and predict outcomes. George Kelly (1955), another cognitive–behavioral theorist, contributed the concept of *personal constructs* to underline the importance of each individual's perception of events in the environment. He believed that the same events are viewed differently by different persons because each individual interprets them through a unique set of personal constructs. Therefore, environmental stimuli, no matter how neutral they appear, will evoke totally different responses in different human beings, including some that are typical of behavior associated with EBDs.

In a similar vein, Julian Rotter (1954, 1972) emphasized the construct of *expectancy*, or a person's belief in the probability that a specific behavior will lead to a valued goal. The stronger the value attached to a particular goal, the greater the probability that the behavior will occur. For example, if a child has the expectancy that completing homework will lead to higher grades, the child will do the homework, provided higher grades are a highly valued goal. Thus, the child's cognitions, not the simple relationship between the behavior and the reinforcement, affect the frequency with which the desired behavior will occur.

Like the behaviorists, the cognitive theorists emphasize the importance of learning in the development of personality. However, they also believe that thoughts not only evolve from events learned directly from environmental influences but also generate other thoughts, influence other types of learning, cause negative feelings, and directly affect behavior. For example, an individual who has learned to fear large dogs after being attacked by one (behavioral learning) thinks about the experience, extending the negative affect to all dogs. Although the incident may have occurred years ago, simply thinking about dogs causes feelings of fear and dog-avoidance behavior. From this perspective, negative thinking can cause or at least kindle most negative feelings; therefore, most behavior that deviates from the norm in a manner that is maladaptive for the individual and for others is motivated at least in part by false ideas, distorted perceptions, or illogical thoughts. Changes in critical aspects of these cognitive processes will affect feelings and will result in altered behavior.

Cognitive theorists do not discount the influence of heredity on personality development; however, it is not an important component of their model. Similarly, they do not concern themselves unduly with the assignation of disability labels. Regardless of diagnostic label, the focus of treatment remains the same—changing cognitive processes. Because thoughts, beliefs, attitudes, and so forth are not directly observable and measurable, these theorists depart from the traditional behavioral insistence on dealing only with objective criteria when attempting to assess and treat maladaptive behaviors. They use subjective information, including the individual's self-statements, to identify the erroneous or illogical thinking that is an element influencing maladaptive behavior. Although they are probing the mind, it is the conscious mind, not unconscious forces (as in the psychodynamic model) that is important.

Theories representing a cognitive approach to emotional disturbance illustrate their behavioral heritage in that they do not present global concepts that explain the organization and structure of personality, nor do they discuss the interrelationships among the significant components of personality. Although they expand the behavioral paradigm beyond classic and operant conditioning by emphasizing internal mediation processes, they are primarily concerned with the conditions influencing the acquisition and performance of specific responses. Like the views of behavioral theorists, the ideas of cognitive theorists are most readily accepted for their applied value, that is, for their usefulness in changing behavior in a pragmatic manner. Although theoretical positions and their respective clinical approaches vary, they are uniform in placing the major responsibility for alleviation of problems on the individual. The person must be capable of identifying through introspection the self-talk that precipitates or accompanies negative feelings and maladaptive behavior. The therapist may assist in helping the individual in these efforts initially, but the individual must take responsibility to attempt to continue to identify these thoughts or beliefs in various environmental contexts. Furthermore, the individual must be motivated to self-regulate, that is, to interrupt the thought process and thereby interfere with the ensuing feelings and behaviors.

Important Cognitive Treatment Approaches

An approach to treatment that has had a great impact on special education is Donald Meichenbaum's (1975, 1977) *stress inoculation therapy*, which has been successful in reducing anxiety and in increasing the coping capabilities of individuals who develop problems in stressful situations. His specific strategies for working with emotionally and behaviorally disordered children are presented in Chapter 6 on cognitive therapies. That chapter also discusses Albert Ellis's (1979) *rational-emotive therapy*, one of the earliest cognitive therapies. Ellis's basic premise is that a well-adjusted individual behaves appropriately because his thinking is rational, whereas an emotionally disordered person has internalized a core of irrational beliefs that cause him to engage in maladaptive behaviors. Ellis emphasizes the importance of teaching the individual to think more logically; thus, his approach has value for educators. A third important therapeutic approach, although it has not been applied directly in special education, is Aaron Beck's *cognitive therapy*. Focusing first on the treatment of depression (Hollon & Beck, 1978) and later on anxiety disorders and phobia (Beck, 1985; Beck & Emery, 1985), Beck also identified illogical thinking that causes problems. He wrote that individuals (a) selectively perceive the world as harmful while ignoring evidence to the contrary, (b) overgeneralize negative implications from limited examples, (c) magnify the importance of undesirable events, and (d) engage in absolutistic thinking that causes overreactions to trivial events. His strategies for treatment involve fostering cooperation between therapist and client to formulate hypotheses regarding key illogical beliefs, developing plans for testing the hypotheses in the environment, and planning further strategies to interrupt the illogical thought–irrational behavior relationship.

Impact on Education

Cognitive approaches have made extensive inroads in special education, not only in programming for children with EBDs but also in instructional planning for all children. The reasons for their applicability in schools parallel those that applied to the behavioral approach. First, because the cognitive model is primarily a deviance perspective, there is little emphasis on etiology. The implication that EBDs are caused by conditions that lie outside the understanding of educators is not drawn. Although certain of the problems that contribute to maladaptive behavior emanate from the individual and not the immediate environment, they are reflected in the child's thinking, a process that lies in the purview of teachers. Second, learning is important. Because children have learned to think illogical thoughts, they can learn to identify them and to prevent them from triggering maladaptive behavior. Such learning can take place in a classroom. Third, procedures for intervening can be clearly delineated for use in the classroom. Fourth, cognitive procedures can be used in combination with behavioral strategies for evaluating the effectiveness of each intervention plan in reducing maladaptive behavior.

Cognitive approaches have an additional attraction that behavioral interventions lack; they place much of the responsibility for changing behavior on the individual rather than on external reinforcement. The major question regarding their efficacy at this time is the extent to which children have the capacity to identify negative thinking and alter it in order to change behavior.

Critique and Summary

Cognitive approaches share the popularity and utilitarian aspects of behaviorism, particularly when applied to interventions in schools. They also share an emphasis on the use of research to validate premises. As has been noted previously, many of the principles of the cognitive and behavioral perspectives are being integrated in approaches to treatment. A criticism that is often applied to the behavioral model, that it focuses on relatively simple aspects of behavior, also is leveled against the cognitive model. In addition, it is accused of oversimplifying the cause–effect relationship between thought and behavior, that is, ignoring the issue of which elements among cognitions, feeling, and behavior are causes and which are effects. Finally, as Skinner (1990) reminded his audience in his last major address, cognitions are not observable and measurable phenomena and therefore do not constitute empirical data. His meaning is clear; attempting to analyze internal components (constructs) bears remarkable similarity to defining and measuring psychoanalytic concepts.

The tenets of the cognitive approach can be summarized as follows:

1. It is primarily a deviance approach, focusing on learned behaviors that influence interactions with the environment.

2. It moves away from the behavioral model in emphasizing the importance of cognitions—that is, thoughts, ideas, beliefs, perceptions, and so forth—in affecting feelings and behaviors.

3. Illogical or irrational thinking can be identified by examining self-talk, and its relationship to maladaptive behavior can be illustrated.

4. Individuals can alter their illogical thinking once they have identified it.

5. Interventions are closely associated with new learning and in many cases are appropriate for use in classrooms.

6. Teachers and parents may be trained to implement cognitive interventions.

Sociocultural Model

The sociocultural approach to the study of EBDs is concerned with deviant behavior produced by the impact of social or cultural forces. Much of the information used to construct this model emanates from the disciplines of sociology and anthropology (Muskal, 1991). These disciplines attempt the systematic study of people's collective behavior, that is, the development, structure, and interaction of groups of human beings, both in our society and across cultures.

A second important body of information integrated into this model is social psychological theory, which emphasizes the importance of interpersonal relationships to the development of personality. From this perspective, failure to develop satisfactory social relationships leads to EBDs. Harry Stack Sullivan's *The Interpersonal Theory of Psychiatry* (1953) and Alfred Adler's *The Practice and Theory of Individual Psychology* (1924) are highly representative of this perspective.

Individual Psychology

Adler's Individual Psychology stressed social responsibility and conscious choices in life. People are seen as creative and self-directing. Although they actively strive for superiority, they are concerned with the welfare of others and their strivings are of benefit to society. However, people with emotional disorders are unusually concerned with their self-esteem and personal aggrandizement and lack healthy social interest. Often they are excessively aggressive and seek to dominate others. Personality is shaped by the individual's unique perceptions and interpretations of environmental events. All children experience innate feelings of inferiority that produce either healthy or unhealthy compensatory strivings and the construction of unique life goals. Conceptions about self are gleaned from the attitudes of others and cause the individual to form a lifestyle or self-concept based on mental schema through which all perceptions of future experience are filtered. The healthiest lifestyle or self-concept is defined by social interest.

Healthy lifestyles are strongly influenced by a warm, loving relationships between children and parents, particularly mothers. People develop best when raised in a democratic environment that permits them to prove their value and explore their interests. Learning is influenced by the promise of success, use of reward and encouragement, and the implementation of social consequences for behavior that breaks group rules.

Interpersonal Theory

According to Sullivan (1953), the social forces that determine personality development are projected in interpersonal relationships. In the earliest stages of life, relationships with parents or other significant persons provide the foundation of an individual's personality. Parents, concerned with a child's socialization, communicate society's expectations of behavior and evaluate the extent to which the child meets those expectations. Feedback gained from these important social interactions contributes heavily to the development of the child's self-concept. Although the early interpersonal interactions are the most crucial, relationships throughout the stages of development also are important. As the child matures, feedback gained from peers and other associates contribute to self-perceptions. In other words, the individual's internalized views of others comprise the self.

The essential component of the interpersonal relationship is communication among people. In the absence of supportive, constructive communication, self-concept is inadequate. Early negative or destructive communication from parents raises anxiety in the child. To diminish the discomfort from the anxiety, the child develops perceptions of a "good me" and a "bad me." The greater the child's anxiety, the greater the disparity between the two aspects of "me." The precedents set by these early communications also cause the individual to develop mental images of others, called *personifications*. These mental prototypes determine how current relationships are perceived and account for the continuity in interpersonal problems. An unhealthy personification is carried into each new relationship, distorting perceptions about what occurs. As these distortions shape the individual's behavior toward the other person, they induce reciprocating behavior that confirms the personification. For example, because an individual with a poor self-concept expects others to be rejecting, she perceives herself as rejected in new relationships even when other individuals are nonrejecting. Ultimately, her negative behavior invites rejection.

The concept of *consensual validation* is related to the development of personifications. The probability of developing negative mental prototypes increases when communication about behavior is inconsistent. Individuals closed off from consensual validation do not receive reliable or valid feedback about their behavior and consequently develop distorted perceptions of reality.

The extent to which personifications are healthy enable two individuals to communicate openly with each other and to form an *interpersonal accommodation*. This type of healthy relationship between individuals enables them to meet mutual, complementary needs. Emotional security is dependent on such relationships. Social relationships that are not mutually satisfactory are generally not sustained, or, if they do persist, are unhealthy, because one person's needs remain unfulfilled.

Social Role-Playing Theory

Sullivan's interpersonal theory draws heavily from social role-playing theory introduced by George Herbert Mead in 1934. Mead believed that mental disorders were the direct result of an inability to play the roles required for successful social interaction. Theoretically, individuals define their interpersonal relationships in terms of social roles. Whether in professional or personal relationships, each individual has expectations regarding the behavior of self and of others. Inability to understand social roles limits successful relationships. Faulty role playing prevents effective communication, thereby isolating an individual and causing emotional problems.

Mead's social theories inspired a vast amount of investigation into "taking the role of others." An offshoot of his principles was the development of the concept of deviance and the evolution of labeling theory (Jarlais, 1972). Deviance, as previously discussed, pertains to the manner in which society's agents ostracize rule breakers by designating them as deviant and assigning some type of label to them. The essence of labeling theory is that the label itself carries *social consequences*. Theoretically, once an individual is labeled, she is characterized by that label in the eyes of society. Consequently, the behavior of an individual labeled psychotic, for example, takes on the characteristics of psychosis, because the labeled individual is under social pressure to assume the deviant role. In other words, society expects the individual's behavior to conform to the deviant identity. Behaviors inconsistent with those expectations are ignored, and consistent behaviors are overemphasized.

Anthropological and Sociological Positions

Further support for the sociocultural perspective is drawn from the work of anthropologists who study EBDs in various cultures, investigating the premise of *cultural relativism*. Although anthropologists generally agree that certain disorders (particularly those designated as psychoses) appear to be universal (Comer, 1999), they also offer evidence of cultural relativism by showing that there are higher rates of emotional disturbance in societies that place individuals under a great deal of stress (Sue & Sue, 1987). Also, sociocultural factors appear to influence what disorders develop and who develops them. For example, anorexia nervosa, an eating disorder, is seen only in Western nations, particularly the United States, whereas TKS (Taijin kyofusho), a psychiatric disorder characterized by intense fear of offending other people, occurs only in Japan (Carson & Butcher, 1992). As to who develops emotional disorders, research shows that emotional disorders increase among elderly people in the United States, where aging is perceived negatively, whereas in Ghana, where elderly people maintain their status, no such increase occurs (Feshbach & Weiner, 1986). Finally, there is the issue of how emotional states are interpreted in different cultures. For example, symptoms of depression common in the United States—sadness, unhappiness, apathy, and so forth—are viewed as religiously purifying by Buddhists (Kleinman & Good, 1985).

In addition to studies of other cultures, a variety of investigations have focused on our own society. *Cultural transmission theory* (Sutherland & Cressey, 1966), which grew out of studies of juvenile delinquency and crime, holds that deviant behavior is a form of social learning. Sutherland and Cressey termed this type of social learning *differential association*, in that the behavior an individual regards as socially appropriate is that learned from his closest associates. Deviance is perceived only with regard to the values of a larger community.

A variety of investigations have studied the high rates of deviance in certain geographic areas. Two hypotheses to explain this phenomenon are *social disorganization theory* (Park & Burgess, 1924) and *anomie* (Durkheim, 1951). Social disorganization theory holds that deviant behaviors increase as community institutions break down and no longer meet the needs of the citizens. Anomie is a state of discontent that results when individual needs expand beyond the point at which they can be met in a society—usually in times of rapid social change. Research supporting these premises (Blazer, George, Landerman, Pennybacker, & Melville, 1985; Dooley & Catalano, 1980) has found unusually high rates of emotional disorders in urban areas undergoing drastic social changes. Related research finds a disproportionately high number of psychotic persons coming from lower socioeconomic areas of cities and a consistent relationship between lower social class and mental disorder (Dohrenwend & Dohrenwend, 1982).

Current Theoretical Offshoots

The *psychoeducational approach* to understanding and helping children with EBDs draws from varied theoretical perspectives, including sociocultural theory (Brendtro & Van Bockern, 1998). Peer groups are viewed as primary agents for establishing and changing an individual's values and behavior. The goal is to influence the individual by changing the attitudes of the entire group through *guided group interaction*. The group is empowered as a problem-solving agent that provides specific members with feedback about behavior and proposes positive alternative behaviors. Because many children and youth with EBDs have learned to distrust adults, peers are far more likely to cause changes in thinking. A comprehensive system for altering attitudes, *positive peer culture*, which evolved from the psychoeducational approach (Vorrath & Brendtro, 1985), is used in residential treatment programs (Brendtro & Wasmund, 1989). Training in using positive peer culture is provided by the National Association of Peer Group Agencies (Kern & Quigley, 1994).

A varied tack currently associated with the sociocultural perspective involves the use of society's laws to provide the means of ensuring the rights of the majority of citizens while simultaneously protecting and assisting individuals, including those identified as socially deviant. Maintaining a fair balance between an individual's rights and the general good of the community is at the heart of this approach. The laws of major importance to this position are part of the Bill of Rights—the First, Fourth, and Fourteenth Amendments to the U.S. Constitution. Respectively, these amendments guarantee freedom of speech, religion, and the press; protection from unreasonable searches; and due process of law and equal protection under the law. The application of this legal approach to the issue of social deviance helps ensure that people who express their individual opinions in accordance with their rights are not treated in the same manner as those persons whose behaviors transgress on the rights of others.

Impact on Education

One implication of the sociocultural model is that schools are a part of the environment that contributes to children's EBDs. Although many educators might find this premise less than appealing, it has received considerable attention in recent years. At the most basic level, the ill effects of poor instruction, improper placements, or inappropriate classroom management strategies are obvious and indicate that successful interventions for individuals with EBDs must involve changes in school policies and teacher behaviors. Other school-related issues from a sociocultural perspective include the stigmatizing effects of disability labeling and the possible inappropriateness of instructing children with disabilities in environments other than the general education classroom. Also, increased awareness of the differences between the concepts of deviance and disability decreases the probability that children who display "atypical" behaviors are automatically thought of as impaired. For instance, individuals who speak dialects that vary from standard English are not construed as linguistically disabled, but simply as deviating from a traditional norm.

The final point involves the increasing emphasis on the social milieu as a significant variable in helping children develop and learn. The strategies developed by such ecological theorists as Nicholas Hobbs (1982), William Morse (1985, 1994), Fritz Redl (1959a, 1959b), and William Rhodes (1967, 1992), among others, are especially influential in the treatment of individuals with EBDs.

Critique and Summary

The sociocultural perspective shares its emphasis on the social milieu with both the existential and the phenomenological models, which are discussed in the following sections. It varies from those perspectives in its emphasis on research that documents the cultural forces that relate to and possibly cause the deviant behaviors that are indicative of emotional disorders.

The principal criticism leveled at the sociocultural perspective is that it fails to discriminate among emotional disorders, classifying socially deviant behaviors such as sociopathic acts designed to exploit others with the bizarre, irrational activities associated with psychosis. Critics also argue that the sociocultural perspective does not encompass the etiological differences of these diverse disorders. Much of the data associated with this point of view documents relationships and does not establish causation. Therefore, assumptions such as the conclusion that poor people who live in inner cities develop a higher incidence of emotional disorders because of the stresses associated with their lives may be erroneous. In fact, people with emotional disorders may be poor because they are incapable of holding a job and may gravitate to an inner-city environment.

The basic tenets of the sociocultural model may be summarized as follows:

1. EBDs are not pathological conditions existing within the individual.

2. Behaviors indicative of EBDs deviate from established societal norms.

3. Any individual, given certain community-based conditions, may come to be labeled emotionally or behaviorally disordered.

4. Certain types of EBDs appear to be culturally relative rather than universal.

5. Faulty communication and inappropriate role playing lead to deviant behavior.

6. A person's social milieu contains the significant forces that influence the person's behavior.

7. Treatment incorporates aspects of the social milieu.

Phenomenological Model

The phenomenological model exemplifies a psychological approach stressing the importance of phenomena from all experiential domains as determinants of behavior. Thus, it incorporates tenets associated with both the psychoanalytic and the behavioral models, but with a totally different effect. Phenomenology shares the behavioral concern with environmental factors but does not restrict attention to the immediate relationship between current events and behaviors. This perspective takes a far more global view of environment as the sum total of all events that shape human behavior. These events include the forces that previously shaped personality as well as the pressures of immediate situations. As in the psychoanalytic model, all aspects of human psychological functioning are important. However, unlike the psychoanalysts, phenomenologists pay small regard to a human being's inherited potential, preferring to focus attention on the use made of that potential, that is, the extent to which humans fulfill their heredity. Succinctly, from the phenomenological perspective the behavioral absorption with stimulus–response associations is an oversimplification. It ignores important components of the individual's internal functioning. On the other hand, the psychoanalytic perspective incorporating internal variables is found wanting because it is too biologically oriented and too pessimistic about human potential. The phenomenological approach is probably best described as a conglomerate of theories reflecting a general philosophic perspective of man, rather than a tight, concise set of behavioral principles. It also has been termed *humanistic psychology* because it focuses on helping each unique individual to overcome the constraints and fears that restrict awareness of current experiences, rather than on past events or specific disabilities. According to Feshbach and Weiner (1986), four interrelated principles characterize this approach:

1. The experiencing person is of primary interest. Individuals must be studied in real-life circumstances and described in terms of personal

consciousness, including subjective experience and self-perceptions. The approach is holistic, not focused on specific components of life.

2. Investigations focus on human choice and emphasize healthy functioning.

3. Meaningfulness must precede objectivity in research efforts. Topics should pertain to significant human issues, not small, easily investigated events.

4. The dignity of the person is of ultimate value. All persons are accepted as unique and valuable.

The single most unifying tenet of the phenomenological perspective is the principle of *self*, which has been an important concept in the work of two representative theorists, Carl Rogers (1902–1987) and Abraham Maslow (1908–1970).

Rogers's Perspective

Carl Rogers (1951, 1959, 1961, 1983) may well be the best known psychologist of the self. His theories of human behavior focus on the development of self-concept, just as ego development is a major component of psychoanalytic theory. From his perspective, self incorporates all subjective experiences, including identity and tendencies toward fulfillment of potential. Specifically, Rogers maintained that each individual is an independent entity with a unique identity or self-concept. Individuals' self-concepts determine the idiosyncratic manner in which they view or perceive reality. (Consequently, reality as an absolute does not exist.) In other words, perceptions of the world are unique because all experiences are filtered through the unique self. Reactions to reality, although they may appear bizarre or inappropriate to others, are always consistent with self-concept. Perceived threats to self arouse defenses that cause increased personal rigidity. Such reactions occur despite the fact that human beings are inherently good, purposeful, and directed toward growth and self-actualization. All else being equal, human beings will act constructively. However, a depressed self-concept can pervert behavior.

From this perspective, it is apparent that behavior cannot be understood from the examination of simple, observable events. An interaction as uncomplicated as a teacher praising a child may produce varied results, depending on the child's perceptions of the event. One child may find praise gratifying to his or her self and enjoy it, whereas another may view praise as insincere and be threatened or upset by it. The nature of the interaction cannot be appreciated unless the child's perceptions are understood. Because the child's perceptions are intrinsically related to the child's self-concept, it is the dimension of self that is the critical determinant of behavior.

The all-important development of self-concept comes about as a result of the judgments of others. Growing children internalize the values of those around them. Consequently, it is essential to the development of a healthy self-concept that children be the recipients of positive feelings from others. They must be accorded *unconditional positive regard*, approval regardless of the extent to which specific behaviors are disapproved or approved. Rogers differentiates between criticism of a behavior and criticism of the child, explaining that acceptance that is dependent on the positive or negative evaluation of a person's actions leads to the development of *conditions of worth*. Conditions of worth lead a person to lose contact with his real experience, behaving according to what he "should" feel. In extreme cases the individual may be unaware of his true feelings, a state of events that produces anxiety and blocks emotional stability. In short, unless individuals are made to feel accepted and loved and are treated with respect, they will lack strong identities and a sense of their own worth.

Rogers's view of the emotional distress experienced by children lacking a healthy self-concept is quite similar to that espoused in the psychoanalytic model. Such individuals are easily threatened by external events and develop excessive anxiety. Anxiety precipitates the use of defense mechanisms such as repression, projection, or rationalization to keep the threatening thoughts from awareness. For instance, the use of *denial*, that is, the failure to acknowledge the existence of a thought or event, protects the self. The defensive individual remains out of touch with the forces that influence behavior. Perceptions of events in the environment are incongruent with the perceptions others have of those events. The more depressed the self, the greater the incongruence and the more serious the emotional disorder.

Alterations in self-perceptions can only evolve from introspection and self-discovery. An individual requires acceptance and support from others to gain the trust required to risk examining incongruence in life. According to Rogers, each disturbed person must be studied as an individual. To understand disturbed behavior, one must unearth the singular nature of the individual's perception of the problem. Thus, treatment is client centered or nondirective, devoted to exploring the individual's views of his life situation and encouraging open expression without fear of rejection or censure. Individuals must draw their own conclusions regarding the wisdom or benefits of their behavior and make their own commitments for change.

Another significant aspect of the emphasis on self from the phenomenological perspective is the development of human potential. As noted previously, human beings are viewed as basically rational, cooperative, and constructive. They are motivated to actualize their potential, to make their lives as fulfilling and meaningful as possible. In fact, self-actualization is an inherent trait that influences or motivates behavior. Aggression, cruelty, and other antisocial behaviors are indications of pathology that result when an individual becomes alienated from society. Alienation and the ensuing distortion of an individual's basic positive nature occur when paths to self-actualization are blocked by environmental forces. Such behaviors disappear when the individual is redirected on the path to self-actualization.

Maslow's Perspective

Abraham Maslow's (1962, 1967, 1969) work typifies the phenomenological emphasis on the inherently healthy nature of human beings and their undeniable tendency to seek fulfillment and self-actualization. For Maslow, self-actualization represented the highest class of human need in a hierarchy of five basic categories that range from the lowest—physiological needs—upward to safety, love, esteem, and self-actualization. Lower needs take precedence over higher needs; therefore, physiological conditions must be satisfied first, safety needs second, and so forth before an individual can obtain self-actualization. If physiological needs are unsatisfied, other needs are not acknowledged. For example, if an individual is hungry (physiological need), she is not concerned with creative acts such as writing poetry.

Maslow maintained that the level of human need fulfillment depends on the extent to which the environment is conducive to growth. Although human beings can be stymied by and alienated from prevailing social forces, as environmental changes occur they can be encouraged to move forward. A high level of need fulfillment is indicative of emotional health, and Maslow insisted that psychology must focus on normal, healthy behavior to understand psychopathology. He attempted to demonstrate the properties of self-actualization by studying people who appeared to have obtained that level of need satisfaction. He described these individuals as possessing characteristics such as self-awareness, creativity, spontaneity, flexibility, and self-acceptance. Their lives, he concluded, were exciting, challenging, and meaningful. Although persons suffering from psychopathology display none of these characteristics, they are not abnormal or disabled; they are reacting to the obstructions that interfere with their psychological growth. Maslow deplored what he called the "psychopathology of the normal," that is, the failure of human beings to realize their potential.

As a consequence of emphasizing the development of human potential, the phenomenological position is greatly concerned with social values. Maslow

(1969) wrote that modern science is responsible for producing a "good society," because self-actualization can occur only under optimal social conditions. An individual's values must reflect her own thoughts and needs; they must not signify blind acceptance of existing social values. Society must encourage human growth rather than repress or attempt to modify it. From this perspective, human beings have free will and the potential to make constructive decisions, regardless of their previous learning and conditioning.

The humanistic outlook of the phenomenologists does not mean that they do not regard humans as capable of doing evil. The novelty of their approach comes from their emphasis on the human capability for good. They believe that it is just as accurate and much more optimistic to emphasize the positive aspects of human nature.

Educational Impact

It is fair to say that the phenomenological theory has had a relatively slight impact on education, even though its values are integrated into plans for progressive education produced by the respected educational philosopher John Dewey (1859–1952; Dewey & Dewey, 1915). Periodic efforts to reintroduce humanistic concepts in the schools have been made, and programs designated as "open education," "open classrooms," and "affective education" have enjoyed brief periods of popularity, particularly in the 1960s and 1970s. More current implementation of these principles can be found in the holistic education movement (Kauffman, 1997). The authoritarian structure of many schools, both in their organization and in their approach to instruction, tends to make the implementation of phenomenological principles difficult.

Adherence to a phenomenological approach would result in the following:

1. Elimination of disability labels as justification for providing children with special services: Children simply would receive whatever assistance they required to fulfill their individual needs and help them feel successful.

2. Curriculum and teaching strategies designed to enhance the development of a positive self-concept: Teachers would offer students unqualified acceptance and respect, separating rejection of specific behavior from rejection of the individual. Open classrooms providing diverse opportunities for children to pursue studies of unique interest would be used to promote learning.

3. Students' choosing to learn or not to learn specific material at any given time: Although their level of functioning in the area would be

noted and discussed, no negative consequences (such as poor grades) would follow. Presumably, individuals only learn material that they are motivated to learn. Information they are forced to study is quickly forgotten (as when students forget to use standard English grammar despite repeated efforts to teach it to them).

Critique and Summary

The principal tenet of the phenomenological position makes it unique in the body of theory discussed thus far. For the first time, human beings are depicted as purposeful, independent individuals with inherent integrity. Heretofore, theories have adhered to deterministic positions and described human beings either as machines programmed by their experiences or as inherently pathological creatures. The phenomenological optimism prevails even in the discussion of humanity's disturbed conditions. Not only are human beings consciously aware of their problems, but they also have the motivation and the free will to solve them.

Such a point of view literally begs for acceptance yet is subject to certain astute criticisms. First, there is evidence that individuals do not readily understand themselves and their problems. Their self-perceptions and self-reports are colored by their unconscious defenses. Therefore, their insights may be nothing more than acceptance of anxiety-reducing rationalizations. Second, inexperienced or confused persons may not be aware of the best behavior course to pursue. They may require firm direction to keep them from harm or to introduce learning experiences that they will eventually come to recognize as advantageous. They are not equipped to make sound judgments before they have those experiences. Third, conscious acknowledgment of problems does not always lead to behavior changes. Fourth, self-actualization is a global concept that, although it synthesizes specific components of human beings' motivational systems into a whole, loses specificity of meaning; in other words, although all behavior may be attributed to humanity's drive for self-actualization, little information about the specific impetus for certain acts is uncovered. To behaviorists like Skinner, self-actualization is simply a metaphysical concept, neither observable nor measurable.

Despite criticism, the phenomenological position provides food for thought as an alternative method of approaching the problem of EBDs. Some of the implications of the phenomenological position are as follows:

- Psychopathology is not an inherent disease; it is a response to societal forces that limit the development of self-concept and block self-actualization.

- Psychopathology stems from perceived threats to the self that elevate anxiety. Individuals use defense mechanisms as protective devices.

- Societal restrictions to self-actualization cause relatively healthy individuals to become alienated and emotionally unhealthy.

- There are no irrational behaviors; reality is perceived differently by every individual, and behavior is in accordance with those perceptions.

- Treatment, involving enhancing self-concept and increasing self-awareness, must be directed by the individual.

- Each person is entitled to select his or her own values and should not be judged or directed to abandon them.

- Self-understanding is the only means of removing the defense barriers preventing emotional growth.

- All persons have the will to make choices about the direction of their lives and the ability to seek redress from their problems.

- A warm, accepting, nonthreatening environment is essential for an individual to increase self-awareness and grow psychologically.

Existential Model

Existential theory is an outgrowth of existential philosophy developed by Søren Kierkegaard (1813–1855) and expanded by such writers as Martin Heidegger (1889–1976), Jean Paul Sartre (1905–1980), Albert Camus (1913–1960), and Martin Buber (1878–1965). The collection of ideas and theories of human behavior that may be loosely classified as *existential* are similar to those associated with the phenomenological position. In both instances the individual is depicted as unique, important, and striving for self-fulfillment. Similarly, EBDs result from the thwarting of healthy drives toward self-actualization, not from inherent or learned deficits within the individual. To understand a person's emotional condition, one must understand the forces within the society that shape her position in life. Theoretical differences between these schools of thought relate to the importance attributed to the effect of society on human beings. The existential approach moves away, to some extent, from the study of the individual's psychological perspective to the study of the cultural forces that restrict human development and growth. The existential perspective also represents a less optimistic view, both of human beings and of society.

From the existential perspective, the individual is perverted and tortured, confused by a culture that cannot be understood. The world, particularly the traditional mores and beliefs that provide the foundation for every person's spiritual and emotional well-being, is constantly changing. The individual feels alone and bewildered, unable to pursue the natural tendency toward actualizing her potential. Often the person reacts to this situation by abandoning the healthy striving for a free life and accepting a role as an unquestioning, conforming member of society. This decision renders the individual an emotional cripple, living a meaningless, anxiety-evoking life. The alternative, that of continued pursuit of self-fulfillment despite the pressures of society, is the only road to health and satisfaction. The individual is a free agent with freedom of will and must take the responsibility of making the most of existence.

Principal Tenets

One of the principal tenets of the existential position is the "will to meaning" (Frankl, 1969). This principle depicts humans as being choosing agents with the responsibility for selecting healthy values that guide their lives. Human values reflect the *essence*, or the inner self. Human beings cannot escape selecting the values that underlie their lives. Even a decision to conform to old social patterns reflects a selection of values. Value selection is a difficult matter because it varies with each individual; values that provide one person with meaning may not be appropriate for another. In addition, values must be socially constructive because an individual's life cannot be meaningful if it does not fulfill obligations to fellow beings.

The existentialists regard the individual's existence, her "being-in-the-world" (Binswanger, 1963), as defining "the human condition." The individual is not separate from the environment; the two are a unity. Conditions that diminish this wholeness, such as cold, inhumane treatment by social institutions, stress-inducing social interactions, pressure to surrender healthy values, and so on, lead to feelings of alienation and despair.

Another main tenet of this position is "nonbeing" or "nothingness" (May, 1969). Nonbeing is the opposite of being and ultimately is death. Existential theorists point out that humans are the only creatures aware of the inevitability of death. This awareness or "encounter with nothingness" generates "existential anxiety," the overriding concern about the quality of the life being led. Thus, throughout life we are faced with anxiety-evoking conflicts stemming from decisions over the direction of our lives. For instance, individuals may recognize the need to abandon a current lifestyle for one providing greater self-fulfillment. Such a path is invariably threatening, because it means less security and greater risk. Inability to take the risk elevates existential anxiety because the individual is aware of the meaninglessness of her current lifestyle and has rejected an opportunity to move toward greater self-fulfillment. Therapy involves individual value clarification. The individual must undergo confrontation, that is, face direct challenges to the meaning of existence. This therapeutic approach is often employed in groups such as encounter groups, where participants demand that members evaluate themselves openly.

Important Theorists

The theorists most closely associated with the existential position are Rollo May (1909–1994) in the United States and R. D. Laing (1927–1989) in England. May (1969) uncovers a basic principle of the existential position when he writes of existentialists' unwillingness to discuss persons in terms of forces, dynamisms, or energies, as is common in most psychological theories. To the existentialist, such terms are meaningless unless they are used in the context of the living being. To understand and help another person, the therapist must avoid focusing attention on information about the person, for example, his "problem" or the drives that cause the pathological condition, and must respond entirely to the human being as he exists in this world. Symptoms of emotional disorders should be viewed as an adjustment, not a failure to adjust. Anxiety is an appropriate state for a human being in a struggle against threats to existence. In short, the person must be viewed as a total entity whose behaviors, no matter how bizarre or destructive they appear, signify the will to strive for self-preservation and growth. It is the individual who ceases to struggle and slips into socially conforming roles who surrenders freedom and seeks oblivion.

The unconventional aspects of the existential model were extended by R. D. Laing. Laing (1967) regarded typical social interactions as being responsible for the pathological shaping of personality, describing them as nothing more than games persons play to avoid discovering their true selves. From most perspectives, social interactions are viewed as a civilizing process by which innately savage children are taught beneficial social rules and thereby "normalized." From Laing's (1967, p. 58) view, normalcy is society's desire to turn a new human being into a "half-crazed creature, more or less adjusted to a mad world." He saw psychosis as resulting when an individual can no longer maintain a false dichotomy between the false outer self and the true inner self. Such a person no longer attempts to deal with conflicting social demands, irrational social sanctions, and confusing life situations. Psychotic behavior is not irrational or indicative of illness; it is a meaningful reply to the absurdities of life. Laing (1965, pp. 99–100) wrote the following:

> What is called psychosis is sometimes simply the sudden removal of the veil of the false self, which had been serving to maintain an outer behavioral

normality that may, long ago, have failed to be any reflection of the state of affairs in the secret self. Then the self will pour out accusations of persecution at the hands of that person with whom the false self has been complying for years.

Impact on Education

The impact of this position on education appears more philosophical than practical. Technically, schools should be resources for the selection of values that result in the self-fulfillment of each individual. To establish this type of supportive environment in practice would require a redefinition of the role of the school in society. Schools are perceived by many people as institutions that encourage conformity and, from Laing's perspective, actively shape the half-crazed creatures deemed normal. Redefining education from an existential perspective would involve two shifts in philosophical perspective. First, socialization would have to be redefined. Currently, educators view socializing as a synonym for conforming. That is, they view the socialization process as one that involves teaching conforming behaviors. In so doing, they ignore the fact that truly social behaviors must reflect human nature. Acts that disrupt the status quo, such as fighting, dissenting, defying authority, and so forth, are components of human nature and are social behaviors. Disruption is a social process. Therefore, socialization must be dissociated from conformity, and disharmonious acts must be recognized as natural social behaviors, not indications of antisocial tendencies.

Second, the concept of normality must be abandoned. From the existential perspective there is no such thing as normalcy. The concept is a totally arbitrary artifact designed for the convenient classification of human beings. Individuals have varied types of skills, aptitudes, and competencies that reflect their uniqueness. There is no norm, no mean or average performance that represents a standard by which people may be judged. Educators must shed the notion of the mean and with it the related belief that deviation from the mean implies some type of deficit or abnormality.

The practical implications of changing prevailing ideas about socialization and normality are clear. First, schools would abandon grading, grouping, testing, and all other related activities that are either indexes of expected performance or evaluations based on those expectations. Second, the assignation of disability labels to children who deviate from the norm would be discontinued. The premise underlying labeling is illogical; it reflects the false concept of normality. Third, educators would provide opportunities for children to pursue unique learning activities by exposing them to a multitude of experiences within the community. Schooling need not be confined to a particular building; the entire community should become part of the school. Fourth, teachers would individualize children's instructional programs, that is, teach children at a level in keeping with their needs. Finally, schools would expand the curriculum to include affective materials. Children would be encouraged to recognize and freely examine the forces that really shape their behavior.

Critique and Summary

The existential position is a conglomeration of philosophical principles, but the primary message is clear. Human beings are constantly striving to find a meaning for existence, a means by which they can counter their alienation from society and their fear of death. Human beings are responsible for their behavior and capable of going to any lengths to sustain their principles and values. As is true of all other perspectives, the existential position is subject to certain criticisms. The first point involves the tenet that society dehumanizes and alienates humanity. It is argued that human beings create their society. If we are inherently programmed for self-fulfillment, why do our social systems remain so detrimental to our welfare? The second criticism involves the sense of pessimism that permeates this model. The overwhelming nature of the forces that repress human beings, as well as our obsessive preoccupation with death, constitute a picture not significantly less negative and depressing than the psychoanalytic approach, despite the existential acceptance of human beings as purposeful and self-directed. Third, many of the actual techniques for psychotherapeutic intervention advocated by the existential psychologists, particularly the group-encounter experiences, are novel only to the extent that they confront the subject and forcefully strip away defenses. As with other therapies that recommend the exploration of inner motivational forces, the existentialists accept the assumption that people can recognize their "true" underlying motivation and that dropping socially acceptable roles will aid them in discovering these underlying truths. Some behavioral scientists question the validity of those assumptions.

Although there is no uniform existential theory that pertains to EBDs, the following statements probably represent an acceptable summary of underlying premises:

1. Human beings become alienated because they have problems leading fulfilling lives.

2. Behaviors represented as indicative of EBDs simply may be appropriate indications of people's alienation from society.

3. Many healthy, nonconforming, or deviant behaviors are typically labeled *disordered* by the existing social institutions.

4. People are not inherently disabled, and deviant behaviors are not symptomatic of mental illness.

5. Effective treatment of problems caused by alienation must involve social reorganization.

6. Social reorganization can be accomplished by breaking down the social facades that encourage people to play deceitful, dishonest games with one another in the name of social interaction. Honest communication with emphasis on the real values of living is the means by which true understanding of self and others can be gained.

Conclusion

This chapter presented a discussion of seven perspectives explaining how human beings develop personality, how behavioral problems occur, and how such problems should be treated. Each of these seven diverse positions has proponents who adhere strictly to that one specific perspective. However, many individuals interested in this topic are more eclectic in their thinking and accept premises emanating from a variety of perspectives. Eclecticism (selecting the best in various doctrines) is a positive approach when it is based on a breadth of theoretical knowledge and when intervention strategies are consistent with the goals associated with a specific philosophical approach. Under these conditions, every program, plan, or strategy used to help individuals with EBDs, regardless of its theoretical frame of reference, would be carefully chosen for its proven effectiveness in accomplishing particular goals.

On the other hand, the haphazard use of treatments or intervention strategies, without regard for underlying theory, is not indicative of an eclectic approach. This type of behavior, documented as occurring all too frequently in schools (Beare, 1991; Grosenick, George, & George, 1988), results from too little information about the topic, acquired in a hit-or-miss fashion. Therefore, it is important that prospective teachers understand the conceptual models that spawn various plans or strategies for intervention or treatment.

An eclectic perspective is also useful in evaluating the validity of the theoretical perspectives explaining the etiology of EBDs. Consideration of the numerous diverse conditions encompassed under the rubric of EBDs suggests that their causes are myriad and that no single perspective can explain all causal factors. These relationships will become clearer as the various types of disorders are discussed in later chapters.

In some cases the eclectic process has led to the integration of certain aspects of major conceptual perspectives into relatively new theoretical positions, such as the psychoeducational approach (Brendtro & Van Bockern, 1998) and the social–cognitive–behavioral approach (Bandura, 1995). Undoubtedly, theoretical orientations will continue to evolve as premises are tested empirically and either substantiated as useful or found to be ineffective.

STUDY QUESTIONS

1. Select two theoretical models of EBDs that primarily reflect a disability perspective. Discuss each, noting their similarities and differences.

2. Discuss in detail the theoretical model of EBDs that is based on learning theory.

3. Discuss the theoretical model that depicts human beings optimistically and regards self-actualization as a basic, intrinsic motivating force. Note the impact of this model on education.

4. Discuss the various types of social forces that are components of the sociocultural model.

5. Select the model that you find most appealing. Compare and contrast it to the model you find least appealing.

References

Adler, A. (1924). *The practice and theory of individual psychology*. New York: Harcourt.

Adler, A. (1963). *The problem child*. New York: Capricorn Books.

Amcoff, S. (1980). The impact of malnutrition on the learning situation. In H. M. Sinclair & G. R. Howat (Eds.), *World nutrition and nutrition education* (pp. 304–338). New York: Oxford University Press.

Anderson, G. M., & Hoshino, Y. (1997). Neurochemical studies of autism. In D. J. Cohen & F. R. Volkmar (Eds.), *Handbook of autism and pervasive developmental disorders* (pp. 43–65). New York: Wiley.

Andreasen, N., Nasrallah, H., Dunn, V., Olson, S., & Grove, W. (1996). Structural abnormalities in the frontal system in schizophrenia: A magnetic resonance imaging study. *Archives of General Psychiatry, 43*, 136–144.

Armistead, L., Forehand, R., Steele, R., & Kotchick, B. (1998). Pediatric AIDS. In T. H. Ollendick & M. Hersen (Eds.), *Handbook of child psychopathology* (3rd ed., pp. 27–42). New York: Plenum Press.

Bandura, A. (1965). Behavior modification through modeling procedures. In L. Krasner & L. Ullmann (Eds.), *Research in behavior modification* (pp. 1–45). New York: Holt.

Bandura, A. (1977). *Social learning theory.* Englewood Cliffs, NJ: Prentice Hall.

Bandura, A. (1986). *Social foundations of thought and action: A social-cognitive theory.* Englewood Cliffs, NJ: Prentice Hall.

Bandura, A. (1995). Comments on the crusade against the causal efficacy of human thought. *Journal of Behavior Therapy and Experimental Psychiatry, 26,* 179–190.

Bassett, A. S. (1992). Chromosomal aberrations and schizophrenia: Autosomes. *British Journal of Psychiatry, 161,* 323–334.

Baxter, L., Phelps, M., Mazziotta, J., Schwartz, J., & Gerner, R. (1985). Cerebral metabolic rates for glucose in mood disorders: Studies with positron emission tomography and fluorodeoxyglucose F18. *Archives of General Psychiatry, 42,* 441–447.

Beare, P. L. (1991). Philosophy, instructional methodology, training, and goals of teachers of the behaviorally disordered. *Behavioral Disorders, 16,* 211–218.

Beck, A. (1985). Theoretical perspectives on clinical anxiety. In A. H. Tuma & J. D. Maser (Eds.), *Anxiety and the anxiety disorders* (pp. 183–198). Hillsdale, NJ: Erlbaum.

Beck, A. T., & Emery, G. (1985). *Anxiety disorders and phobias: A cognitive perspective.* New York: Basic Books.

Binswanger, L. (1963). *Being-in-the-world: Selected papers of Ludwig Binswanger* (J. Needleman, Trans.). New York: Basic Books.

Blazer, D., George, L., Landerman, R., Pennybacker, M., & Melville, M. (1985). Psychiatric disorders: A rural/urban comparison. *Archives of General Psychiatry, 42,* 651–656.

Bornstein, R. A., Schwarzkopf, S. B., Olson, S. C., & Nasrallah, H. A. (1992). Third ventricle enlargement and neuropsychological deficit in schizophrenia. *Biological Psychiatry, 131*(9), 954–961.

Braungart-Rieker, J. M., Rende, R. D., Plomin, R., DeFries, J. C., & Fulker, D. W. (1995). Genetic mediation of longitudinal associations between family environment and childhood behavior problems. *Development and Psychopathology, 7,* 233–245.

Brendtro, L. K., & Van Bockern, S. (1998). Courage for the discouraged: A psychoeducational approach to troubled and troubling children. In R. J. Whelan (Ed.), *Emotional and behavioral disorders: A 25 year focus* (pp. 229–252). Denver, CO: Love.

Brendtro, L. K., & Wasmund, W. (1989). The peer culture model. In R. Lyman, S. Prentice-Dunn, & S. Gabel (Eds.), *Residential and inpatient treatment of children and adolescents.* New York: Plenum Press.

Breuer, J., & Freud, S. (1957). On the psychical mechanism of hysterical phenomena. In J. Strachey (Ed.), *Studies on hysteria* (pp. 5–19). New York: Basic Books.

Brown, J. L., & Pollitt, E. (1996). Malnutrition, poverty, and intellectual development. *Scientific American, 274*(2), 38–43.

Buss, A. (1966). *Psychopathology.* New York: Wiley.

Cannon, T., & Marco, E. (1994). Structural brain abnormalities as indicators of vulnerability to schizophrenia. *Schizophrenia Bulletin, 20*(1), 89–102.

Cannon, T., Mednick, S., & Parnas, J. (1989). Genetic and perinatal determinants of structural brain deficits in schizophrenia. *Archives of General Psychiatry, 46,* 883–889.

Carson, R., & Butcher, J. (1992). *Abnormal psychology and modern life.* New York: HarperCollins.

Comer, R. J. (1999). *Fundamentals of abnormal psychology.* New York: Worth.

Deaton, A. V., & Waaland, P. (1994). Psychosocial effects of acquired brain injury. In R. C. Savage & G. F. Wolcott (Eds.), *Educational dimensions of acquired brain injury* (pp. 239–255). Austin, TX: PRO-ED.

Dewey, J., & Dewey, E. (1915). *Schools of tomorrow.* New York: Dutton.

Dohrenwend, B. P., & Dohrenwend, B. S. (1982). Perspectives on the past and future of psychiatric epidemiology. *American Journal of Public Health, 72*, 1271–1279.

Dooley, D., & Catalano, R. (1980). Economic change as a cause of behavioral disorder. *Psychological Bulletin, 87*, 450–468.

Durkheim, E. (1951). *Suicide, a study in sociology*. Glencoe, IL: Free Press.

Edelbrock, C., Rende, R., Plomin, R., & Thompson, L. A. (1995). A twin study of competence and problem behavior in childhood and early adolescence. *Journal of Child Psychology and Psychiatry, 36*, 775–785.

Ellis, A. (1979). The basic clinical theory of rational emotive therapy. In A. Ellis & M. Whitelay (Eds.), *Theoretical and empirical foundations of rational-emotive therapy* (pp. 17–34). Monterey, CA: Brooks/Cole.

Erikson, E. (1947). Ego development and historic change. *Psychoanalytic Study of the Child, 2*, 359–397.

Feshbach, S., & Weiner, B. (1986). *Personality*. Lexington, MA: Heath.

Flint, J. (1996). Behavioural phenotypes: A window into the biology of behaviour. *Journal of Child Psychology and Psychiatry, 37*, 355–367.

Frankl, V. (1969). *The will to meaning: Foundations and applications of logotherapy*. New York: New American Library.

Freud, A. (1946). *The ego and the mechanisms of defense*. New York: International Universities Press.

Gottesman, I., & Bertelson, A. (1989). Confirming unexpected genotypes for schizophrenia: Risks in the offspring of Fisher's Danish identical and fraternal discordant twins. *Archives of General Psychiatry, 46*, 867–872.

Gottesman, I., & Shields, J. (1982). *Schizophrenia: The epigenetic puzzle*. Cambridge, England: Cambridge University Press.

Gottesman, I. I. (1991) *Schizophrenic genesis*. New York: Freeman

Grosenick, J. K., George, N. L., & George, M. P. (1988). Public school services for behaviorally disordered students: Program practices in the 1980s. *Behavioral Disorders, 13*, 108–115.

Hallahan, D. P., Kauffman, J. M., & Lloyd, J. W. (1996). *Introduction to learning disabilities* (3rd ed.). Boston: Allyn & Bacon.

Hashimoto, T., Tayama, M., Murakawa, K., Yoshimoto, T., Miyazaki, M., Harada, M., & Kuroda, Y. (1995). Development of the brainstem and cerebellum in autistic patients. *Journal of Autism and Developmental Disorders, 25*, 1–18.

Hobbs, N. (1982). *The troubled and troubling child*. San Francisco: Jossey-Bass.

Hogan, D. M. (1998). The psychological development and welfare of children of opiate and cocaine users: Review and research needs. *Journal of Child Psychology and Psychiatry, 39*, 609–620.

Hollon, S., & Beck, A. T. (1978). Psychotherapy and drug therapy: Comparisons and combinations. In S. L. Garfield & A. E. Berg (Eds.), *Handbook of psychotherapy and behavior change* (pp. 437–490). New York: Wiley.

Horney, K. (1945). *Our inner conflicts*. New York: Norton.

Jarlais, D. (1972). Mental illness as social deviance. In W. Rhodes & M. Tracey (Eds.), *A study of child variance* (pp. 82–99). Ann Arbor: University of Michigan Press.

Kane, J. M. (1992). Clinical efficacy of clozaphine in treatment of refractory schizophrenia: An overview. *British Journal of Psychiatry, 160*, 41–45.

Kauffman, J. M. (1997). *Characteristics of emotional and behavioral disorders of children and youth*. Columbus, OH: Merrill.

Kelly, G. (1955). *The psychology of personal constructs*. New York: Norton.

Kendler, K. S., McGuire, M., Gruenberg, A. M., & Walsh, D. (1994). An epidemiological, clinical, and family study of simple schizophrenia in County Roscommon, Ireland. *American Journal of Psychiatry, 151*(1), 27–34.

Kern, D., & Quigley, R. (1994). *Developing youth potential* [video]. (Available from National Association of Peer Group Agencies, Woodland Hills, 4321 Allendale Ave., Duluth, MN 55803)

Kinney, D., Woods, B., & Yurgelun-Todd, D. (1986). Neurologic abnormalities in schizophrenic patients and their families: II. Neurologic and psychiatric findings in relatives. *Archives of General Psychiatry, 43,* 665–668.

Klausner, J. D., Sweeney, J. A., Deck, M. D., & Haas, G. I. (1992). Clinical correlates of cerebral ventricular enlargement in schizophrenia: Further evidence of frontal lobe disease. *Journal of Nervous Mental Disorders, 180*(7), 407–412.

Kleinman, A., & Good, B. (1985). *Culture and depression.* Berkeley: University of California Press.

Laing, R. (1965). *The divided self: An existential study in sanity and madness.* Baltimore: Penguin Books.

Laing, R. (1967). *The politics of experience.* New York: Ballantine.

Mahler, M. S. (1952). On child psychosis and schizophrenia. *Psychoanalytic Study of the Child, 7,* 286–305.

Maslow, A. (1962). *Toward a psychology of being.* Princeton, NJ: Van Nostrand.

Maslow, A. (1967). Self-actualization and beyond. In J. Bugental (Ed.), *Challenges of humanistic psychology* (pp. 229–245). New York: McGraw-Hill.

Maslow, A. (1969). Toward a humanistic biology. *American Psychologist, 24,* 734–735.

May, R. (1969). *Love and will.* New York: Norton.

Mead, G. (1934). *Mind, self and society.* Chicago: University of Chicago Press.

Meichenbaum, D. (1975). A self-instructional approach to stress management: A proposal for stress-inoculation training. In C. Spielberger & I. Sarason (Eds.), *Stress and anxiety* (Vol. 2, pp. 1–33). New York: Wiley.

Meichenbaum, D. (1977). *Cognitive-behavior modification.* New York: Plenum Press.

Minshew, N. J., Sweeney, J. A., & Bauman, M. L. (1997). Neurological aspects of autism. In D. J. Cohen & F. R. Volkmar (Eds.), *Handbook of autism and pervasive developmental disorders* (pp. 257–292). New York: Wiley.

Morse, W. (1985). *The education and treatment of emotionally impaired children and youth.* Syracuse, NY: Syracuse University Press.

Morse, W. (1994). Comments from a biased point of view. *The Journal of Special Education, 27,* 531–542.

Muskal, F. (1991). Sociological/ecological theories of emotional disturbance. *Journal of Developmental and Physical Disabilities, 3,* 267–288.

Neale, J., & Oltmanns, T. (1980). *Schizophrenia.* New York: Wiley.

Nicol, S. E., & Gottesman, I. (1983). Clues to the genetics and neurobiology of schizophrenia. *American Scientist, 71,* 396–402.

Park, R., & Burgess, E. (1924). *The city.* Chicago: University of Chicago Press.

Parnas, J., Cannon, T., Jacobsen, B., Schulsinger, H., Schulsinger, F., & Mednick, S. (1993). Lifetime DSM–IIIR diagnostic outcomes in the offspring of schizophrenic mothers. *Archives of General Psychiatry, 50,* 707–714.

Pavlov, I. (1941). *Conditioned reflexes and psychiatry.* New York: International Universities Press.

Pearlson, G., Kim, W., Kubos, K., Moberg, P., Jayaram, G., Bascom, M., Chase, G., Goldfinger, A., & Tune, L. (1989). Ventricle-brain ratio, computed tomographic density, and brain area in 50 schizophrenics. *Archives of General Psychiatry, 46,* 690–697.

Pennington, B. F., & Welsh, M. (1997). Neuropsychology and developmental psychopathology. In D. Cicchetti & D. J. Cohen (Eds.), *Developmental psychopathology* (pp. 458–490). New York: Wiley.

Plomin, R. (1994). Genetic research and identification of environmental influences. *Journal of Child Psychology and Psychiatry, 35,* 817–834.

Plomin, R. (1995). Genetics and children's experiences in the family. *Journal of Child Psychology and Psychiatry, 36*, 33–68.

Plomin, R., & Rutter, M. (1998). Child development, molecular genetics, and what to do with genes when they are found. *Child Development, 69*, 1223–1242.

Pollin, W., Stabenau, J., & Tupin, J. (1968). Family studies with identical twins discordant for schizophrenia. *Psychiatry, 28*, 60–78.

Redl, F. (1959a). The concept of a therapeutic milieu. *American Journal of Orthopsychiatry, 29*, 721–734.

Redl, F. (1959b). The concept of the life space interview. *American Journal of Orthopsychiatry, 29*, 1–18.

Rhodes, W. (1967). The disturbed child, a problem in ecological management. *Exceptional Children, 39*, 449–455.

Rhodes, W. C. (1992). Navigating the paradigm change. *Journal of Emotional and Behavioral Problems, 1*(2), 28–34.

Rimland, B. (1969). Psychogenesis versus biogenesis: The issues and the evidence. In S. C. Plog and R. B. Edgerton (Eds.), *Changing perspectives in mental illness* (pp. 447–460). New York: Holt, Rinehart & Winston.

Rogers, C. (1951). *Client centered therapy*. Boston: Houghton Mifflin.

Rogers, C. (1959). A theory of therapy, personality and interpersonal relationships, as developed in the client-centered framework. In S. Kock (Ed.), *Psychology, a study of science* (pp. 39–68). New York: McGraw-Hill.

Rogers, C. (1961). *On becoming a person*. Boston: Houghton Mifflin.

Rogers, C. (1983). *Freedom to learn for the 80s*. Columbus, OH: Merrill.

Rotter, J. (1954). *Social learning and clinical psychology*. Englewood Cliffs, NJ: Prentice Hall.

Rotter, J. (1972). *Applications of a social learning theory of personality*. New York: Holt.

Rutter, M. (1995). Clinical implications of attachment concepts: Retrospect and prospect. *Journal of Child Psychiatry and Psychology, 36*, 549–571.

Silberman, E., & Tassone, E. (1985). The Israeli high-risk study: Statistical overview and discussion. *Schizophrenia Bulletin, 11*, 138–145.

Skinner, B. (1953). *Science and human behavior*. New York: Macmillan.

Skinner, B. (1975). *Beyond freedom and dignity*. New York: Knopf.

Skinner, B. (1990). Can psychology be a science of mind? *American Psychologist, 45*, 1206–1210.

Snow, J. H., & Hooper, S. R. (1994). *Pediatric traumatic brain injury*. Thousand Oaks, CA: Sage.

Strauss, A., & Lehtinin, L. (1947). *Psychopathology and education of the brain injured child*. New York: Grune & Stratton.

Suddath, R., Christison, G., Torrey, E., Casanova, M., & Weinberger, D. (1990). Anatomical abnormalities in the brains of monozygotic twins discordant for schizophrenia. *New England Journal of Medicine, 322*, 789–794.

Sue, D., & Sue, S. (1987). Cultural factors in the clinical assessment of Asian Americans. *Journal of Consulting Clinical Psychology, 55*, 479–487.

Sullivan, H. (1953). *The interpersonal theory of psychiatry*. New York: Norton.

Sutherland, E., & Cressey, D. (1966). *Principles of criminology*. Philadelphia: Lippincott.

Target, M., & Fonagy, P. (1994). The efficacy of psychoanalysis for children: Prediction of outcome in a developmental context. *Journal of the American Academy of Child and Adolescent Psychiatry, 33*, 1133–1144.

Thase, M., Frank, E., & Kupfer, D. (1985). Biological processes in major depression. In E. E. Beckman & W. R. Leber (Eds.), Handbook of depression: Treatment, assessment, and research (pp. 107–128). Homewood, IL: Dorsey Press.

Thorndike, E. L. (1913). The psychology of learning. New York: Teachers College Press.

Torrey, E. F., Bowler, A. E., Rawlins, R., & Terrazas, A. (1993). Seasonality of schizophrenia and stillbirths. Schizophrenia Bulletin, 19(3), 551–562.

Ullmann, L., & Krasner, L. (Eds.). (1965). Case studies in behavior modification. New York: Holt, Rinehart & Winston.

Vorrath, H., & Brendtro, L. (1985). Positive peer culture (2nd ed.). New York: Aldine du Gruyter.

Watson, J. B. (1919). Psychology from the standpoint of a behaviorist. New York: Norton.

Watson, J. B., & Rayner, R. (1920). Conditioned emotional reactions. Journal of Experimental Psychology, 3, 1–14.

Wender, P., Kety, S., Rosenthal, D., Schulsinger, F., & Ortmann, J. (1986). Psychiatric disorders in the biological and adoptive families of adopted individuals with affective disorders. Archives of General Psychiatry, 43, 923–929.

Woods, B., Kinney, D., & Yurgelun-Todd, D. (1986). Neurologic abnormalities in schizophrenic patients and their families: I. Comparison of schizophrenic, bipolar, and substance abuse patients and normal controls. Archives of General Psychiatry, 43, 657–663.

PART

II

IDENTIFICATION OF EMOTIONAL AND BEHAVIORAL DISORDERS IN CHILDREN

C H A P T E R

3

EMOTIONAL AND BEHAVIORAL DISORDERS IN CHILDREN AND ADOLESCENTS

Introduction

Full recognition of the number and types of emotional and behavioral disorders (EBDs) experienced by children and adolescents is a relatively recent phenomenon. One mark of such recognition is the advent of a new field, *developmental psychopathology* (Wenar, 1990), that deals specifically with these disorders. The need for this increased emphasis is readily apparent. The Office of Technology Assessment (1986) estimated that between 12% and 15% of American children suffer from some type of psychopathological disorder. In cross-cultural studies involving four different foreign countries, prevalence rates, that is, the number or percentage of cases in a population at any specific time, varied from 18% to 26% (Verhulst & Koot, 1992). Although these figures vary from country to country, possibly because of methodological differences in research designs, prevalence figures of 15% to 20% have gained relatively wide acceptance (Costello & Angold, 1995; Weist, 1997). The impact of these statistics is increased by evidence that few of these children and youth receive appropriate treatment. Weist estimated that less than one third of the individuals with EBDs receive sufficient treatment, and Leaf (1996), in a study encompassing four sites in the United States, found that approximately 25% of young people with disorders received mental health services. The significance of this information has helped to increase professional interest in the study of outcomes, that is, the availability of treatment (Epstein, Kutash, & Duchnowski, 1998).

Increased nationwide attention to outcomes is expected to produce more effective treatment options.

Impact of Development

The identification and treatment of EBDs experienced by children and youth is made considerably more complex by the differences in development that separate children from adolescents and adolescents from adults. The following points illustrate how developmental differences affect the manifestation of EBDs among these groups.

1. *There is variation in the clinical patterns for specific disorders according to age.* For instance, anxiety disorders are experienced by children and adults; however, fear of separation from parents is a common manifestation among children. Also, pathological depression is found in all age groups; however, the suicidal impulses commonly associated with adolescent and adult depression usually are not present in childhood depression (Comer, 1999). In addition, many of the symptoms associated with a disorder manifested in childhood, such as attention-deficit/hyperactivity, do not persist into adulthood.

2. *There is an important relationship between age at symptom onset and specific types of problems* (Cantwell & Rutter, 1994). For example, pervasive developmental disorders (PDDs) such as autism, Rett's disorder, and Asperger syndrome onset prior to 36 months of age (Simpson & Zionts, 2000). Other disorders, such as bipolar mood disorder, anorexia, and drug abuse, usually onset with adolescence (Kazdin, 1993).

3. *Children's behavior must be considered in reference to typical problems associated with specific developmental stages.* Psychologists have identified developmental trends in children that pertain to the display of emotions such as anger, fear, and sadness; the cognitive operations that determine behavior, such as ideas of causality, egocentric thinking, and reality testing; the tendencies to display behaviors such as aggression; and the ability to engage in social relationships. The issue of age appropriateness is always a critical consideration in deciding when thoughts and behaviors are indicative of EBDs. Adults unfamiliar with typical, age-appropriate behavior may erroneously identify "problems" that will disappear with age (Verhulst & van der Ende, 1997).

4. *Childhood disorders are often more transitory than those exhibited later in life.* Children lack the rigid personality structure characteristic of adults. Their self-concepts are less stable, and they have had fewer experiences with the realities of living. Consequently, they may perceive an event as more threatening and stressful than an adult would perceive it and have difficulty coping. Although they react disproportionately to immediate incidents and are easily upset by

minor problems, they also tend to recover from emotional upheavals more readily than adults. Therefore, what appears to be a major emotional problem may respond readily to treatment and have a relatively short duration.

5. *It is frequently easier to identify the pattern of psychopathology among adults than it is to discern specific disorders in children.* Children may lack the verbal skills necessary to communicate information that would lead to effective diagnosis of their conditions. Also, they may mask reactions such as depression through acting-out behaviors such as disobedience and running away (Leese, 1968). As children mature, their emotional responses become more differentiated and more consistent.

Classification of Disorders

In Chapter 1, several different types of systems used to classify EBDs were discussed. One system, associated with a disability or medical perspective, involves psychiatric categories of mental diseases and is presented in the latest edition of the *Diagnostic and Statistical Manual of Mental Disorders* (DSM–IV; American Psychiatric Association [APA], 1994). Another system reflects an empirical rather than a clinical approach and is based on the use of research to identify behavioral syndromes typical of individuals with certain types of problems.

Much has been written about the weaknesses of the DSM–IV approach. Problems exist with both interrater reliability (Silverman, 1994), as when an individual is classified differently by different raters, and categorical integrity (Malcarne & Ingram, 1994), as when the same attributes pertain to multiple diagnostic categories and individuals therefore meet the criteria for multiple disorders. Also, these psychiatric categories usually have few implications for treatment (Achenbach, 1985; Merrell, 1994). Despite these weaknesses and the fact that psychiatric categories do not usually determine eligibility for special education, the DSM–IV classification system is widely used and educators should be familiar with it. Consequently, it is used in this book as the primary structure for the ensuing discussion of specific EBDs. In addition, some reference is made to diagnostic categories derived by empirical methods.

Schizophrenia and Pervasive Developmental Disorders

History has been witness to a great deal of confusion over the terms *schizophrenia, autism,* and *pervasive developmental disorder.* A brief discussion of these terms to attempt to simplify matters is in order. Schizophrenia, the oldest of the three terms, was originally applied to adult psychotic disorders. Kraepelin and Bleuler, the men who originally identified the disorders known as schizophrenia in adults, also reported cases that originated in childhood (Cantor, 1988). Subsequently, studies of schizophrenic-like conditions in children commenced and the term *childhood schizophrenia* gained common usage (Rutter & Schopler, 1987). As investigations continued, however, evidence of significant differences between certain psychotic-like childhood conditions and schizophrenia emerged. Other diagnostic labels, particularly the term *autism*, were used with greater clinical accuracy and the term *childhood schizophrenia* was used less frequently. However, the condition known as childhood schizophrenia exists and is diagnosed when symptoms occur by age 12. The symptoms parallel those associated with schizophrenia in adults or adolescents and, when occurring in childhood, usually persist into adolescence and adulthood (J. R. Asarnow & Asarnow, 1996). As was noted in Chapter 1, schizophrenia is included in the federal law as a type of serious emotional disturbance.

In 1943 Leo Kanner identified autism, or "early infantile autism," as a different syndrome from childhood psychosis. The term *autism* denotes the primary characteristic of the disorder, an inability to relate to people, observable very early in life. Despite Kanner's efforts, other individuals often considered the autistic syndrome to be an early manifestation of childhood psychosis or childhood schizophrenia. In recent years, autism has ceased to be considered a psychosis, primarily because identified children, as they mature, do not display hallucinations or delusions. Autism is acknowledged as a neurological disorder that adversely affects various aspects of development, including social skills and communication ability. In 1980 the DSM category *pervasive developmental disorders* (PDD) was created to encompass autism, Asperger's disorder, Rett's disorder, and childhood disintegrative disorder. The federal government excludes autism from the category of serious emotional disturbance and assigns it to a category of its own.

PDD is a category in DSM–IV that includes conditions marked by "severe and pervasive impairment in several areas of development: reciprocal social interaction skills, communication skills, or the presence of stereotyped behavior, interests, and activities" (p. 65). Autism is the best known of the disorders in this category, and on occasion *pervasive developmental disorder* has been used inappropriately as a synonym for *autism*.

Schizophrenia

Schizophrenia is a term used to describe a variety of psychotic conditions. Psychotic conditions are characterized primarily by a loss of contact with reality, as revealed by delusional beliefs (false ideas such as believing you are God), by hallucinations (bizarre sensory perceptions such as hearing God speak to you), and by disorganized speech (bizarre, disassociated speech that reflects bizarre cognition). Although the term *schizophrenia*, coined in 1911 by the Swiss psychiatrist Eugen Bleuler (1950), means "split mind," it refers to the disorganization of thought processes that is characteristic of afflicted persons, not to manifestations of multiple personalities such as those displayed in the films *The Three Faces of Eve* (1957) and *Sybil* (1976).

Characteristics. The DSM–IV lists five major features of schizophrenia: delusions, hallucinations, disorganized speech, disorganized or catatonic behavior, and negative symptoms such as diminished affect, speech content, and goal-directed activities. As mentioned previously, the first three features are also characteristics of psychosis. Disorganized or catatonic behavior is a broad symptom category including behavior such as extreme silliness or agitation, lack of personal hygiene, bizarre motor responses, and catatonic or rigid body posture. These four behaviors are considered *positive symptoms* of the disorders because they do not occur in the typical population. The *negative symptoms* associated with schizophrenic disorders, such as disassociation from daily events, seclusiveness, lack of emotional responsiveness, and inappropriate social behavior are so named because they indicate failure to display behaviors that occur normally. Although these two patterns of symptoms have been referred to in the literature as reactive or positive-symptom schizophrenia and process or negative-symptom schizophrenia, respectively (Andreasen, 1985), it now appears that many afflicted individuals display both types of symptoms (Guelfi, Faustman, & Csernansky, 1989; Kendler, McGuire, Gruenberg, & Walsh, 1994). Carson and Butcher (1992) elaborated on the most persistent characteristics of schizophrenic conditions:

1. *Disturbances of thought,* characterized by delusions such as the belief that one's thoughts are controlled by an evil force (thought control and persecution), that one is the brilliant mind behind government policy (grandiosity), or that a speech by the president of the United States has a specific, ominous, personal meaning (idea of reference)

2. *Deterioration of daily functioning,* marked by reduced efficiency at work or school, as when a good student begins to fail in every subject, and lack of self-care, as when a meticulous individual stops bathing or wearing clean clothing

3. *Disturbances of language,* characterized by *alogia* (a decrease in language usage or poverty of content in usage), by the use of neologisms (new words with obscure meanings, such as "dishwhite" to refer to a clean

dish) and other inappropriate or meaningless syntactic or semantic forms that are indicative of loose cognitive associations (as in defining the word *orange* as "pie in the sky"); also, disorganized speech characterized by derailment (jumping from topic to topic), tangentiality (responses unrelated to a prompt from another person), and illogicality (drawing false conclusions)

4. *Perceptual disorder*, as when the individual is unable to distinguish relevant from irrelevant stimuli and becomes confused or overwhelmed by a bombardment of sensory events (e.g., seeing the surrounding world as a kaleidoscope of color devoid of form or pattern) or when hallucinations (such as auditory, visual, olfactory, or kinesthetic sensations that have no discernible cause) are experienced

5. *Inappropriate emotion*, as in anhedonia (inability to experience pleasure), lack of affect (emotion), or showing emotion such as joy at a sad occasion

6. *Confused sense of self*, as in being unable to distinguish between oneself and the rest of the world (cosmic feelings)

7. *Disrupted volition*, an inability to complete a course of action or a lack of drive

8. *Detachment*, an indifference to the external world and a preoccupation with an illogical inner world (autistic behavior)

9. *Atypical motor behavior*, various responses that include hyperactivity, hypoactivity, ritualistic actions, and rigid posturing

Regardless of the precise pattern of symptoms exhibited, schizophrenic disorders are among the most serious of the psychopathological conditions in terms of the debilitating effect on the individual and the unfavorable prognosis for recovery (Gottesman, 1991). Their impact is made more serious by the fact that they tend to appear early in life, affecting some young children but being particularly prevalent between the ages of 15 and 45 (median age of onset is 30). Locke and Regier (1985) estimated that approximately 1% of the general population over the age of 18 (equal incidence rates for men and women) has been diagnosed as schizophrenic. These disorders tend to recur or become chronic. Outcomes are particularly poor when onset is gradual and occurs at an early age (Werry, 1992).

Notably, all of the characteristics are not present in every case of schizophrenia, with symptoms differing greatly from case to case. Also, an individual may display a variety of different symptoms over a period of time, and certain of the more persistent symptoms may appear to come and go or vary greatly in intensity from one period to another. Thus, a person may appear to be in good contact with reality on one occasion and highly delusional on the next. The characteristics displayed by children under the age of 6 are even more difficult to identify because the immaturity of these children may prevent them from reporting many of the positive symptoms of the condition. This fact may cause prevalence estimates of childhood schizophrenia (i.e., approximately .2% of the general population; the estimate for adults is 1%) to appear lower than they really are (Gooding & Iacono, 1995). Prevalence is lowest below the age of 5, increases during later childhood, and accelerates rapidly during adolescence (McClellan & Werry, 1997). Not surprisingly, a high percentage of children who are identified as schizophrenic manifest psychotic symptoms, particularly hallucinations and, to a lesser extent, delusions. Wicks-Nelson and Israel (2000), evaluating data from four studies of children between the ages of 8 and 11, reported that between 79% and 84% (mean = 81%) experienced auditory hallucinations and between 28% and 47% (mean = 35.5%) experienced visual hallucinations. Other types of hallucinations, such as tactile and olfactory, were rarely recorded. These studies also were relatively consistent in documenting incidence of delusions, reporting their occurrence in between 53% and 86% (mean = 65.5%) of the children. Findings regarding thought disorders, reported as between 40% and 100% (mean = 73%), were less consistent across studies, possibly due to difficulties identifying thought disorders in young children. The results pertaining to hallucinations are substantiated in other research with children and adults (Volkmar, Becker, King, & McGuashan, 1995). The diagnosis of all psychotic symptoms becomes more likely once children reach school age (Green, Padron-Gayol, Hardesty, & Bassiri, 1992).

In recognition of the varied characteristics associated with schizophrenia, the DSM–IV lists five subcategories of the disorder: undifferentiated, catatonic, disorganized, paranoid, and residual. These subcategories are not identified in children but pertain to adolescents and adults. Many experts suspect that, despite an overlap in certain symptoms, these conditions have different causes. Undifferentiated schizophrenia is marked by the display of any variety of the symptoms just discussed but in irregular patterns that do not fit neatly into any of the other diagnostic categories. Catatonic schizophrenia is characterized primarily by atypical motor behavior, including extreme stupor to the point of total unresponsiveness, extreme activity to the point of frenzy, or a mixture of the two extremes. Persons in stupor may be frozen into one posture for hours, whereas a frenzied individual in the course of wild emotional displays may attempt to hurt himself or others. Disorganized schizophrenia (formerly called hebephrenia) is the most severe form, onsetting early and causing the greatest disruption to the personality. Behaviors include preoccupation and brooding, social withdrawal, bizarre speech and thinking that often appear silly and inappropriate, as well as delusions and hallucinations. *Paranoid schizophrenia* is characterized by suspiciousness and poor social relationships, delusions of persecution (my boss is trying to kill me) and grandiosity (I am the king of the universe), and hallucinations. When dealing with issues outside the delusional system, the individual's reasoning may appear unimpaired; however, the psychotic thinking usually clouds judgment and causes erratic and sometimes dangerous behavior. *Residual schizophrenia* pertains to individuals with previous diagnoses who exhibit some, relatively minor symptoms.

Although specific subcategories of childhood schizophrenia are not usually diagnosed, several characteristics often accompanying schizophrenic states appear more obvious in children. One such characteristic is intense anxiety and related panic (Prior & Werry, 1986). In some cases, individuals are aware of their inability to control their perceptions and thoughts, a situation that understandably induces anxiety and a corresponding panic, particularly in young children. As children mature, they learn to cope with their inner feelings without showing panic. Typical defense or coping mechanisms are obsessive-compulsive or ritualistic behaviors. For example, a child with schizophrenia might require 3 to 4 hours to dress because of elaborate ritualistic procedures that he feels compelled to repeat during each small step of dressing. These efforts to cope with the intense anxiety associated with bizarre thoughts and feelings are so essential to the individual that any attempt to interfere with them may be resisted with violent, aggressive outbursts.

Also, it is likely that the language disorders of schizophrenic children may be more varied than those associated with adults, depending on when in the developmental period the schizophrenic process began to appear. Disturbances may include mutism and echolalia (parrotlike repetition of speech), although these conditions are more closely associated with autism. More typical language patterns include neologisms (newly created words), fragmented speech, immature speech patterns, or bizarre speech (Caplan, Guthrie, & Komo, 1996). In some rare cases, speech develops but regresses as the child matures. On occasion, schizophrenic children develop their own language system that they use to speak to imaginary playmates in fantasy worlds or, in the case of twins, to speak to each other. Among older children whose speech and language are well developed before the obvious onset of the disorder, language usage may be fluent but so obscure that it ceases to be meaningful to listeners.

There is a consensus that the earlier the onset of schizophrenia in childhood, the more severe the disturbance in adulthood (Wenar, 1990; Werry, 1992). Kydd and Werry (1982) noted that common childhood symptoms such as preoccupation with objects and excessive fear often grow into compulsive rituals and delusions, respectively, as the child matures. Although there may be periods of remission, the trend is for the disorder to persist into adulthood.

Eggers and Bunk (1997) reported that only about 25% of children with the disorder appear to recover.

Etiology

There has undoubtedly been more written about the causes of schizophrenia than about all of the other psychopathological conditions put together. Investigations have been conducted that demonstrate that schizophrenia results from genetic factors, neurological disabilities, biochemical disorders, deviant developmental patterns, faulty family dynamics, and an interaction between inherited predispositions and environmental stress. Much of the evidence supporting the notion of biological causal factors was presented in Chapter 2 in the discussion of the biological perspective on EBDs. To summarize those data, it appears that there is reliable evidence of a genetic component, of neurological irregularities in the structure of the brain, and of biochemical imbalances as important precursors to schizophrenia. However, there is not as yet a one-to-one, cause-and-effect biological answer to the problem of schizophrenia (R. F. Asarnow et al., 1994; Bassett, 1992). Probably, no such answer will ever be found if, as many theorists believe, the term *schizophrenia* refers to more than one disorder, presumably with different causal agents.

Psychosocial causation theories, the other side of the coin, appear to deal primarily with family conditions that interact with biological factors to precipitate or exacerbate the disorder. The majority of early research into pathogenic family patterns involved aspects of parent personality. One popular theory attributed cause to the "schizophrenogenic mother," a cold, dominating, unfeeling individual who rejects her child (Bettelheim, 1955, 1959; Bowen, 1960; Rank, 1955), and another attributed the schizophrenogenic personality to both parents (Kaufman et al., 1960; Lidz, Fleck, & Cornelison, 1965). This approach to understanding schizophrenia has not been substantiated by more current research and at present is given little credence. More recent studies show high levels of conflict in the families of persons with schizophrenia (Miklowitz, 1994). However, some researchers have concluded that family relationships are mutually pathological and that parents are adversely affected by children with schizophrenia (J. R. Asarnow & Horton, 1990; Carson, 1984; Woo, Goldstein, & Nuechterlein, 1997).

An alternative avenue of investigation into family patterns has focused on parental relationships marked either by extensive discord (*marital schism*), or by one partner's subservience toward the more maladjusted partner (*marital skew*). Roff and Knight (1981) found both these marital patterns to be predictive of poor outcomes for schizophrenic offspring. In addition, vague or misleading communication within a family, termed *communication deviance*, is seen as a contributing factor. Communication deviance practiced by parents in the form of mixed messages (telling the child something and then behaving in a manner that contradicts what was said) was confirmed by J. R. Asarnow, Goldstein, and Ben-Meir (1988) and Goldstein (1985) as predicting the occurrence of adult schizophrenic disorders among offspring.

Although it is difficult to identify the specific types of environmental stressors that precipitate schizophrenia (Dohrenwend & Egri, 1981), studies of individuals who relapse after experiencing remission have identified as important a form of negative communication called expressed emotion (Butzlaff & Hooley, 1998; Hooley, 1985). Expressed emotion is overcritical communication by family members who are overinvolved with the schizophrenic individual. High levels of expressed emotion in a family have been shown to predict the reoccurrence of schizophrenia in adults (Goldstein, 1985; Linszen, Dingemans, Nugter, & Willem, 1997; Mavreas, Tomaras, Karydi, & Economous, 1992) and its occurrence in high-risk adolescents (Valone, Goldstein, & Norton, 1984).

One final area of investigation of the etiology of schizophrenia involves sociocultural studies. Although there is evidence that schizophrenia occurs in all cultures, it is more pronounced in some than in others (Carson & Butcher, 1992). One interpretation of these data is that some cultures are highly stressful and contribute to the incidence of the disorder. For example, in the United States there is a relationship between the incidence of schizophrenia and lower social class status that has been attributed to environmental stress (Dohrenwend, Levav, Shrout, & Schwartz, 1992). Also, approximately 3% of divorced persons (stressful marriages) manifest schizophrenia (Keith, Regier, & Rae, 1991). However, schizophrenia may cause people to move from a higher to a lower socioeconomic class (Munk & Mortensen, 1992) and may increase marital discord.

Treatment. The outlook for individuals with schizophrenia is mixed, depending to a large extent on the age at onset. The younger the person at onset, the more unfavorable the prognosis for recovery (J. R. Asarnow, 1994). Also, the prognosis for recovery is unfavorable when the onset of this disease is slow and insidious, as is usually true of childhood schizophrenia, and when negative symptoms, such as language problems and poor social skills, precede positive or psychotic symptoms that lead to accurate diagnosis (J. R. Asarnow & Asarnow, 1996).

Pharmacotherapy, or drug therapy, usually in the form of antipsychotic drugs (neuroleptics) that are tranquilizers, such as Haldol (haloperidol) or Thorazine (chlorpromazine), is typically prescribed for all age groups (Kane & Freeman, 1994). This class of drugs is expected to reduce the anxiety and agitation that often accompanies psychosis and to gradually decrease the psychotic symptoms of hallucinations, delusions, and thought disorders. Although the research involving children is limited, there are indications that these drugs have been successful in some cases (J. R. Asarnow & Asarnow, 1996). However, their usefulness is reduced because they have negative side effects (Campbell & Cueva, 1995). Currently, newer antipsychotic drugs, such as clozapine, are being tested with children and adolescents (Kumra et al., 1998). Among adults receiving drug therapy, about 60% continue to experience periodic psychotic episodes, approximately 10% remain profoundly disabled, and about 30% appear to function in relatively acceptable fashion (Strange, 1992; Weinstein, 1983). Apparently, antipsychotic drugs are more likely to alleviate the positive symptoms of schizophrenia, such as hallucinations, than the negative symptoms, such as flat affect and loss of volition (Leff, 1992).

Psychotherapy is practiced with late-onset schizophrenia and has become more useful since the discovery of antipsychotic drugs. A study of treatment outcomes by Hogarty and colleagues (1997) found that psychotherapeutic treatments combined with drug therapy were successful in many cases. The most effective forms of psychotherapy were combinations of insight therapy, family therapy, and social therapy (Jeffries, 1995). This conclusion was supported by the results of a recent meta-analysis of multiple studies (Mojtabai, Nicholson, & Carpenter, 1998).

Little information exists pertaining to use of psychotherapy with children diagnosed as schizophrenic. Some pragmatic intervention strategies that focus on improving family and social relationships involve reducing anxiety-related behaviors and helping the child strengthen coping skills. For example, compulsive ritualistic behaviors that a child may use to minimize anxiety may be structured so that they are less interfering with the child's life and less inconvenient to others. This approach makes no attempt to treat the underlying disease.

Ecological approaches to therapy in which the entire environment is therapeutically structured to strengthen the individual's self-reliance in daily living situations also have been attempted. Milieu therapy has been used with people who are hospitalized with schizophrenia, and therapeutic community-based programs have been provided for discharged individuals (Ciompi et al., 1992; Fairweather, 1980). Behavioral interventions such as token economy programs also have been implemented with some success to teach self-help skills and reduce patterns of inappropriate behaviors (Emmelkamp, 1994).

Pervasive Developmental Disorders: Autistic Disorder

In the DSM–IV, the developmental disorder called autism is applied to children who have impairments in social interactions and communication and who

display repetitive, stereotypic, and restricted interests and activities before reaching age 3.

Social interaction impairments include the failure to engage in nonverbal behaviors that facilitate social relationships, such as eye-to-eye contact, appropriate facial expressions and body postures, and social interaction gestures. More important, social interaction impairments also refer to the detached, unresponsive behavior caused by an impaired cognitive awareness of others, that is, the ability to understand how people think and feel, which is the foundation for social relationships. Research has shown that these problems occur very early in life (Adrien et al., 1993; Stone, 1997). Parents report that their children look through rather than at them, smile rarely, and resist being held. As the children mature, they remain detached and aloof, often ignoring others and appearing incapable of understanding the social cues that are essential for interactions with others (Baron-Cohen, Campbell, Karmiloff-Smith, Grant, & Walker, 1995). Social skills as simple as how to play a game with another person must be directly taught (Harris, 1994).

Communication impairments include a lack of spoken language; stereotyped, repetitive, or idiosyncratic language; inability to initiate or maintain conversations; and lack of developmentally appropriate symbolic play activities. Communication disorders and difficulties with socialization are closely related because the purpose of communication is to interact with others. Children with autism have difficulty with all aspects of communication, including appropriate social gestures, speech, and both expressive and receptive language. They often fail to use typical communicative gestures (such as waving hello or goodbye), and their speech may be atonic, monotonic, or unusual in pitch or rate. Approximately 50% of children with autism do not develop meaningful spoken language (Lord & Paul, 1997). They often remain mute or display echolalia (parrotlike repetition of what has been said to them) that is immediate or delayed (Rydell & Prizant, 1995). Other irregularities include pronoun confusion, as when the child refers to others as "I" or "me" and self as "you," "he," or "she." This characteristic may reflect an inability to differentiate self from others. Although measurement is difficult because of autistic disinterest, there is some indication that children with autism do not understand much of the language spoken to them (Lord & Paul, 1997). They perform better on simple comprehension tasks, for example, identifying colors (Ungerer & Sigman, 1987). Among the higher functioning individuals with autism, language is acquired but often not used appropriately in social context. Often, autistic language is marked by an inability to encode relevant meaning, overliteral interpretations of messages, and poor understanding of the relationships between meaningful concepts (Brook & Bowler, 1992). The children may utter sentences or phrases, but they do not hold conversations, possibly because they are not attuned to the responses of listeners (L. K. Koegel & Koegel, 1995). In some cases they can be trained to converse (Loveland & Tunali-Kotoski, 1997), and this type of instruction in pragmatics (using language for social interaction) has become more prevalent in recent years.

Inappropriate behaviors, interests, and activities include stereotyped, restricted patterns of interest that are abnormal in focus or intensity, inflexible adherence to routines and rituals, stereotyped and repetitive motor movements, and persistent preoccupation with objects. Children with autism frequently display stereotyped motor behaviors such as hand waving or flapping; body rocking; head shaking; repetitively rubbing eyes, mouth, or face; lip licking; or repeating a vocalization incessantly. These repetitive behaviors are viewed as forms of self-stimulation (R. L. Koegel & Koegel, 1990) and are extremely reinforcing forms of sensory feedback to individuals with autism. Other, less bizarre preoccupations may be an obsessive interest in one particular topic (e.g., dinosaurs), insistence on specific routines (e.g., paths to school or types of food), or inappropriate use of objects (e.g., spinning the wheels on toy cars). The more severe of these stereotyped behaviors, such as repetitive head banging, can cause serious injury. Even when injury is not a concern, the individual's intense absorption with these obsessive behaviors prevents the learning of other, more beneficial skills. Some researchers have speculated that these "excess behaviors" displayed by persons with autism are forms of unconventional communication (Durand & Carr, 1992; Vollmer, Marcus, & Ringdahl, 1995).

The term *autistic* means absorption in self or in fantasy. Therefore, the most predominant characteristic of the autistic disorder is a lack of responsiveness to the environment, particularly to human beings. As was noted previously, Leo Kanner (1943) was the first person to identify autism as a distinct syndrome occurring in infancy and childhood, differentiated from other syndromes associated with childhood schizophrenia. According to Kanner, autism is manifested at birth and is caused by biological irregularities. Another early investigator, Rutter (1978), identified the major characteristics of autism that have just been discussed, as well as certain additional, less "autistically" distinctive traits, such as an aversion to noise, negativism (e.g., refusal to eat or dress), and preoccupation with inanimate objects such as rocks or keys. Many observations of both Kanner and Rutter have stood the test of time.

Intellectual Potential. There is some dispute about the intellectual potential of children with autism. Most research has found that a minimum of 75% of the children function in the severely, moderately, or mildly retarded range (Campbell & Green, 1985; Newsom, 1998; Prior & Werry, 1986); however, the impact of language deficit on their performance is not fully understood. Research has documented general deficits in memory (Boucher, 1981) and deficits in tasks that require abstract thinking and verbal skills (Minshew, Sweeney, & Bauman, 1997). Kanner (1943) identified some autistic individuals (savants) who had limited intellectual ability in most respects but showed remarkable memory or ability in a specific area, such as mathematical calculations. Others (O'Connor & Hermelin, 1990; Pring & Hermelin, 1993) have confirmed the presence of this characteristic in certain people with autism.

Prevalence. Estimates of the prevalence of autism vary, but most studies have shown it to be a relatively rare disorder. Recent surveys have suggested that it occurs about 4 to 5 times in every 10,000 children, that it is more common in males than females (4 to 1), and that it appears with equal frequency in all social classes (Fombonne, du Mazaubrun, Cans, & Grandjean, 1997; Klinger & Dawson, 1996; Ritvo et al., 1989; Steffenberg & Gillberg, 1986). However, Simpson and Zionts (2000) stated that the condition is becoming more common, because ever-increasing numbers of children are being identified. They cited prevalence figures of 15 times per 10,000 births, supplied by the Autism Society of America.

Etiology. Theoretical perspectives attributing autism to faulty parenting, particularly mothering (Bettelheim, 1967), have been largely discredited. Recent research has suggested that autism is a biological disorder whose specific cause is still unknown. There is evidence of a relationship between neurological problems and autism, specifically of reduced number of cells and reduced cell density in the limbic system of the brain (Minshew et al., 1997). Other, more specific neural dysfunctions cited involve the vestibular pathway (Colbert, Koegler, & Markham, 1979) and the reticular formation (Rimland, 1964). More recent evidence has documented abnormality early in brain development (often during fetal development), including underdeveloped portions of the cerebellum (R. Courchesne & Courchesne, 1997) and a deficiency of Purkinje's cells (E. Courchesne, 1988). According to E. Courchesne, lack of Purkinje cells makes individuals with autism abnormally sensitive to stimulation in the environment. Autistic and repetitive behaviors reflect an effort to cope with excessive stimulation.

Related approaches to investigating biological causation involve studies of brain metabolism and brain biochemistry (Ornitz, Atwell, Kaplan, & Westlake, 1985; Rumsey, Rapoport, & Sceery, 1985) and for the most part have documented the existence of differences in the brains of individuals with autism and individuals without autism. Biochemical studies have shown high levels of serotonin in 25% to 50% of cases (G. M. Anderson & Hoshino, 1997), but the implications of that result is not clear. In addition, brain dysfunction in the form of epilepsy (25%–35% of cases; Volkmar & Nelson,

1990) and abnormal EEGs (50% of cases) has been associated with autism (Dawson & Castelloe, 1992; Minshew et al., 1997), but the cause of those abnormalities is unknown. Many researchers have attributed autism to multiple biological causes (Martineau, Barthelemy, Jouve, & Muh, 1992).

Efforts to understand the causal agent or, more probably, agents involved in autism have focused on genetic variables. One approach has been to investigate genetic abnormalities, such as Fragile X syndrome, a disorder caused by irregularities in parts of the X chromosome. Rutter, Bailey, Simonoff, and Pickles (1997) reported that approximately 3% of persons with autism have Fragile X syndrome. Another approach has been to look at family relationships. Studies of twins have shown much higher rates of the disorder in identical twins (69%–91%) than in fraternal twins or the general population (Bailey et al., 1995). In addition, research has shown the prevalence of autism among the siblings of a child with autism to be 6 to 8 per 100 (Piven et al., 1997), and family members also tend to develop various cognitive, linguistic, and social disorders that are less serious than autism (Piven et al., 1997). Wicks-Nelson and Israel (2000) suggested that genetic factors predispose family members to a broad band of related disorders that includes the most serious condition, autism.

Prognosis. Many specialists in the study of autism have concluded that the effects of the disease are generally pervasive and largely irreversible (DeMyer et al., 1983). As some children progress from early childhood to childhood, there is improvement in language and social skills, but deficits still exist (Sigman, 1998; Volkmar, Kim, & Cohen, 1997). Studies of adolescents with the disorder have been contradictory but, on the whole, not particularly encouraging (Klinger & Dawson, 1996; Sigman, 1998). Rumsey, Andreasen, and Rapoport (1986) found that adults with autism continue to display unusual behaviors and stereotyped movements and to have serious problems with social interactions. Although there may be some improvement in language skills, for most individuals language deficits remain. Adaptive functioning is so limited that most individuals are cared for by their families (Rumsey, Rapoport, & Sceery, 1985). On a more optimistic note, autism varies in severity, and individuals with relatively mild cases, who are not mentally retarded and who can use language in a meaningful way, tend to make the best adjustments. Some are able to attend college, gain employment, and live independently when they reach adulthood.

Treatment. Approaches to treatment usually include a pharmacological component. Tsai (1998) cited advances in medication designed to treat symptoms by reducing the bizarre behaviors, such as stereotypy and self-injury, that interfere with learning. Drugs of choice include those of the neuroleptic group (tranquilizers or antipsychotic drugs), such as Haldol, although they are not effective with everyone. The sedative group (e.g., Valium) has not been effective, and there have been mixed findings for the use of Naltrexone, an opiate antagonist.

In addition to drug therapy, popular forms of treatment have involved educational and behavioral therapy and a focus on communication skill. Lovaas (1987) used behavior modification techniques to teach language and to raise the intellectual functioning of children with autism. The progress, however, was slow and tedious, requiring round-the-clock efforts of teams of highly trained teachers. Often, learning did not generalize to natural settings. A more current language-based program, Receptive Labeling, developed by Newsom (1998), is sequenced in levels of complexity, designed to teach generalization skills and encourage natural communication. Indeed, the focus of most current instructional interventions is on exploiting the natural environment to build communication skills and enhance social skills.

A comprehensive treatment model, Treatment and Education of Autistic and Related Communication Handicapped Children (TEACCH), takes a holistic approach to working with individuals with autism (Mesibov, 1994). Families are a vital part of the treatment procedures, which are based primarily on the use of cognitive and behavioral strategies, particularly operant conditioning, to provide a highly structured environment for persons with autism. TEACCH also advocates community services, such as vocational training, in addition to school-based programs. A significant strength of the TEACCH program is an ongoing effort to provide empirical verification of its procedures. Thus far, research has tended to support use of the program (Schopler, 1997). In addition, TEACCH's early emphasis on parental involvement in treatment has gained wide acceptance in the field and is currently recognized as essential for success (Kauffman, 1997).

Despite numerous behavioral interventions focused on teaching language, approximately 50% of children with autism remain mute. In these cases various nonvocal forms of communication are taught. These include sign language and augmentative communication systems. Augmentative communication systems are communication boards or computers that present a display of pictures or symbols that the child points to in an effort to communicate. For some children with autism, these methods of communication are quite helpful.

One augmented communication system, however, has led to unfortunate consequences. As is true of any serious disorder, periodically extravagant claims are made for specific treatments of autism. These claims usually involve a great deal of media hype and influence the thinking of the general public for a time. Because there is rarely any empirical evidence to substantiate such treatments, they do not stand the test of time and scientific scrutiny. This type of circumstance occurred with the "facilitated communication" procedure introduced in the early 1990s. Supposedly, the use of a facilitator to guide children's hands when they used communication boards enabled those children to produce elaborate meaningful communications. This procedure, wildly acclaimed for a period of time, has been discredited by any number of research studies (Kauffman, 1997).

Other Pervasive Developmental Disorders

In addition to autism, other PDDS include Asperger's disorder, Rett's disorder, childhood disintegrative disorder (Heller's syndrome), and "PDD not otherwise identified." Many of the symptoms associated with these conditions overlap with the symptoms of autism. In the past these conditions have rarely been identified, and Rett's disorder was not even included in the category until DSM–IV was published in 1994. Of late, interest in Asperger's disorder appears to be increasing in the United States, and children with this diagnosis are entering school-based education programs (L. K. Koegel & Koegel, 1995). However, many professionals still consider the condition to be a mild form of autism (Smith-Myles & Simpson, 1998).

Asperger's disorder, named for the Austrian physician who identified it in 1944, is characterized (like autism) by impaired social interactions but (unlike autism) not by withdrawal. Motor skills may be poor, and, unlike most cases of autism, language may be slow to develop, but does progress as children mature. Language problems tend to occur in pragmatics, the use of language for social interaction, and in voice rhythm. Children have difficulty holding conversations and may talk about bizarre or pedantic topics of little interest to the listener. Intelligence levels are in the average range; however, problems with academic achievement are common. Smith-Myles and Simpson (1998) attribute these problems to characteristics such as narrowly defined interests, inflexibility, literal thinking, and poor organizational skills. The prevalence of Asperger syndrome is estimated to be 71 out of 10,000 births (Gillberg, 1993). Other characteristics pertaining to this disorder parallel those that pertain to autism, except that the prognosis appears more favorable.

Rett's disorder, a rare condition that affects only females, onsets at ages 1 to 2. Normal growth usually occurs for the first 6 months of life, after which head growth decelerates and motor skills deteriorate. Stereotypic hand-washing movements appear, and language does not develop. Mental retardation and social withdrawal are typical. Skill loss is permanent, and prognosis is poor.

Heller's syndrome, or childhood disintegrative disorder, is similar to autism in all respects except age of onset. Affected children experience normal development for at least the first 2 years of life, then, before age 10, experience a drastic regression in previously acquired skills, including language, social behavior, play, and motor functioning. The problems remain relatively constant throughout life, and prognosis is poor.

PDD not otherwise specified is a catch-all category for children who do not meet the criteria for the other four categories.

Organic Mental Disorders

Damage to the brain may produce any of a variety of disorders, ranging from relatively mild behavioral deficits to gross impairments that affect all aspects of functioning, including language, memory, cognition, emotional control, learning, ethical conduct, and orientation in space. Brain damage can be caused by numerous circumstances, many of which are correlated with aging (strokes, Alzheimer's disease). Although Eisenberg (1990) noted that the statistical risk to children is slight, negative changes in the environment suggest that certain causal factors, specifically traumatic brain injury, the AIDS virus, brain tumors, and drug abuse have increasingly important implications for children.

Traumatic Brain Injury

Concern about traumatic brain injury (TBI) in children and youth has led the federal government to create a separate special education category. TBI is not an unusual condition. Any blow to the head can result in sufficient damage to the brain to cause impaired functioning, occasionally including psychopathological complications. According to Chance (1986), each year more than a million people in the United States suffer head injuries in accidents, shootings, muggings, child abuse incidents, and so forth. Significant brain damage is sustained in about 300,000 of these cases. The ramifications of the injury are usually determined by the seriousness of the brain damage. When injuries result in unconsciousness, the individual usually experiences amnesia in regard to the events that immediately preceded the injury. More serious injuries may cause more prolonged unconsciousness or coma. An additional complication is the possibility of intracerebral hemorrhage that damages brain cells and causes irreversible damage. Aftereffects of brain injury may range from mild symptoms of temporary fatigue and mental confusion to more serious complications such as lasting impairment of memory and cognition, depression, heightened anxiety, and increased irritability, and may cause gross personality changes characterized by such bizarre, irrational behavior that the individual no longer seems to be the same person. In some cases posttraumatic epilepsy occurs. Most children with TBI require special education services (Mira & Tyler, 1991). In addition to medical treatment, which usually does not reverse the effects of TBI, interventions designed to help children control behavioral and educational problems are essential.

AIDS Virus

HIV-1, the virus associated with AIDS, attacks the immune system of individuals, making them susceptible to a wide variety of infections. In 1983 Snider and colleagues revealed evidence that HIV could destroy brain cells (before the manifestation of AIDS), paving the way for the identification of two types of brain pathology: aseptic meningitis (inflammation of the meninges) and the AIDS dementia complex. The more deadly of the two, the AIDS dementia complex, attacks brain cells and nerve fibers and in the early stages causes symptoms that include psychomotor slowing, poor concentration, and memory problems. Rapid progression leads to mental confusion, psychotic thinking, apathy, and withdrawal (Navia, Jordan, & Price, 1986). Autopsies of AIDS patients show that approximately 80% suffered neurological damage. Although no studies have been done specifically with children infected with HIV, the possibility of neurologically caused behavioral disorders among them must be considered.

Brain Tumors

Children suffering from brain tumors are not considered to have TBI, because the injury to the brain is not caused by an external force. Brain tumors may be benign or malignant. Even benign tumors create intracranial pressure and cause symptoms such as headaches, vomiting, memory impairment, depression, and convulsive seizures. As the tumor grows, symptoms worsen to include mental confusion, disorientation as to time and place, irritability, hallucinations, apathy, and impairment of intellectual functions. In rare cases the individual may experience euphoria. Emotional disorders may include loss of spontaneity, disinhibition, lability of affect (unstable or highly changeable emotions), and forced emotions. When surgical intervention is feasible, 40% of tumors are curable, and in cases where there is little loss of surrounding tissue, recovery seems almost complete. In about 20% of the cases the disease is arrested for several years, and in the remainder of cases it is quickly fatal. Children tend to recover more readily than adults to insults to the brain, although the prognosis is unpredictable (Comer, 1999).

Drug Abuse

Various psychoactive drugs affect mental functioning: alcohol, barbiturates, hallucinogenics, amphetamines, heroin, cocaine, and marijuana. Any of these drugs cause physiological changes in the brain, which in turn affect all aspects of behavior. Once thought to be solely an adult problem, drug abuse is now recognized as a problem of some preadolescent children and a significant number of adolescents.

Alcohol abuse. Alcohol is a depressant that affects judgment, lowers self-control, and causes motor impairment. Alcohol abuse is the most prevalent form of drug dependence in the United States. Up to 10% of adults in the United States may abuse or be dependent on alcohol (Anthony, Arria, & Johnson, 1995). Abusers drink such large amounts of alcohol that they experience problems in their social and professional lives (Coambs & McAndrews, 1994). Persons dependent on alcohol develop a physical tolerance to it and must drink ever-increasing amounts to experience its effects (Thompson, Gillin, Golshan, & Irwin, 1995). Alcohol abuse is a serious problem among the young (Scheien & Botwin, 1997). Its abuse has been associated statistically with suicides (Comer, 1999) and attempts at suicide (Black, Yates, Petty, Noyes, & Brown, 1986). Increased rates of suicide among children and youth have been attributed in large measure to alcohol (Murphy, 1988). Its excessive use has also been connected to violent crime, including homicide (Goodman et al., 1986). Prolonged drinking over time followed by withdrawal of alcohol or a prolonged drinking spree can result in an acute psychotic-like reaction, alcohol withdrawal delirium (formerly called delirium tremens). Symptoms include insomnia, agitation, disorientation (e.g., inability to recognize friends), hallucinations (e.g., seeing small animals such as rats), fear, tremors of the hands and lips, heavy perspiration, and rapid heartbeat.

There is evidence of genetic predisposition to abuse alcohol (Cloninger, Reich, Sigvardsson, Von Knorring, & Bohman, 1986) and an alcohol-risk personality (Finn, 1990), which is marked by impulsiveness, emotional instability, and poor planning ability. Also, alcohol addiction has been linked with antisocial personality (Alterman, 1988) and with depression (Lutz & Snow, 1985). Overindulgence in alcohol by pregnant women can damage the fetus. Fetal alcohol syndrome, the resulting disorder, is characterized by permanent physical and neurological damage to the child.

Approaches to treating alcohol abuse include medications to reduce withdrawal symptoms; group therapy; behavioral therapy, which may involve either aversive conditioning (the administration of an emetic with alcohol) or cognitive retraining; and Alcoholics Anonymous group discussions. Treatment is more effective when alcohol abuse is not associated with any other disorder (Rounsaville, Weissman, & Prusoff, 1987). Prevention of relapse is an important component of treatment.

Cocaine. Use of cocaine in the United States increased so significantly in the 1980s that it was considered epidemic (National Institute of Drug Abuse, 1990). Use of powerful forms of cocaine has caused the annual number of cocaine-related emergency room incidents in the United States to increase from approximately 4,000 cases in 1982 to 140,000 cases in 1996 (Drug Abuse Warning Network, 1997). Cocaine, especially an extremely potent variety of the drug, called crack, stimulates the cortex of the brain, energizing the individual and heightening awareness of events in the environment. Crack, a highly addictive drug, causes an immediate state of euphoria or a "high." Problems associated with the drug include antisocial or criminal behaviors committed to secure money to purchase it; failure to meet daily responsibilities in families, jobs, or schools; depressed symptoms when the drug is not available; and, when the drug is chronically abused, acute psychotic symptoms similar to those in schizophrenia. Also, death due to excessive dosages may occur. Use of crack by pregnant women is known to have detrimental effects on the fetus, causing varied degrees of organic impairment that result in serious cognitive, learning, and behavioral problems ("crack babies").

Opium, morphine, and heroin. Opium, morphine, and heroin are narcotics that sedate the user. Although their use was epidemic in the 1960s, the number of people using them has declined steadily since that time (W. Smith, 1989), probably in correlation to the increased popularity of cocaine. They produce an immediate high, followed by a relaxed, euphoric state, followed by a negative state characterized by depression. Users develop physiological cravings for the drugs and require greater and greater dosages as their tolerance for them increases. Symptoms of withdrawal include a running nose, tearing eyes, restlessness, perspiration, and increased respiration rate. In time, vomiting, cramping, tremors, and pains throughout the body develop. Death can result from cardiovascular collapse. Withdrawal symptoms subside after 7 or 8 days, although a craving for the drugs appears to remain. As is true of alcohol and crack, addiction to these drugs by pregnant women causes organic damage to the fetus. Addiction also causes the types of social problems associated with addiction to cocaine. Students have been found to abandon their interests in scholastics and athletics, appearing to lack competitiveness and ambition. In addition to the usual withdrawal and psychotherapeutic approaches to treatment, the administration of a synthetic narcotic, methadone hydrochloride, is often employed and has been found to be effective whether or not it is accompanied by psychotherapy.

Barbiturates. Barbiturates are sedatives that depress the action of the central nervous system. The user feels relaxed and pleasantly drowsy. Excessive use causes physiological and psychological addiction and leads to sluggishness, impaired comprehension, mood shifts, motor incoordination, and depression. Also known as downers, barbiturates are commonly used with alcohol and are particularly lethal in that combination. Barbiturate withdrawal is characterized by anxiety, apprehension, tremors of the hands and face, insomnia, nausea, vomiting, cramps, rapid heart rate, and elevated blood pressure. Convulsions may occur, and an acute psychosis often occurs.

Amphetamines. Amphetamines are synthetic drugs that speed up the central nervous system, producing heightened alertness and high energy. Two popular types are Dexedrine and the more potent Methedrine (speed). Common usages are for weight control, narcolepsy (sleep disorder), and treatment of hyperactive children (on whom they have a calming rather than stimulating effect). Amphetamines are not physiologically addictive, but users develop psychological dependencies that cause them to ingest hundreds of tablets in short periods of time. Abusers suffer a variety of physiological effects, including elevated blood pressure, enlarged pupils, unclear speech, tremors, confusion, and excitability. Chronic abuse causes brain damage and a psychotic condition that is similar to paranoid schizophrenia. Because these drugs are not physiologically addictive, withdrawal is not excessively difficult.

Hallucinogens. Hallucinogens cause hallucinations by creating sensory images or by distorting perceptions of the environment. Popular hallucinogens, often called psychedelics, are LSD (lysergic acid diethylamide), mescaline (peyote), and PCP (angel dust). LSD appears to be the most often used of these drugs. A very small amount causes hallucinatory experiences, both pleasant (a "good trip") and unpleasant (a "bad trip"), for about 8 hours. In some cases flashbacks or reoccurrences of the hallucinations take place long after the person has taken the drug. Although LSD has been touted as a mind-expanding boon to creativity, no evidence exists to that effect. LSD is not physiologically addictive, and withdrawal can be accomplished with relative ease.

Marijuana and hashish. Marijuana and hashish, the leaves and flowers and resin of the hemp plant (*Cannabis sativa*), are mild hallucinogens. Marijuana use became so popular in the United States in the 1970s that from 70% to 75% of young people surveyed reported using it (Kandel, Davies, Karus, & Yamaguchi, 1986). When smoked or inhaled, it produces a state of mild euphoria and a floating sensation. Its effects appear rapidly but dissipate within several hours. Physiological effects include increased appetite, dry mouth, slow reaction time, and increased heart rate. Negative effects, including extreme anger and fear, have been reported. These drugs are not physiologically addictive, and the effects of long-term use have not been established.

Mood Disorders: Depression and Mania

Disorders of emotion include states of extreme excitement and euphoria called mania and, much more frequently, states of sadness and despair called depression. The disorders characterized by these emotions and particularly by depression vary greatly in seriousness. For example, depression can range from relatively normal feelings of sadness and melancholy—a familiar state to most individuals—to psychosis (a loss of contact with reality marked by delusions and hallucinations).

Feelings of mild depression usually are related to some type of environmental stress. Frequently such stress is rooted in a sense of loss, for example, of loved ones through death or marital breakup, of status or power, of good health, of a job or a home. Typical depressed behaviors appear in four areas: *affect*—feelings of despair; *motivation*—passive, dependent behavior; *physical and motor*—loss of appetite, insomnia, fatigability; and *cognitive*—ideas of personal worthlessness. More specifically, depression involves a markedly diminished interest in people and events; feelings of sadness often marked by weeping, sleep disruption, or excessive sleeping (in about 9% of the cases); decreased efficiency and productivity; apathy and a low energy level; feelings of inadequacy and helplessness; negative views of the future; and a general tendency to devalue oneself (Ballenger, 1988; Metalsky, Joiner, Hardin, & Abramson, 1993; Parker et al., 1993). In addition, depression may be accompanied by physical ailments such as headaches, dizzy spells, and generalized pain. Often, in the early stages of the disorder, depression is misdiagnosed as a medical problem (Kirmayer, Robbins, Dworkind, & Yaffe, 1993).

Symptoms associated with feelings of mild depression often do not involve each of the four areas just discussed and usually subside within a few months. However, the time for recovery varies with the individual's circumstances, such as socioeconomic status, social contacts, opportunities for stimulation, and so forth. People with strong social support systems fare better than those who are isolated (Paykel & Cooper, 1992). When feelings of depression do not lift within several months, the clinical picture is altered and the individual may be experiencing a more pathological mood disorder (Clayton, 1982).

Because it is often difficult to distinguish between typical and pathological states of depression, the DSM–IV offers diagnostic guidelines that include (a) severity of symptoms (the extent to which the problem adversely affects the individual's ability to function), (b) types of symptoms (whether symptoms include a wide variety of feelings and are characteristic of mania as well as depression), and (c) duration of symptoms (the extent to which the problem is chronic or intermittent). Notably, the DSM–IV does not present diagnostic criteria specifically for children and adolescents. Instead, with minor alterations, the diagnostic criteria used with adults are applied. Depending on the severity, types, and duration of symptoms, categories of mild to moderate disorders are called cyclothymia, dysthymia, or adjustment disorder with depressed mood.

• *Cyclothymia* disorders are bipolar in type and involve fluctuations in mood— from sad, depressed states to euphoric, manic states—that are not directly precipitated by environmental events. These cyclical mood alternations are similar to those experienced by persons afflicted with more serious psychotic mania– depression bipolar disorders, but the symptoms are less intense and do not involve delusions or hallucinations. However, in some cases these disorders are predictive of the more serious conditions (Goplerud & Depue, 1985; Klein, Depue, & Slater, 1985). Although the duration of the disordered functioning is at least 1 year in children and 2 years in adults, the individual may experience episodes of normal functioning periodically. The occurrence of this disorder in children and youth has not been greatly researched (Nottelmann & Jensen, 1995).
• *Dysthymia*, a unipolar disorder, refers to chronic states of nonpsychotic depression (without mania) with symptoms lasting at least 1 year for children and 2 years for adults. Although no identifiable precipitating events need be present, they frequently are. Included in the symptoms are depressed mood (or irritable mood in children and adolescents), poor appetite or overeating, sleep disturbance, low energy or fatigue, low self-esteem, problems with concentration, and feelings of hopelessness.
• *Adjustment disorder with depressed mood* involves symptoms similar to either dysthymia or cyclothymia, but they are less severe, lasting no more than 6 months and precipitated by an identifiable stressor within 3 months of the onset of the depression. There are no manic counterparts to adjustment disorder with depressed mood.

More severe mood disorders are subsumed under two classifications: major depression (a unipolar disorder) and bipolar disorder.

• *Major depression* disorder involves symptoms of depression that are overwhelming and unrelenting. Usually children and adolescents are diagnosed as displaying an irritable mood rather than a depressed mood (Goodyer & Cooper, 1993). Loss of interest in life and inability to experience pleasure are marked. Feelings of worthlessness are prevalent, and a preoccupation with thoughts of death and suicide becomes dominant and persistent. Delusions and hallucinations may be present. If so, they involve themes of personal guilt, punishment, worthlessness, death, and so forth. The most severe form of this disorder is marked by depressive stupor, a state of extreme immobility and unresponsiveness. Major depression may be diagnosed from a single episode or from recurrent episodes when no evidence of manic feeling or behavior is present. Although episodes tend to last about 6 months, there is evidence that this disorder tends to reoccur (Lewinsohn, Zeiss, & Duncan, 1989), with the probability of relapse being related to the severity of the initial disorder. Also, between major episodes it appears that between 10% and 15% of the afflicted suffer less serious feelings of depression (Akiskal & Simmons, 1985). Dysthymia often precedes a major depression episode.

• *Bipolar disorder* involves intense feelings of depression and mania occurring in cycles. Frequently, depressed feelings are most prevalent, although occasionally mania dominates, and in other cases both states occur with similar regularity. The depressed state is identical with that associated with major depression. The manic state is characterized by little or no sleep, wild feelings of excitement and euphoria, excessive activity, and inflated self-esteem that often involves delusions of grandeur and power. Like major depression, this disorder is episodic; however, its onset (ages 25 to 30) is earlier than that of major depression (ages 40 to 45), and it reoccurs more often. Those afflicted with this disorder have a higher mortality rate from suicide (Perris, 1982) and a limited possibility of full recovery (about 40%).

Prevalence

Estimating the prevalence of mood disorders among children and adolescents is difficult and complex. Children and youth may go undiagnosed because they lack the maturity to understand and communicate their feelings. Parents and teachers may lack the sophistication to recognize symptoms of depression in young people. Diagnostic criteria developed for adults may not be completely applicable for younger individuals. Empirical approaches (research based) to diagnoses of disorders in children and adolescents inform us that depressive symptoms usually cluster with symptoms of an anxiety disorder and are prevalent in children identified as conduct disordered (Harrington, Rutter, & Fombonne, 1996; Newcomer, Barenbaum, & Pearson, 1995). Possibly, young people and adults manifest depression differently. Some researchers believe that all young people who exhibit symptoms of depression in their daily lives should receive treatment regardless of whether or not they meet DSM–IV criteria (Kazdin & Marciano, 1998).

If DSM criteria are applied, bipolar and cyclothymic (manic-depressive) disorders have not been diagnosed with any regularity in children and occur in only approximately 1% of adolescents. The serious unipolar conditions occur less frequently in childhood than in adolescence, when incidence rates increase significantly (Fleming, Offord, & Boyle, 1989; Rutter, 1986), and are most prevalent among adults (ages 25 to 65). *Major depressive disorder*, diagnosed in 80% of the cases, is the most prevalent form of affective disorder among children and adolescents. By age 19, approximately 35% of adolescent females and 19% of adolescent males will have had at least one episode of major depressive disorder (Lewinsohn, Rohde, & Seeley, 1998). Wicks-Nelson and Israel (2000) pointed out that approximately one in four individuals experience a diagnosable depressive disorder in childhood or adolescence. Before age 12 there are no differences in prevalence between males and females. At adolescence, however, depression among females increases rapidly and twice as many females as males manifest the disorder. This disparity in prevalence based on gender continues throughout adulthood (Hankin et al., 1998; Wing & Bebbington, 1985).

Age

Age is an important variable in the diagnosis of depression. As children mature, their symptoms of depression become phenomenologically similar to depression in adults, particularly if the onset occurs at adolescence (Friedman, Hurt, Clarkin, Corn, & Aronoff, 1983; Reynolds & Graves, 1989). The same range of unipolar disorders, that is, adjustment disorder with depressed mood, dysthymic depression, and major depression occur (Kovacs et al., 1984), are of lasting duration, and are highly persistent over time. Also, some adolescents with major depressive disorder develop bipolar disorder later in life (Kovacs, 1989, 1996). When adolescents were diagnosed with bipolar disorder (1%), the duration of the disease was significantly longer than the duration of symptoms for those diagnosed with unipolar disorders.

Suicide

The high incidence of depression among young people causes particular concern because of the relationship between depression and suicide. The risk of suicide is about 1% during an initial depressed episode but rises to about 15% when there are recurrent episodes (Klerman, 1982). Suicide among young people apparently is an international problem (Marttunen, Henriksson, Heikkinen, Isomestsa, & Lonnqvist, 1995), although countries vary greatly in the general incidence of suicide. Hungary, Germany, Austria, and Denmark have very high rates (27 per 100,000 annually); Egypt, Mexico, Greece, and Spain have relatively low rates (5 per 100,000); and the United States is in between (12–13 per 100,000; Diekstra, 1990). In the United States, suicide ranks among the first 10 causes of death and is the third leading cause of death (after accidents and homicides) among

15- to 19-year-olds (Hawton, 1986). Since the mid-1950s, suicides and attempted suicides among adolescents have tripled (Fremouw, de Perczel, & Ellis, 1990; Harter & Marold, 1994). Every year, more than 2,000 teenagers (11 of every 100,000) commit suicide and approximately 250,000 attempt suicide (National Center for Health Statistics, 1991; Spirito, Brown, Overholser, & Fritz, 1989). These teenagers may have poor or affluent backgrounds (M. Miller, Chiles, & Barnes, 1982), but often they either have long-term stress in their lives (e.g., poor relationships with parents, family conflict, social isolation) or cannot cope with an immediate stressful situation (e.g., loss of a loved one; Adams, Overholser, & Lehnert, 1994; de Wilde, Kienhorst, Diekstra, & Wolters, 1992). Performance in school is generally poor, and a history of emotional and behavior problems is not unusual (Bryant, Garrison, Valois, Rivard, & Hinkle, 1995; D. Miller, 1994). Lack of strong parental support and loss or absence of important relationships are common precipitating factors (Heikkinen, Aro, & Lonnqvist, 1992). Also, thinking patterns marked by preoccupation with feelings of abandonment, loneliness, hopelessness, and helplessness are powerful predictors of suicide (Levy, Jurkovic, & Spirito, 1995; Shneidman, 1993). Just as distorted, pessimistic cognition characterizes depression, individuals contemplating suicide become preoccupied with their problems and believe that their present circumstances will not change (Klingman & Hochdorf, 1993). Frequently, problems are exacerbated by substance abuse, particularly alcohol (Merrill, Milner, Owens, & Vale, 1992). The statistics pertaining to suicide are made even more staggering if, as many researchers believe, many suicides by young people are officially recorded as accidental deaths to spare parents further grief (Guetzloe, 1991; Hawton, 1986; Poland, 1989).

Although females make more suicide attempts than males, three times as many men as women commit suicide. The incidence of suicide in children under the age of 15 is relatively rare but has been increasing during the past two decades. Approximately 250 children in that age bracket commit suicide every year (National Center for Health Statistics, 1993). Although some people argue that young children do not really understand the implications of death, researchers have reported that children successful in committing suicide have expressed a clear wish to die (Carlson, Asarnow, & Orbach, 1994; Pfeffer, 1993).

Etiology

The cause of mood disorders has been attributed to biological, psychosocial, and sociocultural factors. Adhering to the notion of *biological* causation are those who attribute the disease to genetic factors and biochemical irregularities. Genetic research includes studies of family pedigrees, twins, and adoptions. Family pedigree studies support the premise that depression is inherited. As many as 20% of the relatives of depressed persons suffer depression; the rate for the general population is 5% to 10% (Harrington et al., 1993). Prevalence rates among first-degree relatives (brothers, sisters, and parents) of depressed children and adolescents exceed rates of depression experienced by more distant relatives (Kovacs, Devlin, Pollack, Richards, & Mukerji, 1997). In addition, studies of twins have supported the heritability component (Kendler, Neale, Kessler, & Heath, 1992), and adoption studies have revealed a genetic factor in severe cases of unipolar depression (Wender et al., 1986).

Biochemical explanations of depression have focused largely on the effect of neurotransmitters (chemicals in the brain that transmit messages from one neuron to another). Reduced activity of two neurotransmitters, norepinephrine and serotonin, has been connected to unipolar depression (Yazici et al., 1993). The fact that antidepressant drugs, which increase norepinephrine or serotonin activity, alleviate depression substantiates this premise. However, recent research suggests that the patterns of biochemical interactions are extremely complex and that research results that apply to adults cannot be generalized to children and adolescents (Ivanova, 1998). Even for adults, the research is not definitive, because of technological limitations in measuring the levels of the neurotransmitters (Katz, Lott, Landau, & Waldmeier, 1993).

Another avenue of investigation into biochemical causation of depression involves studies of sleep disorders. Sleep disorders, caused by biochemical irregularities and marked by specific EEG patterns during sleep, have long been associated with clinical depression (Kupfer & Reynolds, 1992). However, these sleep characteristics are not present in children diagnosed with major depressive disorders. Wicks-Nelson and Israel (2000) suggested that either the child and the adult disorders are different or there are age-related biochemical differences in the same disorder.

The *psychosocial* position views mood disorders as reactions to stressful life situations. There is some evidence that prolonged exposure to stressful situations actually causes changes in brain functioning (Thase, Frank, & Kupfer, 1985). It also appears probable that states of mild depression and serious depressive or manic-depressive conditions have different causal agents and that the mild conditions are stress induced. Evidence that the drugs that reduce symptoms associated with bipolar disorder and major depression do not affect mild depressions support this premise.

Among those adhering to the psychosocial position, psychodynamic theorists focus on the premise that depression is caused by experiencing major loss early in life (American Psychiatric Association [APA], 1993). The depressed reaction may not be experienced immediately; individuals may be predisposed to depression later in life (Barnes & Prosen, 1985; Roy, 1985). An extension of this premise holds that children develop depression if their family stability deteriorates after loss of a loved one (Parker, 1992; West, Sandler, Pillow, Baca, & Gersten, 1991). This idea is supported by evidence that relatively few individuals who face early losses manifest depression (Paykel & Cooper, 1992).

Cognitive–behavioral theory also advances a psychosocial perspective of mood disorders. Cognitive–behavioral theorists attend to the manner in which depressed individuals think about themselves and the world. One avenue of thought is that depression results when individuals receive too little social reinforcement and withdraw from social interactions (C. Peterson, 1993). Another, more influential cognitive–behavioral approach examines the negative thoughts and attitudes that cause people to consistently denigrate themselves and to engage in self-defeating behavior (Beck, 1997; Beck & Freeman, 1990). Research with children has found evidence of the distorted thinking proposed by Beck (Kendall, Stark, & Adams, 1990).

A slightly different theoretical slant, the theory of learned helplessness, is proposed by Seligman (1992). When individuals learn through failure that they are helpless to change negative situations, they internalize a belief in their lack of control over their lives and become depressed. This theory has been expanded to include the concept of attribution. When individuals perceive a lack of control over their lives, they may attribute it to an internal cause that is global and stable, that is, that they can never alter the outcome (Abramson, Metalsky, & Alloy, 1989).

The *sociocultural* approach deals with social forces that define roles for individuals in the society and the social pressures that harm people. When individuals such as ethnic minorities and women are confronted with social barriers to self-fulfillment, they may become depressed. Similarly, people who do not understand their role in life, or who are in transition from one role to another, may develop feelings of depression. From a sociocultural perspective, depression occurs in an interpersonal context that must be understood if the person is to recover (Comer, 1999).

Treatment

Mild depressions may be treated solely with psychotherapy (Rounsaville et al., 1987). As has been noted, however, treatment of the serious mood disorders usually involves antidepressant drugs, including MAO (monoamine oxidase) inhibitors and tricyclics for unipolar disorders and lithium for bipolar disorders. MAO is an enzyme produced by the body and apparently contributes to depression. When treated with an inhibitor, approximately 50% of persons with unipolar disorder improve (Davis, 1980). The tricyclics (e.g., imipramine), developed to treat schizophrenia, were discovered instead to be very effective in treating unipolar depression (Montgomery, Bebbington,

Cowen, & Deakin, 1993). For bipolar disorders, lithium, an element found in mineral salts, is the drug of choice. Its effectiveness has been extensively documented (Prien, 1992).

In some rare cases where individuals are unresponsive to drugs and are considered high risks to commit suicide, the very controversial electroconvulsive therapy is used (Fink, 1992). This therapy uses electrical current to cause convulsions. Patients typically have some memory loss, but in the majority of cases their depression improves (Buchan, Johnsone, McPherson, & Palmer, 1992). Despite its apparent effectiveness, the use of electroconvulsive therapy has diminished in recent years (Foderaero, 1993).

Research reviewed by Hollon and Garber (1990) suggested that drug therapy accompanied by psychotherapy is most effective in preventing the reoccurrence of depressed episodes. Among the most effective psychotherapy is the cognitive–behavioral approach devised by Beck and his colleagues (Beck, 1997; Beck, Rush, Shaw, & Emery, 1979).

Among children, symptoms associated with depression may abate without treatment. Often the adjustment of environmental stressors, particularly family relationships, is an important part of interventions with children and youth.

Anxiety Disorders

Anxiety disorders, formerly referred to as neurotic conditions, are characterized by feelings of fear and anxiety (feelings akin to fear). Fear is the body's physical, emotional, and cognitive response to a perception of serious threat, whereas anxiety refers to a similar response to a vague, rather nebulous sense of threat to one's well-being. Like fear, anxiety is experienced when the autonomic nervous system is activated by some type of stressor. Typical anxiety responses include increased perspiration, rapid breathing, muscle tenseness, rapid heartbeat, pallor, goose bumps, nausea, and feelings of horror, dread, and panic. Anxiety differs from fear in that fear is usually associated with a specific menacing environmental circumstance (being confronted by a large, angry dog), whereas the trigger for anxiety is less obvious. All people experience both fear and anxiety; however, some individuals are afflicted with such intense and persistent feelings of fear and anxiety that they are unable to lead contented, productive lives. These people have anxiety disorders.

Recently, anxiety disorders have been recognized as the most common mental disorders in the United States, affecting from 15% and 17% of the adult population (Kessler et al., 1994; Zajecka, 1997). These types of conditions are equally common among children and adolescents and often are classified by empirically devised categorical systems as internalizing disorders (characterized by fearful, withdrawn, unhappy, self-injurious behaviors). In children and youth, anxiety often is identified as coexisting with other disorders, particularly depression (P. Cohen et al., 1993; Newcomer et al., 1995; Nottelmann & Jensen, 1995). Diagnosis of anxiety disorders in young children is complicated by the issue of comorbidity with other conditions and also by the normal fears experienced by children as they mature (such as fear of the dark or of monsters). Usually, the intensity and duration of symptoms differentiate between typical and pathological fear (termed *phobia*). Most clinical diagnoses of anxiety disorders in children and youth are made according to DSM–IV criteria rather than empirically developed instruments.

DSM–IV Criteria

DSM–IV includes one anxiety disorder, *separation anxiety disorder*, that is diagnosed before adulthood. Individuals with this disorder resist separation from significant persons (such as parents) and avoid situations that cause separation (such as attending school). Children also experience any of six other anxiety disorders identified by DMS–IV. *Phobic disorders* occur when people experience intense, irrational fear of an object, activity, or situation. *Panic disorder* is characterized by recurrent attacks of fear that approach terror. *Generalized anxiety disorder* involves general and persistent feelings of anxiety. *Obsessive-compulsive disorder* is marked by repeated irrational thoughts that elevate anxiety and trigger performance of repetitive, irrational actions. *Posttraumatic stress disorder* and *acute stress disorder* are characterized by anxiety linked to catastrophic or traumatic events.

Phobias. Phobias are persistent irrational fears that can be activated by simply thinking about a particular object, activity, or situation (Thorpe & Salkovskis, 1995). These conditions are common, occurring every year in approximately 10% to 11% of adults in the United States (Magee, Eaton, Wittchen, McGonagle, & Kessler, 1996). Estimates of the prevalence of phobias among children and youth vary, but phobias are the most commonly diagnosed anxiety disorder among that population. Phobic disorders are more common in females than males (2 to 1; Regier et al., 1993). Types of phobias vary with age at onset; for example, children often fear monsters, young adults develop fear of heights, and older adults are more likely to express fear of crowds (Ost, 1987).

DSM–IV classifies three categories of phobias: *agoraphobia* (fear of public places), *social phobias* (fears of social situations), and *specific phobias* (all other phobias). Individuals afflicted with agoraphobia develop a fear of leaving their houses, often because they have experienced *panic attacks* in public places. Panic attacks involve symptoms such as heart palpitations, dizziness, faintness, and shortness of breath. These attacks usually do not occur in the home, where persons with this disorder feel secure.

The diagnostic label *agoraphobia* is not applied to children. However, children experience a disorder termed *separation anxiety* that is similar to agoraphobia in some respects. Like agoraphobia, separation anxiety is characterized by resistance to leaving a secure situation (in this case, home and parents), and it involves dramatic symptoms such as dizziness, panic, somatic ailments, and fears of parental death or injury when separation occurs. Often, children with separation anxiety refuse to attend school and withdraw from other social activities outside the home. Other symptoms include repeated nightmares involving the theme of separation, fear of sleeping away from a significant adult, and fears of being removed from significant adults, that is, getting lost or kidnapped. Notably, not all children with separation anxiety refuse to attend school, and not all children who refuse to attend school suffer from separation anxiety. Some children avoid school because of specific phobias such as fear of tests or fear of public speaking (Kearney, Eisen, & Silverman, 1995).

The diagnostic label *separation anxiety disorder* is applied only to individuals under the age of 18. It is an extremely prevalent disorder, affecting approximately 5% of preadolescent children in the United States. Prevalence rates decline after childhood, and the disorder is rarely found in adolescents (Clark, Smith, Neighbors, Skerlec, & Randall, 1994).

Social phobia—persistent, unreasonable fears of social situations and public embarrassment—affects children, adolescents, and adults. A social phobia may be general, encompassing many types of social situations, or specific to a particular activity such as eating in public or public speaking (Norton, Cox, Hewitt, & McLeod, 1997). Either type of social phobia interferes significantly with an individual's life (Stein, Walker, & Forde, 1994). Children and adolescents with social phobias often have problems in a variety of situations (Beidel & Randall, 1994) and have particular difficulty interacting with peers (Ginsburg, LaGreca, & Silverman, 1998). Individuals with social phobias tend to avoid the situations that trigger them.

Specific phobias refer to fears of specific objects or situations such as insects (entomophobia), heights (acrophobia), or illness (nosemaphobia). Exposure to the fear-inducing object or event immediately generates intense anxiety. Children express this anxiety by crying, having tantrums, or clinging to adults and trying to avoid the source of the phobia. Adults and adolescents (but not children) are aware that their fear is excessive and unrealistic, and they also attempt to avoid the precipitating circumstance. Every year, approximately 9% of the people in the United States (2 females to every male) develop symptoms of a specific phobia (Kessler et al., 1994). Also, as many as 5% of children are judged as displaying specific phobias (Silverman & Ginsburg, 1998). Many individuals experience more than one phobia at a time (Magee et al., 1996). Some specific phobias cause more distress than others because the source of the fear is difficult to avoid. For example, it is easier to avoid snakes than dogs; therefore, cynophobia (dogs) usually is more disruptive than ophidiophobia (snakes). Aerophobia (flying) is a devastating disorder for a person whose job involves frequent global travel.

Among the phobias, specific phobias (except for claustrophobia) onset the earliest, tending to develop in childhood. However, they may occur at any time of life (Kendler et al., 1992). Some phobias that begin in childhood disappear without treatment before adulthood. Specific phobias that persist into adulthood or appear during adulthood tend not to dissipate without therapy.

Generalized Anxiety Disorder. Generalized anxiety disorder is characterized by excessive worry and anxiety that, unlike phobias, do not appear to be caused by any specific object or circumstance. Often termed *free-floating anxiety*, the symptoms of this distressing disorder include muscle tension, sleep disruption, irritability, edginess, restlessness, fatigue, difficulty concentrating, inability to relax, and physical symptoms such as chills, diarrhea, sweating, and dry mouth. The pattern of excessive worry exhibited by individuals with generalized anxiety disorder includes rumination over decisions, fear of errors or of performing in a substandard manner, and fear of what the future holds. These individuals often suffer from a mild depression as well (Barlow, 1988).

This common condition usually appears first in childhood or adolescence (before the publication of DSM–IV, the term *overanxious disorder of childhood and adolescence* was used) but may persist into adulthood. In addition to manifesting adult-type symptoms, these children lack the typical joyous, enthusiastic characteristics associated with childhood and are excessively dependent on adults. They encounter social problems because their apprehensions and dependency makes them appear infantile to their peers. Also, they cry easily and complain frequently, traits that do not add to their popularity.

Approximately 4% of the U.S. population is diagnosed with generalized anxiety disorder (Kessler et al., 1994). In children, estimates of the disorder vary, but it is relatively common, particularly in girls (Cohen et al., 1993; Keller et al., 1992). Between the ages of 10 and 20, rates decline steadily for boys (to about 5%) but remain high for girls (at about 14%). As with phobias, twice as many women as men suffer from generalized anxiety disorder. Generally this disorder is of long duration, persisting for many years, particularly when symptoms are severe (Keller et al., 1992). The severity of the symptoms appears to increase with age, becoming more debilitating in adolescence and often coexisting with phobia and depression (Wicks-Nelson & Israel, 2000).

Panic Disorder. Panic disorder is characterized by recurrent and unpredictable panic attacks, feelings of terror that overwhelm an individual and cause symptoms such as shortness of breath, chest pains, choking sensations, dizziness, heart palpitations, and notions that one is either dying or going crazy. Usually there is no obvious reason for the sudden onset of these symptoms. They pass quickly, but the attacks reoccur and the individual experiencing the disorder lives in fear of each attack. Individuals with any type of anxiety disorder may experience panic attacks when exposed to something they dread. The diagnosis of panic disorder is reserved for those people who experience panic attacks frequently, unpredictably, and without apparent reason and whose behavior is altered because of persistent worry about the reoccurrence and significance of the attacks.

According to Weissman, Bland, Canino, and Faravelli (1997), in any given year approximately 2% of people in the United States experience panic disorder. A compilation of research lists typical age at onset at 15 to 35 years and female-to-male ratio at 5:2 (Comer, 1999). The occurrence of panic disorder in prepubertal children is not reliably documented, but both adolescents and children are subject to panic attacks (Ollendick, 1998). In fact, panic attacks are relatively common in adolescents (N. J. King, Gullone, Tonge, & Ollendick, 1993), although many adolescents do not seek treatment, despite the intensity and frequency of the attacks (Ollendick, 1998). Regarding children, there is some speculation that separation anxiety develops into panic disorder (Mattis & Ollendick, 1997).

Obsessive-Compulsive Disorders. Obsessive-compulsive disorders involve unwanted, persistent, preoccupying thoughts, ideas, or images (obsessions) and irresistible impulses to engage in certain repetitive behaviors (compulsions). Both obsessions and compulsions are involuntary; adolescents and adults with this problem recognize that these ideas and actions are maladaptive but cannot control them. Obsessions vary greatly and include wishes (the death of a superior), impulses (an urge to spit on someone's shoes), images (burning down houses), ideas (being hated by everyone), and doubts (having engaged in improper behavior). Common basic themes are dirt, germs, violence, orderliness, religion, and sexuality (Comer, 1999). Compulsive behavior also varies and may be cognitive, as in reciting the words of a song before entering a room, or may involve motor rituals such as repeatedly washing one's hands throughout the day. Common compulsions involve cleaning (Tallis, 1996), checking activities (such as locked doors and windows), organization (items in particular places), touching objects, counting objects, and repeating verbal remarks or chants (Comer, 1999). Typically, obsessions elevate anxiety, which the individual tries to reduce through the compulsive activity (Pato & Pato, 1997). Consequently, most individuals experience both problems; however, it is clinically possible for persons to manifest only obsessions or compulsions. In studies involving children and youth, compulsive rituals occur more frequently than obsessions (Henin & Kendall, 1997).

Most people experience some level of obsessive thinking and compulsive behavior, as when a catchy tune invades consciousness or a lawn must be mowed in a precise, unvarying pattern. A diagnosis of obsessive-compulsive disorder may be warranted when these ideas and actions become excessive, difficult to dismiss, and intrusive; cause anxiety or distress; and literally consume the individual, occupying a great deal of time and preventing him from engaging in more adaptive behaviors.

There is some evidence that obsessive-compulsive disorders are on the increase in the United States, affecting more than 2% of the population in any given year (Karno, Golding, Sorenson, & Burnarn, 1988; Regier et al., 1993). The disorder usually onsets by young adulthood (Regier et al., 1993), and children develop it in the same manner as adults, displaying many of the same symptoms (Swedo, Rapoport, Leonard, Lenane, & Cheslow, 1989). Estimates of prevalence among adolescents also approach 2% (Flament et al., 1988). Unlike the case with other anxiety disorders, incidence figures do not differ significantly for males and females. The symptoms of this disorder appear to be persistent but to fluctuate over time (Flament, Koby, Rapoport, & Berg, 1991).

Posttraumatic and Acute Stress Disorders. Stress-related disorders result from experiencing a traumatic or catastrophic event, such as the death of a parent in an automobile crash, the loss of one's home in a fire, a sexual assault, and so forth. Symptoms of posttraumatic stress disorder include reexperiencing the traumatic event, avoiding activities that are reminiscent of the event, becoming less responsive to other people and activities that formerly were pleasurable, and experiencing signs of increased arousal, such as sleep disturbance, irritability, and inability to concentrate (Taylor, Kuch, Koch, Crockett, & Passey, 1998). Symptoms that appear within 4 weeks of the traumatic event and disappear within 1 month are diagnosed as *acute stress disorder* (APA, 1994). When symptoms continue beyond 1 month, the problem is more serious and the term *posttraumatic stress disorder* is applied.

Posttraumatic stress disorder may occur at any age, and an estimated 8% of the people in the United States experience this disorder at some time in their lives (Kessler, Sonnega, Bromet, Hughes, & Nelson, 1995). The problem is more prevalent among women, with approximately 20% of females and 8% of males exposed to stress developing the disorder (Kessler et al., 1995). The most common causes of posttraumatic stress disorder are combat, disasters, abuse, and victimization. Of these causes, the latter three directly affect children and youth.

Abuse and victimization are prevalent causes of stress disorders (Lemieux & Coe, 1995). Rape and other types of sexual abuse are among the leading forms of abuse in our society. An astounding number of people, approximately 500,000, are raped each year (U.S. Department of Justice, 1995). Almost all victims are female, and the majority are children and adolescents: 29% are under 11 years of age, 32% are between the ages of 11 and 17, and 29% are between the ages of 18 and 29. More than 80% of these individuals are raped by acquaintances or relatives (U.S. Department of Justice, 1995). Research shows that rape victims not only suffer stress immediately after the attack but also have symptoms of stress that persist for 18 months or longer (Moncrieff, Drummond, Candy, Checinski, & Farmer, 1996), and they are prone to long-term health problems (Leserman, Drossman, Li, & Toomey, 1996). The effects of sexual abuse on children who are raped by trusted adults are particularly devastating and related to serious dissociative personality disorders, including multiple personality disorder (Putnam, Guroff, Silberman, Barban, & Post, 1986; Ross, Norton, & Wozney, 1989).

Other types of child abuse causing stress disorders appear to be related to poverty and dysfunctional families (Putnam, 1996). Also, parents of children with stress disorders tend to have stress disorders themselves.

In addition to suffering stress disorders caused by abuse and victimization, evidence exists that, like adults, children exposed to both natural and accidental disasters experience symptoms of posttraumatic stress disorder (Vogel & Vernberg, 1993). Even when children do not meet all of the specific criteria for posttraumatic stress disorder, they develop some of the symptoms, and many display increased fearfulness of situations or events related to the original trauma-inducing circumstance, for example, swimming after a drowning incident. The severity of the disorder among children varies greatly. LaGreca, Silverman, and Wasserstein (1998) suggested that symptom severity and persistence are influenced by the interaction of four variables: degree of exposure to the traumatic event, the characteristics of the child, the child's coping skills, and the degree of social support available. Many experts believe that the prognosis for recovery is generally favorable if psychotherapy is provided, although the outcome is influenced by the psychological health of the individual before the event (Brom, Kleber, & Defares, 1989).

Etiology of Anxiety Disorders

The diverse disorders included in this category undoubtedly have many different causal agents. Since the famous "little Albert" research conducted by J. B. Watson and Rayner (1920), behaviorists have attributed the development of fears or phobias to learning through classical conditioning. Classical conditioning occurs when two stimuli, one innocuous (such as a toy bunny) and the other fear inducing (such as a loud, startling noise), are introduced to an individual at the same time. The individual associates the stimuli and responds in the same way (fearfully) to both. Another behavioral theory is that fear is learned by observing and imitating (modeling) the behavior of another person. Of late, these explanations have been challenged as insufficient to explain the way phobias are typically acquired (Hofmann, Ehler, & Roth, 1995). More current theory reflects a combined biological–behavioral perspective, holding that individuals are genetically predisposed or "prepared" to acquire certain phobias (Graham & Gaffan, 1997; Ohman & Soares, 1993). Predispositions are fulfilled by negative environmental circumstances. For example, overprotective, intrusive parents have been identified as likely to produce fearful, anxious children (Dumas, LaFreniere, & Serketich, 1995).

Similarly, biological explanations have become extremely influential in explaining the development of generalized anxiety disorder. Research exploring the effectiveness of benzodiazepines, drugs that reduce anxiety (Valium and Xanax), has led to an understanding of the biochemical and neurological activity that triggers fear (Brawman-Mintzer & Lydiard, 1997; Haefely, 1990). Basically, states of increased neurological excitability increase fear, which in turn activates biochemicals to reduce excitability so that the fear subsides (Costa, 1995). When this system does not function properly, anxiety does not abate (Lloyd, Fletcher, & Minchin, 1992).

An alternative cognitive perspective holds that anxiety is produced by maladaptive or irrational thinking. In short, people constantly have negative, self-destructive thoughts about themselves and others that cause them to experience intense anxiety (Calvo, Eysenck, & Castillo, 1997; Ellis, 1995). Possibly, children with certain biologically determined predispositions are programmed to focus their attention on negative or threatening events.

Panic disorder also is attributed, at least in part, to biological factors, primarily because symptoms often are controlled by antidepressant drugs (Jefferson, 1997). Some researchers believe that faulty cognitive operations also play a role, in that anxiety-sensitive persons focus on bodily sensations and view them as harmful (Cox, 1996; Cox, Endler, & Swinson, 1995).

Biological explanations for obsessive-compulsive disorder focus on low activity of the neurotransmitter serotonin and on abnormal activity in the brain, either the orbital frontal cortex (located above the eyes) or the caudate nuclei (located in the basal ganglia; Comer, 1999). Drugs that increase serotonin activity reduce obsessive-compulsive symptoms (Klerman et al., 1994; Rapoport, 1991). PET (positron-emission tomography) scans of individuals with obsessive-compulsive disorder show excessive activity in both the orbital frontal cortex and the caudate nuclei (Pato & Pato, 1997) that might be caused by low serotonin activity. Both of these biological irregularities may have a genetic basis. Obsessive-compulsive disorder occurs more frequently in children who have first-degree relatives with the disorder than in the general population (March & Mulle, 1998).

Among anxiety-related conditions, stress disorder appears to be most closely related to environmental circumstances. However, people vary in their ability to cope with stress and overcome traumatic and catastrophic experiences. Research has identified biochemical differences in trauma victims that appear related to the extent of stress they experience (Resnick, Yehuda, Pitman, & Foy, 1995; Yehuda, Kahana, Binder-Brynes, & Southwick, 1995). Also, a genetic component may be involved in the equation; identical twins in combat situations appear to develop similar stress symptoms (True, Rice, & Eisen, 1993).

Treatment of Anxiety Disorders

Psychotherapy is the treatment of choice for most anxiety disorders, particularly for children and youth. Behavioral therapies have a history of great success with all types of phobias. Also, cognitive therapies that focus on reshaping irrational thinking and teaching coping skills and self-management strategies have been effective (Kendall, Panichelli-Mindel, Sugarman, & Callahan, 1997). In some cases, pharmacological treatments also are employed, although they are more likely to be introduced for adolescents than for children. Drugs in combination with cognitive–behavioral therapy that emphasizes learning to resist obsessions and compulsions are particularly useful for treating obsessive-compulsive disorder (Leonard, Swedo, Allen, & Rapoport, 1994).

The development of community therapy reflects an attempt to help victims of traumatic events and minimize the effects of stress. The Disaster Response Network was created in 1991 by the American Red Cross and the American Psychological Association to provide immediate assistance to people affected by natural disasters (Comer, 1999). Rape crisis counseling is another example of the use of trained volunteers to help people cope with trauma.

Attention-Deficit and Disruptive Behavior Disorders

Included in the DSM–IV category *attention-deficit and disruptive behavior disorders* are *oppositional defiant disorder*, *conduct disorder*, and *attention-deficit/*

hyperactivity disorder. These disorders typically first appear in childhood and adolescence.

Oppositional Defiant Disorder and Conduct Disorder

Oppositional defiant disorder (ODD) and conduct disorder (CD) are similar syndromes in that they are characterized by overt, acting-out behaviors that create problems for other people. Empirical research that does not conform to DSM–IV criteria identifies behaviors associated with ODD and CD as part of a broad-based, externalizing (as opposed to internalizing) syndrome (Achenbach, 1993). Children with ODD display a pattern of hostile, resentful behavior marked by resistance to adult authority. Symptoms include arguing with adults, defying adult requests or rules, deliberately annoying others, blaming others for one's own misbehavior, and being easily annoyed, quickly angered, and prone to vindictiveness. To warrant this diagnosis, children must display at least four of these symptoms more frequently than is typical for most children of the same age. The average age of onset for ODD is 6 years, and the condition is more common in boys than in girls when diagnosed before adolescence. The consistent, noncompliant behavior associated with ODD not only presents immediate problems for parents and teachers but also may represent the earliest indication of a lifelong tendency toward antisocial behavior (Hinshaw, Lahey, & Hart, 1993).

CD represents a more serious pattern of behavior that repeatedly violates the rights of others. Individuals with CD display symptoms of hostile behavior in four categories: aggression toward people and animals, destruction of property, deceitfulness or theft, and serious violations of rules. Examples of aggression include fighting using a weapon, being physically cruel to people (mugging) and animals (microwaving, hanging, burning), stealing while confronting a victim (armed robbery), and forcing someone into sexual activity (rape). Destruction of property includes setting fires to cause serious damage (Jacobson, 1985) and deliberately destroying property. Deceitfulness or theft involves breaking into homes, cars, and other property, lying to obtain goods or favors, and stealing. Serious violations of rules include truancy, running away from home, and staying out at night despite parental prohibitions. To be diagnosed with CD, an individual under the age of 18 must exhibit three or more of the symptomatic behaviors in a 12-month period and one behavior within the past 6 months. Also, the behavior must significantly interfere with social, academic, or job-related functioning and not be caused by aversive environmental conditions such as living in high-crime neighborhoods (APA, 1994).

Most cases of CD begin before age 10 (referred to as childhood-onset CD) (average age at onset is age 9), and occur predominantly in males.

Adolescent-onset CD, occurring after age 10, is less frequent, involves a higher ratio of females, features more nonaggressive than aggressive behaviors, and is less likely to persist into adulthood (McGee, Feehan, Williams, & Anderson, 1992; Moffitt, 1993). The prevalence of CD is reported as 6% to 16% of boys and 2% to 9% of girls (APA, 1994). Most (about 95%) individuals diagnosed with CD also meet standards for ODD diagnosis; however, in accordance with DSM–IV guidelines, only the CD diagnosis is used. A minority of children diagnosed with ODD are later diagnosed with CD (Hinshaw et al., 1993). The extensive comorbidity of the two disorders causes some speculation that ODD is a developmental precursor to CD (Wicks-Nelson & Israel, 2000).

In addition to ODD, CD is comorbid with attention-deficit/hyperactivity disorder (ADHD), with between 30% and 50% of children with ADHD developing CD (Johnston & Ohan, 1999). CD also coexists with a variety of other problems, including depression (Dishion, French, & Patterson, 1995), anxiety (Nottelmann & Jensen, 1995), social rejection (Newcomb, Bukowski, & Pattee, 1993), and cognitive/academic deficits (Maughan & Rutter, 1998).

The seriousness of CD appears closely related to the individual's age at onset. Those children with onset of CD before age 10 engage in more aggressive, destructive behaviors and are more likely to persist in antisocial activity as adults than are those with later onset (Patterson, DeBarsyshe, & Ramsey, 1989; Patterson, Reid, & Dishion, 1992; H. M. Walker, 1995; Zeitlin, 1986). Frequently, behaviors become progressively more harmful as the child matures and may culminate in murder. In fact, the profiles of serial killers often show an early history of CD and a progression of increased violence in their antisocial behaviors as they grow older (Douglas & Olshaker, 1995).

The seriousness of CD also is influenced by the types of conduct disordered behaviors displayed. Quay (1986) found different patterns in the types of conduct disordered behaviors committed by individuals and differentiated between socialized and undersocialized CD. Undersocialized individuals engage in more overtly violent, aggressive behaviors, such as fighting, arguing, swearing, boasting, disobeying, being cruel to animals, showing irritability, and attacking others. Socialized individuals are prone to transgress more covertly, through stealing, setting fires, keeping bad company, joining gangs, playing truant, abusing alcohol, and lying. Some individuals, potentially most harmful to others, display both types of CD (Kauffman, 1997).

Juvenile Delinquency

An obvious relationship exists between CD and juvenile delinquency. *Delinquency* is a legal term that refers to breaking the law, and *juvenile* refers to anyone under the age of 18. Young lawbreakers commit two classes of crimes, *index offenses* and *status offenses.* Index crimes are illegal for persons of all ages and include both misdemeanors (shoplifting, vandalism) and felonies (rape, murder, aggravated assault). Status crimes pertain only to juveniles and include events such as sexual promiscuity, running away from home, drinking alcoholic beverages, and truancy. Status crimes are related to so-called incorrigible behavior or behavior that parents cannot control.

The incidence of delinquent behavior among adolescents is quite high, reported at 80% to 90% in self-report surveys. However, a much lower rate of official delinquency is documented (15% to 35% for males and 2% to 14% for females; *Uniform Crime Reports,* 1989). "Official" delinquency requires that a child be judged as delinquent in court by being officially convicted of a crime. Obviously, many delinquent behaviors go undetected or unreported to authorities. Even when an illegal event is reported, police may choose not to prosecute the case or the court may choose not to officially convict the individual. In any given year, about 3% of minors are judged as officially delinquent (Siegel & Senna, 1994). The designation usually is applied to adolescents rather than to young children, although the average age of youthful offenders may be decreasing. When children begin delinquent acts before the age of 12 and when they repeat those types of acts, they are more likely than other individuals to engage in criminal activities as adults (Farrington, 1995). Juvenile delinquents who commit violent crimes are likely to commit violent crimes as adults (Lattimore, Visher, & Linster, 1995). Unfortunately for society, official juvenile delinquency is increasing, and the nature of the offenses is becoming increasingly more violent (Kinnear, 1995). Males commit most offenses, particularly the index crimes. Females usually commit status crimes and, because of gender bias, are more likely to be tried and convicted for behaviors that would be ignored in young males (e.g., sexual promiscuity).

As in the case of CD, empirical research has produced evidence of several subtypes of delinquency (Achenbach, 1982; Quay, 1986), *socialized-subcultural, unsocialized-psychopathic,* and *disturbed-neurotic.* Socialized delinquents do not display characteristics of emotional disturbance but join gangs and relate well with peers in their delinquent subculture. Unsocialized-psychopathic delinquents are indiscriminately aggressive and assaultive. They do not establish sincere social relationships, even with delinquent peer groups, because they view others as objects to victimize and exploit. Disturbed-neurotic delinquents are shy, withdrawn individuals with emotional problems.

Attention-Deficit/Hyperactivity Disorder

DSM–IV presents symptoms of inattention and hyperactivity–impulsivity under the umbrella heading ADHD. For the most part, the crux of this disorder currently is viewed as attention problems that may or may not be accompanied by hyperactive behavior. Symptoms of the attention disorder include distractibility; forgetfulness; and problems organizing tasks, listening when spoken to, sustaining attention, attending to details, following through on instructions or duties, holding on to things necessary for tasks or activities, and avoiding careless mistakes.

Symptoms of hyperactivity include being "on the go" constantly and the inability to sit still (not fidget or squirm), stay seated at appropriate times, play quietly or enjoy quiet activities, and curb incessant talk. Impulsivity is characterized by blurting out answers before the questions are completed, having difficulty waiting a turn, and interrupting or intruding on others. Depending on the types of symptoms exhibited, the individual can be diagnosed as (a) ADHD predominantly inattentive type, also called ADD (six or more symptoms of attention deficit); (b) ADHD predominantly hyperactive–impulsive type (six or more symptoms of hyperactive–impulsive deficit); or ADHD combined type (six or more symptoms of both categories).

As might be expected, individuals with ADHD usually have problems in school, both with academic achievement and social behaviors. As a group, their performance on intelligence tests is slightly lower than that of peers without ADHD, but the intellectual ability of individuals varies and includes giftedness (Barkley, 1998). Their academic underachievement usually is attributed to their problems attending and concentrating. Many children with ADHD require special education services. ADHD is not a specific category for services; consequently, most of these children are identified as "learning disabled" (29%) or "behaviorally disordered" (52%; Reid, Maag, & Vasa, 1994). Disability labeling aside, there appears to be a great deal of overlap between ADHD and learning disabilities, particularly in clinic populations (Anastopoulos & Barkley, 1992).

Some students with ADHD, most often those who display hyperactivity and impulsivity, develop patterns of behavior associated with ODD and CD, possibly as a result of their failure to adjust to the requirements of school (Barrett & Stanford, 1996). Jordan (1998) points out that, unlike individuals with CD and ODD, most children with ADHD annoy or antagonize others without harmful intent and regret their behavior when it is pointed out to them. Regardless of intent, however, difficulties with social interactions are common, particularly for children displaying hyperactive–impulsive behavior. Although most of the hyperactive children want to relate positively with others, the excessiveness of their behavior (e.g., loud, rough, disruptive, rule ignoring, lacking self-control) causes their peers to reject them (Hinshaw, 1998).

The subgroup of children with ADD, who are predominantly inattentive and not hyperactive, differ greatly from their hyperactive peers. They process information slowly and less efficiently, manifest more anxiety and depression, have fewer overt behavior problems, and experience more academic difficulty (Barkley, 1998; Jordan, 1998). They tend to withdraw from social interactions and be ignored by others (Hinshaw, 1998). The characteristics of their disorder more closely fit the internalizing syndrome, whereas the characteristics of the hyperactive–impulsive children are more closely aligned with the externalizing syndrome.

There is considerable disagreement about the prevalence of ADHD. Some people believe that many prevalence estimates are inflated because the ADHD label is applied in an indiscriminate way to children who underachieve and act out because of poor parenting or poor instruction. In the school-age population, figures range from 2% to 30% (Dowdy, Patton, Smith, & Polloway, 1998), reflecting the differing opinions about identification criteria. Jordan (1998) indicated that a 5% figure is accurate if symptoms of hyperactivity are necessary for identification but that 10% to 13% is more realistic when the individuals with attention deficit without hyperactivity are included in the count. ADHD is usually perceived as far more common among boys than girls, with a ratio of four to nine boys to one girl (APA, 1994). Identification of the condition declines with adolescence.

Most experts believe that ADHD is a serious developmental disorder that onsets early in life (before age 7; Kauffman, 1997). Some of the symptoms of ADHD, such as impulsiveness and attention deficit, are also associated with other serious developmental disabilities, such as autism. In some cases, hyperactivity lessens with maturity; however, it is most typical for ADHD-related social, emotional, and achievement problems to persist into adulthood (Slomkowski, Klein, & Mannuzza, 1995).

Etiology of Disruptive Behavior Disorders

The conditions included in the diagnostic category *disruptive behavior disorders* are diverse and have different causes. Unlike the case in ADHD, aggressive behaviors lie at the heart of the ODD and CD categories, and the primary causes of aggression often are attributed to social learning. Early research by Bandura (1965, 1973) that demonstrated how aggressive behavior is imitated by young children remains relevant in a society that is experiencing ever-increasing levels of violently aggressive behavior by children and youth. Children who are exposed to aggression at home will exhibit aggressive behavior (Kashani, Daniel, Dandoy, & Holcomb, 1992). Aggressive behaviors become the norm in families marked by marital discord and aggression between parents (Davies & Cummings, 1994). Children labeled delinquent tend to have family members who have engaged in criminal behavior (Kazdin, 1985).

The tendency to learn aggression by imitating aggressive models also extends to media portrayals of violent behavior (Sprafkin, Gadow, & Adelman, 1992). People gain vicarious reinforcement from observing high-status models rewarded for aggressive behavior, as when the movie hero is acclaimed for killing his enemies. Also, the impact of violent behavior is diminished by repeated exposure to media violence. People begin to believe that the killings, beatings, and other threatening behaviors that they view frequently on television are an appropriate means for solving problems. Children, who are still forming the cognitive schemata that determine their behavior, are particularly vulnerable to this type of exposure. Adler (1994) quantified the extent of the exposure, finding that an average child has watched approximately 8,000 murders and 100,000 violent acts on television before finishing elementary school.

Children also learn to aggress when parents have inadequate management skills. Research by Patterson and colleagues (1992) focused on parental management skills that produce coercive interactions, as when parents are inconsistent with discipline, fail to reward compliant behavior, and inadvertently reinforce children for noncompliant behavior, such as having tantrums, by giving in. When poor management skills occur in the context of a stressful environment (e.g., financial pressure, employment problems, or illness), aggression is more likely to result (Paschall & Hubbard, 1998).

In addition to investigating the relationship between aggression and environmental conditions, investigators have examined biological factors. Research exploring neurological and biochemical differences between highly aggressive persons and typical individuals has uncovered variations in heart rate and skin conductance responses that may signify biological causal factors in the most severely affected persons with lifelong conduct disorder (Quay, 1993). However, this premise and others that explore neurological deficits require further investigation before they are of any practical value to persons interested in curbing excessive aggression. Also, despite the significant tendency for children to display aggressive behavior if other family members do, there is no strong evidence of a genetic component (Wicks-Nelson & Israel, 2000). It seems clear that if genetic factors predispose certain individuals to excessive aggression, they are triggered by interactions with unfavorable environmental conditions (Rutter, Silberg, O'Connor, & Simonoff, 1999).

Etiology of ADHD

The causes of ADHD have not been clearly identified, but most existing research evidence points to some type of biological basis for the disorder. Early theories attributed the problem to immature functioning of the central nervous system or "minimal brain dysfunction" (Jenkins, 1970) and regarded so-called poor perceptual–motor coordination as evidence of "soft neurological signs" or neural pathology (Caputo & Mandell, 1970; Wikler, Dixon, & Parker, 1970). Over the years, these terms have been discarded, and more recent research has associated various types of brain irregularities, including structural differences in the right frontal lobe (Tannock, 1998), with ADHD. There also is some evidence, albeit inconclusive, of atypical biochemical reactions in the brain, particularly with chemicals that affect neurotransmissions (Anastopoulos & Barkley, 1992).

Other biological causation theories have advanced the premise that various foods, particularly sugar, dyes, tomato products, refined white wheat products, and preservatives, are implicated in ADHD. Although this premise has had wide public acceptance, its validity for a majority of children with ADHD has not been confirmed by empirical research (McLoughlin & Nall, 1994; Wolraich, Wilson, & White, 1995). However, food intolerance may produce symptoms of ADHD in a small number of children with specific food allergies.

The most consistent evidence of biological causation lies in genetic research. Studies of twins have shown significantly high concordance rates, and family studies have shown that between 10% and 35% of first-degree family members develop ADHD. However, the manner in which ADHD is inherited has not been determined (Neuman et al., 1999; Wicks-Nelson & Israel, 2000). As with so many other disorders, the variety of symptoms that comprise ADHD probably have multiple causes.

Poor or inappropriate parenting of children with ADHD, particularly those with hyperactivity, may also contribute to the problems associated with the condition. Managing the behavior of a child with ADHD is exhausting and demands the cooperative efforts of both parents using effective strategies to maintain discipline without creating a coercive environment. Not surprisingly, family conditions that are problematic in some manner exacerbate the symptoms of ADHD.

Treatment of Disruptive Behavior Disorders

The use of drugs to treat children is always a highly controversial issue. Critics point out that medications often have negative side effects (e.g., insomnia, headaches, and tics) and that the long-term effects of drugs on a developing brain are not fully understood (Barkley, 1998; DuPaul, Barkley, & Connor, 1998; Whalen & Henker, 1991). For ADHD, however, drugs are a common component of treatment. Stimulants such as Ritalin and Dexedrine have been found to calm the excessive behaviors of children with ADHD and are the drugs of choice. Research supports their effectiveness in reducing impulsivity and hyperactivity and increasing learning for a large majority of children with ADHD

(DuPaul & Stoner, 1994; Whalen & Henker, 1998). Additionally, improved behavior often leads to better social relationships (Jordan, 1998).

Stimulant medication works by arousing the prefrontal cortex, usually within 30 minutes of administration. The drug is effective for 3 to 4 hours, so unless it is given in a slow release capsule, it must be taken periodically throughout the day. When mood disorder, particularly depression, coexists with ADHD or ADD, antidepressant medication (Norpramin, Tofranil, Elavil) also is administered and appears to double the effectiveness of stimulants alone (Barkley, 1995).

Other types of treatment include training parents and teachers to use empirically validated behavior management strategies such as token reinforcement, response cost, and time-out to control noncompliant, defiant, excessive behavior. These strategies are effective in helping children with ODD, CD, and ADHD. Specific information about these procedures is presented in Chapter 5.

Promising treatment programs for individuals with CD and ODD draw upon social learning theory and emphasize training parents to use proven behavioral strategies (Kazdin, 1997) to build a more positive climate in the home. In addition, children are taught cognitive problem-solving strategies to learn to recognize and alter their irrational beliefs and to take responsibility for their behavior. Some of the strategies employed include self-instruction (talking to oneself about the task or behavior) and self-monitoring (evaluating one's own performance; Kazdin, 1997). Specific information about these and other cognitive procedures is presented in Chapter 6. Apparently, treatments involving problem-solving strategies and parental training are most effective for children with CD and ODD when they are combined (Kazdin, Siegel, & Bass, 1992). However, for children with ADHD, cognitive strategies have not proved to produce lasting benefits (Hinshaw, Klein, & Abikoff, 1998).

Physical Disorders

Physical disorders affect eating, sleeping, elimination, sexual functioning, and physical movement. Although these conditions are not classified as anxiety disorders, elevated anxiety is often associated with many of them.

Eating Disorders

Problems related to eating are not uncommon in a society where thinness is worshiped, bizarre diets are the rule, and food abounds. Unfortunately, many of these problems develop into full-blown disorders with serious consequences for the individuals they afflict. The disorders that cause the most concern are *anorexia nervosa, bulimia nervosa, obesity, rumination,* and *pica* (Mizes, 1995).

Anorexia Nervosa. Anorexia nervosa is a condition marked by intense fear of becoming overweight and a distorted self-image that causes misperceptions of body weight. People with this disorder drastically restrict their intake of food and often engage in excessive, compulsive exercise until they become so seriously underweight (15% or more below normal) that, in the case of females, they cease to have menstrual cycles. A subtype of these individuals also binge, then purge themselves through forced vomiting and use of laxatives or diuretics (Russell, 1995). Almost all cases of anorexia nervosa (90% to 95%) occur in females, with peak onset between ages 14 and 19 (Fombonne, 1995). The incidence of this disorder appears to be increasing (Lucas & Holub, 1995). In the United States and other Western countries, approximately 1% to 4% of adolescent girls and young women develop the disorder. Most individuals recover; however, approximately 10% become seriously ill and die from medical problems (anemia, cardiovascular disease, hormonal irregularities) caused by starvation (Nielson et al., 1998; Slade, 1995) or suicide (Pike, 1998; Steiner & Lock, 1998).

The characteristics associated with anorexia nervosa include preoccupation with food (G. A. King, Polivy, & Herman, 1991), which may be caused by starvation. These individuals also have distorted thought processes, in that they dislike their bodies, overestimate their body size (Rushford & Ostermeyer, 1997), and set unrealistic, perfectionistic standards for themselves (DeSilva, 1995). Other problems coexisting with anorexia nervosa include low self-esteem, sleep disturbances, mild depression, and obsessive-compulsive patterns (Casper, 1995; Halmi, 1995; Thiel, Brooks, Ohlmeier, & Jacoby, 1995).

Bulimia Nervosa. Bulimia nervosa differs from anorexia nervosa in that body weight is not below normal and binge eating/purging is typical (10 episodes per week is average; Mizes, 1995). The binge/purge cycle appears to be related to high levels of anxiety and self-disgust (DeSilva, 1995). A subtype of persons with bulimia nervosa substitutes fasting and/or excessive exercise for purging.

Bulimia nervosa appears in 1% to 4% of adolescent or young women. Unlike the profile for anorexia nervosa, persons with this condition tend to suffer mood swings, be unable to control their impulses, and frequently abuse drugs or alcohol (Sanftner & Crowther, 1998; Wiederman & Pryor, 1996). More than one third of these individuals also suffer from personality disorder (Braun, Sunday, & Halmi, 1995).

The causes of anorexia and bulimia are not completely understood; however, most researchers attribute them to multiple factors, including social and family pressures, psychological problems, and biological influences. Social factors include the tendency to equate thinness with beauty in women (Nichter & Nichter, 1991) and prejudice against overweight people (Tiggeman & Wilson-Barrett, 1998). Theories about the role of families in anorexia and bulimia range from a broad perspective of fundamental dysfunction (Vandereycken, 1994) to a narrow view of excessive emphasis on thinness and dieting (Hart & Kenny, 1995). The psychological problems involved include severe cognitive disturbances, for example, lack of self-reliance, independence, and self-respect and a tendency to rely excessively on the views of others (Parker et al., 1993; Vitousek & Manke, 1994). There also is evidence of a relationship between anorexia and bulimia and obsessive-compulsive disorder (Thiel et al., 1995). Biological theorists regard the hypothalamus as the key to eating disorders (Liebowitz & Hoebel, 1998). Centers of the hypothalamus are activated by chemicals that both stimulate and suppress appetite. When those centers malfunction, eating irregularities result.

Treatment of these disorders involves restoring normal eating by using forced feeding in the most serious cases, cognitive therapy (Garner, 1986), behavioral approaches to reinforce eating (Agras, Schneider, Arnow, & Raeburn, 1989), and supportive nursing care (Andersen, 1995; Treasure, Todd, & Szmukler, 1995). Additionally, efforts are made to place individuals with aneroxia and bulimia in therapeutic treatments to alter the cognitive distortions that underlie the conditions.

Obesity. Excessive body weight is a serious problem in the United States, where prevalence rates for obesity have increased 54% among young children and 39% among adolescents since the mid-1960s (Campaigne et al., 1994; Wicks-Nelson & Israel, 2000). This disorder creates significant difficulties—physically, psychologically, and socially—for youngsters that tend to persist into adulthood (Boodman, 1995; Pierce & Wardle, 1993). Obesity is related to low self-confidence, poor self-concept, and inadequate social relationships. Causes of obesity are complex and include social, psychological, and biological factors (Leibel & Hirsch, 1995). Genetics plays an important role in creating a propensity for obesity, which may be exacerbated by family eating habits (Price, 1995). Poor dietary habits are learned from parents, as are patterns of too little exercise and underactivity. Cultural forces such as television trumpet the availability of unhealthy, fat-producing food and provide an inactive pastime for children. Obesity can be countered by developing new, lifelong eating habits that involve fewer calories and less fat and by making increased activity and exercise a part of each day. Fad or crash diets to lose weight quickly are counterproductive because they often slow metabolism and result in further weight gain when they are abandoned.

Rumination and Pica. Rumination is voluntary regurgitation that lacks an organic cause. It occurs most often in infants and individuals with mental retardation. The condition is more prevalent in males (Kerwin & Berkowitz, 1996) and can be dangerous to health, particularly in infants. Information regarding the cause of rumination is sparse and speculative. For infants, increasing parent–child interactions is helpful in curbing the behavior. For individuals with mental retardation, aversive procedures such as shock have been employed.

Pica involves eating inedible substances, such as hair, paper, dirt, paint, and fabric. It is usually diagnosed in children ages 2 to 3 and in individuals with mental retardation (McAlpine & Singh, 1986). Little is actually known about causal factors. Behavioral treatments, including reinforcing eating habits incompatible with pica, have been used to counter the problem.

Other Eating Disturbances. Many children engage in feeding games with adults by refusing to eat at mealtime or agreeing to eat only certain foods. Adults who overreact to these behaviors by insisting that children eat may contribute to negative responses to food that persist into adulthood. Increased parental indifference to the child's eating habits plus withholding of preferred foods, such as desserts and candy, usually bring about a more successful outcome.

Sleep Disorders

Sleep disturbances are common in human beings of all ages. Mindell (1993) reports that approximately 25% of children below the age of 6 have some type of sleep disturbance. Adolescents also suffer sleep problems that may be frequent and persistent (Morrison, McGee, & Stanton, 1992). DSM–IV identifies two main types of sleep disorders, *dyssomnias* and *parasomnias*.

Dyssomnias. Dyssomnias involve disturbances in the amount, quality, or timing of sleep (APA, 1994). Insomnia, hypersomnia, narcolepsy, breathing-related sleep disorder, and disturbed circadian rhythm are types of dyssomnias. Insomnia, difficulty falling and staying asleep, is the most common dyssomnia. It affects between 30% and 40% of adults each year (Comer, 1999) and occurs frequently in children and adolescents. Parents complain of children who have difficulty falling asleep and sleeping through the night. However, research has shown that children with sleeping problems wake no more frequently than children without sleeping problems. When awake, children with sleep problems disturb their parents instead of going back to sleep as other children do (Minde et al., 1993). In children, insomnia often is treated by behavioral strategies that reinforce going to bed and staying in bed when awakened (Minde, Faucon, & Faulkner, 1994).

Hypersomnia is excessive sleepiness that lasts for at least 1 month. Narcolepsy is characterized by attacks of REM (rapid eye movement) sleep during the day. A narcolepsy sufferer may fall asleep while taking a test or driving a car. Breathing-related sleep disorder is caused by lack of oxygen to the brain. Afflicted individuals awaken repeatedly during the night to breathe. Circadian rhythm sleep disorder is variation between the sufferer's sleep–wake pattern and the pattern of most other people in the environment, as when an individual works a night shift.

Parasomnias. Parasomnias are abnormal events that occur during sleep, such as nightmares, sleep terror, and sleepwalking (APA, 1994). Nightmares are the most common of these disorders, affecting people of all ages. Children between the ages of 3 and 6 years are particularly vulnerable to these frightening dreams. They occur during REM sleep (in the middle or later part of the night) and often reflect fears or problems that the child has experienced during the day. Children are easily aroused from nightmares and often remember the episodes. Parents can attempt to pinpoint the source of their anxiety and help them cope with it.

Sleep terror is a more serious condition that occurs relatively rarely (1% to 6%) (Wilson & Haynes, 1985) during the first third of the evening sleep. Individuals awaken suddenly, screaming in a state of panic, often incoherent. Usually the episode is not remembered the next day. Sleep terrors most often appear in children between the ages of 4 and 12 years and disappear during adolescence (APA, 1994).

Sleepwalking involves leaving the bed and walking around without being conscious of doing so or remembering it later. These episodes also occur in the first third of the evening sleep. Usually these individuals avoid physical injury, although accidents do happen on occasion. Approximately 1% to 5% of all children experience this disorder, and up to 30% have occasional episodes. The problem usually disappears before age 15. Stress, fatigue, and physical illness all influence sleepwalking (APA, 1994). Family patterns of sleepwalking also suggest a genetic causal factor.

Elimination Disorders

Elimination disorders include *enuresis* and *encopresis*. Enuresis, the more common of the two disorders, is repeated urination in bed or clothing, during the day or at night, that is not caused by physical illness. The DSM–IV diagnosis is not used unless the child is at least 5 years of age, and the problem occurs with frequency that varies with age. APA (1994) statistics indicate that enuresis is found in 7% of boys and 3% of girls age 5 but decreases to 3% of boys and 2%

of girls at age 10 and to 1% of 18-year-olds. However, other estimates of prevalence are higher (15% to 20% of 5-year-olds and 7% to 15% of 7-year-olds). Bed-wetting, or nocturnal enuresis, occurs more frequently than wetting during the day, or diurnal enuresis. In most cases, the individuals have never been continent (primary enuresis), but 15% develop the problem after a period of continence (secondary enuresis; Walker, Kenning, & Faust-Campanile, 1989).

No single cause for enuresis has been identified. Theories featuring premature toilet training have never been empirically substantiated; however, any variety of poor parenting skills may be involved. There is some evidence that the condition coexists with other behavioral problems (Siegel & Smith, 1991). However, family stress and negative parent–child interactions, which often produce maladaptive behaviors, may be caused in part by the enuresis. Other evidence from family histories and studies of twins suggests that a genetic component may predispose a child for enuresis, and an avenue of biological theory focuses on slow development of the urinary system (Erickson, 1992).

Many cases of enuresis clear up with maturation, without treatment. Also, a variety of behavioral interventions have been effective, including a classical conditioning approach that involves wiring the bed with an alarm system activated by urine (Howe & Walker, 1992; Whelen & Houts, 1990). Drug therapy, particularly use of antidepressants, has achieved some success but is highly controversial because of possible side effects (Ondersma & Walker, 1998).

Encopresis is repeatedly defecating into clothing or other inappropriate places when no physical illness exists. For diagnosis, the behavior must occur at least once a month and the child must be at least 4 years of age (APA, 1994). This condition is less common than enuresis, rarely occurs at night during sleep, occurs primarily in boys, affects about 2% to 3% of children ages 5 to 7, and decreases with age (APA, 1994; Ondersma & Walker, 1998).

Children with encopresis are embarrassed by the condition and experience serious social problems. There is no clear evidence of coexisting psychopathology; however, the condition has not been greatly studied (Comer, 1999). Theories regarding causation include inadequacies in the physical and developmental processes that produce bowel control (Doleys, 1989), faulty training, and stress. Treatment combines behavioral and medical approaches and combinations of the two (Ronen, 1993). These include modifications in diet, use of laxatives, reinforcement for appropriate defecation, and child responsibility for cleanup (Ondersma & Walker, 1998).

Stereotyped Movement Disorders

Stereotyped movements are involuntary, repetitive motor acts. They are seen in children with pervasive developmental disorders, such as autism (e.g., hand waving). The most common type of this disorder is usually referred to as a *tic*. Tics are involuntary muscle movements or spasms, frequently affecting the face, as with eye blinking, lip licking or smacking, and grimacing, and to a lesser extent the body, as with neck twisting and shoulder shrugging. Tics also may be vocal, as with throat clearing and repetition of words or sounds. These problems range from mild to severe in intensity and occur most frequently between the ages of 6 and 14, primarily among males (Schowalter, 1988). In some cases they persist into adulthood. Often the individual is unaware of the tic and experiences increased tension when made aware of it. Occasionally, tics occur as reactions to a specific fatiguing or stressful situation and disappear when the situation alters, for example, when a very tired person finishes writing a paper.

Most tics are caused by stress; however, a more severe condition, *Tourette's syndrome*, is a neurological disorder. Tourette's syndrome, which onsets before age 18, is characterized by multiple motor tics and at least one verbal tic occurring frequently throughout the day for more than 1 year (APA, 1994). It occurs in 4 to 5 persons per 10,000 and more frequently in males. In some cases the tics are extremely obvious (loud barking) and socially inappropriate (shouting obscenities), and sufferers often experience social rejection and may be misidentified as being conduct disordered. However, recent publicity about Tourette's syndrome has educated the public about the condition and to some degree has mitigated negative responses to children displaying the symptoms (Kauffman, 1997).

The cause of Tourette's syndrome is not known; however, it often coexists with other neurological disorders, particularly attention-deficit/hyperactivity disorder and obsessive-compulsive disorder. Like most other conditions, the syndrome is exacerbated by stress (Silva, Munoz, Barickman, & Friedhoff, 1995). Treatment usually is a combination of drugs and cognitive–behavioral therapy and involves family and school.

Psychosocial–Physical Disorders

Psychosocial–physical disorders are bodily illnesses or problems that, for the most part, are caused by psychological or sociocultural factors. This category of disorders includes *factitious disorder*, *somatoform disorders*, and *psychophysiological disorders*.

Factitious Disorders

Individuals who fake physical symptoms because they want to be sick—in situations that do not involve financial gain—may receive the diagnosis of factitious disorder. These individuals do not simply lie about their condition but actually take drugs, use laxatives, apply substances such as feces to open wounds, and so forth to produce illnesses (Feldman, Ford, & Reinhold, 1994). They also endure painful medical tests, surgery, and extensive physical discomfort to appear ill. This type of disorder is difficult to diagnose because the individuals resist any implication that their symptoms are factitious (Bauer & Boegner, 1996). The most severe, long-term type of factitious disorder is *Munchausen syndrome*. Individuals diagnosed with Munchausen syndrome have long histories of hospitalizations and extensive medical records of serious diseases and injuries. According to the APA (1994), the disorder is most common among people who have had a true physical disorder, close relationships with the medical profession in some manner, and an underlying personality disorder. Age at onset is difficult to determine, but the condition is believed to begin in adolescence or early adulthood. Causation is unknown, and no effective treatments have been developed (Feldman & Feldman, 1995; Feldman et al., 1994).

A related form of factitious disorder, *Munchausen syndrome by proxy*, has particularly serious implications for children. In this case, parents (usually mothers) cause physical injury or illnesses in their offspring, often subjecting them to repeated surgery. The most common symptoms of the victims are bleeding, seizures, comas, suffocation, vomiting, diarrhea, poisonings, infections, fevers, and sudden infant death syndrome (Boros, Ophoven, Anderson, & Brubaker, 1995; K. Smith & Killam, 1994). Approximately 10% to 30% of the children die (Boros et al., 1995; Von Burg & Hibbard, 1995), and many survivors are either disfigured or physically impaired (Von Burg & Hibbard). In many cases, siblings of the primary victim also are victimized (Skau & Mouridsen, 1995). Apprehending mothers who commit acts of this type is no easy task because they usually appear totally dedicated to their children. Often, professional health-care workers become suspicious only after a child has endured repeated injuries or illnesses. Typically, parents protest their innocence; however, children's symptoms disappear when they are removed from their mother's care. Not surprisingly, despite their psychological disorder, these parents often are treated as criminals and prosecuted for child abuse (Schreier & Libow, 1994).

Somatoform Disorders

Individuals who complain repeatedly about a variety of physical ailments that have no apparent medical cause may be diagnosed with a somatoform disorder. These individuals genuinely believe that their conditions are medical problems and seek relief; they do not consciously make themselves ill, as is the case with persons with factitious disorders. DSM–IV identifies two types of somatoform disorders, *hysterical* and *preoccupation*. Hysterical disorders involve actual physical changes and resemble true organic medical problems so closely that they often are difficult to diagnose (Kroenke, Spitzer, deGruy, & Hahn, 1997). *Conversion, somatization,* and *pain associated with psychological factors disorders* are hysterical disorders. People with preoccupation disorders have obsessive interest in their bodies and overreact to minor symptoms, perceiving illnesses that do not exist. *Hypochondriasis* and *body dysmorphic disorders* are preoccupation disorders.

• *Conversion disorder.* Conversion disorder involves dramatic physical symptoms of abnormal neurological or sensory functioning. Typical symptoms are blindness, deafness, paralysis, or loss of feeling. This disorder harkens back to Freud's early work with female sufferers of hysteria, and although it may have occurred with some regularity in the Victorian era, it is extremely rare now (at most 3 of every 1,000 persons). Diagnosis requires acute observation of abnormalities in the individual's physical condition. For example, in cases of paralysis, loss of function may not follow neural pathways, and muscles may not atrophy (APA, 1994; Tiihonen, Kuikka, Vinamaki, & Lehtonen, 1995). Conversion disorder begins between late childhood and early adulthood, occurring twice as often in women as in men (Tomasson, Kent, & Coryell, 1991). Onset usually is associated with immediate stress, and symptoms quickly disappear (within several weeks).
• *Somatization disorder.* Somatization disorder involves numerous recurring physical ailments marked by pain, gastrointestinal (nausea, diarrhea), sexual (impotence, menstrual abnormalities), and neurological (double vision, difficulty swallowing) symptoms not having an organic basis. To be diagnosed, the individual must have symptoms in all four categories (APA, 1994). Afflicted individuals, mostly women, spend an inordinate amount of time visiting doctors and often suffer anxiety and depression (Fink, 1995). This problem begins between adolescence and young adulthood (Eisendrath, 1995), persists for years (Kent, Tomasson, & Coryell, 1995), and runs in families, afflicting 10% to 20% of close female family members. Adolescents with this condition have a history of frequent absences from school due to illness and when in school pay frequent visits to the school nurse.
• *Pain associated with psychological factors disorders.* Pain disorders associated with psychological factors involve persistent, severe pain that has no apparent physical basis. Another problem that afflicts more women than men, pain disorder may onset at any age and persist for years (APA, 1994). Although the problem may begin when the individual experiences minor pain associated with a genuine ailment or injury, pain increases after apparent recovery and

patients suffer greatly. Physicians are unable to identify physical causes for the pain.

• *Hypochondriasis*. Hypochondriasis is diagnosed when people worry that minor changes in physical functioning are due to a serious disease. For example, an individual may develop a muscle ache in the shoulder and attribute it to cancer. Some sufferers are aware that their concerns are unrealistic, but many are not receptive to that information. Even those people who develop insight about their behavior continue to consult physicians frequently and to worry excessively about their physical conditions. When not seeing physicians, they frequently self-medicate. Hypochondriasis can onset at any age and affects males and females in equal numbers (APA, 1994).

• *Body dysmorphic disorder*. Body dysmorphic disorder is characterized by excessive worry that some aspect of one's physical appearance is defective. This problem begins in adolescence but may be kept secret for a time. Individuals with this disorder are far different from the majority of human beings who voice dissatisfaction with some aspect of their physical appearance. They become obsessed by what they perceive as intolerable physical flaws on their faces or bodies (wrinkles, facial hair, large mouth, big feet, small breasts) or by odors from their bodies (sweat, breath) and focus excessive amounts of their attention and energy on hiding or changing the flaws. Their self-perceptions defy logic, reaching the level of delusional thinking. Phillips, McElroy, Keck, Pope, and Hudson (1993) found that 30% of individuals with this disorder were housebound and 17% had attempted suicide.

Etiology and Treatment. Behavioral theorists attribute the development of somatoform disorders to early conditioning that positively reinforces illness or to modeling the behavior of another (Whitehead, Cromwell, Heller, & Robinson, 1994). Cognitive theorists point to irrational thinking that oversensitizes the individual to symptoms of illness (Warwick, 1995). They also believe that individuals with these disorders are unable to express their emotions in typical fashion and use physical symptoms to communicate their feelings (Fry, 1993). Another line of thought holds that children, who have limited ability to express their emotions verbally, are particularly likely to use ailments or physical problems as a form of communication (Garralda, 1996).

Psychotherapeutic treatment is rarely sought by people with these disorders, and when it is (usually at the behest of physicians or family), it is often hampered by a lack of effort on the part of the patient. Various cognitive, behavioral, and psychodynamic therapeutic approaches are available, but their effectiveness has not been fully documented (Avia, Ruiz, Olivares, & Crespo, 1996; Bower, 1995).

Stress and Illness

DSM–IV includes a category of psychological factors affecting medical conditions that previously had been referred to as psychosomatic disorders or psychophysiological disorders. These conditions are illnesses that result from an interaction of both psychosocial and organic factors (Comer, 1999). Asthma, characterized by shortness of breath, wheezing, coughing, and a choking sensation, is a classic example of a problem of this type that usually onsets in childhood (DeAngelis, 1994). In a majority of childhood asthma cases, problems caused by a weakened respiratory system interact with environmental pressures, such as troubled family relationships and high dependency needs, to produce the symptoms of the disease (Carr, 1998; Godding, Kruth, & Jamart, 1997). Other conditions in this category include chronic headaches, tension headaches, migraine headaches, hypertension (chronic high blood pressure), coronary heart disease, and coronary arteries (E. H. Johnson, Gentry, & Julius, 1992; Julius, 1992; McDaniels, Moran, Levenson, & Stoudemire, 1994; Park, 1996; A. L. Peterson, Talcott, Kelleher, & Haddock, 1995). In each of these disorders, psychosocial causes produce stress that contributes greatly to the physical problems.

Stress. Since the late 1960s, a great deal of research has documented the relationship between stressors in the environment and a wide range of physical conditions. Investigators have been able to quantify the levels of stress in *life change units* (LCUs) using various modifications of the *Social Adjustment Rating Scale* originally developed by Holmes and Rahe in 1967. For example, the death of a spouse receives the maximum LCU score of 100, whereas moving to a new house receives a score of 20 LCUs. When yearly LCU scores for individuals who develop diseases are compared with those of healthy peers, the results clearly illustrate the relationship between stress and any number of physical disorders (Kiecolt-Glaser, Dura, Speicher, Trask, & Glaser, 1991; Pillow, Zautra, & Sandler, 1996). In turn, this information has led to investigations of the impact of stress on the immune system, called psychoneuroimmunology. This research has demonstrated that stress interferes with the activity of lymphocytes, the white blood cells that circulate through the lymph system and bloodstream to destroy foreign antigens such as bacteria, viruses, and parasites (S. Cohen & Herbert, 1996). Consequently, the individual becomes increasingly vulnerable to viral and bacterial infections (Ader, Felten, & Cohen, 1991; Sternberg & Gold, 1997). Apparently, the stress–disease relationship is modified by personality style, because people who respond to life with optimism and who take control of their lives appear to have better immune systems than those who are less positive and less assertive (Everson, Goldberg, Kaplan, & Cohen, 1996).

Psychological treatments for stress-related physical disorders have increased greatly in recent years (Compas, Haaga, Keefe, Leitenberg, & Williams, 1998). These include hypnosis, support groups, cognitive interventions, insight therapy, and training in relaxation, biofeedback, and meditation strategies (Barber, 1993; Carrington, 1993; Compas et al., 1998; Dubbert, 1995; Smyth, 1998).

Personality Disorders

Every human being has a personality, a unique, consistent pattern of perceiving and reacting to the world. Our personality traits are thought to result from a combination of inherited characteristics and learning (Watson, Clark, & Harkness, 1994). Social interactions are greatly influenced by perceptions of personality, that is, individuals tend to associate with persons they view as having agreeable personalities and disassociate from those they perceive with less favor. In healthy persons, personality characteristics are flexible enough to permit successful interactions in a variety of social circumstances. When individuals present extremely rigid patterns of personality and demonstrate behavior that varies from what is expected by others, they may be identified as having a *personality disorder*.

Personality disorders usually are recognized in adolescence or early adulthood, although some are obvious in childhood (APA, 1994). They are characterized by rigid styles of thinking and behaving that disrupt the individual's life and cause serious problems for others. Persons with personality disorders usually do not view themselves as having problems, because they attribute difficulties in their lives to the behaviors and attitudes of others. Consequently, this class of disorders is highly resistant to treatment. In addition, personality disorders tend to remain constant throughout life, with no periods of improvement. People with these disorders also tend to develop other types of disorders (C. Johnson & Wonderlich, 1992), such as depression or anxiety, and the presence of the personality disorder reduces the probability that the other condition will respond to treatment (Costello, 1996).

DSM–IV presents 10 personality disorders, although there is some debate about their validity as independent conditions (Costello, 1996). These disorders are grouped into three clusters: *odd behaviors*, consisting of *paranoid*, *schizoid*, and *schizotypal* disorders; *dramatic behaviors*, including *antisocial*, *borderline*, *histrionic*, and *narcissistic* disorders; and *high-anxiety behaviors*, consisting of *avoidant*, *dependent*, and *obsessive-compulsive* disorders. For a person to be diagnosed with any of these disorders, the characteristic attitudes and behaviors must be extreme and self-defeating, because the characteristics associated with them are present in milder or less intense forms in most personalities (Maher & Maher, 1994).

Carson and Butcher (1992) identified the prevalent features of common personality disorders as follows: disrupted personal relationships, persistent display of behavior that is troublesome to others, negative life outcomes such as crime or drug addiction, repetition of a maladaptive pattern with no ability to learn from experience, a bad reputation among others, and lack of desire to change.

Odd Personality Behaviors

Odd personality disorders are marked by bizarre thinking and behavior, and their symptoms resemble those associated with the psychosis schizophrenia. In fact, some clinical personnel believe that these disorders are milder forms of schizophrenia (Battaglia, Cavallini, Macciardi, & Bellodi, 1997).

• *Paranoid personality disorder.* Persons with paranoid personality disorder are extremely suspicious of others, regarding them as responsible for all of the negative events that may occur in their lives. Their misperceptions of hostility in others are not so bizarre as to be delusional, and thus they are in contact with reality and not psychotic. Their perceptions are distorted further by their inability to evaluate their own shortcomings, extreme sensitivity to criticism, and tendency to bear grudges (Fenigstein, 1996), all of which reinforces their firm conviction that people are no good. Estimates of the prevalence of this disorder range from less than 1% to almost 3% of people (APA, 1994).

• *Schizoid personality disorder.* People with schizoid personality disorder are unable to form social relationships and show little emotional expression. They are true loners, preferring to live without the company of others. If they find jobs that do not require them to work with others, they often can manage adequately. Prevalence figures have not been established, but the disorder is believed to be less common than the paranoid personality disorder (Goldberg, Schultz, & Schultz, 1986).

• *Schizotypal personality disorder.* The most serious of the "odd" disorders, the schizotypal condition is more closely linked to schizophrenia (Siever, 1986, 1992). The individual with this diagnosis is not only withdrawn but also eccentric. Symptoms include bizarre language (digressive speech and loose associations), magical thinking (extrasensory abilities and control over others), and ideas of reference (belief that unrelated events pertain specifically to oneself), as in schizophrenia, but the person remains in contact with reality. The seriousness of the thought disorder and the bizarre nature of the individual's behavior usually results in an aimless, unproductive life (Millon, 1990).

Dramatic Personality Disorders

Dramatic personality disorders are the most commonly diagnosed personality disorders (Fabrega, Ulrich, Pilkonis, & Mezzich, 1991), possibly because they tend to wreak havoc with other people. However, with the exception of the antisocial personality, they have not been widely researched.

• *Histrionic personality disorder.* Individuals with histrionic personality disorder are unstable, dependent, very excitable, and prone to engage in rather wild attention-seeking behavior (such as dancing a striptease at a party). They love "drama" and live to be recognized by others. Like small children, they are self-centered, cannot delay gratification for long, and overreact to minor frustrations (Comer, 1999). Estimates of prevalence rates range from 2% to 3% of the population (APA, 1994).

• *Narcissistic personality disorder.* Narcissists suffer from grandiose ideas about themselves and feed on the acclaim of others. Although they are basically superficial and unconcerned about the welfare of others, they are often socially charming and skilled at saying things that impress others, characteristics that make them appear more intelligent than they actually are. Because their need for attention and the admiration of others is insatiable, they develop many shallow relationships and are usually sexually promiscuous. Less than 1% of the general population is diagnosed with this disorder, and about 75% of those are men (Grilo, Becker, Fehon, & Walker, 1996).

• *Antisocial personality disorder.* Individuals with antisocial personality disorder have no moral conscience (Lykken, 1995), that is, they exploit others without qualm or remorse, either through aggressive behavior or by conning them. Also called *psychopathic personality* or *sociopathic personality*, their most prominent characteristics are a complete lack of ethics or moral values and an inability to form an honest, trusting bond with another person (Birtchnell, 1996). Antisocial personality disorder is diagnosed in 3.5% of the population (APA, 1994). Mostly male (3:1 ratio; Robins et al., 1984), these people display patterns of antisocial behavior before age 15, including physical cruelty to animals or people. They often run afoul of the law, and many go to jail. They lie repeatedly (Seto, Khattar, Lalumiere, & Quinsey, 1997), have difficulty holding jobs, fail to pay their debts, and plot to get what they want from their victims, whom they regard as weak and deserving of exploitation (Lykken, 1995). Persons with conning personalities are usually more intelligent than those who specialize in overt physical aggression and may appear extremely likeable until the depth of their exploitation is revealed. The more violent types of sociopaths act out against others in seemingly senseless ways, without regard for consequences.

Many of their acts appear to be motivated by a need for excitement (Sher & Trull, 1994). Often, the pattern of behaviors is established in early childhood by lying, cheating, and other exploitive behavior.

• *Borderline personality disorder.* Some clinical personnel regard this personality disorder as a borderline psychosis (O'Connell, Cooper, Perry, & Hoke, 1989). Primary characteristics include mood shifts; self-destructive behaviors, including self-mutilation and alcohol abuse; low frustration tolerance; manipulative suicide attempts; and episodes of loss of contact with reality (delusions). Individuals with this problem are unstable and impulsive, prone to bouts of anger (Gardner, Leibenluft, O'Leary, & Cowdry, 1991), and at times to physical aggression (Lish, Kavoussi, & Coccaro, 1996) toward themselves and others. Given these personality characteristics, it is not surprising that their social relationships are unstable (Barrett & Stanford, 1996). Often, persons with this disorder misjudge the intensity of relationships and are moved to excessive, destructive behavior when other people fail to meet their expectations (Gunderson, 1996). Approximately 2% of the general population is diagnosed with this condition, and about 75% of those individuals are women (Grilo et al., 1996).

Anxious Personality Disorders

Fear is the primary characteristic displayed by people with anxious personality disorders. Symptoms are similar to those associated with the anxiety and mood disorders; however, no direct connection between these conditions has been found (Weston & Siever, 1993). Among all the personality disorders, persons with these conditions respond most favorably to treatment.

• *Avoidant personality disorder.* People with this disorder desperately desire affection and acceptance from others, but their feelings of inadequacy and hypersensitivity to rejection and ridicule make them so consistently uncomfortable in social situations that they avoid social interactions. Avoidant personality is similar to the social phobias, and many individuals with one diagnosis qualify for the other (Fahlen, 1995). This relatively rare disorder (less than 1%) affects men and women equally.

• *Dependent personality disorder.* A primary characteristic of dependent personality disorder is terror at the thought of being alone. Individuals with this problem fear separation from partners, and many subjugate themselves to a dominant person, maintaining the subordinate relationship even in the face of harsh physical and psychological abuse. When a partner ends a relationship, they immediately attempt to seek out another partner. Individuals with this disorder lack confidence in their judgment and become totally dependent on a significant other to make decisions for them (Overholser, 1996). Their excessive fear

of rejection causes them to try to please others at any cost. Despite their efforts, they are unhappy and at risk for depression (Overholser, 1996). Prevalence of this disorder is estimated at 2% of the general population (APA, 1994).
• *Obsessive-compulsive personality disorder.* People diagnosed with obsessive-compulsive personality disorder are overinhibited, overconscientious, overdutiful, preoccupied with orderliness and perfectionism, and rigid. Despite their desire for perfection, their stubborn rigidity, fear of erring, and obsessive attention to detail interfere with their ability to achieve. Approximately 1% to 2% of the general population, mostly white, married, educated, and employed men, receive this diagnosis (APA, 1994). These people are at risk to develop other disorders, particularly obsessive-compulsive disorder.

Etiology

Personality disorders differ greatly in type; therefore, it is reasonable to assume different causal factors. There is some inconclusive evidence of a genetic component influencing these disorders, particularly for paranoid personality (Fenigstein, 1996; Kendler & Gruenberg, 1982), schizotypal personality (Trestman, Horvath, Kalus, & Peterson, 1996), borderline personality (Loranger, Oldham, & Tulis, 1982; Spoont, 1996), and antisocial personality (Zuckerman, 1996), but the importance of environmental influences is not minimized. Most research in this area has involved antisocial personalities. Some of it has focused on family issues such as family poverty, family violence (Luntz & Widom, 1994), loss of a parent or modeling of a psychopathic parent (Farrington, 1991), lack of parental affection (Lahey, Hartdagen, Frick, & McBurnett, 1988), and unintentional reinforcement of aggressive behavior (Capaldi & Patterson, 1994) as important causes of this type of disorder. Less empirical evidence of the environmental role in causing the other disorders is available; however, many theorists point to stressful early environments marked by family disruption and inappropriate parenting as a key causal variable.

Treatment

Personality disorders tend to be resistant to treatment, primarily because the afflicted individuals rarely regard themselves as requiring treatment and are not usually motivated by discomfort to change. Even when they experience discomfort, they tend to externalize the cause. Many of these individuals may be considered psychologically blind, without much awareness of what makes them tick, and without much desire to learn. Except for persons with histrionic personality disorder, who tend to seek out treatment (Nestadt et al., 1990), when individuals with these conditions enter therapy, it is usually at the behest of another person (Beck & Freeman, 1990). They take little responsibility for achieving a successful outcome and tend to drop out quickly (Beck, 1997; Goldberg et al., 1986). The most promising forms of treatment appear to be cognitive and behavior therapy (Beck & Freeman, 1990). People with anxiety-related personality disorders are most likely to benefit from treatment. Antisocial and narcissistic personality disorders are the most resistant to treatment.

Summary

The DSM–IV classification system is one way of organizing and understanding the great variety of EBDs that afflict children and adolescents. As schools become increasingly inclusive, educators must increase their knowledge about these disorders, particularly those that do not cause difficulty for others. Research suggests that school authorities focus their attention on students who externalize their problems, that is, who act out or disrupt the classroom (such as persons who are conduct disordered), and often overlook those who internalize their feelings (such as children who are depressed or anxious; Forness, 1988). Also, school-based services for children and adolescents identified as emotionally and behaviorally disordered tend to be relatively restricted, that is, they are usually not organized on the basis of the types of disorders experienced by individuals, and the groupings may be detrimental to some individuals (e.g., depressed or highly anxious students do not benefit from being grouped with individuals who are aggressive and conduct disordered).

Many of the disorders that have been discussed in this chapter have serious consequences, both for the individuals who manifest the problems and for society. The identification of these diverse problems in school-age individuals not only underlines the need for increased resources devoted to their treatment, but also illustrates both the overwhelming social problems involving the families of these young people and the increased need for social programs that address those problems.

STUDY QUESTIONS

1. Discuss the types of anxiety disorders affecting children and adolescents.

2. Consider autism and childhood schizophrenia. Discuss the ways in which the conditions differ.

3. Discuss the symptoms of depression in children and adolescents.

4. Discuss how children's emotional disorders differ from those of adults.

5. Discuss how attention-deficit/hyperactivity disorder differs from conduct disorder.

References

Abramson, L. Y., Metalsky, G. I., & Alloy, L. B. (1989). Hopelessness depression: A theory-based subtype of depression. *Psychological Review, 96*(2), 358–372.

Achenbach, T. M. (1982). *Developmental psychopathology* (2nd ed.). New York: Ronald Press.

Achenbach, T. M. (1985). *Assessment and taxonomy of child and adolescent psychopathology.* Beverly Hills, CA: Sage.

Achenbach, T. M. (1993). *Empirically based taxonomy: How to use syndromes and profile types derived from the CBCL/4-18, TRF, and YSR.* Burlington: University of Vermont, Department of Psychiatry.

Adams, D. M., Overholser, J. C., & Lehnert, K. L. (1994). Perceived family functioning and adolescent suicidal behavior. *Journal of the American Academy of Child and Adolescent Psychiatry, 33*(4), 498–507.

Ader, R., Felten, D. L., & Cohen, N. (Eds.). (1991). *Psychoneuroimmunology* (2nd ed.). New York: Academic Press.

Adler, J. (1994, January 10). Kids growing up scared. *Newsweek,* 43–50.

Adrien, J. L., Lenoir, P., Martineau, J., Perrot, A., Hameury, L., Larmande, C., & Sauvage, D. (1993). Blind ratings of early symptoms of autism based upon home movies. *Journal of the American Academy of Child and Adolescent Psychiatry, 32,* 617–626.

Agras, W., Schneider, J., Arnow, B., & Raeburn, S. (1989). Cognitive-behavioral and response-prevention treatments for bulimia nervosa. *Journal of Consulting and Clinical Psychology, 57,* 215–221.

Akiskal, H., & Simmons, R. (1985). Chronic and refractory depressions: Evaluation and management. In E. E. Bechan & W. R. Leber (Eds.), *Handbook of depression: Treatment, assessment, and research* (pp. 587–605). Homewood, IL: Dorsey Press.

Alterman, A. (1988). Patterns of familial alcoholism, alcoholism severity, and psychopathology. *Journal of Nervous Mental Disorders, 176,* 167–175.

American Psychiatric Association. (1993). *Practice guideline for major depressive disorder in adults.* Washington, DC: Author.

American Psychiatric Association. (1994). *Diagnostic and statistical manual of mental disorders* (4th ed.). Washington, DC: Author.

Anastopoulos, A. D., & Barkley, R. A. (1992). Attention-deficit hyperactivity disorder. In C. E. Walker & M. C. Roberts (Eds.), *Handbook of clinical child psychology* (pp. 20–233). New York: Wiley.

Andersen, A. E. (1995). Sequencing treatment decisions: Cooperation or conflict between therapist and patient. In G. Szmukler, C. Dare, & J. Treasure (Eds.), *Handbook of eating disorders: Theory, treatment and research* (pp. 164–190). Chichester, England: Wiley.

Anderson, G. M., & Hoshino, Y. (1997). Neurochemical studies of autism. In D. J. Cohen & F. R. Volkmar (Eds.), *Handbook of autism and pervasive developmental disorder* (pp. 43–65). New York: Wiley.

Andreasen, N. (1985). Positive vs. negative schizophrenia: A critical evaluation. *Schizophrenia, 11,* 380–389.

Anthony, J. C., Arria, A. M., & Johnson, E. O. (1995). Epidemiological and public health issues for tobacco, alcohol, and other drugs. In J. M. Oldham & M. R. Riba (Eds.), American Psychiatric Press review of psychiatry (Vol. 14, pp. 94–119). Washington, DC: American Psychiatric Press.

Asarnow, J. R. (1994). Childhood-onset schizophrenia. Journal of Child Psychology and Psychiatry, 35, 1345–1371.

Asarnow, J. R., & Asarnow, R. F. (1996). Childhood-onset schizophrenia. In E. J. Mash & R. A. Barkley (Eds.), Child psychopathology (pp. 591–597). New York: Guilford Press.

Asarnow, J. R., Goldstein, M. J., & Ben-Meir, S. (1988). Parental communication deviance in childhood onset schizophrenia spectrum and depressive disorders. Journal of Child Psychology and Psychiatry, 29, 825–838.

Asarnow, J. R., & Horton, A. A. (1990). Coping and stress in families of child psychiatric inpatients: Parents of children with depressive and schizophrenic spectrum disorders. Child Psychiatry and Human Development, 21(2), 145–157.

Asarnow, R. F., Asamen, J., Granholm, E., Sherman, T., Watkins, J. M., & Williams, M. E. (1994). Cognitive/neurological studies of children with a schizophrenic disorder. Schizophrenia Bulletin, 20, 647–669.

Avia, M. D., Ruiz, M. A., Olivares, E., & Crespo, M. (1996). Shorter communications. The meaning of psychological symptoms: Effectiveness of group interventions with hypochondriacal patients. Behavior Research and Therapy, 34(1), 23–31.

Bailey, A., Le Couteur, A., Gottesman, I., Bolton, P., Simonoff, E., Yuzda, E., & Rutter, M. (1995). Autism as a strongly genetic disorder: Evidence from a British twin study. Psychological Medicine, 25, 63–78.

Ballenger, J. C. (1988). The clinical use of carbamazepine in affective disorders. Journal of Clinical Psychiatry, 49, 13–19.

Bandura, A. (1965). Influence of models' reinforcement contingencies on the acquisition of imitative responses. Journal of Personality and Social Psychology, 1, 589–595.

Bandura, A. (1973). Aggression: A social learning analysis. Englewood Cliffs, NJ: Prentice Hall.

Barber, T. X. (1993). Hypnosuggestive approaches to stress reduction: Data, theory, and clinical applications. In P. M. Lehrer & R. L. Woolfolk (Eds.), Principles and practice of stress management (2nd ed., pp. 182–202). New York: Guilford Press.

Barkley, R. A. (1995). Taking charge of ADHD: The complete, authoritative guide for parents. New York: Guilford Press.

Barkley, R. A. (1998). Attention-deficit/hyperactivity disorder. New York: Guilford Press.

Barlow, D. (1988). Anxiety and its disorders: The nature and treatment of anxiety and panic. New York: Guilford Press.

Barnes, G., & Prosen, H. (1985). Parental death and depression. Journal of Abnormal Psychology, 94, 64–69.

Baron-Cohen, S., Campbell, R., Karmiloff-Smith, A., Grant, J., & Walker, J. (1995). Are children with autism blind to the mentalistic significance of the eyes? British Journal of Developmental Psychology, 13, 379–398.

Barrett, E. S., & Stanford, M. S. (1996). Impulsiveness. In C. G. Costello (Ed.), Personality characteristics of the personality disordered (pp. 364–398). New York: Wiley.

Bassett, A. S. (1992). Chromosomal aberrations and schizophrenia: Autosomes. British Journal of Psychiatry, 161, 323–334.

Battaglia, N., Cavallini, M. C., Macciardi, F., & Bellodi, L. (1997). The structure of DSM–III–R schizotypal personality disorder diagnosed by direct interviews. Schizophrenia Bulletin, 23(1), 83–92.

Bauer, M., & Boegner, F. (1996). Neurological syndromes in factitious disorder. Journal of Nervous Mental Disorders, 184(5), 281–288.

Beck, A. T. (1997). Cognitive therapy: Reflections. In J. K. Zeig (Ed.), The evolution of psychotherapy: The third conference (pp. 157–170). New York: Brunner/Mazel.

Beck, A. T., & Freeman, A. (1990). *Cognitive therapy of personality disorders*. New York: Guilford Press.

Beck, A. T., Rush, A., Shaw, B., & Emery, G. (1979). *Cognitive therapy of depression: A treatment manual*. New York: Guilford Press.

Beidel, D. C., & Randall, J. (1994). Social phobia. In T. H. Ollendick, N. J. King, & W. Yule (Eds.), *International handbook of phobic and anxiety disorders in children and adolescents* (pp. 111–130). New York: Plenum Press.

Bettelheim, B. (1955). *Truants from life*. Glencoe, IL: Free Press.

Bettelheim, B. (1959). Joey: A mechanical boy. *Scientific American, 200*, 116–127.

Bettelheim, B. (1967). *The empty fortress*. New York: Free Press.

Birtchnell, J. (1996). Detachment. In C. G. Costello (Ed.), *Personality characteristics of the personality disordered*. New York: Wiley.

Black, D., Yates, W., Petty, G., Noyes, R., & Brown, K. (1986). Suicidal behavior in alcoholic males. *Comprehensive Psychiatry, 27*(3), 227–233.

Bleuler, E. (1950). *Dementia praecox or the group of schizophrenias*. New York: International Universities Press. (Original work published 1911)

Boodman, S. G. (1995, June 13). Researchers study obesity in children. *The Washington Post*, pp. 10, 13, 15.

Boros, S., Ophoven, J., Anderson, R., & Brubaker, L. (1995). Munchausen syndrome by proxy: A profile for medical child abuse. *Australian Family Physician, 24*(5), 768–773.

Boucher, J. (1981). Memory for recent events in autistic children. *Journal of Autism and Developmental Disabilities, 11*(3), 293–301.

Bowen, M. (1960). A family concept of schizophrenia. In D. D. Jackson (Ed.), *The etiology of schizophrenia*. New York: Basic Books.

Bower, B. (1995, August 26). Hurting to feel better. *Science News, 148*, 143.

Braun, D. L., Sunday, S. R., & Halmi, K. A. (1995). Psychiatric comorbidity in patients with eating disorders. *Psychological Medicine, 51*, 236–238.

Brawman-Mintzer, O., & Lydiard, R. B. (1997). Biological basis of generalized anxiety disorder. *Journal of Clinical Psychiatry, 58*(Suppl. 3), 16–25.

Brom, D., Kleber, R., & Defares, P. (1989). Brief psychotherapy for posttraumatic stress disorders. *Journal of Consulting and Clinical Psychology, 57*, 607–612.

Brook, S. L., & Bowler, D. M. (1992). Autism by another name? Semantic and pragmatic impairments in children. *Journal of Autism and Developmental Disabilities, 22*, 61–62.

Bryant, E. S., Garrison, C. Z., Valois, R. F., Rivard, J. C., & Hinkle, K. T. (1995). Suicidal behavior among youth with severe emotional disturbance. *Journal of Child and Family Studies, 4*, 429–443.

Buchan, H., Johnsone, E. C., McPherson, K., & Palmer, R. L. (1992). Who benefits from electroconvulsive therapy? Combined results of the Leicester and Northwick Park trials. *British Journal of Psychiatry, 160*, 355–359.

Butzlaff, R. L., & Hooley, J. M. (1998). Expressed emotion and psychiatric relapse. *Archives of General Psychiatry, 55*, 547–552.

Calvo, M. G., Eysenck, M. W., & Castillo, M. D. (1997). Interpretation bias in test anxiety: The time course of predictive inferences. *Cognitive Emotions, 11*(1), 43–63.

Campaigne, B. N., Morrison, J. A., Schumann, B. C., Faulkner, F., Lakatos, E., Sprecher, D., & Schreiber, G. B. (1994). Indexes of obesity and comparisons with previous national survey data in 9- and 10-year old black and white girls: The National Heart, Lung, and Blood Institute Growth and Health Survey. *Journal of Pediatrics, 124*, 675–680.

Campbell, M., & Cueva, J. E. (1995). Psychopharmacology in child and adolescent psychiatry: A review of the past seven years. Part I. *Journal of the American Academy of Child and Adolescent Psychiatry, 34*, 1124–1132.

Campbell, M., & Green, W. (1985). Pervasive developmental disorders of childhood. In H. I. Kaplan & B. J. Sadock (Eds.), *Comprehensive textbook of psychiatry* (pp. 13–40). Baltimore: Williams & Wilkins.

Cantor, S. (1988). *Childhood schizophrenia.* New York: Guilford Press.

Cantwell, D. P., & Rutter, M. (1994). Classification: Conceptual issues and substantive findings. In M. Rutter, E. Taylor, & L. Hersov (Eds.), *Child and adolescent psychiatry: Modern approaches* (pp. 217–234). Boston: Blackwell Scientific.

Capaldi, D. M., & Patterson, G. R. (1994). Interrelated influences of contextual factors on antisocial behavior in childhood and adolescence for males. In D. C. Fowles, P. Sutker, & S. H. Goodman (Eds.), *Progress in experimental personality and psychopathology research* (pp. 243–264). New York: Springer.

Caplan, R., Guthrie, D., & Komo, S. (1996). Conversational repair in schizophrenic and normal children. *Journal of the American Academy of Child and Adolescent Psychiatry, 35,* 941–949.

Caputo, D., & Mandell, D. (1970). Consequences of low birth weight. *Developmental Psychology, 3*(3), 363–383.

Carlson, G. A., Asarnow, J. R., & Orbach, I. (1994). Developmental aspects of suicidal behavior in children and developmentally delayed adolescents. In G. G. Naom & S. Borst (Eds.), *New directions for child development, no. 64—Children, youth, and suicide: Developmental perspectives* (pp. 191–209). San Francisco: Jossey-Bass.

Carr, R. E. (1998). Panic disorder and asthma: Causes, effects and research implications. *Journal of Psychosomatic Research, 44*(1), 43–52.

Carrington, P. (1993). Modern forms of meditation. In P. M. Lehrer & R. L. Woolfolk (Eds.), *Principles and practice of stress management* (2nd ed., pp. 155–178). New York: Guilford Press.

Carson, R. (1984). The schizophrenias. In H. E. Adams & P. B. Sutker (Eds.), *Comprehensive handbook of psychopathology.* New York: Plenum Press.

Carson, R., & Butcher, J. (1992). *Abnormal psychology and modern life* (9th ed.). New York: HarperCollins.

Casper, R. C. (1995). Biology of eating disorders. In A. F. Schatzberg & C. B. Nemeroff (Eds.), *The American Psychiatric Press textbook of psychopharmacology* (pp. 55–86). Washington, DC: American Psychiatric Press.

Chance, P. (1986, October). Life after head injury. *Psychology Today, 20,* 62–69.

Ciompi, L., Dauwalder, H., Maier, C., Aebi, E., Trutsch, K., Kupper, Z., & Rutishauser, C. (1992). The pilot project "soteria berne": Clinical experiences and results. *British Journal of Psychiatry, 161,* 145–153.

Clark, D. B., Smith, M. G., Neighbors, B. D., Skerlec, L. M., & Randall, J. (1994). Anxiety disorders in adolescence: Characteristics, prevalence, and comorbidities. *Clinical Psychology Review, 14,* 113–137.

Clayton, P. (1982). Bereavement. In E. S. Paykel (Ed.), *Handbook of affective disorders.* New York: Guilford Press.

Cloninger, C., Reich, T., Sigvardsson, S., Von Knorring, A., & Bohman, M. (1986). The effects of changes in alcohol use between generations on the inheritance of alcohol abuse. In *Alcoholism: A medical - disorder.* Proceedings of the 76th annual meeting of the American Psychopathological Association.

Coambs, R. B., & McAndrews, M. P. (1994). The effects of psychoactive substances on workplace performance. In S. MacDonald & P. Roman (Eds.), *Research advances in alcohol and drug problems.* New York: Plenum Press.

Cohen, P., Cohen, J., Kasen, S., Velez, C. N., Hartmark, C., Johnson, J., Rojas, M., Brook, J., & Streuning, E. L. (1993). An epidemiological study of disorders in late childhood and adolescence: I. Age-and-gender-specific prevalence. *Journal of Child Psychology and Psychiatry, 34,* 851–867.

Cohen, S., & Herbert, T. B. (1996). Health psychology: Psychological factors and physical disease from the perspective of human psychoneuroimmunology. In J. T. Spence, J. M. Darley, & D. J. Floss (Eds.), *Annual review of psychology* (Vol. 47, pp. 261–282). Palo Alto, CA: Annual Reviews.

Colbert, E., Koegler, R., & Markham, C. (1979). Vestibular dysfunction in childhood schizophrenia. *Archives of General Psychiatry, 1*, 600–617.

Comer, R. J. (1999). *Fundamentals of abnormal psychology* (2nd ed.). New York: Worth.

Compas, B. E., Haaga, D. A. F., Keefe, E. J., Leitenberg, H., & Williams, D. A. (1998). Sampling of empirically supported psychological treatments from health psychology: Smoking, chronic pain, cancer, and bulimia nervosa. *Journal of Consulting and Clinical Psychology, 66*(1), 89–112.

Costa, E. (1995). Benzodiazepine–GABA interactions: A model to investigate the neurobiology of anxiety. In A. H. Juma & J. Maser (Eds.), *Anxiety and the anxiety disorders.* Hillsdale, NJ: Erlbaum.

Costello, C. G. (1996). The advantages of focusing on the personality characteristics of the personality disordered. In C. G. Costello (Ed.), *Personality characteristics of the personality disordered* (pp. 3–37). New York: Wiley.

Costello, E. J., & Angold, A. (1995). Developmental epidemiology. In D. Cicchetti & D. J. Cohen (Eds.), *Developmental psychopathology* (pp. 411–433). New York: Wiley.

Courchesne, E. (1988). Brain abnormalities as factors in autism. *New England Journal of Medicine, 5*, 26–30.

Courchesne, R., & Courchesne, E. (1997). From impasse to insight in autism research: From behavioral symptoms to biological explanations. *Developmental Psychopathology, 45*, 111–119.

Cox, B. J. (1996). The nature and assessment of catastrophic thoughts in panic disorder. *Behavior Research and Therapy, 34*(4), 363–374.

Cox, B. J., Endler, N. S., & Swinson, R. P. (1995). An examination of levels of agoraphobic severity in panic disorder. *Behavior Research and Therapy, 33*(1), 57–62.

Davies, P. T., & Cummings, E. M. (1994). Marital conflict and child adjustment: An emotional security hypothesis. *Psychological Bulletin, 116*, 387–411.

Davis, J. M. (1980). Antidepressant drugs. In H. I. Kaplan, A. M. Freedman, & B. J. Sadock (Eds.), *Comprehensive textbook of psychiatry III*, (pp. 157–181). Baltimore: Williams & Wilkins.

Dawson, G., & Castelloe, P. (1992). Autism. In C. E. Walker (Ed.), *Clinical psychology: Historical and research foundations* (pp. 105–141). New York: Plenum Press.

DeAngelis, T. (1994, March). Poor kids are focus of asthma studies. *APA Monitor, 25*(3), 26–27.

DeMyer, M., Barton, S., DeMyer, W., Norton, J., Allen, J., & Steele, R. (1983). Prognosis in autism: A follow-up study. *Journal of Autism and Childhood Schizophrenia, 3*, 199–246.

DeSilva, P. (1995). Cognitive-behavioural models of eating disorders. In G. Szmukler, C. Dare, & J. Treasure (Eds.), *Handbook of eating disorders: Theory, treatment and research* (pp. 108–138). Chichester, England: Wiley.

De Wilde, E. J., Kienhorst, I. C., Diekstra, R. F., & Wolters, W. H. (1992). The relationship between adolescent suicidal behavior and life events in childhood and adolescents. *American Journal of Psychiatry, 149*, 45–51.

Diekstra, R. F. (1990). An international perspective on the epidemiology and prevention of suicide. In S. J. Blumenthal & D. K. Kupfer (Eds.), *Suicide over the life cycle* (pp. 115–136). Washington, DC: American Psychiatric Press.

Dishion, T. J., French, D. C., & Patterson, G. R. (1995). The development and ecology of antisocial behavior. In D. Cicchetti & D. J. Cohen (Eds.), *Developmental psychopathology, Vol. 2: Risk, disorder and adaptation* (pp. 128–153). New York: Wiley.

Dohrenwend, B., & Egri, G. (1981). Recent stressful life events and episodes of schizophrenia. *Schizophrenia Bulletin, 7*, 12–23.

Dohrenwend, B., Levav, I., Shrout, P., & Schwartz, S. (1992). Socioeconomic status and psychiatric disorders: The causation-selection issue. *Science, 255*, 946–952.

Doleys, D. M. (1989). Enuresis and encopresis. In T. H. Ollendick & M. Hersen (Eds.), *Handbook of child psychopathology* (2nd ed., pp. 14–36). New York: Plenum Press.

Douglas, J., & Olshaker, M. (1995). *Mind hunters: Inside the FBI's elite serial crime unit.* New York: Simon & Schuster.

Dowdy, C. A., Patton, J. R., Smith, T. E., & Polloway, E. A. (1998). *Attention-deficit/hyperactive disorder in the classroom.* Austin, TX: PRO-ED.

Drug Abuse Warning Network. (1997). Highlights from 1996 report. Washington, DC: Author.

Dubbert, P. M. (1995). Behavioral (life-style) modification in the prevention and treatment of hypertension. *Clinical Psychology Review, 15*(3), 187–216.

Dumas, J. E., LaFreniere, P. J., & Serketich, W. J. (1995). "Balance of power": A transactional analysis of control in mother-child dyads involving socially competent, aggressive, and anxious children. *Journal of Abnormal Psychology, 104,* 104–113.

DuPaul, G. J., Barkley, R. A., & Connor, D. F. (1998). Stimulants. In R. A. Barkley (Ed.), *Attention-deficit hyperactivity disorder* (pp. 132–166). New York: Guilford Press.

DuPaul, G. J., & Stoner, G. (1994). *ADHD in the schools: Assessment and intervention strategies.* New York: Guilford Press.

Durand, V. M., & Carr, E. G. (1992). An analysis of maintenance following functional communication training. *Journal of Applied Behavior Analysis, 25,* 777–794.

Eggers, C., & Bunk, D. (1997). The longterm course of childhood-onset schizophrenia: A 42-year follow-up. *Schizophrenia Bulletin, 23,* 105–117.

Eisenberg, H. (1990). Behavioral changes after closed head injury in children. *Journal of Consulting and Clinical Psychology, 58,* 93–98.

Eisendrath, S. J. (1995). Psychiatric aspects of chronic pain. *Neurology, 45*(Suppl. 9), 526–534.

Ellis, A. (1995). Rational emotive behavior therapy. In R. J. Corsini & D. Wedding (Eds.), *Current psychotherapies* (5th ed., pp. 31–54). Itasca, IL: Peacock.

Emmelkamp, P. M. (1994). Behavior therapy with adults. In A. E. Bergin & S. L. Garfield (Eds.), *Handbook of psychotherapy and behavior change* (4th ed., pp. 177–195). New York: Wiley.

Epstein, M. H., Kutash, K., & Duchnowski, A. (1998). *Outcomes for children and youth with behavioral and emotional disorders and their families: Programs and evaluation.* Austin, TX: PRO-ED.

Erickson, M. T. (1992). *Behavior disorders of children and adolescents.* Englewood Cliffs, NJ: Prentice Hall.

Everson, S. A., Goldberg, D. E., Kaplan, G. A., & Cohen, R. D. (1996). Hopelessness and risk of mortality and incidence of myocardial infarction and cancer. *Psychosomatic Medicine, 58,* 113–121.

Fabrega, H., Ulrich, R., Pilkonis, P., & Mezzich, J. (1991). On the homogeneity of personality disorder clusters. *Comprehensive Psychiatry, 32*(5), 373–386.

Fahlen, T. (1995). Personality traits in social phobia: I. Comparisons with healthy controls. *Journal of Clinical Psychiatry, 56*(12), 560–568.

Fairweather, G. (Ed.). (1980). *The Fairweather Lodge: A twenty-five year retrospective.* San Francisco: Jossey-Bass.

Farrington, D. P. (1991). Psychological contributions to the explanations of offending. *Issues in Criminology and Legal Psychology, 1*(17), 7–19.

Farrington, D. P. (1995). The development of offending and antisocial behaviour from childhood: Key findings from the Cambridge Study in Delinquent Development. *Journal of Child Psychology and Psychiatry, 36,* 929–964.

Feldman, M. D., & Feldman, J. M. (1995). Tangled in the web: Countertransference in the therapy of factitious disorders. *International Journal of Psychiatric Medicine, 24*(4), 389–399.

Feldman, M. D., Ford, C. V., & Reinhold, T. (1994). *Patient or pretender: Inside the strange world of factitious disorders.* New York: Wiley.

Fenigstein, A. (1996). Paranoia. In C. G. Costello (Ed.), *Personality characteristics of the personality disordered* (pp. 235–272). New York: Wiley.

Fink, M. (1992). Electroconvulsive therapy. In E. S. Paykel (Ed.), *Handbook of affective disorders* (pp. 83–99). New York: Guilford Press.

Fink, P. (1995). Psychiatric illness in patients with persistent somatisation. *British Journal of Psychiatry, 166,* 93–99.

Finn, P. (1990, March). Dysfunction in stimulus-response modulation in men at high risk for alcoholism. Paper presented at a symposium on the *Genetics of Alcoholism: Recent Advances* at the annual meeting of the Research Society on Alcoholism, Montreal, Canada.

Flament, M. F., Koby, E., Rapoport, J. L., & Berg, C. J. (1991). Childhood obsessive-compulsive disorder: A prospective follow-up study. *Archives of General Psychiatry, 492*(10), 977–983.

Flament, M. F., Whitaker, A., Rapoport, J. L., Davies, M., Berg, C. Z., Kalikow, K., Sceery, W., & Shafer, D. (1988). Obsessive-compulsive disorder in adolescence: An epidemiological study. *Journal of the American Academy of Child and Adolescent Psychiatry, 27,* 764–771.

Fleming, J., Offord, D., & Boyle, M. (1989). Prevalence of childhood and adolescent depression in the community: Ontario Health Study. *British Journal of Psychiatry, 155,* 647–654.

Foderaero, L. W. (1993, August 12). Electroshock therapy makes a comeback. *Anchorage Daily News,* p. D3.

Fombonne, E. (1995). Eating disorders: Time trends and possible explanatory mechanisms. In M. Rutter & D. J. Smith (Eds.), *Psychosocial disorder in young people* (pp. 447–491). Chichester, England: Wiley.

Fombonne, E., du Mazaubrun, C., Cans, C., & Grandjean, H. (1997). Autism and associated medical disorders in a French epidemiological survey. *Journal of the American Academy of Child and Adolescent Psychiatry, 36,* 1561–1569.

Forness, S. (1988). School characteristics of children and adolescents with depression. In R. Rutherford, C. M. Nelson, & S. Forness (Eds.), *Bases of severe behavioral disorders in children and youth* (pp. 177–204). Boston: College-Hill.

Fremouw, W., de Perczel, M., & Ellis, T. (1990). *Suicide risk: Assessment and response guidelines.* Elmsford, NY: Pergamon Press.

Friedman, R., Hurt, S., Clarkin, J., Corn, R., & Aronoff, M. (1983). Symptoms of depression among adolescents and young adults. *Journal of Affective Disorders, 5,* 37–43.

Fry, R. (1993). Adult physical illness and childhood sexual abuse. *Journal of Psychosomatic Research, 37*(2), 89–103.

Gardner, D. L., Leibenluft, E., O'Leary, K. M., & Cowdry, R. W. (1991). Self-ratings of anger and hostility in borderline personality disorder. *Journal of Nervous and Mental Disorders, 179*(3), 157–161.

Garner, D. (1986). Cognitive-behavioral therapy for eating disorders. *Clinical Psychologist, 39*(2), 36–39.

Garralda, M. E. (1996). Somatisation in children. *Journal of Child Psychology and Psychiatry, 37*(1), 13–33.

Gillberg, C. (1993). Autism and related behaviors. *Journal of Intellectual Disability Research, 37,* 343–372.

Ginsburg, G. S., LaGreca, A. M., & Silverman, W. K. (1998). Social anxiety in children with anxiety disorders: Relation with social and emotional functioning. *Journal of Abnormal Psychology, 26,* 175–185.

Godding, V., Kruth, M., & Jamart, J. (1997). Joint consultation for high-risk asthmatic children and families with pediatrician and child psychiatrist as co-therapist: Model and evaluation. *Family Process, 36,* 265–280.

Goldberg, S., Schultz, C., & Schultz, P. (1986). Borderline and schizotypal personality disorders treated with low-dose thiothexene vs. placebo. *Archives of General Psychiatry, 43,* 680–686.

Goldstein, M. (1985). Family factors that antedate the onset of schizophrenia and related disorders: The results of a fifteen year prospective longitudinal study. *Acta Psychiatry Scandinavia, 71*(Suppl. 319), 7–18.

Gooding, D. C., & Iacono, W. G. (1995). Schizophrenia through the lens of a developmental psychopathology perspective. In D. Cicchetti & D. J. Cohen (Eds.), *Developmental psychology* (Vol. 2, pp. 435–474). New York: Wiley.

Goodman, R., Mercy, J., Loya, F., Rosenberg, M., Smith, J., Allen, N., Vargas, L., & Kolts, R. (1986). Alcohol use and interpersonal violence: Alcohol detected in homicide victims. *American Journal of Public Health*, 76(2), 144–149.

Goodyer, I. M., & Cooper, P. (1993). A community study of depression in adolescent girls: II. The clinical features of identified disorder. *British Journal of Psychiatry*, 163, 374–380.

Goplerud, E., & Depue, R. (1985). Behavioral response to naturally occurring stress in cyclothymia and dysthymia. *Journal of Abnormal Psychology*, 94, 128–139.

Gottesman, I. I. (1991). *Schizophrenic genesis*. New York: Freeman.

Graham, J., & Gaffan, E. A. (1997). Fear of water in children and adults: Etiology and familial effects. *Behavior Research and Therapy*, 35(2), 91–108.

Green, W. H., Padron-Gayol, M., Hardesty, A. S., & Bassiri, M. (1992). Schizophrenia with childhood onset: A phenomenological study of 38 cases. *Journal of the American Academy of Child and Adolescent Psychiatry*, 31, 968–976.

Grilo, C. M., Becker, D. F., Fehon, D. E., & Walker, M. L. (1996). Gender differences in personality disorders in psychiatrically hospitalized adolescents. *American Journal of Psychiatry*, 153(8), 1089–1091.

Guelfi, G., Faustman, W., & Csernansky, J. (1989). Independence of positive and negative symptoms in a population of schizophrenic patients. *Journal of Nervous and Mental Diseases*, 177, 285–290.

Guetzloe, E. C. (1991). *Depression and suicide: Special education students at risk*. Reston, VA: Council for Exceptional Children.

Gunderson, J. G. (1996). The borderline patient's intolerance of aloneness: Insecure attachments and therapist availability. *American Journal of Psychiatry*, 153(6), 752–758.

Haefely, W. (1990). Benzodiazepine receptor and ligands: Structural and functional differences. In I. Hindmarch, G. Beaumont, S. Brandon, & B. E. Leonard (Eds.), *Benzodiazepines: Current concepts* (Pt. 1, pp. 129–152). Chichester, England: Wiley.

Halmi, K. A. (1995). Current concepts and definitions. In G. Szmukler, C. Dare, & J. Treasure (Eds.), *Handbook of eating disorders: Theory, treatment and research*. Chichester, England: Wiley.

Hankin, B. L., Abramson, L. Y., Moffitt, T. E., Silva, P. A., McGee, R., & Angell, K. E. (1998). Development of depression from preadolescence to young adulthood: Emerging gender differences in a 10-year longitudinal study. *Journal of Abnormal Psychology*, 107, 128–140.

Harrington, R. C., Fudge, H., Rutter, M. L., Breenkamp, D., Groothues, C., & Pridham, J. (1993). Child and adult depression: A test of continuities with data from a family study. *British Journal of Psychiatry*, 162, 627–633.

Harrington, R. C., Rutter, M., & Fombonne, E. (1996). Developmental pathways in depression: Multiple meanings, antecedents, and endpoints. *Development and Psychopathology*, 8, 601–616.

Harris, S. L. (1994). Treatment of family problems in autism. In E. Schopler & G. B. Mesibov (Eds.), *Behavior issues in autism* (pp. 161–175). New York: Plenum Press.

Hart, K., & Kenny, M. E. (1995, August). *Adherence to the superwoman ideal and eating disorder symptoms among college women*. Paper presented at the meeting of the American Psychological Association, New York.

Harter, S., & Marold, D. B. (1994). Psychosocial risk factors contributing to adolescent suicide ideation. In G. G. Noam & S. Borst (Eds.), *New directions for child development, no. 64—Children, youth, and suicide: Developmental perspectives* (pp. 389–415). San Francisco: Jossey-Bass.

Hawton, K. (1986). *Suicide and attempted suicide among children and adolescents*. Beverly Hills, CA: Sage.

Heikkinen, M., Aro, H., & Lonnqvist, J. (1992). Recent life events and their role in suicide as seen by the spouses. *Acta Psychiatrica Scandinavica*, 86(6), 489–494.

Henin, A., & Kendall, P. C. (1997). Obsessive-compulsive disorder in childhood and adolescence. In T. H. Ollendick & R. J. Prinz (Eds.), *Advances in clinical child psychology* (Vol. 19, pp. 76–112). New York: Plenum Press.

Hinshaw, S. P. (1998). *Is ADHD an impairing condition in childhood and adolescence?* Chapter prepared for NIH Consensus Development Conference on Attention-Deficit Hyperactivity Disorder (ADHD): Diagnosis and Treatment. Bethesda, MD.

Hinshaw, S. P., Klein, R. G., & Abikoff, H. (1998). Childhood attention deficit hyperactivity disorder: Non-pharmacological and combination treatments. In P. E. Nathan & J. E. Gorman (Eds.), *A guide to treatments that work* (pp. 209–229). New York: Oxford University Press.

Hinshaw, S. P., Lahey, B. B., & Hart, E. L. (1993). Issues of taxonomy and comorbidity in the development of conduct disorder. *Development and Psychopathology, 5,* 31–49.

Hofmann, S. G., Ehler, A., & Roth, W. T. (1995). Conditioning theory: A model for the etiology of public speaking anxiety? *Behavior Research and Therapy, 33*(5), 567–571.

Hogarty, G. E., Greenwald, D., Ulrich, R. F., Kornblith, S. J., DiBarry, A. L., Cooley, S., Carter, M., & Flesher, S. (1997). Three year trials of personal therapy among schizophrenic patients living with or independent of family, II: Effects on adjustment of patient. *American Journal of Psychiatry, 154*(11), 1514–1524.

Hollon, S., & Garber, J. (1990). Cognitive therapy for depression: A social cognitive perspective. *Personality and Social Psychology Bulletin, 16,* 139–149.

Holmes, T. H., & Rahe, R. H. (1967). The Social Readjustment Rating Scale. *Journal of Psychosomatic Research, 11,* 213–218.

Hooley, J. (1985). Expressed emotion: A review of the critical literature. *Clinical Psychology Review, 5,* 119–139.

Howe, A., & Walker, C. E. (1992). Behavioral management of toilet training, enuresis, and encopresis. *Pediatric Clinics of North America, 39*(3), 413–432.

Ivanova, M. Y. (1998). *Dysregulation of the hypothalamic-pituitary-adrenocortical system in childhood and adolescent major depression: Evidence for biological correlates?* Unpublished manuscript, State University of New York, Albany.

Jacobson, R. (1985). Child firesetters: A clinical investigation. *Journal of Child Psychology and Psychiatry, 26*(5), 759–768.

Jefferson, J. W. (1997). Antidepressants in panic disorder. *Journal of Clinical Psychiatry, 58*(Suppl. 2), 20–24.

Jeffries, J. J. (1995). Working with schizophrenia: A clinician's personal experiences. *Canadian Journal of Psychiatry, 40*(3, Suppl. 1), S22–S25.

Jenkins, R. (1970). Diagnostic classification in child psychiatry. *American Journal of Psychiatry, 127*(5), 140–141.

Johnson, C., & Wonderlich, S. A. (1992). Personality characteristics as a risk factor in the development of eating disorders. In J. H. Crowther, D. L. Tennenbaum, S. E. Hobfoll, & M. A. P. Stephens (Eds.), *The etiology of bulimia nervosa: The individual and familial context* (pp. 364–383). Washington, DC: Hemisphere.

Johnson, E. H., Gentry, W. D., & Julius, S. (1992). *Personality, elevated blood pressure, and essential hypertension.* Washington, DC: Hemisphere.

Johnston, C., & Ohan, J. L. (1999). Externalizing disorders. In W. K. Silverman & T. H. Ollendick (Eds.), *Developmental issues in the clinical treatment of children.* Boston: Allyn & Bacon.

Jordan, D. R. (1998). *Attention deficit disorder: ADHD and ADD* (3rd ed.). Austin, TX: PRO-ED.

Julius, S. (1992). Relationship between the sympathetic tone and cardiovascular responsiveness in the course of hypertension. In E. H. Johnson, W. D. Gentry, & S. Julius (Eds.), *Personality, elevated blood pressure, and essential hypertension.* Washington, DC: Hemisphere.

Kandel, D., Davies, M., Karus, D., & Yamaguchi, K. (1986). The consequences in young adulthood of adolescent drug involvement. *Archives of General Psychiatry, 43,* 746–754.

Kane, J. M., & Freeman, H. L. (1994). Towards more effective antipsychotic treatment. *British Journal of Psychiatry, 165*(Suppl. 25), 22–31.

Kanner, L. (1943). Autistic disturbances of affective content. *Nervous Child, 2,* 217–240.

Karno, M., Golding, J., Sorenson, S., & Burnam, M. (1988). The epidemiology of obsessive-compulsive disorder in five US communities. *Archives of General Psychiatry, 45,* 1094–1099.

Kashani, J. H., Daniel, A. E., Dandoy, A. C., & Holcomb, W. R. (1992). Family violence: Impact on children. *Journal of the American Academy of Child and Adolescent Psychiatry, 31,* 181–189.

Katz, R. J., Lott, M., Landau, P., & Waldmeier, P. (1993). A clinical test of noradrenergic involvement in the therapeutic mode of action of an experimental antidepressant. *Biological Psychiatry, 33,* 261–266.

Kauffman, J. M. (1997). *Characteristics of emotional and behavioral disorders of children and youth.* Upper Saddle River, NJ: Merrill.

Kaufman, I., Frank, T., Heims, L., Herrick, J., Reiser, D., & Willer, L. (1960). Treatment implications of a new classification of parents of schizophrenic children. *American Journal of Psychiatry, 116,* 920–924.

Kazdin, A. E. (1985). *Treatment of antisocial behavior in children and adolescents.* Homewood, IL: Dorsey Press.

Kazdin, A. E. (1993). Adolescent mental health. Prevention and treatment programs. *American Psychologist, 48,* 127–141.

Kazdin, A. E. (1997). Practitioner review: Psychosocial treatments for conduct disorder in children. *Journal of Child Psychology and Psychiatry, 38,* 161–178.

Kazdin, A. E., & Marciano, P. L. (1998). Childhood and adolescent depression. In E. J. Mash & R. A. Barkley (Eds.), *Treatment of Childhood Disorders* (2nd ed., pp. 48–90). New York: Guilford Press.

Kazdin, A. E., Siegel, T. C., & Bass, D. (1992). Cognitive problem-solving skills training and parent management training in the treatment of antisocial behavior in children. *Journal of Consulting and Clinical Psychology, 60,* 733–747.

Kearney, C. A., Eisen, A., & Silverman, W. K. (1995). The legend and myth of school phobia. *School Psychology Quarterly, 10,* 65–85.

Keith, S. J., Regier, D. A., & Rae, D. S. (1991). Schizophrenic disorders. In L. N. Robins & D. A. Regier (Eds.), *Psychiatric disorders in America: The Epidemiological Catchment Area Study* (pp. 211–248). New York: Free Press.

Keller, M. B., Lavori, P. W., Wunder, J., Beardslee, W. R., Schwartz, C. E., & Roth, J. (1992). Chronic course of anxiety disorders in children and adolescents. *Journal of the American Academy of Child and Adolescent Psychiatry, 31,* 595–599.

Kendall, P. C., Panichelli-Mindel, S. M., Sugarman, A., & Callahan, S. A. (1997). Exposure to child anxiety: Theory, research, and practice. *Clinical Psychology: Science and Practice, 4,* 29–39.

Kendall, P. C., Stark, K. D., & Adams, T. (1990). Cognitive deficit or cognitive distortion in childhood depression. *Journal of Abnormal Child Psychology, 18,* 255–270.

Kendler, K., & Gruenberg, A. (1982). Genetic relationship between paranoid personality disorder and the "schizophrenic" spectrum disorders. *American Journal of Psychiatry, 139*(9), 1185–1186.

Kendler, K. S., McGuire, M., Gruenberg, A. M., & Walsh, D. (1994). An epidemiological, clinical, and family study of simple schizophrenia in County Roscommon, Ireland. *American Journal of Psychiatry, 151*(1), 27–34.

Kendler, K. S., Neale, M. C., Kessler, R. E., & Heath, A. C. (1992). Generalized anxiety disorder in women: A population-based twin study. *Archives of General Psychiatry, 49*(4), 267–272.

Kent, D. A., Tomasson, K., & Coryell, W. (1995). Course and outcome of conversion and somatization disorders: A four-year follow-up. *Psychosomatics, 36*(2), 138–144.

Kerwin, M. E., & Berkowitz, R. I. (1996). Feeding and eating disorders: Ingestive problems of infancy, childhood, and adolescence. *School Psychology Review, 25,* 316–328.

Kessler, R. C., McGonagle, K. A., Zhao, S., Nelson, C. B., Hughes, M., Eshleman, S., Wittchen, H. U., & Kendler, K. S. (1994). Lifetime and 12-month prevalence of DSM–III–R psychiatric disorders in the United States. *Archives of General Psychiatry, 51,* 8–19.

Kessler, R. C., Sonnega, A., Bromet, E., Hughes, M., & Nelson, C. B. (1995). Posttraumatic stress disorder in the National Comorbidity Survey. *Archives of General Psychiatry, 52,* 1048–1060.

Kiecolt-Glaser, J. K., Dura, J. R., Speicher, C. E., Trask, O. J., & Glaser, R. (1991). Spousal caregivers of dementia victims: Longitudinal changes in immunity and health. *Psychosomatic Medicine, 53,* 345–362.

King, G. A., Polivy, J., & Herman, C. P. (1991). Cognitive aspects of dietary restraint: Effects on person memory. *International Journal of Eating Disorders, 10*(3), 313–321.

King, N. J., Gullone, E., Tonge, B. J., & Ollendick, T. H. (1993). Self-reports of panic attacks and manifest anxiety in adolescents. *Behavior Research and Therapy, 31*(1), 111–116.

Kinnear, K. L. (1995). *Violent children: A reference handbook.* Santa Barbara, CA: ABC-CLIO.

Kirmayer, L. J., Robbins, J. M., Dworkind, M., & Yaffe, M. J. (1993). Somatization and the recognition of depression and anxiety in primary care. *American Journal of Psychiatry, 150*(5), 734–741.

Klein, D., Depue, R., & Slater, J. (1985) . Cyclothymia in the adolescent offspring of parents with bipolar a affective disorder. *Journal of Abnormal Psychology, 94,* 115–127.

Klerman, G. (1982). Practical issues in the treatment of depression and mania. In E. S. Paykel (Ed.), *Handbook of affective disorders* (pp. 21–37). New York: Guilford Press.

Klerman, G. L., Weissman, M. M., Markowitz, J., Glick, I., Wilner, P. J., Mason, B., & Shear, M. K. (1994). Medication and psychotherapy. In A. E. Bergin & S. L. Garfeil (Eds.), *Handbook of psychotherapy and behavior change* (4th ed., pp. 59–85). New York: Wiley.

Klinger, L. G., & Dawson, G. (1996). Autistic disorder. In E. J. Mash & R. A. Barkley (Eds.), *Child psychopathology* (pp. 11–36). New York: Guilford Press.

Klingman, A., & Hochdorf, Z. (1993). Coping with distress and self harm: The impact of a primary prevention program among adolescents. *Journal of Adolescent Psychology, 15,* 121–140.

Koegel, L. K., & Koegel, R. L. (1995). Motivating communication in children with autism. In E. Schopler & G. B. Mesibov (Eds.), *Learning and cognition in autism* (pp. 23–40). New York: Plenum Press.

Koegel, R. L., & Koegel, L. K. (1990). Extended reductions in stereotypic behavior of students with autism through a self-management treatment package. *Journal of Applied Behavior Analysis, 23,* 119–127.

Kovacs, M. (1989). Affective disorders in children and adolescents. *American Psychologist, 44,* 209–215.

Kovacs, M. (1996). Presentation and course of Major Depressive Disorder during childhood and later years of the life span. *Journal of the American Academy of Child and Adolescent Psychiatry, 35,* 705–715.

Kovacs, M., Devlin, B., Pollack, M., Richards, C., & Mukerji, P. (1997). A controlled family history study of childhood-onset depressive disorder. *Archives of General Psychiatry, 54,* 613–623.

Kovacs, M., Feinberg, T., Crouse-Novak, M., Paulauskas, S., Pollock, M., & Finkelstein, R. (1984). Depressive disorders in childhood. II. A longitudinal study of the risk for a subsequent major depression. *Archives of General Psychiatry, 41,* 643–649.

Kroenke, K., Spitzer, R. L., deGruy, F. V., III, & Hahn, S. R. (1997). Multisomatoform disorder: An alternative to undifferentiated somatoform disorder for the somatizing patient in primary care. *Archives of General Psychiatry, 41,* 352–358.

Kumra, S., Jacobsen, L. K., Lenane, M., Smith, A., Lee, P., Malanga, C. J., Karp, B. I., Hamburger, S., & Rapoport, J. L. (1998). Case series: Spectrum of neuroleptic-induced movement disorders and extrapyramidal side effects in childhood-onset schizophrenia. *Journal of the American Academy of Child and Adolescent Psychiatry, 37,* 221–227.

Kupfer, D. J., & Reynolds, C. F. (1992). Sleep and affective disorders. In E. S. Paykel (Ed.), *Handbook of affective disorders* (2nd ed.). New York: Guilford Press.

Kydd, R., & Werry, J. (1982). Schizophrenia in children under 16 years. *Journal of Autism and Developmental Disorders, 12,* 43–57.

LaGreca, A. M., Silverman, W. K., & Wasserstein, S. B. (1998). Children's predisaster functioning as a predictor of posttraumatic stress following Hurricane Andrew. *Journal of Consulting and Clinical Psychology, 66,* 883–892.

Lahey, B. B., Hartdagen, S. E., Frick, P. J., & McBurnett, K. (1988). Conduct disorder: Parsing the confounded relation to parental divorce and antisocial personality. *Journal of Abnormal Psychology, 97*(3), 334–337.

Lattimore, P. K., Visher, C. A., & Linster, R. L. (1995). Predicting rearrest for violence among serious youthful offenders. *Journal of Research in Crime and Delinquency, 32,* 54–83.

Leaf, P. J. (1996). Mental health service use in the community and schools: Results from the four-community MECA Study. *Journal of the Academy of Child and Adolescent Psychiatry, 35,* 889–897.

Leese, S. (1968). The multivariant masks of depression. *American Journal of Psychiatry, 124*(11), 35–40.

Leff, J. (1992). Schizophrenia and similar conditions. *International Journal of Mental Health, 21*(2), 25–40.

Leibel, R. L., & Hirsch, J. (1995). The molecular biology of obesity. In K. D. Brownell & C. G. Fairburn (Eds.), *Eating disorder and obesity: A comprehensive handbook* (pp. 360–375). New York: Guilford Press.

Lemieux, A. M., & Coe, C. L. (1995). Abuse related posttraumatic stress disorder: Evidence for chronic neuroendocrine activation in women. *Psychosomatic Medicine, 57*(2), 105–115.

Leonard, H. L., Swedo, S. E., Allen, A. J., & Rapoport, J. L. (1994). Obsessive-compulsive disorder. In T. H. Ollendick, N. J. King, & W. Yule (Eds.), *International handbook of anxiety disorders in children and adolescents* (pp. 275–291). New York: Plenum Press.

Leserman, J., Drossman, D. A., Li, Z., & Toomey, T. C. (1996). Sexual and physical abuse history in gastroenterology practice: How types of abuse impact health status. *Psychosomatic Medicine, 58*(1), 4–15.

Levy, S. R., Jurkovic, G. L., & Spirito, A. (1995). A multisystems analysis of adolescent suicide. *Journal of Abnormal Child Psychology, 23,* 221–234.

Lewinsohn, P., Rohde, P., & Seeley, J. R. (1998). Adolescent psychopathology: III. The clinical consequences of comorbidity. *Journal of the American Academy of Child and Adolescent Psychiatry, 34,* 510–519.

Lewinsohn, P., Zeiss, A., & Duncan, E. (1989). Probability of relapse after recovery from an episode of depression. *Journal of Abnormal Psychology, 98,* 107–116.

Lidz, T., Fleck, S., & Cornelison, A. (1965). *Schizophrenia and the family.* New York: International Universities Press.

Liebowitz, S. F., & Hoebel, B. G. (1998). Behavioral neuroscience of obesity. In G. A. Bray, C. Bouchard, & P. T. James (Eds.), *The handbook of obesity* (pp. 85–99). New York: Dekker.

Linszen, D. H., Dingemans, P. M., Nugter, M. A., & Willem, A. J. (1997). Patient attributes and expressed emotion as risk factors for psychotic relapse. *Schizophrenia Bulletin, 23*(1), 119–130.

Lish, J. D., Kavoussi, R. J., & Coccaro, E. F. (1996). Aggressiveness. In C. G. Costello (Ed.), *Personality characteristics of the personality disordered* (pp. 33–54). New York: Wiley.

Lloyd, G. K., Fletcher, A., & Minchin, M. C. (1992). GABA agonists as potential anxiolytics. In G. D. Burrown, S. M. Roth, & R. Noyes, Jr. (Eds.), *Handbook of Anxiety* (Vol. 5, pp. 167–198). Oxford: Elsevier.

Locke, B., & Regier, D. (1985). Prevalence of selected mental disorders. *Mental Health, United States, 1985* (pp. 1–6). Washington, DC: U.S. Government Printing Office.

Loranger, A., Oldham, J., & Tulis, E. (1982). Familial transmission of DSM–III borderline personality disorder. *Archives of General Psychiatry, 39*(7), 795–799.

Lord, C., & Paul, R. (1997). Language and communication in autism. In D. J. Cohen & F. R. Volkmar (Eds.), *Handbook of autism and pervasive developmental disorders* (pp. 213–235). New York: Wiley.

Lovaas, O. (1987). Behavioral treatment and normal educational and intellectual functioning in young autistic children. *Journal of Consulting and Clinical Psychology, ss(1)*, 3–9.

Loveland, K. A., & Tunali-Kotoski, B. (1997). The school-age child with autism. In D. J. Cohen & F. R. Volkmar (Eds.), *Handbook of autism and pervasive developmental disorders* (pp. 236–266). New York: Wiley.

Lucas, A. R., & Holub, M. I. (1995). The incidence of anorexia nervosa in adolescent residents of Rochester, Minnesota, during a 50 year period. In H. C. Steinhausen (Ed.), *Eating disorders in adolescence: Anorexia and bulimia nervosa* (pp. 352–365). Berlin, Germany: Walter de Gruyter.

Luntz, B. K., & Widom, C. S. (1994). Antisocial personality disorder in abused and neglected children grown up. *American Journal of Psychiatry, 151*(5), 670–674.

Lutz, D., & Snow, P. (1985). Understanding the role of depression in the alcoholic. *Clinical Psychology Review, 5*, 535–551.

Lykken, D. T. (1995). *The antisocial personalities.* Hillsdale, NJ: Erlbaum.

Magee, W. J., Eaton, W. W., Wittchen, H. U., McGonagle, K. A., & Kessler, R. C. (1996). Agoraphobia, simple phobia, and social phobia in the National Comorbidity Survey. *Archives of General Psychiatry, 53*, 159–168.

Maher, B. A., & Maher, W. B. (1994). Personality and psychopathology: A historical perspective. *Journal of Abnormal Psychology, 103*(1), 72–77.

Malcarne, V. L., & Ingram, R. E. (1994). Cognition and negative affectivity. In T. H. Ollendick & R. J. Prinz (Eds.), *Advances in clinical child psychology* (Vol. 16, pp. 104–120). New York: Plenum Press.

March, J. S., & Mulle, K. (1998). *OCD in children and adolescents: A cognitive-behavioral treatment manual.* New York: Guilford Press.

Martineau, J., Barthelemy, C., Jouve, J., & Muh, J. P. (1992). Monoamines (serotonin and catecholamines) and their derivatives in infantile autism. Age related changes and drug effects. *Developmental and Medical Child Neurology, 34*(7), 593–603.

Marttunen, M. J., Henriksson, M. M., Heikkinen, M. E., Isomestsa, E. T., & Lonnqvist, J. K. (1995). Suicide among female adolescents: Characteristics and comparison with males in the age group 13–21 years. *Journal of the American Academy of Child and Adolescent Psychiatry, 34*, 1297–1307.

Mattis, S. G., & Ollendick, T. H. (1997). Panic disorder in children and adolescents: A developmental analysis. In T. H. Ollendick & R. J. Prinz (Eds.), *Advances in clinical child psychology* (Vol. 19, pp. 113–134). New York: Plenum Press.

Maughan, B., & Rutter, M. (1998). Continuities and discontinuities in antisocial behavior from childhood to adult life. In T. H. Ollendick & R. J. Prinz (Eds.), *Advances in clinical child psychology* (Vol. 20, pp. 46–61). New York: Plenum Press.

Mavreas, V. G., Tomaras, V., Karydi, V., & Economous, M. (1992). Expressed emotion in families of chronic schizophrenics and its association with clinical measures. *Social Psychiatry, 27*(1), 4–9.

McAlpine, C., & Singh, N. N. (1986). Pica in institutionalized mentally retarded persons. *Journal of Mental Deficiency Research, 30*, 171–178.

McClellan, J., & Werry, J. (1997). Practice parameters for the assessment and treatment of children and adolescents with schizophrenia. *Journal of the American Academy of Child and Adolescent Psychiatry, 33*, 616 635.

McDaniels, J. S., Moran, M. G., Levenson, J. L., & Stoudemire, A. (1994). Psychological factors affecting medical conditions. In R. E. Hales, S. C. Yudofsky, & J. A. Talbott (Eds.), *The American Psychiatric Press textbook of psychiatry* (2nd ed., pp. 338–365). Washington, DC: American Psychiatric Press.

McGee, R., Feehan, M., Williams, S., & Anderson, J. (1992). DSM–III disorders from age 11 to age 15 years. *Journal of the American Academy of Childhood and Adolescent Psychiatry, 31*, 50–59.

McLoughlin, J. A., & Nall, M. (1994). Allergies and learning/behavioral disorders. *Intervention in School and Clinic, 29*, 198–207.

Merrell, K. W. (1994). *Assessment of behavioral, social, and emotional problems: Direct observation and objective methods for use with children and adolescents.* New York: Longman.

Merrill, J., Milner, G., Owens, J., & Vale, A. (1992). Alcohol and attempted suicide. *British Journal of Addiction, 87*(1), 83–89.

Mesibov, G. B. (1994). A comprehensive program for serving people with autism and their families: The TEACCH model. In J. L. Matson (Ed.), *Autism in children and adults* (pp. 397–408). Pacific Grove, CA: Brooks/Cole.

Metalsky, G. I., Joiner, T. E., Jr., Hardin, T. S., & Abramson, L. Y. (1993). Depressive reactions to failure in a naturalistic setting: A test of hopelessness and self-esteem theories of depression. *Journal of Abnormal Psychology, 102*(1), 101–109.

Miklowitz, D. J. (1994). Family risk indicators in schizophrenia. *Schizophrenia Bulletin, 20*(1), 137–149.

Miller, D. (1994). Suicidal behavior of adolescents with behavior disorders and their peers without disabilities. *Behavioral Disorders, 20*, 61–68.

Miller, M., Chiles, J., & Barnes, V. (1982). Suicide attempts within a delinquent population. *Journal of Consulting and Clinical Psychology, 50*, 491–498.

Millon, T. (1990). The disorders of personality. In L. A. Pervin (Ed.), *Handbook of personality theory and practice* (pp. 21–44). New York: Guilford Press.

Minde, K., Faucon, A., & Faulkner, S. (1994). Sleep problems in toddlers: Effects of treatment on their daytime behavior. *Journal of the American Academy of Child and Adolescent Psychiatry, 33*, 1114–1121.

Minde, K., Popiel, K., Leos, N., Faulkner, S., Parker, K., & Handley-Derry, M. (1993). The evaluation and treatment of sleep disturbances in young children. *Journal of Child Psychology and Psychiatry, 34*, 521–533.

Mindell, J. A. (1993). Sleep disorders in children. *Health Psychology, 12*, 151–162.

Minshew, N. J., Sweeney, J. A., & Bauman, M. L. (1997). Neurological aspects of autism. In D. J. Cohen & F. R. Volkmar (Eds.), *Handbook of autism and pervasive developmental disorders* (pp. 267–284). New York: Wiley.

Mira, M. P., & Tyler, J. S. (1991). Students with traumatic brain injury: Making the transition from hospital to school. *Focus on Exceptional Children, 23*(5), 1–12.

Mizes, J. S. (1995). Eating disorders. In M. Hersen & R. T. Ammerman (Eds.), *Advanced abnormal child psychology* (pp. 375–391). Hillsdale, NJ: Erlbaum.

Moffitt, T. E. (1993). Adolescence-limited and life-course-persistent antisocial behavior: A developmental taxonomy. *Psychological Review, 100*, 674–701.

Mojtabai, R., Nicholson, R. A., & Carpenter, B. N. (1998). Role of psychosocial treatments in management of schizophrenia: A meta-analytic review of controlled outcome studies. *Schizophrenia Bulletin, 24*, 569–587.

Moncrieff, J., Drummond, C., Candy, B., Checinski, K., & Farmer, R. (1996). Sexual abuse in people with alcohol problems: A study of the prevalence of sexual abuse and its relationship to drinking behavior. *British Journal of Psychiatry, 169*, 355–360.

Montgomery, S. A., Bebbington, P., Cowen, P., & Deakin, W. (1993). Guidelines for treating depressive illness with antidepressants. *Journal of Psychopharmacology, 7*(1), 19–23.

Morrison, D. N., McGee, R., & Stanton, W. R. (1992). Sleep problems in adolescence. *Journal of the American Academy of Child and Adolescent Psychiatry, 31*, 94–96.

Munk, J. P., & Mortensen, P. B. (1992). Social outcome in schizophrenia: A 13-year follow-up. *Social Psychiatry, 27*(3), 129–134.

Murphy, G. (1988). Suicide and substance abuse. *Archives of General Psychiatry, 45*, 593–594.

National Center for Health Statistics. (1991). Vital statistics of the United States (Vol. 2): Mortality—Part A. Washington, DC: U.S. Government Printing Office.

National Center for Health Statistics. (1993). Advance report of final mortality statistics, 1991. Monthly Vital Statistics Report, Vol. 42(2). Hyattsville, MD: U.S. Public Health Service.

National Institute of Drug Abuse. (1990). Annual report. Washington, DC: U.S. Department of Health and Human Services.

Navia, B., Jordan, B., & Price, R. (1986). The AIDS dementia complex: I. Clinical features. Annals of Neurology, 19, 517–524.

Nestadt, G., Rornanoski, A. J., Chahal, R., Merchant, A., Folstein, M. E., Gruenberg, E. M., & McHugh, P. R. (1990). An epidemiological study of histrionic personality disorder. Psychological Medicine, 29, 413–422.

Neuman, R. J., Todd, R. D., Heath, A. C., Reich, W., Hudzick, J. J., Bucholz, K. K., Madden, P. A., Begleiter, H., Porjesz, B., Kuperman, S., Hesseibruck, V., & Reich, T. (1999). Evaluation of ADHD typology in three contrasting samples: A latent class approach. Journal of the American Academy of Child and Adolescent Psychiatry, 38, 25–33.

Newcomb, A. F., Bukowski, W. M., & Pattee, L. (1993). Children's peer relations: A meta-analysis review of popular, rejected, neglected, controversial, and average sociometric status. Psychological Bulletin, 113, 99–128.

Newcomer, P., Barenbaum, E., & Pearson, N. (1995). Depression and anxiety in children and adolescents with learning disabilities, conduct disorders, and no disabilities. Journal of Emotional and Behavioral Disorders, 3, 27–39.

Newsom, C. (1998). Autistic disorder. In E. J. Mash & R. A. Barkley (Eds.), Treatment of childhood disorders (pp. 416–467). New York: Guilford Press.

Nichter, M., & Nichter, M. (1991). Hype and weight. Medical Anthropology, 13(3), 249–284.

Nielson, S., Moller-Madsen, S., Isager, T., Jorgensen, J., Pagsberg, K., & Theander, S. (1998). Standardized mortality in eating disorders: A quantitative summary of previously published and new evidence. Journal of Psychosomatic Research, 14(3/4), 413–434.

Norton, G. R., Cox, B. J., Hewitt, P. L., & McLeod, L. (1997). Personality factors associated with generalized and non-generalized social anxiety. Personal and Individual Differences, 22(5), 655–660.

Nottelmann, E. D., & Jensen, P. S. (1995). Comorbidity of disorders in children and adolescents: Developmental perspectives. In T. H. Ollendick & R. J. Prinz (Eds.), Advances in clinical child psychology (Vol. 17, pp. 307–334). New York: Plenum Press.

O'Connell, M., Cooper, S., Perry, J., & Hoke, L. (1989). The relationship between thought disorder and psychotic symptoms in borderline personality disorders. Journal of Nervous and Mental Diseases, 177, 273–278.

O'Connor, N., & Hermelin, B. (1990). The recognition failure and graphic success of idiot-savant artists. Journal of Child Psychology and Psychiatry, 31, 203–215.

Office of Technology Assessment. (1986, December). Children's mental health: Problems and services (OTA Publication No. OTA-BP-H-33). Washington, DC: U.S. Government Printing Office.

Ohman, A., & Soares, J. J. (1993). On the automatic nature of phobic fear: Conditioned electrodermal responses to masked fear-relevant stimuli. Journal of Abnormal Psychology, 102(1), 121–132.

Ollendick, T. H. (1998). Panic disorder in children and adolescents: New developments, new directions. Journal of Clinical Child Psychology, 27, 234–245.

Ondersma, S. J., & Walker, E. (1998). Elimination disorders. In T. H. Ollendick & M. Hersen (Eds.), Handbook of child psychopathology (3rd ed., pp. 26–40). New York: Plenum Press.

Ornitz, E., Atwell, C., Kaplan, A., & Westlake, J. (1985). Brain-stem dysfunction in autism. Archives of General Psychiatry, 42, 1018–1025.

Ost, L. (1987). Age of onset in different phobias. *Journal of Abnormal Psychology, 96,* 123–145.

Overholser, J. C. (1996). The dependent personality and interpersonal problems. *Journal of Nervous and Mental Diseases, 184*(1), 816.

Park, A. (1996, September 18). Health roundup: The human condition. *Time,* 82.

Parker, G. (1992). Early environment. In E. S. Paykel (Ed.), *Handbook of affective disorders* (pp. 431–449). New York: Guilford Press.

Parker, G., Hadzi-Pavlovic, D., Brodaty, H., Boyce, P., Mitchell, P., Wilhelm, K., Hickie, I., & Eyers, K. (1993). Psychomotor disturbance in depression: Defining the constructs. *Journal of Affective Disorders, 27,* 255–265.

Paschall, M. J., & Hubbard, M. L. (1998). Effects of neighborhood and family stressors on African American male adolescents' self-worth and propensity for violent behavior. *Journal of Consulting and Clinical Psychology, 66,* 825–831.

Pato, M. T., & Pato, C. N. (1997). Obessive-compulsive disorder in adults. In L. J. Dickstein, M. B. Riba, & J. M. Oldham (Eds.), *Review of Psychiatry* (Vol. 16, pp. 235–262). Washington, DC: American Psychiatric Press.

Patterson, G., DeBarsyshe, B., & Ramsey, E. (1989). A developmental perspective on antisocial behavior. *American Psychologist, 44,* 329–335.

Patterson, G. R., Reid, J. B., & Dishion, T. J. (1992). *Antisocial boys.* Eugene, OR: Castalia.

Paykel, E. S., & Cooper, Z. (1992). Life events and social stress. In E. S. Paykel (Ed.), *Handbook of affective disorders* (pp. 450–469). New York: Guilford Press.

Perris, C. (1982). The distinction between bipolar and unipolar affective disorders. In E. S. Paykel (Ed.), *Handbook of affective disorders* (pp. 45–57). New York: Guilford Press.

Peterson, A. L., Talcott, G. W., Kelleher, W. J., & Haddock, C. K. (1995). Site specificity of pain and tension in tension-type headaches. *Headache, 35*(2), 89–92.

Peterson, C. (1993). Helpless behavior. *Behavior Research Therapy, 31*(3), 289–295.

Pfeffer, C. R. (1993). Suicidal children. In A. A. Leenaars (Ed.), *Suicidology* (pp. 56–57). Northvale, NJ: Aronson.

Phillips, K. A., McElroy, S. L., Keck, P. E., Pope, H. G., & Hudson, J. I. (1993). Body dysmorphic disorder: 30 cases of imagined ugliness. *American Journal of Psychiatry, 150*(2), 302–308.

Pierce, J. W., & Wardle, J. (1993). Self-esteem, parental appraisal and body size in children. *Journal of Child Psychology and Psychiatry, 34,* 1125–1136.

Pike, K. M. (1998). Long-term course of anorexia nervosa: Response, relapse, remission, and recovery. *Clinical Psychology Review, 18,* 447–475.

Pillow, D. R., Zautra, A. J., & Sandler, I. (1996). Major life events and minor stressors: Identifying mediational links in the stress process. *Journal of Personality and Social Psychology, 70*(2), 381–394.

Piven, J., Palmer, P., Jacobi, D., Childress, D., & Arndt, S. (1997). Broader autism phenotype: Evidence from a family history study of multiple-incidence autism families. *American Journal of Psychiatry, 154*(2), 185–190.

Poland, S. (1989). *Suicide intervention in the schools.* New York: Guilford Press.

Price, R. A. (1995). The search for obesity genes. In D. B. Allison & F. X. Pi-Sunyer (Eds.), *Obesity treatment: Establishing goals, improving outcomes, and reviewing the research agenda.* New York: Plenum Press.

Prien, R. F. (1992). Maintenance treatment. In E. S. Paykel (Ed.), *Handbook of affective disorders.* New York: Guilford Press.

Pring, L., & Hermelin, B. (1993). Bottle, tulip, and wineglass: Semantic and structural picture processing by savant artists. *Journal of Child Psychology and Psychiatry, 34,* 1365–1385.

Prior, M., & Werry, J. (1986). Autism, schizophrenia, and allied disorders. In H. C. Quay & J. S. Werry (Eds.), *Psychopathological disorders of childhood* (3rd ed., pp. 156–210). New York: Wiley.

Putnam, F., Guroff, J., Silberman, E., Barban, L., & Post, R. (1986). The clinical phenomenology of multiple personality disorder: Review of 100 recent cases. *Journal of Clinical Psychiatry, 47*, 285–293.

Putnam, F. W. (1996). Posttraumatic stress disorder in children and adolescents. In L. J. Dickstein, M. B. Riba, & J. M. Oldham (Eds.), *Review of Psychiatry* (Vol. 15, pp. 189–216). Washington, DC: American Psychiatric Press.

Quay, H. C. (1986). Conduct disorders. In H. C. Quay & J. S. Werry (Eds.), *Psychopathological disorders of childhood* (3rd ed., pp. 35–72). New York: Wiley.

Quay, H. C. (1993). The psychobiology of undersocialized aggressive conduct disorder: A theoretical perspective. *Development and Psychopathology, 5*, 165–180.

Rank, B. (1995). Intensive study and treatment of preschool children who show marked personality deviations or "a typical development" and their parents. In G. Caplan (Ed.), *Emotional problems of early childhood* (pp. 169–184). New York: Basic Books.

Rapoport, J. L. (1991). Recent advances in obsessive-compulsive disorder. *Neuropsychopharmacology, 5*(1), 1–10.

Regier, D. A., Narrow, W. E., Rae, D. S., Manderscheid, R. W., Locke, B. Z., & Goodwin, F. K. (1993). The de facto US Mental and Addictive Disorders Service System: Epidemiologic Catchment Area prospective 1-year prevalence rates of disorders in services. *Archives of General Psychiatry, 50*, 85–94.

Reid, R., Maag, J. W., & Vasa, S. F. (1994). Attention deficit hyperactivity disorder as a disability category: A critique. *Exceptional Children, 60*, 198–214.

Resnick, H. S., Yehuda, R., Pitman, R. K., & Foy, D. W. (1995). Effect of previous trauma on acute plasma cortisol level following rape. *American Journal of Psychiatry, 152*(11), 1675–1677.

Reynolds, W., & Graves, A. (1989). Reliability of children's reports of depressive symptomatology. *Journal of Abnormal Child Psychology, 17*, 647–655.

Rimland, B. (1964). *Infantile autism: The Syndrome and its implications for a neural theory of behavior*. New York: Appleton-Century-Crofts.

Ritvo, E., Freeman, B., Pingree, C., Mason-Brothers, A., Jorde, L., Jenson, W., McMahon, W., Peterson, P., Mo, A., & Ritvo, A. (1989). The UCLA-University of Utah epidemiologic survey of autism: Prevalence. *American Journal of Psychiatry, 146*, 194–199.

Robins, L., Helzer, J., Weissman, M., Orvaschel, H., Gruenberg, E., Burke, J., & Regier, D. (1984). Lifetime prevalence of specific psychiatric disorders in three sites. *Archives of General Psychiatry, 41*, 949–958.

Roff, J., & Knight, R. (1981). Family characteristics, childhood symptoms, and adult outcome in schizophrenia. *Journal of Abnormal Psychology, 90*, 510–520.

Ronen, T. (1993). Intervention package for treating encopresis in a 6-year-old boy: A case study. *Behavioral Psychotherapy, 21*, 127–135.

Ross, C., Norton, G., & Wozney, K. (1989). Multiple personality disorder: An analysis of 236 cases. *Canadian Journal of Psychiatry, 34*, 413–418.

Rounsaville, B., Weissman, M., & Prusoff, B. (1987). Psychotherapy with depressed outpatients: Patient and process variables as predictors of outcome. *American Journal of Psychiatry, 138*, 67–74.

Roy, A. (1985). Early parental separation and adult depression. *Archives of General Psychiatry, 42*, 987–991.

Rumsey, J., Andreasen, N., & Rapoport, J. (1986). Thought, language, communication, and affective flattening in autistic adults. *Archives of General Psychiatry, 43*, 771–777.

Rumsey, J., Rapoport, J., & Sceery, W. (1985). Autistic children as adults. *Journal of the American Academy of Child Psychiatry, 24*, 465–473.

Rushford, N. M., & Ostermeyer, A. (1997). Body image disturbances and their change with video feedback in anorexia nervosa. *Behavior Research and Therapy, 35*(5), 389–398.

Russell, G. F. M. (1995). Anorexia nervosa through time. In G. Szmukler, C. Dare, & J. Treasure (Eds.), *Handbook of eating disorders: Theory, treatment and research*. Chichester, England: Wiley.

Rutter, M. (1978). Diagnosis and definition. In M. Rutter & E. Schopler (Eds.), *Autism: A reappraisal of concepts and treatment*. New York: Plenum Press.

Rutter, M. (1986). The developmental psychopathology of depression: Issues and perspectives. In M. Rutter, E. E. Izard, & P. B. Read (Eds.), *Depression in young people: Developmental and clinical perspectives* (pp. 3–32). New York: Guilford Press.

Rutter, M., Bailey, A., Simonoff, E., & Pickles, A. (1997). Genetic influences and autism. In D. J. Cohen & F. R. Volkmar (Eds.), *Handbook of autism and pervasive developmental disorders* (pp. 92–130). New York: Wiley.

Rutter, M., & Schopler, E. (1987). Autism and pervasive developmental disorders: Concepts and diagnostic issues. *Journal of Autism and Developmental Disorders, 17*, 159–186.

Rutter, M., Silberg, J., O'Connor, T., & Simonoff, E. (1999). Genetics and child psychiatry: II. Empirical research findings. *Journal of Child Psychology and Psychiatry, 40*, 19–55.

Rydell, P. J., & Prizant, B. M. (1995). Assessment and intervention strategies for children who use echolalia. In K. A. Quill (Ed.), *Teaching children with autism: Strategies to enhance communication and socialization* (pp. 51–70). New York: Delmar.

Sanftner, J. L., & Crowther, J. H. (1998). Variability in self-esteem, moods, shame, and guilt in women who binge. *International Journal of Eating Disorders, 23*, 391–397.

Scheien, L. M., & Botwin, G. F. (1997). Expectancies as mediators of the effects of social influences and alcohol knowledge on adolescent alcohol use: A prospective analysis. *Psychology of Addictive Behavior, 11*(1), 48–64.

Schopler, E. (1997). Implementation of TEACCH philosophy. In D. J. Cohen & F. R. Volkmar (Eds.), *Handbook of autism and pervasive developmental disorders*. New York: Wiley.

Schowalter, J. (1988). Tics. *Pediatrics in Review, 2*, 55–57.

Schreier, H., & Libow, J. (1994). Munchausen by proxy syndrome: A clinical fable for our times. *Journal of the American Academy of Child and Adolescent Psychiatry, 33*(6), 904–905.

Seligman, M. E. (1992). Wednesday's children. *Psychology Today, 25*(1), 61.

Seto, M. C., Khattar, N. A., Lalumiere, J. R., & Quinsey, V. L. (1997). Deception and sexual strategy in psychopathology. *Personal and Individual Differences, 22*(3), 301–307.

Sher, K. J., & Trull, T. J. (1994). Personality and disinhibitry psychopathology: Alcoholism and antisocial personality disorder. *Journal of Abnormal Psychology, 103*(1), 92–102.

Shneidman, E. S. (1993). *Suicide as psychache: A clinical approach to self-destructive behavior*. Northvale, NJ: Aronson.

Siegel, L. J., & Senna, J. J. (1994). *Juvenile delinquency: Theory, practice, and law* (5th ed.). St. Paul, MN: West.

Siegel, L. J., & Smith, K. E. (1991). Somatic disorders. In T. R. Kratochwill & R. J. Morris (Eds.), *The practice of child therapy* (2nd ed., pp. 29–45). New York: Pergamon Press.

Siever, L. (1986). Schizoid and schizotypal personality disorders. In J. R. Lion (Ed.), *Personality disorders: Diagnosis and management* (pp. 32–64). Malabar, FL: Kreiger.

Siever, L. J. (1992). Schizophrenia spectrum personality disorders. In A. Tasman & M. B. Riba (Eds.), *American Psychiatric Press review of psychiatry* (Vol. 11, pp. 29–50). Washington, DC: American Psychiatric Press.

Sigman, M. (1998). Change and continuity in the development of children with autism. *Journal of Child Psychology and Psychiatry, 39*, 817–828.

Silva, R. R., Munoz, D. M., Barickman, J., & Friedhoff, A. J. (1995). Environmental factors and related fluctuation of symptoms in children and adolescents with Tourette's disorder. *Journal of Child Psychology and Psychiatry, 36*, 305–312.

Silverman, W. K. (1994). Structured diagnostic interviews. In T. H. Ollendick, N. J. King, & W. Yule (Eds.), *International handbook of phobic and anxiety disorders in children and adolescents* (pp. 410–425). New York: Plenum Press.

Silverman, W. K., & Ginsburg, G. S. (1998). Anxiety disorders. In T. H. Ollendick & M. Hersen (Eds.), *Handbook of child psychopathology* (3rd ed., pp. 69–109). New York: Plenum Press.

Simpson, R. L., & Zionts, P. (2000). *Autism: Information and resources for parents, families, and professionals.* Austin, TX: PRO-ED.

Skau, K., & Mouridsen, S. (1995). Munchausen syndrome by proxy: A review. *Acta Psychiatrica Scandinavica, 84*, 977–982.

Slade, P. (1995). Prospects for revention. In G. Szumkler, C. Dare, & J. Treasure (Eds.), *Handbook of eating disorders: Theory, treatment and research* (pp. 416–429). Chichester, England: Wiley.

Slomkowski, C., Klein, R., & Mannuzza, S. (1995). Is self-esteem an important outcome in hyperactive children? *Journal of Abnormal Child Psychology, 23*, 303–315.

Smith, K., & Killam, P. (1994). Munchausen syndrome by proxy. *American Psychologist, 19*, 214–221.

Smith, W. (1989). *A profile of health and disease in America.* New York: Facts on File.

Smith-Myles, B., & Simpson, R. (1998). Inclusion of students with autism in general education classrooms: The autism inclusion collaboration model. In R. L. Simpson & B. Smith Myles (Eds.), *Educating children and youth with autism* (pp. 241–256). Austin, TX: PRO-ED.

Smyth, J. M. (1998). Written emotional expression: Effect sizes, outcome types, and moderating variables. *Journal of Consulting and Clinical Psychology, 66*(1), 174–184.

Snider, W., Simpson, D., Nielsen, S., Gold, J., Metroka, C., & Posner, J. (1983). Neurological complications of acquired immune deficiency syndrome: Analysis of 50 patients. *Annals of Neurology, 14*, 403–418.

Spirito, A., Brown, L., Overholser, J., & Fritz, G. (1989). Attempted suicide in adolescence: A review and critique of the literature. *Clinical Psychology Review, 9*, 335–363.

Spoont, M. R. (1996). Emotional instability. In C. G. Costello (Ed.), *Personality characteristics of the personality disordered* (pp. 90–109). New York: Wiley.

Sprafkin, J., Gadow, K. D., & Adelman, R. (1992). *Television and the exceptional child: A forgotten audience.* Hillsdale, NJ: Erlbaum.

Steffenberg, S., & Gillberg, C. (1986). Autism and autistic-like conditions in Swedish rural and urban areas: A population study. *British Journal of Psychiatry, 149*, 81–87.

Stein, M. B., Walker, J. R., & Forde, D. R. (1994). Setting diagnostic thresholds for social phobia: Considerations from a community survey of social anxiety. *American Journal of Psychiatry, 151*(3), 408–412.

Steiner, H., & Lock, J. (1998). Anorexia nervosa and bulimia nervosa in children and adolescents: A review of the past 10 years. *Journal of the American Academy of Child and Adolescent Psychiatry, 37*, 352–359.

Sternberg, E. M., & Gold, P. W. (1997). The mind–body interaction in disease [Special Issue]. *Scientific American Mysteries of the Mind, 20*, 8–15.

Stone, W. L. (1997). Autism in infancy and early childhood. In D. J. Cohen & F. R. Volkmar (Eds.), *Handbook of autism and pervasive developmental disorders* (pp. 423–459). New York: Wiley.

Strange, P. G. (1992). *Brain biochemistry and brain disorders.* New York: Oxford University Press.

Swedo, S., Rapoport, J., Leonard, H., Lenane, M., & Cheslow, D. (1989). Obsessive-compulsive disorder in children and adolescents: Clinical phenomenology of 70 consecutive cases. *Archives of General Psychiatry, 46*, 335–341.

Tallis, F. (1996). Compulsive washing in the absence of phobia and illness anxiety. *Behavior Research and Therapy, 34*(4), 361–362.

Tannock, R. (1998). Attention deficit hyperactivity disorder: Advances in cognitive, neurobiological, and genetic research. *Journal of Child Psychology and Psychiatry, 39*, 65–99.

Taylor, S., Kuch, K., Koch, W. J., Crockett, D. J., & Passey, G. (1998). The structure of posttraumatic stress symptoms. *Journal of Abnormal Psychology, 107*(1), 154–160.

Thase, M., Frank, E., & Kupfer, D. (1985). Biological processes in major depression. In E. E. Beckham & W. R. Leber (Eds.), *Handbook of depression: Treatment, assessment, and research* (pp. 816–913). Homewood, IL: Dorsey Press.

Thiel, A., Brooks, A., Ohlmeier, M., & Jacoby, G. E. (1995). Obsessive-compulsive disorder among patients with anorexia nervosa and bulimia nervosa. *American Journal of Psychiatry, 154*(1), 72–75.

Thompson, P. M., Gillin, J. C., Golshan, S., & Irwin, M. (1995). Polygraphic sleep measures differentiate alcoholics and stimulant abusers during short-term abstinence. *Biological Psychiatry, 38,* 831–836.

Thorpe, S. J., & Salkovskis, P. M. (1995). Phobia beliefs: Do cognitive factors play a role in specific phobias? *Behavior Research and Therapy, 33*(7), 805–816.

Tiggeman, M., & Wilson-Barrett, E. (1998). Children's figure ratings: Relationship to self-esteem and negative stereotyping. *International Journal of Eating Disorders, 23,* 83–88.

Tiihonen, J., Kuikka, J., Vinamaki, H., & Lehtonen, J. (1995). Altered cerebral blood flow during hysterical paresthesia. *Biological Psychiatry, 37*(2), 134–135.

Tomasson, K., Kent, D., & Coryell, W. (1991). Somatization and conversion disorders: Comorbidity and demographics at presentation. *Acta Psychiatrica Scandinavica, 84*(3), 288–293.

Treasure, J., Todd, G., & Szmukler, G. (1995). The inpatient treatment of anorexia nervosa. In G. Szmukler, C. Dare, & J. Treasure (Eds.), *Handbook of eating disorders: Theory, treatment and research.* Chichester, England: Wiley.

Trestman, R. L., Horvath, T., Kalus, O., & Peterson, A. E. (1996). Event-related potentials in schizotypal personality disorder. *Journal of Neuropsychiatry and Clinical Neurosciences, 8,* 33–40.

True, W., Rice, L., & Eisen, S. A. (1993). A twin study of genetic and environmental contributions to the liability for posttraumatic stress symptoms. *Archives of General Psychiatry, 50,* 257–264.

Tsai, L. Y. (1998). Autistic disorder. In M. Wiener (Ed.), *Textbook of child and adolescent psychiatry* (pp. 215–249). Washington, DC: American Psychiatric Press.

Ungerer, J., & Sigman, M. (1987). Symbolic play and language comprehension in autistic children. *Journal of the American Academy of Child Psychiatry, 20,* 318–337.

Uniform Crime Reports. (1989). Federal Bureau of Investigation, U. S. Department of Justice. Washington, DC: U. S. Government Printing Office.

U.S. Department of Justice, Bureau of Justice Statistics. (1995). *Violence against women: Estimates from the Redesigned National Crime Victimization Survey.* Annapolis Junction, MD: Bureau of Justice Statistics Clearinghouse.

Valone, K., Goldstein, M. J., & Norton, J. P. (1984). Parental expressed emotion and psychophysiological reactivity in an adolescent sample at risk for schizophrenia spectrum disorder. *Journal of Abnormal Psychology, 93,* 448–457.

Vandereycken, W. (1994). Parental rearing behaviour and eating disorders. In C. Perris, W. A. Arrindell, & M. Eisemann (Eds.), *Parenting and psychopathology* (pp. 55–73). Chichester, England: Wiley.

Verhulst, F. C., & Koot, H. M. (1992). *Child psychiatric epidemiology.* Newbury Park, CA: Sage.

Verhulst, F. C., & van der Ende, J. (1997). Factors associated with mental health service use in the community. *Journal of the American Academy of Child and Adolescent Psychiatry, 36,* 901–909.

Vitousek, K., & Manke, E. (1994). Personality variables and disorders in anorexia nervosa and bulimia nervosa. *Journal of Abnormal Psychology, 103*(1), 137–147.

Vogel, J. M., & Vernberg, E. M. (1993). Children's psychological responses to disasters. *Journal of Clinical Child Psychology, 22,* 464–484.

Volkmar, F. R., Becker, D. F., King, R. A., & McGuashan, T. H. (1995). Psychotic processes. In D. Cicchetti & D. J. Cohen (Eds.), *Developmental psychopathology* (pp. 117–136). New York: Wiley.

Volkmar, F. R., Kim, A., & Cohen, D. J. (1997). Diagnosis and classification of autism and related conditions: Consensus and issues. In D. J. Cohen & F. R. Volkmar (Eds.), *Handbook of autism and pervasive developmental disorders* (pp. 47–64). New York: Wiley.

Volkmar, F. R., & Nelson, D. S. (1990). Seizure disorders in autism. *Journal of the American Academy of Child and Adolescent Psychiatry, 29,* 127–129.

Vollmer, T. R., Marcus, B. A., & Ringdahl, J. E. (1995). Noncontingent escape as treatment for self-injurious behavior maintained by negative reinforcement. *Journal of Applied Behavior Analysis, 28,* 15–26.

Von Burg, M., & Hibbard, R. (1995). Munchausen syndrome by proxy: A different kind of child abuse. *Indiana Medicine, 88*(5), 378–382.

Walker, C. E., Kenning, M., & Faust-Companile, J. (1989). Enuresis and encopresis. In E. J. Mash & R. A. Barkley (Eds.), *Treatment of childhood behavior disorders* (pp. 181–203). New York: Guilford Press.

Walker, H. M. (1995). *The acting-out child: Coping with classroom disruption* (2nd ed.). Longmont, CO: Sopris West.

Warwick, H. M. C. (1995). Assessment of hypochondriasis. *Behavior Research and Therapy, 33*(7), 845–853.

Watson, D., Clark, I. A., & Harkness, A. R. (1994). Structures of personality and their relevance to psychopathology. *Journal of Abnormal Psychology, 103*(1), 18–31.

Watson, J. B., & Rayner, R. (1920). Conditioned emotional reactions. *Journal of Experimental Psychology, 3,* 1–14.

Weinstein, A. (1983). The mythical readmissions explosion. *American Journal of Psychiatry, 140*(3), 332–335.

Weissman, M. M., Bland, R. C., Canino, G. J., & Faravelli, C. (1997). The cross-national epidemiology of panic disorder. *Archives of General Psychiatry, 54,* 305–309.

Weist, M. D. (1997). Expanded school mental health services: A national movement in progress. In T. H. Ollendick & R. J. Prinz (Eds.), *Advances in clinical child psychology* (Vol. 19, pp. 304–321). New York: Plenum Press.

Wenar, C. (1990). *Developmental psychopathology: From infancy through adolescence* (2nd ed.). New York: McGraw-Hill.

Wender, P. H., Kety, S. S., Rosenthal, D., Schulsinger, F., Ortmann, J., & Lunde, I. (1986). Psychiatric disorders in the biological and adoptive families of adopted individuals with affective disorders. *Archives of General Psychiatry, 43,* 923–929.

Werry, J. S. (1992). Child and adolescent (early onset) schizophrenia: A review in light of DSM-III-R. *Journal of Autism and Developmental Disorders, 22,* 601–624.

West, S. G., Sandler, I., Pillow, D. R., Baca, L., & Gersten, J. C. (1991). The use of structural equation modeling in generative research: Toward the design of a preventative intervention for bereaved children. *American Journal of Community Psychology, 19,* 459–480.

Weston, S. C., & Siever, L. J. (1993, Spring). Biological correlates of personality disorders. *Journal of Personality Disorders* (Suppl.), 129–148.

Whalen, C. K., & Henker, B. (1991). Social impact of stimulant treatment for hyperactive children. *Journal of Learning Disabilities, 24,* 231–241.

Whalen, C. K., & Henker, B. (1998). Attention-deficit and hyperactivity disorders. In T. H. Ollendick & M. Hersen (Eds.), *Handbook of child psychopathology* (pp. 231–241). New York: Plenum Press.

Whelen, J. P., & Houts, A. C. (1990). Effects of a waking schedule on primary enuretic children treated with full-spectrum home training. *Health Psychology, 9,* 164–176.

Whitehead, W. E., Cromwell, M. D., Heller, B. R., & Robinson, J. C. (1994). Modeling and reinforcement of the sick role during childhood predicts adult illness behavior. *Psychosomatic Medicine, 56,* 541–550.

Wicks-Nelson, R., & Israel, A. C. (2000). *Behavior disorders of childhood* (4th ed.). Upper Saddle River, NJ: Prentice Hall.

Wiederman, M., & Pryor, T. (1996). Substance abuse and impulsive behaviors among adolescents with eating disorders. *Addictive Behavior, 21*(2), 269–272.

Wikler, A., Dixon, J., and Parker, J. (1970). Brain function in problem children and controls. *American Journal of Psychiatry, 127*(5), 94–105.

Wilson, C. C., & Haynes, S. N. (1985). Sleep disorders. In P. H. Bornstein & A. E. Kazdin (Eds.), *Handbook of clinical behavior therapy with children* (pp. 290–302). Homewood, IL: Dorsey Press.

Wing, J., & Bebbington, P. (1985). Epidemiology of depression. In E. E. Beckharn & W. R. Leber (Eds.), *Handbook of depression: Treatment, assessment, and research* (pp. 765–794). Homewood, IL: Dorsey Press.

Wolraich, M., Wilson, D. B., & White, J. W. (1995). The effect of sugar on behavior or cognition in children. *Journal of the American Medical Association, 274*, 1617–1621.

Woo, S. M., Goldstein, M. J., & Nuechterlein, K. H. (1997). Relatives' expressed emotion and non-verbal signs of subclinical psychopathology in schizophrenic patients. *British Journal of Psychiatry, 170*, 58–61.

Yazici, O., Aricioglu, F., Gurvi, G., Ucok, A., Tastaaban, Y., Canberk, O., Orguroglu, M., Durat, T., & Sahin, D. (1993). Noradrenergic and serotoninergic depression? *Journal of Affective Disorders, 27*, 123–129.

Yehuda, R., Kahana, B., Binder-Brynes, K., & Southwick, S. M. (1995). Low urinary cortisol excretion in Holocaust survivors with posttraumatic stress disorder. *American Journal of Psychiatry, 152*(7), 982–986.

Zajecka, J. (1997). Importance of establishing the diagnosis of persistent anxiety. *Journal of Clinical Psychiatry, 58*(Suppl. 3), 9–13.

Zeitlin, H. (1986). *The natural history of psychiatric disorder in childhood.* New York: Oxford University Press.

Zuckerman, M. (1996). Sensation seeking. In G. C. Costello (Ed.), *Personality characteristics of the personality disordered* (pp. 223–240). New York: Wiley.

CHAPTER

IDENTIFICATION PROCEDURES
AND AN OVERVIEW OF SERVICES

In the 1990s, issues pertaining to the identification of students with emotional and behavioral disorders (EBDs) became increasingly complex. On one hand, it became more apparent that children and adolescents experience a wide variety of emotional disorders, including depression, schizophrenia, anxiety disorders, personality disorders, and so forth. In the past, many of these types of problems, particularly those that did not result in acting-out behavior, were ignored in school settings, where efforts at diagnosis and intervention focused primarily on disruptive individuals with conduct disorder (CD). As increased awareness of the number and nature of the disorders affecting children and youth made it clear that more effective services for these students were necessary, it became incumbent upon schools to use strategies and procedures that resulted in the immediate identification of individuals who were badly in need of therapeutic services.

On the other hand, with the advent of the regular education initiative, there was an increased emphasis on providing services for problematic students within general education programs. This strategy was designed to minimize the extent to which a student's educational program varied from the norm and to reduce the stigma associated with disability labeling required for special education services. As a result, newly adopted school procedures included many more prediagnostic steps with students, a strategy that retarded the formal identification procedures that precede therapeutic interventions for emotional disorders. Although any policy that delays the identification of students with

EBDs is cause for concern, because these children have been historically under-identified (Ormsbee, Simpson, & Zionts, 1996), these preidentification procedures are viewed as necessary to protect children with relatively mild problems that may be easily rectified by relatively minor adjustments to the children's environment.

Educators caught between these two credible but possibly antagonistic goals have benefited from adapting multistage identification procedures that begin at the earliest stage with strategies that are least likely to mark the student as atypical or deviant and that become progressively more focused on uncovering a specific individual's pathological emotional states in subsequent stages. Several models for school identification procedures have been developed (see Morgan & Jenson, 1988; Walker, Severson, & Haring, 1985). One of the most comprehensive of these is the Iowa Assessment Model (Wood, Smith, & Grimes, 1985), which presents a five-stage plan for identifying and educating individuals with EBDs:

1. Classroom or home adjustments
2. Prereferral activities
3. Referral for special education services—eligibility
4. Referral for special education services—placement
5. Implementation of the special education plan

These steps, which illustrate the necessity of implementing problem-solving strategies in the classroom before referral for special education services, are integrated in a model depicting the teacher's role in the identification process, which is discussed later in this chapter.

The implementation of a comprehensive model for identifying students with EBDs illustrates the fact that a variety of personnel are involved in the process. Opinions about a child's feelings, attitudes, and behaviors may be gathered from the child, peers, parents, teachers, counselors, psychologists, and psychiatrists. A variety of assessment tools and devices exist to aid professionals in formulating valid opinions regarding the type and severity of children's emotional and behavioral problems. These include instruments and strategies frequently used by teachers, such as behavior rating scales; measures of various affective states such as self-concept, anxiety, and depression; techniques for classroom observation, including anecdotal records, sociometric devices, and critical incident reports; and parental interviewing techniques. Also available are a variety of assessment devices used by psychologists and other clinical personnel. These include individualized tests of affective dimensions such as personality traits. Unlike the case with the assessment devices and techniques developed for use by teachers, mental health professionals often administer projective or semiprojective tests that require a level of clinical interpretation. Finally, a variety of professionals, including social workers, psychologists, and psychiatrists, use clinical interviews to gather information that casts light on students' emotional states. These assessment devices are discussed in the following section.

Behavior Assessment Devices and Techniques

A large and varied number of devices and techniques designed to identify students who may have some type of emotional disorder are available to teachers. These range from lists of relatively global characteristics of pathological behavior that provide guidelines for the teacher's subjective judgment of a student's behavior to elaborate norm-referenced rating scales that assess types of behavior that, when displayed often or in abundance, indicate an EBD.

Global Characteristics of Pathological Behavior

Many years ago, Gropper, Kress, Hughes, and Pekich (1968) found that teachers identified 13 principal areas as sources of potential problems. The problem areas remain valid today:

1. Attention to classroom activities: inattention, daydreaming, withdrawal

2. Physical activity: restlessness, hyperactivity, noisemaking

3. Reaction to tension: emotional upsets

4. Appropriateness of behavior: telling tales

5. Meeting work requirements: self-criticism, giving up, not working

6. Interest in work: playing, doodling, drawing

7. Getting along with others: name-calling, fighting, passivity

8. Consideration for group needs: impatient with others, interrupting others, talking out loud

9. Response to teacher requirements or instructions: arguments, rudeness, disobedience

10. Degree of independence: seeking praise, attention, support, currying favor

11. Regard for school rules and conventions: swearing, smoking

12. Regard for general rules: truancy, tardiness, destroying property

13. Integrity: cheating, stealing, tattling

Similar broad guidelines for teacher judgment, listed in Table 4.1, have been developed. The nine criteria included are designed to help teachers evaluate children's behavior with regard to possible emotional disorders. Familiarity with these criteria focus the teacher's attention beyond specific behaviors to the events that evoke them and to students' typical ways of functioning in the environment. The nine criteria help determine the degree of an emotional disturbance as follows:

1. *Precipitating events.* This criterion refers to the extent to which the child's behavior, however undesirable it may appear to be, is directly related to precipitating environmental conditions. The less obvious the relationship be-

TABLE 4.1
Criteria for Determining the Degree of Disturbance

| Criteria | Degree of Disturbance | | |
	Mild	Moderate	Severe
Precipitating events	Highly stressful	Moderately stressful	Not stressful
Destructiveness	Not destructive	Occasionally destructive	Usually destructive
Maturational appropriateness	Behavior typical for age	Some behavior untypical for age	Behavior too young or too old
Personal functionaing	Cares for own needs	Usually cares for own needs	Unable to care for own needs
Social functioning	Usually able to relate to others	Usually unable to relate to others	Not able to relate to others
Reality index	Usually sees events as they are	Occasionally sees events as they are	Little contact with reality
Insight index	Aware of behavior	Usually aware of behavior	Usually not aware of behavior
Conscious control	Usually can control behavior	Occasionally can control behavior	Little control over behavior
Social responsiveness	Usually acts appropriately	Occasionally acts appropriately	Rarely acts appropriately

tween the precipitating event and the child's behavior appears, the more serious the implications for emotional disorder. For example, when teased by classmates, a child may typically respond by fighting. Another child who fights frequently may attack classmates without apparent motivation. Although the first child's response may not be desirable in a classroom and may cause difficulties among peers, it is at least a plausible reaction to causal factors, in this case the ridicule. The second situation involving unprovoked assault is not appropriate to the environmental circumstances. The child's behavior is irrational—he may not know why he attacks others. Such behavior is far more difficult to alter.

2. *Destructiveness.* This component reflects the extent to which the child's behavior is harmful to others or to herself. High levels of destructiveness often indicate severe disorders. Children who engage in sadistic activities, such as killing animals or deliberately injuring other children, have serious emotional problems. Children who threaten others without actually engaging in destructive behaviors usually are less disturbed.

Another equally predictive type of destructiveness involves self-injury. Children with serious problems frequently attempt to hurt themselves. They might be unusually accident prone, or they might engage overtly in masochistic acts by slashing themselves with knives, burning themselves with matches, raking their fingernails over their flesh until they have large sores, tearing out their hair, and so forth. Less severely disturbed children often complain about physical suffering or threaten to hurt themselves.

3. *Maturational Appropriateness.* This gauge indicates the extent to which a child's behaviors are generally considered appropriate for his age group. Children with serious problems frequently show highly regressed behaviors characteristic of younger children. For example, the language of a 5-year-old child who has a psychosis may regress to a 1-year-old level. Other infantile behaviors, such as inability to dress without assistance, also may occur.

On the other end of the scale, children with emotional disorders may display behaviors that appear "too old" for them. For example, an 11-year-old boy might dress and act as though he were 10 years older. The greater the age gap between the child's real and behavioral age, and the more numerous the behaviors that reflect this over- or undermaturity, the more serious the problem.

4. *Personal Functioning.* This criterion refers to the child's capacity to take care of personal needs, including cleaning, dressing, eating properly, finding her way from one place to another, and so forth. A child who is cognitively intact, yet unaware or unconcerned about the routines of daily living, probably has a serious disorder.

5. *Social Functioning.* There are two aspects to this component: the extent to which the child's behaviors prevent the making of friends and the quality of

the behaviors displayed in a group. Usually, the more severe an individual's emotional problems, the more isolated from peers the child will be. The child either ignores peers or rejects them. On occasion, severely disturbed children may relate satisfactorily to a few select peers but demonstrate poor social functioning by a total inability to contribute to a large-group activity. They either withdraw from participation or engage in disruptive behaviors.

6. *Reality Index*. This measure refers to the extent that a child's view of the events that affect his life correspond with objective reality. The greater the gap between an individual's perception of reality and reality as it is perceived by a consensus of others, the greater the severity of the emotional problem. For example, a child with a severe disorder who has a low reality index might feel persecuted and be suspicious of all other persons, including those who consistently treat him with kindness. A person with a less serious problem is less oblivious to the specific events in each environmental situation; thus, he may tend to respond to people with suspicion but learn to trust those who treat him with kindness.

7. *Insight Index*. This index pertains to the child's level of understanding about the behavior that causes problems. A high level of insight suggests that the child is capable of recognizing which behaviors cause problems. Insight, as it pertains to children, does not imply that the child understands the motivation for behavior or that she can change the behavior, but it is regarded by many as a first step toward behavioral change. Children with severe disorders often have little understanding of their behaviors.

8. *Conscious Control*. This component reflects the extent to which the child can control emotions and avoid maladaptive behaviors. Children with mild emotional disorders often exert conscious efforts to stop maladaptive behaviors; for example, a child who fights recognizes that it is a problem and tries to control his temper. Children with more severe problems often act as if they were driven by forces they cannot recognize or control.

9. *Social Responsiveness*. This criterion pertains to the extent to which the child values others. One type of individual lacking social responsiveness is highly egocentric and unwilling to delay the gratification of his own impulses for any reason. Behavior may be indicative either of indifference to others or of contempt for their rights. Because bonds based on love and trust are not formed, there is no external social force that can influence behavior. Another type of individual lacking social responsiveness may structure his environment to avoid dealing with others, as when children live in fantasy worlds. Persons who have less serious disorders may have difficulties with social responsiveness, but they retain their desire for mutually reinforcing interactions with others.

Behavior Rating Scales

Although global criteria for identifying individuals with emotional disorders provide useful frames of reference for teachers, their use requires relatively high levels of clinical judgment and is highly dependent on each teacher's personal level of experience. They do not provide an objective means of differentiating between typical and deviant behaviors, that is, quantitative scores that indicate when behaviors are indicative of a problem and the extent (mild, moderate, or severe) of the problem. Objective information is obtained through the use of standardized, norm-referenced behavior rating scales. These scales are lists of specific behaviors, mostly negative or maladaptive (e.g., "cries easily"), that have been identified as characteristic of emotional problems. Teachers, peers, parents, other knowledgeable persons, or the child may complete a behavioral rating scale by indicating either the absence or presence of each behavior (a true-false format) or the extent or frequency of the behavior (a multipoint Likert scale). The scores are compared to those of children in the normative sample, illustrating the extent of deviation from the norm. Table 4.2 lists and describes many of the most popular behavior rating scales.

Many of the behavior rating scales presented in Table 4.2 have been reviewed in *The Thirteenth Mental Measurements Yearbook* (Impara & Plake, 1998) and in *The Consumer's Guide to Tests in Print* (Hammill, Brown, & Bryant, 1992). The best instruments are those with respectable levels of reliability and validity. For the most part, instruments reporting high reliability and validity coefficients are written in clear, unpretentious language; are simple to use; have been standardized on large, representative groups of students across the nation; and have been validated on samples of children previously identified as having an emotional disorder.

Even when a sound instrument is chosen, however, the user must be aware of the importance of rater bias (Epanchin & Rennells, 1989). Research shows that different raters tend to rate the same individual differently. For example, a child's rating may be quite different from his parent's or his teacher's rating. The most accurate indication of a problem is obtained by ratings from multiple sources. This is best accomplished by using an instrument that provides multiple rating scales standardized on the same sample of subjects, such as the *Behavior Rating Profile* (Brown & Hammill, 1990), which includes teacher, parent, and child scales. However, when agreement among raters does not occur, behavior rating scales can be used in combination with other types of information, such as interview results and anecdotal records, to indicate whether a child requires referral for clinical evaluation. Scales of this type never diagnose the existence of a problem; diagnosis is done by a qualified clinician who interprets evidence from a variety of sources, including behavior rating scales.

TABLE 4.2
Behavior Rating Scales

Name	Purpose	Description
Attention-Deficit/ Hyperactivity Disorder Test (Gilliam, 1995a)	To identify ADHD in persons ages 3–23	Consists of 36 items measuring three ADHD characteristics: hyperactivity, impulsivity, and inattention
Behavior Dimensions Rating Scale (Bullock & Wilson, 1989)	To screen for behavior problems in children ages 5–19	Consists of 43 items (bipolar descriptors that contribute to four scales: Aggressive/Acting Out, Socially Withdrawn, Irresponsible/Inattentive, and Fearful/Anxious)
Behavior Evaluation Scale (2nd ed.) (McCarney & Leigh, 1990)	To identify problem behavior in children in Grades K–12	Teacher rating scale that consists of 76 items that contribute to five scales (corresponding to P.L. 94-142 definition of emotional handicaps): Learning Problems, Interpersonal Difficulties, Inappropriate Behavior, Unhappiness/Depression, and Physical Symptoms /Fears
Behavior Rating Profile (2nd ed.) (Brown & Hammill, 1990)	To screen behavior of children in Grades 1–12; measures home, school, and peer attitudes	Teacher scale: 30 items, 4-point Likert scale; Parent scale: 30 items, 4-point Likert scale; Student scale: 60 items, true-false format; scales yield three subscale scores: school, peer, home (20 items per scale); also yields a sociogram score
Behavioral and Emotional Rating Scale (Epstein & Sharma, 1998)	To measure the personal strengths of children ages 5-0 through 18-11	Contains 52 items measuring five types of strengths: interpersonal, family involvement, intrapersonal, school functioning, and affective
Burks' Behavior Rating Scales (Burks, 1977)	To identify patterns of pathological behavior in primary and junior high school students	Has 110 items that yield 19 scales, such as Excessive Self-Blame, Poor Ego Strength, Excessive Suffering, and Poor Anger Control
Child Behavior Checklist (Achenbach, 1986, 1991)	For parents, teachers, and children to rate a wide range of problem behaviors	Uses an internalizing–externalizing format on teacher, parent, and child forms; also includes a form to record direct observation of behavior

(continues)

TABLE 4.2. *Continued*

Name	Purpose	Description
Comprehensive Behavior Rating Scale for Children (Neeper, Lahey, & Frick, 1990)	To identify learning and behavior problems in children ages 6–14	A 70-item teacher rating format (5-point), with specific scales, including Inattention/Disorganization, Reading Problems, Cognitive Deficits, Oppositional/Conduct Disorder, Motor Hyperactivity, Anxiety, Sluggish Tempo, Social Competence, and Daydreaming
Conners' Rating Scales (Conners, 1997)	To identify children (ages 3–17) with hyperkinetic behavior conduct problems and overindulgent, anxious–passive, asocial, and daydream-attendance problems	Parent and Teacher Forms: Long Parent Form, 93 items; Short Parent Form, 48 items; Long Teacher Form, 39 items; Short Teacher Form, 28 items
Devereux Elementary School Behavior Rating Scale (Spivak & Swift, 1967)	To identify behavioral difficulties in children in Grades K–6 that interfere with successful academic performance	Consists of 47 items that form 11 behavior factors, such as classroom disturbance; items rated on a 7-point scale
The Early Screening Project (Walker, Severson, & Feil, 1994)	To screen preschool children (ages 3–5) for behavior disorders	A downward extension of *Systematic Screening for Behavior Disorders*
Eyberg Child Behavior Inventory (Eyberg, 1980)	For parents to rate problem behaviors in children ages 2–16	Consists of 36 items that yield two scores: Intensity (a cumulative score of problem behaviors on a 7-point scale) and Problems (total number of problem behaviors)
Gilliam Autism Rating Scale (Gilliam, 1995b)	To identify and diagnose autism in persons ages 3–22	Consists of three core subtests (Stereotyped Behaviors, Communication, and Social Interaction) and one optional subtest (Developmental Disturbances)
Hahnemann High School Behavior Rating Scale (Spivak & Swift, 1977)	For teachers to rate behaviors that affect achievement of junior and senior high students	Consists of 45 items that yield 13 behavior factors, all related to achievement
Kohn Problem Checklist (Kohn, 1986)	To assess presence or absence of behavior problems in preschool children	Consists of 49 items that measure dimensions of angry-defiant and apathetic-withdrawn behaviors

(continues)

TABLE 4.2. *Continued*

Name	Purpose	Description
Louisville Behavior Checklist (Miller, 1981)	For parents to rate their children	Has a primary (ages 4–7) and intermediate (ages 7–13) form, each consisting of 164 items that yield three broad and eight specific scales, including a total disability and a prosocial scale, six clinical screening scales, and a scale measuring the tolerance of the raters
Portland Problem Behavior Checklist–Revised (Waksman, 1990)	To rate problem behavior in students in Grades K–12	A teacher rating scale that has female and male forms
Revised Behavior Problem Checklist (Quay & Peterson, 1984)	To rate children's behavior in different situations	Consists of 89 items that contribute to six scales: Conduct Disorders, Socialized Aggression, Attention Problems/Immaturity, Anxiety/Withdrawal, Psychotic Behavior, and Motor Tension Excess
Scale for Assessing Emotional Disturbance (Epstein & Cullinan, 1998)	To identify children and adolescents (ages 5–18) who qualify for the federal special education category Emotional Disturbance	Consists of 52 items measuring seven areas of behavior: inability to learn, relationship problems, inappropriate behavior, unhappiness or depression, physical symptoms or fears, social maladjustment, and overall competence
Social–Emotional Dimension Scale (Hutton & Roberts, 1986)	To screen students ages 5–18 who are at risk for conduct disorders, behavior problems, or emotional disturbance	A 32-item teacher rating scale that yields six subscores: Fear Reaction, Depression Reaction, Avoidance of Peer Interaction, Avoidance of Teacher Interaction, Aggression, and Inappropriate Behavior; includes a Behavior Observation Web to plot student performance graphically
Social Skills Rating System (Gresham & Elliott, 1990)	To screen for social and behavioral problems in children from preschool through Grade 12	Includes student, teacher, and parent forms, each measuring Social Skills (including Cooperation, Assertion, Responsibility, Empathy, and Self-Control), Problem Behaviors (including Externalizing Problems, Internalizing Problems, and Hyperactivity), and Academic Competence

(continues)

TABLE 4.2. *Continued*

Name	Purpose	Description
Systematic Screening for Behavior Disorders (Walker & Severson, 1990)	To help teachers screen elementary-level students for behavior disorders	Involves a three-step identification process: (1) teacher rank-orders students with internalized and externalized problems; (2) teacher completes two checklists for the three highest ranked students on each list; (3) teacher observes those students from Step 2 whose scores exceed cutoffs
Test of Early Socio-Emotional Development (Hresko & Brown, 1984)	To evaluate behavior of children ages 3-0 to 7-11	A downward extension of the *Behavior Rating Profile*; a 30-item student rating scale, a 34-item parent rating scale, and a 36-item teacher rating scale; accompanied by a sociogram
Walker-McConnell Scale of Social Competence and School Adjustment (Walker & McConnell, 1988)	For teachers to rate peer relations and behavior in the classroom	A 43-item teacher rating scale of social skills for students in Grades K–6; subscales measure teacher-preferred social behavior, peer-preferred social behavior, and school adjustment on a 5-point Likert format
Walker Problem Behavior Identification Checklist (Walker, 1983)	To screen for problem behaviors	Consists of 50 items that contribute to total score, with five subscales: acting out, withdrawal, distractibility, disturbed peer relations, and immaturity

Assessment of Self-Concept, Depression, Anxiety, and Other Personality Variables

Other assessment devices tend to focus on a student's feelings and emotions (e.g., "I feel sad often"), instead of or in combination with behavior. These instruments measure characteristics such as self-concept, depression, anxiety, and locus of control. Many of these instruments are self-report scales; however, some also involve forms that are completed by other persons who are well acquainted with the student, such as parents or teachers. A list and brief description of these instruments are presented in Table 4.3.

As is true of the behavior rating scales, these affective states assessment devices vary in their usefulness depending on their reliability and validity, and many have been reviewed in *The Thirteenth Mental Measurement Yearbook* (Impara & Plake, 1998) and in *The Consumer's Guide to Tests in Print* (Hammill et al., 1992). These in-struments differ from the behavior rating scales in that the most significant informant often is the child. Because these devices attempt to assess the child's internal state, that is, attitudes and feelings, as well as overt behaviors, they are more difficult to devise and use than behavioral rating scales. Self-report measures have been criticized because children can convey impressions that are not representative of their true feelings by responding defensively. For example, children may choose to deliberately distort information by lying, as when children who habitually steal for others describe themselves as honest. Other children report their sincere convictions about themselves, but those convictions are erroneous, as when a braggart sees herself as modest and self-effacing. In addition, self-perceptions vary with situational pressures. For example, an individual may depict himself as depressed, withdrawn, and unhappy on a self-rating scale but project a significantly different profile when reassessed at a later time. Finally, self-evaluation may be so threatening to an individual that she unconsciously resorts to denial, as when a person with a consistent record of poor school achievement describes herself as a high achiever despite the fact that she is neither unaware of her academic problems nor deliberately lying. Despite the shortcomings of self-reports, however, research has shown that many children who are not viewed as having problems by their teachers rate themselves as high in the negative feelings associated with depression and anxiety (Newcomer, Barenbaum, & Pearson, 1995). It would appear to be totally inappropriate to ignore their attitudes about themselves.

Notably, more than one third of the instruments presented in Table 4.3 measure some aspect of depression. The increased emphasis on identifying depression in children is a reflection of the concern among many professionals that emotional problems characterized by the internalization of symptoms—that is, feelings of intense worry, fear, anxiety, sadness, and so forth—are often overlooked in school settings, where emotional disorders may be equated with external demonstrations of disruptive behavior. Consideration of the related points—that depression may lead to suicide, and that suicides are increasing among children and adolescents—makes it clear that identification procedures must include instruments that measure internal feelings, such as depression.

TABLE 4.3

Assessment of Affective States

Name	Purpose	Description
Child Depression Scale (Reynolds, 1989)	To measure symptoms of depression in children ages 8–13	Self-report scale that uses a 4-point (*almost never* to *all the time*) response format for 29 items. Item 30 uses five faces looking sad to happy to get a global estimate of general well-being
Children's Depression Inventory (2nd ed.) (Kovacs, 1992)	To measure overt symptoms such as sadness and suicidal ideation	Downward extension of the Beck Depression Inventory (Beck, Ward, Mendelson, Mack, & Erbaugh, 1961). CDI is a self-report scale that consists of 27 items and uses a three-alternative forced-choice format. Short Form is available, which includes 13 items scored on a 4-point scale. Parent Form also available
Children's Depression Scale (Lang & Tisher, 1978)	To measure depression in 9- to 16-year-olds	A 66-item (48 depression and 18 positive) self-report child scale, with a version allowing a parent to describe depressive symptoms of child. Each item is presented on a card sorted by child into five categories: "very wrong" to "very right"
Children's Manifest Anxiety Scale–Revised (Reynolds & Richmond, 1985)	To measure anxiety in children in Grades K–12	A self-report scale consisting of 28 statements and using a yes–no format; has a lie scale and a parent scale
Coopersmith Self-Esteem Inventory (Coopersmith, 1967)	To measure children's (ages 9 and above) feelings of self-worth	Consists of 58 items that consitiute five subscales
Culture-Free Self-Esteem Inventories (2nd ed.) (Battle, 1992)	To measure self-esteem for children in five areas (general, peer, school, parents, and lie scale) and for adults in four areas (general, social, personal, and lie scale)	Three different age-appropriate self-report inventories. Child Form A—60 items; Child Form B—80 items; and Adult Form AD—40 items. Yes–no response format

(continues)

TABLE 4.3. *Continued*

Name	Purpose	Description
Depression and Anxiety in Youth Scale (Newcomer, Barenbaum, & Bryant, 1992)	To measure two clinical dimensions—depression and anxiety—on each of three scales: child, parent, and teacher	Has a 40-item child scale, 45-item parent scale, and 30-item teacher scale. Parent and teacher scales use a true–false format. Child scale uses a 4-point Likert scale
Friendship Questionnaire (Bierman & McCauley, 1987)	To assess children's perceptions of their relationships with peers	Contains 8 open-ended questions about friends and a 32-item self-rating scale (5 point) assessing interactions with peers
Hopelessness Scale (How I Think About the Future) (Kazdin, French, Unis, Esveldt-Dawson, & Sherick, 1983)	To screen for hopelessness, depression, and suicidal intent in children ages 8–13	Consists of 17 items measuring negative attitudes about life. A self-report scale with a true–false format
Index of Personality Characteristics (Brown & Coleman, 1988)	To measure personality characteristics of students ages 8–17	A 75-item self-report instrument that contains eight scales: Academic, Nonacademic, Perception of Self, Perception of Others, Acting On, Acting Out, Internal Locus of Control, and External Locus of Control
Internalizing Symptoms Scale for Children (Merrell & Walters, 1998)	To screen for depression, anxiety, somatic problems, and social withdrawal in children ages 8–13	An individually administered scale used by psychologists, counselors, or teachers to identify potentially serious internalizing disorders
Life Orientation Inventory (Kowalchuk & King, 1988)	To identify potentially suicidal people ages 13 and above	Contains 113 statements about life; half are positive and half are negative. A screening form contains 30 items
Multidimensional Measure of Children's Perceptions of Control (Why Things Happen) (Connell, 1980)	To measure children's (ages 8–14) perceptions of their locus of control	Has two parallel self-report forms, each with 48 items. Uses a 4-point response format to measure four factors: internal control, cognitive, outcomes, and personal reference. Also measures expectations for success or failure
Multidimensional Self-Concept Scale (Bracken, 1992)	To measure global self-concept and six context-dependant self-concept domains: Social, Competence, Affect, Academic, Family, and Physical; for children and adolescents	Consists of six 25-item self-report scales; Likert format

(continues)

TABLE 4.3. *Continued*

Name	Purpose	Description
North American Depression Inventories for Children and Adults (Battle, 1988)	To screen for depression in children ages 6 and above and in adults	Two self-rating scales: a 50-item child form and a 50-item adult form. Both use a yes–no response format
Norwicki-Strickland Locus of Control Scale for Children (Norwicki & Strickland, 1973)	To measure children's (ages 3–12) locus of control	Consists of 40 items that yield one general locus of control score. Uses yes–no response format. Several age-appropriate forms are available
Peer Nomination Inventory for Children (Wirt, Lachar, Kinedinst & Seat, 1977a)	To nominate classmates for depression	Children respond to several specific questions, such as "Who plays alone?" "Who doesn't have much fun?" A child's score is the sum of the nominations received
Personality Inventory for Children (Wirt, Lachar, Kinedinst, & Seat, 1977b)	To measure a multitude (16 scales) of personality traits, including depression and anxiety in children ages 3–16	A 600-item inventory with a true–false format that is completed by parents
Children's Self-Concept Scale (Piers & Harris, 1984)	To measure children's (ages 3–12) attitudes about themselves	Has 80 items that yield a global measure of self-concept and six subscale scores: Behavior, Intellectual and School Status, Physical Appearance and Attributes, Anxiety, Popularity, and Happiness and Satisfaction
Reynolds' Adolescent Depression Scale (Reynolds, 1987)	To measure depression in adolescents	Self-report scale consists of 30 short statements. Responses use a "How often?" format (*almost never, hardly ever, sometimes, most of the time*)
Self-Esteem Index (Brown & Alexander, 1991)	To measure self-esteem of children ages 7–18 as it pertains to academic competence, family acceptance, peer popularity, and personal security	A self-report, 75-item instrument with a 4-point response format. Yields a global Self-Esteem Quotient and four subscale scores
Self-Perception Profile for Children (Harter, 1985)	To measure children's (preschool through adolescence) perceptions about themselves	Consists of 36 items that yield scores on four subscales: Scholastic Competence, Physical Appearance, Behavioral Conduct, and Global Self-Worth. Several age-appropriate versions are available

(*continues*)

TABLE 4.3. *Continued*

Name	Purpose	Description
State-Trait Anxiety Inventory for Children (How I Feel Questionnaire) (Spielberger, Edwards, Lushene, Montuori, & Platzek, 1970)	To measure two types of anxiety: state (current anxiety) and trait (general anxiety) in elementary school children	Two self-report or statement forms measuring trait anxiety and state anxiety; 3-point scale
State-Trait Anxiety Inventory: Form Y (Spielberger, Gorsuch, Lushene, Vagg, & Jacobs, 1977)	To measure two types of anxiety in high school students; upward extension of the How I Feel Questionnaire	A 40-item self-rating scale measuring two types of anxiety; 4-point Likert scale
Stress Impact Scale (Hutton & Roberts, 1990)	To screen students ages 8–19 for stressful events and conditions	A 70-item self-report scale that measures stress occurrence, stress impact differential
Teacher Depression Rating (Lefkowitz & Tesiny, 1980)	To rate depression in children based on four areas of functioning: affective (anxiety and worry), cognitive (self-depreciation), motivational (decreased performance and withdrawal), and vegetative (fatigue, sleep problems)	One global rating
Temperament Assessment Battery (Martin, 1988)	To measure temperaments of children ages 3–7	A multiple-choice paper-and-pencil test using a 7-point rating system; three forms: Teacher (48 items), Parent (48 items) and Clincian (questionnaire); yields three factor scores: Emotionality, Persistence, and Sociability
Tennessee Self-Concept Scale (Fitts & Roid, 1988)	To measure self-concept and self-esteem in persons ages 12 and above	Consists of 100 items that yield a total self-concept score and seven self-esteem scores: Self-Satisfaction, Behavior, Physical Self, Moral-Ethical Self, Personal Self, Family Self, and Social Self

Direct Observation

Observation of students' behavior is the oldest and most obvious means of formulating opinions about them. Good teachers are trained observers; they know what is occurring in their classrooms, even when they appear to their students to be preoccupied with an activity. To document the accuracy of their observations, teachers have been encouraged to keep *anecdotal records* of student behavior. These regular notations of specific behaviors occurring in a particular context relieve the observer of the burden of inaccurate memory and reduce possible tendencies to make inappropriate generalizations or draw inaccurate conclusions about a student. Also, anecdotal records may disclose patterns of behavior over time, such as acting-out episodes on Monday, or problems attending toward the end of the school day. Anecdotal records are a useful supplement to the standardized behavioral rating scales and measures of affect discussed earlier because they provide immediate documentation of a child's specific problematic behavior. Anecdotal records are most useful when they document specific behavior.

Critical incident logs are another means of documenting specific behavior when it is observed. Critical incident logs are written descriptions of important and usually disruptive behaviors, such as fighting, that may not occur on a regular basis. In noting the event, the teacher also records the environmental conditions in which it occurs and attempts to identify the circumstances that trigger the behavior, as well as the consequences that result.

In an effort to increase the reliability of observational techniques, investigators have developed procedures that provide more structure. Observation rating forms have been created to help observers focus on specific behavior. These forms require that each behavior of interest be precisely defined, that specific symbols represent each defined behavior, and that these symbols be recorded on a relatively elaborate chart when each of the specified behaviors occurs (Ormsbee et al., 1996). Use of a prepared observation coding scale of this type is believed to provide a more reliable indication of student behavior than less structured observational strategies. However, investigators have pointed out that observers must be well trained in the use of these structured systems to increase their effectiveness and that excessive complexity of the device may, in fact, reduce accuracy, thereby reducing the reliability and validity of the observation (Hops, Davis, & Longoria, 1995). Also, Wicks-Nelson and Israel (2000) noted that the issue of reactivity (the extent to which awareness of being observed changes behavior) remains a critical problem affecting the accuracy of observational data, even when structured systems are employed. There is evidence that the use of teachers as observers reduces the reactivity effect because their presence in the classroom is not unusual. Further discussion of behavior sampling based on direct observation is provided in Chapter 5.

Sociometric Devices

Increasing emphasis on the ecological aspects of emotional disorders necessitates obtaining data that reflect various aspects of the child's social milieu. Accordingly, a variety of sociometric devices, measures of social or peer relationships, are available for use within the classroom. Among the useful techniques for a quick assessment of a classroom's social climate is the classic sociogram developed by Moreno (1953). Each class member is asked to choose two or three classmates with whom she would most like to share an experience, for example, going to the zoo. Negative affect also can be assessed by having the children choose the individuals with whom they would least like to spend time. The children's selections are plotted graphically, illustrating the popularity of each child and identifying the social isolates. A typical sociogram is represented in Figure 4.1. It shows that Tom and Betty are class stars and that Don is an isolate.

Data of this sort also can be depicted with great clarity on a sociometric matrix, depicted in Figure 4.2. The names of the children are listed horizontally and vertically. Two points are assigned if a child is the first selection of another child, and one point if he is selected second. The children receiving the highest number of points are the most socially influential. The teacher also can determine degrees of peer acceptance; for example, a child might be selected by a number of children, but never as a first choice.

Repeated administration of sociometric measures throughout the school year enables a teacher to assess the possible social growth of certain children as they become more integrated into the social milieu and to identify the possible onset of problems for children who previously were accepted by their peers. However, although these measures indicate peer acceptance, they do not reveal the type of social relationships established by an individual (e.g., conning or manipulating others, intimidating others, buying the favor of others). Also, these measures may encourage students to think negatively about their peers. Their usefulness to identify atypical students who may have an emotional disorder is highly related to the teacher's efforts to encourage typical learners to accept one another and work cooperatively within the classroom.

Parent Interviews

Parents are an important source of information about their children; therefore, teachers who are concerned about their students' emotional welfare are well advised to consult with parents. Although teachers are not expected to conduct clinical interviews, their involvement with the family as the child's teacher may mark them as the least threatening school authority with whom the parent

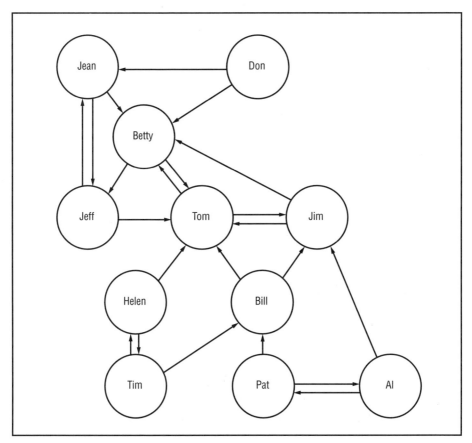

Figure 4.1. Example of Moreno's sociogram.

must deal. Also, it is perfectly appropriate for teachers to discuss a child's class-room problems with parents as part of the first stage of the multistage assess-ment procedure referred to earlier in this chapter.

In conducting a parent interview, teachers should keep in mind two im-portant points. First, information about the child must be conveyed with frank-ness but without negativism and blame. Evoking defensiveness or hostility in a parent is not conducive to a productive interview. Maintaining a highly pro-fessional level of concern for the child's welfare is particularly important in cases where the parent is initially hostile toward the school and possibly the teacher. Negative parents often are mollified in conferences where the empha-sis is on solving their children's problems rather than reporting their faults. Second, the teacher should have a list of issues that require discussion during the interview. Some of those issues are information about family relationships,

	Tom	Betty	Jean	Don	Jeff	Jim	Helen	Bill	Tim	Pat	Al
Tom		2				1					
Betty	1				2						
Jean	2				1						
Don		1	2								
Jeff	2		1								
Jim	2	1									
Helen	2								1		
Bill	1					2					
Tim							2	1			
Pat								2			1
Al						1				2	
Total	8	6	3	0	3	4	2	3	1	2	1

Figure 4.2. Sociometric Matrix.

stresses emanating from the home (financial, legal, medical, etc.), general modes of discipline practiced in the home, the child's behavior in settings other than school, parental willingness to pursue additional help for the child, and any other data that pertain to the particular difficulties being experienced by the child. To aid teachers in conducting parent interviews, Sodac, Nichols, and Gallagher (1985) developed a structured format that is presented as part of the *The Iowa Assessment Model in Behavioral Disorders* (Wood et al., 1985).

Clinical Assessment Devices and Strategies

Assessment devices used most frequently by nonteaching professionals who work with children with EBDs are projective and semiprojective tests. Projective tests are clinical instruments used to probe children's attitudes and feelings (i.e., reflections of conscious and unconscious personality characteristics). They have subjective formats involving ambiguous stimuli that can be interpreted in a variety of ways. Unlike the case with self-report scales, it is difficult for children to recognize the significance of responses, (i.e., whether they are indicative of pathology). Semiprojective devices provide more structured stimuli and, therefore, more clues to appropriate or socially acceptable responses. All projective devices are based on the theoretical premise that individuals project their inner thoughts and feelings onto the ambiguous stimuli, as when one person sees a smoking gun in a cloud formation that another individual views as a bunny rabbit.

Sentence Completion. One form of semiprojective test requires the child to complete a sentence stem, such as "My brother. . . ." or "My trouble is. . . ." Early versions of tests of this type were developed by Ronde (1957) and Rotter (1968). Although the results of this type of test are easier to interpret than the results of projective techniques, children have little difficulty giving socially acceptable responses or avoiding the disclosure of their true feelings.

Drawings. Semiprojective tests of this type include *Draw-A-Person* (Koppitz, 1968; Machover, 1949; Naglieri, McNeish, & Bardos, 1991), the *House-Tree-Person Projective Drawing Techniques* (Buck, 1992; Van Hutton, 1994), the *Draw-A-Family Test* (Deren, 1975), and the *Kinetic Family Drawings* (Burns, 1982). These devices are extremely nonthreatening to most children because children are accustomed to drawing pictures. Hypothetically, the figure drawn provides an index of the child's self-perceptions. Clinical interpretations are based on variables such as the sex of the first figure drawn, the size of the figures, the facial expressions, omission of parts, elaboration of parts, position of the figures, location of the figures on the paper, and so forth. Objective scoring systems have been developed for some of the picture-drawing tests, including those by Koppitz and Naglieri et al. Although assessment tools of this type increase a teacher's knowledge about students' feelings, for the most part they are administered and interpreted by psychologists, because their usefulness is highly related to the clinical experience of the examiner. Even under "ideal" conditions, the use of figure drawings to assess emotional states has been criticized on the basis on unreliability and invalidity. Their advocates argue that they are useful when they are accompanied by other measures of emotional stability.

Apperception Tests. The group of tests that includes the *Thematic Apperception Test* (Murray, 1943), *The Children's Apperception Test* (A. Bellak & Bellak, 1974; L. Bellak, 1993), the *Roberts Apperception Test for Children* (Roberts, 1982), the *Children's Apperceptive Story-Telling Test* (Schneider, 1989), and *The Blacky Pictures* (Blum, 1950) use ambiguous pictures, photographs, or drawings, to elicit stories. The pictures are designed to represent situations that may be problematic to a child, such as the loss of a parent or displacement by a sibling. The child is shown a series of pictures, one at a time, and instructed to make up a story that includes the events that led to the pictured scene, the events happening in the scene, and the outcome of the scene, including a description of what happens to the characters in the picture.

The most venerable of these devices is the *Thematic Apperception Test*, used with adults and children. This instrument consists of 30 pictures, some designed for males and others for females. The child is shown a series of 10 pictures that appear to probe areas of greatest interest to the examiner. Hypothetically, the child identifies with the central figure in the picture and creates a story that projects his feelings about the events. For example, one picture shows a boy staring at a violin. The child's story may describe the boy as depressed because he must practice. Presumably, the child has identified with the boy, and the events in the story represent the child's attitude toward tasks that require practice or hard work.

The *Children's Apperception Test* is a modification of the *Thematic Apperception Test* and uses 10 animal pictures as stimulus cards for children ages 3 to 10. Hypothetically, children identify readily with animals and have less difficulty generating stories when pictures of this type are used. *The Blacky Pictures* uses a rationale and format similar to *The Children's Apperception Test* but features a puppy named Blacky. Twelve cards with cartoon drawings depict Blacky and his dog family in a variety of situations.

The newest of these devices, the *Children's Apperceptive Story-Telling Test*, is designed for children ages 6 through 13. This instrument uses colored-picture stimuli reflective of contemporary family, peer, and school contexts and has stimulus pictures for males and females. In addition, this test differs from the others in that it has an objective scoring system for four major personality characteristics: adaptive, nonadaptive, immature, and uninvested.

For the most part, apperceptive tests are scored by subjective clinical interpretation of the story content. Five common criteria for analyzing stories are the following:

1. The types of individuals with whom the child identifies (e.g., happy, sad, rejected)

2. The needs the key figure or hero manifests (e.g., high achievement, rebellion, love)

3. The environmental influences (e.g., economic deprivation, hostile forces, unhappy home)

4. The interaction between the hero's needs and external pressures (e.g., rebellion against unsympathetic authority figures, lack of opportunity that restricts achievement)

5. The outcome (e.g., victory, defeat, withdrawal)

Historically, projective tests have been criticized on grounds of inadequate empirical substantiation of their reliability and validity (Anastasi & Urbina, 1997). Psychologists who are trained to use these measures note that they are part of a test battery and that clinical diagnosis depends on identifying patterns of responses that are repeated on a variety of tests. Also, the development of objective scoring systems might increase the usefulness of the apperception tests.

Psychodiagnostics. The most unstructured of the projective tests, *Psychodiagnostics* (Rorschach, 1942), consists of 10 symmetrical inkblots printed on a white background. Five blots are achromatic, two are black and red, and three are multicolored. The child or adult administered the test is informed that there are no wrong or right answers and is asked to describe what she sees on a card. Responses are recorded, and the individual may be queried in nondirective fashion to elicit more information. For example, if the person saw a butterfly, she might be asked how the butterfly "seemed" there. The vagueness of the query is to avoid putting ideas into the person's mind. Scoring is based on such criteria as the areas of the blot used in each response (e.g., the whole blot, large details of the blot, small details, the white area); the aspects of the blot that generated the response (e.g., the form, shading, color); the content of the response (e.g., human beings, animals, movement); and the novelty or originality of a response. A variety of approaches to scoring and interpreting Rorschach's test have been developed, and information pertaining to clinical interpretations can be found in Exner and Weiner (1995).

Despite being criticized on grounds similar to those applied to the apperceptive techniques, Rorschach's test remains a very popular clinical assessment tool used extensively by clinical psychologists and other personnel working in mental health settings. Professionals who are trained in the use of this instrument are convinced that it has no rival in uncovering information illustrating an individual's unconscious thoughts and feelings. It is less frequently used in school settings, largely because it is so complex to score and interpret.

Clinical Interviews

The clinical interview, the most commonly used of the assessment techniques discussed here (Watkins, Campbell, Nieberding, & Hallmark, 1995), is an extremely important diagnostic strategy used primarily by psychologists, psychiatrists, and other mental health workers. Although the interviewing strategies used overlap in part with those used by teachers in parent interviews, clinical interviews are characterized by probes into sensitive personal issues affecting a child's emotional stability and by the ability to draw inferences about the individual's affect, level of defensiveness, and ability to cope with reality. Such inferences are based not only on direct responses to questions but also on indirect remarks, nonverbal behaviors, general attitude, and so forth. Clinical interviews may be conducted with children, their parents or parent surrogates, additional family members, and, in some instances, peers. Topics explored include the child's developmental history, data pertaining to medical and physical problems (traumatic injury, sickness, hospitalizations), family (number of children, parents' occupations), family dynamics and relationships, school history, behavior patterns at home and at school, and the type and extent of the child's current problems.

One form of clinical interview is relatively unstructured. Unstructured interviews often are employed with relatively young children or individuals who may be cognitively or linguistically unable or unwilling to respond to direct questioning. The interviewer may use a variety of methods to draw the child into participation, such as figure drawings of self and family, enacting roles with puppets or dolls, or reading a story that depicts a child experiencing emotional difficulty. In many cases, the child is encouraged to engage in symbolic play activities and is asked about the play. For example, if a child, while playing with a doll, remarks that the doll hates school, the interviewer may ask questions about that remark. Leading statements such as "I guess school can really be tough" are often considered more effective probes than direct questions such as "Do you have trouble in school?" The interviewer also may ask questions about the choice of dolls, types of figures drawn, and so forth. Basically, the interviewer determines the direction of the interview by following the child's lead. Although the unstructured interview remains popular, increasing numbers of professionals have expressed a preference for more structured techniques when working with children because the outcomes are less nebulous (Kamphaus & Frick, 1996).

Usually, interviews conducted with older individuals are more highly structured. For example, the interviewer may use a child's responses on a self-report scale as the impetus for discussion with the child or with the parents. In this type of situation, the remarks made by the person being interviewed would be recorded in some manner. Even greater structure in clinical interviews is provided by the use of interview formats that help the interviewer elicit all avenues of significant information pertaining to the seriousness of a child's emotional problems. Kovacs (1985) developed *The Interview Schedule for Children*, a semi-structured, symptom-oriented psychiatric interview for children ages 8 to 17. This interview format explores five areas: major psychopathological symptoms; mental status, such as delusions and hallucinations; signs of pathology observed in the interview; developmental milestones; and clinical impressions about the severity of current symptoms.

Kauffman and colleagues (1997) developed the *Schedule for Affective Disorders and Schizophrenia for School Aged Children*. This semistructured interview is used to measure a wide range of affective disorders in children. A similar semistructured device designed to measure anxiety is the *Anxiety Disorders Interview for Children* developed by Silverman (1994). The *Bellevue Index of Depression* (Petti, 1978) is another semistructured interview, designed for children ages 6 to 12. The child is asked to respond to 40 items that are symptomatic of depression. Each item is rated on two separate 4-point scales: severity (*not at all* to *very much*) and duration (*less than 1 month* to *always*). Symptoms of depression are scored positive if criteria for both degree of severity and duration are met. Finally, Shaffer and colleagues (1996) developed a more highly structured interview form, the *Diagnostic Interview Schedule for Children*.

The major advantage of structuring clinical interviews is increased interrater reliability (raters working independently agree about the absence, presence, or relative severity of a disorder). For example, Petti (1978) found very high positive interjudge agreement among independent raters who used the *Bellevue Index of Depression* as a diagnostic tool.

Teacher's Role in Identification

The information presented thus far in this chapter should make it clear that the identification of children with EBDs is most accurately done in stages. The teacher's role in this process is depicted in Figure 4.3. The stages are represented as levels of an inverted triangle. At the uppermost level of the triangle are all students attending school.

Among these students are some who experience problems (social isolates, underachievers, unusually disruptive and uncooperative children) that concern their teachers. At this level, the teacher's judgment is the primary component in the process of identifying possible emotional disorders. The teacher may use informal observation, including anecdotal records and critical incidence reports, parent interviews, and sociometrics, in addition to close monitoring of achievement to form more accurate impressions about the scope of the students' problems. At the same time, the teacher attempts to help the children accommodate to the school environment and may implement interventions within the classroom that include behavior modification techniques, adjustment of curriculum materials, and reorganization of the classroom setting.

The children whose problems persist move to the second level of the identification triangle. At this level, teachers are more familiar with the children's

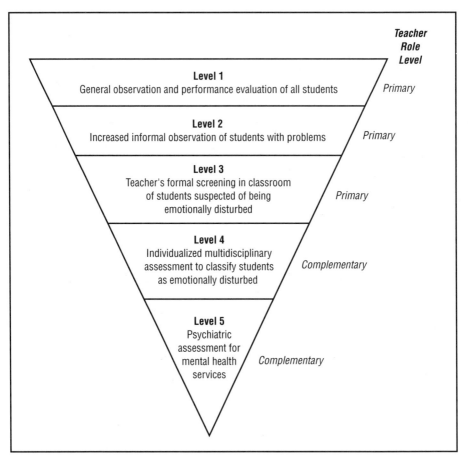

Figure 4.3. Identification of emotionally disturbed children.

difficulties and continue to attempt to alleviate the problems in the course of the general educational program. The identification process continues to be based primarily on teacher judgment; however, the teacher may seek advice and support from other school-based professionals, such as the guidance counselor, reading specialist, school psychologist, or instructional support specialist. Teachers and other specialists may undertake structured direct observations and make more complete evaluations of student academic strengths and weaknesses. Parental involvement also may increase with the implementation of cooperative activities, such as a home–school behavior modification program or homework monitoring. As was true of Level 1, with the exception of parental involvement, efforts to understand and assist children experiencing problems remain within the classroom. The individuals who continue to experience difficulty move to Level 3; they become candidates for teacher-directed screening procedures specifically designed to identify those students whose school-related problems may involve an emotional disorder.

At Level 3, the teacher or appropriate school-based professionals conduct assessment within the classroom by using standardized, norm-referenced behavior rating scales or measures of affective conditions (e.g., anxiety, depression, self-concept). The teacher now has reasonable suspicions that the child's problems cannot be readily remediated within the classroom, although attempts to do so continue. Although the teacher may be assisted at this stage by other school personnel, such as a guidance counselor, the information being gathered reflects the teacher's opinions, and all of the instruments used, including self-report scales, can be interpreted by a teacher. All of the steps taken at the first three levels provide documentation for the next level. Students progressing to Level 4 are those whom the previously gathered data indicate may have an emotional disorder. At this stage, the student is formally referred for special education identification procedures. This step requires a comprehensive evaluation of the student by a multidisciplinary team of professionals, such as a school psychologist, social worker, special education specialist, nurse, and, when deemed necessary, a psychiatrist or neurologist. Parental permission is necessary to proceed with this level, and school districts are mandated to protect students from misidentification by providing assessment in the child's primary language. Students are evaluated on an individual basis, usually outside the classroom, by various members of the multidisciplinary team. Psychological assessment includes standardized measures of intelligence, achievement, aptitude, personality, affect, and attitude. Physical, neurological, and psychiatric evaluations also may occur. Assessment is designed to identify the source of the student's problems and indicate appropriate special education placement when necessary. In most cases, students reaching this level are assigned to special education placements that are mandated by law to be as least restrictive (or as close to the norm) as possible. Although instruments such as projective and semiprojective techniques may be used at this level, the data gathered by the teacher are used to help the team make a decision that may or may not confirm that a particular student has an emotional disorder.

Those individuals who appear to have emotional disorders progress to Level 5. Students identified as having EBDs receive an Individualized Educational Program that must be approved by their parents. Psychiatric services often are recommended, but actual consultation for further psychiatric evaluation and therapeutic services is usually at the discretion of the parents. When parents permit, all relevant information compiled by the teacher and other school personnel may be made available to the psychiatrist.

The funnel-down procedure involved in the identification of individuals with emotional disorders makes clear the teacher's essential role. The procedure acknowledges that children's classroom activities are a vital source of information about children's emotional adjustment. As is true of adults, children's problems are most obvious in the life situations that are most demanding, where they must cope with a variety of stressors. A successful school adjustment depends on a child's ability to assume responsibility and cope with the multiple sources of stress that may be associated with academic achievement, interaction with authority figures, social relationships, conforming to rules, and respecting the rights of the group. Among all professionals, the teacher is most familiar with the child's typical behavior and therefore is uniquely qualified to provide essential information pertaining to the child's emotional well-being. Notably, the identification procedures undertaken by the teacher are simple and straightforward and do not require elaborate training to use. Teachers need not engage in a technical interpretation of data, invade the privacy of the children, or violate good taste. Also, these procedures are not expensive to use.

Overview of Services

The variety of assessment techniques and strategies discussed in this chapter have the common purpose of providing bits and pieces of information about human beings. Their usefulness is directly related to the outcomes of their use—that is, the avenues of treatment or services available for children identified as having EBDs.

Mental Health Services

Mental health agencies are usually identified as the primary source of psychiatric services for children with EBDs. Typically, these agencies have operated independently of the schools, although referral for services often is initiated by school personnel. Mental health agencies are designed to provide psychotherapy, among other social services. Because the classic doctor–patient therapeutic relationship has not been validated as highly successful with children, the best therapeutic efforts involve families and other pertinent individuals. Current theory suggests that an ecologically oriented approach involving interactions between therapists and significant persons at school and at home is a good model for assisting children. However, this type of approach is expensive to implement, and an unfortunate reality concerning mental health resources is that they are too few and those that do exist are not well supported financially by our society. Consequently, mental health facilities fall far short of providing necessary services for children with EBDs (Ormsbee et al., 1996).

Hospital and Residential Facilities

A significant number of children with serious emotional disorders receive treatment in residential facilities, such as private schools and psychiatric hospitals. Although many of these institutions adhere to relatively standard models of doctor–patient therapeutic interaction, there is an increasing effort to involve families in treatment programs. Educational programs are conducted in these facilities, although in hospital settings they are not closely integrated with the general treatment program. However, some hospitals and residential facilities have developed cooperative programs with local school districts that provide educational services outside the residential setting for the children as they begin to function more adaptively. Curry (1986) reported that 60% to 80% of the children treated in psychiatric hospitals and residential treatment facilities make satisfactory adjustments when returned to their typical environments. Although these statistics are encouraging, they must be viewed with caution. Many children, regardless of the severity of their emotional disorders, do not receive hospital and residential services. Large numbers of students with serious emotional disorders are never identified (Kauffman, 1997), approximately 40% of students who have been identified drop out of school (U.S Department of Education, 1990), and significant numbers of children with emotional disorders who reside in temporary foster care situations receive little or no service (Bauer, 1993). The cost of services provided by hospitals and residential facilities is a significant factor limiting the availability of those resources.

Public School Facilities

As was noted previously, children formally diagnosed as having an EBD are eligible for special education services, and the majority of these children are educated in public schools. These services may be provided in self-contained classrooms taught by teachers certified to work with individuals classified as emotionally and behaviorally disordered. Although technically speaking, these classes are available for children with all types of emotional problems, in actuality most of the children enrolled have some type of externalizing disorder (Jennings, Mendelsohn, May, & Brown, 1988). For the most part, the goal of most school-based intervention has been to help children curb their impulses to act out and to increase their academic skills. Although segregated classes limit the opportunities for individuals with emotional disorders to interact with and learn from nondisturbed individuals in more normalized settings, the negative impact of their behavior on the learning of other students often has made self-contained placements necessary.

Children whose emotional disorders are less serious, or less likely to disrupt the learning environment, often remain in general education placements and receive special education services either through any of a variety of pull-out programs on a part-time basis or through classroom support programs. In pull-out programs, the student leaves the general classroom and receives special services in another setting. The most widely used of these program involves the use of resource rooms, a facility for learners with special needs in which a special teacher provides direct remedial or supplemental instruction in academic areas (often in reading in elementary settings). Classroom support programs feature collaboration between the general classroom educator and an instructional support specialist (special teacher, behavior management specialist, etc.) within the general classroom. The classroom support model has become extremely popular because it is cost-effective and purports to program effectively for students with EBDs within the general classroom, without significantly diminishing the quality of the instruction afforded to other children. Unfortunately, research suggests that support for students with EBDs within the general classroom is largely inadequate (Myles & Simpson, 1992).

Teacher's Responsibility for Treatment

Both the current trends in education and the lack of alternative social service community resources make it clear that in our society public school teachers are expected to bear a great deal of responsibility for assisting children with EBDs. It is highly significant that the emphasis in education in the 21st century requires that both general classroom educators and special education teachers not only instruct children in academic subjects but also use strategies that promote emotional adjustment. Although good general classroom teachers have always attended to their students' states of emotional well-being, the expectation that they act to remediate significant emotional or adjustment problems in their students has never been greater. The implications of this movement in education are particularly significant in light of the increased information that is available about the variety of emotional disorders experienced by children and the differing needs associated with those disorders. As for special educators, there is evidence that the current interest in the problems experienced by the children who are "internalizers" rather than "externalizers" will create a need for different approaches to educating children with EBDs. Although behavior modification techniques have traditionally been the treatment of choice in many programs focused primarily on modifying children's acting-out or disruptive behavior, other approaches may be more appropriate for helping seriously depressed or highly anxious children. Clearly, the special education teacher must have a sufficient level of knowledge both to recognize the varied needs of children and to implement a variety of therapeutic approaches.

The designation of the teacher as a therapist does not imply that she is expected to take on the role of psychiatrist or clinical psychologist in treating children with emotional problems and provide in-depth traditional psychotherapy. It simply recognizes the significance of the teacher's role in the shaping of children and acknowledges that children's ability to function adaptively in one of their principal ecosystems, the classroom, is an important predictor of their chances of leading successful lives. To aid the teacher in developing strategies to function as a classroom therapist, the next section of this book contains discussions of a variety of therapeutic methods, techniques, and procedures that are useful in educational settings.

 ## STUDY QUESTIONS

1. Discuss the inverted triangle process for identifying children with EBDs.

2. Discuss the theory behind the use of projective techniques. Give a detailed description of two specific instruments.

3. Discuss two types of sociometrics that can aid in identifying social isolates. Apply one type with a group of children or, if none is available, a group of friends.

4. Take a position on the question of whether teachers are qualified to identify children with EBDs. Support your position with information from this chapter.

5. List and discuss four types of identification tools or strategies that are used by teachers.

References

Achenbach, T. (1986). *Child Behavior Checklist for Ages 2–3*. Burlington: University of Vermont, Department of Psychiatry.

Achenbach, T. (1991). *Manual for the Child Behavior Checklist/4-18 and 1991 profile*. Burlington: University of Vermont, Department of Psychiatry.

Anastasi, A., & Urbina, S. (1997). *Psychological testing*. Upper Saddle River, NJ: Prentice Hall.

Battle, J. (1988). *North American Depression Inventories for Children and Adults*. Austin, TX: PRO-ED.

Battle, J. (1992). *Culture-Free Self-Esteem Inventories* (2nd ed.). Austin, TX: PRO-ED.

Bauer, A. M. (1993). Children and youth in foster care. *Intervention, 28*, 134–142.

Beck, A. T., Ward, C. H., Mendelson, M., Mack, J., & Erbaugh, J. (1961). An inventory for measuring depression. *Archives of General Psychiatry, 4*, 561–571.

Bellak, A., & Bellak, S. (1974). *The Children's Apperception Test*. New York: CPS.

Bellak, L. (1993). *The T.A.T, C.A.T., and S.A.T. in clinical use* (5th ed.). Boston: Allyn & Bacon.

Bierman, K., & McCauley, E. (1987). Children's descriptions of their peer interactions: Useful information for clinical child assessment. *Journal of Clinical Child Psychology, 16*, 9–18.

Blum, G. (1950). *The Blacky Pictures: Manual of instructions*. New York: Psychological Corp.

Bracken, B. (1992). *Multidimensional Self-Concept Scale*. Austin, TX: PRO-ED.

Brown, L., & Alexander, J. (1991). *Self-Esteem Index*. Austin, TX: PRO-ED.

Brown, L., & Coleman, M. (1988). *Index of Personality Characteristics*. Austin, TX: PRO-ED.

Brown, L., & Hammill, D. (1990). *Behavior Rating Profile* (2nd ed.). Austin, TX: PRO-ED.

Buck, J. N. (1992). *House-Tree-Person Projective Drawing Techniques*. Los Angeles: Western Psychological Services.

Bullock, L., & Wilson, M. (1989). *Behavior Dimensions Rating Scale*. Allen, TX: Developmental Learning Materials.

Burks, H. (1977). *Burks' Behavior Rating Scales*. Los Angeles: Western Psychological Services.

Burns, R. (1982). *Self-growth in families: Kinetic Family Drawings research and application*. New York: Bruner/Mazel.

Connell, J. (1980). *A new measure of children's perceptions of control: Individual differences, situational determinants and developmental change*. Unpublished manuscript, University of Rochester, Rochester, New York.

Conners, C. K. (1997). *Conners' Rating Scales*. Austin, TX: PRO-ED.

Coopersmith, S. (1967). *Coopersmith Self-Esteem Inventory*. San Francisco: Freeman.

Curry, J. (1986, August). *Outcome studies of psychiatric hospitalization and residential treatment of youth: Conceptual and research implications*. Paper presented at the annual meeting of the American Psychological Association, Washington, DC.

Deren, S. (1975). An empirical evaluation of the validity of the *Draw-A-Family Test*. *Journal of Clinical Psychology, 31*, 47–52.

Epanchin, B., & Rennells, M. (1989). Parents' and teachers' sensitivity to unhappiness reported by undercontrolled children. *Behavior Disorders, 14*, 166–174.

Epstein, M. H., & Cullinan, D. (1998). *Scale for Assessing Emotional Disturbance*. Austin, TX: PRO-ED.

Epstein, M. H., & Sharma, J. M. (1998). *Behavioral and Emotional Rating Scale*. Austin, TX: PRO-ED.

Exner, J. E., & Weiner, I. B. (1995). *The Rorschach: A comprehensive system*. New York: Wiley.

Eyberg, S. (1980). Eyberg child behavior inventory. *Journal of Clinical Child Psychology, 9*, 29.

Fitts, W., & Roid, S. (1988). *Tennessee Self-Concept Scale*. Los Angeles: Western Psychological Services.

Gilliam, J. (1995a). *Attention-Deficit/Hyperactivity Disorder Test*. Austin, TX: PRO-ED.

Gilliam, J. (1995b). *Gilliam Autism Rating Scale*. Austin, TX: PRO-ED.

Gresham, F., & Elliott, S. (1990). *Social Skills Rating System*. Circle Pines, MN: American Guidance Service.

Gropper, G., Kress, G., Hughes, R., & Pekich, J. (1968). Training teachers to recognize and manage social and emotional problems in the classroom. *Journal of Teacher Education, 19*, 477–485.

Hammill, D., Brown, L., & Bryant, B. (1992). *The consumer's guide to tests in print*. Austin, TX: PRO-ED.

Harter, S. (1985). *Self-Perception Profile for Children*. Denver: University of Denver, Psychology Department.

Hops, H., Davis, B., & Longoria, N. (1995). Methodological issues in direct observation: Illustrations with the Living in Familial Environments (LIFE) coding system. *Journal of Clinical Child Psychology, 55,* 341–346.

Hresko, W., & Brown, L. (1984). *Test of Early Socio-Emotional Development*. Austin TX: PRO-ED.

Hutton, J., & Roberts, T. (1986). *Social-Emotional Dimension Scale*. Austin, TX: PRO-ED.

Hutton, J., & Roberts, T. (1990). *Stress Impact Scale*. Austin, TX: PRO-ED.

Impara, J. C., & Plake, B. S. (Eds.). (1998). *The thirteenth mental measurements yearbook*. Lincoln: University of Nebraska Press.

Jennings, R., Mendelsohn, S., May, K., & Brown, G. (1988). Elementary students in classes for the emotionally disturbed: Characteristics and classroom behavior. *American Journal of Orthopsychiatry, 58,* 65–76.

Kamphaus, R. W., & Frick, P. J. (1996). *Clinical assessment of child and adolescent personality and behavior*. Boston: Allyn & Bacon.

Kauffman, J. (1997). *Characteristics of emotional and behavioral disorders of children and youth* (6th ed.). Upper Saddle River, NJ: Prentice Hall.

Kauffman, J., Birmaher, B., Brent, D., Rao, U., Flynn, C., Moreci, P., Williamson, D., & Ryan, N. (1997). Schedule for affective disorders and schizophrenia for school aged children: Initial reliability and validity data. *Journal of the American Academy of Child and Adolescent Psychiatry, 36,* 980–988.

Kazdin, A., French, N., Unis, A., Esveldt-Dawson, K., & Sherick, R. (1983). Hopelessness, depression, and suicidal intent among psychiatrically disturbed inpatient children. *Journal of Consulting and Clinical Psychology, 51,* 504–511.

Kohn, M. (1986). *Kohn Problem Checklist*. San Antonio, TX: Psychological Corp.

Koppitz, E. (1968). *Psychological evaluation of children's human figure drawings*. New York: Grune & Stratton.

Kovacs, M. (1985). *The Interview Schedule for Children*. Pittsburgh, PA: University of Pittsburgh.

Kovacs, M. (1992). *Children's Depression Inventory* (2nd ed.). Pittsburgh, PA: University of Pittsburgh.

Kowalchuk, B., & King, J. (1988). *Life Orientation Inventory*. Austin TX: PRO-ED.

Lang, M., & Tisher, M. (1978). *Children's Depression Scale*. Victoria, Australia: Australia Council for Educational Research.

Lefkowitz, M., & Tesiny, E. (1980). Assessment of childhood depression. *Journal of Consulting and Clinical Psychology, 48,* 43–60.

Machover, K. (1949). *Personality projection in the drawing of the human figure*. Springfield, IL: Thomas.

Martin, L. (1988). *Temperament Assessment Battery*. Los Angeles: Western Psychological Services.

McCarney, S., & Leigh, J. (1990). *Behavior Evaluation Scale* (2nd ed.). Austin, TX: PRO-ED.

Merrell, K. W., & Walters, A. S. (1998). *Internalizing Symptoms Scale for Children*. Austin, TX: PRO-ED.

Miller, L. (1981). *Louisville Behavior Checklist*. Los Angeles: Western Psychological Services.

Moreno, J. (1953). *Who shall survive? Foundations of sociometry, group psychotherapy, and sociodrama* (2nd ed.). New York: Beacon House.

Morgan, D., & Jenson, W. (1988). *Teaching behaviorally disordered students: Preferred practices*. Columbus, OH: Merrill.

Murray, H. A. (1943). *Thematic Apperception Test*. Cambridge, MA: Harvard University Press.

Myles, B. S., & Simpson, R. L. (1992). General educators' mainstreaming preferences that facilitate acceptance of students with behavior disorders and learning disabilities. *Behavioral Disorders, 17,* 305–315.

Naglieri, J., McNeish, T., & Bardos, A. (1991). *Draw A Person: Screening Procedure for Emotional Disturbance*. Austin, TX: PRO-ED.

Neeper, R., Lahey, B., & Frick, P. (1990). *Comprehensive Behavior Rating Scale for Children*. San Antonio, TX: Psychological Corp.

Newcomer, P., Barenbaum, E., & Bryant, B. (1992). *Depression and Anxiety in Youth Scale*. Austin, TX: PRO-ED.

Newcomer, P., Barenbaum, E., & Pearson, N. (1995). Depression and anxiety in children and adolescents with learning disabilities, conduct disorders, and no disabilities. *Journal of Emotional and Behavioral Disorders, 3*, 27–39.

Norwicki, S., & Strickland, B. (1973). A locus of control scale for children. *Journal of Consulting and Clinical Psychology, 40*, 148–154.

Ormsbee, C., Simpson, R., & Zionts, P. (1996). Preassessment, referral, assessment, and placement. In P. Zionts (Ed.), *Teaching disturbed and disturbing students: An integrated approach* (2nd ed., pp. 71–118). Austin, TX: PRO-ED.

Petti, T. (1978). Depression in hospitalized child psychiatry patients. *Journal of American Academic Child Psychiatry, 17*, 49–59.

Piers, E., & Harris, D. (1984). *Children's Self-Concept Scale (The Way I Feel About Myself)*. Nashville, TN: Counselor Recordings and Tests.

Quay, H., & Peterson, D. (1984). *Revised Behavior Problem Checklist*. Coral Gables, FL: Psychological Assessment Resources.

Reynolds, C., & Richmond, B. (1985). *Revised Children's Manifest Anxiety Scale*. Los Angeles: Western Psychological Services.

Reynolds, W. (1987). *Reynolds' Adolescent Depression Scale*. Odessa, FL: Psychological Assessment Resources.

Reynolds, W. (1989). *Child Depression Scale*. Odessa, FL: Psychological Assessment Resources.

Roberts, G. (1982). *Roberts Apperception Test for Children*. Los Angeles: Western Psychological Services.

Ronde, A. (1957). *The sentence completion method*. New York: Ronald.

Rorschach, H. (1942). *Psychodiagnostics*. New York: Grune & Stratton.

Rotter, J. (1968). *Manual: The Rotter Incomplete Sentence Blank*. New York: Macmillan.

Schneider, M. (1989). *Children's Apperceptive Story-Telling Test*. Austin, TX: PRO-ED.

Shaffer, D., Fisher, P., Dulcan, M., Davies, M., Piacentini, J., Schwab-Stone, M., Lahey, B., Bourdon, K., Jensen, P., Bird, H., Canino, G., & Regier, D. (1996). The NIMH Diagnostic Interview Schedule for Children: Description, acceptability, prevalence rates, and performance in the MECA study. *Journal of American Academy of Child and Adolescent Psychiatry, 27*, 675–687.

Silverman, W. K. (1994). Structured diagnostic interviews. In T. H. Ollendick, N. J. King, & W. Yule (Eds.), *International handbook of phobic and anxiety disorders in children and adolescents* (pp. 219–316). New York: Plenum Press.

Sodac, D., Nichols, P., & Gallagher, B. (1985). Pupil behavioral data. In G. H. Wood, C. R. Smith, & J. Grimes (Eds.), *The Iowa Assessment Model in Behavioral Disorders: A training manual* (pp. 51–69). Des Moines: Iowa Department of Public Instruction.

Spielberger, C., Edwards, C., Lushene, R., Montuori, J., & Platzek, D. (1970). *State-Trait Anxiety Inventory for Children*. Palo Alto, CA: Consulting Psychology Press.

Spielberger, C., Gorsuch, R., Lushene, R., Vagg, P., & Jacobs, G. (1977). *State-Trait Anxiety Inventory, Form Y*. Palo Alto, CA: Consulting Psychology Press.

Spivak, G., & Swift, M. (1967). *Devereux Elementary School Behavior Rating Scale*. Devon, PA: Devereux Foundation.

Spivak, G., & Swift, M. (1977). Hahnemann High School behavior rating scale. *Journal of Abnormal Child Psychology, 5*, 299–307.

U.S. Department of Education. (1990). *Twelfth annual report to Congress on the implementation of the Education of the Handicapped Act.* Washington, DC: U.S. Government Printing Office.

Van Hutton, T. (1994). *House-Tree-Person Technique.* Odessa, FL: Psychological Assessment Resources.

Waksman, S. (1990). *Portland Problem Behavior Checklist–Revised.* Austin, TX: PRO-ED.

Walker, H. (1983). *Walker Problem Behavior Identification Checklist.* Los Angeles: Western Psychological Services.

Walker, H., & McConnell, S. (1988). *Walker–McConnell Scale of Social Competence and School Adjustment.* Austin, TX: PRO-ED.

Walker, H., & Severson, H. (1990). *Systematic Screening for Behavior Disorders (SSBD): A Multiple Gating Procedure.* Longmont, CO: Sopris West.

Walker, H., Severson, H., & Feil, E. (1994). *The Early Screening Project: A proven child-find process.* Longmont, CO: Sopris West.

Walker, H., Severson, H., & Haring, N. (1985). *Standardized screening and identification of behavior disordered pupils in the elementary age range: Rationale, procedures and guidelines.* Eugene: University of Oregon.

Watkins, C. E., Campbell, V. L., Nieberding, R., & Hallmark, R. (1995). Contemporary practice of psychological assessment by clinical psychologists. *Professional Psychology: Research and Practice, 26*, 54–60.

Wicks-Nelson, R., & Israel, A. (2000). *Behavior disorders of childhood* (4th ed.). Upper Saddle River, NJ: Prentice Hall.

Wirt, R., Lachar, D., Kinedinst, L., & Seat, P. (1977a). *Peer Nomination Inventory for Children.* Los Angeles: Western Psychological Services.

Wirt, R., Lachar, D., Kinedinst, L., & Seat, P. (1977b). *Personality Inventory for Children.* Los Angeles: Western Psychological Services.

Wood, F., Smith, C., & Grimes, J. (1985). *The Iowa Assessment Model in Behavioral Disorders: A training manual.* Des Moines, IA: State Department of Public Instruction.

PART

III

THERAPY AND INTERVENTIONS

CHAPTER

BEHAVIORAL THERAPY

Phyllis L. Newcomer and Christina Ager

Behavioral therapy has evolved over the past 100 years from its origins in classical and instrumental conditioning, through applied research on reinforcement and punishment, and more recently into the areas of functional behavioral assessment, using instructional principles to teach appropriate behaviors and systems models designed to maximize appropriate behaviors in particular settings. Although behaviorism has expanded its arena, methodology, and treatment options, the guiding principles of behavioral therapy remain the same: the use of experimental principles to assess situations, develop treatment options, and evaluate effectiveness.

Historical Background and Chapter Framework

The term *behavioral therapy* appears to have been introduced in the 1950s, first by Lindsley (1954), then with more popular impact by Lazarus (1971). Its earliest roots were the investigations into classical and instrumental conditioning undertaken by the Russian psychologists Ivan Pavlov (1927, 1928), Vladimir Bekhterev (1932), and A. G. Ivanov-Smolensky (1927, 1928) and by the Americans Edward L. Thorndike (1898), J. B. Watson (1916), B. F. Skinner (1953), and others. Interestingly, although much of the early research into conditioning principles was conducted with animals (Pavlov's famous salivating dog experiment), many of the fathers of behavioral therapy, including Pavlov (1932, 1934) and Watson (with Rayner, 1920; the equally famous "little Albert" experiments), applied those principles directly to humans. Thus, behavioral therapy existed in practice long before it existed in name.

Later in the 20th century, experimental psychology and behavioral therapy began to encompass general theories of learning theory. Theoretical models of learning based on the principles of conditioning enabled investigators to formulate more comprehensive hypotheses for the study of abnormal behavior. The work of Clark Hull (1943, 1952) appears of particular importance in this respect. Of equal significance is the work of Albert Bandura (1969), who in *Principles of Behavior Modification* incorporated theoretical data on symbolic and cognitive processes into a behavioral model and developed social learning theory (Bandura, 1977).

During the 1950s the application of behavior principles to clinical cases began in earnest. Theorists such as Dollard and Miller (1950) and Mowrer (1950) translated psychodynamic constructs into the terminology of learning theory. To a large degree, however, the way was led by B. F. Skinner, who demonstrated the effectiveness of operant conditioning with psychotic patients at the Metropolitan State Hospital in Waltham, Massachusetts, and published his important book *Science and Human Behavior* (1953).

In England the work of H. J. Eysenck and M. B. Shapiro at the psychology department of the Institute of Psychiatry moved behavior therapy one step further. Eysenck (1949, 1950, 1964a) was among the first to cogently critique the medical approaches to the study of abnormal behavior. He perceived clinical personnel as behavioral researchers who must apply methods of scientific inquiry to the solution of behavioral disorders. Similarly, Shapiro (1951, 1961, 1966) developed clinical procedures for assessment and treatment of problematic conditions based on hypothesis formation and testing, rather than on the traditional administration of psychodynamic tests. This emphasis on the use of experimental strategies in applied settings constitutes the foundation of an experimental–clinical approach to behavioral disorders.

In the United States, Joseph Wolpe, later joined by Arnold Lazarus, drew from Hull's conceptualizations to formulate clinical procedures based on the theory of reciprocal inhibition. Their work encompasses many specific techniques associated with behavioral therapy and are discussed in great length later in this chapter.

As this brief history suggests, behavioral therapy did not emanate from one particular source. In fact, the multiplicity of behavioral foundations has generated a certain amount of dispute regarding the definition of the term. Some individuals view behavioral therapy as the application of learning theory in clinical situations. For example, Eysenck (1964b) defined behavioral therapy as "the attempt to alter human behavior and emotion in a beneficial manner according to the laws of modern learning theory." Other experts have disputed this definition, finding it too limiting. Yates (1970,) typifies this attitude with his definition.

> Behavioral therapy is the attempt to utilize systematically that body of empirical and theoretical knowledge which has resulted from the application of the experimental method in psychology and its closely related disciplines (physiology and neurophysiology) in order to explain the genesis and maintenance of abnormal patterns of behavior; and to apply that knowledge to the treatment or prevention of those abnormalities by means of controlled experimental studies of the single case, both descriptive and remedial. (p.18)

Yates's position emphasizes three related points: (a) behavioral therapy involves the formulation and testing of unique experimental hypotheses for each specific individual, (b) these hypotheses should be based on far more than learning theory, and (c) behavioral therapy requires controlled experimental investigations of the single case to determine treatment effectiveness. With this process-oriented definition, any technique such as role playing or therapeutic art may be integrated into the behavioral intervention, provided it is applied in accordance with the experimental method.

Early on, some theorists rejected this "generalist" definition (Wolpe, 1976); however, the current state of behavioral therapy aligns itself with Yates. Methods of intervention have broadened, but the hallmark of behavioral therapy is the process by which behaviors are observed and analyzed and the ways in which treatments are developed and tested. Although, the application of any technique that alters behavior can be referred to as behavioral therapy, in this chapter use of the term is largely restricted to the principles derived from conditioning, learning theory, and functional assessment; therefore, the primary frame of reference is stimuli (observable events in the physical environment) and responses (observable reactions to stimuli) and the principles of reinforcement that influence or alter responses. Although the tenets of behaviorism are expanding rapidly, increasingly encompassing the internal cognitive operations that occur between stimuli and responses, most of these principles are examined in Chapter 6, "Cognitive Therapy," which also discusses cognitive–behavioral interventions such as social skills training, interpersonal problem-solving training, and moral-reasoning training. The cognitive information in this chapter extends only to the concepts involved in Bandura's Social Learning Theory. Even with these restrictions, the reader will find the discussion of behavioral therapy to be far more complex than many of the therapies presented in other chapters of this book, for example, drama, art, and music. Those chapters refer primarily to therapeutic techniques, whereas behavioral therapy constitutes a distinct approach, a methodology for studying behavior.

Consequently, this necessarily long chapter is divided into five major sections, which discuss (a) applied behavioral procedures, such as applied behavioral analysis (ABA) and behavior modification; (b) functional behavioral assessment; (c) specific behavioral interventions based on function; (d) school-based applications, including schoolwide and classroom applications of behavioral therapy; and (e) clinical applications, addressing applied procedures more generally associated with interventions in clinical settings. This distinction is obviously arbitrary, as both educational and clinical applications involve common procedures, that is, the practical application of behavioral theory. The information in this chapter will be more clearly understood if the reader is familiar with the rationale and major concepts associated with behavioral psychology. Those persons lacking such familiarity might wish to consult the Appendix for a brief discussion of behavioral principles.

Applied Behavioral Procedures

For ease of understanding, the term *applied behavioral analysis*, or ABA, is used predominantly in this section and encompasses many of the procedures associated with the more common term *behavior modification*. The techniques discussed pertain primarily to procedures that are generally applicable in educational settings to affect behaviors. Although ABA once focused exclusively on challenging or inappropriate behaviors, over the past 20 years, research and application has reoriented toward promoting adaptive and socially appropriate behaviors. In addition, because behaviorism has adopted a functional approach, we no longer refer to problematic or challenging behaviors as "maladaptive"; although acting-out behaviors, anxiety, and even withdrawal are "maladaptive" from an outsider's point of view, these behaviors actually function in an adaptive way for the client. Instead, we use the terms *inappropriate* or *problematic* to denote that the behavior is not acceptable or causes problems for the client, or the term *challenging* to focus attention on changing the behavior.

ABA is defined by Sulzer-Azaroff and Mayer (1977, p. 6) as "a systematic, performance-based self-evaluative method of changing behavior." Essentially, the principles of conditioning and learning, particularly reinforcement, are applied to manipulate behavior, to establish new behavior, to maintain satisfactory behavior, to increase or reduce behavior, and to extend or restrict behavior to specific settings. The four main components of ABA involve (a) focusing attention on specific activities or behaviors, (b) direct observation and recording of these behaviors and supporting variables, (c) formulation of behavioral objectives and goals from observation, and (d) treatment or intervention based on experimental analysis and data collection.

Focusing on Specific Behaviors

Regarding the first step, focusing attention on specific behaviors, ABA requires that terms denoting internal feelings, such as *anger* or *sadness* be operationalized as specific behaviors. Thus, rather than describe an individual as "angry," the interventionist might specify behaviors such as fights with peers, has temper tantrums, throws stones at passing cars, or uses profanity. Any or all of these behaviors may denote anger, or emotions related to anger, such as fear, anxiety, or frustration. Anger is a construct that is neither directly observable nor directly measurable. Unless it is defined operationally, in terms of specific behaviors, it cannot be incorporated into therapeutic interventions dependent on objective verification of behavioral change. In other words, the fact that an individual is less angry is best demonstrated by the performance of fewer angry behaviors. The behaviors selected to be modified are called *target behaviors*. A target behavior may be an existing behavior that needs to be increased (e.g., completing independent work assignments) or decreased (e.g., fighting less often), or it may be a behavior not exhibited that needs to be developed (e.g., following directions).

Often when children behave inappropriately in school, numerous behaviors require modification. Changing behavior is difficult, as the reader might recall from personal attempts to lose weight, give up smoking, or exercise regularly. It is not desirable to target more than one or two behaviors at one time. Therefore, the interventionist must select the behavior that is most problematic to focus on initially. Behaviors given priority status are those that involve risk of injury to the child or others, those that greatly affect the individual's general well-being, those that occur with great frequency, and those that are intense and of long duration. Information from parents, teachers, and the children themselves will help determine which behaviors to target initially. Changing a behavior to one that is of value to these key individuals can lead to feelings of success, additional support, and a belief in the process.

Direct Observation and Recording of Behavior and Environmental Variables

The second component of ABA, the direct observation and recording of the target behaviors identified in the first step provides the backbone of ABA because it involves the techniques that are used to obtain objective data for development of goals and strategies for behavioral change. Alberto and Troutman (1990) identified six types of data that can be recorded: rate, duration, latency, topography, force, and locus. *Rate* is the frequency of a behavior in a specific time period. It involves discrete, countable responses, for example, as in the number of times a student gets out of his chair in a 15-minute period. *Duration* is temporal data involving measures of how long a behavior lasts once it begins. Examples are the amount of time the child remains out of his seat once he has left his chair or the duration of a temper tantrum. *Latency* also is temporal data, but it involves the time that lapses between a cue for a response to begin and the beginning of the response. In other words, the time of importance is that which elapses between the teacher's instructions to return to the seat or to begin an academic task and the child's efforts to comply. *Topography* refers to the quality of behavior. To return again to the out-of-seat example, the teacher may want to measure what a child does when he is out of seat (e.g., walk around the room, sit in a corner, play with objects, or hit other students). *Force* pertains to the intensity or severity of a response, as in the severity of a temper tantrum or the intensity of aggression toward self or others. A rating of force may be very useful when trying to change a high-intensity behavior that occurs fairly infrequently. *Locus* of behavior pertains to where and when it occurs. A child's frequency of fighting might be greater in relatively unstructured situations such as lunch or recess. (The locus of behavior is examined further under the section on functional behavioral assessment.) All of these data are gathered through a variety of sampling techniques.

Sampling. The sampling technique used to gather data depends on whether the behavior to be measured is transitory or permanent. Behaviors such as the number of homework assignments completed or the number of arithmetic problems finished are readily observable because they are recorded permanently. Homework or arithmetic papers are samples of behavior and may be evaluated to determine frequency of response, rate of responding, accuracy, items completed, and even intensity of damage during a temper tantrum. The number of pieces of trash left on a classroom floor or in the school yard can also be collected, counted, and used as permanent product data to alter littering behaviors. Photographs of graffiti on a school building may become permanent data concerning vandalism.

The observation and measurement of transitory behaviors, however, is far more difficult. Behaviors such as fighting or swearing leave no permanent record of their occurrence that may be assessed at a later time. They must be measured when they occur and recorded for later analysis. This type of observation usually requires a live observer or some type of taped record. The observation may be done by event, duration, or interval time sampling.

Event sampling simply involves counting the number of times a specific behavior occurs in a specific interval of time. It is useful for measuring the frequency of discrete responses, such as correct answers, hand raising, or getting out of seat. For example, an event recording might reveal that in four hour-long intervals, George got out of his seat 6, 14, 3, and 8 times.

Duration sampling focuses on the length of time a behavior occurs. Examples include the time required to complete an academic task or the length of a temper tantrum. A clock is used to measure how long it takes Jane to complete her mathematics assignment or a stopwatch to determine how long Jason's temper tantrums last.

Interval time sampling is employed in two situations: (a) when behaviors are not clearly discrete and it is difficult to tell where they begin and end and (b) when behaviors occur at such a high frequency that they are difficult to count. For example, a teacher may need baseline data on a child's out-of-seat behavior. However, if the behavior occurs 10, 20, or 30 times in an hour, it is virtually impossible to collect this data while teaching. Using an interval time sampling method, the teacher might simply record every 10 minutes if the child left her seat without permission. If it is necessary to know if a behavior occurred throughout an entire interval, a *whole-interval system* is established. Thus, if Joey cried for an entire 10-minute interval or Keisha was out of her seat the entire time, the behavior would be recorded as having occurred. If Joey stopped crying or Keisha returned to her seat halfway through the interval, it would not be recorded. With a *partial interval sampling* technique, the behavior need only occur once during the 10-minute interval to be recorded. Therefore, if Keisha got out of her seat at any time during the interval, the behavior would be recorded. This technique is useful to chart fleeting behaviors such as swearing. Whole-interval time sampling tends to underestimate behavior, whereas partial interval sampling often overestimates occurrence. The most accurate estimate is often obtained by using *momentary time sampling*. In momentary time sampling the behavior is charted if it is observed when a signal cues the observer to record. This cue could be a tape-recorded beep or a timer set to go off every 10 minutes. If Joey cried for 14 of 15 minutes in the interval, stopping 1 minute before the end of the interval, the behavior would not be recorded. However, if he began crying just as the signal to record sounds, it would be recorded. This strategy is useful for reoccurring and relatively persistent behaviors such as thumb sucking. Although less accurate than event recording (the behavior might occur nine times during the interval but be absent in the last minute), time-sampling techniques are less demanding of the rater because the teacher need check for the occurrence of a behavior only periodically, rather than counting every occurrence during the time period. Finally, a *coded interval* can be used to sample several behaviors simultaneously. Each important behavior is assigned a letter on a recording sheet. If the behavior occurs during the time interval, the observer puts a slash through the letter. Interval time sampling of any type is best used with frequent behavior. As a rule of thumb, it should not be used if the behavior occurs on an average of less than once in 15 minutes (Arrington, 1943).

Obviously, time is an important component for effective sampling. If data are not gathered continuously, that is, recorded 24 hours a day over extended time periods, various formulas can be used to determine when to sample. These are generally referred to as fixed and randomized sampling. *Fixed sampling* is undertaken at a set time period every day. With *randomized sampling*, data are gathered at various periods of time throughout the day. The latter approach usually yields more accurate and reliable information because it is likely to tap more representative behavior, thus reducing the possibility of sampling error, an important consideration in evaluating observational data. Intervention programs based on inaccurate observations obviously are of little value, either to the child or the teacher.

According to Hawkins and Dotson (1975), there are three sources of error that can influence the accuracy of observations. First, it is important that the definition of the response be clear and sufficiently detailed so that the observer is not unsure when a response has occurred. For example, a teacher recording the frequency of out-of-seat behavior might be unsure whether rising briefly from the chair to see the blackboard should be counted as a response, unless it is clearly specified that rising from the chair for any reason without permission constitutes out-of-seat behavior. If a definition is not ambiguous, any number of different observers will agree in identifying a response, indicating that the results of the observation are reliable and can be used with confidence. A desirable level of agreement among raters is between 80% and 100% (Kazdin, 1980). Second, environmental conditions can interfere with accurate observation. An observer might be distracted from seeing or hearing certain responses. For instance, a teacher attending to another child's needs might miss the display of a target behavior, particularly if the response is not extremely obvious. Finally, an observer may lack the motivation to stay with the task or may find it to be too difficult. Inexperienced individuals who are unfamiliar with the process of direct observation of behavior usually find the task more demanding than those who have used the process previously.

Additional sources of error are related to the use of inappropriate data-gathering procedures. It is not unusual for behavior to change when some aspect of the environment is altered. Therefore, it is not surprising that an individual usually will behave differently when she becomes aware that she is being observed closely and that her behavior is being recorded. The investigator must try to ensure that the recorded data have not been biased by the implementation of the observational system. The appropriate strategy in gathering observational data is to allow for an *adaptation period* before recording representative behavior. This period is designed to allow the subject of the observation to accommodate to the process. Once this accommodation occurs, she will resume her typical behavior. Adaptation occurs more rapidly when the observational process involves minimal disruption to usual classroom activities. For example, data gathering by the classroom teacher is less disruptive to normal routine than data gathering by an outside observer. Once the adaptation period has passed, the data gathered from consistent observation of typical or representative behavior are referred to as *baseline measurements*. These data serve as a standard for evaluating the effects of the treatment to follow. Once the intervention has begun in the *treatment phase*, the data gathered over a prescribed period of time are compared with the baseline measurements. The extent that treatment phase data differ from the individual's typical behavior before treatment illustrates the success or failure of the intervention; thus, it is essential that baseline data be accurate. Also, the baseline data as well as treatment data serve as standards for a *follow-up phase*, when data are gathered after the intervention has been terminated to determine the extent to which the improved behavior has persisted.

Displaying and Interpreting Data. Once gathered, the data are generally portrayed in the form of a graph or chart. The curves provide a visual representation of behavior that is readily interpretable. The vertical line, or ordinate, represents the behavior measurement, such as number or rate of responses, and the horizontal line, or abscissa, reflects units of time when data are taken. Figure 5.1 is a graph of Keisha's out-of-seat behavior that shows the frequency or rate of occurrence of that behavior during an adaptation period, a baseline phase, a treatment phase, and a follow-up phase.

The data in Figure 5.1 show that the challenging behavior decreased with the advent of the intervention and that the reduction in out-of-seat behavior persisted when compared to baseline data during the follow-up phase. Therefore, these hypothetical data suggest that the intervention was successful. Often, however, effectiveness of the treatment is not so easy to determine. For example, suppose Keisha's rate of out-of-seat behavior decreased, but only on an average of twice per day. The teacher might regard the improvement as too slight and consider implementing another type of intervention. Also, suppose the improved rate of behavior was not maintained during the follow-up phase. Because a new response, in-seat behavior, has not been learned, the intervention cannot be regarded as successful.

Another method of displaying and analyzing data is through sequence analysis (Goodwin, 1969). Called the "ABC" of behavior analysis, it involves three categories: antecedent stimuli (A), problem behavior (B), and consequences of behavior (C). Antecedent stimuli are events that precede the response or problem behavior and include variables such as the child's activity, his location

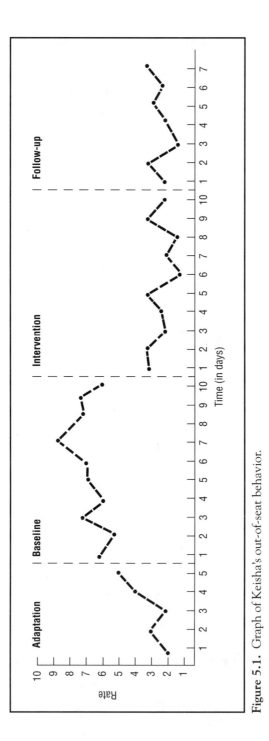

Figure 5.1. Graph of Keisha's out-of-seat behavior.

in the room, the activities of classmates and teacher, the time of day, and so forth. The problem behavior refers to the child's response—both the frequency and the duration. The consequences include events such as the teacher's reaction and peer response, as well as other activities in the room. A sequence chart for Keisha is presented in Figure 5.2.

With this type of chart all of the environmental variables that pertain to the behavior are identified. The contingencies or relationship between the target behaviors and the antecedent stimuli and consequences are portrayed. Events not considered are those occurring inside the child, that is, what he thinks or feels about the situation. This type of cognitive information is not included in the ABC analysis, because it is not considered pertinent for the implementation of treatment. The ABC approach reflects the principles of operant conditioning (see Appendix). The treatment depends on manipulation of reinforcement, that is, adjustment of external environmental events. Altering the consequences of Keisha's behavior should change its occurrence, regardless of her thoughts or ideas about the situation. Presumably, once Keisha is no longer engaging in challenging behavior and is receiving positive reinforcement from teacher and peers for more constructive activities, she will develop better feelings and thoughts about herself.

Setting Goals and Objectives

As portrayed thus far, the name of the game in ABA, behavior modification, and functional behavioral assessment is specificity, not only in the procedures used to identify target behaviors that require change or in the observation and recording of behaviors but also in the formulation of a plan for the intervention that includes both goals and objectives. The key to an effective behavioral intervention is that both the client and the interventionist have clear and precise knowledge about what must be accomplished.

According to Sulzer-Azaroff and Mayer (1977, p. 28), "a behavioral goal ought to be selected to provide both immediate and long term benefits to the client." In that case, the goals of the behavioral intervention designed to help Joey would include increasing his popularity with his peers, increasing his academic skills, and increasing his enjoyment of the day-to-day events associated with attending school. These general statements provide an orientation for an intervention but require further elaboration if they are to be operationalized, that is, defined in a manner that makes it possible to observe and measure outcomes. The clarity and usefulness of such goals are ensured by refining them into behavioral objectives.

A behavioral objective clarifies a goal by specifying the *desired response*, the *conditions* or *situation* in which it should occur, and the *criteria* for evaluating

Antecedents	Behavior	Consequences

Activity:
  Reading Lesson
	Inappropriate Laughter	Teacher:
		  Criticizes Child

Location:
  Front of room,
  reading circle
	Ridiculing remarks to peers	Peers:
		  Distracted, make
		  negative remarks

Time:
  10 to 11 A.M.
	Frequency:
	  3 remarks, 4 outbursts
	  of Laughter
		Activity:
		  Work is interrupted
		  negative remarks

Peer Activity:
  Independent reading
	Time:
	  1 hour	

Figure 5.2. Sequence chart for Keisha.

whether the objective has been met (Mager, 1962). Sulzer-Azaroff and Mayer (1977) noted that the desired response may be delineated as to its characteristics, including *topography*—where the response must be given (e.g., words must be written on the appropriate line of the paper with appropriate spacing between the letters), *intensity*—how strong the response must be (e.g., answer must be loud enough to be heard), *frequency*—how often the response must occur (e.g., hand must be raised before each remark), *duration*—how long the response must persist (e.g., 30 minutes of seatwork), and *accuracy*—what constitutes a correct response (e.g., 98% correctly spelled words). As often as possible, interventionists are encouraged to target increasing the alternative adaptive response in the behavioral objective rather than decreasing the inappropriate response. For example, targeting an increase in in-seat behavior will be more effective than targeting a decrease in out-of-seat behavior.

The second attribute of a behavioral objective, specifying the conditions or situation in which the response should occur, adds further precision to the planned intervention. When these components are added, the individual knows precisely when and how the adaptive response is to be demonstrated. In Keisha's case, she is expected to stay in her seat during independent and large-group work activities. Simon would be expected to ask to take a break when frustrated during a writing task.

Specifying the criteria for evaluating whether the objective has been met is the third characteristic of a behavioral objective. Both terminal and intermediate criteria need to be developed. Terminal criteria specify the final desired outcome (e.g., for Keisha to stay in her seat 95% of the required time). Intermediate criteria serve as stepping-stones to the terminal criteria. The criterion level for determining success must be realistic and feasible. Basing terminal criteria on the performance of children who do not display challenging behaviors is helpful. For example, if the average child in the fourth-grade class gets out of her seat without permission twice a day, that would be a reasonable terminal criterion for Keisha. However, it would be harmful to plan an intervention that made reinforcement contingent on behavior the child could not possibly display. Because an objective must be attainable to be effective, the guiding rule in establishing a criterion level is to set minimum acceptable levels. The child who is in her seat only 20% of the day will probably fail if the criterion is set at 80% during the initial intervention. If the child fails, the behavior is not reinforced, and the desired behavior is less likely to be demonstrated again. A 10% to 15% increase in alternative behavior (or decrease for problematic behavior) over baseline levels is thought to be obtainable for initial goal setting. So, the child is more likely to be successful at the 35% level, which, because it represents a substantial increase over the baseline rate of behavior, should be agreeable to the interventionist. As the in-seat response becomes stronger, the criterion level can be elevated to a final acceptable level of, say, 95% of the day.

With the exception of basic life skills (crossing the street after looking both ways, recognizing poison labels), very basic academic skills (recognizing numbers and letters), and aggressive behaviors (not punching the principal), a 100% criterion for any behavior is probably inappropriate because most people do not perform most tasks at the level of perfection. An intervention designed to increase in-seat behavior will probably fail if a criterion level of 100% is established for success.

Involving children in the development of their behavior modification plan can prove beneficial. Listing behaviors that children are good at, along with behaviors that "cause them trouble," can be very helpful in focusing the children and the interventionist on both the strengths and weaknesses. The interventionist should then translate those behaviors into specific goals and objectives. Returning to the students, they can then prioritize and choose which goal to work on first. The best method of establishing a cooperative, mutually agreeable plan of behavioral objectives and goals is through behavioral contracting. A contract is a formal agreement between individuals that indicates their commitment to behavioral change. The contract specifies what adaptive behaviors will be demonstrated, how and by whom they will be monitored, what sanctions will accompany failure to display them, what privileges will be earned, and what time dimensions apply. For example, Keisha and her teacher might formally contract to increase her in-seat behavior. A written agreement is drawn up with terms calling for a progressive increase in the adaptive response over a 2-week period. The teacher agrees to monitor on an hourly basis. Tokens are to be awarded when the behavioral specifications are met and withheld when they are not met. If Keisha proves unable to meet her commitment, the contract will be evaluated to determine its feasibility. Readjustment in the schedule of reinforcement might be necessary. In effect, the contract is renegotiated. Samples of behavioral contracts are presented later in this chapter.

Treatment Based on Experimental Analysis and Data Collection

The last step in applying the principles associated with ABA and behavior modification involves treatment. This step is consistent with those that precede it, in that it is based on the application of scientific principles. For the most part, treatments used in educational settings should be informed by the function of the behavior and should either alter the antecedents of the behavior or use the principles of reinforcement associated with operant conditioning (see Appendix).

Reinforcement. Simply stated, reinforcers are the consequences of behavior that either increase or decrease the incidence of its occurrence (Morris, 1985). Primary reinforcers such as food and drinks (also called tangible reinforcers) reduce drive states (hunger and thirst). Secondary reinforcers such as praise, facial expressions, and gestures (also called social reinforcers); tangible reinforcers such as money, prizes, or tokens; activity reinforcers such as free time; and graphic reinforcers such as grades are consequences whose reinforcement value is learned. Positive reinforcers occur after a behavior has been displayed and increase the probability that the behavior will occur again. For example, Joshua receives a happy-face sticker every time he finishes his arithmetic problems in the allotted time and required manner. Negative reinforcers are aversive stimuli that when removed increase the probability that a desired behavior will occur. In this case, Joshua's successful completion of his arithmetic paper causes his teacher to permit him to leave an isolation desk where he had been working and return to his regular seat. Negative reinforcement differs from another behavioral consequence, punishment. Punishment involves the addition of an aversive stimulus as when Joshua completes his arithmetic paper during recess when it is not finished during the appropriate time period. Additional specific information about the uses of each type of reinforcer, as well as punishment, will be provided in the ensuing section of this chapter that deals with classroom applications of behavior modification strategies.

The success of a behavioral intervention based on reinforcement is directly related to adherence to generally accepted principles of reinforcement. Walker and Shea (1991) presented five principles or rules to guide educators in planning and implementing a behavior modification program: (a) Reinforce the target behavior only; (b) in the first stages of a behavioral intervention, reinforce immediately after the behavior is displayed; (c) in the early stages of the intervention, reinforce every time the behavior is exhibited; (d) when a target behavior reaches the desired level of frequency, reinforce intermittently; and (e) always use social reinforcers with other (tangible, activity, or graphic) reinforcers.

Although the first rule regarding the target behavior seems obvious, implementation is more complex than it appears. Frequently, nontargeted behaviors are unwittingly reinforced in classrooms. For instance, a child's teacher might respond to his out-of-seat behavior by reprimanding him, assuming that negative comments will diminish the behavior. However, if the child regards any attention as reinforcing, following his out-of-seat behavior with negative remarks (attention) will increase the frequency of the behavior. As a corollary to this point, if the teacher discontinues the negative attention (stops the reinforcement) and ignores the behavior for a sufficient period of time, the behavior eventually will be *extinguished* (not occur). However, because the child has become accustomed to reinforcement, when attention is withdrawn the incidence frequency might increase briefly before the lack of reinforcement becomes apparent and the extinction process begins.

Another violation of the first principle occurs when an interventionist awards a reinforcer when the target behavior has not been displayed in accordance with the agreed-upon behavioral contract. If a child's response falls short of the established criterion, for example, if he completes 9 arithmetic problems instead of the required 10, the behavior is not reinforced, regardless of excuses, protests, or any desire on the teacher's part to be supportive of effort. If the criterion is too difficult, it must be modified to a more appropriate level. However, if it is appropriate, the stated standards for behavioral response must be enforced.

The second and third principles illustrate the relationship between behavior and its consequence. When a new behavior is being learned, it is learned more efficiently if reinforcement follows it immediately and is given consistently. Delays in reinforcement create the possibility that nontargeted behavior may intervene and become associated with the reinforcer. Also, the consistent use of reinforcement following a target behavior strengthens the bond between those two events. For example, a student who is given a token and praise (reinforcers) every time she raises her hand before she speaks in class learns this response most efficiently when the positive consequences occur consistently and immediately. If much time elapsed, the student might associate an alternative response, such as not answering the teacher's questions, with the reinforcement. If the reinforcement is not consistent, the student will take longer to internalize the relationship between behavior and consequence or may never learn the desired response.

Once a behavior is demonstrated with acceptable frequency, the fourth principle becomes relevant. It appears that consistent reinforcement diminishes in effectiveness and that the probability of the desired behavior continuing to appear at the appropriate level is increased when the individual is unsure whether or not she will earn the reinforcement. In the case of our student, she raises her hand hoping to be reinforced and so long as reinforcement occurs on occasion, she raises her hand regularly. It is also true that she responds even when she receives only praise and is no longer given a token, a point that illustrates the fifth and last principle. Because social reinforcers are always paired with tangible reinforcers, it is possible to phase out the latter consequence over time and establish a response that can be generalized to a variety of situations.

Although behavioral treatments are accomplished by the systematic application of the principles of function, antecedent control, and reinforcement, the successful application of these techniques is not a matter of speculation. The adherence of this approach to scientific methodology mandates the use of research designs to investigate the effectiveness of each intervention. The interventionist plans and implements treatment strategies in such a way that their effectiveness can be evaluated objectively. In other words, the treatment itself must be an experiment that demonstrates that the intervention used was responsible for the behavioral change that occurred. Otherwise, even when behavior improves, the interventionist cannot be certain why. Applied experimental treatments of this type have been classified into two major categories: intrasubject and intersubject designs (Alberto & Troutman, 1990; Craighead, Kazdin, & Mahoney, 1976).

Experimental Designs. In *intrasubject design*, an individual's or group's performance is measured under varied circumstances. No comparisons with other persons or groups are required. For example, John's rate of computing arithmetic problems may be assessed in the presence and absence of the reinforcer, a complimentary note to his parents. If he is more efficient when reinforced, it can be assumed that the note to parents is an effective treatment. To ensure the validity of the conclusion, there should be alternating periods of reinforcement and no reinforcement.

Intersubject design involves between-group comparisons. Two or more groups are exposed to different treatments and their performances are compared. For example, John and his classmates might receive notes for parents whenever they solve arithmetic problems, whereas a control group receives no special reinforcement for that activity. The average performance of each group is compared. If John's group's average performance is significantly better than that of the control group, the effectiveness of the treatment is supported.

Both intrasubject and intersubject designs have been used extensively in behavioral treatment. As the examples given above demonstrate, intrasubject designs permit the interventionist to draw conclusions about specific individuals, whereas intersubject or group research does not. In other words, in intrasubject research, when John's performance on arithmetic problems was analyzed under two conditions, a complimentary note to his parents and no special reinforcer, the conclusion drawn pertained specifically to John. However, when the performance of two groups was compared, the conclusion pertained only to the group's responses; no assumptions could be made about group member John's specific response to the reinforcement. Even if he appeared subjectively to perform well, there is no evidence that he would not have done as well or better if he had been in the group that was not reinforced with a note to parents. Therefore, group or intersubject research is particularly valuable in demonstrating the general validity of an experimental assumption, for example, that children do better work when they receive positive notes to show to their parents. In contrast, intrasubject research tests whether an assumption applies in each unique case; thus, it minimizes the significance of individual differences in determining reinforcement or treatment strategies. When the treatment goal is the modification of an individual's specific problem behavior, intrasubject experimental design is extremely useful.

Four types of intrasubject research designs have been used in educational settings: (a) *reversal-replication*, or ABAB, design; (b) *multiple-baseline* design; (c) *changing-criterion* design; and (d) *multielement* design.

Reversal-Replication Design. The reversal, or ABAB, design is based on the premise that behavior change is contingent on the absence or presence of the reinforcer. Therefore, the occurrence of the behavior is measured under reinforced and nonreinforced conditions (as in the intrasubject example testing John's response to a positive note to his parents). The initial data recorded, Step 1(A), was briefly discussed earlier in the chapter; termed a *baseline*, it is evidence of the frequency or strength of the behavior without intervention. For example, John's usual performance on arithmetic problems can be measured as the number of problems completed correctly in one 30-minute period for 5 successive days. The amount of time required to establish a baseline varies with the behavior being assessed. However, care must be taken that the period of adaptation has passed, and the pattern of performance of the behavior should be relatively stable.

Step 2(B) is the treatment phase. The planned intervention is now implemented. John is reinforced for completing arithmetic problems in one 30-minute

228 ◇ Therapy and Interventions

period for 5 successive days. No change in John's production suggests that the treatment is ineffective. John may not respond well to the note to his parents as a reinforcer, or other variables may be interfering with the effectiveness of the reinforcer in this instance. An increase in John's production suggests but does not signify that the reinforcer was effective. John may do better simply because of novelty effect (a new experience), or Hawthorne effect (the tendency for individuals to perform better when they receive any type of special attention), or because of any number of other confounding variables.

At this point, Step 3(A), a return to Step 1(A) is implemented, and the program is reversed. The treatment is withdrawn, and the conditions existing before treatment are reestablished. If John's performance again returns to his baseline rate, there is increased evidence that the treatment may be a causal factor in his improvement. Finally, the last step to complete one replication, 4(B), is the reinstitution of the treatment. Once again, John's performance should accelerate to previously obtained heights if the treatment is effective. However, if the evidence supporting the value of the reinforcer is still not conclusive, for example, if John's performance in Step 4(B) improved but did not reach levels obtained in Step 2(B), or if the interventionist would like to evaluate results over longer periods of time, the replication can be repeated by returning to baseline conditions in Step 5(A) and treatment conditions in Step 6(B).

There are several variations of the reversal design. One involves no initial baseline measure and is used in instances where the individual has never demonstrated the target behavior. For example, an individual who cannot speak English has a zero baseline rate for uttering English sentences. The reversal design to be used is BAB. Another variation pertains to behaviors that cannot be reversed or returned to baseline conditions. If a child learned 100 new reading words under the experimental treatment condition of praise, the words will not be forgotten when the reinforcement is withdrawn. In these cases, the effectiveness of the reinforcer can be tested by withholding it from reading activities and applying it to a variety of other achievement activities, such as spelling, arithmetic, and so forth. If the child's level of performance on the reading activities diminishes, but the degree of efficiency on other activities increases, it would appear that the reinforcer is effective.

Although the reversal design is used often in educational research, it has certain limitations that frequently prevent the formation of definitive conclusions regarding treatment effectiveness. Kazdin (1975) demonstrated that behavior usually does not return to baseline rate during the repetition of Step A. The higher level of response without reinforcement may suggest that the treatment was not responsible for the change in behavior. However, it also may indicate that the treatment resulted in other associations that tend to keep responses accelerated. For example, John might have received parental rewards for better arithmetic production during Step 2(B). Although the teacher's positive note to his parents initiated his new response, its withdrawal does not diminish the other reinforcers that might have developed.

Another persistent problem is the continued possibility of results caused by the Hawthorne effect. If the effects were due to being singled out for treatment, rather than caused by the reinforcer, the predicted decrease and acceleration in performance during Steps 3(A) and 4(B), respectively, would still be likely to occur. This problem is always true in single-case ($N = 1$) studies and is more serious where the efficacy of treatments other than praise or attention is being evaluated.

A final problem, most significant for an interventionist who would apply this design in schools or clinics, pertains to ethics. Once an individual shows improved behavior, it often is not ethical to deliberately reverse the treatment and bring about an increased incidence of problem behavior. Obviously, there is a firm line between applied research with human beings and experimental laboratory investigations with animals that cannot be crossed in the name of science. Therefore, in using this design, the interventionist must maintain a clear vision of the general goal of behavioral therapy, to help the individual involved. If there is a question about the relative effectiveness of various reinforcers in increasing a child's adaptive behavior, it is perfectly reasonable to use the reversal steps in the design. In the long run, finding the best reinforcer will be in the child's best interest. Similarly, the reversal design may be used legitimately when the reversed step results in nothing more extreme than a brief period of decreases in academic achievement. The child will quickly regain accelerated levels in Step 4(B). The design is inappropriate when a child has improved control over debilitating behaviors such as fighting, stealing, setting fires, and so forth. Obviously, any technique that results even in a brief reoccurrence of those activities is not beneficial to the individual involved.

Multiple-Baseline Design. The multiple-baseline design, by introducing treatment at different points in time, demonstrates the causal relationship between treatment and behavior without returning to baseline conditions (Baer, Wolf, & Risley, 1968). One type of strategy, termed *multiple-baseline across behaviors*, involves two or more behaviors simultaneously. After baseline data have been gathered, treatment is provided for one behavior while the others remain untreated. When the treated behavior changes, the intervention is extended to the second problem behavior, and so on, until all problem behaviors are modified. If each behavior changes when the treatment is introduced, it is assumed that the treatment has caused the improvement. An example of this strategy might involve increasing John's achievement in reading and spelling as well as arithmetic. After his typical baseline performance is graphed in all three achievement areas, the treatment, a note to his parents, is applied initially to increase performance on arithmetic tasks. If performance improves, the treatment is maintained for arithmetic and extended to reading activities. Once reading improves, the treatment is extended to spelling tasks. Because his performance in each of these areas improved only when John received the treatment, it can be concluded that the reinforcer was responsible for the changes in his behavior.

A slightly different version of this type of design is termed *multiple-baseline across individuals*. In this type of application, data are gathered on a single behavior for two or more persons. Treatment is applied to one person while the others continue at the baseline rate. If the first person's behavior changes, the treatment is extended to another person, and so on until all persons receive the treatment. For example, the teacher might decide to help Leroy, Briana, and Ludwig improve their reading achievement. Reading is demonstrated by their ability to read short stories at 90% accuracy and answer correctly five comprehension questions. The treatment, reinforcement with tokens, is applied first to Leroy. If his efficiency improves, the treatment is extended to Briana. If Briana also improves in reading, the treatment is extended to Ludwig.

A third version of this design is *multiple-baseline across situations*. This strategy involves one behavior, any number of individuals, and several situations. For example, the reading program for the three children above might be conducted twice daily. In one situation, the token reinforcement system is used with all three and their behavior is recorded. In the other situation, no reinforcement is provided. Presumably, the children will be more productive in the first situation. After a period of time, reinforcement is introduced in the second situation with a predictable acceleration in achievement.

Although multiple-baseline designs avoid the ethical problems associated with reversal designs, they are not free from problems. There is some indication that reinforcement of one behavior indirectly affects the performance of other behaviors (Buell, Stoddard, Harris, & Baer, 1968). For example, Leroy may be reinforced only for achievement in mathematics, but his performance in other academic areas may also accelerate. Therefore, the evidence that the reinforcement caused his improved achievement is confounded.

Similarly, reinforcement provided for one individual may affect the behavior of others. When Leroy earns tokens for his efforts, Briana and Ludwig may try harder, even though they are not being given direct reinforcement. The same effect may be observed in varied situations, because behavior reinforced in one place may be demonstrated in another situation.

Clearly, these problems are more important to the behavioral scientist seeking a precise method of validating the effectiveness of the treatment than they are to the practitioner, who is more concerned about improved behavior. The fact that the effects of direct reinforcement may spread to other persons' behaviors or situations is an important positive benefit of treatment. It suggests that the notion of reinforcement is far more complex than it might initially appear to be and that individuals may begin patterns of self-reinforcements that are more powerful than the external variables controlled or manipulated by the interventionist. Possibly, the most significant effect of direct overt reinforcement is to "turn the tide" toward a more generalized demonstration of adaptive behaviors.

Changing-Criterion Design. The third intrasubject design, changing-criterion (Axelrod, Hall, Weis, & Rohrer, 1974), demonstrates the effectiveness of treatment by showing that it continues to change behavior when the criterion for reinforcement is altered. For instance, a single behavior, such as making negative remarks to others, may be selected for treatment. The initial criterion may be established at 50% of the average baseline utterances, which are 10 per school day. Reinforcement, a token, is awarded every time the behavior is not demonstrated more than 5 times. As the behavior diminishes, the criterion for reinforcement is established at 20% of the baseline utterances. To earn the token, the child must not utter more than two negative remarks per day. Ultimately, the criterion may preclude any negative remarks. The fact that the child decreases negative utterances to meet each new criterion level suggests that the treatment caused the behavioral change.

The changing-criterion design is extremely useful for gradually modifying behaviors. It reflects the behavioral emphasis on solving problems in small, sequenced steps rather than attempting to effect all-or-nothing changes in behavior. Although it appears to validate the effects of treatment, as with the other intrasubject designs, the evidence is not definitive. It is possible that initial changes in behaviors evoke reinforcement from other sources that are responsible for the continued behavioral modification. For example, the child who reduces his negative utterances may receive positive reinforcement from other sources, such as peer or parent approval with the token system having relatively little to do with the eventual discontinuation of the behavior. These treatment validation problems are difficult to overcome in single-case studies.

Multielement Design. The final intrasubject design to be discussed is called the multielement or alternating treatments design (Barlow & Hayes, 1979). This approach uses the strategy of random application of alternative treatments in varied situations with the same individual to establish causal relationships between treatment and behavior. For example, the teacher might wish to examine the effectiveness of four reinforcement strategies for altering Betty's inappropriate out-of-seat behavior. The teacher may devise Treatment A, a token for 100% in-seat behavior every hour; Treatment B, 5 minutes of free time at the end of the day for 100% in-seat behavior every hour; Treatment C, a note home to parents informing them of Betty's progress if she avoids inappropriate out-of-seat behavior for 4 hours of the school day; and Treatment D, no treatment or baseline conditions. The treatments are applied independently of Betty's behavior, on a random basis each day. Betty is informed each morning which treatment is in effect, and her inappropriate out-of-seat behavior is tabulated under each treatment condition over an extensive period of time. A comparison of her performance under each treatment condition reveals the relative effectiveness of each approach.

The multielement design has been found effective for investigating complex behaviors, such as motivating a class of hard-core underachievers to attempt academic tasks. Among the intrasubject intervention designs, it provides the most valid data about the causal relationship between treatment and behavior. It also provides objective information regarding the relative strength of alternative interventions. A disadvantage of this design is that the effects of any treatment may be influenced by the other treatments. For example, Betty may perform less competently when receiving tokens or free time because she prefers to be reinforced by a note to her parents. If any of the reinforcers were used alone, there might be very little difference in the rate of behavior they produce. Another disadvantage to this design is that it is elaborate and time-consuming to implement.

For the most part, intrasubject designs are easily applied by teachers in classroom situations. In fact, many teachers have probably used strategies such as the multiple-baseline across individuals in an informal way. For instance, the teacher finds that awarding John the privilege of being teacher's helper reduces his disruptive behavior, so she extends that reinforcer to another disruptive child. To apply such techniques more objectively requires only closer attention to data recording. The teacher no longer relies solely on impressions about treatment effectiveness but instead bases conclusions on recorded events.

Intersubject Designs. The alternative approach to empirical investigation of treatment effectiveness, intersubject designs, is less likely to be used by teachers because such designs do not provide data that are directly applicable to the solution of a specific individual's problems. However, the most basic design, control-group design, is not difficult to implement and should be more widely used in classroom situations.

The control group design compares the performance of at least two discrete groups of people. The treatment is administered to only one group (experimental group), while the other (control group) is maintained under normal or preexperimental conditions. The differences in the average performance of the experimental and control groups indicate the effectiveness of the treatment. For this technique to be used most effectively, children must be randomly assigned to each group. Random assignment ensures that preestablished differences in variables other than the treatment will not affect the outcome. For example, all kindergarten students in a school are randomly assigned to two classes. The techniques usually employed to assign children to kindergarten classes, such as their area of residence, are not employed to ensure that variables such as socioeconomic status do not influence the investigation. The experimental group is to receive concentrated instruction in oral language skills, while the control group receives the typical play-oriented kindergarten experience. At the end of the year, the respective oral language competence of the groups is measured and compared. If the treatment was effective, the experimental group will exceed their nontreated peers in oral language skills.

The control group design has distinct advantages over the typical educational approach used to measure children's gains in skill, pre–post testing. In school settings children are usually tested on a variable such as oral language ability, given a particular instructional intervention, and tested again at the end of the school year. Their gains in oral language skills are attributed to the instruction, and it is concluded that the instructional approach is an effective method of teaching. Both the attribution and conclusion may be erroneous, however, because the gains may have been due to extraneous variables such as maturation or increased test-taking skill. Also, without establishing a control group as a basis of comparison, it is impossible to know whether or not the children would have made greater gains from an alternative instructional approach.

This brief discussion of control group design barely scratches the surface. Much more information could be provided about this design, as well as other intersubject designs, but it is beyond the scope of this book. The interested reader should consult Campbell and Stanley (1963). The intent of this discussion is to suggest that it is not beyond the teacher's capabilities to conduct simple group studies. For instance, a teacher who suspects that children behave better when they are given 15 minutes of strenuous physical exercise after every hour of academic instruction can test that premise by randomly assigning students to an experimental or a control group, giving the experimental group physical exercise and the control group a passive activity, and comparing their behavior on any number of criteria. This simple experiment should verify the teacher's impressions about how to best manage the students.

The principles used in observing, recording, and modifying an individual's behavior as it occurs constitute the backbone of behavioral therapy. The impact of this approach has been particularly pronounced in special education, and many examples of techniques that have proved valuable in school settings are available. Recently, an extension of ABA emerged as a powerful tool. Functional behavioral assessment is used to determine specific variables that either trigger or maintain behaviors, as well as to design effective behavioral interventions.

Functional Behavioral Assessment

Functional behavioral assessment (FBA) is based on the idea that all behaviors serve a function, otherwise they would not be maintained. FBA denotes a significant shift and advancement in the field of behavioral therapy. Dunlap and colleagues (1993) defined FBA as "a process of identifying functional relationships between environmental events and the occurrence and nonoccurrence of a target behavior." Effective positive interventions require valid preintervention data about the functions of problem behaviors (Carr, Robinson, & Palumbo, 1990). Although direct observation is the preferred method of identifying these relationships, rating scales and interviews have also been used.

One primary goal of FBA is to derive accurate hypotheses connecting the target behaviors and the environment. Two major categories of relationships are identified: (a) the operations of a reinforcement contingency, including positive reinforcement or negative reinforcement, and (b) a controlling antecedent stimulus (Dunlap et al., 1993). An example of an undesirable behavior being maintained by a positive reinforcement contingency is classroom personnel's giving attention to a child who is disrupting others by swearing, walking around the room, or taking other students' materials. If a negative reinforcement relationship is in operation, these same behaviors may be maintained by the disruptive student's escaping an unpleasant task, for example, not completing his math work. A controlling antecedent might be influencing the behavior if it occurs during a specific activity (lunch, reading), a specific time period (midmorning), or with certain personnel (the music teacher).

FBA is usually conducted in four stages. Stage 1 begins with initial observations focusing on the child's behaviors and contributing environmental factors. During Stage 2 a team meeting is conducted during which principal players such as the teachers and the school psychologist brainstorm possible controlling variables and develop hypotheses. Stage 3, called functional analysis, involves manipulation in the classroom to test the hypotheses and determine experimentally which variables are actually associated with the occurrence or nonoccurrence of the target behavior. Stage 4 results in intervention development based on the function of the behavior (Dunlap et al., 1993).

Stages 1 and 2: Initial Observations and Brainstorming

FBA is an extension of ABA and so uses the same methodologies, strategies, and categories of observation. Stage 1, making initial observations, is an expanded version of the ABC analysis. Rather than the three-column, antecedent–behavior–consequence observation form, FBA utilizes a six-column data collection form as shown in Figure 5.3. Stage 2, includes a team meeting designed to review the initial observations and brainstorm ideas about controlling variables, consequences, possible functions, and alternative skills. At the end of Stage 2, the team should have completed the FBA form.

Setting Events and Antecedents. Both setting events (or slow triggers) and antecedents (or fast triggers) occur prior to the target behaviors and therefore are antecedents. The distinction is that setting events set the stage for the behavior to occur; they make it more likely that the target behavior may occur but are not the direct catalyst. If we think of the child as a pot of water on a stove, the setting events are what set the pot to simmer. For example, if refusal to do work, which escalates into disruption of class, are the target behaviors, setting events that may result in the child's being more likely to engage in these behaviors may include environmental variables (the room's being too hot or a substitute teacher), interpersonal variables (an argument at home or on the bus on the way to school), instructional variables (a writing task, large-group instruction), or internal variables (not getting enough sleep, feeling sick). In contrast, antecedents occur immediately before the target behavior. Examples of antecedents are levying consequences, giving corrective feedback, refusing a student's request to use the bathroom, and giving a direction to begin work. A typical scenario might play out like this: A student may enter the classroom in a bad mood after not having enough sleep and having a fight on the bus (setting events). However, the teacher, using good management skills, asks the student what is wrong, helps him talk about the fight, and gets him to sit in his seat and begin work. However, an hour later during language arts when the student is required to engage in a writing task, which he does not enjoy, frustration mounts (antecedent). The student leaves his desk and begins walking around the room and making noises (target behavior). Then the vice principal enters the classroom and tells the student to report for detention after school due to the fight on the bus (antecedent). In response to the fast trigger, the student tips over a desk and leaves the room (target behaviors).

Different types of setting events may affect the probability of the occurrence of challenging behaviors by students with emotional and behavioral problems. Internal or medical setting events include lack of sleep, hunger, thirst, illness, needing medication, and such conditions as obsessive-compulsive

Setting events (slow triggers)	Antecedents (fast triggers): What happens before the behavior occurs?	Problem behaviors:	Consequences: What happens after the behavior occurs? (adults, peers, tasks)	Possible functions: What does the student get or avoid by doing the behavior?	Alternative skills: What are the appropriate behaviors to be demonstrated?

Figure 5.3. Functional behavioral assessment observation form.

disorder, posttraumatic stress, and attention-related problems. Non–school-based setting events include a chaotic home life, parentalization, feeling stressed or overwhelmed, rushed morning routines, oversleeping, and conflict prior to leaving for school. General school-related setting events include forgetting homework, failing a test, getting in an argument with another student, facing changes in routine or schedule, having a substitute teacher, and being in rooms that are too hot or too noisy. Specific environments may serve as setting events. For example, behavior problems are more likely to occur in the hallway, playground, and cafeteria and during wait or transition times. Classroom-based or instructional setting events found to be related to problem behaviors in children with emotional and behavioral problems include low versus high levels of praise, no self-monitoring versus self-monitoring, not ignoring versus ignoring, no attention versus attention, no choice versus low-versus high-preference tasks, long versus short tasks, far versus near teacher proximity, and purposeful and specific instructional tasks (e.g., spelling or math) versus analogue tasks (Dunlap et al., 1993). Antecedents that frequently trigger behavioral outbursts include teacher direction, denial of a request, corrective feedback, levying consequences, student errors, peer insults or teasing, and the assignment of work that the student feels is too difficult.

Problem Behaviors and Consequences. In FBA problem or target behaviors are defined in the same way as in ABA. They need to be operationalized as specific behaviors that are observable and measurable. Consequences—what happens after the behavior occurs—are also similar to those observed in ABA. They require direct observation of adults, peers, and task demands. Possible consequences are redirection by teacher, peer attention, a visit to the counselor's office, or a substitute assignment.

Possible Functions. Functions can be categorized into two major types: what is gotten or what is avoided. Target behaviors can get children access to adult or peer attention, access to desired activities, material rewards, control, status, or sensory stimulation. Target behaviors can also result in students being able to avoid undesirable activities, adult or peer attention, loss of status, frustration, failure, embarrassment, or sensory stimulation. Upon reviewing this list of functions, most adults will agree that the functions themselves are reasonable. Most adults want attention, access to desired activities, material rewards, control over their lives, status, and sensory stimulation. Similarly, adults generally want to avoid undesirable activities, contact with people they do not like, frustration, failure, and embarrassment; at times, adults also want to relax and avoid stimulation. Therefore, it is not the functions of the behaviors that are problematic but the inappropriate behaviors students engage in to obtain the functions.

In attempting to determine the function of a target behavior, if the behavior is followed consistently by peer attention, one might hypothesize that the behavior is maintained by getting peer attention. However, if the student is sent to the counselor's office, the function may be either to escape work or gain the attention of a desired adult, the counselor.

Alternative Skills. Recent work in FBA has shown the benefit in using an instructional or skill-building model to develop appropriate skills to take the place of inappropriate target behaviors. For example, negotiating a less frustrating task would be an alternative skill if the function of the disruptive behavior was escaping the task. Asking to see the counselor would be an effective alternative skill if the function was to gain access to a desired adult. Focusing on alternative skills has three primary benefits. First, it allows teachers to apply an instructional model to changing behavior; teaching students what to do is consistent with their role as teachers. Second, teaching alternative skills prepares students to function more effectively in their environments. Finally, focusing on alternative skills development avoids the use of a reductive approach to behavior change, where the emphasis is on eliminating problem behaviors without providing students with an adaptive way to get what they need. Reductive approaches stem from a control model, which has proved ineffective. Using the functional model, one can assume that challenging behaviors will persist or change topographies unless the child or adolescent is provided with an adaptive alternative that will enable him to meet the function of the behavior. The logic underlying a functional model, which has proved experimentally and practically sound, is also the logic behind establishing communicative alternatives to socially motivated problem behaviors (Doss & Reichle, 1989).

Hypothesis Development. Developing accurate hypotheses concerning the controlling variables is critical to developing effective intervention strategies. The hypothesis statement takes the following form: When (*slow and fast triggers*), the student will (*target behavior*) to get/avoid (*function*). For example, the following four hypotheses might be generated about a student's behavior:

- When tired and assigned an undesirable task (writing), Simon will leave his seat and make noises to escape from the task.
- When assigned an undesirable task, Simon will leave his seat and make noises to get positive attention from his peers.
- When in a fight and then given consequences, Simon will physically act out and leave the classroom to express anger and avoid fighting with the teacher.

- When in a fight and then given consequences, Simon will physically act out and leave the classroom to gain access to the guidance counselor and her office.

Stage 3: Functional Analysis

Dunlap and colleagues (1993) used functional analysis in the classroom to determine experimentally which variables are associated with the occurrence or nonoccurrence of the target behavior. By manipulating classroom variables such as high-demand versus low-demand tasks, near versus far teacher proximity, short versus long tasks, choice versus no choice, and attention versus no attention, they were able to determine under which conditions the target behavior was most likely to occur. Although this step may be cumbersome and may require additional personnel, school faculty can adapt this procedure to provide important information about the true associations between target behaviors and environmental factors. For example, if the teacher alters writing tasks with nonwriting tasks across a number of language arts lessons and observes the frequency of out-of-seat and disruptive behaviors, she will be able to determine whether writing tasks are fast triggers. Teachers can also easily alter proximity and amounts of praise systematically to examine their effects on behavior. Once the associations are established, goals and objectives can be established and interventions can be developed.

Stage 4: Intervention Development

Although behavioral interventions are still sometimes classified by the topography of the behavior, a more useful approach is to base and address intervention development on the function of the behavior. For example, traditionally the interventionist might have looked at interventions designed to stop tantrums, disruption, or refusal to do work. However, a variety of diverse behaviors such as throwing tantrums, fighting, disrupting class, getting out of seat, avoiding tasks, and withdrawing socially may require similar intervention plans if the behaviors serve the same function, for example, getting attention. Similarly, the same behavior in two different situations or children will require different interventions if the functions they serve differ across settings or children. For example, out-of-seat behavior may serve to gain teacher attention in one setting, whereas in another it may serve to give the student access to social time with peers or to escape from work. In this second case, different interventions will be required to effectively address the different functions out-of-seat behavior serves.

Teachers of students with emotional and behavioral problems are presented daily with a host of challenging behaviors that will require remediation, intervention, and instruction. These behaviors may include calling out, refusal to do work, getting out of seat, crying, throwing tantrums, cursing, making sarcastic or derogatory remarks, leaving the room, thumb-sucking, elective mutism, isolated or withdrawn behavior, excessive movement, destruction of property, self-abuse, and aggression. Other issues that may arise include behaviors associated with hysteria, depression, obsession, psychosis, compulsion, and phobias. School personnel should remember to look initially at the schoolwide, situation-specific, and classroom management systems that are operating. These behavior management systems should ensure that general environmental conditions serve to support appropriate positive behaviors and to reduce problem behaviors. If these management systems are well developed and implemented and behavior problems persist, then school personnel must turn their attention to ABA, individual functional assessment, and development of an individual behavior plan for the target student.

Whatever the behavior or the function of the behavior, the goals of behavioral interventions are (a) to engineer the environment to both decrease the probability of the occurrence of a problem behavior and increase the likelihood of the occurrence of the alternative prosocial behavior and (b) to teach students more appropriate behaviors to get what they need from the environment (obtain the function). In essence, the goal is to render the inappropriate challenging behaviors ineffective and replace them with more effective, appropriate behaviors that serve the same function.

Antecedent Interventions. During this final stage of FBA, interventions are developed based on observed associations delineated in the hypotheses. Although they often are not as widely used, antecedent interventions are far more powerful than consequential interventions. Antecedent interventions are designed around the slow and fast triggers prompting challenging behaviors to occur. For example, in the case of Simon, discussed in the previous section, if fighting at home is identified as a setting event (slow trigger) for Simon's disruptive behaviors, then an antecedent intervention can be designed to address his response to the fighting at home. For example, the teacher might provide a safe, quiet space for Simon to go to upon arriving at school; take the time to talk to Simon about the fight; and teach him strategies to deal with the feelings of fear, anger, or anxiety prompted by the fight. Relaxation training and journal writing might also prove effective antecedent interventions.

Students who respond aggressively to being told what to do often benefit from antecedent interventions that provide choices such as "Would you like to do the odd or even math problems on page 67?" Providing academic tasks at the child's instructional level (rather than frustration or mastery level) is a very effective antecedent strategy resulting in reduced behavior problems. Another example is having a student who exhibits problem behaviors in the hallways repeat the hall rules before leaving the room. Teachers can alter how they give directions and corrective feedback as part of an antecedent intervention.

Because the antecedents take place prior to the occurrence of the behavior, manipulating them may result in the elimination of problem behaviors, rather than their reinforcement, which may be the result with consequential interventions. For example, if it is determined that Simon's out-of-seat and noisemaking behaviors are motivated by escaping writing activities, alternatives for writing (using a word box or magnetic poetry kit, dictating into a tape recorder, using a computer for word processing) could be substituted. Also, the writing task could be followed with high-preference activities that are motivating. Simon could also be taught a more adaptive alternative response, such as asking to take a break when he begins to be frustrated during a writing task. If however, his out-of-seat and noisemaking behaviors serve the function of gaining positive peer attention, then the other students should be taught to ignore and provide more appropriate avenues for Simon to get the attention of the class. The intervention must be paired to the function of the target behavior to be effective. Similarly, if leaving the room provides a way of expressing anger and avoiding fighting with the teacher, Simon will need to be taught more appropriate ways to express anger. If, however, Simon leaves the room to gain access to the counselor, sit in her office, listen to her talk to other students, and gain a "friendly ear," then his access to the counselor will have to be barred for inappropriate behaviors and opportunities provided for him to visit the counselor when he behaves appropriately.

In addition to allowing manipulation of the antecedents of problem behaviors and thus the behavior's elimination, antecedent interventions have several other advantages, including the following: (a) the teacher or interventionist may be in direct control of antecedent stimuli; (b) antecedent interventions are more instructional in approach and therefore more consistent with the role of the teacher; and (c) they provide strategies for children and adolescents to use that are portable or generalizable to other situations.

Functions of Behaviors and Intervention Approaches

Access to Adult or Peer Attention

A large number of disruptive behaviors may be maintained by the target childs' gaining access to adult or peer attention. One sign is that the occurrence of the problem behavior is followed by attention from either the teacher, teacher assistant, or fellow students. Common problem behaviors include calling out, being out of seat, being the "class clown," and disrupting instruction. To help determine if a problem behavior may serve the function of gaining access to adult attention, teachers can concentrate on giving students high levels of attention for appropriate behaviors and observe whether or not problem behavior decreases. Ignoring problem behavior may also be tried as a functional manipulation, but a response burst (temporary increase in the behavior) may occur. In addition, if the behavior serves to get attention and attention is denied, the child may escalate the behavior to where attention must be given or a new problem behavior may emerge as a way for the child to get the attention he needs. Once it is determined that attention is the primary function of the behavior, an intervention must be developed that will replace inappropriate attention-getting behavior with more appropriate attention-getting behavior. For example, Mr. Andrew may decide to ignore Collin's calling-out behavior (ignoring) and give him scheduled attention every 10 minutes for appropriate behaviors. In this way Collin gets what he needs, attention, for acceptable behaviors and is denied attention for unacceptable behaviors.

To develop effective interventions for behaviors maintained by attention, it must be determine whose attention is critical. If, for example, Collin's peers laugh when he becomes the class clown, then the intervention would have to target peer behavior, as well as address Collin's need to be the center of attention. Mr. Andrew could offer Collin a daily or weekly comedy spot for which he could prepare material and practice during the school day. Language arts, mathematics, politics, and history might be incorporated into this creative project. In addition, the class could be given a reward (10 points a period) for ignoring Collin's clowning, and a larger reward at the end of the week if 250 points are earned. Collin has been given an acceptable way of gaining peer attention but has been denied attention for unacceptable behaviors. If clowning occurs only during certain time periods, such as mathematics period or in the afternoon, then the behavior plan need only target those times. Another source of attention is from ancillary school personnel such as the teaching assistant, guidance counselor, or principal. Often teachers send very disruptive students out of the room for discipline reasons, to talk to someone, or simply to cool down. If the disruptive behavior is maintained by the attention of ancillary personnel, then the behavior will persist. Scheduling time with these favorite people a few times a week, teaching students to ask to go see them appropriately, and developing a behavior plan that reduces the disruption may be helpful in these situations.

Escaping Attention

Students may also wish to avoid contact or attention with certain individuals, including professional staff and peers. If the teacher and the student or the student and a classmate have a particularly difficult relationship, then behaviors that result in the removal of the student or classmate from the room may be maintained. In these cases, teachers must examine their own verbal and instructional behavior to determine whether they are communicating negative messages or a lack of confidence to the student. Conflict resolution and relationship-building activities may need to be built into the behavioral program to reestablish positive interactions between the teacher or peer and the target student. In Chapter 10, "Play Therapy," play activities are discussed as a means of establishing rapport or renegotiating difficult relationships.

Achieving Access to Desired Activities or Material Rewards

Children and adolescents may also engage in challenging behaviors to gain access to desired activities or material rewards. Often this access is accidentally provided, as in the case of a child's being sent to the office for cursing at a teacher. The attention of the secretary, being able to listen in on the workings of the hub of the school, and even getting to deliver messages or stuff mailboxes are all examples of inadvertently reinforcing the inappropriate behavior with desired activities. Another example is allowing a student to work on the computer after she refuses to do the assigned task and disrupts the class. Material awards can also be inadvertently provided, as in the case of the in-school suspension room teacher who gives out food treats for good behavior in the room. To address these situations requires behavioral interventions that provide opportunities for the student to get access to the desired activities or to get material rewards in appropriate ways, most effectively by engaging in behaviors that are incompatible with the challenging behavior, for example, completing work or raising her hand. Another example is when a child leaves the classroom and runs around the halls. For some students, the act of running or running and being chased is the desired activity. In these cases, teachers should build physical activity into the schedule. For young children for whom it is developmentally appropriate, teachers may even provide opportunities to play "catch me."

Impromptu behavior management tools can also lead to students' gaining desired activities or rewards for inappropriate behaviors. These impromptu plans are usually established with the student after she acts out and generally take the form of a negotiation: "If you do the rest of your math without disrupting class, you can earn two pretzels." The student quickly learns that if she acts out, she can bargain for a desired activity or material reward. In these situations behavioral interventions must be developed proactively, not reactively or "on the spot."

The difference between skill and performance deficits also must be considered when addressing problem behaviors (see Chapter 7, "Educational Therapy," for additional information). Some children do not know how to seek attention appropriately (skill deficit) and will require instruction. Behavioral plans for students who know how to behave appropriately but who still engage in challenging behaviors (performance deficit) can be developed around reinforcement rather than instruction.

Quality-of-life issues need to be considered when developing interventions addressing the function of behaviors. Children must have regular access to opportunities to engage in desired activities or obtain material rewards. For students with poor quality of life (i.e., minimal opportunities at home or school), establishing time both earned and unearned to have fun and meet developmental needs is critical and can go a long way in alleviating behavioral difficulties.

Avoiding or Escaping Tasks

Like many adults, children are likely to attempt to avoid or escape certain tasks for various reasons. Believing the task is too difficult, not knowing how to start, having experienced previous failures, or simply not liking the task are all reasons for task-avoidant behaviors. Task avoidance can take many forms, including verbal refusal, getting up and walking around the room, starting a fight with a peer or the teacher, engaging in other tasks, procrastination, and disrupting instruction. One key to deciding whether a behavior serves the function of task avoidance is if it ceases when the task is withdrawn ("Why don't you help me with the bulletin board instead?"), delayed ("You can do this later"), or modified ("OK, just do the even numbers). Another indication that the function of a challenging behavior is avoidance is if the behavior frequently occurs during particular academic subjects or particular academic tasks (e.g., writing or cooperative learning). Behavioral interventions designed to help students who escape tasks include teaching or providing them with appropriate ways to take brief breaks when frustrated, chunking (helping them break down a task into manageable components), and providing them with choices of work when appropriate. Behavioral goals such as "Joshua will begin academic work within 30 seconds after directions are given" can be assigned, monitored, and rewarded. It is critical that academic tasks be presented at the student's instructional level in each subject to avoid frustration and boredom, which are frequent antecedents for acting-out behavior in students with EBDs. Contingencies for task completion and accuracy, including daily grades in each subject area, are critical and should be provided immediately for students who frequently act out to avoid work. Teachers should also circulate and provide positive and corrective feedback for all students in the first few moments of independent seat work to avoid students' finishing part of the assignment incorrectly and needing to redo work. Using the Premack principle by following the completion of an unpreferred activity with a highly preferred one can be helpful, as can alternating preferred and nonpreferred tasks.

Some students, especially those with a "tough" image, may prefer to avoid tasks they are not good at rather than risk loss of status in front of their peers. Defiant, disruptive, and even aggressive behaviors may be engaged in, even to the extent of being removed from the classroom, thus successfully avoiding the task. In this way their status as tough and willing to stand up to the teacher is maintained without the risk of failure or embarrassment in front of peers. This is often the case for students who read or do mathematics well below grade level, whose abilities may embarrass them. Interventions in these cases must be designed to help the students maintain their status as leaders while still receiving the instruction they need.

Extreme cases of task avoidance or escaping school include cutting class or being absent or truant. Behavioral interventions for these situations need to address what is so aversive about the school or class environment and how to alleviate those aversive situations. Providing students with purposeful instruction and success must be considered as integral components of such a plan.

Control

At times, students will engage in behaviors to gain control over a situation or some part of their lives. An indicator that problem behaviors may be control driven is the students' initially refusing to begin a task or follow a direction but later, at a self-chosen time, doing so willingly. Self-determination and autonomy are important and positive attributes often denied students with special needs, whose days are often regimented and predetermined. Control-based interventions generally involve the use of choice. Giving directions in the form of simple choices rather than commands may alleviate a significant percentage of challenging behaviors that are control driven. Commands such as "Do the first 20 problems on page 82" or "Write two paragraphs in your journal" tend to result in refusals. Substituting questions like "Would you like to do the odd- or even-numbered problems?" or "Would you like to use markers or pens to complete your journal today?" or "Would you like to read at your desk or on the carpet?" can go a long way to reducing problem behaviors.

A student who needs control in his life may also be allowed to schedule his work at certain times of the school day or decide which tasks to complete when presented with a series of independent practice activities. Additionally, giving students important and complex jobs that they can organize and carry out (such as helping younger students or developing a bulletin board or learning center) may also help meet the need for control. Instruction in self-control strategies also may prove beneficial in these situations.

Status

Many students with EBD are known throughout the school. Although their status may be negative in orientation, it is nonetheless status. Status includes components of recognition, leadership, belonging, and prestige and is especially important in middle school and high school. Behaviors that elicit or maintain negative status may take the shape of defiance, disruption, refusal, cursing, and disrespecting or insulting teachers or peers. Students who engage in these behaviors to gain status require interventions that enable them to "not lose face" and help them to establish positive status. Giving them high-status jobs or important leadership positions can often prove very effective.

In a middle school in Philadelphia, a student who engaged in high levels of disrespectful, disruptive, and verbally aggressive behaviors was given the job of "school greeter." The job did not exist before and was created as part of his behavior plan based on a functional assessment indicating status as the controlling variable. The job required training in how to greet guests and dignitaries at the door, reciting a brief history of the school, and giving a tour of the school facilities. On days when he was to serve as greeter, he was expected to wear a shirt and tie. He also was required to carry a walkie-talkie to communicate with the principal as to his and the visitors' location. Although not required to earn the job initially, because it was part of his behavior plan, he was required to stay out of trouble (come to school on time, act respectfully, complete schoolwork, and not engage in verbal aggression) to do the job. The intervention proved highly effective; the student engaged in only one instance of problem behavior in the 2 years he held the job of school greeter. Some school staff were initially opposed to his being "rewarded" for his problem behaviors, believing the job should have gone to a "good" student. However, the effectiveness of the intervention proved the power of functional assessment. Just as we would not withhold appropriate academic intervention from a student with learning disabilities, students with EBDs have the right to effective behavioral interventions.

Sensory Stimulation or Physical Release

Some students engage in challenging behaviors because those behaviors increase or decrease sensory stimulation or provide necessary physical release. Behaviors serving these functions may be as diverse as self-stimulation (finger-flicking, noisemaking), self-soothing (rocking or obsessively touching clothing or other appealing textures), masturbation, high levels of activity (frequent getting out of seat, running around the room, playing with objects), and physical aggression toward objects or people. Although the topographies of these behaviors differ, they all may serve the function of bringing the physical body back to stasis. All people, including students with emotional and behavioral challenges, have optimal levels of stimulation and relaxation that are individual specific. Self-regulatory behaviors, such as turning down the radio or getting up to stretch one's legs while studying, are examples. For students with autism or mental retardation, obsessive-compulsive disorder, attention-deficit disorder, hyperactivity, or posttraumatic stress, self-stimulatory and self-soothing mechanisms are critical for feelings of safety and comfort. The goal for interventions designed to address issues of physical stimulation is to provide students with socially appropriate, nondisruptive ways to either increase or decrease their activity. Altering the topography of the behavior or substituting socially appropriate behaviors for socially unacceptable behaviors is one approach to intervention development. For example, Sally may be given a lollipop to suck on to replace thumb-sucking; Steven may rub a worry stone rather than play with objects in his desk. Teaching students to engage in relaxation exercises or to use verbal self-soothing statements may be effective. Listening to a Walkman playing classical music may substitute for constant noisemaking. For students who need increased levels of physical activity, teachers can incorporate workout times into the schedule. Workouts should be simple and able to be performed in the classroom and may include sit-ups, push-ups, or yoga and meditation, depending on the goal of the intervention.

For some students, aggression or destruction may serve to release emotional and physical energy. This is often the case with students whose teacher reports that "you can watch his anger build and build, then he explodes, and after that he is fine." In this case, teaching students to engage in aggression replacement training or to do release-type physical activity prior to exploding may be helpful.

School-Based Applications

The bulk of the research into the effectiveness of behavioral interventions in schools supports their usefulness in general and also presents additional information about the methodological procedures that have proved particularly beneficial in facilitating behavioral change. School-based applications of behavioral therapy can be categorized into four overlapping areas: (a) schoolwide positive behavior management, (b) situation-specific behavior management, (c) classroom management, and (d) individual behavior plans. Traditionally, a great deal of research has focused on the development of individual behavior plans for students displaying severe behavioral or emotional challenges. However, managing students' problem behaviors, or instilling "discipline," has been consistently identified by the public and school personnel as the single most troublesome issue confronting schools (Center & McKittrick, 1987; Nelson & Colvin, 1996; Walker et al., 1996). Because, the incidents of severe problem behaviors in schools has increased remarkably over the past 10 years, researchers have begun to broaden their perspective and apply behavioral principles to general school-based interventions. Recently, some researchers have begun to develop a systems model of behavioral therapy for schools (Colvin, Kameenui, & Sugai, 1993; Nelson, 1996; Nelson & Colvin, 1996; Walker et al., 1996). Schools are viewed as interwoven systems in which the behavior of students needs to be effectively managed. Three general systems—schoolwide, situation specific, and classroom management—form the foundation to effectively promote positive, and minimize negative, behaviors in schools.

Schoolwide Positive Behavior Management

The past decade has seen a proliferation of schoolwide programs whose goal is to support and increase prosocial and socially desirable behaviors (Colvin et al., 1993; Nelson, 1996; Nelson & Colvin, 1996; Walker et al., 1996). These programs were developed in response to the ineffective punishment-oriented and reactive approaches traditionally used in schools. These traditional approaches ignored appropriate behaviors and punished inappropriate behaviors through the use of reprimands, loss of privileges, calls or notes home, detention, suspension, and expulsion. Those strategies have proved to be more destructive than constuctive.

Positive schoolwide programs are designed to be proactive. They establish systematic and consistent approaches to increase appropriate or desired behaviors and decrease problem behaviors. Packaged school discipline programs such as Assertive Discipline (Canter, 1976) and positive discipline (Clarizio, 1981; Nelson, 1987) have been employed by a number of schools. Although theoretically these programs have much to offer, they often leave the details of procedural implementation unaddressed. As Colvin and colleagues (1993) pointed out, the details about how to establish criteria, what format awards and their presentation should take, program dissemination, and how to obtain consistency of implementation are not included.

More recently, several empirically validated programs have emerged that deal directly with how to implement schoolwide programs designed to build and maintain appropriate behaviors. Project PREPARE (Colvin et al., 1993), developed by the University of Oregon, is one such program. The two major goals of Project PREPARE are (a) to develop preservice and inservice models of staff development to ensure effective and consistent implementation of the schoolwide program and (b) to apply valid instructional principles to managing and maintaining behaviors in schools. Project PREPARE has six guidelines and a curriculum model for establishing a schoolwide proactive system. The six guidelines are as follows:

1. *Establish agreement among staff on a basic approach to managing behavior.* Researchers and practitioners recommend an instructional approach to behavioral problems that conceptualizes managing social behavior problems in much the same way as teachers manage instructional problems. When a student makes an academic error, correction procedures are implemented, resulting in additional instruction, practice, and feedback. If academic problems become persistent, teachers diagnose the problems, alter instruction, and provide still more practice and feedback. Teachers who accept the remedial approach to academic instruction will understand and appreciate its application to social behavior and view it, rather than the punishment approach, as more consistent with their role as a teacher (Walker et al., 1996).

2. *Establish school discipline as an instrument for student success.* The schoolwide plan serves the primary function of allowing learning to take place effectively and efficiently. Positive approaches are more likely than negative approaches to remove behavior problems as impediments to teaching and learning.

3. *Utilize and rely on proactive approaches.* The trend in managing behavior at the school level is toward positive, preventive, and problem-solving approaches and away from punitive approaches. Students are more responsive to positive approaches, and both school personnel and students rate them as more desirable.

4. *The principal must provide visible and supportive leadership.* Schoolwide programs must be systematically planned and adopted and implemented by all staff in order to be effective. Strong leadership and ongoing support from the principal is required to accomplish these goals.

5. *Staff must rely on collegial commitment.* To be effective, school-based plans must be implemented with a high degree of fidelity by all school staff. A united

commitment to the program is required for success. Gersten, Walker, and Darch (1988) pinpointed three critical variables to establishing collegiality: (a) staff working together, (b) a comprehensive framework or philosophy, and (c) concrete, specific plans. Project PREPARE is a template for school staff to use to establish a schoolwide positive behavior management plan that is specific to the school and that all staff can commit to.

6. *Utilize effective staff development and teacher change practices.* Implementation of any schoolwide program of behavior management requires staff development and staff behavior change. The teachers' belief that the program will bring about the desired change and their collegiality have been identified as critical variables in producing changes in teacher behavior (Colvin, Tobin, & Schacker, 1994).

The Project PREPARE curriculum model specifies five major components of schoolwide programs. The first component, a *statement of purpose*, spells out the reason for the program. Most schoolwide discipline plans are established to develop student behaviors and organizational structures that ensure an orderly learning environment. The second component, *behavior expectations*, are rules about desired behaviors or actions that facilitate the teaching and learning process. Expectations are developed for both general and specific settings. For example, a general expectation is that students will behave in a safe manner, whereas noise and activity expectations may differ across settings (library, hallway, playground). Five guidelines are delineated for establishing behavior expectations:

1. The number of behavioral expectations should be limited to three or four.

2. Behavioral expectations should be short, stated in positive terms, and use common language.

3. Identify specific behaviors to illustrate the range of acceptable variability.

4. Identify positive and negative examples.

5. Define a clear process and specific timelines for establishing the expectations, including who will decide (all staff, departments, students), how decisions will be made (small or large group), and the specific plan for training students and staff and disseminating information about the program.

Examples of general behavioral expectations might include managing one's self and respecting others' rights and property. Setting specific expectations for the cafeteria might include maintaining your voice at a conversational level and disposing of your trash after eating.

The third curriculum component is a continuum of *procedures for teaching schoolwide behavioral expectations*. This includes acknowledging students who demonstrate expected behavior, teaching students to demonstrate desired behaviors, and identifying ways to maintain or increase the rate of acceptable behaviors. Instructional procedures, including instruction, modeling, practice, error correction, and rewards, are used to teach desired behaviors. Award systems are developed with specific criteria for earning the award, when awards will be presented, and how awards and expectations will be communicated or disseminated to both the school community and the community at large.

A continuum of *procedures for correcting problem behaviors* constitutes the fourth component and includes defining and categorizing the problem behaviors and systematic procedures for changing those behaviors. Procedures are presented for correcting minor behavior problems, beginning with ignoring paired with praise of a student who is displaying the expected behavior, redirecting paired with positive reinforcing compliance, teach–practice–reinforce, delivering warning, and, finally, delivering penalty or revoking privileges. Finally, *procedures for record keeping, evaluation, and dissemination* are presented to track student performance and evaluate the schoolwide program.

Lewis (1997) developed both a schoolwide system for behavioral support and a system for training teachers to implement it. Lewis's Effective Behavioral Support (EBS) reinforces the need for teacher commitment and delineates staff responsibilities concerning system implementation and monitoring of one another's behaviors. Two other behavior management programs are Project DESTINY (Cheney, Barringer, Upham, & Manning, 1995) and Project ACHIEVE (Knoff, Batsche, & Knoster, 1997). All of the projects adopt a behavioral therapy approach requiring observation and recording of behavior, intervention development, and analysis of intervention results. Results from these projects indicate that schoolwide systems of positive behavioral support are extremely effective ways to increase appropriate school behaviors and decrease problem behaviors.

Situation-Specific Behavior Management

Schoolwide behavior management systems address multiple settings, such as the cafeteria, playground, and hallways. These specific situations or settings can be analyzed using applied behavioral analysis principles and behavioral therapies as well. For example, observing the lunchroom may show that many problems occur when students leave their seats to retrieve forgotten items (straws, napkins, forks). If lunchroom monitors wear aprons with large pockets and carry those items, students can raise their hands and request the item without leaving their seats. Also, in an elementary school in Philadelphia, teaching staff to use, and students to respond to, a transition device called a color wheel helped students to discern the appropriate times for getting food (green), eating (yellow), and cleaning up (red). Within 2 weeks, lunchtime discipline referrals had decreased by 65% (Ager, personal correspondence). Instituting organized recess, placing recess before rather than after lunch, and strategizing effective arrival and dismissal procedures are other simple changes that have been shown to significantly reduce behavior problems in situation-specific settings (Nelson, 1996).

Classroom Management

Bullock, Ellis, and Wilson (1994) identified the need for teachers, particularly teachers of children with emotional and behavioral problems, to be competent classroom managers as the major competency required for success. Classroom management strategies "provide the structure for implementation of behavior management strategies" to decrease inappropriate behaviors and increase appropriate behaviors (Gunter & Denny, 1996, p. 15). In other words, effective behavioral therapy is contingent on effective classroom management. Ager (2000) delineated eight classroom management strategies or behavior basics based on behavioral principles that lead to success:

• *Be proactive.* One of the basic laws of behavior is that: the best predictor of future behavior is past behavior. Therefore, teachers must be proactive in dealing with behavioral problems. If every day for the past 2 weeks Tanya has returned to the classroom after lunch being noisy and picking on other students, then tomorrow she is likely to engage in the same behaviors. Teachers too often rely on the "hope technique," hoping that today Tanya will return to class quietly and appropriately. This outcome is unlikely, and the hope technique is a very ineffective way to manage behavior. Accepting that the best predictor of future behavior is past behavior, the teacher should proactively establish a contract with Tanya that helps her enter the classroom quietly and appropriately.
• *Monitoring and consistency.* Effective behavioral control is predicated on the teacher's ability to monitor behavior and consistently implement consequences. Most serious behavior problems occur as part of a behavior chain that

begins with more minor challenging behaviors. For example, fighting does not usually occur when students are appropriately engaged in work. It is precipitated by other antagonistic behavior, as when Jason, who is known for fighting during lunchtime, begins by making faces at Ian and progresses to calling Ian names, walking over to Ian's table, and finally taking Ian's food. When Ian resists, Jason throws a punch. Effective behavioral control means that the teacher monitors Jason's behavior closely and intervenes when the behavioral chain begins (i.e., when Jason makes a face at Ian). To wait too long in the behavioral chain results in escalating behaviors and the need for more extreme interaction.

Providing consistent responses to inappropriate behavior is critical if students are going to pair consequences with behavior rather than with the teacher's level of tolerance or with chance. This rule is especially true for students with emotional and behavioral problems who tend toward an external locus of control. If consequences are to result in behavior change, they must be levied every time the behavior occurs, rather than sporadically or when the teacher's tolerance runs out.

• *Effective rules.* Classroom rules are critical to good behavior management. They should be limited to four to six and be observable and measurable and stated in positive terms. The rules should be posted and visible from across the room. If students cannot read, pictures or drawings should be substituted for words. Different situations may require different rules so that the class may have rules for large-group instruction, cooperative learning activities, and hallway movement. Rules should be taught and reviewed periodically. Students should be given the opportunity to practice and receive feedback for appropriate rule-following behaviors. Table 5.1 provides examples of effective and ineffective rules.

TABLE 5.1
Classroom Behavior Management Rules

Effective Rules	Ineffective Rules
Keep hands and feet to yourself	Respect others
Walk in the school building	Don't run
Use an inside voice	No yelling
Compliment others	Be nice

• *Teacher interactions.* Probably the most potent behavioral tool teachers possess is their interaction with students. Most students want teacher attention, and many students who display challenging behaviors have learned that the quickest and easiest way to get teacher attention is to act out. Positive attention, in the form of verbal and nonverbal praise, sets the best class climate and makes the day most enjoyable for teachers and students. Therefore, teachers must be conscious of how they provide positive attention. Many teachers ignore appropriate classroom behaviors, responding instead to inappropriate behavior, as when students get out of their seats, do not follow directions, or become disruptive. *Positive feedback* is praise or thanks for a specific appropriate behavior. Marking correct answers is one way that teachers can engage in a positive interaction. Most often, teachers ignore correct answers and put check marks by incorrect responses. Placing a C next to the right answers is more reinforcing and more behaviorally appropriate. *Corrective feedback* involves telling the student what to do. Corrective feedback is delivered in a neutral or positive tone of voice and conveys the expectation that the student will comply. *Negative feedback* criticizes students, draws attention to negative behaviors, and uses a negative, nasty, or sarcastic tone of voice. A good teacher will provide hundreds of feedback statements in a day, and effective behavior managers tally a 5:1:0 ratio of positive to corrective to negative feedback. Examples for similar situations are shown in Table 5.2.

In addition to providing positive attention, teachers need to ensure that the content of the vast majority of their interactions are academic in orientation and are directed to students who are on task rather than off task. Teachers are encouraged to record data on their verbal behaviors in the form of frequency counts. These data will help them determine the type of feedback and attention they are using with their students.

TABLE 5.2
Student Behavior Feedback

Positive Feedback	Corrective Feedback	Negative Feedback
Joshua is ready.	Please get your book out.	Stop looking around.
Tiesha and Jamal are quiet.	Quiet down now.	Shut up.
James, thanks for raising your hand.	I call on students with their hands raised.	Don't call out!
Numbers 2, 3, and 4 are correct.	Try number 1 again, remember to carry the one.	Number 1 is wrong.

A small minority of students with emotional and behavioral problems have difficulty accepting positive feedback because it contradicts their negative self-image. This is not unlike replying, "No I don't" to the comment "You look beautiful in that suit." However, in more extreme cases students with these problems may stop doing the appropriate behavior they were praised for and immediately become aggressive or disruptive. If a student demonstrates this inability to accept positive praise, teachers should begin a program of behavioral shaping with the student. Initially the teacher may walk by the student's desk and, without making eye contact, give the student a thumbs-up. This could be followed by saying, "Nice job" as she walks by, still without making eye contact. Once the child has acclimated to these forms of praise, the teacher might begin stopping by briefly to say "good job" and eventually progress to direct praise with eye contact. Some students may require an entire academic year to become accustomed to receiving positive reinforcement.

- *Proximity.* The teacher should be a presence throughout the room. Ineffective teachers often appear to be anchored to the front of the room or spend too much time sitting at their desks. Proximity to a student provides a nonverbal method of getting students back on task, helps subdue small behavior problems, enables teachers to give corrective feedback in a private and respectful manner, and avoids setting up power plays between teachers and students. Teachers should circulate throughout the room while lecturing and teaching small groups. During independent seat-work activities, proximity allows teachers to grade students' papers as they work on them, providing immediate feedback and error correction.
- *Routines.* Routines are an effective way to manage the mechanics of the classroom. At a minimum, teachers should use routines for arrival and dismissal and handing out and handing in work. Established routines save time and aggravation, provide a sense of organization and safety, and minimize wait and transition times. Like rules, routines should be established the first day of school, modeled, practiced, and reviewed periodically.
- *Transition and wait time.* Research shows that 25% to 33% of the average American school day is eaten up in transition and wait time. In general this is problematic, but it is unacceptable for students with emotional and behavioral issues, who are frequently one to three grade levels behind instructionally. Wait time is most effectively minimized by good teacher planning. Teachers should arrive at school each morning completely prepared for the day ahead. Effective transition strategies include using a color wheel to indicate a new activity, playing "beat the clock," using transition buddies, and marking the end point of the transition with a fun or rewarding activity.

• *Academic planning for success.* No matter how effectively a teacher uses behavior management principles, effective control of students is almost impossible unless instruction is interesting and designed to promote student success. Students with emotional and behavioral problems do not deal well with boredom or frustration. Chapter 7, "Educational Therapy," provides an in-depth look at instructional planning.

Teachers who use these eight classroom management strategies will minimize potential behavior problems and maximize the use of appropriate behaviors. Behavior problems that persist despite good classroom management require the use of a problem-solving approach such as ABA or FBA to determine the controlling antecedent and consequent variables and to develop effective interventions.

In addition to using the classroom management strategies just discussed, teachers should be aware of four additional general strategies for using behavior management in the classroom (Blackham & Silberman, 1975). They represent the optimal effects of combining certain behavior principles and are discussed in detail here:

• *Extinction and positive reinforcement.* The teacher should alter undesirable behavior by simultaneously decreasing it and increasing a desirable behavior. If the teacher wants Mary to decrease the amount of time she spends daydreaming, she should provide a substitute behavior, such as working on assignments that can be reinforced as the daydreaming is decreased. This principle is similar to what has been termed the "praise and ignore" technique (Drabman, 1976), which simply involves reinforcing socially appropriate behavior with praise and attention while simultaneously ignoring inappropriate behavior. Patti's behavior is marked by her inability to play with others, and observation proves that she receives most adult attention when she demonstrates behaviors incompatible with social play, such as sitting alone. The treatment involves withholding adult attention when she is not interacting socially and reinforcing with praise and attention when she engages in social play. A multitude of studies exist that attest to the efficiency of the praise and ignore technique. Among the behaviors successfully modified are hyperactivity (Allen, Henke, Harris, Baer, & Reynolds, 1967), excessive fantasy play (Bijou & Baer, 1967), attending school (Copeland, Brown, & Hall, 1974), cooperation with peers (Hart, Reynolds, Baer, Brawley, & Harris, 1968), crying (Harris, Wolf, & Baer, 1984), and paying attention (Hawkins, McArthur, Rinaldi, Gray, & Schafternaur, 1967). The pitfalls associated with this procedure are that some behaviors are too disruptive or dangerous to ignore. If peer reinforcement supersedes teacher responses and reinforces the behavior the teacher is trying to ignore, classmates can be taught to effectively ignore behaviors. Prompts to ignore banging or yelling, praise for continued task performance, and reward systems designed to reinforce ignoring have all proven highly effective in reducing behaviors maintained by peer attention.

• *Modeling and positive reinforcement.* The teacher may use a combination of modeling and positive reinforcement to effectively introduce a new behavior into the child's repertoire and simultaneously increase the probability of its occurrence. If the teacher wants the class to walk quietly in the halls, the teacher would model the behavior, have the students practice, and then praise them for appropriate hallway behavior. Also, a behavioral contract can be developed in which the class earns 5 points each time the students walk quietly in the halls. When the class has earned 50 points, the students can play math bingo during math time. In addition to direct teacher modeling of the desired behavior, the teacher can make use of peer models to set a good example (Bandura, 1965). In the case of relatively complex behaviors, such as employment interviewing, the teacher can make use of videotaped simulations to demonstrate the behaviors that must be imitated by the children (Bandura, 1965).

• *Role shift and positive reinforcement.* In role shift and positive reinforcement, an individual is reinforced for demonstrating behavior that is opposite to and incompatible with a problem behavior. For example, Tommy, a child who often makes unfriendly remarks to his classmates, is reinforced for smiling and making friendly remarks. The reinforced behaviors are not compatible with the problem behavior. Although the problem behavior is not deliberately extinguished, its incidence of occurrence decreases.

• *Behavior contracts, positive reinforcement, and withdrawal of reinforcement.* A fourth behavioral management procedure involves using behavior contracts to specify the consequences of both adaptive and challenging behavior. The association of these techniques permits the child to contrast the pleasurable results of adaptive behavior with the cost of problem behavior. In effect, it supports the old truism that you don't miss what you don't have, but you hate to lose what you have. Thus, if Jason contracts with his teacher to avoid fighting in school or on the playground, he earns an extra 10-minute free time period each day he is successful but pays the price in loss of this free time on days when he is not successful. Although the withdrawal of positive reinforcement is not synonymous with punishment, children generally perceive it as punishing (Baer, 1962), and it depresses the incidence of inappropriate behaviors (Wolf, Risley, & Mees, 1964).

Figures 5.4, 5.5, and 5.6 show how contracts can be used in this fashion.

Charles (1989) provided two additional strategies, the rules-ignore-praise approach and the rules-reward-punishment approach. In the former the teacher

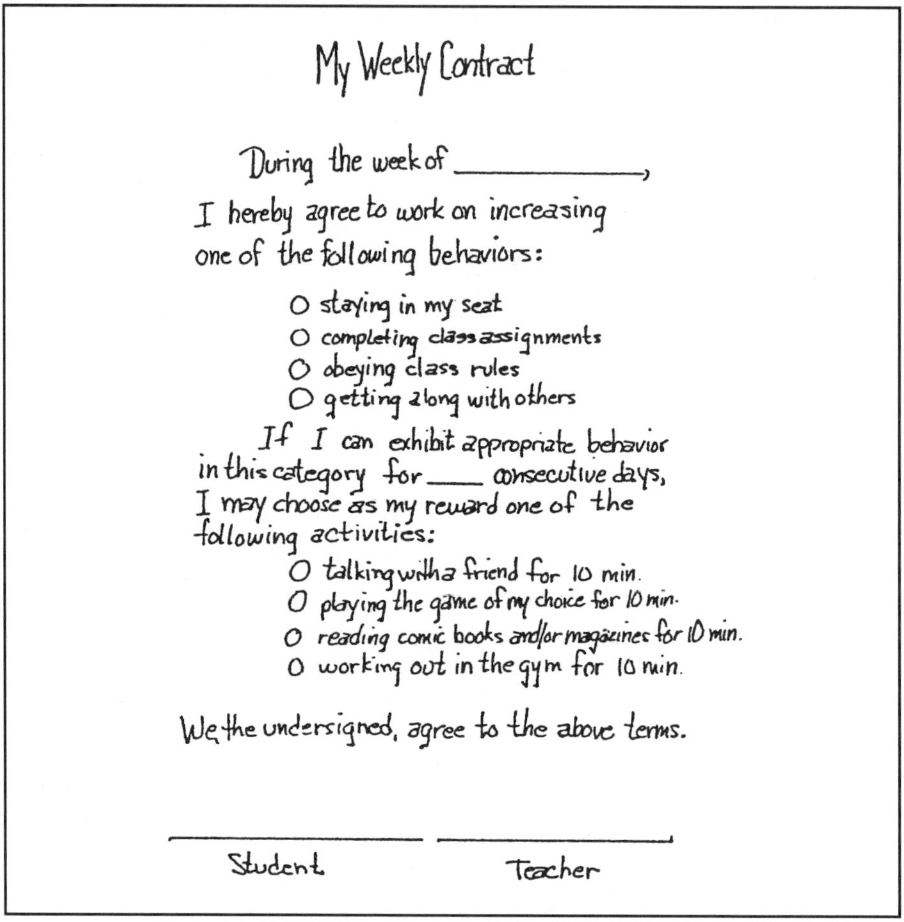

My Weekly Contract

During the week of _____,
I hereby agree to work on increasing
one of the following behaviors:

O staying in my seat
O completing class assignments
O obeying class rules
O getting along with others

If I can exhibit appropriate behavior
in this category for ____ consecutive days,
I may choose as my reward one of the
following activities:

O talking with a friend for 10 min.
O playing the game of my choice for 10 min.
O reading comic books and/or magazines for 10 min.
O working out in the gym for 10 min.

We the undersigned, agree to the above terms.

_____   _____
Student   Teacher

Figure 5.4. Secondary-level contract.

and students formulate class rules (approximately five), which are written on a chart and posted. Students who comply with rules are consistently praised and those who do not are ignored (when possible). When a rule is broken (e.g., a child leaves her seat without permission), the teacher praises another student for complying with the rule and does not pay attention to the rule breaker. This system is recommended only for elementary-level students.

The rules-reward-punishment approach also begins with rules and involves rewards, but it incorporates punishment for inappropriate behavior. Rules, formulated by the teacher and his students, are written and displayed as in the rules-ignore-praise approach, and students who follow them understand that

Figure 5.5. Intermediate-level contract.

they will receive any of a number of reinforcers—praise, tokens, notes to parents, and so forth. Consequences for rule breaking also are established by the teacher and students and discussed often. When a student chooses to break a rule, she is aware of the consequences and they are enforced immediately. This approach is useful for older children and those with behavior problems. A particular advantage is that the teacher is not choosing to punish the child; rather, the contingencies of rule breaking have been defined previously by the class, and the student is aware of the consequences of her behavior.

Alternative strategies for decreasing problem behavior were presented by Martin and Pear (1999). These include situational inducement; instruction,

Figure 5.6. Primary-level contract.

modeling, and role playing; adjusting a chain; stimulus control and partial elimination; and overcorrection.

• *Situational inducement.* Situational inducement involves adjusting the stimulus that is evoking a challenging response. For example, a student with emotional difficulties, Jason, responded to any form of verbal reprimand made audibly in front of his classmates (including gentle reminders made in a soft, controlled voice) by engaging in angry, retaliatory behaviors such as shouting obscenities, throwing books, and, on several occasions, running from the classroom. The adjustment to the stimulus involved having the teacher take Jason aside when he was not conforming to class rules and speak to him privately. When addressed privately, Jason never displayed acting-out behavior and typically resumed appropriate classroom activity.

• *Instruction, modeling, and role playing.* Instruction, modeling, and role playing are useful individual or small-group strategies. When students have consistent difficulty coping with a particular situation, the teacher discusses the problem with them and suggests responses that might help them avoid violating school rules. The teacher models the more adaptive behavior and uses role playing to help students learn new responses. For example, a relatively young group of special education junior high school students were having difficulty in the lunchroom, where older students were taunting them about their special class status and on occasion threatening to throw food at them. The special education students showed their anger by displaying clearly visible acting-out behavior, such as fighting, throwing food, shouting obscenities, and so forth, and usually one or more of the group members encountered difficulty with lunchroom monitors that culminated in some form of punishment. The teacher suggested that the students try to avoid the taunters but if that was not possible that they try to ignore their remarks and continue to eat and talk to one another. The teacher modeled the behavior, asking various students to play the role of the taunters, then he played the taunters' role while the students practiced their response. The results were encouraging, with the frequency of punishment associated with lunchroom behavior diminishing. Periodically the teacher and students reviewed and rehearsed the coping response.

• *Adjusting a chain.* Often it is possible to use indirect strategies to alter an undesirable response by eliminating a component of the sequence or chain of behaviors that lead up to it. To use this strategy, the teacher must be able to identify the sequence that typically leads to the undesired response. For example, a child who invites the ridicule of her peers by telling them outrageous falsehoods typically exhibits this behavior when her classroom performance has not earned positive recognition by the teacher. The teacher finds that praising her for some performance early in the day usually eliminates her need to gain attention by impressing her classmates with fabricated stories.

• *Stimulus control and partial elimination.* Stimulus control and partial elimination of a challenging behavior are used in situations when it is impossible to extinguish an inappropriate response completely. This circumstance might occur when a variety of individuals are involved with a child and the teacher cannot control the contingencies on all occasions. For example, a teacher on recess duty might find it impossible to get students to stop playing and line up to return to class at the appropriate time—when the bell rings. Consequently, some students are late for class. Punishment does not extinguish the behavior, because the variety of teachers involved with the children deal with both problems—failure to line up promptly and lateness to class—differently; therefore, negative contingencies are not applied consistently. The teachers on recess duty agree to alter the stimulus by using a whistle 5 minutes before the bell to alert students to line up. Students are made aware that a minimum of 5 minutes of playtime must be devoted to the line-up process. Also, they are told that when they respond immediately to the bell, the whistle will not be used and their recess will not be shortened. On occasions when any of the students do not respond immediately to the bell, the whistle signal is reinstituted for the following 5 days.

• *Overcorrection.* A form of punishment known to decrease undesirable behaviors is a method called overcorrection (Azrin & Besalel, 1980). One component of this method, positive practice, requires that an individual who engages frequently in a challenging behavior be required to repeat a desirable alternative behavior over and over. An associated component, restitution, involves rectifying any destruction to the environment. For example, a child who scribbles on his desk with a black pen is required to practice using the pen appropriately for significant periods of time every day for 2 weeks. He also is required to clean not only his own desktop but also the tops of every desk in the classroom.

Reinforcers

The topic of reinforcers was briefly introduced earlier in this chapter. Classroom teachers faced with decisions regarding which type of reinforcer to use should be familiar with their benefits and limitations.

Primary reinforcers such as food reduce drive states and are therefore highly reliable. Obviously, all persons get hungry and are susceptible to the reinforcement value of food. One limitation of using primary reinforcers is that individuals satiate quickly, so the reinforcers may lose their effectiveness. However, many students with emotional and behavioral problems do not get the nutrition they need and are often hungry, making food an effective reward. Healthy snacks such as raisins and pretzels are preferable to candy or cookies. Generally, primary reinforcers have been used in the initial stages of a modification program to establish a stable adaptive response. At that point they usually are paired with social reinforcement (see next section) to sustain the response. Primary reinforcers are also useful with persons with more severe disabilities such as schizophrenia (Lovaas et al., 1966) and moderate to severe mental retardation (Hundziak, Maurer, & Watson, 1965), who may have difficulty responding to alternative types of reinforcement. Even in these cases, however, some form of secondary reinforcement is paired with the primary reinforcement.

Social reinforcement uses such reinforcers as attention, gestures, social recognition, and praise. It is used most frequently by teachers because it involves little effort and no cost. It is also less artificial in school settings than alternative types of reinforcement. Social reinforcement is effective when the function of the target behavior is to gain attention, status, or recognition. Social recognition has been found to be successful when used with children with behavioral challenges (Zimmerman & Zimmerman, 1962), nursery-school students (Brown & Elliott, 1965), a nontalking boy (Brison, 1966), elementary school children (Barclay, 1967), high school students (McAllister, Stachowiak, Baer, & Conderman, 1969), and a variety of others. Similarly, praise and other verbal behaviors have been shown to be powerful enough to influence classes of verbal responses (Binder, McConnell, & Sjoholm, 1957; Vogel-Sprott, 1964), self-reference statements (Krasner, 1965), and information-seeking and decision-making responses (Krumboltz & Thorensen, 1964).

Although social recognition is an effective reinforcer of desired behavior, it is an equally effective reinforcer of problem behavior (Hall, Lund, & Jackson, 1968). If Lilly goes into a tantrum in class and the teacher responds with attention, even critical or negative attention, Lilly may be reinforced for her tantrum and exhibit the behavior again. Therefore, as has been noted previously, teachers must carefully analyze their reactions to children's challenging behaviors to ensure that they are not inadvertently reinforcing them.

The major disadvantage of social reinforcement is that it may not be a sufficiently powerful contingency, particularly at the beginning stages of an intervention. Some children do not attend to social reinforcement or do not regard it as particularly rewarding. In cases when a social reinforcer such as praise does not increase the probability that a behavior will occur, it is not a positive reinforcer. In addition, the effectiveness of social reinforcement is related to the status of the agent supplying it. Praise from a highly valued individual may determine behavior more readily than similar remarks from a low-status person. This is particularly true among adolescents, who value peer approval far more than adult approval and behave accordingly.

Token reinforcement is a system that has the advantage of combining the principles of immediate and delayed gratification. Desired responses are reinforced immediately with tokens that may be exchanged at a later time for backup reinforcer items or events. The immediate reinforcement increases the probability that the desired behavior will be repeated, and the use of backup reinforcers helps the student learn to save for a desired object or event. For example, a child may earn one token every hour she works without calling out. After accruing a certain number of tokens, the child may choose to exchange them for a backup reinforcer such as candy, the privilege of running the film projector, extra recess, or a free time period, or the child may decide to delay gratification, earn additional tokens, and exchange them for a more costly backup reinforcer such as lunch with her teacher or a toy. Possibilities for backup reinforcers are extensive, because they need not be delivered immediately after the desired response is exhibited.

When a system of token reinforcement is applied to a group, the effect is to establish an economy similar to that based on money. In effect, children earn tokens as a salary, which they use to purchase items that give them pleasure. They can spend their tokens in a class store that may be nothing more than a box stored in the classroom. Because tokens are associated with a variety of backup reinforcers, they have very powerful reinforcement value. Flexibility and administrative convenience are added advantages of token economies. The system is flexible in that it permits the behavior modifier to make simple adjustments in the rate or duration of responses necessary to earn the token reinforcer. Also, the price of backup reinforcers may be raised so that the child must work harder for the privilege or item. Administratively, the behavior modifier need not be concerned with problems such as satiation that accompany the direct use of primary reinforcers or with practical difficulties of having to select a reinforcer appropriate for a particular child.

Generally this system is particularly useful in school settings because it often works with children who do not respond to social reinforcement. Token systems are also easy to employ. Martin and Pear (1999) summarized 12 suggested requirements for successful programs.

1. The target behaviors that will earn tokens must be discussed thoroughly by the teacher and the students involved, clearly specified, and written on a chart or blackboard. If both individual and group token systems are used, the individual target behaviors and the reinforcement contingencies should be represented by a formal written contract, and the behaviors being modified should be posted on the student's desk. The rules governing individual and group contingencies should be reviewed frequently with the students.

2. The student must be able to perform the target behaviors for which tokens will be given.

3. The backup reinforcers for which tokens are exchanged must be appealing to the students and should not be readily available outside the token system. The teacher should prepare a list of backup reinforcers that includes a variety of items or events, such as toys, school supplies (pencils, pens), sweets, free time, extra recess, classroom jobs, notes to parents, lunch with the teacher, special seating privileges, and so forth. The list should be made available to the students.

4. The number of tokens earned must be consistent with the difficulty or effort required to perform the behavior, and the cost of backup reinforcers

should be based on their therapeutic value to the child. For example, if a student has great difficulty controlling his aggression, reinforcement for nonaggressive behavior must be sufficient to provide a potent incentive for proper behavior. Similarly, if a child is typically shy and nonverbal, a backup reinforcer that enables her to lead the class in the pledge of allegiance to the flag should cost very few tokens.

5. If possible, the teacher should keep a record of tokens earned by each child (and the group when a group system is used). Student incentive is often enhanced when the number of tokens earned is recorded on a chart displayed for the entire class to see.

6. If the response cost (token fines) is also used, the exact conditions under which tokens will be earned or lost should be clearly communicated to the students. When tokens are given or taken away, the teacher should relate the action to the student behavior involved. The teacher's statement should be to the point, and arguments regarding token loss should be avoided at all costs. Response cost is a punishment and is subject to the problems inherent in the use of any punishment. However, when it is used sparingly, as a contingency for specific behavior (defined and discussed previously by the class), it has been shown to help students acquire the ability to accept reprimands without extreme anger (Phillips, Phillips, Fixsen, & Wolf, 1973).

7. The frequency with which backup reinforcers are made available should vary. Early in the program, the frequency should be high, for example, once or twice per day for approximately the first 3 or 4 days. As the program progresses, store time should occur less frequently, until it occurs only once per week, usually on Friday afternoon, by the third week of the token economy. Token exchange for the backup reinforcer should be held at the end of the school day. If the backup reinforcer is a toy or a game and is given to a student during the school day, he is likely to be distracted by it and to distract other students from appropriate task behavior. In cases where a student's needs are such that he requires the opportunity to exchange his tokens for a backup reinforcer without a prolonged delay in gratification, permit him to select an item but indicate to the child that his name tag will be placed on it so he can have it at the end of the day.

8. Extend token reinforcement so that the target behavior will be encouraged in a wide range of situations (classroom, physical education class, playground). Desirable behavior is not likely to generalize to nonreinforced settings.

9. Devise the token system so that a student competes with himself rather than other students (i.e., on the basis of desirable improvements in his own performance and behavior).

10. Always combine praise with tokens so that social reinforcement ultimately can be used to maintain desirable academic and social behavior.

11. A well-devised token system should gradually withdraw material reinforcers and rely on reinforcing activities and events. Ultimately, social reinforcement and reinforcing events should maintain the desired behavior.

12. The token system should be simple, functional, and not distract from learning. Tangible tokens (chips, stamps) can be used, although the teacher must take care to minimize opportunities for children to play with them in class. (They might be stored in a coffee-can bank.) Also, these types of tokens are easily traded or stolen, disrupting the reinforcement system. To avoid this problem, some teachers use a different-colored chip for each child. However, in school situations, check-mark tokens may be the easiest to use. Each student is issued a card with his name on it. As he earns points or check marks, they are recorded on the card and initialed by the teacher. If the card is taken by another student, he cannot use it to obtain backup reinforcers. If it is destroyed, the teacher can re-create the card if she has wisely maintained her own records of the tokens awarded each day.

The token economy system is extremely popular. It has been used in one form or another with children with mental retardation (Birnbrauer, Wolf, Kidder, & Tague, 1965; Zimmerman, Zimmerman, & Russell, 1969), autism (Craighead & Meyers, 1973; Martin, England, Kaprowy, Kilgour, & Pilek, 1968), attention-deficit disorder (Quay, Sprague, Werry, & McQueen, 1967), schizophrenia (Drabman, 1973), emotional problems (O'Leary & Becker, 1967), and delinquency (Meichenbaum, Bowers, & Ross, 1968). It may be used with groups as well as individuals. A token economy called The Good Behavior Game (Barrish, Saunders, & Wolf, 1969) was used to decrease the out-of-seat and talking-out behavior of an entire class. The procedure involves dividing the class in half and having the two teams compete for tokens. Research suggests that group procedures, although less time-consuming, are as effective as individual programs (Drabman, Spitalnik, & Spitalnik, 1974; Herman & Tramontana, 1971).

Contingency management is a reinforcement technique based on the Premack principle (1959, 1965) that a low-probability behavior can be increased in frequency when its execution is followed by a high-probability behavior. More simply, Homme (1969) calls this principle "Grandma's Law: first eat your vegetables, then you may have your dessert." With contingency management, a child is reinforced for completing a low-probability task, such as an arithmetic assignment, with a high-probability task, such as reading a mystery story.

There are two methods of implementing contingency management. One method simply permits the student free time to pursue a reinforcing activity after he completes an assigned task. The time allowed for completion of the assignment is not specified but is always followed by a set period of free time. A second, more precise method establishes specific time periods for each assignment. If the assignment is completed before the time elapses, the reinforcement is free time for the remainder of the time period. For example, the school day may be divided into 60-minute periods. An arithmetic assignment is estimated to take 55 minutes. Children who complete the task in 55 minutes have 5 minutes of time to engage in a pleasurable activity. Children who fail to complete the assignment gain no free time reinforcement.

The key to using a contingency management system effectively is to ensure that the time periods allotted are fair to all students. Some individuals might be expected to complete 20 arithmetic problems in 55 minutes, whereas others might be capable of doing 50 problems. If assignments were not individualized, the contingency system would penalize the slower, less capable students, who are in the greatest need of effective reinforcement.

The system is also more effective if the teacher provides a separate reinforcing events area in the room that contains a variety of appealing games, toys, books, and gadgets. The stock of this area should be changed periodically to prevent boredom. A good practice is to have the children suggest the items for the reinforcing events area. They also may contribute items.

In addition to the management tasks connected with this system, which obviously require effort and planning, implementation requires a spacious room. Also, reinforcing events activities may distract other students; therefore, the program must be carefully introduced to the children, and they must understand the limits to reinforcing events activities.

The contingency management system, although not used as extensively as alternative reinforcement systems, has been applied successfully with children who are retarded (Daley, 1969), as well as with typical learners (Homme, 1966). It appears to be more effective when integrated with a token economy (Nolen, Kunzelmann, & Haring, 1967; Wasik, 1970).

Reinforcing Agents

There is evidence that peers can administer token economies (Martella, Marchand-Martella, Miller, Young, & Macfarlane, 1995). The effectiveness of peer-delivered social reinforcement is less clear, but it appears to be influenced by the social relationships among the children. When peers are friends, social reinforcement is less effective (Hartup, 1964; Titkin & Hartup, 1964). Parents have also been trained as reinforcing agents (Bijou, 1965; O'Leary, O'Leary, & Becker, 1967; Russo, 1964), and the importance of parental involvement appears to be achieving greater recognition among educators.

Finally, investigations have demonstrated that both children with and children without behavior problems can control their own token economies and self-manage their behaviors with minimum training (Sugai & Horner, 1994).

Punishment

For the most part, behavior interventions are predicated on the use of functional assessment, antecedent strategies, or reinforcement. In a few circumstances, however, reinforcement systems are ineffective in modifying particularly harmful or disruptive behavior and stimulus control programs also are ineffective, so the use of punishment is considered. As has been noted previously, punishment is an aversive contingency designed to decrease the incidence of a behavior. Punishment, like positive reinforcement, is defined by its effect on the target behavior. An aversive stimulus must decrease the frequency or probability of a behavior occurring to be considered a punisher.

Because punishment-based interventions result in increases in aggression, vandalism, truancy, and absenteeism (Martin & Pear, 1999), they should be used only as a last resort and only with behaviors that are extremely harmful, dangerous, or likely to result in the child's exclusion from the current educational setting. Before resorting to using punishment, teachers should try every other conceivable intervention. Once a punishment-based intervention is implemented, teachers need to be absolutely certain the aversive stimuli is having the desired effect. Many teachers persist in using an aversive stimulus (calling home, detention, withholding recess) even though the behavior does not decrease. If a "punisher" is not working—the target behavior is not decreasing—then the intervention should be abandoned.

Martin and Pear (1999) provided guidelines to enhance the effectiveness of punishment when it must be used. First, it is important that an appropriate punisher be selected. The most appropriate punishers are those that can be used shortly after the undesirable behavior has occurred and that are not associated in any way with positive reinforcement. In school, the teacher must select a circumstance she has control over (e.g., denying recess, modification of lunch privileges, reduction of free time, detention after school), make the punishment fit the crime, and make sure that her attention is not providing the child with positive reinforcement. For example, a teacher may choose to attempt to decrease the incidence of fighting on the playground by withholding recess privileges (paired with teaching conflict resolution strategies) but would be ill advised to punish a violator by depriving her of recess for a week, because that length of time is excessive. Also, if the child receives teacher attention during the period she is not at recess, it may act as a positive reinforcer and the punisher will not be effective.

Often teachers use a verbal reprimand as a punisher. Although verbal reprimands can be effective, a great deal of research has shown that often they do not really diminish the frequency with which a challenging behavior occurs. A typical example was reported by Madsen, Becker, Thomas, Koser, and Plager

(1970), who tested the effectiveness of the teacher utterance "sit down" in reducing children's out-of-seat behavior. Using a modified reversal design, they established a baseline of typical teacher "sit down" comments, had the teacher triple the frequency of those comments, returned to a baseline level, returned to the elevated frequency, and finally had the teachers praise behaviors incompatible with out-of-seat behavior. They found a 37% increase in out-of-seat behavior during the high-frequency periods. The last stage, praising incompatible behaviors, resulted in a 33% decrease in those behaviors. These results show the limitations of verbal reprimands in reducing out-of-seat behavior. Apparently, however, the manner of delivery is a factor, because quiet reprimands have been shown to be more effective than loud reprimands (O'Leary & Becker, 1968; O'Leary, Kaufman, Kass, & Drabman, 1970).

Additional research has shown that verbal reprimands are most effective when they are consistently backed up by a stronger punisher. For example, a child who is warned that detention will be assigned after school if a behavior does not cease must be assigned the detention immediately if that behavior continues. Even when this contingency occurs, the strength of the detention as a punisher will depend on how it is conducted. The experience should be aversive; the child should spend the time sitting quietly and not be permitted to socialize or complete schoolwork (positive reinforcers that negate the impact of the punishment). Also, the child must remain after school on the day the behavior occurred, not at a convenient time.

A second important rule regarding punishment is that it must be delivered consistently. If the child demonstrates the challenging behavior upon her return to school the following day, the punishment must follow. Research (Kircher, Pear, & Martin, 1971) has shown that occasional punishment is not as effective as punishment that follows every instance of the undesirable behavior.

Generally, in school settings the types of punishment most frequently recommended for use are response cost and time-out. *Response cost* is the response-contingent withdrawal of positive reinforcement. A child loses a positive reinforcer contingent on inappropriate behavior. For example, a student may lose the privilege of eating lunch in the cafeteria with his friends (positive reinforcement) because of throwing food. Response cost also is employed as a component of token economies: The child must give back a previously earned token. Recent studies have shown that response cost interventions are very effective for students with impulsivity and high levels of inappropriate behaviors, such as children with attention-deficit/hyperactivity disorder or attention-deficit disorder.

Time-out is short for "time-out from positive reinforcement." This procedure may involve ignoring an individual for a brief period of time, as when a teacher simply looks away from a child seeking attention. In its more severe form, time-out calls for placing a child engaging in extremely disruptive behavior, such as throwing a tantrum, in social isolation for a given period of time. Technically, the child is prevented from experiencing positive reinforcement during that period. This punishment may be accomplished through the use of a time-out space in the classroom, such as a study carrel or a "time-out room," which is devoid of all furniture or equipment that might stimulate the individual and therefore contains nothing that is positively reinforcing. Return to the classroom or to the group is determined by passage of time (usually about 5 to 10 minutes) and appropriate behavior during the last minutes of the time period. If the child's behavior remains inappropriate after passage of the allotted time, the period of isolation is extended. Studies have demonstrated the usefulness of the time-out procedure in conjunction with positive reinforcement (Walker, Mattson, & Buckley, 1968; Whelan & Haring, 1966). In these instances, the child is praised when the problematic behavior has ceased and she has been released from the time-out room. Drabman and Spitalnik (1973) used time-out procedures exclusively to reduce the incidence of out-of-seat behavior and aggression among children residing in a psychiatric hospital.

Dangers of Punishment. A great deal of research into the effects of punishment have revealed data clearly indicating that it should be used only when all other methods of intervention have failed (Azrin & Holz, 1966). Often punishment produces unpleasant side effects such as crying or fearful behavior. Also, it has been documented that strong punishment causes aggressive behavior directed in random fashion—even toward individuals who had nothing to do with the administration of the punishment. One explanation of this response is that children often model the behavior adults apply to them (Bandura, 1969).

Possibly the most significant danger associated with punishment lies in its long-term effects. Although it may decrease a challenging behavior, the effects of punishment often generalize to other aspects of the environment where it occurred. For example, if a child is punished often in school, she may develop negative affect toward a variety of elements associated with school, such as interacting with teachers, reading books, interacting with classmates, and so forth. This type of response happens all too frequently to children who are punished by being scolded, criticized, ridiculed, or addressed sarcastically for making a mistake in an academic task such as arithmetic computation. The criticism is counterproductive because it diminishes the probability that the child will want to attempt the academic task again. When criticism of this type is repeated, the child's negative or aversive feelings about a particular academic task often generalize to other subject matter, and yet another individual who "hates" attending school has been developed.

In light of the problems associated with the use of punishment, it is important that the teacher use it judiciously—and always to benefit the child. Punishment is most effective if the child has been made aware previously that it will always follow the display of certain specified behavior and has agreed that the punishment is a fair consequence. Punishment should never be associated with extreme anger or hostility on the teacher's part. The teacher must remain calm and reasonable, stressing the relationship between the child's specific behavior and the punishing consequence.

Commercial Programs Using Behavioral Principles

The principles associated with behavioral therapy have been integrated into comprehensive commercial programs available for use in schools and in homes. Among the most popular of the school programs is *Assertive Discipline: A Take-Charge Approach for Today's Educator*, authored by Lee Canter (1976) with input from Marlene Canter. Their philosophy—that teachers can create a classroom environment most conducive to learning and to the personal growth of their students by using behavioral strategies to deal assertively with discipline—is shared by York, York, and Wachtel in *Toughlove* (1982) and by Silberman and Wheelan in *How To Discipline Without Feeling Guilty: Assertive Relationships with Children* (1980). Because the approaches are similar, only *Assertive Discipline* is discussed in this text. The Canters' key ideas focus on the right of teachers to insist on appropriate, responsible behavior from students and the right of students to learn in an environment as free from disruption as possible. They believe that failure in the classroom is increased when teachers fail to assert themselves in establishing appropriate discipline. To aid teachers in being more assertive, they suggest the following procedures (after Charles, 1989):

1. Identify expectations clearly.
2. Say, "I like that" and "I don't like that."
3. Persist in stating expectations and feelings.
4. Use a firm tone of voice.
5. Maintain eye contact.
6. Use nonverbal gestures in support of verbal statements.
7. Use hints, questions, and "I" messages, rather than demands, for appropriate behavior.

8. Follow through with promises that are reasonable consequences and were previously established, rather than threatening.

9. Be assertive in confrontations with students by making statements of expectations, indicating the consequences that will occur, and noting why action is necessary.

The first procedure, identifying expectations clearly, pertains to the establishment of behavioral limits, written rules that specify consequences for violations. Items 2 through 6 involve teacher behaviors that reflect an assertive demeanor. Teachers should make personal statements to their students about appropriate and inappropriate behaviors. Persistence in stating rules is referred to as "the broken record" technique. The teacher is advised to repeat a message when a student does not attend or attempts to divert her. For example, a teacher may remark, "Bobby we do not leave our seats without permission," only to have Bobby offer an explanation for his behavior; "I need to sharpen my pencil." The teacher says, "I see your pencil needs sharpening, but we do not leave our seats without permission." The repetition may be repeated three times before the teacher should follow through with appropriate consequences. All remarks are delivered in a firm, businesslike tone of voice—the teacher should never be harsh, sarcastic, or abusive. The teacher should look straight into the student's eyes when speaking and should accompany her remarks with appropriate gestures, such as hand movements and facial expressions. Also, sometimes physical touch, such as light hand placement on the shoulder, is effective.

The seventh item, using hints, questions, and "I" messages, helps remind students through hints and personal reference statements to return to work, without focusing attention on a specific child. For example, a teacher observing a child beginning to whisper while taking a test might remind the class that there is no talking during the test or comment, "I hear talking when everyone should be silent." The final two points indicate how to follow through on limits. Promises are vows to take an action that has been carefully explained in advance to the students. Students choose to behave appropriately or inappropriately and are aware of the positive and negative consequences that follow. Promises are an example of assertive interactions with students—definite statements of rules for appropriate behavior. Assertive Discipline contrasts this type of interaction to nonassertive teacher responses in which the teacher passively pleads with the students to behave more appropriately and to hostile teacher responses that are characterized by sarcasm, threats, and shouts and are designed to intimidate. To assertively enforce consequences, teachers are advised to follow a progressive sequence that begins with writing the student's name on the board while reaffirming his violation of the behavior rule. This step warns the misbehaving student that further misbehavior will entail negative consequences. Continued misbehavior warrants a check beside the name and an automatic 15-minute detention. For a third incident, the child receives another check and a 30-minute detention; yet another incident involves a third check, a 30-minute detention, and a student phone call to parents to explain his misbehavior. The fifth incident warrants a fourth check and adds a meeting with the principal to the other consequences. Finally, if a sixth incident occurs, the student is suspended from school.

The foregoing procedures are initiated at the beginning of each day. In addition to the strategies for discipline, Assertive Discipline emphasizes positive consequences, suggesting reinforcement strategies previously discussed in this chapter. Assertive Discipline has been widely used nationally, probably because it is relatively easy to implement. The most serious criticism of it suggests that it ignores methods for improving the quality of instruction and discourages the teacher from examining the specific classroom events that may be involved in the child's challenging behavior. In a review of the literature investigating its effectiveness, Emmer and Aussiker (1987) found little substantiation of positive effects on student behavior and attitudes, little effect on teacher behavior, and the greatest effect on teachers' attitudes regarding improved discipline in the classroom. Render, Padilla, and Krank (1989) in their review of the literature also found no lasting benefits adhering to the schoolwide use of Assertive Discipline. It would appear that behavioral principles are most effective when they are used with flexibility, that is, when some specific strategies are used to attempt to resolve certain problems and others are used in different circumstances. It is wise to remember that behavioral interventions are predicated on the principles of scientific validation. In each application, when data do not substantiate that an intervention is working, it must be changed. Unfortunately, when certain of the strategies are packaged and used in routinized fashion in classrooms, much of the benefit of the approach may be lost.

Clinical Applications of Behavioral Therapy

Thus far we have explored the general applications of behavior principles through ABA, FBA, behavior modification, and environmental manipulation. The emphasis has been on depicting strategies typically used by teachers in a classroom. These strategies and others based on behavioral theory also are applied in clinical settings—that is, those that might be termed psychotherapeutic, if it were not for behavior therapists' insistence on distinguishing between traditional psychotherapies, such as Freudian analysis, and behavioral therapy.

The separation of behavior modification from what is referred to in this section as clinical–behavioral therapy is arbitrary. It will become apparent in the discussion of clinical treatments that many of the simpler strategies are implemented by teachers in classrooms as well as by caretakers in homes. In fact, cross-setting problems such as anxiety, depression, self-injury, and anti-social behaviors require behavioral therapy to be implemented across settings to be effective (Watson & Gresham, 1998).

Anxiety-Reducing Therapies

As was discussed earlier in this book, the DSM–IV (APA, 1994) lists 13 different types of anxiety disorders, including the following seen in children: generalized anxiety disorder/overanxious disorder, separation anxiety disorder, obsessive-compulsive disorder, panic disorder, and phobias. Children suffering from *generalized anxiety disorder* or *overanxious disorder* worry excessively about daily affairs, such as getting to school on time, whether they are doing a good job, what will happen next, and much more. These excessive concerns reveal their concern about safety and generally result in their asking many questions, becoming withdrawn or hyperactive, and requiring frequent reassurance. *Separation anxiety*, fear of leaving a parent or primary caregiver, interferes with school attendance and forming relationships with peers and other adults. Behavior therapy is very successful in helping children with this type of problem.

Obsessions, persistent, intrusive thoughts such as preoccupation with death, and *compulsions*, repetitive acts or rituals, such as excessive hand washing or cleaning, have been successfully treated by a variety of behavioral interventions. Obsessive-compulsive disorders are not uncommon in children. Although compulsive behaviors or rituals are relatively easy to identify, obsessive thoughts that are equally debilitating may require careful observation to be uncovered. Children experiencing such thoughts are often too frightened to discuss them. The obsessed child requires reassurance that she is not "crazy" and that the condition can be treated.

Panic disorders add the element of physical or psychological panic reactions (shortness of breath, chest pains, crying, hysteria, paralysis) to anxiety disorders or phobic reactions. Children who suffer from panic disorders generally require behavioral therapy along with cognitive interventions to address internalized verbal behaviors that contribute to the panic reaction.

Phobias, exaggerated, unrealistic fears, are relatively commonplace experiences for many individuals throughout their lifetime. In cases where they either become so intense as to be more than an inconvenience, or persist in duration, behavior therapy has proved effective in eliminating them. Historically, behavioral treatments of fear responses began with Jones's (1924) classic efforts to decondition fear of animals in children by pairing the introduction of the feared object with an alternative stimulus, food (the principle of reciprocal inhibition used later by the psychiatrist Joseph Wolpe). Currently, systematic desensitization, implosion, and flooding are the preferred methods of treating phobic conditions, and phobias have also been successfully treated with imagining and in vivo techniques.

Fear of attending school is apparently commonplace. In many instances, school phobia is associated with a cluster of neurotic responses, including anxiety over separation from the mother and somatic complaints (Last, 1991). In others cases, aggression, running away, noncompliance, and tantrums form the cluster of behaviors surrounding school nonattendance (Cooper, 1986). Behavioral treatments have involved soliciting parental assistance in forcing school attendance, providing positive social reinforcement when the child enters school, and ignoring somatic complaints (Kearney & Tillotson, 1998; Leventhal, Weinberger, Stander, & Sterns, 1971). Functional assessment surrounding the reasons for school phobia have proved effective in developing interventions that return students to school (Kearney & Tillotson). Systematic desensitization techniques (in vivo) have been applied by leading a child, step by step, through the behaviors of entering school (Garvey & Hegrenes, 1966; Kearney & Silverman, 1990). Occasionally, parents and teachers have been used to provide positive reinforcement for all independent behavior during periods of systematic desensitization (Patterson, 1965). Generally, behavior therapy has been very effective in combating school phobia.

Joseph Wolpe, one of the foremost behavioral therapists specializing in the reduction of anxiety associated with phobic conditions, based his intervention strategy, *systematic desensitization*, on the principle of reciprocal inhibition—that "an anxiety response habit can be weakened by evoking a response incompatible with anxiety in the presence of the anxiety-evoking stimulus" (Wolpe, 1976, p. 17). In other words, it is more difficult for an individual to experience anxiety in a situation that usually evokes that response if an alternative response is evoked. The alternative response inhibits the anxiety response.

Wolpe (1961, 1973) identified three main categories of incompatible responses that inhibit anxiety: the *assertive, sexual,* and *relaxation* responses. Assertive responses are defined as "any overt expression of spontaneous and appropriate feelings other than anxiety." They are used primarily to overcome anxiety that is evoked in interpersonal situations and that inhibits verbal responses to others. The individual is taught to verbalize feelings that are customarily inhibited, such as anger and affection. The verbal responses weaken the anxiety response habit. Treatments for sexual responses are used when anxiety pertains to sexual situations. Sexual excitation is controlled by the parasympathetic nervous system, and anxiety by the sympathetic nervous system. The arousal of one response inhibits the other. From Wolpe's perspective, however, the most important and useful inhibitor of anxiety is deep-muscle relaxation, a process originally recognized by Jacobson (1938), who developed strategies for progressive relaxation in disturbing situations.

Systematic Desensitization. The current behavioral perspective regarding the theoretical basis of systematic desensitization is that it is used to extinguish challenging behavior that is negatively reinforced—that is, reinforced by avoidance of a painful, anxiety-evoking situation. For example, a child who is afraid of school and stays away is negatively reinforced by the avoidance of both school and the anxiety and fear associated with school. Negatively reinforced behavior is more difficult to extinguish than positively reinforced behavior because the individual withdraws from the situation as soon as anxiety elevates and does not learn whether the aversive consequences associated with the situation (rejection or bullying by peers) ever occur. Also, the avoidance behavior reduces anxiety and is therefore reinforced. The procedures used in systematic desensitization involve developing a ranked list or hierarchy of fears, ordered according to how much fear they evoke, and systematically deconditioning each sequenced fear response, proceeding from low fear to high fear. For example, a hierarchy of fear of dogs might at the lowest or least fear-evoking step involve a picture of a dog, progress through sequenced steps that are progressively more anxiety inducing, such as viewing a live dog, and culminate with the most fear-evoking step, holding a dog. Although the fear of dogs example involved real life or in vivo experiences, that is, the person handled a real dog, systematic desensitization of complex fears may be conducted by having the client imagine situations that typically arouse anxiety. Thus, a claustrophobic person whose hierarchy pertains to fear of closed spaces need only imagine himself in a series of anxiety-evoking situations, such as being trapped in an elevator, to be desensitized.

Wolpe noted (1976) that most people with emotional and behavioral disorders require desensitization for more than one fear hierarchy. In fact, the identification and construction of the hierarchies is a critical step in effective treatment. Hierarchies are constructed from four main sources of information: the patient's clinical history (the onset and vicissitudes of the challenging reaction); the patient's case history (family background, childhood experiences); responses and reactions to probing questions; and responses to questionnaires such as the *Fear Survey Schedule for Children–Revised* (Ollendick, 1983), the *Social Anxiety Scale for Children–Revised* (LaGreca & Stone, 1993), and the *Depression and Anxiety in Youth Scale* (Newcomer, Barenbaum,

& Bryant, 1994). The hierarchies are not restricted to the patient's obvious or stated fears but may be developed for less apparent problems gleaned from the questionnaires or interviewing techniques. They may be thematic, as in the fear of dogs hierarchy that sequences steps involving reactions to the basic theme "dogs," or they may be of temporal–spatial design (Yates, 1970). The steps of temporal–spatial hierarchies move the individual through various time and space settings. For example, fear of leaving home may be desensitized by a hierarchy including sequences such as walking toward the door, opening the door, stepping outside for 5 seconds while holding the doorknob, walking down the outside steps, walking to the edge of the curb, and so on. Often, temporal–spatial and thematic designs are combined.

When relaxation is used as the anxiety-inhibiting response in conjunction with systematic desensitization, the patient is trained in relaxation techniques as the hierarchies are being formed. The traditional technique involves the relaxation of various muscle groups through concentration. In some cases hypnosis is used to induce relaxation. Koeppen (1974) and Ollendick and Cerny (1981) developed relaxation scripts for children because those developed for adults have proved too difficult for children to learn. Relaxation scripts for children are shorter and require the isolation of fewer distinct muscle groups (Francis & Beidel, 1995). Sessions are recommended twice weekly and may use common experiences to teach the difference between tense and relaxed muscles, such as imagining biting down on a jawbreaker and then relaxing the jaw (Laurent & Potter, 1998, Ollendick & Cerny).

When the individual is able to relax deeply, the weakest, least fear-evoking scene or event from the hierarchy is presented. The child must imagine the scene briefly, then concentrate again on relaxation. The alternate pairing of imaginary experiences and relaxation is continued until the initial scene no longer evokes anxiety. At that point, the next step on the hierarchy is introduced and the procedures are repeated. Theoretically, as each item is desensitized, the item above in the hierarchy becomes less threatening and also can be desensitized through the inhibiting effects of relaxation. Therefore, each scene of the hierarchy can be presented without causing the child discomfort. When the final scene, which before treatment was the most anxiety-evoking event in the hierarchy, is presented, it too can be inhibited through relaxation procedures. The success of the procedure depends on beginning with an imagined stimuli that stimulates a weak anxiety response, that is, one that can be inhibited by relaxation. Relaxation and other anxiety-inhibiting responses will not immediately inhibit strong anxiety responses. Thus, if the individual experiences discomfort when confronted with a scene or event, the item must either be reduced into smaller steps on the hierarchy or must be presented in a different way to build up desensitization.

Wolpe (1976) reported that the deconditioning of anxiety in imaginary situations is associated with an abatement of anxiety in corresponding real-life situations. These positive outcomes occur even when clients employ *automated systematic desensitization*, that is, use of tape recordings to practice relaxation and desensitization to hierarchical scenes at home. Wolpe's conclusions were confirmed by Kennedy and Kimura (1974), who reported that clients experience a reduction in avoidance behaviors even when they do not complete the entire fear hierarchy.

Other behavioral therapists (Bouman & Emmelkamp, 1996; Craske, 1993; Goldstein, 1969; Hamilton & Schroeder, 1973; Lang, 1969; Paul, 1969; Yates, 1970), however, have questioned the efficacy of deconditioning through imaginary situations, pointing out that research indicates that real or in vivo experiences produce better results than are gained through the use of imagery. Differing results seem to be emerging for various types of anxiety and phobic disorders. For example, in vivo behavioral treatment for agoraphobia has proved significantly more effective than imagery-based interventions (Bouman & Emmelkamp; Craske); this result has also been obtained for school phobic reactions (Laurent & Potter, 1998). However, if the nature of a person's fears makes it difficult or impractical to use in vivo procedures, Emmelkamp (1986) reports that treatments using imagery are usually successful.

Additional criticisms of systematic desensitization pertain to each component of Wolpe's method: the accuracy of the theory of reciprocal inhibition, the importance of relaxation, the necessity of constructing sequenced hierarchies, and the necessity of systematic progression through the hierarchies (Yates, 1975). Currently, many behaviorists reject the theory of reciprocal inhibition and view systematic desensitization as an example of extinction therapy, the process of limiting a response through nonreinforcement.

Regarding the importance of relaxation, Lazarus and Abramovitz (1962) modified the procedures by using alternative anxiety-inhibiting responses in addition to relaxation with systematic desensitization. They introduced *emotive imagery*, imagined events that arouse feelings of self-importance, joy, pride, and so forth. When the individual generated good feelings through emotive imagery, a minimal anxiety-arousing stimulus for the hierarchy was introduced. Yates (1975) reviewed relevant research into the role of relaxation and concluded that systematic desensitization is effective whether or not relaxation training is part of the program. In response, Wolpe (1973) noted that muscle relaxation is but one technique to inhibit anxiety. He pointed out that the emotion generated by the traditional patient–therapist relationship tends to inhibit anxiety when it is a weak response, and he attributed the beneficial effects of 40% of psychotherapy (nonbehavioral) to this fact. He asserted that the efficiency of a specific system must be tested by recoveries above that 40% baseline level and that systematic desensitization combined with relaxation is effective for resistant patients.

The importance of specific, individualized hierarchy construction has been questioned by Cotler (1970), Donner and Guerney (1969), McGlynn (1971), and Nawas, Fishman, and Pucel (1980), who found standard or group hierarchies as effective as individualized hierarchies, even when the standard items were in random order. *Group desensitization*, introduced by Lazarus (1961), involves use of a standard fear hierarchy with a group that progresses systematically to higher anxiety-inducing levels when every member is ready for the next step.

More important, desensitization has been found to work when the sequence of low-anxiety items is presented first (Cohen, 1969; Edelman, 1971a; Suinn, Edie, & Spinelli, 1970) and when high-anxiety items are presented first (Krapfl & Nawas, 1970). These results suggest that it may not be necessary to proceed through step-by-step desensitization and that high-anxiety responses may be diminished when low-anxiety responses are ignored. The conclusion is supported by research that denotes the effectiveness of massed desensitization procedures, that is, moving quickly through the hierarchy, as opposed to the slow, cautious progress that characterizes standard desensitization procedures (Hall & Hinkle, 1972; Robinson & Suinn, 1969).

Implosive Therapy and Flooding. The foregoing evidence has led to the increased popularity of two alternative techniques based on classic extinction theory—implosive therapy and flooding. In implosive therapy the individual imagines and relives anxiety-evoking scenes or events. Unlike systematic desensitization, however, the imagery is designed to elicit a massive "implosion" of anxiety. When the feared aversive consequences fail to occur in the safe therapeutic setting, the power of the stimulus to evoke anxiety is diminished. Repeated exposure to the imagined stimulus further reduces its anxiety-evoking potential until it no longer causes avoidance behavior in real life.

Flooding is an in vivo procedure in which the anxious individual is placed in a real-life situation that typically evokes anxiety. As is true of implosive therapy, no attempt is made to systematically sequence the experiences to avoid overwhelming the individual nor is relaxation involved. The individual's exposure to the real-life anxiety-arousing situation on repeated occasions reveals that feared consequences do not occur, and the stimulus no longer evokes avoidance behavior. According to Wolpe (1973, pp. 193–200), research suggests that implosive and flooding procedures are useful for treatment of compulsive neuroses based on fear of contamination (Rachman, Hodgson, & Marks 1971) but are generally less effective than systematic desensitization and more prone to relapse (DeMoor, 1970; Mealiea & Nawas, 1971; Willis & Edwards, 1969). However, more current reviews of research (Emmelkamp, 1986) have supported the premise that both implosive and flooding procedures are as effective as systematic desensitization and are more efficient to use. Also, flooding appears to be superior to implosive therapy.

Flooding and implosion have been found to produce significant amounts of distress in children, especially young children; consequently, it is critical that they understand the rationale behind the treatment and what will occur (Francis & Beidel, 1995). Flooding has been particularly effective in treating obsessive-compulsive disorder. Combining imaginal flooding, in vivo flooding, and response prevention, McCarthy and Foa (1988) effectively treated a 13-year-old boy who had obsessive thoughts related to harming his family, failure in school, and ridicule by others, which were heightened by repetitive motions. Both the ritualistic behaviors and the obsessive thoughts were decreased, and effects maintained at 1-year follow-up. Sessions were conducted in the clinic and at home, and school personnel were informed of the treatment. These researchers stressed that involving primary caregivers and school personnel is critical for treatment success.

Modeling. Modeling is learning based on observing another person's behavior (Bandura, 1977), and filmed, live, and participant-observation formats have been used successfully to help children overcome anxiety (Laurent & Potter, 1998). In all three formats, children observe another person demonstrating nonfearful and appropriate behaviors in response to stimuli that produce anxiety or fear in the child. After observation the child engages in practicing the nonfearful responses and is given feedback and reinforcement based on performance (Ollendick & Francis, 1988). Modeling is generally most effective in treating simple phobias. Johnson and McGlynn (1988) effectively treated with filmed and guided participant observation a 6-year-old girl who had a balloon phobia.

Assertiveness Therapy. The strategies associated with assertiveness training are useful for individuals who are often taken advantage of by others, as well as those who are extremely inhibited in social situations. The crux of the behavioral approach is to teach assertive responses through modeling and other instructional techniques such as prompting (Bandura, 1977) and to reinforce the person for demonstrating the newly learned responses. Assertiveness is the ability to express one's thoughts and feelings without violating the rights of others. In therapy the individual learns to recognize the difference between assertive and nonassertive responses in typical social situations or interpersonal relationships.

The individual practices in the therapeutic setting, then is encouraged to practice in real-life situations. According to Wolpe (1976), assertiveness reduces anxiety; therefore, the individual is more comfortable and confident in social interactions. Research into the effectiveness of assertiveness therapy finds it to be most relevant in cases where the individual's fear is related to personal encounters in social situations (Wolpe, 1973).

Aversion Therapy. According to Wolpe (1976), aversion therapy is useful in inhibiting inappropriate and unhealthy emotional responses other than anxiety, particularly those that are pleasurable, such as pedophilia, alcoholism, and drug addiction. An aversive response such as electric shock is paired with the unadaptive pleasurable response and inhibits its occurrence. Thus, a pedophile would be encouraged to imagine himself engaging in deviant sexual activities and would be shocked as this behavior began. The response to the shock would interfere with the excitation response to the sexual imagery. A form of aversion therapy based on instrumental conditioning involves the application of an unpleasant stimulus that is terminated when the patient ceases the challenging behavior. For example, an individual may be shocked each time she smokes a cigarette, but the shock is terminated as soon as the cigarette is discarded. A less drastic aversive technique involves aversive imagery. The patient is encouraged to imagine unpleasant scenes in response to the pleasure-evoking stimulus. For example, an alcoholic may imagine the unpleasant effects of a hangover in response to a bottle of alcohol.

Attempting to spread a word of caution about the use of aversive techniques, Wolpe pointed out that many inappropriate habits like excessive drinking and drug addiction usually are secondary to neurotic anxiety, and he noted that "aversion therapy should never be used before every attempt has been made to decondition the anxiety. If the basic anxiety is removed, the behaviors that stem from it will usually disappear, and there will be no need for aversive therapy" (1973, pp. 216, 238).

Habit Disorders and Tics

Watson and Sterling (1998) offered this definition of *habit*: "a benign, learned, persistent, volitional, topographically repetitive behavior that is maintained by reinforcement and evoked by many discriminative stimuli" (p. 431). Most people engage in habitual behavior, and unless there is considerable cost to the individual in terms of physical, psychological, social, academic, or work problems, most habits go untreated (Hansen, Tishelman, Hawkins, & Doepke, 1990). Habit disorders and tics are classified in DSM–IV as impulse-control disorders. Habits may be directly reinforced, may become conditioned reinforcers, or may be negatively reinforced if they are associated with a reduction in anxiety (such as in the case of some thumb-sucking behaviors). Tics are rapid and brief stereotypic movements or vocalizations and are often considered under involuntary control (Watson & Sterling, 1998). Treatment for tics is more often sought because they generally evoke negative attention and result in negative stigma.

Functional assessment models have been used effectively to evaluate the antecedents and consequences associated with habits and tics and to plan successful interventions. Antecedents commonly associated include the presence of certain individuals (e.g., they are more likely to occur when the father is in the room), commands ("go clean your room"), and specific settings (while in the car). Consequential analysis reveals social attention, negative reinforcement, and automatic reinforcement to be maintaining variables.

Treatment using antecedent interventions generally follows the pattern of identifying nonevocative stimuli, arranging the environment so that those stimuli are prevalent, and heavily reinforcing all appropriate behaviors other than the habit or tic. After a reduction in the target behavior, evocative stimuli can be paired with nonevocative stimuli. For example, if tics occur during command situations but not during compliments, the parent might pair a compliment with a command, "Nice to see you helping your brother. Please go clean up your room." If social attention is maintaining the behavior, then ignoring (extinction) is employed along with social attention for incompatible behaviors. For example, habitual throat clearing would be ignored and making no throat-clearing noise would be reinforced. If the habit or tic is maintained by escape or avoidance of aversive stimuli (negative reinforcement), then escape extinction is paired with allowing the child to escape the aversive situation for displaying appropriate behaviors. For example, a student whose tic results in escape from work would not have work withdrawn in the presence of the tic but could earn work withdrawal in its absence. Adding a tangible reinforcer for not engaging in the habit or tic behavior is likely to increase the strength of the interaction (Watson & Sterling, 1998).

Automatic reinforcement is presumed to be a primary maintainer of many habit and tic behaviors. In these cases interventions must either prevent the behavior from occurring or punish the behavior. Watson and Allen (1993) attached a splint to the thumb of a child whose thumb-sucking had become problematic, thus preventing the child from engaging in the behavior. Automatic negative reinforcement may also be at play in many instances. Examples include vocal tics that follow a feeling of tightness in a child's chest and nail biting that reduces anxious feelings. Relaxation training can relax the chest muscles and reduce anxiety. However, Peterson, Campose, and Azrin (1994) found relaxation training to be insufficient by itself, but pairing it with mild punishment (point loss or nasty-tasting nail polish) increased intervention effects. If a habit has become a conditioned reinforcer, then treatment should follow a differential reinforcement and mild punishment paradigm.

Finally, a nonspecific treatment (seemingly independent of function), *habit reversal*, has proved effective in reducing bruxism (Peterson, Dixon, Talcott, & Kelleher, 1993), tics (Azrin & Peterson, 1990), stuttering (Wagaman, Miltenberger, & Andorfer, 1993), and nail-biting (Silber & Haynes, 1991), among others. Miltenberger and Fuqua (1985) found that five components of habit reversal were critical to effective treatment: (a) self-monitoring, (b) competing response, (c) relaxation training, (d) social support, and (e) habit inconvenience review. Research on children has been very effective but has suggested that a sixth component—reinforcement for completing the treatment procedures—is required.

Massed negative practice is based on the theory of reactive inhibition (Hull, 1943), which states that the repetition of a response generates fatigue, which acts to inhibit the occurrence of that response. Thus, unadaptive motor habits such as tics and stuttering may be eliminated by having the patient deliberately repeat the behavior. This approach is one of the most often cited treatments for tics; however, research has reported very mixed efficacy results, with some studies showing high success rates and others showing little or no success (Peterson et al., 1994; Watson & Sterling, 1998).

Other Conditions Addressed by Behavioral Therapies

Many other pathological conditions of childhood have been addressed successfully using the techniques of ABA, FBA, and other therapies based on behavioral principles (Watson & Gresham, 1998). These include attention and concentration problems (DuPaul & Hoff, 1998), speech disfluencies (Miltenberger & Woods, 1998), child abuse and neglect (Donohue, Ammerman, & Zelis, 1998), sleep problems (Durand, Mindell, Mapstone, & Gernet-Dott, 1998), elimination disorders (Friman & Jones, 1998), recurrent pain (Allen & Matthews, 1998), eating disorders (Williamson, Womble, & Zucker, 1998), depression (Watson & Robinson, 1998), self-injury (Mace, Vollmer, Progar, & Mace, 1998), and antisocial behaviors (Sprague, Sugai, & Walker, 1998). Although the scope of this chapter limits addressing these behaviors, persons interested in additional information are encouraged to review the literature.

This discussion of interventions used with specific problem behaviors was designed to demonstrate the effectiveness of behavioral strategies for modifying a variety of inappropriate behaviors, including many encountered by teachers of children with social and emotional difficulties. For the most part, research supports the effectiveness of this approach to treatment (Marks, 1982; Watson & Gresham, 1998), and outcomes compare favorably with those obtained when other approaches are used (Smith, Glass, & Miller, 1980). Although there are limits to the effectiveness of behavioral therapy, the simplicity, economy, and efficacy of the behavioral approaches argue for their use in educational settings. This conclusion is not presented to suggest that the classroom teacher undertake all of the treatment strategies discussed in this chapter, or that she is responsible for the treatment of complex conditions such as conversion hysteria, depression, and stuttering. The intent of revealing the extensive uses of behavioral therapy is to inform and thus to reduce the teacher's anxiety, confusion, or frustration when she encounters children manifesting serious emotional disorders in the classroom.

However, teachers often must be prepared to cope personally with behaviors such as head banging, enuresis, phobic reactions, elective mutism, and so on. The evidence that operant principles may be applied to reduce the occurrence of these behaviors just as they are used to change more typical challenging classroom behaviors, such as disruptive behavior and poor academic achievement, should increase the teacher's confidence in her ability to provide a therapeutic environment for children with emotional and behavioral problems.

STUDY QUESTIONS

1. List and discuss the four main components of ABA. Then develop a plan to use ABA with a student, friend, or relative.

2. Discuss FBA. Why is it important to know the function of the behavior? What interventions match which functions?

3. Discuss the types of reinforcement systems and the type of punishment that can be used with disturbed children in school situations.

4. Plan a token economy.

5. Compare and contrast systematic desensitization and flooding interventions.

6. Discuss the advantages and disadvantages of a behavioral approach to helping students with emotional and behavioral problems. Integrate information from the behavioral section in Chapter 2.

References

Ager, C. L. (2000). *BEST Program: Staff handbook.* Glenside, PA: Arcadia University.

Alberto, P., & Troutman, A. (1990). *Applied behavior analysis for teachers* (3rd ed.). Columbus, OH: Merrill.

Allen, K., Henke, L., Harris, F., Baer, D., & Reynolds, N. (1967). The control of hyperactivity by social reinforcement of attending behavior in a preschool child. *Journal of Educational Psychology, 58,* 231–237.

Allen, K. D., & Matthews, J. R. (1998). Behavior management of recurrent pain in children. In T. S. Watson & F. M. Gresham (Eds.), *Handbook of child behavior therapy* (pp. 263–286). New York: Plenum Press.

American Psychiatric Association. (1994). *Diagnostic and statistical manual of mental disorders* (4th ed.). Washington, DC: Author.

Arrington, R. (1943). Time-sampling in studies of social behavior: A critical review of techniques and results with research suggestions. *Psychological Bulletin, 40,* 81–124.

Axelrod, S., Hall, R., Weis, L., & Rohrer, S. (1974). Use of self-imposed contingencies to reduce the frequencies of smoking behavior. In M. Mahoney & C. Thorensen (Eds.), *Self-control: Power to the person* (pp. 77–85). Belmont, CA: Brooks/Cole.

Azrin, N., & Besalel, V. (1980). *How to use over-corrrection.* Lawrence, KS: H and H Enterprises.

Azrin, N., & Holz, W. (1966). Punishment. In W. Honig (Ed.), *Operant behaviors: Areas of research and application* (pp. 380–447). New York: Appleton-Century-Crofts.

Azrin, N., & Peterson, A. L. (1990). Treatment of Tourette syndrome by habit reversal: A waiting list control group comparison. *Behavior Therapy, 21,* 305–318.

Baer, D. (1962). Laboratory control of thumbsucking by withdrawal and representation of reinforcement. *Journal of Experimental Analysis of Behavior, 5,* 525–528.

Baer, D., Wolf, M., & Risley, T. (1968). Some current dimensions of applied behavior analysis. *Journal of Applied Behavioral Analysis, 1,* 91–97.

Bandura, A. (1965). Influence of models' reinforcement contingencies on the acquisition of imitative responses. *Journal of Personality and Social Psychology, 1,* 589–595.

Bandura, A. (1969). *Principles of behavior modification.* New York: Holt, Rinehart & Winston.

Bandura, A. (1977). *Social learning theory.* Englewood Cliffs, NJ: Prentice Hall.

Barclay, R. (1967). Effecting behavior change in the elementary classroom: An exploratory study. *Journal of Counseling Psychology, 14,* 240–247.

Barlow, D., & Hayes, S. (1979). Alternating treatment design: One strategy for comparing the effects of two treatments in a single subject. *Journal of Applied Behavior Analysis, 2,* 199–210.

Barrish, H., Saunders, M., & Wolf, M. (1969). Good behavior game: Effects of individual contingencies for group consequences on disruptive behavior in a classroom. *Journal of Applied Behavior Analysis, 2,* 199–124.

Bekhterev, V. (1932). *General principles of human reflexology.* New York: International Universities Press.

Bijou, S. (1965). Experimental studies of child behavior, normal and defiant. In L. Krasner & L. Ullmann (Eds.), *Research in behavior modification* (pp. 56–81). New York: Holt, Rinehart and Winston.

Bijou, S., & Baer, D. (1967). *Child development: Readings in experimental analysis* (Vol. 3). New York: Appleton-Century-Crofts.

Binder, A., McConnell, D., & Sjoholm, N. (1957). Verbal conditioning as a function of experimenter characteristics. *Journal of Abnormal and Social Psychology, 55,* 309–314.

Birnbrauer, J., Wolf, M., Kidder, J., & Tague, C. (1965). Classroom behavior of retarded pupils with token reinforcement. *Journal of Experimental Child Psychology, 2,* 219–235.

Blackham, G., & Silberman, A. (1975). *Modification of child and adolescent behavior.* Belmont, CA: Wadsworth.

Bouman, T. K., & Emmelkamp, P. M. G. (1996). Panic disorder and agoraphobia. In V. B. Van Hasselt & M. Hersen (Eds.), *Sourcebook of psychological treatment manuals for adult disorders* (pp. 23–64). New York: Plenum Press.

Brison, D. (1966). A nontalking child in kindergarten: An application of behavior therapy. *Journal of School Psychology, 4,* 65–69.

Brown, P., & Elliott, R. (1965). The control of aggression in a nursery school class. *Journal of Experimental Child Psychology, 2,* 103–107.

Buell, J., Stoddard, P., Harris, F., & Baer, D. (1968). Collateral social development accompanying reinforcement of outdoor play in a preschool child. *Journal of Applied Behavior Analysis, 1,* 167–173.

Bullock, L. M., Ellis, L. L., & Wilson, M. J. (1994). Knowledge/skills needed by teachers who work with students with severe emotional/behavioral disorders: A revisitation. *Behavioral Disorders, 19,* 108–125.

Campbell, B., & Stanley, J. (1963). Experimental and quasi-experimental designs for research and teaching. In N. Gage (Ed.), *Handbook of research on teaching* (pp. 171–246). Chicago: Rand McNally.

Canter, L. (1976). *Assertive discipline: A take-charge approach for today's educator.* Seal Beach, CA: Canter and Associates.

Carr, E. G., Robinson, S., & Palumbo, L. W. (1990). The wrong issue: Aversive vs. nonaversive treatment. The right issue: Functional vs. nonfunctional treatment. In A. C. Repp & N. N. Singh (Eds.), *Perspectives on the use of nonaversive and aversive interventions for persons with developmental disabilities* (pp. 362–379). Sycamore, IL: Sycamore Press.

Center, D. B., & McKittrick, S. (1987). Disciplinary removal of special education students. *Focus on Exceptional Children, 20*(2), 1–9.

Charles, C. (1989). *Building classroom discipline.* White Plains, NY: Longman.

Cheney, D., Barringer, C., Upham, D., & Manning, B. (1995). Project DESTINY: A model for developing educational support teams through interagency networks for youth with emotional or behavioral disorders. *Special Services in the Schools, 10*(2), 57–76.

Clarizio, H. F. (1981). *Toward positive classroom discipline.* New York: Wiley.

Cohen, R. (1969). The effects of group interaction and progressive hierarchy presentation on desensitization of test anxiety. *Behavior Research and Therapy, 7,* 15–26.

Colvin, G., Kameenui, E., & Sugai, G. (1993). Reconceptualizing behavior management and schoolwide discipline in general education. *Education and Treatment of Children, 16*(4), 361–381.

Colvin, G., Tobin, T., & Schacker, L. (1994). *Technical report: Archival data.* Unpublished document, Project PREPARE, College of Education, University of Oregon, Eugene.

Cooper, M. (1986). A model of persistent absenteeism. *Educational Research, 28,* 14–20.

Copeland, R., Brown, R., & Hall, R. (1974). The effects of principal-implemented techniques on the behavior of pupils. *Journal of Applied Behavior Analysis, 7,* 77–86.

Cotler, S. (1970). Sex differences and generalization of anxiety reduction with automatic desensitization and minimal therapist interaction. *Behavior Research and Therapy, 8,* 273–285.

Craighead, W., Kazdin, A., & Mahoney, M. (1976). *Behavior modification.* Boston: Houghton Mifflin.

Craighead, W., & Meyers, A. (1973). *Behavioral modification with the autistic child in the classroom setting.* Paper presented at the meeting of the Association for Advancement of Behavior Therapy, Miami.

Craske, M. G. (1993). Assessment and treatment of panic disorder and agoraphobia. In A. S. Bellack & M. Hersen (Eds.), *Handbook of behavior therapy in the psychiatric setting* (pp. 229–250). New York: Plenum Press.

Daley, M. (1969). The reinforcement menu: Finding effective reinforcers. In J. Krumboltz & C. Thorensen (Eds.), *Behavioral counseling, case studies and techniques* (pp. 42–45). New York: Holt, Rinehart & Winston.

DeMoor, W. (1970). Systematic desensitization versus prolonged high intensity stimulation (flooding). *Journal of Behavior Therapy and Experimental Psychiatry, 1,* 45–52.

Dollard, J., & Miller, N. (1950). *Personality and psychotherapy.* New York: McGraw-Hill.

Donner, L., & Guerney, B. (1969). Automated group desensitization for test anxiety. *Behavior Research and Therapy, 7,* 1–13.

Donohue, B., Ammerman, R. T., & Zelis, K. (1998). Child physical abuse and neglect. In T. S. Watson & F. M. Gresham (Eds.), *Handbook of child behavior therapy* (pp. 183–202). New York: Plenum Press.

Doss, S., & Reichle, J. (1989). Establishing communication alternatives to the emission of socially motivated excess behavior: A review. *Journal of the Association for Severely Handicapped, 14*(2), 101–112.

Drabman, R. (1973). Child versus teacher administered token programs in a psychiatric hospital school. *Journal of Abnormal Child Psychology, 1,* 66–87.

Drabman, R. (1976). Behavior modification in the classroom. In W. Craighead, A. Kazdin, & M. Mahoney (Eds.), *Behavior modification* (pp. 227–242). Boston: Houghton Mifflin.

Drabman, R., & Spitalnik, R. (1973). Social isolation as a punishment procedure: A controlled study. *Journal of Experimental Child Psychology, 16,* 236–249.

Drabman, R., Spitalnik, R., & Spitalnik, K. (1974). Sociometric and disruptive behavior as a function of four types of token economies. *Journal of Applied Behavior Analysis, 1,* 93–101.

Dunlap, G., Kern, L., dePerczel, M., Clarke, S., Wilson, D., Childs, K., White, R., & Falk, G. (1993). Functional analysis of classroom variables for students with emotional and behavioral disorders. *Behavioral Disorders, 18*(4), 275–291.

DuPaul, G. J., & Hoff, K. E. (1998). Attention/Concentration problems. In T. S. Watson & F. M. Gresham (Eds.), *Handbook of child behavior therapy* (pp. 99–126). New York: Plenum Press.

Durand, V. M., Mindell, J. A., Mapstone, E., & Gernet-Dott, D. H. (1998). Sleep problems. In T. S. Watson & F. M. Gresham (Eds.), *Handbook of child behavior therapy* (pp. 203–220). New York: Plenum Press.

Edelman, R. (1971a). Desensitization and physiological arousal. *Journal of Personality and Social Psychology, 17,* 259–266.

Edelman, R. (1971b). Operant conditioning treatment of encopresis. *Journal of Behavior Therapy and Experimental Psychiatry, 2,* 71–73.

Emmelkamp, P. (1986). Behavior therapy with adults. In S. L. Garfield & A. E. Bergin (Eds.), *Handbook of psychotherapy and behavior change* (3rd ed., pp. 385–442). New York: Wiley.

Emmer, E., & Aussiker, A. (1987). *School and classroom discipline programs: How well do they work?* Paper presented at the annual meeting of the American Educational Research Association, Washington, DC.

Eysenck, H. (1949). Training in clinical psychology: An English point of view. *American Psychologist, 4,* 173–176.

Eysenck, H. (1950). Function and training of the clinical psychologist. *Journal of Mental Science, 96,* 710–725.

Eysenck, H. (1964a). The effects of psychotherapy. *International Journal of Psychiatry, 1,* 99–144.

Eysenck, H. (1964b). *Experiments in behavior therapy.* New York: Pergamon Press.

Francis, G., & Beidel, D. (1995). Cognitive-behavioral psychotherapy. In J. S. March (Ed.), *Anxiety disorders in children and adolescents* (pp. 321–340). New York: Guilford Press.

Friman, P. C., & Jones, K. M. (1998). Elimination disorders in children. In T. S. Watson & F. M. Gresham (Eds.), *Handbook of child behavior therapy* (pp. 239–260). New York: Plenum Press.

Garvey, W., & Hegrenes, J. (1966). Desensitization techniques in the treatment of school phobia. *American Journal of Orthopsychiatry, 36*, 147–152.

Gersten, R., Walker, H., & Darch, C. (1988). Relationship between teachers' effectiveness and their tolerance for handicapped students. *Exceptional Children, 54*, 433–438.

Goldstein, A. (1969). Separate effects of extinction, counter-conditioning and progressive approach in overcoming fear. *Behavior Research and Therapy, 7*, 47–56.

Goodwin, D. (1969). Consulting with the classroom teacher. In J. Krumboltz & C. Thorensen (Eds.), *Behavioral counseling cases and techniques*. New York: Holt, Rinehart & Winston.

Gunter, P. L., & Denny, R. K. (1996). Research issues and needs regarding teacher use of classroom management strategies. *Behavioral Disorders, 22*(1), 15–20.

Hall, R., & Hinkle, J. (1972). Vicarious desensitization of test anxiety. *Behavior Research and Therapy, 10*, 407–410.

Hall, R., Lund, D., & Jackson, D. (1968). Effects of teacher attention on study behavior. *Journal of Applied Behavior Analysis, 1*, 1–12.

Hamilton, M., & Schroeder, H. (1973). A comparison of systematic desensitization and reinforced practice procedures in fear reduction. *Behavior Research and Therapy, 11*, 649–652.

Hansen, D. J., Tishelman, A. C., Hawkins, R. P., & Doepke, K. J. (1990). Habits with potential as disorders: Prevalence, severity, and other characteristics among college students. *Behavior Modification, 14*, 66–80.

Harris, F., Wolf, M., & Baer, D. (1984). Effects of social reinforcement of child behavior. *Young Children, 20*, 8–17.

Hart, B., Reynolds, N., Baer, D., Brawley, E., & Harris, F. (1968). Effects of contingent and noncontingent social reinforcement on the cooperative play of a preschool child. *Journal of Applied Behavior Analysis, 1*, 73–76.

Hartup, W. (1964). Friendship status and the effectiveness of peers as reinforcing agents. *Journal of Experimental Child Psychology, 1*, 154–162.

Hawkins, R., & Dotson, V. (1975). Reliability scores that delude. In E. Ramp & G. Semp (Eds.), *Behavior analysis: Areas of research and application* (pp. 359–376). Englewood Cliffs, NJ: Prentice Hall.

Hawkins, R., McArthur, M., Rinaldi, P., Gray, D., & Schafternaur, L. (1967). *Results of operant conditioning techniques in modifying the behavior of emotionally disturbed children.* Paper presented at the 45th annual meeting of the International Council for Exceptional Children Convention, St. Louis.

Herman, S., & Tramontana, J. (1971). Instructions and group versus individual reinforcement in modifying disruptive group behavior. *Journal of Applied Behavior Analysis, 4*, 113–119.

Homme, L. (1966). Human motivation and environment. In N. Haring & R. Whelan (Eds.), *The learning environment: Relationship to behavior modification and implications for special education.* Kansas Studies in Education, Vol. 16. Lawrence: University of Kansas Publications, 30–39.

Homme, L. (1969). *How to use contingency contracting in the classroom.* New York: Research Press.

Hull, C. (1943). *Principles of behavior.* New York: Appleton-Century-Crofts.

Hull, C. (1952). *A behavior system.* New Haven, CT: Yale University Press.

Hundziak, M., Maurer, R., & Watson, L. (1965). Operant conditioning in toilet training of severely mentally retarded boys. *American Journal of Mental Deficiency, 70*, 120–124.

Ivanov-Smolensky, A. (1927). Neurotic behavior and the teaching of conditioned reflexes. *American Journal of Psychiatry, 84*, 483–488.

Ivanov-Smolensky, A. (1928). The pathology of conditioned reflexes and the so-called psychogenic depression. *Journal of Nervous and Mental Disease, 67*, 346–350.

Jacobson, E. (1938). *Progressive relaxation*. Chicago: University of Chicago Press.

Johnson, J. H., & McGlynn, F. D. (1988). Simple phobia. In M. Hersen and C. G. Last (Eds.), *Child behavior therapy casebook* (pp. 45–53). New York: Plenum Press.

Jones, M. (1927). A laboratory study of fear: The case of Peter. *Journal of Genetic Psychology, 31*, 308–315.

Kazdin, A. (1975). *Behavior modification in applied settings*. Homewood, IL: Dorsey Press.

Kazdin, A. (1980). *Research design in clinical psychology*. New York: Harper & Row.

Kearney, C. A., & Silverman, W. K. (1990). A preliminary analysis of a functional model of assessment and treatment for school refusal behavior. *Behavior Modification, 14*, 340–366.

Kearney, C. A., & Tillotson, C. A. (1998). School attendance. In T. S. Watson & F. M. Gresham (Eds.), *Handbook of child behavior therapy* (pp. 143–161). New York: Plenum Press.

Kennedy, T., & Kimura, H. (1974). Transfer, behavioral improvement, and anxiety reduction in systematic desensitization. *Jounal of Consulting and Clinical Psychology, 42*, 720–728.

Kircher, A., Pear, J., & Martin, G. (1971). Shock as punishment in a picture-naming task with retarded children. *Journal of Applied Behavior Analysis, 4*, 227–233.

Knoff, H., Batsche, G., & Knoster, E. (1997). School-wide behavioral management systems. *Research Connections in Special Education, 1*(1), 2–8.

Koeppen, A. S. (1974). Relaxation training for children. *Elementary School Guidance and Counseling, 9*, 14–21.

Krapfl, J., & Nawas, M. (1970). Client–therapist relationship factor in systematic desensitization. *Journal of Consulting and Clinical Psychology, 33*, 435–439.

Krasner, L. (1965). Verbal conditioning and psychotherapy. In L. Krasner & L. Ullmann (Eds.), *Research in behavior modification* (pp. 211–228). New York: Holt, Rinehart & Winston.

Krumboltz, J., & Thorensen, C. (1964). The effect of behavioral counseling in group and individual settings on information-seeking behavior. *Journal of Counseling Psychology, 11*, 324–333.

LaGreca, A. M., & Stone, W. L. (1993). Social anxiety scale for children–revised: Factor structure and concurrent validity. *Journal of Clinical Child Psychology, 22*, 17–27.

Lang, P. (1969). The mechanics of desensitization and the laboratory study of human fear. In C. M. Franks (Ed.), *Behavior therapy: Appraisal and status* (pp. 160–191). New York: McGraw-Hill.

Last, C. G. (1991). Somatic complaints in anxiety disordered children. *Journal of Anxiety Disorders, 5*, 125–138.

Laurent, J., & Potter, K. I. (1998). Anxiety-related difficulties. In T. S. Watson & F. M. Gresham (Eds.), *Handbook of child behavior therapy* (pp. 371–392). New York: Plenum Press.

Lazarus, A. (1961). Group therapy of phobic disorders by systematic desensitization. *Journal of Abnormal and Social Psychology, 66*, 504–510.

Lazarus, A. (1971). *Behavior therapy and beyond*. New York: McGraw-Hill.

Lazarus, A., & Abramovitz, A. (1962). The use of "emotive imagery" in the treatment of children's phobias. *Journal of Mental Science, 4*, 209–212.

Leventhal, T., Weinberger, G., Stander, R., & Sterns, R. (1971). Therapeutic strategies with school phobias. *American Journal of Orthopsychiatry, 37*, 64–70.

Lewis, T. (1997). *Responsible decision making about effective behavioral support*. (Eric Document Reproduction Service No. 305 961)

Lindsley, O. (1954). *Studies in behavioral therapy: Status report III.* Waltham, MA: Metropolitan State Hospital.

Lovaas, O., Freitag, G., Kinder, M., Rubenstein, B., Schaeffer, B., & Simmons, J. (1966). Establishment of social reinforcers in two schizophrenic children on the basis of food. *Journal of Experimental Child Psychology, 4,* 109–125.

Mace, F. C., Vollmer, T. R., Progar, P. R., & Mace, A. B. (1998). Assessment and treatment of self-injury. In T. S. Watson & F. M. Gresham (Eds.), *Handbook of child behavior therapy* (pp. 413–432). New York: Plenum Press.

Madsen, C., Becker, W., Thomas, D., Koser, L., & Plager, E. (1970). An analysis of the reinforcing function of "sit down" commands. In R. K. Parker (Ed.), *Readings in educational psychology* (pp. 265–278). Boston: Allyn & Bacon.

Mager, R. (1962). *Preparing instructional objectives.* Palo Alto, CA: Fearon.

Marks, I. (1982). Toward an empirical clinical science: Behavioral psychotherapy in the 1980's. *Behavioral Therapy, 13,* 63–81.

Martella, R. C., Marchard-Martella, N. E., Miller, T. L., Young, K. R., & Macfarlane, C. A. (1995). Teaching instructional aides and peer tutors to decrease problem behaviors in the classroom. *Teaching Exceptional Children, 27*(2), 53–56.

Martin, G., England, G., Kaprowy, W., Kilgour, K., & Pilek, V. (1968). Operant conditioning of kindergarten-class behavior in autistic children. *Behavior Research and Therapy, 6,* 281–294.

Martin, G., & Pear, J. (1999). *Behavior modification: What it is and how to do it* (6th ed.). Englewood Cliffs, NJ: Prentice Hall.

McAllister, L., Stachowiak, J., Baer, D., & Conderman, L. (1969). The application of operant conditioning techniques in a secondary school classroom. *Journal of Applied Behavior Analysis, 2,* 277–285.

McCarthy, P. R., & Foa, E. B. (1988). Obsessive-compulsive disorder. In M. Hersen & C. G. Last (Eds.), *Child behavior therapy casebook* (pp. 55–69). New York: Plenum Press.

McGlynn, F. (1971). Individual versus standardized hierarchies in the systematic desensitization of snake-avoidance. *Behavior Research and Therapy, 9,* 1–5.

Mealiea, W., & Nawas, M. (1971). The comparative effectiveness of systematic desensitization and implosive therapy in the treatment of snake phobia. *Journal of Behavioral Therapy and Experimental Psychiatry, 2,* 85–94.

Meichenbaum, D., Bowers, K., & Ross, R. (1968). Modification of classroom behavior for institutionalized female adolescent offenders. *Behavior Research and Therapy, 6,* 343–353.

Miltenberger, R. G., & Fuqua, R. W. (1985). A comparison of contingent vs. non-contingent competing response practice in the treatment of nervous habits. *Journal of Behavior Therapy and Experimental Psychiatry, 16,* 195–200.

Miltenberger, R. G., & Woods, D. W. (1998). Speech disfluencies. In T. S. Watson & F. M. Gresham (Eds.), *Handbook of child behavior therapy* (pp. 127–142). New York: Plenum Press.

Morris, R. (1985). *Behavior modification with exceptional children: Principles and practices.* Glenview, IL: Scott, Foresman.

Mowrer, O. (1950). *Learning theory and personality dynamics.* New York: Ronald Press.

Nawas, M., Fishman, S., & Pucel, J. (1980). A standardized desensitization program applicable to group and individual treatments. *Behavior Research and Therapy, 8,* 49–56.

Nelson, J. (1987). *Positive discipline.* New York: Ballantine.

Nelson, J. (1996). Designing schools to meet the needs of students who exhibit disruptive behavior. *Journal of Emotional and Behavioral Disorders, 4*(3), 147–161.

Nelson, J. R., & Colvin, G. (1996). Designing supportive school environments. *Special Services in the Schools*, *11*(1/2), 169–186.

Newcomer, P. L., Barenbaum, E. M., & Bryant, B. R. (1994). *Depression and Anxiety in Youth Scale*. Austin, TX: PRO-ED.

Nolen, P., Kunzelmann, H., & Haring, N. (1967). Behavior modification in a junior high learning disabilities classroom. *Exceptional Children*, *34*, 163–168.

O'Leary, K., & Becker, W. (1967). Behavior modification of an adjustment class: A token reinforcement program. *Exceptional Children*, *33*, 637–642.

O'Leary, K., & Becker, W. (1968). The effects of intensity of a teacher's reprimands on children's behavior. *Journal of School Psychology*, *7*, 8–11.

O'Leary, K., Kaufman, K., Kass, R., & Drabman, R. (1970). The effects of loud and soft reprimands on the behavior of disruptive students. *Exceptional Children*, *37*, 145–155.

O'Leary, K., O'Leary, S., & Becker, W. (1967). Modification of a deviant sibling interaction pattern in the home. *Exceptional Children*, *33*, 521–526.

Ollendick, T. H. (1983). Reliability and validity of the revised fear survey schedule for children (FSSC–R). *Behaviour Research and Therapy*, *21*, 685–692.

Ollendick, T. H., & Cerny, J. A. (1981). *Clinical behavior therapy with children*. New York: Plenum Press.

Ollendick, T. H., & Francis, G. (1988). Behavioral assessment and treatment of childhood phobias. *Behavior Modification*, *12*, 165–204.

Patterson, G. (1965). An application of conditioning techniques to the control of a hyperactive child. In L. Ullmann & L. Krasner (Eds.), *Case studies in behavior modification* (pp. 370–375). New York: Holt.

Paul, G. (1969). Outcome of systematic desensitization: Background procedures and uncontrolled reports of individual treatment. In C. M. Franks (Ed.), *Behavior therapy: Appraisal and status* (pp. 63–104). New York: McGraw-Hill.

Pavlov, I. (1927). *Conditioned reflexes*. London: Oxford University Press.

Pavlov, I. (1928). *Lectures on conditioned reflexes*. New York: International Universities Press.

Pavlov, I. (1932). Neurosis in man and animals. *Journal of the American Medical Association*, *99*, 1012–1013.

Pavlov, I. (1934). An attempt at a physiological interpretation of obsessional neurosis and paranoia. *Journal of Mental Sciences*, *80*, 187–197.

Peterson, A. L., Campose, R. L., & Azrin, N. H. (1994). Behavioral and pharmacological treatments for tic and habit disorders: A review. *Journal of Development and Behavioral Pediatrics*, *15*, 430–441.

Peterson, A. L., Dixon, D. L., Talcott, G. W., & Kelleher, W. J. (1993). Habit reversal treatment of temporomandibular disorders: A pilot investigation. *Journal of Behavioral Therapy and Experimental Psychiatry*, *24*, 49–55.

Phillips, E., Phillips, E., Fixsen, D., & Wolf, N. (1973). Behavior-shaping for delinquents. *Psychology Today*, *7*, 74–108.

Premack, D. (1959). Toward empirical behavior laws: I. Positive reinforcement. *Psychological Review*, *66*, 219–233.

Premack, D. (1965). Reinforcement theory. In D. Levin (Ed.), *Nebraska symposium on motivation* (pp. 123–180). Lincoln: University of Nebraska.

Quay, H., Sprague, R., Werry, J., & McQueen, M. (1967). Conditioning visual orientation of conduct problem children in the classroom. *Journal of Experimental Child Psychology*, *5*, 512–517.

Rachman, S., Hodgson, R., & Marks, I. (1971). The treatment of chronic obsessive compulsive neurosis. *Behavior Research and Therapy*, *9*, 237–248.

Render, G., Padilla, J., & Krank, H. (1989). What research really shows about assertive discipline. *Educational Leadership, 46*, 72–75.

Robinson, C., & Suinn, R. (1969). Group desensitization of a phobia in masses sessions. *Behavior Research and Therapy, 7*, 319–321.

Russo, S. (1964). Adaptations in behavioral therapy with children. *Behavior Research and Therapy, 2*, 43–47.

Shapiro, M. B. (1951). An experimental approach to diagnostic psychological testing. *Journal of Mental Science, 97*, 748–764.

Shapiro, M. B. (1961). A method of measuring psychological changes specific to the individual psychiatric patient. *British Journal of Medical Psychology, 34*, 255–262.

Shapiro, M. B. (1966). The single case in clinical-psychological research. *Journal of General Psychology, 74*, 3–23.

Silber, K. P., & Haynes, C. E. (1991). Treating nailbiting : A comparative analysis of mild aversion and competing response therapies. *Behavior Research and Therapy, 30*, 15–22.

Silberman, M., & Wheelan, S. (1980). *How to discipline without feeling guilty: Assertive relationships with children.* Champaign, IL: Research Press.

Skinner, B. F. (1953). *Science and human behavior.* New York: Macmillan.

Smith, M., Glass, G., & Miller, T. (1980). *The benefits of psychotherapy.* Baltimore: Johns Hopkins University Press.

Sprague, J., Sugai, G., & Walker, H. (1998). Antisocial behavior in schools. In T. S. Watson & F. M. Gresham (Eds.), *Handbook of child behavior therapy* (pp. 451–474). New York: Plenum Press.

Sugai, G., & Horner, R. (1994). Including students with severe behavior problems in general education settings: Assumptions, challenges, and solutions. *Oregon Conference Monograph, 6*, 109–120.

Suinn, R., Edie, C., & Spinelli, P. (1970). Accelerated massed desensitization: Innovation in short-term treatment. *Behavior Therapy, 1*, 301–311.

Sulzer-Azaroff, B., & Mayer, G. (1977). *Applying behavior-analysis procedures with children and youth.* New York: Holt, Rinehart & Winston.

Thorndike, E. (1898). Animal intelligence: An experimental study of the associative process in animals. *Psychological Review Monograph Supplement.*

Titkin, S., & Hartup, W. (1965). Sociometric status and the reinforcing effectiveness of children's peers. *Journal of Experimental Child Psychology, 18*, 50–64.

Vogel-Sprott, M. (1964). Response generalization under verbal conditioning in alcoholics, delinquents and students. *Behavior Research and Therapy, 2*, 135–141.

Wagaman, J. R., Miltenberger, R. G., & Andorfer, R. E. (1993). Analysis of a simplified treatment for stuttering in children. *Journal of Applied Behavior Analysis, 26*, 53–62.

Walker, H., Mattson, R., & Buckley, N. (1968). Special class placement as a treatment alternative for deviant behavior in children. In F. Benson (Ed.), *Modifying deviant social behaviors in various classroom settings* (pp. 115–142). Eugene: University of Oregon.

Walker, H. M., Horner, R. H., Sugai, G., Bullis, M., Sprague, J., Bricker, D., & Kaufman, M. (1996). Integrated approaches to preventing antisocial behavior patterns among school-age children and youth. *Journal of Emotional and Behavioral Disorders, 4*(4), 194–209.

Walker, J., & Shea, T. (1991). *Behavior management: A practical approach for educators* (5th ed.). New York: Merrill.

Wasik, B. (1970). The application of Premack's generalization on reinforcement to the management of classroom behavior. *Journal of Experimental Child Psychology, 10*, 33–43.

Watson, J. B., & Rayner, R. (1920). Conditioned emotional reaction. *Journal of Experimental Psychiatry, 3*, 1–14.

Watson, J. B. (1916). Behaviorism and the concept of mental disease. *Journal of Philosophical, Psychological Scientific Methods, 13*, 587–597.

Watson, T. S., & Allen, K. D. (1993). Elimination of thumb-sucking as a treatment for severe trichotillomania. *Journal of the American Academy of Child and Adolescent Psychiatry, 32*, 830–834.

Watson, T. S., & Gresham, F. M. (Eds.). (1998). *Handbook of child behavior therapy*. New York: Plenum Press.

Watson, T. S., & Gresham, F. M. (1998). Current issues in child behavior therapy. In T. S. Watson & F. M. Gresham (Eds.), *Handbook of child behavior therapy* (pp. 499–504). New York: Plenum Press.

Watson, T. S., & Robinson, S. L. (1998). A behavior analytic approach for treating depression. In T. S. Watson & F. M. Gresham (Eds.), *Handbook of child behavior therapy* (pp. 393–412). New York: Plenum Press.

Watson, T. S., & Sterling, H. E. (1998). Habits and tics. In T. S. Watson & F. M. Gresham (Eds.), *Handbook of child behavior therapy* (pp. 431–450). New York: Plenum Press.

Whelan, R., & Haring, N. (1966). Modification and maintenance of behavior through systematic application of consequences. *Exceptional Children, 32*, 281–289.

Williamson, D. A., Womble, L. G., & Zucker, N. L. (1998). Cognitive behavior therapy for eating disorders. In T. S. Watson & F. M. Gresham (Eds.), *Handbook of child behavior therapy* (pp. 335–356). New York: Plenum Press.

Willis, R., & Edwards, J. (1969). A study of the comparative effectiveness of systematic desensitization and implosive therapy. *Behavior Research and Therapy, 7*, 387–395.

Wolf, M., Risley, T., & Mees, H. (1964). Application of operant conditioning procedures to the behavior problems of an autistic child. *Behavior Research and Therapy, 1*, 305–312.

Wolpe, J. (1961). The systematic desensitization treatment of neuroses. *Journal of Nervous and Mental Disorders, 132*, 189–203.

Wolpe, J. (1973). *The practice of behavior therapy*. New York: Pergamon Press.

Wolpe, J. (1976). *Theme and variations: A behavior therapy casebook*. New York: Pergamon Press.

Yates, A. J. (1970). *Behavior therapy*. New York: Wiley.

Yates, A. J. (1975). *Theory and practice in behavior therapy*. New York: Wiley.

York, P., York, D., & Wachtel, T. (1982). *Toughlove*. New York: Doubleday.

Zimmerman, E., & Zimmerman, J. (1962). The alteration of behavior in a special classroom situation. *Journal of Experimental Analysis of Behavior, 5*, 59–60.

Zimmerman, E., Zimmerman, J., & Russell, C. (1969). Differential effects of token reinforcement on instruction-following behavior in retarded students instructed as a group. *Journal of Applied Analysis, 2*, 101–112.

CHAPTER

6

COGNITIVE THERAPY

Phyllis L. Newcomer and Christina Ager

Cognitive therapies share a theoretical perspective that internal cognitive thoughts, ideas, beliefs, perceptions, and attitudes influence emotions and determine behavior. Mental functions such as problem-solving strategies, attribution of causes to events, perceptions of threat, and self-verbalizations play a large part in determining the quality of an individual's adaptation to the environment. Although all therapeutic approaches are designed to alter an individual's thoughts and ideas, cognitive therapies are distinguished by the *directness* of concentration on these events. In other words, whereas other approaches eventually may help an individual develop new ideas through indirect techniques, such as the development of insight or the release of repressed emotion, cognitive therapies focus directly on cognitive restructuring or reorganization, holding that cognitive changes must produce behavioral changes. Because the most often used and thoroughly researched of these therapeutic approaches are concerned with behavioral outcomes as well as cognitive changes, many of the principles associated with behavioral therapy (see Chapter 5) have been integrated into their theoretical foundations, and they are frequently referred to as cognitive–behavioral therapies. In some cases they are extensions of behavioral therapy that emphasize the internal mediating factors affecting the perception of stimuli and influencing responses. They are the natural outgrowth of the movement among behaviorists away from strict adherence to theories attributing all behavior to overt stimuli and responses. A good example is the work of Albert Bandura (1977), a social learning theorist who discussed individuals' expectations as a factor influencing behavior and emphasized the importance of selective modeling in learning new behaviors.

Phillip Kendall (2000) presented a guiding theory for cognitive–behavioral therapy with children and adolescents, noting that "for clinical work, the most direct and useful theories are those that propose to explain the processes of change" (p. 3). His theory and recent research into the ways in which cognitive processes co-occur and mediate behavior advance the field of cognitive interventions. Cognitive therapies have always incorporated behavior change into their strategies and goals, including internal verbal behavior and beliefs (e.g., rational-emotive therapy, cognitive therapy, self-instructional training, problem-solving training) and covert and overt physical behaviors (e.g., anxiety management training, aggression control training, relaxation training). These theories hold that "behavioral events, associated anticipatory expectations and post-event attributions, and ongoing cognitive information processing and emotional states combine to influence behavior change" (pp. 3, 4).

Cognitive therapies orient toward a problem-solving approach that is both an indicator of successful childhood adjustment and a component of many empirically validated psychological treatments for child and adolescent disorders (Kazdin & Weisz, 1998; Ollendick & King, 1998). As problems arise throughout life, cognitive information processing critically affects how we make sense of the world. Dysfunctional cognitive information processing necessitates mediation and modification (e.g., Ingram, Miranda, & Segal, 1998). Positive emotional states have been shown to influence cognitive and behavioral abilities (Diener & Lucas, 1999), whereas negative emotional arousal lessens our abilities to problem solve, exercise self-control, and demonstrate appropriate social behaviors. Southam-Gernow and Kendall (2000) found that clients must understand emotional experience and its modification to engage in effective cognitive problem solving. In other words, clients must be able to recognize and identify emotions as well as link them to triggers in the external world.

Almost all cognitive and cognitive–behavioral therapies follow a structured approach to therapy and many use a manual-based approach. The structure of these manual-based approaches includes ways to develop goals, as well as the pacing and sequenced steps required to reach those goals. Examples of such manual-based cognitive therapies include the *Stop and Think Workbook* (Kendall, 1992a), which addresses impulsivity, and the *Coping Cat Workbook* (Kendall, 1992b), which deals with anxiety.

Cognitive therapies are performance-based interventions designed to bring about changes in thoughts, feelings, and behaviors. They attempt to teach skills or remediate skills deficits in cognition, emotion, or behavior. A vital component of these interventions is practice of newly acquired skills or alternative ways of thinking and behaving. Discussion, modeling, practice, and feedback are generally considered critical steps in the therapeutic process.

Because cognitive–behavioral therapies analyze and work with children's internal and external environments, they use an *integrationist perspective* (Meichenbaum, 1977). This perspective emphasizes learning processes "while underscoring the centrality of the individual's mediating/information processing style in the development and remediation of psychological distress" (Kendall, 2000, p. 6). The interplay between the internal environment (including emotions and cognitions) and behaviors is complex, and the contribution of each varies with the presenting psychological problem. Addressing the external environment necessitates considering the social context in which the child must function (i.e., home, school, community settings). Expected roles and rules that are often determined by families and school authorities need to be analyzed and considered to plan goals for treatment. Family involvement in therapy, either as consultants or co-clients, is a critical component of successful treatment. This often requires changing the family's interpersonal systems, especially for treatment of anxiety disorders, attention-deficit/hyperactivity disorders, oppositional defiant disorders, and conduct disorders (Ollendick & King, 2000). Consequently, therapists using a cognitive–behavioral approach are diagnosticians who determine what the specific problems are and what primary systems need addressing during treatment. Additionally, their roles have also been constructed as educator and coach. In these capacities they learn the client's strengths and weaknesses, identify and help modify internal dialogues, model behavior, encourage change, and provide information and feedback.

Cognitive Concepts and Therapy

Over the past two decades an extensive range of research on cognition has led to a greater understanding of the cognitive mechanisms that contribute to both the development and the treatment of psychological disorders. There is some evidence that it is advantageous to view cognition not as a singular concept but as a set of components including cognitive structures, processes, content (events), and products. Such discrimination leads to better understanding and aids in diagnosis and treatment (Ingram & Kendall, 1987; Kendall & Ingram, 1987, 1989). Following is a brief overview of these components of cognition.

Memory and the ways in which information is represented in memory are considered *cognitive structures*. Cognitive structures or schemas (also called templates) screen and filter new experiences through existing memory. For example, the cognitive schema for anxious individuals is threat, and the schema for aggressive individuals is provocation. Experiences get processed through these structures. What is contained in the cognitive structures—what is actually experienced, remembered, or represented—is called *cognitive content*. After a number of experiences, individuals with psychological problems may respond in a characteristic way to most events. These limited cognitive structures become so ingrained that new events trigger automatic cognitive content (e.g., fear, anger), and information processing or learning alternatives are limited. The way people perceive and interpret these experiences illustrates their *cognitive processes*. Results that occur from the interaction of information and cognitive structures, content, and processes are the *cognitive products*. Attributions, internal statements of anger, and decisions about future events are all examples of cognitive products.

An example may help to make the interplay of these components clearer. Imagine that a group of sixth-grade students are getting off the school bus to go to a play one winter morning. The sidewalk outside the theater is icy. A number of students fall on the ice. Initially most of the students will react by saying, "Oh, no!" or something similar. However, individual students will process the event very differently. Some will be embarrassed; others will become self-denigrating ("I am such an idiot. So clumsy."); others may get angry; and still others will laugh, get up, and not process the event cognitively.

Students who do process the event will then move on to making conclusions about the causes of the fall and assign causal attributions, a cognitive product. Depending on their cognitive structures, students will vary in their perceptions of the event. Many students may check to see who witnessed the event, realize many classmates have fallen too, and think no more about it. Another person, however, may process the event as a highly personal embarrassment and develop specific cognitive content such as anxiety about going on class trips or going out in icy weather. The student who is self-denigrating may attribute the fall to her inability to do anything right. This type of stable judgmental internal attribution is characteristic of depression (Abramson, Seligman, & Teasdale, 1979; Stark, Sander, Yancy, Bronik, & Hoke, 2000). A student who becomes angry and blaming is attributing the event to intentional provocation by others. This type of cognitive processing reflects aggressive retaliatory behavior disorders (Lochman, Whidby, & FitzGerald, 2000). A healthy attribution might include accurate assessment of the situation ("It was icy. Nothing bad happened.") and acceptance of minor responsibility ("Next time I should be more careful.").

Cognitive and cognitive–behavioral interventions are designed to challenge children's and adolescents' existing cognitive structures and aid them in seeing how cognitive content and products are related to their interpretations of events, rather than to the events themselves. Dysfunctional cognitive processes are generally divided into cognitive deficiency and cognitive distortion. The absence of thinking or cognitive processing is indicative of deficiencies associated with undercontrolled or externalizing disorders such as impulsivity, acting out, and attentional problems. Cognitive distortions are characterized by dysfunctional (irrational or maladaptive) processes. Distortions often play lead roles in overcontrolled disorders such as anorexia and internalized childhood disorders such as depression and anxiety. Aggressive youth have difficulties with both cognitive distortions (provocative attributions) and deficiencies (interpersonal problem solving; Kendall, Ronan, & Epps, 1990; Lochman & Dodge, 1998). According to Kendall (2000), research has supported the importance of distinguishing among (a) overcontrolled and undercontrolled disorders, (b) distortions and deficiencies, and (c) the need to recognize the relationship between the type of disorder and the type of processing problem.

Cognitive–behavioral therapy includes a fairly diverse number of approaches, all designed to restructure cognitions, solve problems, and enhance the ability to cope with problem-evoking events. Historically, cognitive-restructuring methods emerged first, and they provide the theoretical bases for later work in the field. Because these methods have implications for educational application, representative theories are discussed in some detail in this chapter. Following discussion of cognitive-restructuring approaches, various coping skills and problem-solving therapies are examined. These approaches employ sets of strategies to teach individuals specific skills and how to apply those skills in difficult situations. Next, anger management training and moral reasoning instruction are discussed. Then, recent uses of cognitive and cognitive–behavioral therapies in the treatment of emotional and behavioral disorders manifested by children and adolescents are reviewed. Specific suggestions for teachers and a discussion of several behavior management programs that integrate cognitive principles into their theoretical base conclude the chapter.

Cognitive-Restructuring Methods

By far the most elaborate theoretical perspectives associated with cognitive–behavioral therapy feature cognitive-restructuring methods. Three of the most recognized are Albert Ellis's rational-emotive therapy, Aaron Beck's cognitive therapy, and Donald Meichenbaum's self-instructional training. Most coping-skills and problem-solving therapies rely on critical aspects of these theories.

Rational-Emotive Therapy

Developed in 1955 by Albert Ellis, a disenchanted psychoanalytical therapist, rational-emotive therapy (RET) is an active-directive treatment approach predicated on the premise that emotionally disturbed states and conditions are caused primarily by distorted cognition. Ellis (1962, 1979) wrote that human beings engage in irrational thinking that, by causing them to experience distressing emotional states and engage in maladaptive behavior, prevents them from achieving their long-range hedonistic goals to live well and be happy. Ellis presented these basic assumptions of RET: "that man is a uniquely rational, as well as a uniquely irrational animal; that his emotional or psychological disturbances are largely a result of his thinking illogically or irrationally; and that he can rid himself of most of his emotional or mental unhappiness, ineffectuality and disturbance if he learns to maximize his rational and minimize his irrational thinking" (1962, p. 36).

Implicit in Ellis's assumptions is the notion that *thinking* and *emotion* are not two distinct processes; rather, they are interrelated. More succinctly, thinking and feeling are so closely related that they cannot realistically be considered independently. Ellis explained that emotion is caused by several noncognitive events, such as sensorimotor stimulation (the sight of a large animal causes fear), and biophysical stimulation through the autonomic nervous system and hypothalamus (electric shock causes fear). However, the most important cause is the thinking process (anticipation of meeting a large animal or of being shocked causes fear). Thinking also involves the recirculation of previous emotional experiences that regenerate feeling (thoughts about an angry encounter experienced last week evoke fresh anger). Thus, emotion and emotional thought (i.e., strongly evaluative or biased thought, or attitudes) are closely related.

Similarly, emotions can be controlled by a variety of means, including use of biochemicals (tranquilizing or sedative drugs), the sensorimotor system (exercises or controlled breathing), existing emotional feeling (well-established feelings for someone), and, most critically, cerebral processes (thinking, or telling the self to calm down). RET does not negate the importance of sensorimotor or biophysical techniques, as is reflected by the inclusion of the word *emotive* in the title; however, the obvious emphasis is on the cognitive techniques used to alter feeling and behavior by altering thinking.

According to RET, individuals become emotionally or psychologically disordered because they make *absolutistic evaluations* of the events in their lives. Absolutistic evaluations are cognitive distortions and figure prominently in psychological problems stemming from distorted processing. Borrowing from Horney (1967), Ellis cited the importance of the "tyranny of the 'shoulds'," a type of thinking that leads to the setting of unrealistic standards for perfection in behavior. The "shoulds" and "musts" of absolutistic thinking influence the development of other irrational thought processes, including "awfulizing," "I-can't-stand-it-itis," and "damnation." Awfulizing is the process of viewing events as catastrophic; I-can't-stand-it-itis refers to believing that one's life will be destroyed if a particular event occurs; and damnation involves rating self or others with extreme harshness for failing to perform a "should." The following are other cognitive distortions that characterize emotional disturbance (after Dryden & Ellis, 1988):

- *All-or-none thinking.* If I am not totally lovable, I must be totally unlovable.

- *Jumping to conclusions and negative non sequiturs.* Others are aware of my limitations and view me as incompetent.

- *Fortune-telling.* When others become aware of my imperfections, they will despise me forever.

- *Focusing on the negative.* Because something goes wrong, nothing good ever happens in my life.

- *Disqualifying the positive.* When people compliment me, they are unaware of my real weaknesses or are simply being kind and over-looking my failings.

- *Allness and neverness.* When circumstances are bad, they will always be that way.

- *Minimization.* My accomplishments are due to luck and are trivial, but my mistakes are my fault and are awful.

- *Emotional reasoning.* My poor performance makes me feel awful and proves I'm no good.

- *Labeling and overgeneralization.* A poor effort on my part categorizes me with the bums of the world.

- *Personalizing.* I'm so awful, people are whispering about me and laughing at me.

- *Phonyism.* Although others may appear to admire me, I'm a phony, and if they knew the real me they would despise me.

- *Perfectionism.* I should do a task perfectly, and if I don't I'm incompetent.

RET differentiates between healthy preferences or desires and dogmatic, absolutistic musts and must nots. It also differentiates between appropriate negative emotions that help orient people toward new goals and escalated negative feelings generated by irrational beliefs that block personal growth, thus contrasting, for example, sadness with depression, concern with anxiety, disappointment with shame, regret with guilt, and annoyance with anger. For example, desires for success and acceptance by others are healthy, appropriate goals. Therefore, failure at a task or rejection by a friend may evoke sadness, concern, disappointment, and so forth, which are feelings appropriate to the circumstances. Responding to failure or rejection with thoughts dominated by absolute musts or shoulds, however, escalates desires into demands and generates extreme, pathological emotion, such as feelings of hopelessness, self-hate, self-denigration, and intense hostility.

Because individuals with emotional difficulties use negative, self-defeating thoughts and self-talk to create and maintain their unhappy state, treatment includes delineating the person's past and present illogical thinking and self-defeating remarks by "1. Bringing them forcefully to his attention or consciousness, 2. Showing him how they cause and maintain his disturbance, 3. Identifying the logical links in his internalized sentences, and 4. Teaching him how to rethink and re-verbalize these internalized thoughts" (Ellis, 1962, p. 59). Examples of typical irrational ideas produced by cognitive distortions include the following (Ellis, 1962):

- "The idea that it is a dire necessity for an adult human being to be loved or approved of by virtually every significant other person in his community" (p. 61).

- "The idea that one should be thoroughly competent, adequate, and achieving in all possible respects if one is to consider oneself worthwhile" (p. 63).

- "The idea that certain people are bad, wicked or villainous and that they should be severely blamed and punished for their villainy" (p. 65).

- "The idea that it is awful and catastrophic when things are not the way one would very much like them to be" (p. 69).

- "The idea that human unhappiness is externally caused and that people have little or no ability to control their sorrows and disturbance" (p. 72).

- "The idea that if something is or may be dangerous or fearsome one should be terribly concerned about it and should keep dwelling on the possibility of its occurring" (p. 75).

- "The idea that it is easier to avoid than to face certain life difficulties and self-responsibilities" (p. 78).

- "The idea that one should be dependent on others and needs someone stronger than oneself on whom to rely" (p. 80).

- "The idea that one's past history is an all-important determiner of one's present behavior and that because something once strongly affected one's life, it should indefinitely have a similar effect" (p. 82).

- "The idea that one should become quite upset over other people's problems and disturbances" (p. 85).

- "The idea that there is invariably a right, precise, and perfect solution to human problems and that it is catastrophic if this perfect solution is not found" (p. 86).

RET does not offer elaborate explanations regarding the origins of emotional disturbance; however, Ellis (1979) used an ABC model of emotional disturbance to describe how psychological problems are perpetuated. People do not understand the cause–effect relationships between their absolutistic beliefs (B) and psychological pathology (C). Rather, they believe that events in their lives, or more precisely their inferences about the events in their lives (A), cause problems. For example, Richard attributes his extremely high level anxiety (C)—in accordance with his inferences and perceptions—to the impossible demands of his teacher (A), whereas his anxiety is caused by his irrational belief that he must perform with perfection and never make a mistake (B).

Another reason problems are perpetuated is that, even when an individual recognizes the existence of irrational beliefs, he searches for the antecedents of the beliefs rather than concentrating on changing them. Focusing on the past and searching for deeply hidden causal factors in the unconscious mind is viewed as counterproductive. Present events are of primary importance. The third reason why many people fail to change is that they are unwilling to work hard enough to counter their irrational thinking. In Ellis's terms, they have low *frustration tolerance* and give up when therapy proves to be other than a soothing experience.

In RET, therapeutic change can occur at various levels. The most desirable level involves philosophical restructuring of the irrational beliefs—that is, change at Level B. When changes occur at Level B, an individual often is able to spontaneously alter distorted perceptions and inferences at Level A. For example, if Richard works to correct his beliefs involving his perfectionism, he might be able to view school tasks more realistically, cease making faulty attributions about his teacher ("she hates me"), stop overreacting to mistakes, and so forth. However, if change at Level B appears unobtainable for some reason, changes can be made at the inferential level (A) exclusively. Richard may alter his negative perceptions about his teacher's attitudes and may display a more positive affect toward her, which in turn is reciprocated and is positively reinforcing to Richard. Therefore, his level of anxiety is lessened even though his absolutistic thought system regarding perfection is unaffected.

Advocates of RET believe that philosophical changes at Level B are far superior to inferential changes at Level A, even if symptoms are not reduced as rapidly. A principal approach to therapy is a logico-empirical method of scientific questioning, challenging, and debating (Ellis, 1979, p. 20), as when an individual forms a hypothesis that challenges an inference or belief, formulates a strategy for testing it, and evaluates the outcome. For example, Richard's decision to challenge his negative attributions regarding his teacher by engaging in friendly behaviors represents the formulation and testing of a hypothesis. The positive feedback he receives validates the hypothesis. Other therapeutic strategies include the use of rationally oriented coping self-statements; relaxation; problem solving; and skill-training methods. Although RET involves the use of multimodal therapeutic techniques influencing cognition, emotion, and behavior, those affecting cognition are most important. As might be expected in an active–directive therapy, those cognitive strategies involving active disputing of irrational beliefs are preferred over those emphasizing cognitive distraction (e.g., relaxation exercises).

Dryden and Ellis (1988), in discussing the major cognitive, emotive, and behavioral therapeutic techniques associated with RET, provided a typical approach to the most important strategy: actively disputing irrational beliefs. They indicated that, after helping an individual identify an irrational belief, the therapist actively debates with the client regarding its validity, often using questions associated with the Socratic method, such as "Where is the evidence that you must have this?" Thus, the individual is forced to provide logical verification of the belief. Also, the psychologically disturbed person is expected to do homework, that is, to practice disputing irrational beliefs. This person is assisted in the process by reading appropriate books and articles (Ellis & Becker, 1982), listening to audiotapes of RET lectures, and practicing RET with friends.

Other cognitive techniques are the use of more positive (less catastrophic) language (e.g., saying "that's too bad" instead of "that's horrible") and the use of imagery techniques. The language of self-talk influences feeling; therefore, monitoring the extent to which it accurately reflects the implications of a negative situation and correcting it when it describes an unfortunate event as a tragedy is therapeutic.

In the use of imagery, an individual is asked to produce an image of a Level A experience (having an essay returned that needs editing) while he attempts to refute his Level B ideas (that he must be perfect) and change his Level C emotions (anxiety). Lazarus (1984) developed time-projection imagery methods that also are used. When an individual is convinced that an event is awful, he is asked to imagine what life would be like at various intervals after the event has occurred. The goal is to challenge the irrational belief by helping him see that life goes on and people recover from negative experiences.

RET's emotive therapeutic techniques have received less attention than those used for cognitive restructuring and involve the therapist's use of humor and self-disclosure. Humor is used to help the client take the world less seriously. Self-disclosure illustrates that all human beings err and that the client is not alone in experiencing certain kinds of problems. Other emotive strategies include asking clients to role-play their rational selves, and in some cases to engage in risk-taking exercises. Risk taking involves engaging in a feared activity, as when an individual afraid of appearing foolish or ignorant is encouraged to speak in public.

RET behavior strategies include homework assignments, which are used frequently to practice cognitive restructuring and often involve in vivo desensitization and flooding, in which the individual practices refuting irrational thinking in a real-life situation (see Chapter 5). Other strategies include antiprocrastination exercises, designed to help the client stop avoiding difficult tasks that pertain to the problem, and the use of rewards and penalties (e.g., fines). (The use of penalties is relatively unusual in therapeutic situations.)

According to Ellis (1962), the therapist is a "frank counter-propagandist" who uses the didactic method to "encourage, persuade, cajole, and occasionally even insist" (p. 95) that the troubled person act in some manner that will counteract illogical thoughts. Although the therapist unconditionally accepts the client regardless of behavior, because therapy should not involve the assignment of blame, the therapeutic environment is not warm and loving. The therapist's primary obligation is to vigorously and consistently reiterate the illogical ideas at the root of the client's problems. The client must not be permitted to evade or elude the essence of the problems by dwelling on superficial aspects or by hiding behind the rationalizations that are part of irrational defenses against reality. For example, an adolescent who maintains that he fails in school because his teacher dislikes him must be convinced that his negative self-talk pertaining to feelings of inadequacy and fear of failure contribute more to the problem than does the teacher's attitude. He also must learn to dismiss the irrational notion that because he dislikes a task, he need not deal with it. He must accept responsibility for his life situation. Unless he resolves these basic problems, even a superficial modification of current school performance would have no lasting effect on behavior.

Rebuttals to Early Criticism. Having forcefully stated how therapy should be conducted, Ellis (1962, 1970) was equally forceful in answering criticisms of his approach and of cognitive therapies in general. One of the most prevalent attacks is that cognitive therapies, particularly those such as RET that emphasize cognitive restructuring, are too "intellectualized" and "ooververbal." In response, Ellis noted that RET does not ignore feelings and in fact the client is asked to discuss feelings about events, not to talk about his conceptions of his condition. When negative, self-harming feelings are recognized, the client is led to identify the cognitive sources. RET emphasizes the relationship between emotion and thinking and shows how cognitive changes produce changes in emotion.

A second criticism is that the use of realism is limited in human affairs; that is, realism is not the only authority in determining opinions or behaviors. Ellis agreed, but found the statement irrelevant. He maintained that cognitive restructuring approaches are based on the idea that attitudes are not necessarily developed from realistic, external events but instead spring from internal interpretations of external forces. RET employs clear, logical thought processes to alter those internal, subjective interpretations.

A third attack is that RET is superficial and depends solely on suggestion and "positive thinking." Because it is not designed to uncover the patient's deep unconscious thoughts; RET results in symptom removal rather than in a real cure. In response, Ellis argued that RET is designed to alter an individual's basic philosophy of life and as such is not superficial. The suggestions used in treatment pertain to underlying irrational thoughts, not to the superficial problems that may be espoused by the patient.

Also, the unconscious emotions that underlie disturbed states are identified and introduced to conscious awareness in RET through examination of an individual's self-talk. This process is decidedly different from that associated with "positive thinking" techniques (Peale, 1952) that simply involve the repetition of positive statements, such as "I am a loved person." In RET, understanding and analyzing thoughts is a prelude to replacing them with more constructive or realistic ideas.

A fourth attack charges that RET is too directive and authoritarian. Ellis responded that all psychotherapy involves authoritarian attempts to control behavior. RET simply takes a more open, direct path to helping the individual alter the attitudes and behaviors troubling him. The more efficiently the therapist can accomplish this task, the more effective the therapy. It must be expected that the therapist will impose values on the patient and that presumably the client needs to acquire new values, because he is not doing well with those previously acquired.

Finally, cognitive restructuring therapies are attacked as being ineffective with clients who are extremely disturbed or mentally limited. Ellis argued that RET can be more effective with such individuals than other approaches because the techniques are directive and systematic.

Efficacy of RET. Some research has documented the use of RET techniques with client populations manifesting a wide variety of problems and compared the RET techniques with other therapeutic techniques (Dryden & Ellis, 1988; Lyons & Woods, 1991). However, there is considerable controversy over the methodological adequacy of these early studies (Haaga & Davison, 1995). Hollon and Beck (1986) summed up this critical point of view: "RET appears to have the least clear empirical support of any of the major variants [of cognitive–behavioral therapy], although that state of affairs may derive . . . from the fact that the bulk of the trials . . . were earlier, less rigorously conducted efforts" (p. 476).

Two main sources of criticism are (a) insufficient testing of unique RET hypotheses and (b) inattention to acceptable research methods (Haaga & Davison, 1989, 1995). Specifics include failure to isolate or investigate hypothetical constructs and nonreporting of clinically significant treatment effects, follow-up results, and attrition. The most serious criticism of the RET research is that it systematically fails to specify or measure RET itself. This failure to report on the specifics and integrity of the treatment methods calls into serious question most research favoring this approach (Haaga & Davison, 1995).

Applicability of RET. Ellis has continued to promote the theories behind RET (Ellis, 1995), stating that the application of its principles will lead to a more "self-actualized and self-fulfilled existence" (p. 73). Although the efficacy of RET is questionable, its philosophical basis and the cognitive distortions and irrational thoughts isolated by Ellis as contributing to psychological problems continue to be recognized and treated by most forms of cognitive–behavioral therapy. Ellis has made clear that the use of RET techniques is not restricted to psychotherapists. He has authored many books for public consumption, such as *A New Guide to Rational Living* (Ellis & Harper, 1975), *A Guide to Personal Happiness* (Ellis & Becker, 1982), *Rational-Emotive Approaches to the Problems of Childhood* (Ellis & Bernard, 1983), and *How to Stubbornly Refuse to Make Yourself Miserable About Anything—Yes, Anything!* (Ellis, 1988), and with his colleagues at the Institute for Rational-Emotive Therapy has developed videocassettes, audiocassettes, and programmed material for mass use, maintaining that individuals who read about RET techniques may apply them to improve their own lives and to help others lead more productive lives.

Cognitive Therapy

Cognitive therapy (CT) is a comprehensive theoretical approach for cognitive restructuring that evolved from Aaron Beck's early work with depressed individuals (Beck, 1963). Like Ellis, Beck became disgruntled with psychoanalytic therapy, and like RET, his approach to therapy focuses primarily on the content and processes of cognition. He describes cognitive therapy as "the application of the cognitive model of a particular disorder with the use of a variety of techniques designed to modify the dysfunctional beliefs and faulty information processing characteristic of each disorder" (Beck, 1993, p. 194). This statement clarifies how CT can be used to help individuals identify and counter problems at two cognitive levels. The first level involves the individual's belief system, that is, the way she typically views the world in expectations, evaluations, and attributions of causality. Unlike the hard-to-access unconscious processes emphasized by the psychoanalytic approach, an individual's belief system is relatively easy to access. These typical ways of responding to events in the environment are so characteristic of an individual that they are referred to as *automatic thought*. Once they are identified, the individual is encouraged to distance or dissociate from these beliefs by regarding them more objectively, not as facts, but as hypotheses. Next, the client is helped to scrutinize these beliefs and formulate a more adaptive view.

The second, deeper level of CT involves identifying the client's typical *schema*, or the underlying cognitive structures that influence perceptions of events (Beck & Weishaar, 1989; Hollon & Kriss, 1984). Called core *beliefs*, these are similar to Ellis's irrational beliefs (Level B in the ABC paradigm) and are stated as "if-then" propositions. Although core beliefs are more difficult to identify than automatic thoughts, once accessed, they are challenged in the same manner.

DeRubeis and Beck (1988) identified six types of cognitive errors that occur at both the automatic thought and the core belief levels:

1. *Arbitrary inference.* Drawing conclusions without supporting evidence or in spite of contradicting evidence.

2. *Selective abstraction.* Ignoring the majority of features in a situation and basing a conclusion about the entire event on a detail.

3. *Overgeneralization.* Drawing a general rule or conclusion from isolated incidents and applying the rule in related and unrelated situations.

4. *Magnification and minimization.* Making errors in judging the magnitude of an event, thus distorting its significance.

5. *Personalization.* Relating events to self when there is no reason for doing so.

6. *Dichotomous thinking.* Placing experiences in two opposite, extreme categories, such as glorious or horrendous, and applying the negative categorization to self.

Clinical Techniques. As noted, CT is a cognitive–behavioral therapy, and a variety of behavioral methods are used to help bring about cognitive change. These include self-monitoring, scheduling activities, chunking (breaking down a task into smaller segments), and using graded tasks (after DeRubeis & Beck, 1988). In CT the client is instructed to self-monitor behavior by recording hourly any information that pertains to pertinent activities. In some cases, the client also is asked to record the degree of mastery or pleasure associated with an activity, often on a scale ranging from 0 (*worst*) to 100 (*best*). The therapist uses this record to learn how the client spends time, to generate questions about the client's thoughts during specific activities, and to identify consistent patterns of events associated with good or bad feelings.

CT is an active-directive therapy (although less directive than RET); consequently, the client and therapist collaborate in scheduling activities that the client must plan to accomplish. These activities include those that are reported in self-monitoring as generating good feelings, or those that once were rewarding but currently are avoided, or those that have the potential to be rewarding. Obstacles related to activity scheduling are discussed in therapy. When clients avoid performing activities (usually those that are associated with the clients' problems), the cognitions associated with the incident are discussed in therapy.

For difficult activities, chunking is used. For example, the task of writing a paper may begin with preparing an outline for the paper. The client also may grade or sequence tasks so that simpler aspects are presented first, for instance, choosing a topic for the paper. Although behavior strategies are important, the techniques that provide the backbone of CT are designed to directly change cognition. These include keeping a daily record of dysfunctional thoughts, asking three types of questions, using the *downward arrow* procedure, identifying cognitive errors, and identifying schemata.

The principal goal of CT is to help the client to be aware of thoughts, images, and inferences she makes when in a situation that evokes unpleasant emotion and to learn to question their accuracy. Therefore, the client is asked to complete a daily record of dysfunctional thoughts (Beck, Rush, Shaw, & Emery, 1979), either with assistance by the therapist during a session or independently, for later discussion in therapy. The daily record is a relatively simple form that includes a column for the date, a second column to describe the situation (either the actual event or the stream of thoughts leading to an unpleasant emotion), and a third column to describe the emotion and rate the degree of intensity on a scale ranging from 1 (*a trace*) to 100 (*the most intense possible*). In the fourth column, the individual attempts to record the automatic thoughts that preceded the emotions and rate her belief in those thoughts on a scale ranging from 0% (*not at all*) to 100% (*completely*). The fifth column is used to record a rational response to the automatic thoughts and to rate extent of belief on a 0% to 100% scale. The sixth and final column is used to re-rate the client's belief in the automatic thoughts after they are examined and for noting and rating subsequent emotions.

Use of the record of dysfunctional thoughts enables the therapist to spot breakdowns in any stage of the therapeutic process—in identifying problematic cognitions, in the degree of belief that remains after examination, and in the value or appropriateness of rational response that is chosen. Once clients have experience evaluating their thinking, the record can be dispensed with; however, clients' knowledge of the process or the sequence of steps that comprise it enables them to practice CT throughout their lives.

As suggested, the keystone of this approach is to teach the client to question her faulty cognitions. To do so, three types of questions are taught:

1. What is the evidence for and against the belief?
2. What are the alternative interpretations of the event or situation?
3. What are the real implications, if the belief is correct?

In some instances, when the client appears unable to distance from an inference and is too upset by an emotionally disturbing incident to formulate alternative hypotheses to explain it, the therapist uses the downward arrow technique, skipping the first two types of questions and helping the client examine the implications of the disturbing event if her interpretation of it is correct. The object of the questions is to elicit the personal meaning attached to the inference, until the client's responses reveal a related inference that is more readily attacked with the CT format. For example, a depressed young man is convinced that his girlfriend's decision to take a vacation without him is evidence of diminished love. He appears unable to truly believe any alternative explanation for her behavior. When questioned about the implications of his inference if it were true, he reveals that he believes her rejection is inevitable because he is not a lovable person and ultimately is always rejected by others. These core beliefs can be challenged with the entire CT questioning process.

In addition to the use of questions, the client is helped to identify the type of cognitive errors that he is prone to make, such as overgeneralization (i.e., perceiving himself as totally unlovable because he experienced rejection in the past) or magnification (i.e., equating his girlfriend's preference for an independent vacation with a lack of love). The client's schema—the amalgamation of cognitive processes typically used to view and respond to events in the world—is identified by the consistent pattern of beliefs that he associates with his psychological problems. For example, a client may consistently reason that "if I am not perfect, I am a total failure." Therefore, unlike RET, the CT approach does not assume that the therapist can readily identify the basic irrational thoughts (Level B of the ABC paradigm) that trigger maladjustment, but rather that the client ultimately will identify them in the therapeutic process. Once faulty cognitive processes are identified a healthier schema can be identified, practiced, and reinforced.

CT Applied. As noted, CT grew from Beck's interest in depression. Beck (1972) proposed that a negative self-schema caused biased information processing, influencing the individual's memories of past events and distorting current views. This "negativity hypothesis" of the cognitive model of depression is strongly supported by clinical results (Ernst, 1985; Haaga, Dyck, & Ernst, 1991). An initial step in treatment, assessment of the individual's cognitive schema, is accomplished by measuring attitudes. Beck found that depressed persons had rigid attitudes about their self-worth, tending to evaluate themselves in response to external events, such as the approval of others and achievement. Also, they minimized their accomplishments and practiced *phonyism* (Ellis's term), believing that others would reject them if they really knew them.

In addition to assessment, the early stages of treatment are devoted to didactic explanation of the cognitive model of depression. Clients often are asked to read *Coping with Depression* (Beck & Greenberg, 1974), and the ensuing discussion of the book often begins the process of curbing the client's feelings of hopelessness associated with depression. Treatment progresses with the use of the behavioral and cognitive strategies discussed above, as the client progresses from understanding the cognitive model, to using the techniques to alter thoughts and attitudes with the support of the therapist, to integrating the techniques into her cognitive repertoire to be used whenever necessary in daily living.

As cognitive theories have gained credibility and acceptance, CT has been used to treat other types of disorders, including panic disorders, generalized anxiety disorders, phobias, hypochondriasis, obsessive-compulsive disorders, eating disorders, and even multiple-personality disorders (Beck, 1993). For example, Ottaviani and Beck (1987) applied the strategies to eliminate panic disorders in 30 persons who had been experiencing an average of 4.5 attacks per week. Panic disorder, including the familiar agoraphobia (morbid fear of large, open places), is an intense manifestation of anxiety triggered by psychosocial or physical stress that is characterized by physical sensations such as pain in the chest, shortness of breath, increased heart rate, light-headedness, and numbness or tingling in extremities. These sensations evoke ideas and images of physical catastrophe, such as death, heart attack, and fainting, and mental or behavioral catastrophe, such as loss of control or going crazy. Sometimes these symptoms are accompanied by memory lapse or difficulty in reasoning. When the symptoms commence, the individual's irrational fear of catastrophic consequences reduces the ability to think about less serious causation. As catastrophic ideation increases, physical symptoms intensify, and panic as well as other phobic behavior results. Fear of symptoms and the situation in which symptoms occur constitute the basis of phobias.

CT treatment of this condition is designed to show the client that physical sensations prior to and during panic attacks are not dangerous. The steps to accomplish this include the following:

1. Conducting a thorough physical examination

2. Providing the client with information about panic disorders

3. Helping the client identify the misattributions or erroneous thoughts occurring during an attack (fear of heart attack)

4. Reinterpreting those thoughts (pain in the chest does not signify heart attack)

5. Helping the client switch focus from internal sensations and catastrophic thoughts to external reality

6. Teaching relaxation or controlled-breathing techniques (used only in the early stages of an attack)

7. Teaching other cognitive distraction techniques (in early stages, to focus attention on conversation, the environment, a puzzle, etc.)

8. Inducing a mini–panic attack in the office (usually with hyperventilation) to show the client that the attack can be stopped

9. Helping the client to visualize the anxiety-evoking situation or deliberately experience it in real life, while applying the CT strategies to prevent an attack

CT also has been applied to more generalized types of anxiety disorders (Beck & Rush, 1975; Blowers, Cobb, & Mathews, 1987; Butler, Fennell, Robson, & Gelder, 1991; Durham & Turvey, 1987). Beck noted that, unlike phobia and panic disorders, which have an acute onset of anxiety, disorders marked by chronic onset of anxiety are fueled by cognitions that involve criticism, rejection, and failure. In these cases, anxiety is induced by a broader class of stimuli that occur more frequently, are more difficult to identify, and are less frequently avoided. Stimuli are more frequently internal, because danger-related ideation is part of the individual's stream of consciousness. However, in both cases, anxiety, an emotion, is triggered by fear, a type of ideation that signals danger. Just as phobia is a fear of consequences (fear of a rat is fear of being bitten by a rat), chronic anxiety is produced by fear of catastrophic outcomes that dominates the client's cognitions as he scans both internal and external stimuli for "dangerous" properties.

Treatment for chronic anxiety follows the format used to treat panic attacks: making self-observations that reveal ideations (automatic thoughts and fantasies) that evoke anxiety; regarding these ideations as hypotheses and questioning their accuracy (distancing); identifying the beliefs or assumptions that underlie these faulty hypotheses; and demonstrating that these assumptions are incorrect.

Finally, Beck (1982) applied the principles of CT to manage stress. Pretzer, Beck, and Newman (1989) reported on that application. Stress, defined as external and internal demands that tax adaptive capacity, is cognitively mediated (Forsythe & Compas, 1987). Through CT's guided discovery approach, the client is alerted to the processes of selective attention, automatic (unreflective) thoughts, and unrealistic beliefs that play a central role in stress development and provoke emotional and physiological responses. Intervention results in the revision of important cognitions about notions of personal risk, resources to cope with risk, and the probability of success entailed by alternative courses.

Efficacy of CT. Two major claims made by the advocates of CT are that it is effective in solving immediate problems and that, once trained in its use, clients can apply strategies throughout their lives, thus preventing the reoccurrence of a problem or the development of new psychological disorders. These benefits have been supported by research into depression, anxiety, and panic disorders. Research has shown cognitive therapy to be more effective in treating unipolar depression and more resistant to relapses than other forms of treatment, including psychotherapies and pharmacological interventions (Beck, Hollon, Young, Bedrosian, & Budenz, 1985; Dobson, 1989; Elkin, 1994; Hollon & Najavits, 1988; Shea, Elkin, & Imber, 1992).

Generalized anxiety disorders have been effectively treated using cognitive therapy techniques, including anxiety-management training and cognitive–behavioral interventions (Blowers et al., 1987; Durham & Turvey, 1987). Three studies have compared cognitive therapy–based interventions with pharmacological interventions, with results in all three favoring cognitive therapy during treatment and at follow-up (Butler et al., 1991; Lindsay, Gamsu, McLaughlin, Hood, & Elspie, 1984; Power, Jerrom, Simpson, Mitchell, & Swanson, 1989).

Research has also found effective treatment using cognitive therapy for bulimia (Fairburn et al., 1991) and panic disorders (Clark, 1991; Newman, Beck, Beck, Tran, & Brown, 1990). DeRubeis and Beck (1988) and Beck (1993) both cited the need for additional research to demonstrate the effectiveness of the theory for use with these and other conditions.

Finally, another perceived benefit of CT is that the model is well defined and the related strategies used in therapy are clearly presented. Therefore, therapists can be carefully trained in its use and their effectiveness can be measured. A variety of third-party rating forms have been developed for this purpose. Research has shown that when the rating forms are used by expert raters, interrater reliability is excellent (DeRubeis & Beck, 1988; Hollon, Emerson, & Mandell, 1982). Thus, the possibility of treatment failure due to therapist error is reduced.

A final line of research involves predicting client response to treatment, that is, which individuals will benefit from CT as opposed to other strategies. A study by Simons, Murphy, Levine, and Wetzel (1986) identified persons high on the *Rosenbaum's Self-Control Scale* (Rosenbaum, 1980) as good risks for CT. These individuals tend to use thinking or planning to improve their lives.

Self-Instructional Training

Unlike Ellis and Beck, Meichenbaum is a behavioral therapist who described his approach to cognitive restructuring, called self-instructional training (SIT; Meichenbaum & Goodman, 1971), as a form of cognitive–behavioral modification. His primary interest has been the relationship between covert verbal self-instructions and overt behavior and, to a lesser extent, emotions. He attributed his interest in the role of cognitive factors in behavior modification (Meichenbaum, 1977, 1979; Meichenbaum & Cameron, 1973) primarily to the influence of Luria (1961) and Vygotsky (1962), who held that the development of voluntary control over behavior evolves gradually from external regulation by others to self-regulations that result from internalization of verbal commands. Meichenbaum's concepts also were influenced by the work of Mischel (1974), who examined the effectiveness of self-generated strategies in reducing frustration.

The thrust of SIT differs from that of RET and CT in that it was designed to counteract cognitive *deficiency* rather than cognitive distortions. Specifically, rather than concentrating on erroneous inferences and harmful beliefs that lead to distortion and misinterpretation of events, and that characterize *internalized* disorders such as depression, SIT focuses on the absence of constructive self-statements that lead to adaptive behavior—a characteristic of *externalized* disorders. In fact, SIT was initially developed to help impulsive or hyperactive children overcome mediational deficits. Important goals involve teaching children to generate appropriate verbal self-commands; to use those commands to structure their behavior, that is, to serve as cues for the recall of appropriate behavior or to aid in correcting behavior errors; and to reinforce themselves when they behave appropriately. Hypothetically, self-instructions interrupt automatic behavioral or cognitive chains, strengthen an individual's mediational processes, and enable her to respond more effectively and appropriately to events in the environment.

Meichenbaum (1977) presented three phases of SIT. The first phase, a cooperative venture between therapist and client, consists primarily of gathering information needed to conceptualize the problem. During this phase, the client may use imagery to relive problematic situations and self-monitoring assignments (e.g., homework) to identify the inappropriate covert language that occurs when problems are experienced. It is important that therapist and client develop a common conceptualization of the problem. The second phase involves testing the accuracy of the conceptualization of the problem and generating more adaptive self-statements. The third phase is devoted to active attempts to change self-statements and behavior. Standard procedures developed to intervene with impulsive children but useful in modifying other problematic behaviors are applied. These include (a) modeling and talking through a task while the child observes, (b) having the child perform the task while the model gives verbal instructions, (c) having the child perform the task while instructing himself aloud, (d) having the child perform the task while whispering instructions, and (e) having the child perform the task while instructing himself covertly. Modeling and practice of relevant skills are essential behavioral components of SIT.

From its initial application with impulsive children, the use of SIT has been expanded to a variety of clinical disorders, including schizophrenia (Meichenbaum & Cameron, 1973), anxiety (Meichenbaum & Turk, 1976), and phobia (Mahoney, 1974), and great significance has been attached to self-instruction in the use of problem-solving strategies. In current applications, Meichenbaum (1985, 1986, 1990) emphasized the cognitive concepts involved in self-regulation, discussing the development of schemata through activities that give an active role to the learner. These instructional activities include collaborative learning, reciprocal teaching, discovery opportunities, scaffolding, and practice opportunities (see Chapter 7). Also emphasized are the cognitive steps that comprise self-instruction: problem definition, problem approach, attention focusing, coping statements, error-correcting options, and self-reinforcement (Kendall, 1985). These steps resemble components of Ellis's and Beck's theories. DeRubeis and Beck (1988) pointed out that, because Meichenbaum's approach is based on a learning theory–derived system, thoughts are treated more as behaviors and less emphasis is placed on the meaning of the thoughts. Also, the client is provided with specific coping statements to use in problematic situations rather than trained to actively question her inferences.

Clinical Application. SIT is probably best known and most thoroughly researched in regard to its use with children in educational settings. It has been applied to help children control aggression, pay attention, complete assignments, be less disruptive, and perform a variety of academic tasks, such as reading and writing, more effectively. A typical application was reported by Braswell and Kendall (1988), who documented its use with an impulsive, aggressive, underachieving fourth-grade student. The therapist applied the five sequenced steps that comprise SIT to help the child control his aggressive behavior and complete his academic tasks. However, self-instruction techniques applied to school-related activities were ineffective. The child appeared to say the appropriate words (self-talk) without understanding the underlying concepts they represented, so the therapist applied the strategies to problems occurring in ice hockey games (the child's consuming interest). When the child understood the purpose of the self-instructional steps in this context, the therapist transferred the strategies to school-related behaviors with far greater success.

Efficacy of SIT. As noted previously, the efficacy of SIT with children has been investigated extensively. Braswell and Kendall (1988) presented a concise review of that literature. Although the results are equivocal, sufficient data indicate that the approach is effective, particularly in improving performance in specific situations. A more important issue regarding its effectiveness concerns generalization—that is, the client's ability to use the self-instructional strategies in general contexts. This issue has not yet been resolved, because a substantial amount of research both supports and disputes this premise. The general conclusions drawn from efficacy research are more encouraging than discouraging.

Application of Cognitive-Restructuring Approaches

SIT has been used in a variety of educational settings to alter children's cognitions by providing them with self-talk that is conducive to the display of adaptive behavior. Braswell and Kendall (1988) pointed out that much of this training is noninteractive, because the therapist only tells the children what to do or say. Interactive SIT is typified by Meichenbaum's (1979) work, with the therapist teaching, through modeling and guided practice opportunities, the self-verbalizations that are designed to alter behavior. Kendall, Chu, Pimentel, and Choudhury (2000) demonstrated the effectiveness of the interactive approach in increasing the self-control and reducing the hyperactivity of disruptive children. Mansdorf and Lukens (1987) used an interactive self-instructional approach to successfully treat two school-phobic children, helping them return to school within 2 weeks of training.

Interactive SIT also has been used effectively with groups of first- and third-grade students to teach adaptive classroom behaviors (Manning, 1988). This application emphasized modeling, using both adult models and videotapes of peer models to demonstrate and verbalize the desired behaviors. For example, a model would raise his hand while saying, "If I yell out the answer, others will be disturbed. I'll raise my hand and wait." After observing the models, the children practiced the behaviors and verbalizations. The self-talk was gradually faded until it was covert. Finally, numerous research studies have revealed the effectiveness of SIT in improving the academic achievement of children with learning disabilities, particularly when it is combined with social and cognitive problem-solving tasks (Graham, 1983; Leon & Pepe, 1983; Scardamalia, Bereiter, & Steinbach, 1984).

Other applications of cognitive-restructuring techniques have focused on altering children's attributions, that is, their attitudes and beliefs about why they have problems. Research has shown that children who perform poorly academically make attributions that contribute to their poor performance (Butkowsky & Willows, 1980; Pearl, 1985); that is, they expect to fail or attribute failure to their stupidity. Training involves teaching children to link a more adaptive attributional statement (e.g., "If I try harder, I'll do it") with their specific behavioral effort (e.g., solving math problems). The approach is successful when children have the ability to perform the task or when the teacher is in the process of teaching the necessary skills; it is not successful when children's failure is not due to their faulty attributions, but to a skill deficit. Also, the type of attribution appropriate for each child must be identified; for example, a child may need to remind himself that if he works more slowly or checks his work, he will be successful. As Braswell and Kendall (1988) pointed out, "attributions of causality must be reality based and accurate" (p. 192).

Cognitive SIT has proved effective in changing impulse control and attentional difficulties in children (Finch, Spirito, Imm, & Ott, 1993; Hinshaw, 2000) and is a critical component of most coping skills approaches, including social skills training, anger management training, and problem-solving training (Finch, Nelson, & Ott, 1993; Goldstein, 1999; Kendall, 2000).

Coping-Skills Therapies

Cognitive interventions that emphasize coping skills are less theoretical than those associated with cognitive restructuring. The latter approach involves a comprehensive attempt to analyze cognitions—that is, belief systems, thought patterns, attitudinal biases, and so forth—in order to identify the causes of an individual's unique and personal psychological disorders. Coping skills approaches are far less analytical and are designed to provide an individual with a set of strategies that will increase ability to function satisfactorily in various problematic situations. Coping skills may be components of cognitive-restructuring approaches or may be used alone. They are a quick, efficient means of improving an individual's adjustment without providing extensive training. Stress inoculation training, social skills training, problem-solving training, and anger control training are four examples of approaches that emphasize the use of coping skills as the principal means of intervening.

Stress Inoculation Training

Stress inoculation training, also called stress management training and, less frequently, relaxation training, is the process of helping individuals learn to deal more effectively with stressful events through techniques that target physiological arousal and cognitions. Many children and adolescents experience various levels of stress over issues of school, friendships, family, work, sexuality, and drugs (Frydenberg, 1997). Magnusson (1982) studied anxiety-provoking situations in 12- to 18-year-olds. He discovered that preadolescents feel most stressed by the physical properties of the situation (the event itself, physical consequences, and sanctions). In contrast, older adolescents reported the psychological consequences (shame, guilt, separation) as the primary bases for stress. Stress has been demonstrated to have serious psychological consequences, including problems with school adjustment and performance (Eccles, Lord, & Miller-Buchanan, 1996; Ianni & Orr, 1996), delinquency (Sullivan, 1996), suicide (Cohen-Sandler, Berman, & King, 1982), depression (Frydenberg), drug use (Bachman, Johnson, O'Malley, & Wadsworth, 1996), eating disorders (Schwartz & Johnson, 1985), and general maladjustment (Cowen, Weissberg, & Guare, 1984).

The theoretical premise underlying stress inoculation training is that individuals who learn to cope with mild levels of stress are better able to cope with more intense levels in the future (Mason, 1980; Orne, 1965). In effect, their beliefs about their ability to function are altered by the training, and they are more likely to feel in control of potentially stressful situations. Using this theory, Cameron and Meichenbaum (1982) organized stress inoculation training into three stages. The first stage, didactic training, is to educate the individual about stress-related reactions. Several theoretical approaches to stress reactions may be presented to enable the client to understand his personal reactions. Fear reactions involve two major components: heightened physiological arousal and cognitive events (e.g., images and thoughts) that create anxiety (Cameron & Meichenbaum; Stoyva & Anderson, 1982). Treatment should involve reducing the physiological arousal and interfering with the anxiety-evoking images and thoughts (self-statements).

The second stage of training involves therapist–client discussion of various behavioral and cognitive coping skills. These include such techniques as relaxation exercises (progressive relaxation training, yogaform stretching, breathing exercises, somatic focusing, thematic imagery, and meditation); changing negative self-statements to a more adaptive self-talk; realistically exploring the risks in the stressful situation; discussing more realistic expectations; considering alternative responses; using imagery to view pleasant or nonthreatening aspects of the stressful event; and self-reinforcement. These coping skills should vary depending on the individual's needs and the situation but should always include mental rehearsal of strategies that interfere with the experience of stress or reduce its effect. The client can select three or four of the strategies that he finds most appealing or easiest to use. These should be rehearsed in role-playing situations until the client feels proficient using them.

The third stage is devoted to behavioral rehearsal, in which the client applies the coping skills in graduated stressful situations, beginning with minimally threatening events. Coping responses can be practiced in therapy, using imagery and in vivo stressors, then in real life. Exposure to the most threatening stressor should be postponed until the client is comfortable using the strategies in less threatening circumstances.

Application and Efficacy. Evidence of the efficacy of stress inoculation training and stress management training is widespread and convincing across conditions as diverse as test taking, migraine headaches, hypertension, school anxiety, insomnia, and pain (see Goldstein, 1999). The application of these strategies to reduce pain is based on the premise that pain is experienced because of a combination of physiological and sensory-discriminative factors, motivational–affective components, and cognitive–evaluative components (Varni, LaGreca, & Spirito, 2000). The influence of motivational–affective components can be demonstrated by the absence of pain in certain situations, as when an athlete feels pain only after a competition. The cognitive–evaluative components are demonstrated by the fact that an individual's evaluation of the severity of pain is related to her previous experience with pain. Thus, what is minor pain to one individual may be major pain to another. Another indication of the cognitive role in pain is the fact that thinking about pain often heightens its intensity. For example, when an individual is stimulated by an interesting conversation, she forgets about a headache that was extremely painful before the conversation began.

Teaching individuals to cope with pain follows the sequence of intervention strategies previously discussed. The client chooses from a variety of coping strategies those that she perceives as most useful, practices them with help in minimal pain situations, then attempts to use them in more stressful pain-related situations. Research conducted using multicomponent coping skills to curb stress and manage pain has proved them to be successful (Varni et al., 2000).

In another successful intervention, Hains and Szyjakowski (1990) used Meichenbaum's (1985) stress inoculation training to diminish anxiety and anger and increase the self-esteem and the number of reported positive cognitions of 21 adolescent males. Treatment gains were maintained at a 10-week follow-up.

Social Skills Interventions

Deficits in age-appropriate prosocial behavior are well recognized as characteristic of children identified as having EBDs (Camp & Ray, 1984; Goldstein, 1999; Kendall & Morison, 1984). These children also may exhibit aggressive or socially isolated behaviors that are associated with serious adolescent and adult maladjustment, such as juvenile delinquency, dropping out of school, and mental health problems later in life (Asher, Oden, & Gottman, 1977; Gersten, Langer, Eisenberg, Simacha-Fagan, & McCarthy, 1976; Goldstein, 1999; McGinnis & Goldstein, 1997a, 1997b).

Social skills that enable children and adolescents to interact appropriately with peers and adults are related both to friendship development and acceptance in peer groups (Gresham & Lemanek, 1983). Peer socialization is critical in the process of child development because it serves as an arena for mastery of aggressive impulses, cognitive and moral development, the learning of sex roles, and achievement of social competence (Hartup, 1979). Social competence has been defined by Epanchin (1991) as "possessing age-appropriate social skills that enable [the child] to determine what is expected in a given social situation, to behave in the expected manner, and to satisfy her own needs and wishes in the situation" (p. 415).

Three types of social incompetence have been identified (Hughes & Hall, 1987): behavioral skills deficits, cognitive deficits, and cognitive–behavioral deficits. Behavioral skills deficits involve inability to perform the appropriate social behaviors. Children with behavioral skills deficits know what they should do (e.g., be friendly) but do not know how to do it (smile, make eye contact). Children with cognitive deficits have distortions or delays in their thinking about social information, selective attention and retention, and distorted belief systems and self-statements. Many students with social and emotional disturbance are inaccurate in their appraisal of social situations; for example, they may perceive a neutral stimulus as aggressive and respond aggressively, much to another person's surprise. Finally, most children and adolescents have difficulty with both behavior and the cognitive process, manifesting cognitive–behavioral deficits.

The most promising instruction in social skills and social-problem-solving skills has been cognitive–behavioral in nature (Hughes, 1988; Kendall & Braswell, 1993). Cognitive–behavioral techniques generally include instruction, modeling, practice, feedback, self-instruction, and social problem solving as part of a packaged approach. Those packages that include adequate instruction time and some means to generalize the use of skills to home or community situations, such as homework and using significant others as confederates, have been most successful (Ager & Cole, 1991). Teachers also should pay attention to using models that are as similar to the students as possible; for example, a socially skilled peer or an older same-sex student who is seen as "cool" will be much more effective as a model than the teacher. (For more detailed information on social skills instruction, see Gallagher, 1988; Goldstein, 1988; Paul & Epanchin, 1991).

Important social skills include entering and exiting social interactions, holding a conversation, receiving and giving both positive and negative feedback, perspective taking, negotiation, sharing, and resisting peer pressure. The *Skills Streaming* series (McGinnis & Goldstein 1997a, 1997b) delineates 50 to 60 skills to be mastered depending on a student's age. Epanchin (1991) identified seven general skills that children and adolescents need to be considered socially competent, stating that they should be able to do the following:

1. Read social rules and expectations
2. Interpret social and interpersonal cues
3. Communicate effectively in social situations
4. Initiate social interactions in an age-appropriate manner
5. Establish and maintain friendships
6. Solve problems when they arise
7. Negotiate tactfully and successfully with others

Social skills instruction, like academic instruction, should be individualized if it is to be most effective. However, by their nature, social skills and social-problem-solving skills must be taught using at least dyads or small groups. Also, social skills must be taught throughout the curriculum and addressed throughout the day for students to be most successful. Setting aside time to instruct social skills is important; however, opportunities to practice must be provided throughout the entire school day.

A large number of social skills curricula have been developed and are currently available. These include ACCEPTS (Walker et al., 1983), ACCESS (Walker, Todis, Holmes, & Horton, 1987), I Can Behave (Mannix, 1986), Personal Power (Wells, 1987, 1988, 1989), The PREPARE Curriculum (Goldstein, 1999), Skill Streaming the Elementary School Child (McGinnis & Goldstein, 1997b), Skill Streaming the Adolescent (McGinnis & Goldstein, 1997a), Think Aloud (Camp & Bash, 1981), and Waksman Social Skills Curriculum (Waksman, Messmer, & Waksman, 1988).

Students need to possess both a myriad of social skills and the social-problem-solving ability to determine which social skills are appropriate for a given situation. Although they are dealt with separately in this chapter, social skills and social problem solving are actually integrally interwoven and must be used together to promote significant clinical outcomes that both maintain over time and generalize to everyday situations.

Problem-Solving Approaches

Various models of social problem solving, also called social information processing, have been recommended as ways in which we can conceptualize how children interact (Dodge, 1986; Hughes & Hall, 1987). Hughes and Hall's system is a very simple three-step model: reading, generating, and applying. Basic questions address each step: Can the students "read" the social situation? Can they "generate" appropriate problem-solving strategies in a particular situation? Can they "apply" these strategies appropriately? Problem-solving therapy was introduced by D'Zurilla and Goldfried (1971) in their important article "Problem-Solving and Behavior Modification" and expanded by Spivack, Platt, and Shure (1976) in their book The Problem-Solving Approach to Adjustment. D'Zurilla and Goldfried regarded problem solving as overt or cognitive processes that provide an individual with a variety of options for responding to problem situations and increase the possibility of an effective response. Their theoretical perspective, problem-solving therapy, along with Spivack et al.'s perspective, interpersonal cognitive problem solving, aptly depict the problem-solving approach to cognitive therapy.

Problem-Solving Therapy

D'Zurilla and Goldfried's (1971) approach to therapy involves providing the client with an arsenal of problem-solving techniques that will enable him to function as a therapist when dealing with problematic situations in daily living. They identified five overlapping stages as representative of the problem-solving process (D'Zurilla, 1988):

1. Problem orientation
2. Problem definition and formulation
3. Generation of alternative solutions
4. Decision making
5. Solution implementation and verification

According to D'Zurilla (1988), information about problem orientation helps the individual to increase sensitivity to problems; focus attention on problem solving and away from unproductive thinking, such as worrying; persist in the face of obstacles and stress; and minimize disruptive emotional distress while maximizing positive emotional states. Involved in problem orientation are problem perception (recognizing and labeling problems), problem attribution (attributing the cause of problems to changeable forces rather than to an unchangeable internal defect), problem appraisal (viewing a problem as a challenge or an opportunity for growth rather than as a potentially harmful threat), personal control (perceiving a problem as soluble and viewing self as capable of reaching the solution), and time and effort commitment (estimating the time for problem solution correctly and devoting the necessary time).

The second step in the problem-solving process, problem definition and formulation, teaches the client an assessment process: gathering relevant information, clarifying the nature of the problem, setting realistic goals, and reevaluating the importance of the problem for personal well-being. The third step, generating alternative solutions, is based on learning the quality principle (evaluate the quality of solutions), the variety principle (generate many solutions), and the deferment-of-judgment principle (avoid jumping to conclusions) in order to produce better ideas about the solution. The fourth component of problem solving, decision making, is based on expected utility theory (Beach & Mitchell, 1978) and prospect theory (Tversky & Kahneman, 1981). Expected utility theory holds that choices are based on a rational benefit–cost (positive outcome–negative outcome) analysis, and prospect theory maintains that an individual's solutions are influenced by subjective factors, such as the way problems are formulated and outcomes are conceived. The final stage of this model, solution implementation and verification, the empirical step in the sequence, is based on the cognitive–behavioral concept of self-control (Bandura, 1971). The client tries her selected solution to the problem; evaluates its effectiveness; and, depending on the extent to which it matches expectations, either returns to the problem-solving process or self-reinforces.

D'Zurilla (1986) reported that emotional responses are extremely important variables affecting problem solving. High levels of emotion negatively affect thinking and also may influence problem recognition, goals, alternative solutions, and assessment of outcomes. When excessive emotion is a factor, training must include coping skills, such as cognitive-restructuring activities (correcting misconceptions, irrational beliefs, or faulty attributions); self-instruction (coping self-directions and positive self-talk); and relaxation techniques.

A main thrust of this approach has been to solve social problems. D'Zurilla (1986) indicated that the ability to solve social problems corresponds with social competence and is inversely related to psychological maladjustment and maladaptive behavior. Research supporting this premise has shown that individuals have fewer signs of stress and engage in fewer maladaptive behaviors when they feel they have the ability to control or predict the outcome of a problem situation (Geer, Davison, & Gatchel, 1970; Hiroto & Seligman, 1975). Another avenue of research has shown that individuals who rate themselves as effective problem solvers are appraised as having fewer social problems and being better adjusted than people who regard themselves as ineffective at solving problems (Heppner, Neal, & Larson, 1984).

Clinical Applications of Problem-Solving Therapy

The first step in problem-solving therapy involves assessment of the individual's problem-solving ability and problem-solving performance. A variety of questionnaires and tests are available for this purpose, including the *Problem Solving Inventory* (Heppner & Petersen, 1982) and the *Means-Ends Problem-Solving Procedure* (MEPS) (Platt & Spivack, 1975). Observational assessment also is used. D'Zurilla (1986) recommended teaching clients the Problem-Solving Self-Monitoring model, in which the client is asked to record precise details of the problematic situation, all of her feelings and emotions when it occurred (intensity is rated on a 9-point scale), alternative solutions considered, reasons for solution choice, and what happened when the solution was implemented (rated on a 10-point scale).

The assessment process determines whether the client is likely to be a good candidate for problem-solving therapy. Logically, those who would benefit most from learning problem-solving strategies experience emotional problems or display maladaptive behaviors because they have inadequate problem-solving skills. They may be individuals who typically blame themselves for creating problems because they are stupid, unlucky, or abnormal in some respect; perceive a problem as a significant threat but minimize the benefits of solving it while maximizing the cost; have no real hope of coping with their problems effectively, either because they think most problems cannot be solved or they lack the competence to solve them and need someone else to intervene; or believe that failure to solve a problem quickly (as most people do) indicates incompetence.

Once the first step has been accomplished, the next step, problem definition, focuses on teaching the client to avoid cognitive distortions when appraising his problematic situation. The client learns to conceptualize a problem in terms of the discrepancy between present circumstances ("what is") and the conditions he desires or demands ("what should be") and to identify the barriers to reducing the discrepancy. The client also learns to set problem-solving goals that are specific and concrete, as well as realistic and obtainable (D'Zurilla, 1988).

Defining and formulating a problem may be a relatively simple operation, as in isolating circumstances that are specific antecedents of maladaptive responses. For example, perception of rejection by others may trigger depression. However, the formulations also may be extremely complex, as when the most obvious problem is not the basic problem. The obvious problem may be caused by the basic problem or may be a small part of the basic problem, for example, when low self-esteem causes perceptions of rejection as well as other maladaptive cognitions, such as heightened fear of failure. Treatment plans can focus on the basic problem or on the smaller components of the basic problem. Another important distinction at this stage is between *problem-focused* formulations and *emotion-focused* formulations. The former approach is designed to improve the problematic situation, whereas the latter is aimed at changing personal reactions to the situation to reduce stress. For example, a person who is consistently ridiculed and harassed by a superior at work may not be able to change the situation, so problem formulation must be emotion focused to change the employee's responses to the superior's demeaning behavior.

The third step in problem-solving therapy, generating alternative solutions, is accomplished by having the client brainstorm, that is, think of and write down as many diverse solutions as possible without rejecting any ideas or attempting to judge their value. The next step, decision making, involves screening the list, eliminating inferior or impractical ideas (too risky, too costly, etc.), and anticipating solution outcomes for the surviving options in terms of expected benefits (positive outcomes) and costs (negative outcomes). After anticipating outcomes, each solution is evaluated on four criteria: problem resolution, emotional well-being, amount of time and effort required, and overall personal–social well-being. After considering each solution in regard to those criteria, the client asks three questions: Is the problem solvable? Do I need more information before I select and implement a solution? What solution should I choose to implement? If the answers to the first two questions are yes and no, respectively, the client chooses a solution.

As the client moves to the last step in treatment and implements the solution, he is helped to monitor his performance, noting information—such as lack of motivation or too much emotional stress—that impedes the client's ability to apply the chosen solution to the problem. If the client is experiencing difficulty, he may select an alternative solution or attempt to rectify the problems blocking the success of the plan being used. If the solution meets the expectations the client established when the plan was formed, the client has achieved the goal and terminates the activity with self-reinforcement (a reward of some type). Later sessions are devoted to helping the client apply the entire process to alternative problems so that he becomes increasingly capable of using the strategies without outside assistance.

Depending on the severity of a specific case, problem-solving therapy might be included as part of a broader cognitive treatment approach or used as the sole treatment. In either circumstance, treatment is two-pronged, featuring attempts to identify problems that are antecedents of maladaptive responses but also emphasizing the teaching of general problem-solving skills that can be used in other circumstances.

Interpersonal Cognitive Problem Solving

The model developed by Spivack et al. (1976), interpersonal cognitive problem solving, is essentially the same as the problem-solving theory approach just discussed. According to these theorists, effective interpersonal problem solving involves the ability to (a) recognize the range of possible problem situations in the social environment, (b) generate multiple alternative solutions to interpersonal problems, (c) plan a series of steps necessary to achieve a given goal, (d) foresee the short-term and long-term consequences of a given alternative, and (e) identify the motivational elements related to one's actions and the actions of others (Dobson & Block, 1988). Unlike problem-solving theory, however, the focus of this model is on children. Spivack et al. developed a series of training programs that use interpersonal cognitive problem solving to educate children, including preschoolers and those labeled as emotionally disordered, in performing the skills associated with each of the above steps. After the trainer discusses each problem-solving skill and provides the children with examples, the children engage in structured activities that require them to apply the strategies to hypothetical and actual problems. *The*

PREPARE Curriculum (Goldstein, 1999) uses this model as the basis for its training in problem solving, as do other coping skills packages.

Efficacy of ICPS

Numerous reviews of the literature have reported that interpersonal cognitive problem solving, problem-solving therapy, and other related problem-solving interventions have been used effectively with individual clients suffering from a broad spectrum of emotional and social disorders, including depression, anxiety, obesity, academic underachievement, and adolescent adjustment problems (Durlak, 1983; D'Zurilla, 1986; D'Zurilla & Nezu, 1982; Kirschenbaum & Ordman, 1984; O'Donohue & Noll, 1995). Problem-solving therapy also has been reported to be effective when used in group therapy with individuals without emotional or social disorders who want to improve their general problem-solving skills and function socially with greater effectiveness (Heppner, Reeder, & Larson, 1983; Schinke, Blythe, & Gilchrist, 1981).

Researchers of interpersonal cognitive problem solving have investigated the relationship between social-problem-solving abilities and psychopathology with the *Means-End Problem-Solving Procedure* (Platt & Spivack, 1975) a self-report device. The device is a series of story stems depicting situations in which a problem occurs at the beginning of the story and is solved at the end. The client must complete the story by supplying the events that brought about the solution of the problem. Researchers (Platt, Scura, & Hannon, 1973; Platt, Spivack, Altman, Altman, & Peizer, 1974) have shown that emotionally maladjusted children are less able than typical children to formulate plans to reach their desired goals. Poor performance on the *Means-End Problem-Solving Procedure* also correlates with low scores on the *Beck Depression Inventory* (Beck, 1967b). However, there is no definitive empirical evidence of a significant relationship between adjustment and skills in interpersonal cognitive-problem-solving skills (Kendall, 1985; Kendall & Fischler, 1984).

Problem-solving interventions with elementary school children with emotional problems have been applied effectively by Robin, Schneider, and Dolnick (1976). Termed the *turtle technique*, this approach is designed to limit aggressive responses through a four-step process. In Step 1 children are taught to mimic a turtle's responses when provoked by drawing in their limbs and lowering their heads. Step 2 involves learning relaxation skills to be used while acting like a turtle. During Step 3 the children learn to generate solutions other than aggression and to consider the consequences of those solutions. At Step 4, children are rewarded for practicing the first three steps. Kazdin, Bass, Siegel, and Thomas (1989) found problem-solving training to be more effective than relational therapy in diminishing the antisocial behavior of children (ages 7 to 13) with severe conduct disorders. However, the maladaptive behaviors of most of the youth remained outside the normal range.

Although efforts to teach problem-solving strategies to children with emotional problems are laudable, difficulties remain. Frequently, in interventions where problem solving is taught separately from other coping or social skills, cognitions change, but behavior does not improve. Also, solutions taught in one circumstance do not generalize unless generalization skills are specifically taught (Meichenbaum, 1991). Mounting evidence suggests that problem-solving strategies are most effective when part of a comprehensive cognitive–behavioral treatment package designed to address cognitive difficulties along with emotional and behavioral deficits.

Anger-Management Training and Aggression-Replacement Training

One of the most important applications of problem-solving strategies has been directed toward the control of anger and related aggression. Although anger, in and of itself, is not a problematic emotion, anger is frequently and convincingly implicated in many destructive and aggressive acts, including threats, violence, weapons offenses, vandalism, and murder (U.S. Office of Juvenile Justice and Delinquency Prevention, 1994). The origins of anger control training can be found in the work of Luria (1961), a Russian psychologist, who researched the ways children learn to regulate overt behaviors using internal speech. Little and Kendall (1979) took Luria's work further, examining the developmental sequence by which we learn to use verbal behavior to develop self-control. Meichenbaum and Goodman (1971) explored issues of self-control in impulsive youngsters, and Novaco (1975) began to utilize SIT to manage anger and aggression in youth. Novaco's conceptualization of anger (pp. 252–253) shows how it is largely a cognitive process:

> The arousal of anger is . . . an affective stress reaction. That is, anger arousal is a response to perceived environmental demands—most commonly, aversive psychosocial events. . . . Anger is thought to consist of a combination of physiological arousal and cognitive labeling of that arousal as anger. Anger arousal results from particular appraisals of aversive events. External circumstances provoke anger only as mediated by their meaning to the individual.

Eva Feindler and her colleagues elaborated on Novaco's work and developed and refined anger control training through a substantial body of research (e.g., Feindler, 1979; Feindler & Fremouw, 1983; Feindler, Marriott, & Iwata, 1984). The intervention chain they developed includes triggers, cues, reminders, reducers, and self-evaluation. *Triggers* are provocations to anger arousal. Both external events and internal appraisals can serve as triggers for anger. Because anger is mediated by internal verbal statements, a statement such as "I can't believe he did that to me; he is such a jerk, I'm going to get him" is much more likely to lead to anger than "Wow, I wonder if that was an accident; maybe I should go talk to him." *Cues* are the physical sensations that tell an individual that he or she is getting angry. *Reminders* are self-instruction statements, and *reducers* are relaxation techniques, and both are designed to reduce anger arousal. Finally, *self-evaluation* affords the individual the opportunity to either self-correct or self-reinforce, depending on the self-assessment.

In the first stages of anger control training, children and adolescents learn to identify what external events are most likely to act as triggers for their anger and to identify what self-statements they are making that reinforce or further provoke anger arousal. Next they learn to identify their body's cues. Flushed cheeks, tense jaw muscles or fists, tears, squinting the eyes, and grinding the teeth are all common cues indicating anger. Internal appraisals of anger can be mediated through the use of statements that soothe and calm rather than provoke; these reminders are self-instructions such as "Relax," "Stay calm," and "Don't get angry." They can also be specific to the situation, for example, "It's okay, I'll do better on the next test," or "He's just trying to make me angry by calling me names; I don't have to respond." Reducers are relaxation techniques designed to reduce the physical sensations accompanying anger. Common reducers are counting backward, deep breathing, and pleasant imagery. Self-assessment and homework assignments conclude the training and allow participants to predict upcoming events that might produce anger and evaluate their performance in everyday situations. Arnold Goldstein has developed two programs using this anger management sequence, *Anger Control Training* (Goldstein, 1999) and *Aggression Replacement Training* (Goldstein, Glick, & Gibbs, 1998). *Anger Control Training* is the simple version, addressing anger using the five steps just outlined. *Aggression Replacement Training* is a comprehensive system that incorporates social skills training, instruction in interpersonal problem solving, moral reasoning, and anger control training in an attempt to comprehensively address the growing level of aggression among youth. The *Anger Coping Program* (Lochman et al., 2000) is a briefer version of the *Coping Power Program* (Lochman & Wells, 1996), both of which are cognitively based interventions with multiple components and include cognitive restructuring, social problem solving, social skills, and SIT.

Efficacy of Anger Control Training

There is substantial evidence that impulsive, angry, aggressive individuals too frequently recall anger-evoking situations and sometimes add aggressive acts and hostile intentions when recalling those situations (e.g., Lochman & Lampron, 1986). In addition, they are more likely to appraise as anger other feelings, such as fear and anxiety, and less likely to have angry feelings without acting on them in a hostile manner (Lochman et al., 2000; Nelson & Finch, 2000; Polyson & Kimball, 1993). These researchers also have found that anger control training needs to include multiple components for intervention effectiveness. Although information on the effectiveness of the various anger control programs is scarce, there is substantial evidence that cognitive–behavioral interventions incorporating relaxation training, cognitive restructuring, and self-instruction are effective in reducing anger and aggression (see Kendall, 2000; Lochman et al., 2000; Nelson & Finch).

Moral-Reasoning Instruction

Another cognitive–behavioral approach to the treatment of hostile or aggressive acts involves the development of moral reasoning. Moral reasoning, the ability of individuals to think through the moral aspects of situations and to make decisions that will benefit them while preserving the rights of others tends to be underdeveloped in children and adolescents with emotional or behavioral problems (Sigman, Ungerer, & Russell, 1983; Swarthout, 1988; Thoma, Rest, & Barnett, 1986). Consequently, these individuals make decisions that violate the rights of others and do not resolve interpersonal conflicts well. Research on moral development of children with emotional problems has increased over the past 15 years and shows considerable promise. Researchers have found that training leads to advances in moral-reasoning stages (Arbuthnot & Gordon, 1986; Gibbs, Arnold, Ahlborn, & Cheesman, 1984; Niles, 1986; Rosenkoener, Landman, & Mazak, 1980) as well as improvements in absenteeism, behavioral referrals, and academic performance (Arbuthnot & Gordon, 1986).

Typically, the aims of moral-reasoning instruction are to teach children how to critically think about the moral components of situations and how to make good decisions; goals that resemble those associated with problem-solving therapy and interpersonal cognitive problem solving. The most frequent type of moral-reasoning instruction employs the moral discussion group. Students, in groups of 5 to 10, discuss moral dilemmas. Through discussion, conflict, modeling of advanced levels of reasoning, and consensus, students gain knowledge and reasoning abilities. Cognitive restructuring, SIT, and social decision making are all incorporated into moral-reasoning instruction.

Although initially most of the moral dilemmas used in this type of instruction were hypothetical (e.g., a woman is dying of cancer, and her husband cannot afford the life-saving drug), the use of real-life, relevant situations has been recommended (Maag, 1989; Niles, 1986). Therapists and teachers should attempt to use situations familiar to children, such as deciding whether to cheat on a test or steal food from a convenience store. Other important issues include obligations and loyalty to friends, resisting peer pressure, and responding to authority figures. Readers are referred to *The PREPARE Curriculum* (Goldstein, 1999) for a more extensive presentation of these techniques. Maag recommended the use of moral-reasoning training in conjunction with training in social skills and social problem solving, because all three are critically interwoven.

Cognitive–Behavioral Therapy with Children and Adolescents

Although certain cognitive therapy approaches, such as Meichenbaum's self-instructional activities and Spivack et al.'s interpersonal cognitive problem solving, have been developed specifically for use with children, originally most cognitive therapies were developed for adults. Over the past 15 years, however, researchers and clinicians have modified existing techniques and developed additional ways to use cognitive–behavioral interventions with older children and adolescents who display a wide range of psychological difficulties (Dattilio & Freeman, 2000; Finch et al., 1993; Kendall, 2000; Wilkes, Belsher, Rush, & Frank, 1994). Adaptations of cognitive–behavioral strategies are available for children as young as 5 to 7 years of age (e.g., Lochman, FitzGerald, & Whidby, 1999). However, the usefulness of these therapies is limited with young children, whose cognitive abilities differ from those of adults. Braswell and Kendall (1988) summarized issues requiring consideration when cognitive strategies are considered for use with young children.

The most obvious issue is the extent to which children understand the premises associated with certain strategies, particularly those used to correct cognitive distortions. For example, identifying faulty attributions and differentiating logical from illogical thinking may be difficult for many children. Another issue is that children and adolescents have much less control over variables at home and at school that will contribute to psychological adjustment. So, although they may change their thinking and behavior, they are unlikely to be in situations where they can directly influence the interactions and behaviors of those around them.

A related issue is that children also differ from adults in the extent to which the opinions and attitudes of parents and peers influence their responses to therapy. Research suggests that the involvement of significant others in children's therapy greatly increases the probability that the intervention will be successful (Howard & Kendall, 1987; Kendall & Williams, 1986). Children and adolescents are usually referred to therapy by adults (parents, teachers), rather than seeking treatment themselves, a phenomenon that likely has clinical implications, although they have not been determined.

Although the difficulties of using cognitive therapy with children must be considered, several advantages also should be noted. Children's personality traits are quite flexible compared with those of adults. Therefore, children are more open to new concepts and less resistant to change. Also, even when psychologically troubled, many children surpass adults in their ability to form the type of trusting relationship that is essential for successful therapy. Finally, children are creatures of the present. Unlike many adults who fixate on past events as the sources of their difficulties, children respond quickly to changes in the "here and now."

Initially, most cognitive techniques were used to address "internalizing" problems, disorders that primarily affected the child rather than persons around the child. Internalizing disorders include anxiety, depression, eating disorders, and somatic disorders. More recent research has established that children and adolescents with "externalizing" disorders such as attention deficit, hyperactivity, anger, and aggression are responding to these treatments.

Cognitive–Behavioral Techniques with Externalizing Disorders

Anger and Aggression. Concern over anger, aggression, and violence in children and adolescents has increased dramatically during the last decade. This phenomenon is not limited to youth; the United States ranks first in the world for rates of interpersonal violence (American Psychological Association, 1993). However, increases in youth violence are much higher than increases in adult violence (Snyder & Sickmund, 1995). Abundant evidence supports the relationship between aggression in children and adult crime, alcoholism, divorce, drug abuse, mental illness, and unemployment (e.g., Farrington, 1995; Horne & Sayger, 1990; Robins, 1966). Anger and aggression also affect other individuals as victims, as well as the community at large. Loeber and Hay (1997) defined *aggression* as behavioral acts that inflict mental or bodily harm on others, and *violence* is defined as aggressive acts that cause serious harm (Loeber & Stouthamer-Loeber, 1998). Therefore, the difference between aggression and violence is one of degree.

Nelson and Finch (2000) adapted Price's (1996) clinical classification system for relevant dimensions of anger, aggression, and violence. These dimensions are presented in Table 6.1. Descriptors of each level are as follows:

Level 1: The Impatient/Annoying/Irritating Child. These children whine, complain, and become enraged when they are told "no," do not get their own way, or are challenged. They may yell and/or hold their breath. Generally their anger is "controlled," and they may turn it against themselves, saying they are stupid or that they hate themselves.

Level 2: The Stubborn/Dramatic Child. These children refuse to follow directions or comply with requests or demands. They engage in verbal aggression such as swearing, name-calling, and insulting others. This verbally assaultive behavior may be interpreted by parents and teachers as being on the verge of violent behavior, and their dramatic behaviors contribute to the feeling that

TABLE 6.1
Clinical Classification System for Externalizing Disorders

Relevant Dimensions	Level 1	Level 2	Level 3	Level 4	Level 5	Level 6
Anger	X	X	X	X	X	X
Verbal aggression directed at self	X	X	X	X	X	X
Verbal aggression directed at others		X	X	X	X	X
Physical aggression against inanimate objects			Minimal damage	Severe damage	Severe damage	Severe damage
Physical aggression against others					Unintentional harm	Intentional harm
Violence						Intentional harm

Note. From "Managing Anger in Youth: A Cognitive–Behavioral Intervention Approach," by W. M. Nelson and A. J. Finch, 2000, in P. C. Kendall (Ed.), *Child and Adolescent Therapy: Cognitive-Behavioral Procedures* (pp. 129–172), New York: Guilford Press. Copyright 2000 by Guilford Press. Reprinted with permission.

they are "out of control" when in fact they are expressing their anger only through verbal means. A teenage boy who steps toward a teacher and calls him a bastard is acting at Level 2.

Level 3: The Threatening Child and the Beginning of Damage. The frequency and intensity of Level 3 anger is higher than that at Level 2 and involves verbal aggression that includes threatening harm, injury, or death to others. However, Level 3 youngsters have never harmed another living thing but have caused minor damage to objects such as trash cans, chairs, and so on. These children are still exercising some control and are cognizant of the undesirability of engaging in more harmful forms of aggression.

Level 4: The "Taking It Up a Notch" Child. These children purposely and intentionally display their anger by seriously damaging or destroying objects. They may break valuable objects and throw things through windows. They often threaten others with an available weapon (e.g., knife, scissors, baseball bat); however, they keep a distance between themselves and those they are angry with, often exiting the situation when approached. Although they are still exhibiting some control by not engaging in aggression against others, they are perceived as very dangerous and out of control.

Level 5: The Assaultive Child. At this level, children exhibit verbal aggression, threats, and physical aggression, including pushing, shoving, hitting, and throwing objects at people that will not cause physical harm. Injuries caused by children and adolescents at Level 5 are still unintentional.

Level 6: The Violent Child. These children exhibit violent behavior that is dangerous and causes intentional physical harm. At this stage, caregivers and teachers feel intimidated and even abused and believe the situation is hopeless and out of their control. The intentionality of the aggression is the critical determiner of Level 6 behavior.

Research has shown that children and adolescents with anger and aggression problems have difficulty with cognitive products, including social–cognitive appraisal; social problem solving; appraisal of internal arousal and emotional reactions; cognitive operations; schematic propositions; and mediating physiological arousal (Finch, Nelson, & Moss, 1993; Lochman et al., 2000; Nelson & Finch, 2000). Both cognitive distortions and cognitive deficiencies are present in children with high levels of anger or aggression. Additionally, angry and aggressive youth often have problems with depression, anxiety, and self-esteem.

Effective cognitive–behavioral treatment for angry and aggressive youth includes aspects of RET, behavior modification, and cognitive therapy and contains multiple intervention components (Lochman et al., 2000; Nelson & Finch, 2000). The interventions generally include (a) instruction in social-problem-solving and social-skills instruction; (b) coping models, including relaxation training; (c) role playing; (d) in vivo experiences and assignments; (e) affective education; (f) homework assignments; and (g) operant conditioning, most typically response–cost (Kendall & Braswell, 1993). Programs found to have positive results with aggressive, angry children include the *Anger Coping Program* (Lochman et al., 2000) and the *Coping Power Program* (Lochman & Wells, 1996). Both are cognitively based interventions using cognitive restructuring to address deficiencies and distortions in functioning and to effect behavioral change.

Attention-Deficit/Hyperactivity Disorder. Research has documented that, although cognitive procedures alone are ineffective for children with attention and activity disorders, cognitive additions to behaviorally based programs hold more promise (Finch, Spirito, et al., 1993; Hinshaw, 2000). Hinshaw discussed the fact that the terms *attention deficit disorder* (ADD) and *attention-deficit/hyperactivity disorder* (ADHD) are umbrella terms for a wide variety of symptoms. In fact, as many as 2,000 symptom variations are possible given the criteria for these disorders. In addition, Hinshaw noted the strong levels of comorbidity for ADHD and ADD with other disorders, including aggression, anxiety, depression, and learning disabilities. Comorbidity affects the use of cognitive–behavioral interventions for these youngsters in two ways: (a) interventions must be tailored to address the individual child's particular presenting problems, and (b) interventions effective in treating these other disorders may be effective with children comorbid for ADD and ADHD.

Outcome research on the use of cognitive–behavioral interventions with children with clinical levels of ADD or ADHD has produced mixed results. Some researchers have found these types of procedures helpful (Braswell & Bloomquist, 1991; Hinshaw, 2000; Kendall & MacDonald, 1993), but other studies have found cognitive–behavioral interventions to be ineffective (Abikoff, 1991). Hinshaw noted that relevant procedures affecting outcome include social skills, self-instruction, self-evaluation, and anger management, coupled with behavioral interventions addressing immediate feedback and contingency management procedures.

Many children and adolescents with attention/activity or anger/aggression disorders pose a challenge for treatment because they display symptoms of both externalizing disorders (e.g., lack of attention, hyperactivity, aggression) and internalizing disorders (e.g., anxiety, depression).

Cognitive–Behavioral Techniques with Internalizing Disorders

Anxiety Disorders. Anxiety and fear become pathological when they are disproportionate to the actual environmental threat and when they infringe on everyday functioning. Along with feelings of fear and anxiousness, these disorders often include physical symptoms and persistent, sometimes obsessive worrying; thus, anxiety has emotional, somatic, and cognitive components. Children and youth who experience anxiety disorders generally suffer from cognitive distortions rather than cognitive deficiencies. Research has found that their thinking contains negative cognitions that center around danger and threat and that cause fear of being hurt or scared and self-critical thoughts (Barrios & Hartmann, 1988; Daleiden & Vasey, 1997; Prins, 1986; Treadwell & Kendall, 1996). It is the frequency and persistence of negative self-statements that is predictive of each individual's psychological condition (Kendall et al., 2000). Cognitive–behavioral interventions have been shown to reduce negative thinking and increase ability to function (Treadwell & Kendall, 1996). Research has found that family variables are strongly implicated in the development and maintenance of anxiety in children, with issues of autonomy, parental anxiety, and control at the center of many problems (Kendall et al., 2000).

The "Coping Cat" Approach. A cognitive–behavioral therapy for anxiety, developed by Kendall and colleagues (Kendall, 1992b; Kendall, Kane, Howard, & Siqueland, 1989), is designed to teach children to recognize signs of anxiety reactions and to use those signs to cue their use of anxiety management techniques. This program emphasizes coping, modeling, identification and modification of anxious self-talk, exposure to anxiety producing situations, role playing, contingent rewards, homework, affective education, bodily awareness, and relaxation training. These strategies are applied and practiced in situations that are increasingly anxiety provoking, using both imaginal and in vivo techniques. *The Coping Cat Workbook* (Kendall, 1992b) accompanies the intervention.

Anxiety Management Training. A second, related approach, anxiety management training, was developed by Suinn and colleagues (Suinn, 1986; Suinn & Deffenbacher, 1988; Suinn & Richardson, 1971) during a period when many behaviorally trained clinicians were attempting to move beyond situation-specific interventions and identify general therapeutic strategies useful to alleviate a variety of psychological problems in diverse circumstances. These clinicians were particularly concerned with the limitations of systematic desensitization (see "Behavioral Therapy," Chapter 5), regarding it as a time-consuming, unnecessarily long treatment approach. As a more effective alternative, they developed a concise, easily learned series of coping strategies to combat anxiety. Their approach is based on the premise that anxiety is an acquired drive—a series of learned responses that in turn act as stimuli for avoidance behavior. For example, a person who has a phobia of dogs is cued to scream, run, experience panic, and go to any extreme to avoid dogs, not by a dog (a stimulus), but by the anxiety (an acquired drive state) associated with cognitions about dogs. Thus, the key to overcoming phobia is to teach the person to control anxiety, regardless of the anxiety-evoking stimulus. Once learned, these coping strategies may be applied in any circumstance when anxiety is evoked.

Like systematic desensitization (Wolpe, 1976), anxiety management training uses deep-muscle relaxation as a basis for coping with anxiety. After learning relaxation techniques, the client practices visualizing scenes that arouse anxiety. Unlike systematic desensitization, no attempt is made to sequence anxiety-evoking events from mild states to progressively more severe states. Also, the anxiety-coping skills are applied to a wide variety of potentially threatening events to ensure that the strategies are internalized and useful in diverse circumstances. Although the simplicity of anxiety management training makes it attractive, there is limited empirical evidence supporting the efficacy of this technique (Grace, Spirito, Finch, & Ott, 1993; Suinn, 1986). Stress inoculation training has also been used effectively to reduce anxiety in children and adolescents across anxiety-provoking situations. Research has demonstrated effectiveness for test anxiety, medical and dental procedures, and general fears and phobias (Grace et al., 1993).

Childhood and Adolescent Depression. Cognitive–behavioral programs designed to treat childhood and adolescent depression have addressed unipolar depressive disorder in children 9 years of age and older. Children with learning disabilities, medical conditions, and other psychological problems have much higher prevalence rates of depression than other children (Stark et al., 2000). Stark and colleagues, along with other cognitive theorists, have begun to integrate cognitive and interpersonal theories as a model of depression development (Baldwin, 1992; Rudolph, Hammen, & Burge, 1997; Shirk, 1998; Stark, Schmidt, & Joiner, 1996). Prevailing models have used either Beck's (1993) cognitive theory or Abramson's (1999) learned helplessness theory of depression with interpersonal theories. Stark's model integrates Beck's cognitive theory of depression with attachment theory. Beck's model provides hypotheses and empirical validation of the cognitive disturbances present in depressed youth. Attachment theory describes the process by which these cognitive disturbances may originate in very young children and subsequently influence development.

Cognitively, depressive disorders are linked to negative cognitive distortions about the self, the world, and the future that are triggered by a specific vulnerability to stress. Recent evidence shows that depressed youth are lacking in positive schemas about the self and may have stronger negative self-schemas than nondepressed youth have (Hammen & Zupan, 1984; Zupan, Hammen, &

Jaenicke, 1987). The absence of a positive self-schema leads to an imbalance in information processing. Fewer interpretations of a positive self are processed and internalized, which in turn reinforces negative cognitive distortions about self, the world, and the future. Because the first schema to develop is the self-schema, it affects all other cognitive schemas.

Cognitive representations of relationships guide cognitive processing that is ultimately related to the child's sense of self (Rudolph, Hammen, & Burge, 1995). Secure or insecure attachments are based on the coherence and organization of the relationships between the child, the primary caregiver, and the family in general (Main, 1996). Insecure and anxious attachment fosters a self-schema as unlovable, and Beck (1993) hypothesized that an unlovable self-schema is at the core of depression. Research supports the influence of early learning and experience within the family in forming core schema (Stark et al., 1996).

In other words, a child is depressed due to distortions in information processing stemming from early learning experiences around attachment and the self-schema. This child, when faced with a stressful situation, is more likely to find the situation threatening and to negatively assess her ability to deal with the stress. Also, depressed individuals are less likely to seek out social support when dealing with stressful situations because they are more likely to have negative schema about others' ability to help and about the ability to affect the future. These negative cognitions lead to even greater depression.

Cognitive–Behavioral Treatment. Stark and Kendall (1996) developed a 30-session treatment plan to address childhood depression. They note that the intervention must include parents, family, and school for a variety of reasons, including (a) to support the child's therapy; (b) to encourage the development of new, more adaptive schemas and information-processing mechanisms; (c) to encourage the use of coping skills in everyday situations; and (d) to change everyday situations that contribute to the depressive symptoms. The basic components of the program are as follows:

- *Affective education* that targets the identification and labeling of pleasant and unpleasant emotions and links emotions and related thoughts

- *Self-monitoring* pleasant and unpleasant emotions and depressing thoughts that enables youngsters to note their occurrence as well as identify situations likely to lead to each type of emotion or thought

- *Purposeful scheduling* that includes daily scheduling of enjoyable and goal-directed activities that allow children access to pleasant emotions and feelings of competence

- *Problem solving* that centers on the actual issues in a given situation, the alternative interpretations that may exist, and playing the "What if" game

- *Assertiveness training and coping skills training* to teach children to use their mood as a cue to engage in coping mechanisms and to feel capable of dealing with difficult or stressful situations

- *Identifying personal standards, goal setting, and self-evaluation training* to enable youngsters to set their own goals based on personal values and then evaluate how they cope and behave relative to their goals

The components of this treatment program are designed to address both the cognitive and mood disturbances present in depressed youngsters. Initial research into this program and other related cognitive–behavioral interventions indicates that they are effective in treating depressed youngsters (see Stark et al., 2000). Stark, Kaslow, and Reynolds (1985) taught a group of depressed children (ages 9 to 12) to set more realistic standards for performance, self-monitor pleasant activities, use self-reinforcement, and examine their attributions. The subjects experienced significant reductions in symptoms of depression, indicating that they had the necessary developmental maturity to use cognitive-restructuring strategies. It appears that success is greater when modeling and role playing are used to teach the strategies and when effective behavioral contingencies are used to reinforce the learning of the new cognitive skills. Additional research into the cognitive and interpersonal variables contributing to depression should lead to fine-tuning these programs and increase their efficacy.

Application of Cognitive–Behavioral Strategies in Schools

Clearly, it is appropriate for members of the mental health community associated with school settings (psychiatrists, psychologists, social workers, and counselors) to use cognitive strategies to help children and youth with psychological difficulties. It also is clear that some of these strategies (particularly the approaches developed by Meichenbaum [1977, 1979, 1986, 1990] and by Spivack et al. [1976]) have been designed for use by teachers in classrooms to assist children in overcoming a variety of learning and behavioral problems, just as behavior modification strategies have been refined for that purpose. The following suggestions are intended to provide further guidelines for teachers who are interested in applying cognitive strategies in their classrooms.

• *Teach cognitive concepts.* Many adolescents are capable of understanding the concepts associated with cognitive therapy, even those basic to cognitive restructuring, the most challenging of the cognitive approaches. Younger children also may be taught strategies for solving problems, identifying attributions, altering self-verbalizations, differentiating between rational and irrational thoughts, and so forth, if the concepts are introduced in interesting formats (e.g., games), expressed concretely (e.g., "An irrational thought is a weed; a rational thought is a flower"), illustrated with numerous examples, practiced with teacher guidance, and applied in structured situations—in short, if the concepts are taught properly and if children are positively reinforced for learning them.

Stark, Rouse, and Livingston (1991) reported on a cognitive-restructuring and self-evaluative program for depressed children that has been implemented successfully in schools. The first step is an affective education program consisting of a sequenced series of games designed to teach important vocabulary and concepts. The initial game, Emotive Vocabulary I, involves a deck of cards containing the names of emotions. Children draw the cards and are reinforced for describing how the emotion feels. At the next level, Emotive Vocabulary II, children draw the cards and are reinforced when they can describe how a person experiencing the emotion might be thinking and behaving. For the third game, Emotive Charades, the children earn reinforcement when they act out emotions named on the cards. They also discuss experiencing the emotions. Emotive Statues, the fourth game, requires the children to take turns being a statue or a sculptor. The sculptor draws a card and shapes the statue to show the emotion. Discussion involves experiencing the emotion in real life. The fifth game, Emotive Expression, involves expressing emotions on the cards vocally, but without words. The children identify the emotions, then discuss the thoughts and feelings associated with them.

The second step in this program was designed to teach self-control. The children learn to monitor their behaviors, that is, to distance and observe themselves in problematic situations; to evaluate how their behaviors have met their goals and expectations; and to reinforce themselves for adaptive responses. Teachers use cognitive modeling to demonstrate behaviors while verbalizing irrational thoughts, then present a series of more adaptive thoughts that the child might substitute to prevent maladaptive behavior. In turn, children role-play each episode. Many of the activities are based on the children's homework, that is, their daily records of significant incidents that involve good and bad consequences.

• *Set realistic goals for children.* Children show individual differences in their abilities to learn this type of content, just as they do for all other types of content. Encourage children who appear to grasp the strategies rapidly to apply them in a variety of situations, at home as well as at school. For those who are less responsive, persist in helping them apply one procedure, such as problem solving, in one specific context. Also, if certain individuals are unable to use problem solving or the cognitive-restructuring techniques, teach them to use simpler cognitive distracters such as relaxation and deep breathing to help them remain calm.

• *Teach these strategies to all children*, not only to those who evidence emotional disorders. All children would benefit from learning how to solve problems more effectively; alter their self-derogatory or self-defeating thoughts and self-talk; understand the relationships between thinking, feeling, and emotion; and cope with stress. As Ellis (1962) pointed out, the people who gain most from therapy are the people who least need it.

• *Share cognitive explanations of behavior and feelings with parents.* Cognitive concepts such as problem solving, altering misperceptions, and thinking more adaptive thoughts are not threatening to people. They do not suggest that the teacher is intent on "playing Freud." Familiarity with these premises may help parents understand their children better and may improve their parenting skills. Parents also may become more aware of how their own faulty cognitions contribute to their problems.

• *Use cognitive strategies with individuals experiencing specific problems as well as with groups.* Like a behavior modification program, these strategies may be applied to help a child experiencing a specific problem. Similarly, they may be used with intact classes or with small groups of children who share specific types of problems, such as an inability to meet their responsibilities or aggression.

An illustrative treatment program was described by Lochman, White, and Wayland (1991), who successfully taught a group of aggressive fourth- and fifth-grade boys to cope with anger. They used discussion, observation, modeling, and role playing to help the boys identify the affective and physiological cues of anger arousal. They explored the situations at home and at school that caused anger. Then they showed a videotape of an angry boy while directing attention to the signs of his anger and speculating on his feelings. Each student talked about his own unique physiological response, such as muscle tension, pulse rate, and facial expressions, and his thoughts when angry. When the group members were able to identify the signs of anger arousal in themselves, they focused on identifying their self-talk and explored its relationship to anger arousal or reduction. Finally, verbal taunts were used to enable the boys to practice self-talk that reduced anger. At first, puppets were used to make the verbal taunts. When the boys were able to consistently demonstrate good coping skills in that context, peers made verbal taunts.

• *Model and role-play cognitive strategies.* Show the children how you use cognitive strategies. For example, reveal how your thoughts might have influenced your perception of an event and subsequently your behavior. Provide instances of catastrophic thinking (e.g., "Getting a traffic ticket is the end of the world") and other maladaptive self-talk that perpetuate bad feelings (e.g., "I should never break anything; if I do, I'm a fool") and examples of altering those thoughts with more constructive self-verbalizations. Your frank disclosure will show how pervasive such thinking is and encourage openness among the children. Encourage them to discuss similar thoughts and feelings they have experienced.

Also use modeling and role playing to help solve problematic situations in school. Discuss a problem with the class; then model the maladaptive behavior while verbalizing thoughts that instigate it. Substitute more adaptive thoughts and have class members role-play. For example, if certain children are prone to make insulting remarks to others, discuss the problem in a general way with the class; then model a typical situation where insults are exchanged. Point out the thoughts that might influence behavior ("He doesn't like me" or "She never plays with me"). Have a child role-play by responding verbally to the insult and help her identify her thoughts. Discuss how thinking about being disliked causes feelings of anger and insulting behavior. Model the situation, verbalizing more adaptive thinking ("She's busy right now; maybe we'll play later") that causes better feelings and does not lead to insults. Have pairs of children role-play similar episodes.

• *Experiment with a variety of cognitive approaches.* Students differ, depending on their emotional needs, maturity, intelligence, and so forth, in their ability to benefit from particular aspects of cognitive therapy. For some, learning to cope with anger is essential, whereas others might be helped more by a problem-solving approach or by evaluating their irrational thoughts.

Even the more complex cognitive strategies can be presented with an informal instructional format. For example, Stark et al. (1991) recommended a game called Thought Detective to teach cognitive restructuring. Children are taught to "detect" thoughts that influence their behavior, evaluate the evidence that the thoughts are true, consider alternative thoughts, and think about real outcomes if undesirable events occur. Initially, children are presented with a hypothetical problem, such as a shy student who has difficulty making friends. The detectives brainstorm to identify possible maladaptive thoughts that cause social isolation, such as fears of rejection ("Others will be mean") or feelings of inferiority ("I'm not smart enough"). Evidence about the truth of each maladaptive possibility is discussed, illustrating that the student's thinking may be erroneous. Then the detectives generate alternative thoughts to help the student feel more confident about interacting with others. Finally, the class explores the actual ramifications of trying to make friends and being rebuffed. Once children learn to be good thought detectives, they can use the strategies to deal with real-life problems.

• *Be an active–directive agent for change.* Teaching usually is regarded as an active–directive occupation. A teacher presents information appropriate for students and tries to ensure that it is learned. Relatedly, teachers are not passive when students have problems that restrict learning; they try to change the situation. Cognitive–behavioral therapies are active–directive approaches to changing problematic situations and thus are useful tools for teachers. To illustrate the point, consider the concept of homework.

Homework is assigned to children to give them the opportunity to practice skills. Logically, children with adjustment problems need to practice skills that will help them behave more adaptively. Therefore, when an appropriate behavior is identified by student and teacher, the child's homework is to practice it in certain circumstances, record his efforts, and discuss them with the teacher or class. For example, shy individuals might be asked to speak to a certain number of strangers each day and to record the episodes. Phobic children might practice anxiety-evoking imagery and relaxation several times each day. Children in conflict with parents might make a certain number of positive statements to them every evening. Children who are overdependent on adults might practice completing simple tasks without adult support or advice. Children who are irresponsible might be assigned a number of chores to complete each day. Overcompetitive children might be made responsible for helping other children improve in certain skills. Children who are disliked because they make unfriendly, hostile, or supercilious remarks to others might practice making positive, supportive remarks to a certain number of peers each day. This simple but useful strategy is particularly effective when children's successful efforts are rewarded in some fashion. The entire process appears totally in keeping with teacher–student roles.

• *Encourage the children to teach cognitive strategies to one another.* Once the students become familiar with therapeutic techniques and accustomed to discussing them, they may work with one another to, for example, problem solve or remind one another of irrational thinking. This step may be particularly important for adolescents, because they are far more prone to listen to their peers than to adults. Cognitive therapists encourage autonomy and self-reliance and recommend the use of educational aids to increase independence. One such educational aid is the Disputing Irrational Beliefs instruction sheet (Ellis & Harper, 1975, p. 216). This sheet is simply a format that requires an individual to write down answers to questions about her irrational beliefs, such as "What irrational belief do I want to dispute and surrender?" The following questions pertain to the falseness or truthfulness of this belief. As the individual thinks about the belief in order to answer, she becomes better able to recognize and combat the force of the irrational idea.

• *Use overt behavior to evaluate the effectiveness of cognitive strategies.* What an individual says can be deceptive and misleading; what the person does is a far more reliable index of where he is psychologically. Even with internalized states such as depression, a person's actions reveal whether or not he feels less depressed.

Cognitive-Oriented Behavior Management Programs*

Glasser's Perspective

The theory and methodology that constitute William Glasser's initial approach to behavior management, *reality therapy*, are presented in two books, *Reality Therapy* (1965) and *Schools Without Failure* (1969). Like Ellis and Beck, Glasser was trained in traditional psychoanalytic philosophy and procedures but found them inadequate. Unlike Ellis's and Beck's approaches, Glasser's is more practically oriented. The tenets of reality therapy are fairly simple, aimed primarily at avoiding the "whys" of emotional disturbance and, instead, adopting the behavioristic perspective of focusing on altering behavior. However, Glasser deviated from a strict behavioral perspective by emphasizing the role of cognitions in the emotional and behavioral problems. He placed great importance on the idea that human beings are rational change agents capable of controlling their behavior. When they make bad choices, they consciously decide to behave in ways that are irresponsible, exploitive of others, and unrealistic in regard to perceptions of consequences. Glasser espoused a rationale for behavior change that involves the use of discipline to help students develop feelings of responsibility for their behavior and a commitment to behave more appropriately.

Glasser (1965) believed that emotional disturbance evolves when an individual is unable to fulfill two basic needs, "the need to be loved and to love and the need to feel that we are worthwhile to ourselves and to others" (p. 9). This failure is caused when an individual does not behave in a manner that is realistic, responsible, and right (the three R's).

The right–wrong aspects of reality therapy hold for all traditional classifications of psychological disorders—anxiety, depression, psychosis, and psychopathic and delinquent behavior. Individuals with emotional disorders behave inappropriately and engage in rationalizations, justifications, and other exploitive activities that enable them to maintain their inappropriate patterns

---

* This section of the chapter begins with a perspective on behavior management strategies that, to some extent, is designed to alter thoughts and ideas underlying student misbehavior in the classroom. The perspective is William Glasser's two-pronged model, consisting initially of reality therapy and control theory. The chapter concludes with a brief discussion of a comprehensive program built on Glasser's model to address behavior and resolve conflict in schools, *Developing Emotional Intelligence* (Bodine & Crawford, 1999).

of behavior. Their behavior problems are related to the most important of Glasser's basic tenets—responsibility.

Responsibility is "the ability to fulfill one's needs, and to do so in a way that does not deprive others of the ability to fulfill their needs" (Glasser, 1965, p. 13). Glasser believed that all persons with emotional disorders are "ill" because they are irresponsible, in contrast to the traditionally accepted psychiatric position that they are irresponsible because they are ill. Because they are irresponsible, they cannot earn the respect or admiration of others and cannot maintain a sense of their own self-worth. Thus, in time, because their basic needs for love and respect remain unfulfilled, they must suffer emotionally.

According to Glasser, acquiring responsibility is a complicated, lifelong process that must be learned. Learning is accomplished best as children of loving parents who teach them with appropriate affection and discipline. Parents who love their children and want what is best for them must discipline them. Discipline differs from punishment in that it is simply the enforced consequences of the child's behavior; a child who does not complete the assigned homework does not go outside to play baseball. Unlike punishment, discipline need not cause pain and always is limited to a specific behavior. It teaches the child to behave according to society's standards, to meet obligations, and to not infringe on the rights of others.

Another R concept, realism, is related to those concepts discussed previously. Glasser noted that persons with psychological problems have another common characteristic: They all deny the reality of the world around them. In other words, the symptoms of their disturbance—breaking laws, being disagreeable with others, justifying their behavior—all reflect the individuals' inability to recognize and accept the manner in which society functions. They deny that certain behaviors evoke certain consequences, whether they like it or not. Thus, they cannot be excused when they ignore reality and blame their problems on other people or on external events. They must be brought to recognize the long-term impacts or consequences of their actions and be forced to become responsible.

Educational Applications. Glasser (1978) believed that teachers are duty bound to maintain effective discipline in the classroom. Effective discipline is defined as helping students make good choices about their behavior. Glasser listed six functions required for an effective discipline program:

- Setting and enforcing classroom rules
- Consistently stressing student responsibility to meet obligations and to obey rules

- Rejecting excuses and rationalizations for bad choices

- Making value judgments about student behavior

- Helping students choose adaptive alternate behavior

- Associating logical consequences with good and bad choices

Function 1 stems from Glasser's view that discipline begins with classroom rules designed to promote effective learning. Rules should be generated by both the students and the teacher. There should be relatively few, and they should be simply stated (so they can be understood by all students) and displayed in the classroom. Once established, they must be enforced. Function 2 emphasizes the importance of constantly stressing children's responsibility for their own behavior. Teachers should hold regular classroom meetings to discuss issues of responsibility, such as failure to complete work on time, or lateness to class, and should encourage students to provide suggestions to remedy these problems. Function 3 signifies Glasser's insistence on the necessity of holding children to their commitments. Teachers must accept no excuses when a child fails to do what she has agreed to do, including obey class rules.

Function 4 reflects Glasser's belief that it is perfectly appropriate to estab-lish behavioral standards that reflect certain values (e.g., Fighting is inappro-priate) and, when a child exhibits inappropriate behavior, to make a value judgment about the behavior by questioning (e.g., "What is going on?" "Is it against the rules?" "Is it helpful to you or others?").

Function 5 refers to the necessity of teaching the child to make better choices. When an individual's behavior is inappropriate, he is asked to suggest a more realistic, beneficial alternative with questions such as "What could you do that would be more helpful?" When the child responds honestly to that question, he is making decisions and beginning to accept responsibility. As in Function 3, once the child makes a value judgment and a commitment to change, no excuse is accepted for not following through.

Function 6 is the most important component in the process for establishing discipline. When students make bad choices, they must face realistic conse-quences that have been previously associated with those choices. For example, if they are late, they lose free time. Similarly, when they make good choices, a desirable consequence should follow. Glasser pointed out that the teacher should never permit students who are irresponsible to avoid negative conse-quences. However, those consequences should neither be physically punishing nor involve caustic or sarcastic language.

Although the use of a questioning format in this behavior management plan is important, the teacher never asks, "Why are you doing that?" Glasser believes this question is irrelevant, that the person's motivation for the behavior (even if known) is of little significance. In fact, because "why" questions usually elicit justifications for behavior, they should be avoided.

Another important strategy involves the teacher's response when the child cannot make an accurate value judgment about her behavior. The child may be convinced that the behavior is acceptable or may be unwilling to cooperate with the questioning process. In either case, the child is resisting responsibility for her behavior, and the teacher should not tell the child what she is doing is wrong. The child simply must take the social consequences of misbehavior.

If the child is aware that the behavior is inappropriate but cannot make a better choice of behavior, the teacher should offer alternatives. However, the child should choose the actual course to be pursued from the options suggested by the teacher. For example, a child who fights constantly at recess may be able to formulate a plan to control this behavior. The teacher may suggest options, such as going to recess with another class, remaining inside and helping the office staff with errands, or joining in recess activities but leaving the playground when angry feelings begin to develop. The child must select a preferred course of action and, in so doing, accept responsibility for avoiding fights.

These simple procedures are predicated on the establishment of a supportive relationship between the child and the teacher. It is essential that the child recognize that discipline does not convey dislike and that, in fact, the teacher enforces discipline because he cares enough about the child to want her to change. Thus, to be effective, the teacher must avoid displaying anger or outraged indignation when a child fails to keep a commitment. The child is involved in a painful process of new learning that cannot succeed if she is not secure about the teacher's positive regard.

In *Schools Without Failure*, Glasser (1969) moved beyond the concept of discipline and presented a plan for redirecting the focus of modern education that is a forerunner to his most recent book, *Control Theory in the Classroom* (1985). He believed that many emotional problems are instigated and nurtured by modern instructional procedures, which he sees as deemphasizing thinking and problem solving in favor of rote memory activities. He offered a model of group meetings designed to teach children concepts such as decision making, social responsibility, and cooperation, in short, concepts that currently are deemphasized in competitive, achievement-oriented classrooms. His model involves three types of classroom meetings: *social-problem-solving* (the most important for the purpose of this book), *open-ended*, and *educational diagnostic*.

The first type, social-problem-solving, deals with the individual and group problems of the class and school. These meetings are vehicles for altering children's cognitions and helping them assume a degree of control over their destiny. Issues such as class attendance, grades, and individual behavior problems all may be introduced. The discussion should be directed toward problem solving; it should not affix blame, provide an outlet for griping, or culminate in punishment. Specific problem behavior by a given child is a legitimate topic but should not remain a topic of discussion over additional meetings unless the problem child has done something positive that deserves recognition. Meetings should not seek to find perfect answers to problems but should make clear that many problems have no perfect solution and must be met with the alternatives that are most helpful. Children benefit from problem-solving opportunities, a function usually denied them in modern education.

Open-ended meetings are not directed at problem solving but are for the discussion of any thought-provoking questions related to the children's lives. In these situations the teacher is not looking for factual answers but is trying to stimulate thought.

Educational-diagnostic meetings are related directly to content being studied by the class. They provide a means other than objective testing to ascertain whether the children are mastering the information being taught. They also provide an atmosphere for free discussion and relieve the children of the burden of being wrong. These meetings should never be used to grade children but simply to learn how much the children really understand.

To conduct these meetings, Glasser recommended that the teacher and students be seated in a tight circle. The teacher should sit in a different place each day and should arrange the children to reduce the possibility of problems arising. The meetings should be short (10 to 30 minutes for primary age children and 30 to 45 minutes for older children) and should be held regularly (once a day for elementary students and two to three times a week for secondary students). Topics for discussion may be introduced by the teacher or by the children. Initially, the teacher may need to take much of the responsibility for topic selection because the children will be reticent until they become familiar with the operation. In addition, the teacher should be prepared for initial difficulty in eliciting open discussion by the children. They are not accustomed to having an open format for their opinions in school, and it takes them some time to learn to contribute. Open-ended questions such as "Suppose I were to select two children to accompany me to the zoo; whom would I select?" serve to stimulate discussion. Another method is to use argumentative questions, such as "Are poor people lazy?" or "What would you do if you had a million dollars?"

Practical issues such as when to talk can be solved by having the children raise their hands. This method also prevents certain children from dominating the sessions. Also, reluctant speakers who fail to volunteer might be brought into the discussion by a remark such as "You are listening carefully; would you like to comment?" It is important that the teacher always be supportive of the children's efforts and that no attempt be made to criticize them. Children whose remarks are too personal or boring to the group may be stopped with a polite, "Thank you for your comments; let's hear from someone else now."

Glasser's relatively simple techniques were designed for application in schools because he believed that teachers have an advantage over other professionals who work with children with psychological problems: Teachers see their students on a daily basis and have the opportunity to establish a trusting relationship with them. His later work, presented in *Control Theory in the Classroom* (1985), showed no decrease in his attitude about the importance of the school in helping these children but revealed a different perspective on his attitude toward discipline. In this perspective he responded to the extensive apathy toward learning displayed by an ever-increasing number of students, particularly adolescents. He voiced great concern (extending the themes introduced in *Schools Without Failure*) that schools functioning in the traditional manner no longer met students' inherent basic needs, which he defined as the need to survive, the need to belong (to be accepted by the group), the need for power (to control one's life), the need for freedom (to be self-reliant), and the need for fun. He believed that discipline can work only in a classroom where students' needs are satisfied. Therefore, he advocated organizing the classroom to promote cooperative learning (see Chapter 7, "Educational Therapy").

Organizing students into small learning groups (about four persons) uses the powerful influence of peers to motivate students to achieve and frees students from overdependence on teachers (satisfying the need for freedom). The needs for belonging and fun are met because the cooperative group functions as a unit in a variety of situations, both academic and nonacademic. The need for power is met when students help one another and contribute to the group's undertakings. Glasser believed that cooperative learning reduces discipline problems and improves academic achievement. However, children who cannot respond to the cooperative classroom environment and who still present discipline problems will require the approach discussed in Glasser's (1965) *Reality Therapy*.

Developing Emotional Intelligence

Bodine and Crawford (1999) expanded and extended Glasser's work on reality therapy and control theory into a comprehensive program, *Developing Emotional Intelligence*, designed to address conflict in schools. The basis of their approach can be summed up as follows:

Accepting that much, if not all, of what is viewed as misbehavior in schools is actually conflict for which a constructive resolution has not yet been advanced provides a framework for dealing with unacceptable and nonproductive behaviors. Conflict is a discord of needs, drives, wishes, and/or demands. Three basic categories of conflict exist: Intrapersonal conflict involves an internal discord, interpersonal conflict involves discord between two parties, intergroup conflict is discord within a group of people or between groups of people. Each of these types of conflict has an impact on schools. (p. 65)

Bodine and Crawford (1999) also note that interpersonal conflict between students and teachers is actually, at times, conflict between the students and the school systems. *Developing Emotional Intelligence* is designed to address all three categories of conflict by assuming that conflict is natural and that the key to resolution is to apply the principles of creative resolution to human relationships rather than attempting to use extrinsically motivated management practices such as rewards and punishments, which they see as essentially coercive and subsequently problematic. Reflecting Glasser, they see responsible behavior as the keystone behavior. Management programs must foster responsible behavior by allowing each individual (adults included) to continually build on his or her understanding of the hows and whys of his or her own behavior.

Building on Glasser's basic needs (the need to survive, the need to belong, the need for power, the need for freedom, and the need for fun), they postulate that conflict is inevitable because these basic needs will sometimes come into conflict intrapersonally as well as interpersonally. Behavior, then, is viewed as the actions we take to resolve those conflicts. Humans, they postulate, will always choose the behavior they believe to be the best available option to either alleviate pain or to fulfill pleasure. All behavior, then, is simply behavior, and they argue that "misbehavior" is a label given to behaviors that cause conflict between people. Furthermore, by using the term *misbehavior*, most classroom systems slide into a coercive approach and lose the appropriate focus for finding effective solutions, conflict resolution.

At the heart of conflict resolution (and responsibility) is making choices that protect one's rights without infringing on another person's, that is, enabling oneself to meet one's needs while not impairing someone else's opportunities to meet their needs. Bodine and Crawford (1999) conceptualize behavior as *total behavior*, which has four components. *Doing, thinking, feeling,* and *physiology* always occur simultaneously. For people to satisfy their needs, they must be able to sense what is going on inside themselves and around them and be able to act on that information. Once people understand that it is possible to choose behaviors, they will understand that they can change behavior.

Bodine and Crawford see the ability to change the doing and thinking behaviors as leverage points; thus, this program reflects a cognitive–behavioral model. Behavior management programs should be designed to enable or assist the individual child to focus attention on satisfying his or her basic needs by using the thinking component to plan for the doing component.

Managing the classroom for developing emotional intelligence is based on two foundations. The first is building a supportive environment using Glasser's reality therapy approach. Bodine and Crawford (1999) recommend all components of reality therapy including (a) focusing on the person's total behavior, (b) asking him what he wants now, (c) asking the person to evaluate whether his present behavior is likely to get him what he wants, (d) helping him make a new plan with new behaviors, (e) agreeing on the plan, and (f) not giving up on his ability to acquire a more responsible and satisfying life.

The second foundation is establishing a behavior management system to create responsible learners. This involves focusing on *teachable abilities* and *facilitative probes*. Teachable abilities are attitudes, ways of thinking, and skills that when mastered lead to changes in behavior. Teachable abilities are taught using facilitative probes, a question or statement that prompts the child to evaluate his behavior and focus on his developing ability to change or choose new behaviors. According to Bodine and Crawford (1999, p. 84), self-awareness is a critical element in the behavior management program and is designed to teach students to

- examine how they make judgments and assessments;
- tune in to the sensory data available to them;
- get in touch with their feelings;
- gain awareness of their intentions; and
- attend to their actions.

This program uses a community-based rather than an individual model of control, suggesting that the "we" of the group is smarter and more powerful in facilitating change than the "me" of the individual. Thus, the emphases are on sharing, cooperating, helping others, recognizing good in ourselves and others, thinking win–win, and working together to meet students' individual and group needs. It is a *sense-based* rather than a *rule-abundant* system, because it is centered on responsibilities and rights rather than rules. The focus of interactions to foster teachable abilities involves questions such as "What right did you violate?" or "Did you act responsibly?"

Classroom components include class meetings, life rules, CARE (Communication About Responsibility Education) Time, and time-out. Class meetings function in much the same ways as Glasser's meetings; they introduce behavioral expectations; help students understand psychological needs, wants, responsibilities, rights, and choices; introduce and teach about conflict; and provide a forum to resolve problems. Life rules follow the basic tenets of good rule development: They must be few and positive, make sense, be enforceable, help create a sense of community, and have consequences. CARE Time is designed to help students focus on how they are acting, feeling, and thinking; what they want; whether they are acting responsibly; and what choices they can make to change the outcome of the situation. CARE Time may be scheduled but should also be woven into the day to provide a forum for dealing with problems as they occur. Time-out is used to temporarily remove youngsters if they are disrupting learning and is designed to facilitate self-evaluation rather than to serve as punishment. An additional component, teaching conflict resolution strategies, is useful to facilitate a process whereby the parties in conflict come to successful resolution without outside interference.

Developing Emotional Intelligence is a program that uses empirically based cognitive–behavioral interventions, including self-management, coping skills instruction, problem-solving strategies, and cognitive restructuring, in practical ways. It is one of the most promising programs available to help teachers manage classrooms in ways that ensure students' needs are met, including the need to develop responsible behavior as a means of leading a successful life.

 ## STUDY QUESTIONS _____

1. Discuss cognitive restructuring. Give examples of its usefulness in treating children and youth with emotional problems.

2. Compare and contrast the tenets underlying cognitive therapy with those underlying behavioral therapy. Explain how they can act in tandem for more effective interventions.

3. Discuss cognitive–behavioral interventions for anger and aggression.

4. According to Glasser, how are reality, responsibility, and right and wrong, related to emotional disturbance?

5. What are the major steps in Meichenbaum's self-instruction therapy?

6. Discuss the application of two coping skills strategies.

7. Explain the major components of Developing Emotional Intelligence and how they may be useful in today's school environment.

References

Abikoff, H. (1991). Cognitive training in ADHD children: Less to it than meets the eye. *Journal of Learning Disabilities, 24,* 205–209.

Abramson, L. Y. (1999). *Developmental maltreatment and cognitive vulnerability to depression.* Paper presented at the spring meeting of the Society for Research in Child Development, Albuquerque, NM.

Abramson, L. Y., Seligman, M. E. P., & Teasdale, J. D. (1979). Learned helplessness in humans: Critique and reformulation. *Journal of Abnormal Psychology, 87,* 49–74.

Ager, C. L., & Cole, C. L. (1991). A review of cognitive-behavioral interventions for children and adolescents with behavioral disorders. *Behavioral Disorders, 16,* 276–287.

American Psychological Association. (1993). *Summary report of the American Psychological Association Commission on violence and youth: Vol. 1. Violence and youth: Psychology's response.* Washington, DC: Author.

Arbuthnot, I., & Gordon, D. A. (1986). Behavioral and cognitive effects of a moral reasoning development intervention for high-risk behavior disordered adolescents. *Journal of the American Psychological Association, 54,* 208–216.

Asher, S. R., Oden, S. L., & Gottman, I. M. (1977). Children's friendships in school settings. In L. Katz (Ed.), *Current topics in early childhood education* (Vol. 1, pp. 123–167). Norwood, NJ: Ablex.

Bachman, J. G., Johnson, L. D., O'Malley, P. M., & Wadsworth, K. N. (1996). Transition in drug use during late adolescence and young adulthood. In J. A. Graber, J. Brooks-Gunn, & A. C. Petersen (Eds.), *Transitions through adolescence.* Mahwah, NJ: Erlbaum.

Baldwin, M. W. (1992). Relational schemas and the processing of social information. *Psychological Bulletin, 112,* 461–484.

Bandura, A. (1971). Vicarious and self-reinforcement process. In R. Glasner (Ed.), *The nature of reinforcement.* New York: Academic Press.

Bandura, A. (1977). Self-efficacy: Toward a unifying theory of behavioral change. *Psychological Review, 84,* 191–215.

Barrios, B. A., & Hartmann, D. B. (1988). Fear and anxieties. In E. J. Mash & L. G. Terdal (Eds.), *Behavioral assessment of childhood disorders* (2nd ed., pp. 196–264). New York: Guilford Press.

Beach, L., & Mitchell, T. (1978). A contingency model for the selection of decision strategies. *Academy of Management Review, 3,* 439–449.

Beck, A. T. (1963). Thinking and depression: Idiosyncratic content and cognitive distortions. *Archives of General Psychiatry, 9,* 324–333.

Beck, A. T. (1967a). *Depression: Causes and treatment.* Philadelphia: University of Pennsylvania Press.

Beck, A. T. (1967b). *Depression: Clinical, experimental, and theoretical aspects.* New York: Harper and Row.

Beck, A. T. (1982). Cognitive approaches to stress. In C. Lehrer & R. Woolfolk (Eds.), *Clinical guide to stress management.* New York: Guilford Press.

Beck, A. T. (1993). Cognitive therapy: Past, present, and future. *Journal of Consulting and Clinical Psychology, 61* (2), 194–198.

Beck, A. T., & Greenberg, R. (1974). *Coping with depression.* New York: Institute for Rational Living.

Beck, A. T., Hollon, S., Young, J., Bedrosian, R., & Budenz, D. (1985). Treatment of depression with cognitive therapy and amitriptyline. *Archives of General Psychiatry, 42,* 142–148.

Beck, A. T., & Rush, A. (1975). A cognitive model of anxiety formation and anxiety resolution. *Issues in Mental Health Nursing, 7,* 349–365.

Beck, A. T., Rush, A., Shaw, B., & Emery, G. (1979). *Cognitive therapy of depression*. New York: Guilford Press.

Beck, A. T., & Weishaar, M. E. (1989). Cognitive therapy. In D. Wedding & R. Corsini (Eds.), *Current psychotherapies* (4th ed.). Itasca, IL; Peacock.

Blowers, C., Cobb, J., & Mathews, A. (1987). Generalized anxiety: A controlled treatment study. *Behaviour Research and Therapy, 25,* 493–502.

Bodine, R. J., & Crawford, D. K. (1999). *Developing emotional intelligence: A guide to behavior management and conflict resolution in schools*. Champaign, IL: Research Press.

Braswell, L., & Bloomquist, M. L. (1991). *Cognitive-behavioral therapy with ADHD children: Child, family, and school interventions*. New York: Guilford Press.

Braswell, L., & Kendall, P. (1988). Cognitive-behavioral methods with children. In K. S. Dobson (Ed.), *Handbook of cognitive-behavioral therapies* (pp. 167–213). New York: Guilford Press.

Butkowsky, I., & Willows, D. (1980). Cognitive-motivational characteristics of children varying in reading ability: Evidence for learned helplessness in poor readers. *Journal of Educational Psychology, 72,* 408–422.

Butler, G., Fennell, M., Robson, P., & Gelder, H. (1991). Comparison of behavior therapy and cognitive behavior therapy in the treatment of generalized anxiety disorder. *Journal of Consulting and Clinical Psychology, 59,* 167–175.

Cameron, R., & Meichenbaum, D. (1982). The nature of effective coping and the treatment of stress related problems. In L. Goldberger & S. Breynitz (Eds.), *Handbook of stress* (pp. 13–40). New York: Free Press.

Camp, B. W., & Bash, M. A. (1981). *Think aloud*. Champaign, IL: Research Press.

Camp, B. W., & Ray, R. S. (1984). Aggression. In A. W. Meyers & W. E. Craighead (Eds.), *Cognitive behavior therapy with children* (pp. 315–350). New York: Plenum Press.

Clark, D. M. (1991, September). *Cognitive therapy for panic disorder*. Paper presented at the National Institutes of Health Consensus Development Conference on the Treatment of Panic Disorder, Bethesda, MD.

Cohen-Sandler, R., Berman, A. L., & King, R. A. (1982). Life stress and symptomatology: Determinants of suicidal behavior in children. *Journal of the American Academy of Child Psychiatry, 21,* 178–186.

Cowen, E. L., Weissberg, R. P., & Guare, J. (1984). Differentiating attributes of children referred to a school mental program. *Journal of Abnormal Child Psychology, 12,* 397–410.

Daleiden, E., & Vasey, M. W. (1997). An information-processing perspective on childhood anxiety. *Clinical Psychology Review, 17,* 407–429.

Dattilio, F. M., & Freeman, A. (2000). *Cognitive-behavioral strategies in crisis intervention*. New York: Guilford Press.

DeRubeis, R., & Beck, A. (1988). Cognitive therapy. In K. S. Dobson (Ed.), *Handbook of cognitive-behavioral therapies* (pp. 272–306). New York: Guilford Press.

Diener, E., & Lucas, R. (1999). Personality and subjective well-being. In D. Kahneman, E. Diener, & N. Schwarz (Eds.), *Well-being: The foundations of hedonic psychology* (pp. 213–239). New York: Russell Sage Foundation.

Dobson, K. (1989). A meta-analysis of the efficacy of cognitive therapy for depression. *Journal of Consulting and Clinical Psychology, 57,* 414–19.

Dobson, K., & Block, L. (1988). Historical and philosophical bases of the cognitive-behavioral therapies. In K. S. Dobson (Ed.), *Handbook of cognitive-behavioral therapies* (pp. 3–38). New York: Guilford Press.

Dodge, K. A. (1986). A social information processing model of social competence in children. In M. Perlmutter (Ed.), *Cognitive perspectives on children's social and behavioral development*. Hillsdale, NJ: Erlbaum.

Dryden, W., & Ellis, A. (1988). Rational emotive therapy. In K. S. Dobson (Ed.), *Handbook of cognitive-behavioral therapies* (pp. 214–271). New York: Guilford Press.

Durham, R. C., & Turvey, A. A. (1987). Cognitive therapy vs. behavior therapy in the treatment of chronic anxiety. *Behavior Research and Therapy, 25,* 229–234.

Durlak, J. A. (1983). Social problem-solving as a primary prevention strategy. In R. D. Felner, L. A. Jason, J. N. Moutsugu, & S. S. Farber (Eds.), *Preventive psychology.* New York: Pergamon Press.

D'Zurilla, T. (1986). *Problem-solving therapy: A social competence approach to clinical intervention.* New York: Springer.

D'Zurilla, T. (1988). Problem-solving therapies. In K. S. Dobson (Ed.), *Handbook of cognitive-behavior therapies* (pp. 85–135). New York: Guilford Press.

D'Zurilla, T., & Goldfried, M. (1971). Problem-solving and behavior modification. *Journal of Abnormal Psychology, 78,* 107–126.

D'Zurilla, T., & Nezu, A. (1982). Social problem solving in adults. In P. C. Kendall (Ed.), *Advances in cognitive-behavioral research and therapy* (pp. 98–130). New York: Academic Press.

Eccles, J. S., Lord, S., & Miller-Buchanan, C. (1996). School transactions in early adolescence: What are we doing to our young people? In J. A. Graber, J. Brooks-Gunn, & A. C. Petersen (Eds.), *Transitions through adolescence.* Mahwah, NJ: Erlbaum.

Ellis, A. (1962). *Reason and emotion in psychotherapy.* New York: Stuart.

Ellis, A. (1970). Rational-emotive therapy. In L. Hersher (Ed.), *Four psychotherapies.* New York: Appleton-Century-Crofts.

Ellis, A. (1979). The basic clinical theory of rational emotive therapy. In A. Ellis & M. Whitelay (Eds.), *Theoretical and empirical foundations of rational-emotive therapy.* Monterey, CA: Brooks/Cole.

Ellis, A. (1988). *How to stubbornly refuse to make yourself miserable about anything—Yes, anything!* Secaucus, NJ: Stuart.

Ellis, A. (1995). Reflections on rational-emotive therapy. In M. J. Mahoney et al. (Eds.), *Cognitive and constructive psychotherapies: Theory, research and practice* (pp. 69–73). New York: Springer.

Ellis, A., & Becker, I. (1982). *A guide to personal happiness.* North Hollywood, CA: Wilshire Books.

Ellis, A., & Bernard, M. (Eds.). (1983). *Rational-emotive approaches to the problems of childhood.* New York: Plenum Press.

Ellis, A., & Harper, R. (1975). *A new guide to rational living.* Hollywood, CA: Melvin Powers.

Elkin, I. (1994). NIMH treatment of depression collaborative research program: Where we began and where we are. In A. E. Bergin & S. L. Garfiel (Eds.), *Handbook of psychology and behavior change* (4th ed., pp. 31–54) New York: Wiley.

Epanchin, B. C. (1991). Teaching social behavior. In J. L. Paul & B. C. Epanchin (Eds.), *Educating emotionally disturbed children and youth* (2nd ed., pp. 413–448). New York: Merrill.

Ernst, D. (1985). *Beck's cognitive theory of depression: A status report.* Unpublished manuscript, University of Pennsylvania, Philedelphia.

Fairburn, C. G., Jones, R., Peveler, R. C., Carr, S. J., Solomon, R. A., O'Connor, M. E., Burton, J., & Hope, R. A. (1991). Three psychological treatments for bulimia nervosa. *Archives of General Psychiatry, 48,* 463–469.

Farrington, D. P. (1995). The development of offending and antisocial behavior from childhood: Key findings from the Cambridge study in delinquent development. *Journal of Child Psychology and Psychiatry, 36,* 929–964.

Feindler, E. L. (1979). *Cognitive and behavioral approaches to anger control training in explosive adolescents.* Unpublished doctoral dissertation, West Virginia University, Morgantown.

Feindler, E. L., & Fremouw, W. J. (1983). Stress inoculation training for adolescent anger problems. In D. Meichenbaum & M. E. Jaremko (Eds.), *Stress reduction and prevention*. New York: Plenum Press.

Feindler, E. L., Marriott, S. A., & Iwata, M. (1984). Group anger control training for junior high school delinquents. *Cognitive Therapy and Research, 8*, 299–311.

Finch, A. J., Nelson, W. M., & Moss, J. H. (1993). Childhood aggression: Cognitive-behavioral therapy strategies and interventions. In A. J. Finch, W. M. Nelson, & E. S. Ott (Eds.), *Cognitive-behavioral procedures with children and adolescents: A practical guide* (pp. 148–205). Boston: Allyn & Bacon.

Finch, A. J., Nelson, W. M., & Ott, E. S. (1993). *Cognitive-behavioral procedures with children and adolescents: A practical guide*. Boston: Allyn & Bacon.

Finch, A. J., Spirito, A., Imm, P. S., & Ott, E. S. (1993). Cognitive self-instruction for impulse control in children. In A. J. Finch, W. M. Nelson, & E. S. Ott (Eds.), *Cognitive-behavioral procedures with children and adolescents: A practical guide* (pp. 233–256). Boston: Allyn & Bacon.

Forsythe, C., & Compas, B. (1987). Interaction of cognitive appraisals of stressful events and coping: Testing the goodness of fit hypothesis. *Cognitive Therapy and Research, 11*, 473–485.

Frydenberg, E. (1997). *Adolescent coping: Theoretical and research perspectives*. London: Routledge.

Gallagher, P. A. (1988). *Teaching students with behavior disorders: Techniques and activities for classroom instruction*. Denver, CO: Love.

Geer, J., Davison, G., & Gatchel, R. (1970). Reduction of stress in humans through nonveridical perceived control of aversive stimulation. *Journal of Personality and Social Psychology, 30*, 30–43.

Gersten, J. C., Langer, T. S., Eisenberg, J. B., Simacha-Fagan, O., & McCarthy, E. D. (1976). Stability and change in types of behavioral disturbance of children and adolescents. *Journal of Abnormal Child Psychology, 4*, 111–127.

Gibbs, J. C., Arnold, K. D., Ahlborn, H. H., & Cheesman, F. L. (1984). Facilitation of sociomoral reasoning in delinquents. *Journal of Consulting and Clinical Psychology, 52*, 37–45.

Glasser, W. (1965). *Reality therapy*. New York: Harper & Row.

Glasser, W. (1969). *Schools without failure*. New York: Harper & Row.

Glasser, W. (1978). Disorders in our schools: Causes and remedies. *Phi Delta Kappan, S9*, 331–333.

Glasser, W. (1985). *Control theory in the classroom*. New York: Perennial Library.

Goldstein, A. P. (1988). PREPARE: A prosocial curriculum for aggressive youth. In R. B. Rutherford, Jr., C. M. Nelson, & S. R. Forness (Eds.), *Bases of severe behavioral disorders in children and youth* (pp. 119–142). San Diego, CA: College-Hill.

Goldstein, A. P. (1999). *The PREPARE curriculum: Teaching prosocial competencies*. Champaign, IL: Research Press.

Goldstein, A. P., Glick, B., & Gibbs, J. C. (1998). *Aggression replacement training: A comprehensive intervention for aggressive youth*. Chamapaign, IL: Research Press.

Grace, N., Spirito, A., Finch, A. J., & Ott, E. S. (1993). Coping skills for anxiety control in children. In A. J. Finch, W. M. Nelson, & E. S. Ott (Eds.), *Cognitive-behavioral procedures with children and adolescents: A practical guide* (pp. 257–288). Boston: Allyn & Bacon.

Graham, S. (1983). The effect of self-instructional procedures on LD students' handwriting performance. *Learning Disability Quarterly, 6*, 231–234.

Gresham, F. M., & Lemanek, K. L. (1983). Social skills: A review of cognitive-behavioral training procedures with children. *Journal of Applied Developmental Psychology, 4*, 439–461.

Haaga, D. A. F., & Davison, G. C. (1989). Outcome studies of rational-emotive therapy. In M. E. Bernard & R. DiGiuseppe (Eds.), *Inside rational-emotive therapy: A critical appraisal* (pp. 155–197). San Diego, CA: Academic Press.

Haaga, D. A. F., & Davison, G. C. (1995). An appraisal of rational-emotive therapy. In M. J. Mahoney & D. Michenbaum (Eds.), Cognitive and constructive psychotherapies: Theory, research and practice (pp. 74–86). New York: Springer.

Haaga, D. A. F., Dyck, M. J., & Ernst, D. (1991). Empirical status of cognitive theory of depression. Psychological Bulletin, 110, 215–236.

Hains, A., & Szyjakowski, M. (1990). A cognitive stress reduction intervention program for adolescents. Journal of Counseling Psychology, 37, 79–84.

Hammen, C., & Zupan, B. A. (1984). Self-schemas, depression, and the processing of personal information in children. Journal of Experimental Child Psychology, 37, 598–608.

Hartup, W. W. (1979). The social worlds of childhood. American Psychologist, 34, 944–950.

Heppner, P., Neal, G., & Larson, L. (1984). Problem-solving training as prevention with college students. Personnel and Guidance Journal, 62, 514–519.

Heppner, P., & Petersen, C. (1982). The development and implications of a personal problem solving inventory. Journal of Counseling Psychology, 29, 66–75.

Heppner, P., Reeder, B., & Larson, L. (1983). Cognitive variables associated with personal problem-solving appraisal: Implications for counseling. Journal of Counseling Psychology, 30, 537–545.

Hinshaw, S. P. (2000). Attention-deficit/hyperactivity disorder: The search for viable treatments. In P. C. Kendall (Ed.), Child and adolescent therapy: Cognitive-behavioral procedures (pp. 88–128). New York: Guilford Press.

Hiroto, D., & Seligman, M. (1975). Generality of learned helplessness in man. Journal of Personality and Social Psychology, 31, 311–327.

Hollon, S., & Beck, A. T. (1986). Cognitive and cognitive-behavioral therapies. In S. L. Garfoeld & A. E. Bergin (Eds.), Handbook of psychotherapy and behavior change (3rd ed., pp. 443–482). New York: Wiley.

Hollon, S., Emerson, M., & Mandell, M. (1982). Psychometric properties of the Cognitive Therapy Scale. Unpublished manuscript, University of Minnesota and the St. Paul Ramsey Medical Center, Minneapolis-St. Paul.

Hollon, S., & Kriss, M. (1984). Cognitive factors in clinical research and practice. Clinical Psychology Review, 4, 35–76.

Hollon, S. D., & Najavits, L. (1988). Review of empirical studies on cognitive therapy. In A. J. Frances & R. E. Sales (Eds.), American psychiatric press review of psychiatry (Vol. 7, pp. 643–666). Washington, DC: American Psychiatric Press.

Horne, A. M., & Sayger, T. V. (1990). Treating conduct and oppositional defiant disorders in children. Elmsford, NY: Pergamon Press.

Horney, K. (1967). Feminine psychology. New York: Norton.

Howard, B., & Kendall, P. (1987). Child interventions: Having no peers? Philadelphia: Temple University Press.

Hughes, J. N. (1988). Cognitive behavior therapy with children in schools. New York: Pergamon Press.

Hughes, J. N., & Hall, R. J. (1987). A proposed model for the assessment of children's social competence. Professional School Psychology, 2, 247–260.

Ianni, F. A. J., & Orr, M. T. (1996). Dropping out. In J. A. Graber, J. Brooks-Gunn, & A. C. Petersen (Eds.), Transitions through adolescence. Mahwah, NJ: Erlbaum.

Ingram, R. E., & Kendall, P. C. (1987). The cognitive side of anxiety. Cognitive Therapy and Research, 11, 523–537.

Ingram, R. E., Miranda, J., & Segal, Z. V. (1998). Cognitive vulnerability to depression. New York: Guilford Press.

Kazdin, A., Bass, D., Siegel, T., & Thomas, C. (1989). Cognitive behavioral therapy and relationship therapy in the treatment of children referred for anti-social behavior. Journal of Consulting and Clinical Psychology, 57, 522–535.

Kazdin, A. E., & Weisz, J. R. (1998). Identifying and developing empirically supported child and adolescent treatments. *Journal of Consulting and Clinical Psychology, 66,* 19–36.

Kendall, P. (1985). Toward a cognitive-behavioral model of child psychopathology and a critique of related interventions. *Journal of Abnormal Child Psychology, 13,* 357–372.

Kendall, P., & Braswell, L. (1993). *Cognitive-behavioral therapy for impulsive children* (2nd ed.). New York: Guilford Press.

Kendall, P., & Fischler, G. (1984). Behavioral and adjustment correlates of problem solving: Validational analysis of interpersonal cognitive problem solving measures. *Child Development, 55,* 879–892.

Kendall, P., & Williams, C. (1986). Adolescent therapy: Treating the "marginal man." *Behavior Therapy, 17,* 522–537.

Kendall, P. C. (1992a). *Stop and think workbook* (2nd ed.). Ardmore, PA: Workbook Publishing.

Kendall, P. C. (1992b). *Coping cat workbook.* Ardmore, PA: Workbook Publishing.

Kendall, P. C. (Ed.). (2000). *Child and adolescent therapy: Cognitive-behavioral procedures.* New York: Guilford Press.

Kendall, P. C., Chu, B. C., Pimentel, S. S., & Choudhury, M. (2000). Treating anxiety disorders in youth. In P. C. Kendall (Ed.), *Child and adolescent therapy: Cognitive-behavioral procedures* (pp. 235–290). New York: Guilford Press.

Kendall, P. C., & Ingram, R. E. (1987). The future for cognitive assessment of anxiety: Let's get specific. In L. Michelson & M. Ascher (Eds.), *Anxiety and stress disorders: Cognitive-behavioral assessment and treatment* (pp. 89–104). New York: Guilford Press.

Kendall, P. C., & Ingram, R. E. (1989). Cognitive-behavioral perspectives: Theory and research on depression and anxiety. In P. C. Kendall & D. Watson (Eds.), *Anxiety and depression: Distinctive and overlapping features* (pp. 27–54). New York: Academic Press.

Kendall, P. C., Kane, M., Howard, B., & Siqueland, L. (1989). *Cognitive-behavioral therapy for anxious children: Treatment manual.* Philadelphia, PA: Kendall Department of Psychology, Temple University.

Kendall, P. C., & MacDonald, J. P. (1993). Cognition in the psychopathology of youth and implications for treatment. In K. S. Dobson & P. C. Kendall (Eds.), *Psychopathology and cognition* (pp. 387–427). San Diego, CA: Academic Press.

Kendall, P. C., & Morison, P. (1984). Integrating cognitive and behavioral procedures for the treatment of socially isolated children. In A. W. Meyers & W. E. Craighead (Eds.), *Cognitive behavior therapy with children* (pp. 315–350). New York: Plenum Press.

Kendall, P. C., Ronan, K., & Epps, J. (1990). Aggression in children/adolescents: Cognitive-behavioral treatment perspectives. In D. Pepler & K. Rubin (Eds.), *Development and treatment of childhood aggression* (pp. 341–360). Hillsdale, NJ: Erlbaum.

Kirschenbaum, D. S., & Ordman, A. M. (1984). Preventive interventions for children: Cognitive behavioral perspectives. In A. W. Meyers & W. E. Craighead (Eds.), *Cognitive behavior therapy for children.* New York: Plenum Press.

Lazarus, A. (1984). *In the mind's eye.* New York: Guilford Press.

Leon, J., & Pepe, H. (1983). Self-instructional training: Cognitive behavior modification for remediating arithmetic deficits. *Exceptional Children, 50,* 54–60.

Lindsay, W. R., Gamsu, T. V., McLaughlin, E., Hood, E. M., & Elspie, C. A. (1984). A controlled trial of treatments of generalized anxiety. *British Journal of Clinical Psychology, 26,* 3–16.

Little, V. L., & Kendall, P. C. (1979). Cognitive-behavioral interventions with delinquents: Problem solving, role taking, and self-control. In P. C. Kendall & S. D. Hollon (Eds.), *Cognitive-behavioral interventions.* New York: Academic Press.

Loeber, R., & Hay, D. F. (1997). Key issues in the development of aggression and violence from childhood to early adulthood. *Annual Review of Psychology, 48*, 371–410.

Loeber, R., & Stouthamer-Loeber, M. (1998). Development of juvenile aggression and violence: Some common misconceptions and controversies. *American Psychologist, 53*, 242–259.

Lochman, J., & Dodge, K. (1998). Distorted perceptions in dyadic interactions of aggressive and nonaggressive boys: Effects of prior expectations, context, and boy's age. *Development and Psychopathology, 10*, 495–512.

Lochman, J., White, K., & Wayland, K. (1991). Cognitive-behavioral assessment and treatment with aggressive children. In P. C. Kendall (Ed.), *Child and adolescent therapy* (pp. 25–65). New York: Guilford Press.

Lochman, J. E., FitzGerald, D. P., & Whidby, J. M. (1999). Anger management with aggressive children. In C. Schaefer (Ed.), *Short-term psychotherapy groups for children* (pp. 301–349). Northvale, NJ: Aronson.

Lochman, J. E., & Lampron, L. B. (1986). Situational social problem-solving skills and self-esteem of aggressive and nonaggressive boys. *Journal of Abnormal Child Psychology, 14*, 605–617.

Lochman, J. E., & Wells, K. C. (1996). A social-cognitive intervention with aggressive children: Prevention effects and contextual implementation issues. In R. D. Peters & R. J. McMahon (Eds.), *Preventing childhood disorders, substance use, and delinquency* (pp. 111–143). Thousand Oaks, CA: Sage.

Lochman, J. E., Whidby, J. M., & FitzGerald, D. P. (2000). Cognitive-behavioral assessment and treatment with aggressive children. In P. C. Kendall (Ed.), *Child and adolescent therapy: Cognitive-behavioral procedures* (pp. 31–87). New York: Guilford Press.

Luria, A. (1961). *The role of speech in the regulation of normal and abnormal behavior*. New York: Liveright.

Lyons, L. C., & Woods, P. J. (1991). The efficacy of rational-emotive therapy: A quantitative review of the outcome research. *Clinical Psychology Review, 11*, 357–369.

Maag, J. W. (1989). Moral discussion group interventions: Promising technique or wishful thinking? *Behavioral Disorders, 14*, 99–106.

Magnusson, D. (1982). Situational determinants of stress: An interactional perspective. In L. Goldberger & S. Breznitz (Eds.), *Handbook of stress* (pp. 31–44). New York: Free Press.

Mahoney, M. (1974). *Cognition and behavior modification*. Cambridge, MA: Ballinger.

Main, M. (1996). Introduction to the special section on attachment and psychopathology: 2. Overview of the field of attachment. *Journal of Consulting and Clinical Psychology, 64*, 237–243.

Manning, B. (1988). Application of cognitive-behavior modification: First and third graders' self-management of classroom behaviors. *American Educational Research Journal, 25*, 193–212.

Mannix, D. S. (1986). *I can behave: A classroom self-management curriculum for elementary students*. Austin, TX: PRO-ED.

Mansdorf, L., & Lukens, E. (1987). Cognitive-behavioral psychotherapy for separation anxious children exhibiting school phobia. *Journal of the American Academy of Child and Adolescent Psychiatry, 26*, 222–225.

Mason, L. J. (1980). *Guide to stress reduction*. Los Angeles: Peace Press.

McGinnis, E., & Goldstein, A. (1997a). *Skills streaming the adolescent*. Champaign, IL: Research Press.

McGinnis, E., & Goldstein, A. P. (1997b). *Skills streaming the elementary school child: New strategies and perspectives for teaching prosocial skills* (rev. ed.). Champaign, IL: Research Press.

Meichenbaum, D. (1977). *Cognitive behavior modification*. New York: Plenum Press.

Meichenbaum, D. (1979). Teaching children self-control. In B. B. Lahay & A. E. Kazdin (Eds.), *Advances in clinical child psychology* (Vol. 2, pp. 1–33). New York: Plenum Press.

Meichenbaum, D. (1985). *Stress inoculation training*. New York: Pergamon Press.

Meichenbaum, D. (1986). *Metacognitive methods of instruction: Current status and future prospects*. New York: Hawthorne Press.

Meichenbaum, D. (1990). Cognitive perspective on teaching self-regulation. *American Journal on Mental Retardation, 94*, 367–368.

Meichenbaum, D. (1991). Common themes and unresolved challenges. In P. C. Kendall (Ed.), *Child and adolescent therapy* (pp. ix–xi). New York: Guilford Press.

Meichenbaum, D., & Cameron, R. (1973). Training schizophrenics to talk to themselves. *Behavior Therapy, 4*, 515–535.

Meichenbaum, D., & Goodman, J. (1971). Training impulsive children to talk to themselves. *Journal of Abnormal Psychology, 77*, 115–126.

Meichenbaum, D., & Turk, D. (1976). The cognitive-behavioral management of anxiety, anger, and pain. In P. O. Davidson (Ed.), *The behavioral management of anxiety, depression, and pain*. New York: Brunner/Mazel.

Mischel, W. (1974). Processes in delay of gratification. In L. Berkowitz (Ed.), *Advances in experimental social psychology* (Vol. 7, pp. 34–49). New York: Academic Press.

Nelson, W. M., & Finch, A. J. (2000). Managing anger in youth: A cognitive-behavioral intervention approach. In P. C. Kendall (Ed.), *Child and adolescent therapy: Cognitive-behavioral procedures* (pp. 129–172). New York: Guilford Press.

Newman, C. F., Beck, J. S., Beck, A. T., Tran, G. Q., & Brown, G. K. (1990, November). *Efficacy of cognitive therapy for panic disorder in medicated and nonmedicated populations*. Poster session presented at the meeting of the Association for the Advancement of Behavior Therapy, San Francisco.

Niles, W. J. (1986). Effects of a moral development discussion group on delinquent and predelinquent boys. *Journal of Counseling Psychology, 33*, 45–61.

Novaco, R. W. (1975). *Anger control: The development and evaluation of an experimental treatment*. Lexington, MA: Heath.

O'Donohue, W., & Noll, J. (1995). Problem-solving skills. In W. O'Donohue & L. Krasner (Eds.), *Handbook of psychological skills training: Clinical techniques and applications*. Boston: Allyn & Bacon.

Ollendick, T., & King, N. (1998). Empirically supported treatments for children with phobic and anxiety disorders. *Journal of Clinical Child Psychology, 27*, 156–167.

Ollendick, T., & King, N. (2000). Empirically supported treatments for children and adolescents. In P. C. Kendall (Ed.), *Child and adolescent therapy: Cognitive-behavioral procedures* (pp. 386–427). New York: Guilford Press.

Orne, M. (1965). Psychological factors maximizing resistance to stress with special reference to hypnosis. In S. Klausner (Ed.), *The quest for self-control*. New York: Free Press.

Ottaviani, R., & Beck, A. T. (1987). Cognitive aspects of panic disorders. *Journal of Anxiety Disorders, 1*, 15–28.

Paul, J. L., & Epanchin, B. C. (1991). *Educating emotionally disturbed children and youth. Theories and practices for teachers*. New York: Merrill.

Peale, N. (1952). *The power of positive thinking*. Englewood Cliffs, NJ: Prentice Hall.

Pearl, R. (1985). Cognitive-behavioral interventions for increasing motivation. *Journal of Abnormal Child Psychology, 13*, 443–454.

Platt, J., Scura, W., & Hannon, J. (1973). Problem solving thinking of youthful incarcerated heroin addicts. *Journal of Community Psychology, 1*, 278–281.

Platt, J., & Spivack, G. (1975). *Manual for the means-end problem-solving procedure (MEPS): A measure of interpersonal cognitive problem-solving skill*. Philadelphia: Hahnemann Community Mental Health/Mental Retardation Center.

Platt, J., Spivack, G., Altman, N., Altman, D., & Peizer, S. (1974). Adolescent problem solving thinking. *Journal of Consulting and Clinical Psychology, 42*, 787–793.

Polyson, J., & Kimball, W. (1993). Social skills training with physically aggressive children. In A. J. Finch, W. M. Nelson, & E. S. Ott (Eds.), *Cognitive-behavioral procedures with children and adolescents: A practical guide* (pp. 206–232). Boston: Allyn & Bacon.

Power, K. G., Jerrom, D. W. A., Simpson, R. J., Mitchell, M. J., & Swanson, V. (1989). A controlled comparison of cognitive behavior therapy, diazepam and placebo in the management of generalized anxiety. *Behavioral Psychotherapy, 17*, 1–14.

Pretzer, J., Beck, A. T., & Newman, C. (1989). Stress and stress management: A cognitive view. *Journal of Cognitive Psychotherapy, 3*, 163–179.

Price, J. A. (1996). *Power and compassion: Working with difficult adolescents and abused parents.* New York: Guilford Press.

Prins, P. J. (1986). Children's self-speech and self-regulation during a fear-provoking behavioral test. *Behavioral Research and Therapy, 24*, 181–191.

Robin, A., Schneider, M., & Dolnick, M. (1976). The turtle technique: An extended case study of self-control in the classroom. *Psychology in the Schools, 13*, 449–453.

Robins, L. N. (1966). *Deviant children grown up: A sociological and psychiatric study of sociopathic personality.* Baltimore: Williams & Wilkins.

Rosenbaum, M. (1980). A schedule for assessing self-control behaviors: Preliminary findings. *Behavior Therapy, 11*, 109–121.

Rosenkoener, L. I., Landman, S., & Mazak, S. G. (1980). Use of moral discussion as an intervention with delinquents. *Psychological Reports, 46*, 91–94.

Rudolph, K. D., Hammen, C., & Burge, D. (1995). Cognitive representations of self, family, and peers in school-age children: Links with social competence and sociometric status. *Child Development, 66*, 1385–1402.

Rudolph, K. D., Hammen, C., & Burge, D. (1997). A cognitive-interpersonal approach to depressive symptoms in preadolescent children. *Journal of Abnormal Psychology, 25*, 33–45.

Scardamalia, M., Bereiter, C., & Steinbach, R. (1984). Teachability of reflective processes in written composition. *Cognitive Science, 8*, 173–90.

Schinke, S., Blythe, B., & Gilchrist, L. (1981). Cognitive-behavioral prevention of adolescent pregnancy. *Journal of Counseling Psychology, 28*, 451–454.

Schwartz, S., & Johnson, J. H. (1985). *Psychopathology of childhood: A clinical–experimental approach.* New York: Pergamon Press.

Shea, M. T., Elkin, I., & Imber, S. D. (1992). Course of depressive symptoms over follow-up: Findings from the National Institutes of Mental Health treatment of depression collaborative research program. *Archives of General Psychiatry, 49*, 782–787.

Shirk, S. R. (1998). Interpersonal schemata in child psychotherapy: A cognitive–interpersonal perspective. *Journal of Clinical Child Psychology, 27*, 4–16.

Sigman, M., Ungerer, J. A., & Russell, A. (1983). Moral judgment in relation to behavioral and cognitive disorders in adolescents. *Journal of Abnormal Child Psychology, 11*, 503–512.

Simons, A., Murphy, G., Levine, J., & Wetzel, R. (1986). Cognitive therapy and pharmacotherapy for depression: Sustained improvement over one year. *Archives of General Psychiatry, 43*, 43–48.

Snyder, H. N., & Sickmund, M. (1995). *Juvenile offenders and victims: A national report* (Document No. NCJ-153569). Washington, DC: U.S. Dept. of Justice, Office of Juvenile Justice and Delinquency Prevention.

Southam-Gernow, M., & Kendall, P. C. (2000). Emotion understanding in youth referred for treatment of anxiety disorders. *Journal of Clinical Child Psychology, 29.*

Spivack, G., Platt, J., & Shure, M. (1976). *The problem-solving approach to adjustment*. San Francisco: Jossey-Bass.

Stark, K., Kaslow, N., & Reynolds, W. (1985). *A comparison of the relative efficacy of self-control and behavior therapy for the reduction of depression in children*. Paper presented at the Fourth National Conference on the Clinical Application of Cognitive Behavior Therapy, Honolulu.

Stark, K., Rouse, L., & Livingston, R. (1991). Treatment of depression during childhood and adolescence: Cognitive–behavioral procedures for the individual and family. In P. C. Kendall (Ed.), *Child and adolescent therapy* (pp. 165–206). New York: Guilford Press.

Stark, K. D., & Kendall, P. C. (1996). *Treating depressed children: Therapist manual for "Action."* Ardmore, PA: Workbook Publishing.

Stark, K. D., Sander, J. B., Yancy, M. G., Bronik, M. D., & Hoke, J. A. (2000). Treatment of depression in childhood and adolescence: Cognitive–behavioral procedures for the individual and family. In P. C. Kendall (Ed.), *Child and adolescent therapy: Cognitive-behavioral procedures* (2nd ed., pp. 173–235). New York: Guilford Press.

Stark, K. D., Schmidt, K., & Joiner, T. E. (1996). Depressive cognitive triad: Relationship to severity of depressive symptoms in children, parents' cognitive triad, and perceived parental messages about the child him or herself, the world, and the future. *Journal of Abnormal Child Psychology, 24*, 615–625.

Stoyva, J., & Anderson, C. (1982). A coping-rest model of relaxation and stress management. In L. Goldberger & S. Breznitz (Eds.), *Handbook of stress*. New York: Free Press.

Suinn, R., & Deffenbacher, J. (1988). Anxiety management training. *The Counseling Psychologist, 16*, 31–49.

Suinn, R., & Richardson, F. (1971). Anxiety management training: A nonspecific behavior therapy program for anxiety control. *Behavior Therapy, 2*, 498–510.

Suinn, R. M. (1986). *Manual: Anxiety management training (AMT)*. Fort Collins, CO: Rocky Mountain Behavioral Science Institute.

Sullivan, M. L. (1996). Development transitions in poor youth: Delinquency and crime. In J. A. Graber, J. Brooks-Gunn, & A. C. Petersen (Eds.), *Transitions through adolescence*. Mahwah, NJ: Erlbaum.

Swarthout, D. W. (1988). Enhancing the moral development of behaviorally emotionally handicapped students. *Behavioral Disorders, 14*, 57–68.

Thoma, S., Rest, J., & Barnett, R. (1986). In J. Rest (Ed.), *Moral development: Advances in research and theory*. New York: Praeger.

Treadwell, K. H., & Kendall, P. C. (1996). Self-talk in anxiety-disordered youth: States-of-mind, content specificity, and treatment outcome. *Journal of Consulting and Clinical Psychology, 64*, 941–950.

Tversky, A., & Kahneman, D. (1981). The framing of decisions and the psychology of choice. *Science, 211*, 453–458.

U.S. Office of Juvenile Justice and Delinquency Prevention. (1994). *Juvenile crime, 1988–1992*. Washington, DC: Author.

Varni, J. W., LaGreca, A. M., & Spirito, A. (2000). Cognitive–behavioral interventions for children with chronic health conditions. In P. C. Kendall (Ed.), *Child and adolescent therapy: Cognitive–behavioral procedures* (pp. 291–333). New York: Guilford Press.

Vygotsky, L. (1962). *Thought and language*. Cambridge: Massachusetts Institute of Technology Press.

Waksman, S., Messmer, C. L., & Waksman, D. D. (1988). *The Waksman Social Skills Curriculum: An assertive behavior program for adolescents*. Austin, TX: PRO-ED.

Walker, H. M., McConnell, S., Holmes, D., Todis, B., Walker, J., & Goldnen, N. (1983). *The Walker Social Skills Curriculum: The ACCEPTS program*. Austin, TX: PRO-ED.

Walker, H. M., Todis, B., Holmes, D., & Horton, G. (1987). *The Walker Social Skills Curriculum: The ACCESS program*. Austin, TX: PRO-ED.

Wells, R. H. (1987). *Personal Power I. Succeeding in school: Developing appropriate teacher interaction skills.* Austin, TX: PRO-ED.

Wells, R. H. (1988). *Personal Power II. Succeeding with self: Gaining self-control.* Austin, TX: PRO-ED.

Wells, R. H. (1989). *Personal Power III. Succeeding with others: Peer interaction skills.* Austin, TX: PRO-ED.

Wilkes, T. C. R., Belsher, G., Rush, A. J., & Frank, E. (1994). *Cognitive therapy for depressed adolescents.* New York: Guilford Press.

Wolpe, J. (1976). *Theme and variations: A behavior therapy casebook.* New York: Pergamon Press.

Zupan, B. A., Hammen, C., & Jaenicke, C. (1987). The effects of current mood and prior depressive history on self-schematic processing in children. *Journal of Experimental Child Psychology, 43,* 419–458.

CHAPTER

EDUCATIONAL THERAPY

Christina Ager and Phyllis L. Newcomer

The term *educational therapy* refers to the therapeutic value of typical school-related activities. School success includes both academic and social components. The primary goal of educational therapy is to enable children with emotional and behavioral difficulties to redefine themselves as competent learners and contributing positive members of the school community. Classrooms, as the primary educational environment, must be structured to maximize instructional engagement and academic progress as well as provide a forum in which students can feel like they belong, are safe, and can contribute.

Teachers of students with emotional and behavioral disorders cite four major issues that have a pervasive impact on the instructional environment (Coleman & Vaughn, 2000): (a) the emotional variability of the students, (b) fear of failure, (c) trust issues, and (d) the challenge of motivating the students. The majority of research with students with emotional and behavioral difficulties has focused on social behaviors and skills rather than instructional programming. This chapter is devoted to examining the instructional environment, including assessing, planning, delivering instruction, and monitoring student success. Chapters 5 and 6, on behavioral and cognitive interventions, respectively, provide more extensive information on social and behavioral skills related to school success.

Educationally therapeutic activities include assessment and instructional techniques in academic skill or content areas, such as reading, arithmetic, and written expression, that correct or remediate learning deficits in all children; instructional arrangements or organizational procedures that facilitate learning for children with emotional problems; and general classroom management strategies that effectively reduce maladaptive, disruptive, or unproductive activities by children.

The basic assumptions underlying educational therapy are that affective and cognitive functions are intertwined and that effective teaching improves students' academic skills, increases their feelings of success and self-esteem, and subsequently leads them to exhibit more adaptive nonacademic behaviors. In this context, "teacher" is synonymous with "therapist," and therapy is an ongoing process throughout the day that is designed to facilitate success and increase self-esteem in children.

Academic failure is frequent among children with emotional and behavioral problems (Coleman & Vaughn, 2000; Hewett, 1969). Some children have a variety of developmental, biophysical, or acquired problems that interfere with their ability to absorb subject matter in a typical school environment. Other children show increased symptoms of emotional problems as they progress through school because they cannot achieve successfully in school. These individuals might remain well adjusted were it not for the frustration experienced in school.

The teacher who wants to provide a school experience that is therapeutic must arrange the instructional environment to promote student success, for failure is rarely therapeutic, especially for students with emotional and behavioral problems. To be successful in school, students must meet academic and behavioral expectations. To promote success, teachers must have certain competencies. They must be able to (a) use and interpret various formal and informal tests and assessment techniques, (b) translate the information gained into goals and instructional objectives, (c) monitor and evaluate the students' progress, (d) plan for effective instruction, and (e) deliver effective instruction to the students.

Conducting Assessments

Effective instruction begins with assessment techniques that enable teachers to specify students' academic strengths and weaknesses through the systematic collection of data. The two primary purposes for educational assessment are to specify and verify problems and to make instructional decisions (Salvia & Ysseldyke, 1985). Assessment information is critical to the processes of instructional planning and monitoring of students' progress. A student should be tested in all curricular areas to determine specifically which concepts and skills are already known and which need to be learned. Assessment can be conducted using a variety of methods, including standardized tests, criterion-referenced measures, curriculum-based assessment, skills checklists, and permanent product data and anecdotal data.

Standardized Tests

A sample of frequently administered standardized tests is listed in Table 7.1. Formal evaluations using standardized or norm-referenced tests "yield information of a quantitative nature and tend to compare a specific child's performance with national or regional normative data" (Hammill, 1971, p. 343). Raw scores, usually the total number of correct responses, can be converted to age equivalents, grade equivalents, standard scores, composite scores, or percentiles to make normative comparisons. Generally, teachers use standardized or norm-referenced tests to determine how a student's level of achievement compares with others at the same grade or age level. Standardized test results are most useful for making decisions about special education eligibility, decisions that are based, in part, on the extent to which students' scores deviate from the norm. Although they are helpful tools for this purpose, standardized tests have limitations.

According to Wallace and Larsen (1978, pp. 22–23), "the teacher is provided with little data that can be used in actually teaching the child. The more exact information upon which daily instruction is usually formulated is omitted in the results obtained from most formal assessment instruments." Therefore, norm-referenced tests must be followed by more specific assessment strategies that yield information needed to plan instruction.

Criterion-Referenced Measures

Criterion-referenced tests are designed to assess a student's mastery of specific skills by comparing performance to an absolute standard or criterion of skill performance, such as 90% mastery on a spelling test. These measures allow intrasubject comparisons (comparing changes in performance by the same student over time) rather than the intersubject comparisons (comparisons between children) yielded through standardized or norm-referenced measures. Criterion-referenced tests, often characterized as informal measures, can be used to (a) determine areas of academic strength and weakness, (b) validate or modify the conclusions and recommendations of formal standardized evaluation, (c) specify the student's instructional needs, and (d) inform an instructional program for the student. The object of the assessment is to discover what a particular student does or does not know.

Criterion-referenced tests have been developed by commercial publishers to accompany particular basal reading, math, and spelling textbook series as

TABLE 7.1

Standardized Tests Useful for Formal Assessment

Test	Content Area
Achievement Tests	
Diagnostic Achievement Battery–3 (Newcomer, 2001)	Spoken language, written language, reading mathematics
Diagnostic Achievement Test for Adolescents (Newcomer & Bryant, 1993)	Reading, writing, mathematics, science, social studies, spoken language
Formal Reading Inventory (Wiederholt, 1986)	Reading
KeyMath Diagnostic Arithmetic Test (Connolly, 1988)	Math
Peabody Individual Achievement Test (Dunn & Markwardt, 1981)	Math, reading recognition, reading comprehension, spelling, general information
Stanford Diagnostic Mathematics Test (3rd ed.) (Beatty, Madden, Gardner, & Karlsen, 1984)	Math
Language Tests	
Clinical Evaluation of Language Fundamentals–Revised (Semel, Wiig, & Secord, 1987)	Spoken language
Test of Early Language Development (Hresko, Reid, & Hammill, 1999)	Spoken language
Test of Language Competence–Expanded (Wiig & Secord, 1985)	Metalinguistics
Test of Language Development–Intermediate (TOLD–I:3) (Hammill & Newcomer, 1997)	Spoken language
Test of Language Development–Primary (TOLD–P:3) (Newcomer & Hammill, 1997)	Spoken language
Test of Reading Comprehension–3 (Brown, Hammill, & Wiederholt, 1995)	Reading
Test of Written Language–3 (Hammill & Larsen, 1996)	Written language
Test of Written Spelling–2 (Larsen & Hammill, 1986)	Spelling
Intelligence Tests	
Woodcock-Johnson Psycho-Educational Battery (Woodcock & Johnson, 2000)	Cognitive skills, academic skills, interest inventory
Wechsler Intelligence Scale for Children–Third Edition (Wechsler, 1991)	Intelligence
Comprehensive Test of Nonverbal Intelligence (Hammill, Pearson, & Wiederholt, 1997)	Intelligence

well as content area instruction in social studies and science. These commercial criterion-referenced tests are often referred to as monitoring systems. They may include pretests, which are given before an instructional period; progress tests, given to measure daily achievement; and posttests, given after the instructional period. Most monitoring systems usually include some method of record keeping.

Criterion-referenced tests also can be constructed by teachers. For example, the weekly spelling test may include words that the teacher selects randomly from the child's reading series. Gronlund (1976) proposed the following six simple guidelines to aid teachers in the use of behavioral procedures for test construction:

1. Clearly define and delineate the domain of learning tasks.

2. Express instructional objectives in behavioral terms.

3. Clearly specify a standard of performance.

4. Adequately sample student performance within each performance area.

5. Select test items based on how well they reflect the behavior specified in the instructional objective.

6. Devise a scoring and reporting system that adequately describes student performance on clearly defined learning tasks.

The first guideline refers to the scope of the subject matter to be included on the test. For example, if the subject matter is arithmetic, the teacher must decide if the scope should include only computation or should also involve arithmetic, vocabulary, and problem-solving skills. If the scope is restricted to computation, the teacher must decide what specific computational skills should be included.

The second guideline is discussed in detail in the section of this chapter on writing behavioral objectives. Briefly, it consists of forming instructional objectives that are observable and measurable. For example, a statement such as "The student will be able to recognize and name the numerals 1, 2, and 3 when they are shown on flashcards" specifies precisely what the student must do after being instructed, whereas the statement "The student will learn the numerals 1, 2, and 3" does not.

Objectives stated behaviorally always include a criterion, leading directly to the third guideline, specifying a a standard of performance. This pertains to components such as level of accuracy and rate of response. For example, the statement "The student will be able to recognize and name the numerals 1, 2, and 3, without error, within 5 seconds after viewing each flash card" includes standards.

The fourth guideline pertains to including enough items in each skill area on the test. For example, an arithmetic test of the four basic computational skills must include a representative number of addition, subtraction, multiplication, and division problems. Too few items in one area would preclude the formation of accurate conclusions about the child's skills in that area.

The fifth guideline, also about the selection of test items, suggests that each item used must pertain to the instructional objectives. If an instructional objective pertained to recognition and naming of numerals, it would be poor testing strategy to ask the child to write a numeral on the test.

The final guideline indicates that the teacher should convert test results to charts, graphs, or records that permit the teacher to monitor the child's progress in academic areas. The importance of monitoring student progress, as well as the belief that teachers should test what they teach, led to the development of various curriculum-based assessment models (Deno, 1985; Shapiro, 1989; Shapiro & Lentz, 1985).

Curriculum-Based Assessment

One basic assumption of curriculum-based assessment (CBA) strategies is that instruction is most effective and students most successful when the academic skills to be taught are at the student's instructional level, rather than too difficult (frustrational level) or too easy (mastery level). Other assumptions are that academic skills should be assessed directly, on an ongoing basis, and that resulting assessment data should influence the type of instruction and level of teaching materials used, as well as document the student's progress through the curriculum.

CBA was designed to provide direct measurement of academic skills by evaluating student performance on the materials in the curriculum (Shapiro & Ager, 1992). Deno (1987, p. 41) described CBA as "any set of measurement procedures which use direct observation and recording of a student's performance in the local curriculum as a basis for gathering information to make instructional decisions." A number of different models of CBA have been developed and investigated, including curriculum-based assessment for instructional design (CBA-ID) (Coulter & Coulter, 1989; Gickling & Havertape, 1981; Gickling, Shane, & Croskery, 1989; Gickling & Thompson, 1985; Hargis, 1987), criterion-referenced curriculum-based assessment (Blankenship, 1985; Idol, Nevin, & Paolucci-Whitcomb, 1986), curriculum-based evaluation (Howell & Morehead, 1987), curriculum-based measurement (Deno, 1985, 1986; Shinn, 1989), and a version incorporating an evaluation of the instructional environment as well as student skills (Shapiro, 1987, 1989; Shapiro & Lentz, 1985, 1986). These models differ in terms of the metrics used for measurement, the type and focus of the probes developed from the curriculum, and the emphasis on either assessment or alteration of instruction. Finally, an integrated model of CBA that incorporates elements from other models into a four-step problem-solving approach has been proposed by Shapiro and Ager (1992).

In Step 1 of the integrated model, the teacher examines the educational environment. This step includes reviewing teaching schedules to make sure adequate time is being planned for instruction and examining student work samples to analyze errors and approximate levels of performance. Work samples can also be examined for opportunities to respond; for example, teacher inspection of the student's worksheets on multiplication facts may yield the surprising result that only 3 of 40 problems gave the student practice on the nine-times tables. Classroom contingencies (outcomes) for work completion and accuracy are delineated and examined to determine if they are effective. If possible, this step also includes direct observation of instruction by the teacher or school psychologist to determine the child's on-task behaviors as well as the prevailing types of teacher behaviors. Important teacher behaviors are revealed by determining (a) how many and what type of questions are asked, (b) how instruction is conducted (large group, small group, one-to-one), and (c) what the frequency of teacher attention is when students are on task versus when they are off task. Traditionally, direct observation has been the job of school psychologists; however, increasingly more practical techniques are available that allow teachers to conduct self-observations, peer observations, and student observations. Examples include interval time sampling and the use of cues for observation, such as using kitchen timers and tape recorders.

Step 2 includes direct assessment of the student's academic behavior. Probes are developed from the student's reading, math, and spelling curricula. In reading, 150- to 200-word passages are taken from the student's basal reader and the student is asked to read aloud for 1 minute. The number of words read correctly and incorrectly are identified and compared with either locally developed norms or norms taken from the literature. These comparisons result in determining whether a student is at the frustrational, instructional, or mastery level in the tested material. Similarly, 2-minute probes are developed from the mathematics sequence to determine which skills the student has mastered and which are at the instructional or frustrational level (e.g., two-digit addition with regrouping). Similar procedures are followed to assess spelling, using lists of words taken from the student's spelling curriculum or, if no curriculum is used, from the basal reader. Three-minute writing samples using story starters as prompts are used for assessing written expression. In each subject matter area, measures such as the rate of words read or written correctly and incorrectly (reading and written expression), the rate of digits correct and incorrect (mathematics), and the rate of letter sequences correct (spelling), are used to determine the child's instructional levels.

Long- and short-term instructional objectives are written directly from the CBAs. For example, if a fourth-grade student is instructional at the third-grade level in mathematics and the second-grade level in reading, bringing the student up to grade level in both areas might constitute the general focus of the long-term objectives. Appropriate short-term objectives might include targeting unknown skills in math and increasing both rate and accuracy in reading.

Instructional modifications such as those proposed by Gickling (Gickling & Havertape, 1981; Gickling et al., 1989; Gickling & Thompson, 1985) are made in Step 3. Effective instructional modifications include controlling for known versus unknown content, flash card drill, peer tutoring, extra minutes of instruction, self-management procedures, and so forth. These techniques are used to help students master instructional-level materials and to reduce discrepancies between the performance of students with special needs and those in the mainstream.

Step 4 consists of monitoring student progress and evaluating the effectiveness of instructional modifications. Both long- and short-term goals can be monitored through the use of brief, timed probes (e.g., those described earlier) repeated regularly. Data are then graphed in relation to the goals set for the student so that the teacher and the student can readily assess whether the goals are being met or whether further modifications should be made. A more in-depth discussion of these procedures can be found in Olson and Platt (2000), Shapiro (1996), and Shinn (1989).

Skills Checklists

Skills checklists are another tool for informally evaluating a student's academic abilities. These are lists of skills that a student should be able to demonstrate if she has mastered certain material and is ready to progress to a higher level of instruction. They differ from criterion-referenced tests in that the skills represented on checklists are not defined behaviorally, nor do they involve a specific standard of performance. An example of a skills checklist is the Reading Checklist: Fluent Reading and Writing Stage (Cooper & Kiger, 2001) presented in Figure 7.1. Teachers can construct their own skills checklist by itemizing the tasks that a student must master and providing a place to record whether mastery has been accomplished. An example of a teacher-made checklist is presented in Figure 7.2.

READING CHECKLIST:
FLUENT READING AND WRITING STAGE

Name_____   Grade _____   Age _____

+ = consistently present

− = not present

× = somewhat present; recheck; insufficient evidence

Benchmark	Date	Comments
Behaviors from Almost Fluent Stage		
Word Recognition		
Construction of Meaning		
Grasps genres		
Perceives text structure		
Appreciates levels of meaning		
Varies reading according to purpose		
Uses strategies to construct meaning		
Is aware of own thinking		
Is learning study strategies		
Uses graphic material		
Enjoyment		
Recommends books to others		
Is exploring adult reading		
Sees self as competent reader		
Sets goals/self-evaluates		
Is aware of own purpose		
Research Skills		
Can plan a research project		
Knows how to locate information		
Takes notes/attributes sources		
Synthesizes information		

Instructional Plans:

_____

_____

_____

Figure 7.1. Reading Checklist: Fluent Reading and Writing Stage. *Note.* From *Literacy Assessment—Helping Teachers Plan Instruction,* by J. D. Cooper and N. D. Kiger, 2001, Boston: Houghton Mifflin. Copyright 2001 by Houghton Mifflin. Reprinted with permission.

	Has Mastered	Needs Review	Has Not Mastered
1. Can follow oral directions	☐	☐	☐
a. One specific direction	☐	☐	☐
b. Two specific directions	☐	☐	☐
c. Three specific directions	☐	☐	☐
d. Four or more specific directions	☐	☐	☐
2. Can listen to an oral story	☐	☐	☐
a. Can answer questions concerning the story	☐	☐	☐
b. Can retell the story in his or her own words	☐	☐	☐
c. Can retell the story's events in correct order	☐	☐	☐
3. Recognizes the differences between letters and words	☐	☐	☐
4. Relates his or her experiences verbally	☐	☐	☐
5. Can relate his or her experience in complete sentences	☐	☐	☐
6. Can say the alphabet in order	☐	☐	☐
7. Can say the alphabet while pointing to each letter	☐	☐	☐
8. Can write the alphabet in order	☐	☐	☐
9. Can supply rhyming words for simple poems	☐	☐	☐
10. Can recognize words that begin with the same sound	☐	☐	☐
11. Can recognize words that end alike	☐	☐	☐
12. Knows the sounds of the consonants	☐	☐	☐
13. Knows the sounds of the short vowels	☐	☐	☐
14. Can name the beginning, medial, and final sound of a word	☐	☐	☐
15. Can recognize a c-v-c word after the teacher says each sound	☐	☐	☐
16. Can blend c-v-c words	☐	☐	☐
17. Can substitute beginning and ending sounds in word families	☐	☐	☐
18. Recognizes the sight words a, is, the, I, and, come	☐	☐	☐

Figure 7.2. Prereading and primary reading skills checklist.

Skills checklists are useful for verifying information obtained from standardized tests. For example, a student, Donnie, scored below grade level on the money subtest of the *KeyMath Diagnostic Arithmetic Test* (Connolly, 1988) by missing the four items involving coin identification and making change.

1. Knows the names of:
   penny   dime   nickel   quarter   half-dollar

2. Knows the equivalent in cents for:
   penny   dime   nickel   quarter   half-dollar

3. Can add change involving:
   pennies   dimes   nickels   quarters   half-dollars

4. Uses the signs ¢ and $ properly.

5. Can make change for amounts under 50 cents.

6. Can make change for amounts under $1.00.

7. Can solve computational problems involving a decimal point.

8. Can solve verbal problems involving addition and subtraction of monetary amounts under $1.00.

Figure 7.3. Skills checklist: Money.

Because these four items tap only certain aspects of money knowledge, the teacher may not be sure of the extent of Donnie's problem. The teacher can gather more information by constructing a skills checklist that samples all of the skills involved in identifying coins and making change, such as the one presented in Figure 7.3. The teacher has not only verified Donnie's deficiency in identifying coins and making change but also gathered specific information for writing instructional objectives.

Permanent Product Data and Anecdotal Data

Two final types of informal assessment include permanent product data and daily anecdotal records. Permanent product data are work samples taken from the student's everyday assignments. Performance on daily assignments can be analyzed for errors and resulting information used to plan daily remedial instruction (see Gable & Hendrickson, 1990, for a detailed account of error analysis). In addition, teachers can review the written opportunities to respond provided on the worksheets to gain information on how much work the child completes during the assigned academic period. Because permanent product data are part of daily instruction, no extra effort is required for collection, making it both cost-effective and time-efficient.

Daily anecdotal records are written by the teacher and reference the child's performance in the various academic areas. This relatively informal procedure can be useful if it is done systematically. The accumulated information is helpful in determining whether to reteach a skill, devise a different teaching strategy, or proceed to the next skill. The following authors have provided useful information regarding the construction of informal assessment instruments: Gable and Hendrickson (1990), Overton (1992), Olson and Platt (2000), Shapiro (1996), and Shinn (1989). For assessment devices appropriate for students with emotional or behavioral problems coupled with severe or profound mental retardation, see Browder (1991). Martin (1988) discussed assessment devices appropriate for preschoolers with emotional or behavioral problems.

Annual Goals and Instructional Objectives

After assessing a student's strengths and weaknesses using the informal assessment tools discussed above, the teacher's next task is to construct annual goals and short-term instructional objectives that will guide instruction throughout the school year. Annual goals are written statements covering what the student is expected to gain from his educational program. They generally reflect the progress a student is expected to make in each academic area over the course of a year. Suggestions or prototypes of annual goals can be found in teacher's manuals of published curriculum materials. For example, an annual goal for a fourth-grade student in most mathematics programs is to learn division of whole numbers. To develop annual goals for each learner, the teacher must consider typical developmental and curricular expectations based on chronological age (local or districtwide norms may be available for curriculum-based measures of performance), consult the child's assessment data, examine the child's past learning history, and draw on her own experience working with children. The teacher's goals for each child must realistically reflect the child's capabilities by enabling him to make academic gains and overcome academic and behavioral deficits. Students in special education classes are frequently performing at lower grade levels than their chronological-age peers. When student variables permit, special education teachers should set goals that entail more than 1 year's progress for each academic year; otherwise, students will always remain below grade level. Whenever possible, the focus of instructional planning for special educators should be to increase the use of effective instructional techniques that enable students to make progress toward grade-level performance.

Short-term objectives are based on annual goals. They represent the learning tasks a student must master to reach the annual goal. The number of short-term objectives written for each annual goal will vary depending on the degree of specificity of the objective and the needs of the student. To develop short-term objectives, teachers may draw from published lists of objectives and scope-and-sequence charts, which are provided with most commercial curriculum materials, and they may use targeted rate measures as derived from CBA techniques. CBAs should also be used to determine which scope-and-sequence goals have and have not been mastered so that teachers write objectives only on those not mastered. Additionally, teachers can construct their own sequences of short-term objectives, often referred to as skill hierarchies. To do so, they must perform a *task analysis* of each annual goal. Task analysis is simply the process whereby the annual goal is reduced to its smallest component parts, the short-term objectives. For example, an annual arithmetic goal for a student might be to learn to add and subtract three-digit numbers when regrouping is involved. This annual goal could be task analyzed into the following components or subskills:

1. Can construct and count sets of different numbers
2. Understands number/numeral relationships
3. Can add one-digit numerals
4. Can subtract one-digit numerals
5. Can add two-digit numerals
6. Can subtract two-digit numerals
7. Can add two-digit numerals that require regrouping
8. Can subtract two-digit numerals that require regrouping
9. Can add and subtract two-digit numerals with zeros that require regrouping
10. Can add three-digit numerals
11. Can subtract three-digit numerals
12. Can add three-digit numerals that require regrouping
13. Can subtract three-digit numerals that require regrouping
14. Can add and subtract three-digit numerals with zeros that require regrouping

Depending on the student's characteristics and needs, the annual goal could be task analyzed with regard to the psychomotor skills needed, such as holding a pencil, writing numerals, and working from right to left, or it could be task analyzed in terms of the social–emotional behaviors needed, such as remaining in seat, attending to the task, or completing the task. Once an annual goal has been task analyzed, the teacher consults the assessment data to determine which of the subskills have already been mastered by the student. Short-term objectives are then written for those skills the student needs to learn to reach the annual goal.

As stated earlier, the degree of specificity in writing short-term objectives can vary. The most widely used method of devising instructional objectives was developed by Mager (1962), who refers to them as behavioral objectives. The process involves three components:

1. *What?* Stating the *behavior* to be learned in very specific terms

2. *How and when?* Stating the *conditions* under which the behavior is to occur and when it is to occur

3. *How much?* Stating the *criteria* for acceptable performance

A behavioral objective for Step 11 of the preceding task analysis might be formulated in the following manner:

▶ During a math practice session, when given a pencil and a worksheet with 10 subtraction problems requiring no regrouping, the student will complete them at 90% accuracy in less than 5 minutes.

In the preceding statement, all of the components of a behavioral objective are present.

1. *Behavior.* Write the answers to 10 subtraction problems that have three-digit numbers and do not require regrouping.

2. *Conditions.* The task should be done during a math practice session, using pencil and paper.

3. *Criteria.* Performance should be at 90% accuracy in less than 5 minutes.

Monitoring Student Progress and Performance

Each student's Individualized Education Program (IEP) should contain the annual goals and short-term objectives for the academic year. The IEP then becomes the focal document used by teachers to plan instruction and to monitor student progress and performance. Frequent monitoring of progress and performance is critical and has been shown to increase student achievement by over 25% on both standardized tests and informal measures (D. Fuchs & Fuchs, 1986). Frequent monitoring provides documentation as well as reinforcement for both teachers and students and is considered critical by teachers of students with emotional and behavioral challenges (Coleman & Vaughn, 2000).

Although no consensus exists as to the optimal rate of monitoring, using curriculum-based probes twice weekly has proved very effective and practical. Because of the brevity of these measures, administering and scoring weekly probes in reading, math, written expression, and spelling can take as little as 15 minutes per child.

Math and written expression probes can be given to the entire class at one time, and students can easily be taught to self-correct and self-graph, thus saving the teacher even more time. L. S. Fuchs, Fuchs, and Stecker (1989) reported that teachers who use CBA to monitor reading performance were found to (a) use more specific and acceptable achievement goals, (b) be more realistic about goal achievement, (c) cite more objective sources for deciding whether instruction is adequate or needs modification, and (d) modify students' instructional programs more frequently. In addition, students whose teachers frequently monitored their performance made greater gains in math, spelling, and reading than students in more traditionally run special education classrooms (L. S. Fuchs & Fuchs, 1987). Finally, students in classes where performance is frequently monitored know more about their own academic goals and their progress toward those goals (L. S. Fuchs, Butterworth, & Fuchs, 1989), which may increase motivation and student responsibility for learning.

Two types of monitoring have been discussed in the literature (Olson & Platt, 2000; Shapiro, 1996; Tindal, 1987): performance monitoring and mastery monitoring. Performance monitoring assesses a student's progress on a particular skill (e.g., reading rate) throughout the school year. Both precision teaching and CBA provide four-step models for performance monitoring that include taking a baseline, teaching and testing, graphing scores, and evaluating performance. Rate measures, such as words correct per minute, are the most often used metrics for monitoring student performance.

Mastery monitoring evaluates student progress through the curriculum, testing how well a student has learned what has been taught. In mastery monitoring, the pool of items tested changes each time the curricular unit changes. For example, in language arts, students might encounter units on sentence construction in the fall semester and paragraph writing in the spring. In the fall, mastery monitoring might include the percentage of sentences written with capital letters and correct punctuation, whereas in the spring, mastery might include the percentage of paragraphs containing a topic sentence, one main idea, and a transition sentence to the next paragraph. Mastery monitoring is conducted after teaching and learning of a particular unit has occurred and thus is not performed as frequently as performance monitoring. It allows teachers to monitor and document attainment of IEP objectives. Detailed presentations of how to conduct performance and mastery monitoring can be found in Olson and Platt (2000) and Tindal (1987).

Planning for Instruction

Effective instruction is a form of classroom management. When students are attending to their work and engaged in learning, fewer behavior problems occur. The highest percentages of on-task behaviors and the lowest percentages of disruptive behaviors have consistently been found to be related to providing opportunities for active learning using materials at students' instructional levels (DePaepe, Shores, & Jack, 1996; Greenwood, 1991; Greenwood, Carta, & Atwater, 1991). Teachers who want to develop effective classrooms need to consider a number of factors, including planning and scheduling, human resources, materials, teacher behaviors, and motivational strategies. In addition, teachers need to be conscious of the teacher behaviors that facilitate student learning.

Planning and Scheduling

Planning organizes and guides teachers for the year, the week, the day, and the individual lesson. Planning helps the classroom to run smoothly; reduces wait and transition times, helping to prevent behavior problems; and instills in teachers a sense of confidence and security. The most important resource for special educators' planning is the IEP, and teachers should invest time before school starts becoming familiar with their students' IEPs. Planning is facilitated if teachers coordinate students' goals and objectives so that small- and large-group instruction can be used effectively.

Lesson plans should be completed weekly for all academic subjects. Daily review of instructional planning may be required in reading, language arts, and mathematics to ensure that the current lesson builds on the previous day's performance. For example, if José mastered two-by-two multiplication today, the plan to move on to a new skill might be implemented; if mastery was not accomplished, additional instruction is required.

It is very important that emergency lesson plans be available for a substitute should the teacher be unable to teach; these plans should be detailed enough that someone else can teach from them. Critical components of lesson plans include (a) the date, (b) class time, (c) students involved in the activity or instruction, (d) subject area, (e) the objective on which students are working, (f) type of instruction (teacher-led small group, individual, peer tutoring), and (g) the assignment, including page and problem numbers.

Scheduling enables teachers to accomplish the goals they have planned for the students. Students with learning and emotional problems benefit from a written schedule of the day's or week's activities because it establishes the order of activities and academic expectations in advance (Mercer & Mercer, 1989).

Individual schedules may be placed on students' desks or posted on the blackboard or bulletin board, although the latter necessitates that students get out of their seats to check their schedules. Gallagher (1988) and Olson and Platt (2000) developed general guidelines for teachers to consider when scheduling daily activities:

1. Alternate high-preference and low-preference activities.
2. Provide time cues.
3. Group students by level, interest, and need. Heterogeneous groups are appropriate for some types of instruction, whereas homogeneous groups are better for others.
4. Schedule opportunities for active involvement, independent seatwork, teacher-directed instruction, peer tutoring, and cooperative learning.
5. Stress goals and objectives.
6. Provide feedback on the scheduling sheet.
7. Emphasize the relatedness of special education to regular education.
8. Allot time for the teacher to consult with other teachers and administrators and to visit mainstream classes.

Another important aspect of scheduling is wait time or transition time, the time students spend waiting for an activity to begin after another has ended. Research suggests that transition time can account for as much as one third of every school day and that behavior problems may increase during these times (Greenwood, 1991; Greenwood et al., 1991). Use of concurrent rather than sequential scheduling reduces wait or transition time. With sequential scheduling (used in most classrooms), one activity involving all students ends before another begins. With concurrent scheduling, students may be engaged in numerous activities ending at different times. Each student moves from one activity to another on an individual basis; wait time is minimized and instructional time is maximized.

Two variables that affect scheduling are the use of various instructional arrangements and the use of available resources (discussed in the next section). Instructional arrangements include large- or small-group instruction, individual or one-to-one instruction, and individual seatwork. Activities also can be varied. For example, teachers can have students work at the board, engage in hands-on creative activities, read, write, and use learning stations.

Research with students with EBDs indicates that varying the type of instructional activities is critical to maintaining high levels of student motivation and participation (Williams, Williams, & McLaughlin, 1991).

Typically, more one-to-one instruction and individual seatwork occur in special education settings, whereas more large-group instruction is used in regular education (Greenwood, 1991; Greenwood et al., 1991). Although one-to-one instruction may be a highly beneficial format for certain students with special needs, a number of issues must be considered when using it extensively.

First, although one-to-one instruction may maximize student–teacher interaction when the teacher is with the child, it minimizes interaction when the teacher is engaged with someone else. In many special education classrooms, students receive 5 or 10 minutes of teacher time per subject and then are required to work independently while the teacher works with every other child individually. Organizing students into small groups allows them to model one anothers' responses and permits frequent student responses, direct teacher contact, and teacher-controlled instruction (Gast, Doyle, Wolery, Ault, & Baklart, 1991; Shapiro, 1989).

Finally, a goal of special education placements is to remediate problem areas and enable students to return to the mainstream. Consequently, it is important that students learn to perform well in situations that are similar to those encountered in regular education classrooms. Because large-group instruction is used frequently in regular classes, special educators need to increase their students' time in large-group instruction so that students can practice and hopefully master the skills required. Additionally, choral or group responding can significantly increase the number of opportunities for each child to respond during any given period (Sainato, Strain, & Lyon, 1987).

The varied levels of student performance many special educators encounter in their classes make it more difficult to plan large-group instruction. However, as discussed earlier, the identification of goals and objectives common to a number of students will facilitate the effective and efficient use of various instructional arrangements, including large-group instruction. For example, a teacher might have three students working on a second-grade reading level, five on the third grade level, and two each on the fifth and sixth grade levels. However, large-group instruction is still feasible. The teacher might write a poem on the blackboard and read it with the children. IEP objectives for the fifth and sixth graders might include discussing the meanings of words and concepts and querying the children to determine levels of comprehension of poetic form, content, vocabulary, and so forth. The teacher might follow up by having the group find an example of poems (at their levels) in the library to read to the group. In math an appropriate large-group activity might be to teach all students, using choral responding, to count by 2s, 3s, 4s, 5s, and so on.

This skill is beneficial for addition and subtraction, as well as for multiplication and division, thus covering grade levels from second to sixth.

Human Resources

The smart teacher of children with behavior problems takes all the help she can get. In fact, if help is not offered, the teacher seeks it out or arranges it, using the resources of other professionals, the children, and their parents to improve the instructional program.

Professional Resources. Among the professionals who can be of help to teachers are school principals and assistant principals, resource or consulting teachers, curriculum coordinators, school psychologists, guidance counselors, school-affiliated psychiatrists, and classroom paraprofessionals.

School principals are educational policymakers; thus, their support of special education programs for children with behavior problems is critical. Unfortunately, their interest and attention are focused on many diverse constituents within the school, and often the needs of "problem" children are low-priority items. Many principals also have little education about or experience with special education and especially with alternatives to the standard detention–suspension model for handling acting-out youth. It behooves a teacher of children with disabilities to make sure that her program is not ignored or simply tolerated as a "necessary evil." In effect, the teacher must conduct a proactive campaign to garner administrative support and to educate the school community concerning effective interventions.

One strategy in such a campaign is frequent, brief, teacher-initiated meetings that involve discussions of constructive, positive topics, such as children's progress, or that involve the principal in the instructional program, such as seeking her opinion about an instructional decision or discussing plans for class activities. Another strategy is to interest the principal in visiting the class to observe the children. In the usual course of events, these visits are limited to times when a problem occurs rather than times when typical instruction is occurring. If the principal is familiar with the classroom operations, she can be of greater assistance as a troubleshooter. The third strategy is to involve the principal in classroom functions. She might conduct classroom discussions or serve as a crisis intervention specialist. Obviously, the extent to which these goals can be realized will depend on the attitudes of the individuals involved. At the very least, however, the teacher should try to build a positive rather than a negative relationship.

Two other invaluable assets are the services of a variety of *resource teachers* who might be associated with the school and the *instructional support team*.

Most elementary schools and some secondary schools have resource programs designed to provide corrective and remedial academic instruction to children who experience achievement problems. Resource teachers are available to work with children who are having academic difficulty or to act as consultants to other teachers in the school. Although these programs usually are supplemental to regular education services—that is, they provide support for mainstreamed children—they can and should be used by special educators who teach children with emotional disorders in self-contained classes. Some children, despite efforts to individualize instruction in the regular or self-contained special classroom, will benefit from additional tutorial or small-group instruction. Often, the additional attention the child receives from a "special" teacher adds the necessary impetus for breakthroughs in academic achievement areas. Obviously, such desirable outcomes can occur only when teachers cooperate closely and when instructional programs are planned carefully.

The resource room can also serve as an initial step in a program culminating in the reintegration of the child with emotional problems into the regular classroom. In this circumstance the child must be taught the types of coping skills that will help him or her function in the more normal and more stressful regular class environment. For example, in the resource room the child may be required to self-start independent assignments and to work to completion without teacher attention. Also, the student may need practice controlling behavior while moving from one room to another. The resource teacher, who is usually a special educator, should be a helpful assistant in teaching such coping skills.

Instructional support teams are generally composed of permanent school district employees such as special and regular educators, administrators, psychologists, guidance counselors, reading specialists, speech–language therapists, and occupational therapists. Also, professionals hired on a case-by-case basis, such as psychiatrists, behavioral consultants, and neurologists, may attend. Generally, teachers refer cases to the instructional support team, which may conduct assessments, develop possible interventions, and provide consulting services to the special educator. In addition, members of the instructional support team may observe the child and teacher in the classroom and monitor student progress after the intervention is implemented.

Another use of resource personnel is as a *crisis or helping teacher* (Morse, 1976). This role is based on the idea that crises are critical periods for helping children because intervention provided at the time of a crisis can be extremely effective. Generally this role falls to personnel who already have a variety of roles to play within the school environment, such as an assistant principal, guidance counselor, or small-learning-community coordinator. Theoretically, during a crisis some individuals may be more susceptible to suggestions from others than at other times. The person is less defensive, and the realistic aspects of the problem are more likely to penetrate the individual's consciousness. Thus, the crisis teacher must be available to deal with the child immediately—not, as is usually true in schools, when time happens to be available or when the child has "cooled down." Often the classroom teacher has too many responsibilities to take advantage of an opening in a particular child's defenses. The availability of a backup resource teacher is a valuable addition to the program.

The teacher's interaction with other mental health specialists, including the guidance counselor, school psychologist, and psychiatrist, can be particularly useful in situations where each professional uses the expertise associated with her particular discipline. The teacher should find that the information available in psychological and psychiatric reports increases her knowledge about the children and their problems and provides alternative opinions for problem solutions. Confusion and inefficiency can result from an interdisciplinary approach to problem solving only when the teacher attempts to surrender the responsibility of classroom management to noneducators. These instances usually culminate in the preparation of an elaborate plan of teaching strategies and behavioral management techniques by individuals who have never attempted to teach or manage groups of typical—much less troubled—children. This point is not meant to imply that consultant services by noneducators are not useful. Good advice and assistance in problem solving are valuable resources. Usually, the more familiar ancillary personnel are with the reality of the classroom situation, the more useful their advice is.

Another variable concerning the effective use of nonteaching school personnel is their specific competence and interests. Some guidance personnel and school psychologists function excellently in a crisis-intervention capacity. They also may be willing and able to conduct individual therapy sessions with certain children who need more attention than the teacher can provide. Generally, the professionals who offer the greatest assistance in dealing with the problems of emotional disturbances are those housed in the school, as opposed to those who visit periodically.

Increased use of *paraprofessionals* in special education over recent years also has had positive effects on students with disabilities (Pickett, 1988). A 42% increase in the use of paraprofessionals in special education was reported between 1976 and 1982 (Frith & Lindsey, 1982), and the trend continues. Recently, a new type of paraprofessional, the therapeutic support staffer, has been assigned to many students with emotional and behavioral problems. Generally, a member of the therapeutic support staff acts as a one-to-one support person and a crisis interventionist with an individual client. Because therapeutic support staff are hired by agencies other than the school district, interagency meetings to facilitate planning and implementation become critical so that the teaching staff and the therapeutic support staff can work effectively as a team.

Paraprofessionals can provide a cost-effective means of providing instructional and behavioral support; however, training, planning, and supervision must be conducted in a meaningful way if teachers and paraprofessionals are to work together as an instructional team. Traditionally, paraprofessionals have been used primarily for clerical tasks, such as typing and duplicating. Recently, more paraprofessionals have been providing instructional, behavioral management, and diagnostic support, as well as contributing to classroom organization and even student planning. For example, Martella, Marchand-Martella, Miller, Young, and Macfarlane (1995) successfully taught paraprofessionals to engage in behaviors specifically designed to decrease problem behaviors in the classroom. Matching teachers' needs with paraprofessionals' skills is important. In addition, paraprofessionals can prove invaluable with culturally and linguistically diverse populations if the paraprofessional is fluent in the students' language and culture. On the down side, poorly motivated or untrained paraprofessionals can be a major detriment to a child's instructional program.

Student Resources. Children are often an underutilized resource in their own education. *Student-directed instructional strategies,* such as peer tutoring and cooperative learning (discussed later in this chapter), and *self-management strategies* are critical aspects of a well-functioning classroom. Original work in self-management techniques, possibly the most significant child resource, was carried out by Lovitt (1973) and has been followed up by others who have systematically trained children with emotional or behavior problems to self-manage (Stevenson & Fantuzzo, 1984; Sugai & Rowe, 1984). Using behavior modification principles, Lovitt demonstrated that children can be taught to correct, count, chart, and evaluate their own performance on academic tasks. He also demonstrated that children trained in self-management skills become more highly motivated to achieve. The student involved in Lovitt's program was led, step by step, through eight phases of self-management activity: (a) scheduling morning and afternoon assignments, (b) scheduling the entire day, (c) correcting work, (d) evaluating daily academic response rate, (e) examining his overall record of academic performance, (f) charting achievement data in reading and in math, (g) charting achievement rates in six academic subjects, and (h) setting his own contingencies in three of six academic areas.

The success of self-management activities is increased when the definitions of behaviors to be monitored are clear and taught to the child. Additionally, students need to be trained to self-monitor, self-chart (or self-graph), and self-reinforce. Occasional unannounced checks by the teacher may facilitate accurate and honest self-management. Initially, it may be important to reinforce children simply for agreeing with or matching the teacher's monitoring. As children learn the definitions and routines, independence can be fostered. Recently, Snyder and Shapiro (1997) taught students with behavior problems to help run their own simulated IEP meetings, including introducing the IEP, reviewing past goals, discussing future goals, and closing the IEP meeting. Apparently, it is not beyond the competence of many children with emotional and behavioral problems to accept responsibility for their academic production if they are carefully shown how to do so.

Parental Resources. Parental involvement in programs for children with emotional and behavioral difficulties, after having been regarded with a certain amount of suspicion for many years, is finally gaining rightful recognition as an important ingredient to school success. It has always been obvious that optimal benefits for children occur when school authorities and parents cooperate. The less obvious information pertains primarily to how to arrange such cooperation or, more precisely, how to help parents help their children. Currently, a great deal of information on this topic is available. Beale and Beers (1982) proposed a tripartite approach to soliciting and maintaining parents' involvement in their children's education: (a) parent education, (b) parent volunteering, and (c) parent communication. Parent education programs teach parents ways to manage children's behaviors or ways to teach their children academic skills. Parent volunteer programs provide opportunities for parents to become directly involved in classrooms or school activities by acting as tutors, class mothers, chaperones, and fund-raisers. School–parent contacts form the basis of the parent communication approach and may include conferences, notes, phone calls, and home–school contracts. According to survey information, parents of children of all ages seem to prefer the communication approach (McCarney, 1986; McKinney & Hocutt, 1982; Winton & Turnbull, 1981).

Commercial parent education programs, such as *Parent Effectiveness Training* (Gordon, 2000) and *Systematic Training for Effective Parenting* (Dinkmeyer & McKay, 1997), are available. These resources are useful for planning parent discussion groups, parent tutoring, and group training in effective parenting.

Parent discussion groups are relatively informal meetings held by the teacher and principal and attended by other interested professionals, such as the school psychologist or guidance counselor. These sessions should meet for approximately 1 hour once a month and should deal primarily with problem-solving strategies. Problems at school and at home should be discussed. Parents and educators should develop consistent methods of handling shared problems.

Parent tutorial services pertain to the in-school involvement of parents as tutors. For any child but their own, parents can be a helpful resource if the tutorial program is carefully planned. Typically, parents are far more tolerant and effective in tutoring other people's children. Similarly, the children are more responsive when a comparative stranger offers them help. Using parents as tutors has the combined advantages of permitting them to make a direct contribution to their child's school program and allowing them to learn and practice specific instructional techniques that later might be used at home. As in all other tutorial programs, effectiveness depends on systematic planning and structure. Parent volunteers must be aware of the program's goals and must have observed and practiced sequenced instructional techniques, combined with positive reinforcement methods. Teacher demonstrations may help parent volunteers understand and model the roles they are expected to play.

Group training in effective parenting sessions, conducted by the school psychologist, guidance counselor, or other individual proficient in parenting techniques, involves training parents in all aspects of the parent–child relationship. For example, the goals of *Systematic Training for Effective Parenting* (STEP) by Dinkmeyer and McKay (1997, p. 14) are the following:

1. To help parents understand a practical theory of human behavior and its implications for parent–child relationships

2. To help parents learn new procedures for establishing democratic relationships with their children

3. To help parents improve communication between themselves and their children so all concerned feel they are being heard

4. To help parents develop skills of listening, resolving conflicts, and exploring alternatives with their children

5. To help parents learn how to use encouragement and logical consequences to modify their children's self-defeating motives and behaviors

6. To help parents learn how to conduct family meetings

7. To help parents become aware of their own self-defeating patterns and faulty convictions that keep them from being effective parents who enjoy their children

Presumably, such training will indirectly benefit the teacher, whose job should become far simpler when critical home problems are alleviated or minimized. As effective communication with parents contributes to the school success of children with emotional problems, teachers benefit from viewing parents as partners. Developing an atmosphere of respect and trust will foster parent involvement and is particularly important when working with parents of diverse cultural backgrounds (Chan, 1987; Olion, 1989). African American parents often report lack of respect from teachers and school administrators as a primary reason for their minimal involvement with the educational system (Marion, 1981).

A helpful way of facilitating communication is to begin the school year by phoning parents once a week or once every other week to report on students' progress. The teacher should think about what to discuss prior to making the call and jot down a few notes as a reminder. Parents should be given time to talk, because all too frequently phone calls from school are unidirectional. Initially it is best to emphasize the students' successes. Many parents, having received phone calls from teachers only when there is a problem, become more cooperative when they hear positive information. Phoning home is most effective if the teacher knows the best time for parents to speak on the phone. Teachers often call immediately after school ends, a hectic time in many households, and not ideal for securing parents' full attention.

When it is necessary to discuss a problem, the teacher should use the positive-negative-positive rule, also called the sandwich technique. The teacher should begin the conversation with a positive remark (e.g., "José has been doing very well in spelling; he scored a 95% on this week's test"). The teacher should then introduce the problem ("However, he hasn't been completing his math homework"). After discussing the problem with the parent and coming up with a collaborative solution, the teacher should thank the parent for her help and end the conversation on a positive note ("Thanks so much for discussing José's homework with me. He is such a helpful child; he volunteered twice this week to tutor another student in reading."). This positive-negative-positive formula tends to promote good feelings between parents and teachers.

When calls include discussion of a child's problems, the teacher should remember that the responsibility for the child in school belongs to the teacher. Although teachers should keep parents informed when children have problems and should seek their cooperation, they should be prepared to discuss their attempts to solve those problems when and where they occur and be sure not to convey the impression that they expect the parents to rectify the situation. For example, a teacher who says, "Betty got in trouble today on the playground. What are you going to do about it?" probably is not responding appropriately when the problem occurs and, in suggesting the problem belongs to the parent, is admitting her lack of competence. She might say instead, "Betty had difficulty on the playground today, and I am removing her recess privileges for the rest of the week. I wanted you to know because I am concerned about her problems in getting along with others. How does she get along with other children in your neighborhood?" Teachers who are anxious or insecure about parental conferencing by phone or in person should practice with a friend or colleague. Tape-recording a role-playing situation of this type might provide valuable information about tone of voice, choice of words, and so forth that might convey an attitude of dislike or disrespect that is not intentional.

Notes sent home are also an effective means of communication. They can be used daily or periodically to report progress, homework, and upcoming events. Many teachers use a communication notebook that travels back and forth with the child and promotes two-way communication with the parent. The positive-negative-positive rule is also appropriate for written communication. However, care must be taken to consider the parents' reading ability and to write legibly.

Parent–teacher conferences also provide an effective mechanism for building a collaborative partnership with parents. Successful conferences require the teacher to (a) plan them for mutually convenient times, (b) plan the conference content thoroughly, (c) inform parents about the topics that will be discussed so that parents are prepared, (d) ask parents for input on issues they would like to discuss prior to the meeting so that necessary information can be gathered, and (e) conduct follow-up. The strategies for successful face-to-face conferences are similar to those appropriate for communication by phone or note. Teachers should present both positive and negative information about the child. When problems are discussed, teachers should convey their concerns rather than their dislikes or frustrations. They should present their attempts to solve the problems in school and seek information regarding the child's behavior at home. It is important to focus on constructive steps to be taken at home and school to help the child make a better adjustment.

Use of nonverbal communication and jargon may influence the effectiveness of communication. The Crisis Prevention Institute (1983) reported that 85% of communication is nonverbal. In addition, if there is a discrepancy between the verbal and nonverbal messages, people most often attend to the nonverbal message. Therefore, it is important to pay attention to your own and the parents' facial expressions, posture, and voice (see Hepworth & Larsen, 1990, for more detailed information on nonverbal communication).

Like members of most professions, teachers and other school personnel are often guilty of using jargon that can interfere with communication. Many adults feel uncomfortable asking what words mean or asking for clarification. It is important to use language that is simple and understandable and to do so in a way that is not condescending.

Parents are a valuable resource in the education of students with emotional problems. Teachers who take the time and initiative to establish positive, collaborative partnerships with parents will benefit greatly from the improved relationships.

Materials

Selecting Materials. When selecting materials for teaching, the teacher should consider three factors: (a) the needs of the student, (b) the needs of the teacher, and (c) the dictates of the curriculum (Wilson, 1978). When examining students' needs, the teacher must consider the children's level of academic skill and development, as well as their social and emotional needs. The teacher should select materials that not only teach necessary academic skills but also motivate and arouse the students' interest. Moreover, it is important to investigate which instructional materials have been previously successful with the student and which materials have been associated with anxiety, frustration, and failure. In a therapeutic educational program, it is not wise to reintroduce materials associated with past failure. Using high-interest, age-appropriate materials that reflect the students' real lives will increase student motivation.

Multiethnic materials have become increasingly available over the past decade and should be considered for use. They provide not only additional perspectives on history, science, and language arts but also role models for the development of self-esteem and supply teachers with ways to address the political and everyday realities of students' lives.

The needs of the teacher are also important in selecting materials, for teachers are the main facilitators of instruction (Gallagher, 1988). Their theoretical biases, teaching styles, and levels of teaching competence may influence materials selection; however, it is most important for teachers to select materials that meet student needs. Teachers who are flexible in materials selection, who make modifications appropriate for individual students, and who incorporate a number of different materials to teach concepts will find that they are more successful than teachers who are rigid in their selection and use of materials.

The third factor, dictates of the curriculum, involves the limits imposed on materials selection by the general school curriculum. Students often must master certain skills or certain academic content before they can move to the next grade level. This is especially true at the middle school and high school levels, where certain courses are required for graduation. In cases such as these, instructional materials pertaining to particular subject areas must be identified and purchased.

Other considerations relevant to curriculum are particularly important for special education students. If a student's goals indicate that a return to the mainstream is likely, then use of the mainstream text for that subject in the special education setting is essential, both for generalization and to ensure that the student has the same prerequisite knowledge that her regular education peers do. Also, special education classes often use curricular materials that differ from those used in regular education classes. The benefits of an alternative curriculum must outweigh the cost of students' not using the same materials as their peers. Teachers can make that judgment more accurately by using materials analysis forms to assess the content, organization, and format of published curricular materials (Burnette, 1987; Olson & Platt, 2000). They also should read reviews of curricular materials published in educational journals prior to making selections. In one such review, Carnine (1991) discussed the critical components of mathematics curricula.

Adapting Materials. An important component of individualizing instruction to meet students' academic or emotional needs involves the adaptation of instructional materials. Sometimes a student will not experience success with a particular instructional material. In these instances the teacher must alter or modify the material so that it is more appropriate for the student. Wilson (1976) presented a range of options for adapting and developing materials in a four-level hierarchy that includes (a) altering regular materials, (b) selecting other materials, (c) combining several diverse materials, and (d) developing new materials.

Print materials may be altered in a variety of ways, including modifying readability levels, changing vocabulary, presenting different concepts, simplifying directions, reorganizing content, changing response modes, and providing different types and amounts of practice (Olson & Platt, 2000).

The following are specific suggestions to make materials more appropriate for special education students:

- Limit the length of assignments. The number of pages that students must read or the number of math problems they must work can be reduced.

- Color-code directions. Directions can be highlighted with a marker so that students can find them easily on the page.

- Use outlines and study guides. This is especially important at the secondary level with such subjects as history, health, and literature.

- Rewrite explanations and directions on a lower readability and syntactic level.

- Use tapes and slides to accompany written material. This helps accent important facts and key concepts.

- Place written materials on cassette tapes. Students can hear the reading matter as they follow along in their texts.

- Break skills into smaller steps. A workbook or textbook often teaches a new skill in only one or two pages. Supplementary lessons can be built into the workbook or text to teach the skill in smaller steps and provide for more reinforcement and practice.

If none of these modifications is successful, the teacher can move to the second level of Wilson's (1976) hierarchy and select other materials. The task is to find material that is written at a lower level with a format that is interesting yet easier to understand and that covers the same content or skills as the regular material. Using alternative materials to supplement instruction may prove very beneficial; for example, baseball cards and song lyrics are high-interest materials that can be used for reading instruction.

If no solutions to the curricular problem are found at the first two levels, the teacher must move to the third level of the hierarchy and develop a curriculum by combining several diverse materials. To do this effectively, the teacher must select materials that cover the required content area—for example, regrouping in addition, the life cycle of the toad, or the history of the Equal Rights Amendment—and that are at the same instructional level with regard to format, readability, and interest.

When all else fails, teachers can move to the fourth rung of the hierarchy: developing new materials. Starkel (1978) warned that this task is very time-consuming and may prove surprisingly expensive if the teacher considers the cost of her time. Generally, teacher-made materials work best when limited to instructional games and flash cards intended for drill and reinforcement.

Using students to create some materials can prove invaluable in terms of saving time and also creates a sense of ownership for the students. Students can create flash cards, word searches, and crossword puzzles and help make and assemble learning centers and bulletin boards.

Computers in Instruction. Computers and computer software are rapidly becoming available for use in the classroom. Although some programs may not be appropriate for use with students with special needs, many others are. FrEdWriter (Apple-public domain) is one useful program designed to help students learn to write effective stories, essays, and reports. Teachers develop a shell of questions or lead sentences at the beginning of each paragraph. Students then compose the rest of the story or essay using FrEdWriter on the computer. Public domain software, which can be copied and modified, provides another alternative for use with students with special needs (Chiang, 1986). Chiang recommended making six modifications to enhance traditional instructional software for use with students with handicaps: (a) add a word file editor that allows students to access a word list directly from spelling or language arts programs, (b) provide a performance summary prior to quitting a program, (c) include clear directions that can be viewed at any time, (d) provide opportunities for self-correction, (e) provide prompts to show students where to go next, and (f) control the duration of the display.

In addition to using the computer and computer software for instruction, teachers may find the computer invaluable for classroom organization, student assessment, and student monitoring. Programs are available that give CBA probes and allow students (or teachers) to graph students' performance (L. S. Fuchs & Fuchs, 1990). Also, computerized IEPs enable teachers to more easily organize instruction around common goals and objectives. Databases used for scheduling allow the teacher to enter one modification, which is then reflected on all of the students' schedules. Teachers who gain competence with computers find it saves them valuable time while enhancing their instructional program.

However, caution should be used when turning instruction over to computers. A recent study by Dawson, Venn, and Gunter (2000) compared teacher-led to computer-led instruction in reading. The study found that students with emotional and behavioral problems made the greatest gains in both reading rate and accuracy under the teacher-led instructional model.

Teacher Behaviors

Although the selection and use of appropriate curriculum materials are essential, even the best are ineffective unless the teacher knows how to promote learning. One critical component of effective teaching is providing sufficient opportunities for the student to respond during instruction. Opportunities to respond refer to the number of chances or opportunities a student has to practice a particular skill or fact through some type of response. Responses may be written, oral, or the actual exhibition of a skill, such as carrying out an experiment. Opportunities to respond are the educational variable most significantly related to academic achievement (Greenwood, 1991; Greenwood et al., 1991). Simply stated, the more students practice or repeat a task, the more they learn. Therefore, all teachers, but particularly teachers of students with emotional or behavioral problems that might interfere with learning, must ensure that their charges have sufficient opportunities to practice what they are learning. Reliance on traditional curricula to supply adequate opportunities to respond is not recommended. Carnine (1991), in a review of traditional mathematics curricula, stated that many of these curricula allow for very limited practice for each skill and even less review over time to spur retention of skills.

Two ways to increase opportunities to respond are by increasing the pace of instruction and requiring students to be actively engaged. Researchers have found that rapid pacing of instruction results in higher levels of child engagement than medium or slow pacing, as well as increased opportunities to respond. Teachers can use rapid pacing when presenting a variety of academic materials, such as math facts, spelling words, and vocabulary words. Drill and practice also can be paced rapidly, as can asking questions of the class. The use of choral, in addition to individual, responding may also increase the pace of instruction while increasing the group's opportunities to respond (Sainato et al., 1987).

Teachers also should plan instruction that requires students to be actively engaged as opposed to passively engaged. Student behaviors that are active include reading aloud, answering questions aloud, writing, and manipulation of materials. Passive behaviors include reading silently, attending to the teacher during lectures, and observing others manipulating materials. Active engagement is highly correlated with opportunities to respond and is more highly correlated with student achievement than passive engagement. Teachers can increase achievement by planning instruction that results in students' being active during academic times.

Student interest in instruction may also play an important role in engagement by spurring students to listen attentively and to cognitively manipulate the information presented. A teacher can facilitate attentive listening and active thinking by previewing lectures or demonstrations, informing students of the goals of instruction, and describing the opportunities students will have to display their knowledge after the teacher's presentation.

Teacher Verbalizations. The type and manner of teacher verbalizations have also been found to influence children's performance in the classroom. Nondidactic remarks (verbalizations that are not too instructive or directive), such as encouraging comments, have been found to promote independence, cooperation, and self-esteem (Stallings, 1975), and language that is positive rather than critical has resulted in higher rates of student on-task behavior (Fagot, 1973). Additionally, high levels of praise or approvals given by teachers have been found to be related to increased compliance with requests (Atwater & Morris, 1988).

Praise and approving remarks are examples of the type of feedback teachers provide to students. Feedback lets the children know how they are progressing. Consistent, immediate feedback has been shown to have the most positive effect on student performance (Brophy & Good, 1986). It is particularly useful when students are acquiring new academic skills, because it helps ensure that they are proceeding correctly and prevents them from practicing incorrect skills. It eliminates the type of frustration children experience when, after completing an entire worksheet, they discover a critical error in their work and must redo the page.

Feedback from the teacher is particularly important to students with emotional problems who feel overwhelmed by an assignment. Teachers can create additional opportunities to provide feedback by dividing students' work into smaller segments and giving feedback as they complete each segment. One method is to draw a colored line (perhaps the student's favorite color) on the page, dividing the work into two, three, or more sections. After the children complete a section, they raise their hands, prompting the teacher to check their work and praise them for working so diligently.

As noted, feedback about academics and behavior is best received when it is positive. Thus, teachers might consider marking correct questions with a C and leaving incorrect items blank. This also enables students to correct previously missed items and receive all Cs, which may be very rewarding. Another technique to provide positive feedback is to average the grades of the students' original work and their corrected work. This can serve as an incentive for students, while reflecting initial performance. For example, if a child earns a 70%, then improves it to 90%, the recorded grade is 80%; similarly, if another child's grade is 30% (suppose the child is not interested in trying) and then is improved to 90%, the recorded grade is 60%, denoting a better initial effort for the first child.

Positive feedback often is dependent on good behavior. To promote good behavior, the teacher is encouraged to "catch the students being good." Ignoring inappropriate behavior and praising prosocial behavior are much more effective than giving negative feedback. In addition, teachers should encourage appropriate behavior with prompts that tell students what the teacher wants the students to do (e.g., "Put the papers on the shelf and sit down") rather than what not to do ("Don't wander around"). As for academics, feedback for behavior should be frequent and specific. Behavior-specific feedback is often referred to as labeled praise, denoting that the person providing the feedback labels the behavior being praised (e.g., "Good raising your hand, Jerome" and "Nice standing quietly in line, class"). These types of statements directly connect the praise with the specific behavior appreciated or expected.

When teachers offer more general praise statements, such as "Lionel, you are being so good," students may not be clear about what they are doing that is positive. Additionally, more general statements may be processed by children as an editorial on who they are rather than what they are doing. This is especially true of negative feedback statements, such as "You are so bad today." It is important for teachers to remember to convey that children are neither bad nor good and that their behavior is at issue, not their identity.

Feedback can also be given nonverbally with the use of stickers, feedback notes, certificates of performance, and graphs or charts. All of these forms of feedback may be used for either academics or behavior and provide tangible, visual, and durable means for recognizing student achievement. General feedback is also given more subtly through the class climate and physical space.

Classrooms that display students' work and graphs of progress indicate to students the importance of their productions.

Teachers can also influence students' academic performance and behavior in school by verbal behaviors that precede or follow tasks. Providing directions or instructions prior to an assignment falls into this category. Many teachers use the strategy of saying to students, "This is a hard one" before giving the students a question the teacher is sure the children can answer. In this way the children's sense of self-confidence is increased. Under no circumstances should teachers minimize the difficulty of assigned work. Students who are told that "this problem is an easy one" and then find that they cannot solve it come to believe that they are not capable of successful completion of even very simple work, which undermines their confidence to attempt or persevere with more challenging tasks.

There are a number of other important aspects to giving directions or instructions. Although different situations or teaching styles may call for various levels of directed activities by students, teachers must always give clear and specific directions or instructions. Teachers should delineate steps, if necessary, when using multiple directions, for example, "After you complete your math, line up at the door for gym. Remember to put your book in your desk and your paper in the bin." Writing abbreviated directions on the board or having students review directions orally after they have been given may also help students with emotional or behavioral problems focus on what needs to be done. Because many of these students have trouble following directions, teachers should teach them key words to listen for, such as "underline," "circle," and "choose two." Teaching students to listen for these types of words and phrases will result in fewer problems (e.g., a student's circling when underlining is called for, or another student's completing all of the math word problems instead of choosing two of the three given) and will reduce student frustration.

When a teacher is giving directions or instructions to children, the teacher's proximity to students is also important. Students with emotional or behavior problems are less likely to react negatively if directions or prompts are delivered quietly and discreetly by a teacher who is in close proximity to them than if these remarks are announced from across the room. In addition, teachers who circulate around the room, maintaining proximity to students, generally have greater control over their students.

Motivational Strategies

Many theories of student motivation delineate two primary considerations: students' perceptions of competence and their perceptions of control. Spaulding (1992) presented an excellent detailed account of various motivational strategies to increase competence and control in classroom situations. Included are both intrinsic and extrinsic approaches, as well as strategies that are effective for large- and small-group instruction and individual seatwork.

One central feature of intrinsic motivational strategies is predictability. Creating highly predictable work environments enhances students' self-perceptions of competence and control (Rothbaum, Weisz, & Snyder, 1982) and is related to lower levels of stress-related behaviors and cognitions than are situations in which students feel they have little control (Bandura, 1986). Schedules and daily routines help students feel that school involves a predictable sequence of activities. This is especially critical for students with emotional or behavioral problems who do not adapt well to changes in the environment.

Alternating difficult tasks in which students are learning new material with tasks in which they are competent also increases the likelihood of their feeling motivated to continue a task. Research also suggests that alternating the learning of new concepts with practice of previously acquired material increases the rate of acquisition of the new material (Gickling & Thompson, 1985), further improving motivation.

Extrinsic motivational strategies include the use of reinforcement, both tangible and social. These strategies are discussed in Chapter 5, "Behavioral Therapy."

Choice Making. Providing choice or control opportunities is another way to increase intrinsic motivation (Deci & Ryan, 1985). Research and practice have recently begun to emphasize choice making as an important developmental objective related to personal control and dignity (Bambara, Ager, & Koger, 1994; Cole, Davenport, Bambara, & Ager, 1997; Dunlap et al., 1994). Spaulding (1992) classified classroom choices as optioned or open, social or nonsocial, and involving procedures or content. Optioned choices are those for which the teacher provides alternatives (e.g., "Gabriella, you may read or use the computer"), whereas open choices are not restricted. Social choices involve choosing partners to do an activity or involve a social activity, whereas nonsocial choices pertain to teacher instruction. Choices about procedure allow students to choose how to do a project, such as writing or orally presenting a book report, whereas content choices allow them to determine the subject of the project. Bambara and Ager (1992) found that, for some individuals, choice may be a significant variable in the amount of time spent on task and in the number of disruptive and aggressive behaviors displayed.

Choice making may be a particularly effective strategy for students whose inappropriate behaviors are related to the function of control (see Chapter 5, "Behavioral Therapy," for a further discussion of functional behavioral assessment). Teaching choice making involves teaching problem solving. Students are taught to take some level of control over their school day and are given the opportunity to experience the consequences of their choices.

Teachers should consider the many ways available to provide opportunities for choice to students. For example, appropriate choices might include where to complete their reading assignment (at their desk, sitting on the carpet, or in the reading corner), or when to complete assignments (you can complete your independent seatwork now and then work on the special project after lunch, or vice versa), or in what order they wish to complete their math, science, and language arts independent seatwork for the day. Students might be able to select whether to work alone or with a partner on certain activities and what type of activity to complete to demonstrate knowledge of the causes of the Civil War (write a song, essay, poem, or newspaper article). Students can also be given choices about materials; for example, they could use markers, colored pencils, pastels, or ballpoint pens.

Choices should not just be presented; choice making must be taught as a developmental skill. Teachers of young children know not to stand in the middle of the classroom and ask a 4-year-old, "What do you want to play with?" Instead, closed choices are usually offered to children or adolescents unaccustomed to making choices. For example, "Would you like to play with blocks or the parachute?" might be a more productive question. Many students will need assistance in learning to think through and decide what they want to do. Sampling has been shown to be an important component of choice making. People will rarely choose to do what they have not done before. Providing time for students to try out activities, materials, assignments, or locations will enable them to decide what they like.

Initially, choice making may be frightening for some students. This may be especially true for students with emotional and behavioral issues, who are often fearful of failure or afraid of making the "wrong" choice. Some students who are too passive and conforming may have a strong desire to please the teacher and choose what they believe the teacher would like them to do rather than what they want to do. Providing students with opportunities to make simple choices gives them a level of control and a sense of competence that is beneficial to their development. Allowing students to make choices is not an alternative to instructional planning, however. Incorporating choice making into the educational environment needs to be thoughtfully planned and implemented.

Delivering Effective Instruction

Methods for delivering instruction have been evolving steadily over the past 20 to 25 years as educators have become increasingly concerned with the issue of accountability for student learning. As the responsibility for a student's success in school shifted from the student and the parents to those who plan and implement the educational program, it became increasingly clear that teachers require effective strategies and methodologies for making instruction meaningful to each child.

Inclusion

The trend in special education is toward providing instruction in the general education classroom using a variety of individual interventions, consultation support, and team-teaching approaches. Litigation has supported the right of students, including those with emotional and behavioral problems, to an education in the least restrictive environment (Lewis, Chard, & Scott, 1994). In some instances the least restrictive environment may be the general education classroom. Inclusion works only when adequate educational and behavioral supports are provided to ensure student success.

Guetzloe (1993) found children with emotional and behavioral challenges to be the least welcome in general education classrooms. Teacher attitudes, expectations, willingness to learn new techniques, and participation in professional collaboration greatly affect inclusion efforts. Rife and Karr-Kidwell (1995) listed a number of critical considerations that maximize the success of inclusion programs with children with behavioral problems, including selection of general education teachers, peer tutoring, parental involvement, involvement of a "care team," use of a social skills curriculum, and collaborative teaching. Lewis and others (1994), in an analysis of inclusion for students with emotional and behavioral problems, found that the use of best practices behavioral interventions in the classroom and systematic schoolwide positive approaches to all children with challenging behaviors were critical to a successful inclusion program. Creative instructional strategies, such as team teaching, also help inclusion work.

Team Teaching. Many inclusion models use a collaborative-teaching or team-teaching approach. Generally, in a team-teaching approach a general educator and a special educator are jointly responsible for a class of students containing both general and special education students. Truly effective teaching teams use a variety of instructional formats, with teachers playing a number of different roles, depending on the lesson plan. Teachers should plan lessons together, decide on areas of responsibility during instruction, and share the responsibility for grading.

Team teaching can take a number of forms. Both teachers can co-teach the lesson, or one teacher can present the material initially to the entire group, after which the class is split into two groups with each teacher responsible for one of them. Also, one teacher can present while the second teacher instructs a smaller group of students, manages behavior, or performs a specific activity. It is important for teachers to switch roles regularly so that the students understand that both teachers are responsible for the entire class. Having two desks of equal size will add to the understanding that both professionals are teachers. The typical teacher aide model should be avoided, because both people are professionals and have different areas of expertise. When one professional is reduced to the role of assistant, animosity can develop, damaging the working relationship.

Although team teaching is a new model that requires a period of adjustment to implement, teachers who work well together as a team report impressive benefits, including shared responsibility, the opportunity to observe each other and the students, and exposure to new ideas and the other teacher's areas of expertise. Personality characteristics, teaching styles, and the desire to be involved in a teaching team should be considered when establishing teaching teams.

Multiple Intelligences

Howard Gardner introduced the idea of multiple intelligences as an alternative to traditional models of intelligence that delineate students into those who are intelligent and those who are not. Gardner (1987) found that the primary question is not which students are smart but, rather, how each student is smart. Gardner postulates seven different intelligences and argues that teachers need to teach to and help students develop their strengths and improve their areas of weakness. Schools are often very focused on linguistic and logical–mathematical intelligence to the exclusion of other ways of learning and demonstrating knowledge. By validating different kinds of intelligence, Gardner allows both teachers and students to value difference. Armstrong (1994) described the various intelligences as shown in Table 7.2.

A student's various intelligences can be discerned through observation of preferred activities and areas of excellent performance or through brief checklists. When multiple intelligences are used as an instructional model, students are educated about the various intelligences. A grid may be displayed on a blackboard or bulletin board, and ways of learning and assignments can be developed in conjunction with the students' intelligences. For example, in a class that is studying primates, students who are linguistically oriented may decide to write reports, stories, or plays about primates. Those who are oriented toward logical–mathematical intelligence may examine statistics concerning land-to-population ratios, food consumption, and social circles. Illustrating

TABLE 7.2

Varied Intelligences

Children who are strongly	Think	Love	Need
Linguistic	In words	Reading, writing, telling stories, playing word games	Books, writing materials, journals, discussions, debates, stories
Logical–mathematical	In numbers and through reasoning	Math problems, experiments, logic, questioning, puzzles, analyzing	Math and science materials, puzzles, experiments, logic games, manipulatives
Spatial	In diagrams, images, and pictures	Drawing, designing, doodling, building models, visualizing	Art and building materials, puzzles, illustrations
Bodily–kinesthetic	In movement and through sensation	Dancing, running, jumping, building, gestures, acting	Drama and role play, building and art materials, sports and physical games, miming, tactile experiences
Musical	In melodies, songs, and rhythms	Singing, whistling, playing instruments, humming, listening	Writing songs, concerts, music, instruments
Interpersonal	Through interaction with others	Discussing, leading, or being part of a group; relating, mediating, socializing	Friends, group games, plays or stories about others, community events, clubs, social events, mentors/apprentices
Intrapersonal	Through introspection	Setting goals, meditating, thinking, dreaming, being quiet, planning	Secret places, time alone, self-directed activities, choices

Note. From *Multiple Intelligences in the Classroom*, by T. Armstrong, 1994, Alexandria, VA: Association for Supervision and Curriculum Development. Copyright 1994 by Association for Supervision and Curriculum Development. Reprinted with permission.

these students' works might be the responsibility of those who are more spatial in orientation, and those who favor bodily–kinesthetic approaches may show the class how various primates move around, use their toes to pick up items, and interact socially. Writing a song to teach the class facts about primates or analyzing and comparing the sounds made by gorillas and monkeys might be the job of those with high musical intelligence. Students with intrapersonal intelligence might reflect on how life would be different for a monkey placed in a zoo and write a diary from the monkey's point of view. Finally, those with interpersonal strengths might organize or run work groups, direct the play, or establish a community awareness day around ecological issues affecting primates. Effective teachers can see how using all of their students' intelligences, and hence all of their students' talents, adds to the educational program and self-esteem of the group.

In addition, teachers using the multiple intelligences model will become more adept at presenting information in a variety of ways to key in on the learning strengths of students. Research has shown that this paradigm is an effective way to move educators away from concentrating on what students with disabilities cannot do, a deficit model, toward a competency-based model of what students do well (Armstrong, 1987, 1988). Armstrong (1994) pointed out individuals with emotional or behavioral problems who excelled in diverse intelligences, including Edgar Allan Poe, Charles Darwin, Vincent van Gogh, Robert Schumann, and Harry Stack Sullivan. He also delineated various strategies to bypass or remediate areas of weakness. For example, students' good logical intelligence can use the Internet and electronic bulletin boards as a means of gathering information or interacting with others. Students with kinesthetic strengths can participate in Outward Bound, and those with musical intelligence can join musical groups. An excellent resource for lesson plan ideas using the multiple intelligences model is *Celebrating Multiple Intelligences: Teaching for Success* (New City School, 1994).

Teachers of students with emotional and behavioral needs know that varying instructional presentation and learning activities reduces behavior problems and improves performance. Multiple intelligences provides a theoretical framework through which students can begin to view themselves as capable learners.

Teacher-Directed Instructional Methods

Six types of teacher-directed instructional methods have gained popular acceptance. *Direct instruction* places primary emphasis on antecedent stimuli (teacher wording, examples, presentation of material). Both *precision teaching* and *prescriptive teaching* originally were developed as specific methodologies for use with underachieving students, primarily in special education settings. Their application was later expanded to include general education students. *Active teaching* provides insight into the instructional benefits of actively pursuing instructional goals. *Learning strategy instruction* approaches learning from a cognitive or metacognitive perspective, in which students are taught how to approach various tasks successfully. Finally, *study skills instruction* is presented as a way to teach students how to learn and retain information and how to demonstrate their knowledge on tests and reports.

Direct Instruction. Direct instruction (Engelmann & Carnine, 1982) operates on several basic components common to many educational models with a behavioral emphasis. These components include (a) the use of reinforcement and mastery learning principles, (b) regular and direct assessment, (c) breaking tasks into small components through task analysis, and (d) teaching prerequisite skills (Kinder & Carnine, 1991). The most basic difference between direct instruction and other models is the former's emphasis on the antecedents of instruction, such as teacher directions, instructional statements, and prompts. A number of direct instruction curriculum materials have been developed by Engelmann and colleagues in reading, math, and language arts. These include *Reading Mastery*, formerly *Distar Reading* (Engelmann & Bruner, 1988); *Corrective Mathematics* (Engelmann & Carnine, 1981); *Connecting Math Concepts* (Engelmann & Carnine, 1991); and *Distar Language* (Engelmann & Osborn, 1976). These curriculum materials are often referred to as scripted because they provide actual scripts for teachers to follow when teaching content material.

Scripts include instructional information, prompts for student responses, and feedback about student performance. Scripts are designed for what Kinder and Carnine (1991) referred to as "faultless communication." Four components are at the heart of direct instruction's faultless communication: (a) explicit teaching of rules and strategies, (b) example selection, (c) example sequencing, and (d) covertization. Making the steps in the thinking process overt and observable is at the heart of explicit teaching of rules and strategies. Students are guided through demonstrations of the use of the strategy in which each step in the process is explicitly delineated and elaborated on. Guided practice of the rule or strategy is accomplished through carefully selected examples that differ in relevant attributes but teach are the same strategy (e.g., adding *ing* to single-syllable words ending in a consonant). Examples are sequenced to maximize student learning, sometimes by alternating examples that illustrate the concept and examples that do not illustrate it (e.g., using "running" and "runs" to illustrate doubling the final consonant when adding a suffix beginning with a vowel). Throughout these initial processes, each step is overt; in the final stages, generalization and maintenance for independence are developed through covertization (i.e., the systematic fading of prompts and instructions so that the students' strategies become covert). Delivery of instruction is governed by brisk or rapid pacing and specific correction procedures, principles discussed earlier in this chapter.

Studies have found that direct instruction tends to produce higher academic gains than other forms of instruction for students with special needs (Gersten, 1985; Homer & Albin, 1988; Kinder & Carnine, 1991; White, 1988). A meta-analysis conducted by White examined 25 investigations of direct instruction with students with handicaps. White concluded that direct instruction showed strong and consistent effects across subjects (reading and math), elementary and secondary grade levels, and mild to more severe disabilities. One drawback of direct instruction is the extensive training and practice necessary for teachers to become proficient and natural in its delivery. Estimates are that it takes a full academic year for teachers to achieve mastery of direct instruction techniques.

Precision Teaching. The precision teaching model (Kunzelmann, Cohen, Hulten, Martin, & Mingo, 1970; Lindsley, 1971) was devised as a system for monitoring each student's daily academic progress. This model employs the measurement and data collection procedures of behavior modification, which are to (a) target a response, (b) collect and chart baseline data, (c) devise and implement a change strategy, and (d) continue to chart the resulting response. According to Lindsley, precision teaching differs from behavior modification in that the focus of the change strategy is curricular; that is, it involves the academic skills and concepts the child is trying to master. Precision teaching tries to help the child "do more successful classroom work by making curricular changes . . . rather than trying to jack up a dull curriculum with rewards for doing tasks" (Lindsley, 1971, p. 115).

The use of precision teaching involves the daily measurement of performance rate (frequency divided by time) on various academic tasks. When a student is not making progress, curricular changes are made. These changes might involve lowering the difficulty level of a task, changing the instructional material the student is using, or changing the teaching strategy being used by the teacher. These curricular changes are made in lieu of giving the student tangible incentives such as candy, tokens, or prizes for completing appropriate curriculum tasks.

A principal tool used in precision teaching is the standard behavior chart. The behavior chart has a special six-cycle semilogarithmic design that allows the recording of behavioral data on a frequency-per-minute basis ranging from 0 to 1,000 times per minute. The upper limit for behaviors—1,000 times per minute—represents the time in a day when a person typically is most awake and functioning. A behavior that occurs once a day would occur at a rate of 0.001 times per minute (1 [frequency] divided by 1,000 [minutes]) and would be recorded near the bottom of the chart. A student who correctly worked 20 math problems in 10 minutes would have a math performance rate of 2

(20 [frequency] divided by 10 [time]). A student who correctly read 100 words in 2 minutes would have a reading rate of 50. These behaviors would be recorded in the appropriate place on the chart. The frequency-per-minute chart permits great flexibility in recording a wide variety of behaviors and enables teachers to know exactly how their students are progressing in each academic subject.

Lindsley (1971) stated that precision teaching is a structure imposed on tried-and-true teaching procedures that provides more precise information about a child's rate of progress and indicates how instruction can best be individualized. The basic assumptions and methods of precision teaching closely match CBA's progress-monitoring approach. The major difference is the use of the logarithmic scale for graphs in precision teaching. Some teachers and students find these types of graphs difficult to understand and use. Progress-monitoring graphs are a viable alternative because both methodologies provide teachers and students with data on performance toward very specific learning objectives and allow teachers to make decisions about effective instruction.

Prescriptive Teaching. Prescriptive teaching is "An organization of definable and observable components of the process of instruction to achieve a predetermined or prescribed objective" (Peter, 1972, p. 3). The prescriptive teaching model of individualized instruction is similar to precision teaching, although it is not as rigorous in its methodology. However, like precision teaching, it stresses the systematic application of behavioral learning principles to children's educational experiences.

The conceptual model of prescriptive teaching consists of three elements: (a) elicitors of events occurring before a behavior, (b) the behavioral response itself, and (c) reinforcers, or events occurring after a behavioral response that serve to maintain, strengthen, or weaken the response (see Figure 7.4). For example, a teacher calls a student to the board to work a math problem, the student comes to the board and gets the problem right, and the teacher praises him publicly and shows the class his work. The elicitor is the teacher's calling to the child, the behavioral response is the child coming to the board, and the reinforcer is the correct response and praise. The reinforcer will strengthen the response because it is something the child likes (a positive reinforcer). Had the reinforcer been something the child dislikes, such as getting the problem wrong or ridicule from peers (a punisher), the behavioral response would have been weakened, and in the future the child would be more prone to avoid coming when the teacher calls or perhaps even to doing math at his seat.

Four stages comprise the conceptual model of prescriptive teaching. The first stage involves describing the student's entering behavior, that is, the student's beginning level of academic functioning. This description is obtained

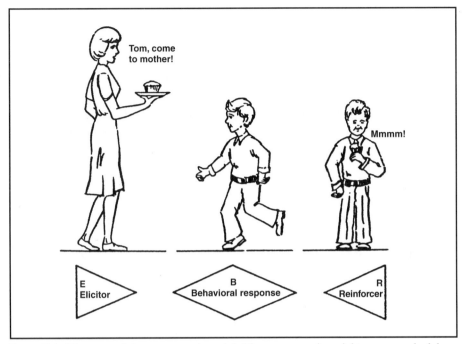

Figure 7.4. Elements of the conceptual model. The conceptual model is composed of these three elements: elicitor (E), behavior (B), and reinforcer (R). *Note:* From *Individual Instruction* by L. Peter, 1972, New York: McGraw-Hill. Copyright 1972 by Wadsworth. Reprinted with permission.

by observing the student in the classroom and by working individually with the student. Direct observation of classroom behavior reveals the maladaptive behaviors that interfere with achievement, as well as their elicitors and reinforcers. Specific academic strengths and weaknesses are assessed through diagnostic teaching on an individual basis. In diagnostic teaching, academic tasks of various degrees of difficulty are presented to the child under varied conditions of reinforcement (e.g., praise, tokens, food). The child's performance should indicate where he functions best academically and which reinforcers are most motivating.

The second stage of prescriptive teaching involves delineating the goals or final outcomes of a student's program. These goals are called terminal objectives and are written according to the elicitor–behavior–reinforcer model of prescriptive teaching. For example, Steve, a fifth-grade student, was having difficulty with social studies. When given an independent assignment to do (seatwork), he would gaze around the room, tap his feet on the floor, drum his fingers on the desk, and wiggle around in his seat. Rarely did Steve finish an assignment. A terminal objective for Steve might be the following: When given the fifth-grade social studies book, Steve will read the assignment and correctly answer on paper the questions at the end of the chapter while receiving only customary teacher attention.

The third phase involves writing en route objective. En route objectives are a series of skills or behaviors that the student must learn or accomplish to move from entering behaviors to the terminal objectives. Usually, the teaching procedures and curricular materials are specified in the en route objectives. En route objectives also are written according to the elicitor–behavior–reinforcer model. (An example of an elicitor–behavior–reinforcer model for Steve is presented in Table 7.3.). This list of objectives should continue until the desired terminal objective is reached.

The fourth stage of prescriptive teaching is the evaluation. The teacher can accomplish evaluation subjectively by simply observing the student in the classroom to see if the terminal objective has been attained. It also can be conducted objectively by observing the student in the classroom and collecting data regarding the frequency of the terminal behavior.

Active Teaching. Active teaching (Rosenshine, 1979) is an instructional approach aimed at keeping students actively involved in learning. It is characterized by five basic elements (Goetz, Alexander, & Ash, 1992):

1. Teaching activities are focused on academics, and goals of instruction are clearly communicated with students.

2. Time established for teaching is sufficient and continuous.

3. Content coverage is extensive and sequenced.

4. Student success is high, and all responses are followed by immediate, academically oriented feedback.

5. Teacher–student interactions are structured but not authoritarian.

The first three elements of Active Teaching are obvious and essential components of good instruction. They mesh well with the idea of a structured approach to instruction specified in the fifth element. The program leads to high student success and provides the opportunity for positive feedback.

The effectiveness of active teaching is supported by research revealing that disruptive behavior rarely occurs in classrooms in which teachers employ active teaching (Heilman, Blair, & Rupley, 1986). A number of additional recommendations for successfully using active teaching have been reported (Goetz et al., 1992). To use this approach, teachers should make sure learning is meaningful and instructionally relevant to students. Students with emo-

TABLE 7.3
Elicitor–Behavior–Reinforcer Model

Elicitor	Behavior	Reinforcer
1. Fifth-grade social studies book	Read one paragraph and answer correctly on paper two questions about the paragraph	Five minutes' free time to listen to the radio
2. Fifth-grade social studies book	Read three paragraphs and answer correctly on paper three questions about the paragraphs	Teacher praise and four minutes' free time to listen to radio
3. Fifth-grade social studies book	Read one page and answer correctly on paper five questions about the content	Teacher praise and good-progress note to take home

tional or behavioral problems are not generally motivated to learn by vague references to possible future usefulness of material, such as "You will need this to get into college." In addition to showing relevancy, instruction should be replete with effective examples, illustrations, and models. Teachers should plan examples and models prior to instruction and evaluate their success following use. Teachers should also provide a variety of materials for practice and application of each skill. Materials should vary in form and content, as well as difficulty level. With materials of various difficulty levels, teachers and students can use some for independent work, some for instruction, and some for exploration.

Two final components of active teaching include ongoing diagnosis of student learning and the extensive use of positive feedback as an integral part of instruction. Student participation in group instruction, performance during independent activities, and academic progress should be assessed, with results used to modify instructional strategies that are ineffective. Positive feedback should be used to direct student learning and behavior, as well as to encourage student participation and success.

Learning Strategy Instruction. Several researchers have investigated the effectiveness of teaching cognitive and metacognitive learning strategies to adolescents with emotional and learning problems (Alley & Deshler, 1979; Armbruster, Echols, & Brown, 1982; Armbruster & Gudbrandsen, 1986; Wong, 1985). Strategy training places the instructional emphasis on teaching students how to learn and how to apply what they have learned in diverse situations.

Although some authors differentiate between cognitive strategies, learning strategies, and metacognition, the distinctions are neither consistent across authors nor critical for their use in the classroom (Paul & Epanchin, 1991). Alley and Deshler (1979) defined learning strategies as "techniques, principles, or rules that will facilitate the acquisition, manipulation, integration, storage, and retrieval of information across situations and settings" (p. 13). This definition incorporates both metacognitive and cognitive strategies (Ellis, Lenz, & Sabornie, 1987). Three rationales are offered by Deshler and Schumaker (1986) for the inclusion of learning strategy training for adolescents:

1. Development and application of learning strategies is significantly related to age; older students have been found to be consistently more proficient than younger students in acquiring and using these structures.

2. Teaching adolescents how to learn will increase their ability to learn outside of school and therefore to adapt to future demands.

3. Students learn to take responsibility for their learning and progress using a learning strategies approach. Taking responsibility increases future commitment and independence.

Learning strategy instruction is often interwoven with self-regulation or self-instruction, for students are taught to monitor their own problem-solving processes (Meichenbaum & Asarnow, 1979). Self-statements that are often part of both processes are "What do I need to do next?" "Reread the instructions," and "I'm doing a good job."

The *Learning Strategies Curriculum* (Schumaker, Deshler, Alley, & Warner, 1983) was developed at the University of Kansas and consists of a collection of learning strategy instructional packets. The curriculum was developed to match the curricular demands of secondary education and centers around three strands. The first strand contains strategies designed to help students acquire information from written material. One example, the *Multipass Strategy* (Schumaker, Deshler, Alley, & Denton, 1982), is used by students to survey materials and to obtain and study critical information in textbook chapters. The second strand focuses on strategies that enable students to identify and remember the most important information. An example is the *FIRST-Letter Mnemonic Strategy* developed by Nagel, Schumaker, and Deshler (1986). The third strand is designed to help students deal with high school demands for written expression and includes the *Assignment Completion Strategy* (Deshler & Schumaker, 1986) and the *Sentence Writing Strategy* (Schumaker & Sheldon, 1985).

Teaching methodology is a critical component of the *Learning Strategies Curriculum*. Acquisition and generalization of the learning strategies are developed through a series of eight steps in which the teacher

1. pretests and obtains a commitment to learn;
2. describes the strategy;
3. models the strategy;
4. verbally rehearses the strategy;
5. controls the practice of the strategy and provides feedback;
6. grades the appropriate practice and provides additional feedback;
7. obtains from the student a commitment to generalize the strategy; and
8. follows up to ensure that generalization has occurred.

Generalization training (training students to use the strategy when it is appropriate in other school contexts) is critical if learning strategy training is to become a tool rather than another curriculum area. Paul and Epanchin (1991) discussed four types of generalization training that are critical if students are to be able to use the learning strategies to improve everyday performance. *Antecedent generalization* occurs prior to direct instruction of the strategy and focuses on providing a clear rationale for the learning of the skill. Included are immediate examples for the use of the skill. *Concurrent generalization* takes place while the student is acquiring the learning strategy and consists of using multiple exemplars, daily reminders, and applications to class assignments. After the learning strategy has been mastered, *subsequent generalization* training occurs. The goal of subsequent generalization is to get students to apply the strategy to other settings and situations in which it is applicable. Finally, *independent generalization* shifts to the student the responsibility for continuing to apply new skills. Self-control procedures, goal-setting techniques, and self-reinforcement are used to teach students to be self-regulated learners.

Study Skills Instruction. Students with emotional and behavioral problems may need instruction in how to study. The use of study skills strategies has been shown to improve school achievement (for a review, see Weinstein, Goetz, & Alexander, 1988). Study skills that need to be considered for instruction include listening, note taking, organization, scheduling, comprehending, textbook usage, memory strategies, test taking, and report writing. Frequently, students report studying for a test but still do poorly. Although some students may not study, many others do not know or use effective means to study school material.

Teachers can build study skills instruction into academic instruction by sequencing or altering assignments, as well as through direct instruction. For example, assignments can be developed around the use of advanced organizers. Teachers can introduce new chapters by using the table of contents, headings, illustrations, and charts, thus providing a model for students to follow in their own studies. Students can be asked, as a group, what a chapter might contain as a way to teach self-questioning. Student worksheets can be sequenced so that initial questions require advanced organizers, whereas later questions request details found within the actual text. Teachers can play study skills games in which students compete in teams to find answers quickly and without in-depth reading.

Shaping listening and note-taking skills is often effective. Initially, teachers may provide students with notes in outline form prior to the lecture; gradually, teachers can eliminate portions of the outline, allowing the students to complete it as they listen to the lecture. Other study strategies include the five-step method and the two-column method for taking notes (Bragstad & Stumpf, 1987), use of advanced organizers (Gleason, 1988), SQ3R (Robinson, 1961), and EVOKER (Pauk, 1984). For more detailed information about study skills instruction, see Olson and Platt (2000) and Wallace and Kauffman (1998).

Student-Directed Instructional Methods

Instructional methods that are student directed require teacher preparation and participation. Teachers are responsible for preparing materials, organizing the sessions, and especially for monitoring and reinforcing students for appropriate cooperative, tutorial, and academic behaviors. Students require guidance and training for student-directed procedures to be successful. Included in student-directed methods are *cooperative learning* and *peer tutoring*.

Cooperative Learning. Use of cooperative learning strategies has been increasing rapidly across all school subjects and grade levels. Cooperative learning strategies are defined by Slavin (1991) as "instructional techniques in which students work in small groups to help one another learn academic material" (p. 105). Underlying the use of cooperative learning to improve student performance are three cognitive theories, which have been delineated by Slavin (p. 108):

1. learning by teaching or cognitive elaboration (Dansereau, 1988; Webb, 1985);

2. Vygotskian or Piagetian theories emphasizing learning through cognitive conflict and students' operating in one another's proximal zones of development (Mugny & Doise, 1978; Murray, 1982); and

3. opportunities for students to provide individualized assessment, immediate feedback, and personally tailored assistance to other group members (Slavin, 1989, 1990).

Two important components of cooperative learning strategies are the cooperative incentive structure and the cooperative task arrangements (Cosden &
Haring, 1992; Slavin, 1983, 1988a, 1991). Cooperative incentive structures
and task arrangements provide opportunities for students to gain group rewards
by working on tasks as a group. Cooperative learning arrangements generally
differ from competitive or individualistic arrangements. In competitive learning situations, students' goal attainments are arranged so that one student can
achieve his goal only when the competing student does not. In this situation,
students' goal attainments are negatively correlated. Common examples of
competitive goal structuring in classroom situations are the spelling bee (only
one student may win, so all the rest must lose) and tests scored on a normal
curve where only a predetermined number of As and Bs are assigned. In individualistic arrangements, which are most common in school settings, students'
goal attainments are independent and unrelated. Individualistic and cooperative strategies are often used concurrently in classrooms. Although two forms
of cooperative learning, Student Teams-Achievement Divisions and Teams-
Games-Tournaments, involve competition, the competition is among groups
of students who need to work cooperatively to attain group goals and rewards.

It is critical for teachers to remember that cooperative learning involves a
set of skills that must be delineated and taught, especially to students with emotional and behavioral challenges. Taking turns, listening to others, stating one's
ideas, negotiating, planning, following directions, and staying on task are some
of the skills required for successful cooperation to take place. These skills must
be taught, prompted, and reinforced for cooperative learning activities to be
effective.

Although many teachers of students with EBDs may doubt the efficacy of
cooperative approaches with their students, Taylor and Larson (1998) found
cooperative learning techniques to be effective with students with attention-
deficit and hyperactive disorders and other behavior problems. These authors
describe a number of valuable techniques that may be used to deal with typical
problems presented by students with behavioral disorders. Table 7.4 provides
a brief overview of these problems and interventions.

According to Slavin (1988a), a strong advocate, the social psychology literature "has shown that people working for a cooperative goal encourage one
another to do their best, help one another do well, and like and respect one
another." Four models of cooperative learning have been developed: (a) the
jigsaw approach, (b) the group project, (c) the competitive teams approach,

TABLE 7.4
Behavioral Problems

Behaviors	Interventions
Argumentative	Encourage ownership of behavior, avoid power struggles, teach to avoid criticizing by offering solutions, provide a safe time-out space, clarify and encourage questions about expectations and directions, teach how to express feelings and ideas with peers
Immaturity	Frequently refer to team rules, pair students with more mature students, planned ignoring, redirection toward task, teach individual responsibility
Misinterpreting social cues	Encourage clarifying questions, reward appropriate social responses, use humor to minimize embarrassment, give clear directions about how to respond to social situations such as receiving a compliment or taking constructive criticism
Peer rejection	Discreetly reward students for working with difficult behaviors, use peer confederates, provide opportunities for students to demonstrate strengths and contribute to the group, form heterogeneous teams, do not allow self-selection of teams, teach socially appropriate behaviors
Overactivity	Establish roles and activities that allow movement, reward with small motor breaks, provide hands-on or active learning activities, allow to stand to work

Note. From "Using Cooperative Learning with Students Who Have Attention Deficit Hyperactivity Disorder," by H. E. Taylor and S. Larson, 1998, *Social Studies and the Young Learner, 10*(4), 1–4. Copyright 1998 by National Council for the Social Studies. Reprinted with permission.

and (d) Team-Accelerated Instruction (formerly Team-Assisted Individualization). The first three models are generic in nature and may be adapted for various content areas, whereas specific math materials are also available for use with Team-Accelerated Instruction.

In the jigsaw approach, one student is assigned one part of the task or material to be completed by the group. For example, if students are completing a skills packet or writing a report about Harriet Tubman, students either elect or are assigned to learn about one aspect of her life. After mastering individual information, each person shares or teaches the rest of the group what she has learned. As a whole, the group then completes the packet or writes the report. The name *jigsaw* is derived from the process: Each person learns a piece of the puzzle, which is shared with the group so as to complete the picture. If absenteeism is a problem, Slavin (1988a) recommended assigning two students from each group to each subtask or developing activities that can be completed in one school day. When working on group projects, students pool their knowledge to complete a project or assignment, such as making a straw tower or building a terrarium. More complex tasks, such as measuring actual rooms, building things, or completing experiments, seem to produce more cooperation than simpler tasks, such as completing a worksheet.

The competitive teams approach combines competition among different groups of students with cooperation within the groups. Students cooperate to learn material and earn team rewards while competing with other classroom-based teams. Two structured formats developed by Slavin and colleagues at Johns Hopkins University are Student Teams-Achievement Divisions (Slavin, 1988b) and Teams-Games-Tournaments (Slavin, 1988b). In Student Teams-Achievement Divisions, the class is divided into learning teams of three to five students. Teachers present new material using lectures and discussions on Mondays and Tuesdays. On Wednesdays and Thursdays, learning teams study worksheets and materials using cooperative strategies. Students may quiz each other, break up into pairs, or develop any technique that will enable all members of the teams to learn the material. On Fridays, students take 30-item quizzes individually. Individual scores are then added to the team score. Slavin (1988a) suggested having students earn points based on increases in quiz grades over previous averages.

Teams-Games-Tournaments is an adaptation of Student Teams-Achievement Divisions. The procedures are identical except that the quiz at the end of the week is replaced by a student tournament. Students work in teams during the week, and on Friday students from various teams who are on similar levels compete at each tournament table for team points. Materials include a quiz, numbered cards, and an answer sheet. Students draw cards, and the per-son with the highest number begins, reading aloud the corresponding question on the quiz. The reader then answers the question. Other players may challenge the answer. Whoever gives the correct answer keeps the card. If the reader is incorrect, no penalty is given; if a challenger is incorrect, she loses a card. Individual team members' card earnings are combined for the team score, and the team with the most cards wins. Students change tournament levels each week according to their prior week's performance.

Team-Accelerated Instruction (Slavin, 1988a) combines cooperative learning and individualized instruction for mathematics. Students are assigned only those skill units in which initial assessments determine they have deficits. Each unit consists of a guide sheet, skill pages, two formative tests, a unit test, and answer sheets for skill pages and tests. Materials are available for addition, subtraction, multiplication, division, decimals, fractions, percentages, statistics, ratios, algebra, and word problems. Each student reads the guide sheet and asks either the teacher or other students for assistance. The student then completes four problems on the first skill page, and another student corrects them. Students who have all four correct proceed to the next skill page. If fewer than four are correct, the student asks for assistance and then completes the next four problems. After completing the skill pages, the student takes a formative test. If the student is correct on 8 of 10 answers, the student takes the unit test. Each student earns points for the team each week based on units completed and scores on tests. (More detailed information can be obtained from Barbara Luebbe, Project Director, Johns Hopkins University Team Learning Project, Center for Social Organization of Schools, 3505 N. Charles St., Baltimore, MD 21218.)

Cooperative learning strategies have been found to increase academic achievement in reading comprehension (Slavin, Stevens, & Madden, 1988), math (Slavin, Leavey, & Madden, 1984), and science and social studies (Slavin, 1988a). Possibly because these groups are generally heterogeneous, including students of various ability levels, genders, and racial or ethnic groups, positive social outcomes have also been found. These include increased acceptance of students with special needs within the classroom setting (Madden & Slavin, 1983; Slavin et al., 1984), increased interactions between typical and special needs students during general school activities (Johnson, Johnson, Warring, & Maruyama, 1986), and improved race relations (Slavin, 1985; Slavin & Oickle, 1981). Cooperative learning has also been found to maximize learning by capitalizing on the cooperative nature of some cultures, such as Mexican American and other Latino cultures (Briganti, 1989; Grossman, 1990).

Peer Tutoring. Peer tutoring is a subset of peer-assisted learning (PAL; Topping & Ehly, 1998). PAL is designed to have students consciously and systematically help other students to learn and in so doing to make academic gains themselves. PAL is built on the success of peer tutoring and includes peer tutoring, peer modeling, peer instruction, peer counseling, peer monitoring, and peer assessment. The designers of PAL describe how disruptive students as well as other students with behavioral issues can be taught to effectively tutor, instruct, monitor, assess, and counsel other students. Programs must be well planned out and monitored. The scope of PAL is broad, but the discussion here concentrates specifically on peer tutoring because the evidence for its success with special education populations is well documented.

The idea of using peer tutoring to help children with emotional and behavioral problems is consistent with the notion of using in-school resources to promote learning. Peer tutoring involves students tutoring other students.

Three peer-tutoring formats have been identified: cross-age, same age, and classwide. In cross-age tutoring, older children help younger students. Research comparing cross-age and same-age tutoring has found equal academic but better social gains for students with EBDs when cross-age tutoring is used (Durrer & McLaughlin, 1995). In classwide peer tutoring an entire class is broken up into two teams of multiple tutoring dyads. Students take turns being the tutor and the tutee, and points are earned for correct responses. At the end of the session, team points are totaled and one team declared the winner.

The keys to success in all three types of formats are training and program structure. Children are able to help other children perform well when they are trained in advance to understand the benefits of positive reinforcement, the content to be taught, and the procedures to be used. It is especially true for students with emotional and behavioral problems that a clear format, close teacher monitoring for appropriate interactions and on-task behavior, and frequent praise are all beneficial to the success of peer tutoring.

In addition to training in advance of the program, the program itself must be well structured. Structure implies that the teacher has identified the goals of the program and has explained them to the tutors. Also, specific behaviors appropriate for the tutor and his charge are clarified. Both children must know what is expected of them. The teacher monitors the session to reinforce appropriate behaviors and provide assistance. In general, implementing peer-tutoring programs includes selecting learning objectives to be targeted, selecting and matching students, preparing materials, determining schedules, planning the procedure, training tutors, and monitoring and evaluating the tutoring sessions. Most peer-tutoring programs are implemented for 15 to 20 minutes a session two or three times a week. (For more detailed information on models and implementation, see Delquadri, Greenwood, Whorton, Carta, & Hall, 1986; Maheady, Sacca, & Harper, 1988; Olson & Platt, 2000.)

Peer tutoring has numerous benefits, both academic and nonacademic. Peer tutoring provides increased individualization, one-on-one instruction, and increased academic and social success in the mainstream (Miller, Baretta, & Heron, 1994). Improvements in learning and achievement have been found for elementary and high school students with special needs, regardless of whether they acted as the tutee or the tutor (Eiserman, 1988; Maheady et al., 1988; Scruggs & Richter, 1986). Peer tutoring has resulted in increases in academic performance across all areas of the curriculum, including reading (Chiang, Thorpe, & Darch, 1980; Eiserman), math (Greenwood, Dinwiddie, et al., 1984; Maheady et al., 1988), spelling (Maheady & Harper, 1987; Mandoli, Mandoli, & McLaughlin, 1982), social studies (Maheady et al., 1988), and language arts (Maher, 1984).

Nonacademic benefits include improved social acceptance and attitudes toward students with special needs (Johnson & Johnson, 1980; Schuler, Ogulthorpe, & Eiserman, 1987), reduced absenteeism and tardiness (Lazerson, Foster, Brow, & Hummel, 1988; Maher, 1982), and reduction in disciplinary referrals (Maher, 1982, 1984). Classwide peer tutoring is one of the instructional strategies recommended for culturally diverse students with special needs who are at risk for special education referral (Maheady, Towne, Algozzine, Mercer, & Ysseldyke, 1983).

Peer tutoring also provides increased opportunities to respond (Delquadri et al., 1986; Greenwood, Delquadri, & Hall, 1984), allows children to practice an adult role of responsibility (Olson, 1982), and provides opportunities for children to feel useful, needed, and competent (Allen, 1976). Frequently, peers are adept at translating the teacher's ideas into meaningful examples or more astute language, and peer tutoring gives students the opportunity to engage in these teaching behaviors. Learning objectives appropriate for peer tutoring include answering comprehension questions, practicing in reading workbooks, learning spelling words, practicing math facts, and learning the meanings of vocabulary words (Delquadri et al., 1986).

STUDY QUESTIONS

1. Discuss six guidelines for teachers to follow when constructing tests.

2. Discuss three factors to be considered when selecting instructional materials.

3. What are the key variables that affect student academic progress?

4. Discuss four aspects of teacher behavior that influence student performance.

5. Discuss the multiple intelligences model. What are the benefits of using such an approach?

6. Discuss several ways in which parents can be involved in programs for students with emotional and behavioral challenges.

7. Compare and contrast teacher-directed and student-directed instructional techniques. What are the advantages of each?

References

Allen, V. L. (1976). The helping relationship and socialization of children: Some perspectives on tutoring. In V. L. Allen (Ed.), *Children as teachers: Theory and research on tutoring*. New York: Academic Press.

Alley, G. R., & Deshler, D. D. (1979). *Teaching students with learning problems* (3rd ed.). Columbus, OH: Merrill.

Armbruster, B. B., Echols, C. H., & Brown, A. L. (1982). The role of metacognition in reading to learn: A developmental perspective. *Volta Review, 84*, 45–56.

Armbruster, B. B., & Gudbrandsen, B. (1986). Reading comprehension instruction in social studies programs. *Reading Research Quarterly, 21*(1), 36–48.

Armstrong, T. (1987). Describing strengths in children identified as "learning disabled" using Howard Gardner's theory of multiple intelligences as an organizing framework. *Dissertation Abstracts International 48*, 08A. (University Microfilms No. 87–25, 844)

Armstrong, T. (1988). Learning differences—not disabilities. *Principal, 68*(1),34–36.

Armstrong, T. (1994). *Multiple intelligences in the classroom*. Alexandria, VA: Association for Supervision and Curriculum Development.

Atwater, I. B., & Morris, E. K. (1988). Teachers' instructions and children's compliance in preschool classrooms: A descriptive analysis. *Journal of Applied Behavior Analysis, 21*, 157–168.

Bambara, L. M., & Ager, C. (1992). Using self-scheduling to promote self-directed leisure activity in home and community settings. *Journal of the Association for Persons with Severe Handicaps, 17*(2), 67–76.

Bambara, L. M., Ager, C., & Koger, F. (1994). The effects of choice and task preference on the work performance of adults with severe disabilities. *Journal of Applied Behavioral Analysis, 27*, 555–556.

Bandura, A. (1986). *Social foundations of thought and action: A social cognitive theory*. Englewood Cliffs, NJ: Prentice Hall.

Beale, A., & Beers, C. S. (1982). What do you say to parents after you say hello? *Teaching Exceptional Children, 15*(1), 34–39.

Beatty, L., Madden, R., Gardner, E., & Karlsen, B. (1984). *Stanford Diagnostic Mathematics Test* (3rd ed.). San Antonio, TX: Psychological Corp.

Blankenship, C. S. (1985). Using curriculum-based assessment data to make instructional management decisions. *Exceptional Children, 42*, 233–238.

Bragstad, B. J., & Stumpf, S. M. (1987). *A guidebook for teaching study skills and motivation*. Boston: Allyn & Bacon.

Briganti, M., (1989). *An ESE teacher's guide for working with the limited English proficient student*. Orlando, FL: Orange County Public Schools.

Brophy, J. E., & Good, T. L. (1986). Teacher behavior and student achievement. In M. L. Wittrock (Ed.), *Handbook of research on teaching* (3rd ed., pp. 328–375). New York: Macmillan.

Browder, D. M. (1991). *Assessment of individuals with severe disabilities: An applied behavior approach to life skills assessment* (2nd ed.). Baltimore: Brookes.

Brown, V. L., Hammill, D. D., & Wiederholt, J. L. (1995). *The Test of Reading Comprehension–3: A method for assessing the understanding of written language*. Austin, TX: PRO-ED.

Burnette, J. (1987). *Adapting instructional materials for mainstreamed students*. Washington, DC: Office of Special Education Programs, United States Department of Education.

Carnine, D. (1991). Reforming mathematics instruction: The role of curriculum materials. *Journal of Behavioral Education, 1*, 37–58.

Chan, D. M. (1987). Curriculum development for limited-English proficient exceptional Chinese children. In M. K. Kitano & P. C. Chinn (Eds.), *Exceptional Asian Children and Youth* (pp. 61–69). Reston, VA: The Council for Exceptional Children.

Chiang, B. (1986). Modifying public domain software for use by the learning disabled student. *Journal of Learning Disabilities, 19*, 315–317.

Chiang, B., Thorpe, H. W., & Darch, C. B. (1980). Effects of cross-age tutoring on word-recognition performance of learning disabled students. *Learning Disabilities Quarterly, 3*(4), 11–17.

Cole, C. L., Davenport, T. A., Bambara, L. M., & Ager, C. L. (1997). Effect of choice and task preference on the work performance of students with behavior problems. *Behavioral Disorders, 22*(2), 65–74.

Coleman, M., & Vaughn, S. (2000). Reading interventions for students with emotional/behavioral disorder. *Behavioral Disorders, 25*(2), 93–104.

Connolly, A. (1988). *KeyMath revised: A diagnostic inventory of essential mathematics.* Circle Pines, MN: American Guidance Service.

Cooper, J. D., & Kiger, N. D. (2001). *Literacy assessment—Helping teachers plan instruction.* Boston: Houghton Mifflin.

Cosden, M. A., & Haring, T. G. (1992). Cooperative learning in the classroom: Contingencies, group interactions, and students with special needs. *Journal of Behavioral Education, 2*, 53–72.

Coulter, A., & Coulter, E. (1989). *Curriculum-based assessment for instructional design.* Unpublished training materials, Directions and Resources Group, New Orleans.

Crisis Prevention Institute. (1983). *CPI workshop materials.* Milwaukee, WI: Author.

Dansereau, D. F. (1988). Cooperative learning strategies. In C. E. Weinstein, E. T. Goetz, & P. A. Alexander (Eds.), *Learning and study strategies: Issues in assessment, instruction, and evaluation* (pp. 103–120). New York: Academic Press.

Dawson, L., Venn, M., & Gunter, P. L. (2000). The effects of teacher versus computer reading models. *Behavioral Disorders, 25*(2), 105–113.

Deci, E., & Ryan, R. (1985). *Intrinsic motivation and self-determination in human behavior.* New York: Plenum Press.

Delquadri, J., Greenwood, C. R., Whorton, D., Carta, J. J., & Hall, R. V. (1986). Classwide peer tutoring. *Exceptional Children, 52*, 535–542.

Deno, S. L. (1985). Curriculum-based measurement: The emerging alternative. *Exceptional Children, 52*, 219–232.

Deno, S. L. (1986). Formative evaluation of individual programs: A new role for school psychologists. *School Psychology Review, 15*, 358–374.

Deno, S. L. (1987). Curriculum-based measurement. *Teaching Exceptional Children, 20*, 41.

DePaepe, P. A., Shores, R. E., & Jack, S. L. (1996). Effects of task difficulty on the disruptive and on-task behavior of students with severe behavior disorders. *Behavioral Disorders, 21*(3), 216–225.

Deshler, D. D., & Schumaker, I. B. (1986). Learning strategies: An instructional alternative for low-achieving adolescents. *Exceptional Children, 52*, 583–590.

Dinkmeyer, D., & McKay, G. (1997). *Systematic training for effective parenting.* Circle Pines, MN: American Guidance Service.

Dunlap, G., dePerczel, M., Clarke, S., Wilson, D., Wright, S., White, R., & Gomez, A. (1994). Choice making to promote adaptive behavior for students with emotional and behavioral challenges. *Journal of Applied Behavior Analysis, 27*, 505–518.

Dunn, L., & Markwardt, F. (1981). *The Peabody Individual Achievement Test.* Circle Pines, MN: American Guidance Service.

Durrer, B., & McLaughlin, T. F. (1995). The use of peer tutoring interventions involving students with behavior disorders. *B. C. Journal of Special Education, 19*(1), 20–27.

Eiserman, W. D. (1988). Three types of peer tutoring: Effects on the attitudes of students with learning disabilities and their regular class peers. *Journal of Learning Disabilities, 21*, 223–229.

Ellis, E. S., Lenz, B. K., & Sabornie, E. S. (1987). Generalization and adaptation of learning strategies to natural environments. Part 2: Research into practice. *Remedial and Special Education, 8*, 6–23.

Engelmann, S., & Bruner, E. C. (1988). *Reading mastery.* Chicago: Science Research Associates.

Engelmann, S., & Carnine, D. (1981). *Corrective mathematics.* Chicago: Science Research Associates.

Engelmann, S., & Carnine, D. (1982). *Theory of instruction.* New York: Irvington.

Engelmann, S., & Carnine, D. (1991). *Connecting math concepts.* Chicago: Science Research Associates.

Engelmann, S., & Osborn, J. (1976). *Distar language.* Chicago: Science Research Associates.

Fagot, B. I. (1973). Influence of teacher behavior in the preschool. *Developmental Psychology, 9*, 198–206.

Frith, G. H., & Lindsey, J. D. (1982). Certification, training, and other programming variables affecting special education and the paraprofessional concept. *The Journal of Special Education, 16*, 229–236.

Fuchs, D., & Fuchs, L. S. (1986). Test procedure bias: A meta-analysis of examiner familiarity. *Review of Educational Research, 56*, 23–26.

Fuchs, L. S., Butterworth, J., & Fuchs, D. (1989). Effects of curriculum-based progress monitoring on student knowledge of performance. *Education and Treatment of Children, 12*, 21–32.

Fuchs, L. S., & Fuchs, D. (1987). *Improving data-based instruction through computer technology: Continuation application.* Unpublished manuscript, Vanderbilt University, Nashville, TN.

Fuchs, L. S., & Fuchs, D. (1990). *Monitoring Basic Skills Progress (MBSP).* Austin, TX: PRO-ED.

Fuchs, L. S., Fuchs, D., & Stecker, P. M. (1989). The effects of curriculum-based measurement on teachers' instructional planning. *Journal of Learning Disabilities, 22*, 51–59.

Gable, R. A., & Hendrickson, J. M. (Eds.). (1990). *Assessing students with special needs: A sourcebook for analyzing and correcting errors in academics.* New York: Longman.

Gallagher, P. A. (1988). *Teaching students with behavior disorders: Techniques and activities for classroom instruction.* Denver, CO: Love.

Gardner, H. (1987). Beyond IQ: Education and human development. *Harvard Educational Review, 57*(2), 187–193.

Gast, D. L., Doyle, P. M., Wolery, A., Ault, M. J., & Baklart, J. L. (1991). Acquisition of incidental information during small group instruction. *Education and Treatment of Children, 14*, 1–18.

Gersten, R. (1985). Direct instruction with special education students: A review of evaluation research. *The Journal of Special Education, 19*, 41–58.

Gickling, E. E., & Havertape, J. (1981). *Curriculum-based assessment* (CBA). Minneapolis, MN: School Psychology Inservice Training Network.

Gickling, E. E., Shane, R. L., & Croskery, K. M. (1989). Assuring math success for low-achieving high school students through curriculum-based assessment. *School Psychology Review, 18*, 344–355.

Gickling, E. E., & Thompson, V. P. (1985). A personal view of curriculum based assessment. *Exceptional Children, 52*, 205–218.

Gleason, M. M. (1988). Study skills: Teaching study strategies. *Teaching Exceptional Children, 20*(3), 52–53.

Goetz, E. T., Alexander, P. A., & Ash, M. J. (1992). *Educational psychology: A classroom perspective.* New York: Merrill.

Gordon, T. (2000). *Parent effectiveness training*. New York: Wyden.

Greenwood, C. R. (1991). Longitudinal analysis of time, engagement, and achievement in at-risk versus non-risk students. *Exceptional Children, 1*(1), 521–534.

Greenwood, C. R., Carta, J. J., & Atwater, J. (1991). Eco-behavioral analysis in the classroom: Review and applications. *Journal of Behavioral Education, 1*, 59–77.

Greenwood, C. R., Delquadri, J., & Hall, R. V. (1984). Opportunity to respond and student academic performance. In W. L. Heward, T. E. Heron, J. Trap-Porter, & D. S. Hill (Eds.), *Focus on behavior analysis in education* (pp. 58–88). Columbus, OH: Merrill.

Greenwood, C. R., Dinwiddie, G., Terry, B., Wade, L., Stanley, S., Thibadeau, S., & Delquadri, J. (1984). Teacher-versus-peer-mediated instruction: An ecobehavioral analysis of achievement outcomes. *Journal of Applied Behavior Analysis, 17*, 521–538.

Gronlund, N. M. (1976). *Measurement and evaluation in teaching*. New York: Macmillan.

Grossman, H. (1990). *Trouble-free teaching: Solutions to behavior problems in the classroom*. Mountain View, CA: Mayfield.

Guetzloe, E. C. (1993). The special education initiative: Responding to changing problems, populations, and paradigms (The Forum). *Behavioral Disorders, 18*(4), 303–307.

Hammill, D. (1971). Evaluating children for instructional purposes. *Academic Therapy, 6*, 341–353.

Hammill, D., & Larsen, S. (1996). *The Test of Written Language–3*. Austin, TX: PRO-ED.

Hammill, D., & Newcomer, P. (1997). *Test of Language Development–Intermediate* (TOLD–I:3). Austin, TX: PRO-ED.

Hammill, D., Pearson, N. A., & Wiederholt, J. L. (1997). *Comprehensive Test of Nonverbal Intelligence*. Austin, TX: PRO-ED.

Hargis, C. H. (1987). *Curriculum-based assessment: A primer*. Springfield, IL: Thomas.

Heilman, A. W., Blair, T. R., & Rupley, W. R. (1986). *Principles and practices of teaching reading* (6th ed.). Columbus, OH: Merrill.

Hepworth, D. H., & Larsen, J. A. (1990). *Direct social work practice: Theory and skills* (3rd ed.). Homewood, IL: Dorsey Press.

Hewett, F. (1969). *The emotionally disturbed child in the classroom*. Boston: Allyn & Bacon.

Homer, R. H., & Albin, R. W. (1988). Research on general-case procedures for learners with severe disabilities. *Education and Treatment of Children, 11*, 375–388.

Howell, K. W., & Morehead, M. K. (1987). *Curriculum-based evaluation for special and remedial education*. Columbus, OH: Merrill.

Hresko, W., Reid, D. K., & Hammill, D. (1999). *Test of Early Language Development*. Austin, TX: PRO-ED.

Idol, L., Nevin, A., & Paolucci-Whitcomb, P. (1986). *Models of curriculum-based assessment*. Austin, TX: PRO-ED.

Johnson, D., & Johnson, R. (1980). Integrating handicapped children into the mainstream. *Exceptional Children, 47*, 90–98.

Johnson, D., Johnson, R., Warring, D., & Maruyama, G. (1986). Different cooperative learning procedures and cross-handicap relationships. *Exceptional Children, 53*, 247–252.

Kinder, D., & Carnine, D. (1991). Direct instruction: What it is and what it is becoming. *Journal of Behavioral Education, 1*, 193–214.

Kunzelmann, H., Cohen, M., Hulten, W., Martin, G., & Mingo, A. (1970). *Precision teaching*. Seattle, WA: Special Child Publications.

Larsen, S., & Hammill, D. (1986). *Test of Written Spelling–2*. Austin, TX: PRO-ED.

Lazerson, D. B., Foster, H. L., Brow, S. I., & Hummel, J. W. (1988). The effectiveness of cross-age tutoring with truant, junior high students with learning disabilities. *Journal of Learning Disabilities, 21,* 253–255.

Lewis, T. J., Chard, D., & Scott, T. M. (1994). Full inclusion and the education of children and youth with emotional and behavioral disorders. *Behavioral Disorders, 19*(4), 277–293.

Lindsley, O. R. (1971). Precision teaching in perspective. *Teaching Exceptional Children, 3,* 114–119.

Lovitt, T. (1973). Self-management projects with children with behavioral disabilities. *Journal of Learning Disabilities, 6,* 15–28.

Madden, N. A., & Slavin, R. E. (1983). Effects of cooperative learning on the social acceptance of mainstreamed academically handicapped students. *The Journal of Special Education, 17*(1), 171–182.

Mager, R. (1962). *Preparing instructional objectives.* Palo Alto, CA: Fearon.

Maheady, L., & Harper, G. F. (1987). A classwide peer-tutoring program to improve the spelling test performance of low income, third- and fourth-grade students. *Education and Treatment of Children, 10,* 120–133.

Maheady, L., Sacca, M. K., & Harper, G. F. (1988). Classwide peer tutoring with mildly handicapped high school students. *Exceptional Children, 55*(1), 52–59.

Maheady, L., Towne, R., Algozzine, B., Mercer, J., & Ysseldyke, J. (1983). Minority overrepresentation: A case for alternative practices prior to referral. *Learning Disability Quarterly, 6*(4), 448–457.

Maher, C. A. (1982). Behavioral effects of using conduct problem adolescents as cross-age tutors. *Psychology in the Schools, 19,* 360–364.

Maher, C. A. (1984). Handicapped adolescents as cross-age tutors: Program description and evaluation. *Exceptional Children, 5*(1), 56–63.

Mandoli, M., Mandoli, P., & McLaughlin, T. F. (1982). Effects of same-age peer tutoring on the spelling performance of a mainstreamed elementary LD student. *Learning Disability Quarterly, 5*(2), 185–189.

Marion, R. L. (1981). *Educators, parents, and exceptional children.* Rockville, MD: Aspen.

Martella, R. C., Marchand-Martella, N. E., Miller, T. L., Young, K. R., & Mactarlane, C. A. (1995). Teaching instructional aides and peer tutors to decrease problem behaviors in the classroom. *Teaching Exceptional Children, 27*(2), 53–56.

Martin, R. P. (1988). *Assessment of personality and behavior problems.* New York: Guilford Press.

McCarney, S. B. (1986). Preferred types of communication indicated by parents and teachers of emotionally disturbed students. *Behavioral Disorders, 11*(2), 118–123.

McKinney, J. D., & Hocutt, A. M. (1982). Public school involvement of parents of learning disabled and average achievers. *Exceptional Education Quarterly, 3*(2), 64–73.

Meichenbaum, D., & Asarnow, V. (1979). Cognitive-behavior modification and metacognitive development: Implications for the classroom. In P. C. Kendall & S. D. Hollon (Eds.), *Cognitive-behavioral interventions: Theory, research, and procedures.* New York: Academic Press.

Mercer, C. D., & Mercer, A. R. (1989). *Teaching students with learning problems* (3rd ed.). Columbus, OH: Merrill.

Miller, A. D., Baretta, P. M., & Heron, T. E. (1994). START tutoring: Designing, training, implementing, adapting, and evaluating tutoring programs for school and home settings. In R. Gardner, III, D. M. Sainato, J. O. Cooper, T. E. Heron, W. L. Heward, J. W. Eshelman, & T. A. Grossi (Eds.), *Behavior analysis in education: Focus on measurably superior instruction* (pp. 265–282). Pacific Grove, CA: Brooks/Cole.

Morse, W. (1976). Crisis intervention in school mental health and special classes for the disturbed. In N. Long, W. Morse, & R. Newman (Eds.), *Conflict in the classroom* (3rd ed.). Belmont, CA: Wadsworth.

Mugny, G., & Doise, W. (1978). Socio-cognitive conflict and structurization of individual and collective performances. *European Journal of Social Psychology, 8*, 181–192.

Murray, F. B. (1982). Teaching through social conflict. *Contemporary Educational Psychology, 7*, 257–271.

Nagel, D., Schumaker, J. B., & Deshler, D. D. (1986). *The learning strategies curriculum: The FIRST-letter mnemonic strategy*. Lawrence, KS: Excel Enterprises.

New City School. (1994). *Celebrating multiple intelligences: Teaching for success*. St. Louis, MO: Author.

Newcomer, P. (2001). *Diagnostic Achievement Battery–3*. Austin, TX: PRO-ED.

Newcomer, P., & Bryant, B. (1993). *Diagnostic Achievement Test for Adolescents*. Austin, TX: PRO-ED.

Newcomer, P., & Hammill, D. (1997). *Test of Language Development–Primary* (TOLD–P:3). Austin, TX: PRO-ED.

Olion, L. (1989). Enhancing the involvement of black parents of adolescents with handicaps. In A. A. Ortiz & B. A. Ramirez (Eds.), *Schools and the culturally diverse exceptional students: Promising practices and future directions* (pp. 96–103). Reston, VA: Council for Exceptional Children.

Olson, J. (1982). Treatment perspectives: Peer tutoring. In B. Algozzine (Ed.), *Problem behavior management* (pp. 40–44). Rockville, MD: Aspen.

Olson, J., & Platt, J. (2000). *Teaching children and adolescents with special needs*. New York: Merrill.

Overton, T. (1992). *Assessment in special education: An applied approach*. New York: Macmillan.

Pauk, W. (1984). *How to study in college*. Boston: Houghton Mifflin.

Paul, J. L., & Epanchin, B. C. (1991). *Educating emotionally disturbed children and youth: Theories and practices for teachers*. New York: Merrill.

Peter, L. (1972). *Individual instruction*. New York: McGraw-Hill.

Pickett, A. L. (1988). *A training program for paraprofessionals working in special education and related services*. New York: National Resource Center for Paraprofessionals in Special Education, New Careers Training Laboratory, City University of New York.

Rife, R. M., & Karr-Kidwell, P. J. (1995). *Administrative and teacher efforts for elementary emotionally disturbed and behaviorally-disordered students: A literary review and recommendations for an inclusion program*. (ERIC Document Reproduction Service No. ED 396 497)

Robinson, F. P. (1961). *Effective study*. New York: Harper & Row.

Rosenshine, B. (1979). Content, time, and direct instruction. In P. L. Peterson & H. L. Walberg (Eds.), *Research on teaching: Concepts, findings, and implications* (pp. 28–55). Berkeley, CA: McCutchan.

Rothbaum, R., Weisz, J., & Snyder, S. (1982). Changing the world and changing the self: A two-process model of perceived control. *Journal of Personality and Social Psychology, 42*, 5–37.

Sainato, D. M., Strain, P. S., & Lyon, S. R. (1987). Increasing academic responding of handicapped preschool children during group instruction. *Journal of the Division of Early Childhood, 12*, 23–30.

Salvia, J., & Ysseldyke, J. (1985). *Assessment in special and remedial education*. Boston: Houghton Mifflin.

Schuler, L., Ogulthorpe, R. T., & Eiserman, W. D. (1987). The effects of reverse-role tutoring on the social acceptance of students with behavioral disorders. *Behavioral Disorders, 13*(1), 35–44.

Schumaker, J. B., Deshler, D. D., Alley, G. R., & Denton, P. H. (1982). Multipass: A learning strategy for improving reading comprehension. *Learning Disability Quarterly, 5*, 295–304.

Schumaker, J. B., Deshler, D. D., Alley, G. R., & Warner, M. M. (1983). Toward the development of an intervention model for learning disabled adolescents. *Exceptional Education Quarterly, 4*, 45–74.

Schumaker, J. B., & Sheldon, J. (1985). *Learning strategies curriculum: The sentence writing strategy*. Lawrence: University of Kansas Press.

Scruggs, T. E., & Richter, L. (1986). Tutoring learning disabled students: A critical review. *Learning Disability Quarterly, 9*(1), 2–14.

Semel, E., Wiig, E., & Secord, W. (1987). *Clinical Evaluation of Language Fundamentals–Revised*. San Antonio, TX: Psychological Corp.

Shapiro, E. S. (1987). *Behavioral assessment in school psychology*. Hillsdale, NJ: Erlbaum.

Shapiro, E. S. (1989). *Academic skills problems: Direct assessment and intervention*. New York: Guilford Press.

Shapiro, E. S. (1996). *Academic skills problems: Direct assessment and intervention* (2nd ed.). New York: Guilford Press.

Shapiro, E. S., & Ager, C. L. (1992). Assessment of special education students in regular education programs: Linking assessment to instruction. *Elementary School Journal, 92*, 283–296.

Shapiro, E. S., & Lentz, F. E. (1985). Assessing academic behavior: A behavioral approach. *School Psychology Review, 14*, 325–338.

Shapiro, E. S., & Lentz, F. E. (1986). Behavioral assessment of academic skills. In T. R. Kratochwill (Ed.), *Advances in school psychology* (Vol. 5, pp. 87–139). Hillsdale, NJ: Erlbaum.

Shinn, M. R. (Ed.). (1989). *Curriculum-based measurement: Assessing special children*. New York: Guilford Press.

Slavin, R. E. (1983). When does cooperative learning increase student achievement? *Psychological Bulletin, 94*, 429–445.

Slavin, R. E. (1985). Cooperative learning: Applying contact theory in desegregated schools. *Journal of Social Issues, 41*(3), 45–62.

Slavin, R. E. (1988a). Cooperative learning and student achievement. *Educational Leadership, 46*(2), 31–33.

Slavin, R. E. (1988b). *Student team learning: An overview and practical guide* (2nd ed.). Washington, DC: National Education Association.

Slavin, R. E. (1989). Cooperative learning and student achievement: Six theoretical perspectives. In M. L. Maehr & C. Ames (Eds.), *Advances in motivation and achievement* (Vol. 6, pp. 161–178). Greenwich, CT: JAI Press.

Slavin, R. E. (1990). *Cooperative learning: Theory, research, and practice*. Englewood Cliffs, NJ: Prentice Hall.

Slavin, R. E. (1991). Cooperative learning and group contingencies. *Journal of Behavioral Education, 1*, 105–116.

Slavin, R. E., Leavey, M., & Madden, N. A. (1984). Combining cooperative learning and individualized instruction: Effects on student mathematics achievement, attitudes, and behaviors. *Elementary School Journal, 84*, 409–422.

Slavin, R. E., & Oickle, E. (1981). Effects of cooperative learning teams on student achievement and race relations: Treatment by race interactions. *Sociology of Education, 54*, 174–180.

Slavin, R. E., Stevens, R. J., & Madden, N. A. (1988). Accommodating student diversity in reading and writing instruction: A cooperative learning approach. *Remedial and Special Education, 9*(1), 60–66.

Snyder, E. P., & Shapiro, E. S. (1997). Teaching students with emotional/behavioral disorders the skills to participate in the development of their own IEPs. *Behavioral Disorders, 22*(4), 246–259.

Spaulding, C. L. (1992). *Motivation in the classroom*. New York: McGraw-Hill.

Stallings, J. (1975). Implementation and child effects of teaching practices in follow-through classrooms. *Monographs of the Society for Research in Child Development, 40* (Serial No. 163).

Starkel, J. (1978). *Selection and adaptation of materials for learning disabled adolescents*. Unpublished manuscript, University of Kansas, Lawrence.

Stevenson, H. C., & Fantuzzo, J. W. (1984). Application of the "generalization map" to a self-control intervention with school-aged children. *Journal of Applied Behavior Analysis, 17*, 203–212.

Sugai, G., & Rowe, P. (1984). The effect of self-recording on out-of-seat behavior of an EMR student. *Education and Training of the Mentally Retarded, 19*, 23–28.

Taylor, H. E., & Larson, S. (1998). Using cooperative learning with students who have attention deficit hyperactivity disorder. *Social Studies and the Young Learner, 10*(4), 1–4.

Tindal, G. (1987). Graphing performance. *Teaching Exceptional Children, 20,* 44–46.

Topping, K., & Ehly, S. (1998). *Peer-assisted learning.* Hillsdale, NJ: Erlbaum.

Wallace, G., & Kauffman, J. M. (1998). *Teaching students with learning and behavior problems* (4th ed.). Columbus, OH: Merrill.

Wallace, J., & Larsen, S. (1978). *Educational assessment of learning problems: Testing for teaching.* Boston: Allyn & Bacon.

Webb, N. (1985). Student interaction and learning in small groups: A research summary. In R. E. Slavin, S. Sharan, S. Kagan, R. Hertz-Lazarowitz, C. Webb, & R. Schmuck (Eds.), *Learning to cooperate, cooperating to learn* (pp. 147–172). New York: Plenum Press.

Wechsler, D. (1991). *Wechsler Intelligence Scale for Children—Third Edition.* San Antonio, TX: Psychological Corp.

Weinstein, C. E., Goetz, E. T., & Alexander, P. A. (1988). *Learning and study strategies: Issues in assessment, instruction, and evaluation.* San Diego, CA: Academic Press.

White, W. A. T. (1988). A meta-analysis of the effects of direct instruction in special education. *Education and Treatment of Children, 11,* 364–374.

Wiederholt, J. (1986). *Formal Reading Inventory.* Austin, TX: PRO-ED.

Wiig, E., & Secord, W. (1985). *Test of Language Competence–Expanded.* San Antonio, TX: Psychological Corp.

Williams, B. F., Williams, R. L., & McLaughlin, T. F. (1991). Classroom procedures for remediating behavior disorders. *Journal of Development and Physical Disabilities, 3,* 349–383.

Wilson, J. (1976). *Adapting instructional materials.* Unpublished manuscript, University of Kansas, Lawrence.

Wilson, J. (1978). Selecting educational materials and resources. In D. Hammill & N. Bartel (Eds.), *Teaching children with learning and behavior problems* (2nd ed.). Boston: Allyn & Bacon.

Winton, P., & Turnbull, A. P. (1981). Parent involvement as viewed by parents of preschool handicapped children. *Topics in Early Childhood Special Education, 1*(3), 11–19.

Wong, B. Y. (1985). Issues in cognitive–behavioral interventions in academic skill areas. *Journal of Abnormal Child Psychology, 13*(3), 441–455.

Woodcock, R. W., & Johnson, M. B. (2000). *Woodcock-Johnson Psycho-Educational Battery.* Allen, TX: DLM Teaching Resources.

PHENOMENOLOGICAL THERAPIES AND APPROACHES TO CLASSROOM MANAGEMENT

In Chapter 2, the phenomenological perspective of emotional disorders was introduced and discussed. This chapter expands on that introduction by discussing (a) the strategies associated with two examples of phenomenological therapy that have particular applicability in educational settings, *gestalt therapy* (Perls, 1969; Perls, Hefferline, & Goodman, 1965) and *client-centered therapy* (Rogers, 1951), and (b) two classroom management approaches that reflect a phenomenological perspective, *teacher effectiveness training* and *peer mediation*. In phenomenological approaches, the major emphasis is on perception—each individual's unique processing of events in the environment—as determining human behavior. Although perception involves cognition, feelings or emotive processes are of primary importance in understanding and treating psychological disorders.

Gestalt Therapy

The German term *gestalt* has no specific equivalent in English but is usually translated to mean "the whole." It evolves from the field of gestalt psychology, the study of perceptual processes (the interpretation of the environment). According to gestalt theory, wholes are more than the sum of their parts, and parts are determined by the intrinsic nature of the whole. When applied to psychological disorders, the term refers to the importance of viewing personality as a whole, not as a series of specific responses to events. To understand the whole personality, perceptions of the external world and the inner self must be examined.

Fritz Perls, officially recognized as the father of gestalt therapy, founded the New York Institute for Gestalt Therapy in 1952 and the Cleveland Institute for Gestalt Therapy in 1954. He was extremely successful in treating individuals with psychological disturbances and developed an elaborate theory that explained the specific problems they exhibited in terms of the gestalt. Many of his principles and techniques are too esoteric to be discussed in this text. Only those that are necessary for understanding his approach and that have relevance for application in school settings are presented.

Perls believed that human beings are unified organisms, that is, that they function as a whole. The processes called thinking, feeling, and behaving are not independent components but are interrelated. Similarly, mind and body are interrelated aspects of an individual. People grow because they are inherently motivated to satisfy needs through contact with the environment. The satisfaction of need states is a conscious process to regain equilibrium (balance or homeostasis) disturbed by the need. For example, frustration fosters growth by creating needs and forcing the individual to learn to manage in the environment and to mature. As children mature, they become increasingly independent; those hindered (spared frustration) by overprotective or overindulgent parents remain dependent and immature.

The maturational process causes anxiety, a reflection of the individual's leaving the now and striving for the future. Also, because a person's interaction with the environment does not always go smoothly, characteristics of psychological disorders develop. For example, an individual who cannot accept part of his personality practices *projection*, that is, attributing those rejected characteristics to others. *Introjection* occurs when one person uncritically accepts others' values, even when they are incompatible with her own. This process works against the development of a stable personality. When growth becomes stagnated because the individual's needs and the needs of the society conflict, neurotic defensive adjustment occurs. Neurotic adjustment is characterized by perceptual distortion—inability to realistically interpret events in the environment and lack of self-awareness. The individual ceases to function as an integrated whole and engages in a wide variety of feelings, thoughts, and behaviors that are punishing to others and to self and that interfere with living in society. In current terminology, neurotic adjustment would encompass all of the disorders experienced by children and adolescents described in the *Diagnostic and Statistical Manual of Mental Disorders* (American Psychiatric Association, 1994) except psychosis and organic or biological diseases.

Therapeutic Goals and Techniques

The goals of gestalt therapy are to help the individual become aware of (cease avoiding) unwanted emotions and to reestablish healthy contact with the environment. Unlike most adherents to cognitive and behavioral approaches (active–directive therapies) that emphasize actions taken by the client to alter maladaptive behavior patterns, Perls (1969) believed that awareness per se can be curative. This notion is closely aligned with the psychoanalytic premise that insight into one's problems is curative. Awareness includes understanding self and accepting reality and is obtained by concentrating on the present, "the here and now." However, understanding self and the external world does not refer solely to cognitive realization (as when one understands the concepts involved in the equation $1 + 1 = 2$). Awareness is a global phenomenon involving all aspects of an individual's internal and external experiences. The individual is led to recognize the significance of his thoughts, feelings, gestures, tone of voice, breathing pattern, and so forth. Notably, although thoughts, ideas, and other cognitions are examined, the emphasis of the gestalt approach is on increasing the client's awareness of present feelings by sharpening his body sense and teaching him to listen to his verbalizations.

Perls believed that therapy should take place in groups because social interactions are psychologically revealing and group input contributes to the development of awareness. He also believed that therapy should be a short-term experience focused on the solution of current problems. Dwelling on past events, a technique associated with psychoanalytic therapy, often permits clients to continue to escape grappling with current events and to avoid taking responsibility for problems. From the gestalt perspective, taking responsibility for problems is the key to successful therapy because it is a necessary component of independence and maturity—the characteristics of psychological health.

As for actual therapeutic techniques, gestalt therapy, like other phenomenological approaches, is relatively nondirective. The therapist does not tell a client what to do but provides a situation in which, because the client feels accepted rather than threatened, he is able to lower defenses and face problems more realistically. Gestaltists believe in the power of human beings to make good choices and decisions when they are not forced to be defensive. They also believe that growth and increased awareness must be internally directed—that it cannot be developed for and transmitted to a person by someone else.

As mentioned previously, in therapy the individual's attention is directed to his manner of expression. Perls believed that nonverbal behaviors are more revealing of true feelings than the content of verbal remarks. For example, the person's posture, facial expressions, and voice tone and pitch all indicate attitudes that must be introduced into the client's awareness. Questioning is a therapeutic technique used to direct the client's attention to these elements. Typical questions ("what" questions, not "why" questions) to promote awareness are "What are you aware of now?" "What are you feeling?" "What are you doing with your hand?" If the individual resists answering, the issue is not pressed, because awareness cannot be forced.

Interestingly, many other theorists with markedly different perspectives share Perls's opinion that avoidance of assuming responsibility for behavior is an important characteristic of psychological disturbance. In gestalt therapy, clients' attempts to blame others for their problems, or to blame their problems in society on their pasts or their emotional difficulties, are immediately challenged by the therapist. To help direct attention to this avoidance of reality and responsibility, the therapist asks the client to use responsible language, such as using "I" instead of "it" when referring to body parts and activities. For example, the client should say, "I broke a lamp" instead of "A lamp (it) got broken." A similar semantic strategy is used to help the client experience events in the here and now. Language is cast in the present, as in "I am angry," rather than "He made me angry." For the purposes of therapy, the past and future do not exist; only "now" exists.

Drawing on the work of Jacob Moreno (whose approach, psychodrama, is discussed in Chapter 11), Perls recommended the use of role-playing techniques to help speed up awareness. However, unlike Moreno, Perls did not involve others in role playing but had the client play every role. According to Patterson (1980), role-playing techniques used in gestalt therapy include the shuttle technique, topdog–underdog dialogue, and the empty chair technique.

The shuttle technique requires that the client's attention be directed back and forth from one experience or activity to another. For example, the person may be asked to talk, then guided to examine what he has said by a question such as "Are you aware of this sentence?" In topdog–underdog dialogues, the client role-plays two opposing aspects of personality that create conflicts. Topdog represents the neurotic "shoulds" that dictate behavior, such as "I should be perfect and never make mistakes" (see discussion about Albert Ellis in Chapter 6), whereas underdog stands for the evasive, irresponsible "yes buts" of behavior (as in "Yes, I knew my paper was due today, but the cat ate it"). In the empty chair technique, the client engages in dialogue with a significant other, changing chairs as he plays himself and the other person.

Other therapeutic techniques or games (Levitsky & Perls, 1970) include taking responsibility, secret guilt, projection, reversal, rehearsal, and exaggeration. To draw a client's attention to taking responsibility, he is asked to follow statements about himself with the sentence "I take responsibility for it." Individuals who comply with this request begin to bring their own perceptions about responsibility in line with those held by others who quite realistically perceive themselves as responsible for their behaviors.

Secret guilt involves thinking of a personal secret that invokes guilt and (without telling others) imagining how others would react if they knew. This strategy forces the client to experience (in imagery) hidden fears about previous behavior, thereby increasing awareness. *Projection* occurs when an individual is asked to attribute his characteristic behavior, emotion, or attitude to another, and to role-play the other person displaying the characteristic.

When *reversal* is used, the client is asked to play a role opposite to his overt behavior, as when an aggressive individual is told to behave passively. The technique called *rehearsal* involves repeatedly sharing thoughts that pertain to social role playing with other members of the group. For example, a withdrawn person interested in dating would discuss thoughts that pertain to that social activity. *Exaggeration* requires the client to repeat an important statement over and over with great emphasis. It is used when he makes an important statement in a casual way, suggesting that he is unaware of its importance, as when a highly aggressive individual casually remarks, "So I punched him in the nose."

Homework (see Chapter 6 for cognitive–behavioral applications of homework) is another therapeutic strategy used in gestalt therapy. Clients are asked to use imagery to relive the therapy session and to try to identify the elements that evoke anxiety or cause discomfort. These elements are explored in ensuing therapy sessions.

Efficacy and Criticism

Gestalt therapy provides general goals that orient practitioners in their attempts to create a climate in which individuals with emotional disorders can become aware of the elements within themselves that prevent them from functioning successfully in society. The specific techniques associated with this approach are not applied systematically, as they are in behavioral interventions and certain cognitive therapies. Rather, they are used in the course of the therapeutic interaction as they are needed to increase a client's understanding or emotional awareness at that moment. Consequently, the effectiveness of the therapy is highly related to the talent of the therapist using the techniques. Therefore, efficacy research has never been viewed by advocates of the approach as an appropriate means of evaluating the effectiveness of therapy; instead, it evaluates the effectiveness of the therapist, and in Perls's case, reports from trained observers indicate that he was extremely effective.

According to Patterson (1980), critics of the gestalt approach are skeptical of the general applicability of the procedures, holding that Perls was successful because of the force of his personality and his clients' desire to please him.

Other criticisms are that this type of therapy is useful only with highly intellectual, overcontrolled, neurotic individuals, and that in reality it is not a process of self-discovery but a highly directive process of manipulation by the therapist.

It is fair to note that all therapeutic approaches, like all teaching approaches, are directive to some degree, and that some are far more directive than others. The phenomenological approaches are among the least directive therapies. As to the general effectiveness of gestalt principles, every human interaction is highly personalized. Successful results in therapy may depend primarily on the extent to which the parties involved trust and have confidence in each other.

Educational Applications

Perls did not address the application of his theory and therapeutic techniques specifically to children. Also, unlike behavioral and cognitive therapies, his phenomenological therapy does not provide a set of highly structured procedures for changing human behavior that have been applied to children by others. It does, however, provide therapeutic guidelines, not for making an individual behave as others behave but for increasing each person's capacity to perceive and choose a more constructive and fulfilling path.

Despite the relative dearth of specific techniques, certain characteristics of gestalt therapy appear useful in educational settings. Foremost among these is the identification of constructive group interactions and experiences as essential for good psychological health. In addition to promoting constructive interactions, the group plays an important part in establishing an environment conducive to growth. The group is a realistic audience, typically judging the roles played by each group member with brutal honesty. The teacher is a member of the group whose role is not to suppress honest response in herself or others but to attempt to help every member respond in a manner that promotes awareness.

Promoting awareness, the purpose of gestalt therapy, is accomplished by reacting to students and helping them react to one another in ways that do not evoke (or provoke) defensive behavior. Threats, punishment, sarcasm, hostile language or acts, negative facial expressions and body language, and harsh tones of voice are reactions that evoke defensive behavior. Students can be made aware of the implications of provocative behaviors by participating in group discussions. Although not a phenomenological theorist, William Glasser (see Chapter 6) provided some guidelines for group sessions within the classroom. Also, later in this chapter, Carl Rogers's ideas on this topic are presented. In addition to group discussions, however, it is essential that teachers avoid using provocative strategies themselves and provide a model for students to emulate, because that is a more powerful teaching device than discussion.

Gestalt therapy teaches that the daily events involved in living are important elements of an individual's perceptual field. By extension, any event occurring in the classroom can serve as a vehicle to promote awareness. Use of the "what" questions discussed previously is a nonthreatening means of directing a student's attention to feelings, thoughts, or behavior that require examination. For example, a student who passes out papers by throwing them on the desk of specific classmates is communicating certain feelings, possibly anger or disdain, without using words. The teacher might respond by reprimanding him, in which case the child might stop, but he does not examine either the behavior or the feelings connected with it. Use of questions such as "What are you doing?" or "What are you feeling when you do that?" asked without anger or annoyance directs the student's attention to both the behavior and the feelings. Even if his response is defensive or evasive, the pattern of directing his attention in this manner provides him with the opportunity to become more aware of his actions and their social implications.

A phenomenological or humanistic approach to education need not be directed solely toward students with emotional disorders. All children benefit from becoming more aware of their feelings and the demeanor they present to others. Their increased self-awareness helps them recognize the relationship between (a) their feelings and the way others view them and (b) the quality of their interactions in society.

The focus of gestalt therapy on solving problems in the present (the here and now) and on taking responsibility for behavior also is important to educators. Although past circumstances in children's lives may have shaped their personalities and determined their typical ways of responding in society, teachers have little choice but to continuously direct attention to current events, thus helping students recognize their responsibility—both for causing those events in the here and now and for making changes that will lead to better lives. As a phenomenologist, Perls viewed human beings as capable of making constructive choices, regardless of the previous negative influences in their lives. The gestalt strategies involving the use of responsible language and language in the present are simple procedures for increasing children's awareness of their responsibility. Once again, the teacher can model the behavior by using responsible language ("I haven't finished correcting your papers" rather than "Your papers aren't finished yet"). Role-playing strategies such as reversal (playing a role opposite the typical overt behavior) also help children recognize aspects of themselves not usually revealed to others. (Role-playing strategies, as well as modifications through the use of puppetry, are discussed in Chapter 12.)

Possibly the greatest impact of this approach for educators pertains to the goals of instruction and the classroom climate. Perls noted that responsibility promotes independence and maturity—characteristics that enable individuals to lead fulfilling lives. By implication, teachers can help children grow and develop into self-actualized human beings by heightening their awareness of their ability to function without teacher support or direction; that is, schools must provide children with the opportunity to participate in planning (taking responsibility for) their instructional program. Teachers and administrators who assume full responsibility for this planning rob students of the opportunity to become involved in their education and to make decisions about their lives. Children who comply and follow teacher direction may remain dependent on support from others and fail to develop the creative initiative characteristic of mature learners. Children who do not comply and resist teacher direction may be communicating their inability to perceive the relevance of the instructional program in their lives.

A related point is that people do not increase awareness because they are told or instructed to do so. As mentioned previously, awareness cannot be forced; it must come from within. Learning involves awareness; therefore, teaching that is dogmatic, undemocratic, or highly directive, and that does not promote awareness and responsibility, cannot result in real learning. Carl Rogers has much more to say about this point, as discussed in the following section.

Client-Centered Therapy

The basic tenets that underlie client-centered therapy were introduced in Chapter 2 of this book. Rogers's approach is explored further here because he was interested in the application of his techniques with children (see *The Clinical Treatment of the Problem Child*, 1939) and in education (see *Freedom to Learn*, 1969).

To briefly reiterate, the basic philosophy associated with Rogers's work is that individuals have the power to make constructive choices and to strive toward self-actualization. Individuals are inherently "good" (cooperative, trustworthy, rational, realistic, forward moving) but can develop emotional problems when their basic needs for love, security, and acceptance are not met and when they are deprived of *unconditional positive regard*. Healthy self-concept and self-regard are related to positive regard from significant others that is not contingent on proving worthiness (conditions of worth). When love and positive regard are not given or are given inconsistently (as when parents withdraw love when they disapprove of behavior), children are unable to develop a healthy level of self-regard. Their perceptions of experiences in the world become distorted or are denied awareness. In Rogers's terms, *incongruence* between self and experience develops; an individual's awareness of events does not conform to reality as it is perceived by others. Internalized constraints limit ability to recognize feelings and impair social interactions.

The more incongruent the individual's self-structure, the greater the probability of threat from without. Incongruent information either elicits anxiety or evokes defensiveness. Highly defensive individuals are closed to input; their perceptions are rigid and inaccurate. In a social encounter, a defensive individual literally may fail to hear or see specific threatening events (block them from awareness) or may use any of a series of defense mechanisms to combat them (denial, rationalization, projection, etc.). For example, a student with poor self-regard may not hear compliments, may perceive neutral remarks as pejorative, or may deny (be unable to recognize) the accuracy of a remark describing her behavior.

Therapeutic Goals and Techniques

The primary goal of Rogerian therapy is to resolve incongruence, thus helping the individual use his inherent tendency toward self-actualization to move toward psychological health. Psychological health is represented by a person's becoming more open to experiences and less defensive, more realistic and objective in perceptions, more effective in problem solving, more accepting of self and others, and more creative (Rogers, 1959). The psychologically healthy individual is a fully functioning person (Rogers, 1969), unafraid to experience life, challenged by events, able to give up the need to be "in control" of all events, and able to do what "feels right." This concept of a fully functioning person is similar to Maslow's concept of a self-actualized person (see Chapter 2).

For an individual to accomplish this goal, the therapeutic environment must be nondirective; the client must define the direction of the therapy. Phenomenological therapy is based on the premise that human beings have the capacity to make good choices, to regulate and control themselves, and to develop a system of constructive values that will guide them to living a socially rewarding life—if they are permitted to explore their inner selves in a warm, accepting, secure environment. The therapist facilitates the client's progress by providing an environment in which positive regard is unconditional, that is, in which the client is accepted without qualification. All of the client's thoughts and feelings are considered relevant and are freely expressed as the therapist attempts to understand the client's internal world. When clients avoid discussing difficult issues or topics related to problems, they have not yet developed the level of trust necessary to explore them. The therapist does not press the clients, because the desire to address these issues must come from within. Each client's subjective experiences are of critical importance because every individual is unique and therefore perceives events differently. Although there may be an objective reality, people live in their personal, subjective worlds, and the ideas that they view as truth (confirmed scientific knowledge) are actually their subjective perceptions of truth.

As with gestalt therapy, the techniques associated with client-centered therapy are less important than the attitude and philosophy of the therapist. Basically, the therapist must develop an empathetic understanding—that is, walk in the client's shoes—and must communicate a sincere attitude of caring to the client. The most important technique to bring about this highly personal, trusting relationship is *reflective* or *active listening*, which involves permitting the client to discuss what is of interest without providing answers, interpreting what is said, or pushing for further information. Other techniques used are *empathetic responses* (Wolfgang, 1999). For example, *questioning* (requests for clarification or amplification) is an empathetic response when it reflects the therapist's real desire to understand (enter the private world of) the client. *Restatement* of the client's remarks also is used to help clarify feelings or ideas; however, the restatement must be nonjudgmental. The therapist is reacting to the client's experience, not reinterpreting it from his own frame of reference. *Encouraging* or *reassuring remarks* may be used sparingly to help the client appreciate that she is understood or supported. Other forms of communication may be postural or vocal (but not verbal); the therapist may nod his head affirmatively or make a sound such as *hmm* to signify interest. No technique is used self-consciously to manipulate the client into providing further information.

The nondirective role played by the therapist communicates that the responsibility for progress lies with the client. Initially, this may be difficult for the client to accept, because it does not conform to the typical roles of "superior doctor" and "inferior patient" associated with society's dominant medical model. Rogers (1961) observed that clients often are discouraged in the early stages of therapy. However, as time passes and they become increasingly open to experiences, they progress through periods of widely conflicting feelings (ups and downs), until eventually they reach a stage of self-acceptance and self-regard that enables them to continue their growth process without further formal therapy.

As is true of gestalt therapy, the client-centered approach focuses on current events rather than the past and places greater emphasis on feelings rather than cognitions. The client's increased awareness of currently existing feelings about self and others promotes greater congruence between his perceptions and reality.

Rogers's approach varies from gestalt therapy in his insistence on positive regard and empathetic understanding of clients without the confrontation used by Perls to force clients to examine their attitudes.

Efficacy and Criticism

Rogers is almost unique among the phenomenological theorists in his interest in empirical research of his psychotherapeutic techniques. He used recordings of therapy sessions to make objective analyses of the processes so that he could study behavior and attitudes throughout the proceedings. However, he regarded the quality of his encounters with his clients as more important than any other variables, including the specific techniques employed. Although the constructs he investigated, such as unconditional positive regard and congruence, are measured in the therapeutic process, they are not related to specific strategies or techniques. Consequently, as was true of Perls, there is evidence that Rogers was successful as a therapist. He created a warm, accepting environment, and his clients gained ability to see themselves and their environments more realistically. However, it is difficult to document the strategies he used so that other therapists could use them successfully. Instead, Rogers implied that any of a variety of strategies can be used, as long as the therapist is nondirective (nondogmatic), holds increasing congruence as a goal, provides unconditional positive regard, and maintains the appropriate empathetic attitude toward the client.

Therapists holding alternative orientations dispute Rogers's opinions regarding the requisite conditions in therapy to bring about a basic change in personality. For example, Ellis (1959) believed that, of Rogers's criteria for successful therapy, only empathy is essential. Other forms of criticism leveled at Rogers's approach involve issues of its applicability with individuals who are not highly verbal and intelligent. For example, critics have questioned the feasibility of expecting a nonverbal, acting-out adolescent to reach into her subjective stream-of-consciousness to discuss feelings that promote incongruence with the environment. Another criticism is that the approach does not focus sufficient attention on cognitions or make sufficient use of the realities of the objective world (as others see it) to help clients accept responsibility and restructure their lives. Finally, although some individuals accept the validity of many of the major premises associated with the nondirective approach, they argue that the therapist's relatively passive role delays the client's growth and that the process takes far longer than would be the case if the therapist were more directive.

Despite criticism of client-centered therapy and its relatively slight emphasis on uniform methodology and procedures, Patterson (1980) pointed out that extensive evidence in the literature indicates that the client-centered approach has been used effectively with a wide variety of individuals with emotional problems.

Educational Application

Rogers was extremely interested in the application of phenomenological principles in education. As a professor of psychology who taught for many years at
various universities and institutes around the country, he saw many potential
parallels between the functioning of a teacher (Rogers preferred the term *facilitator*) and a therapist, and he presented his ideas in *Freedom to Learn* (1969).
Success in both activities is related to the establishment of a warm, supportive
environment that facilitates human growth. Traditional approaches to education characterized by dominant teachers serving as imparters of knowledge to
passive, subordinate learners not only fail to promote learning but also actually
contribute to the loss of self-esteem that constitutes the root of psychological
disturbance.

Rogers believed that, to function in an environment that is constantly
changing, students must be educated in the process of learning, not merely supplied with static knowledge, soon to be outdated. Teachers should be facilitators of learning, just as client-centered therapists facilitate a client's psychological growth. The same phenomenological principles designed to enhance
self-esteem and promote self-actualization apply in each circumstance.

Real learning (not the temporary memorization and regurgitation of facts or
the routine compliance with teacher direction that often passes for learning) is
an inner-directed activity. Simply stated, people learn very efficiently when
they initiate the learning and when learning is experiential. Student-initiated
learning is significant learning, and it occurs only when students see the subject
matter as relevant to their lives. For example, people learn rapidly and efficiently when they perceive that learning will enhance their lives and when they
want to achieve a particular goal (e.g., an adolescent learning to drive a car).

In addition, real learning often involves a change in self-organization
(one's view of oneself), which is threatening. The male student who has internalized sexist attitudes regarding the inherent inferiority of females has difficulty altering those beliefs, regardless of objective evidence to the contrary.
The value that he places on perceiving himself as superior is at risk. Learning
that is threatening to self is more likely to occur when perceptions of external
threats are at a minimum; an accepting environment that permits the student
to arrive at conclusions in his own time, without external pressure, reduces his
defenses of self and enables change to occur.

A large amount of real or significant learning is acquired through doing.
Experiential confrontation with practical, social, ethical, or personal problems
promotes learning. Spending time helping the homeless helps children understand the problems of homelessness. Organizing and conducting an auction for
a charitable cause teaches a variety of useful social and academic skills. Enacting

a play brings drama to life. The more extensive the degree of student involvement in the activities—that is, the more responsibility they assume—the more learning is facilitated. In addition, the more students are involved as whole people—that is, on a feeling level as well as an intellectual level—the more lasting the learning experience.

Finally, real learning is creative learning. Creativity is facilitated when the individual relies on herself, not only to plan and implement a project but also to evaluate her performance. External evaluation does not promote the independence and self-reliance necessary for creative work.

Self-initiated learning is not dependent on the teacher's scholarly knowledge, lectures, curricular planning and so forth but results from the personal relationship between the facilitator and the learner. One quality of the personal relationship that facilitates learning is the realness of the facilitator. Students must see their teachers as real people with real feelings, attitudes, idiosyncratic behavior, and so forth. A real person is not a paragon; she can make mistakes and admit them without concern about playing a "teacher role" and maintaining an image of teacher that is a facade. The facilitator also can show emotion and communicate to students her likes and dislikes without intimidating or rejecting the students.

Other attitudes that facilitate learning are prizing, acceptance, and trust. Rogers explained that these characteristics are nonpossessive caring and acceptance of each student as a separate, worthwhile, trustworthy person. As a unique human being, each student is a conglomerate of positive and negative attitudes, neither more nor less perfect or imperfect than the teacher. Therefore, indications of humanness, such as fear, anger, apathy, and concern about personal adequacy should not be viewed by the teacher as providing a reason to demean, criticize, or otherwise reject the individual. Behaviors and attitudes that reflect human errors and inadequacies (part of the human condition) are altered only when the individual desires to make changes, and that desire is never promoted in a hostile or rejecting environment.

Another element in a facilitative teacher–learner relationship is *empathic understanding*. The teacher must understand what the educational experience is like from the learner's point of view. This ability to stand in another's shoes is dramatically different from the judgmental "I know what's wrong with you" response to children who experience difficulty in school. Rogers believed that teachers should set goals of making one nonevaluative, empathic response per day to a student who is experiencing difficulty.

Structuring the Classroom. Rogers offered specific advice to teachers who are interested in establishing a self-initiated learning approach in their classrooms. An important step in providing such an environment is to discuss with students the problems or issues they regard as real and relevant. Rogers noted that students initially will be confused or resistant to this effort because they rarely are confronted with issues as problems to be solved and have never been exposed to the idea that investigating problems of interest to them is an appropriate learning activity in schools. However, young people have a great deal of intrinsic motivation that may be tapped once they perceive that the teacher is genuine and not willing to accept the traditional teacher role. In time, students will show that they can take responsibility for their learning.

Rogers recommended a variety of strategies and techniques that help children accept the self-initiated approach to learning. One important recommendation is that teachers learn to organize time differently. Rather than devoting inordinate amounts of time to typical activities, such as preparing lesson plans, building examinations, developing units of study, and grading tests, teachers must devote a majority of time to providing resources for learners. In addition to the usual academic materials, such as books, films, and recordings, resources should include speakers, field trips, live animals, plants, and other less typical items and events. Teachers themselves are resources (counselors, lecturers, advisers), to be used by students in any meaningful manner.

In their roles as counselors or advisers to children, teachers should promote the use of the scientific method; that is, they should pose problems and encourage inquiry. The scientific method, in which children formulate questions, conduct investigations, and make autonomous discoveries, is not only an essential tool of self-initiated learning in the classroom but also an approach to learning that facilitates creative discovery throughout life.

A contract is another useful strategy that helps a child plan and implement a learning project. A contract is a written agreement between the student and the teacher that specifies each person's responsibilities. In one type of contract, the student assumes total direction of the learning; the student specifies particular information about the learning task he will undertake, and the teacher agrees to a grade that will be awarded when the obligations are met.

Simulation activities, which are types of experiential learning, also are useful educational activities. Students simulate a component of the social system they are interested in learning about and gain firsthand experience of the processes that occur in real life. For example, after researching and gaining information about political elections, students conduct a simulation, engaging in each related component, such as developing a platform, campaigning, conducting polls, debating, negotiating, deal making, and so forth.

Helping children evaluate their work is yet another facilitative strategy that promotes self-initiated learning. Children should establish criteria that reflect their goals for their projects. Self-evaluation extends their responsibility to include decisions about whether those criteria have been met and expands their experience in functioning as self-sufficient learners.

Strategic grouping of students is an essential strategy in a self-initiated learning classroom. In keeping with Rogers's belief that decisions about learning must come from within, students who choose not to participate in self-initiated learning should not be forced to do so. Teachers can meet their needs by organizing these students into groups and providing conventional instruction, while the self-initiated learners proceed with their own projects. Children might avail themselves of each approach to different degrees and might move from conventional to unconventional learning as they grow more confident from observing the attitudes of their classmates who use the self-initiated approach.

Teachers also should group students whose self-initiated projects indicate common interests. These groups provide an opportunity for students to discuss their unique perspectives, share materials, and cooperate in their learning experiences. Each week, the group should select a chairperson who serves as moderator and a group reporter who notes the group plans. The teacher serves as a consultant to the groups. She also arranges to have personal conferences with students as they plan and proceed with their learning projects in order to help them articulate their specific ideas and clarify the purpose of their endeavors.

In addition to using group formats to facilitate study, teachers should set up encounter groups in which students are permitted to communicate freely about their attitudes, ideas, frustrations, concerns, and so forth. As is true of most activities, students decide whether they will participate in these groups and control the extent of their participation. They also decide about topics for discussion. The stipulation is that everyone's opinion is valued, even if others are not in agreement; no one is censured or rejected. Teachers should participate in these groups on the same basis as the other participants, presenting individual opinions but never dominating or overriding others' points of view. Teachers may take the initiative in sharing thoughts and feelings to provide examples for the students and to establish the climate of frankness and acceptance within the group.

Phenomenological Systems of Behavior Management

The work of Carl Rogers has spawned several structured approaches to managing children's behavior. Two such approaches, Teacher Effectiveness Training and Peer Mediation, are discussed next.

Teacher Effectiveness Training

The developer of Teacher Effectiveness Training (TET), Thomas Gordon (1974, 1988, 1989), studied with Carl Rogers in the 1940s. Gordon was a clinical psychologist whose primary interest was in helping parents (*Parent Effectiveness Training*, 1976) and teachers manage children's behavior using nonauthoritarian methods that avoid power struggles and promote win–win situations. Like Rogers, Gordon believed that power struggles end with either a teacher win or a student win, neither of which results in a constructive solution to a problem. Gordon saw society's reliance on punishment or harsh discipline to train or educate children as a mistake, and he drew upon research showing that severe punishment is related to juvenile delinquency, violent crimes, and aggressive behavior in children to support his position (Gordon, 1989). From Gordon's perspective, authoritarian or controlling teacher behavior can include rewards as well as punishment. Students become dependent on teachers for rewards and fear their loss. Grades and praise are viewed by teachers as forms of reward; in reality, however, grades do not reward anyone but high achievers and may even be detrimental to that group if they cause students to lose their intrinsic desire to learn and they learn only to earn good grades. In like manner, praise is not the reward that teachers believe it to be. Instead, it often is a means to impose the teacher's will on students in order to manipulate and control their behavior. Praise also promotes dependency in students and does not help them learn to take responsibility for their lives and solve their own problems.

To help teachers understand and use Rogerian principles in the classroom, Gordon (1989) reiterated Rogers's basic concepts for effective teaching in reference to a "teacher behavior continuum." The purpose of the continuum is to illustrate strategies that promote open, authentic communication between the teacher and student. Authentic communication involves an honest exchange of thoughts, ideas, and feelings without efforts to control or convince someone of rightness or wrongness. The behaviors in the continuum, arranged from least use of power to most use of power, are as follows:

1. *Silently looking on.* This behavior is used to allow a student time to express a problem. When a student states a concern or opinion, the teacher nods or says "uh-huh" to encourage further remarks. This silence communicates acceptance and encourages sharing.

2. *Nondirective statements.* Nondirective statements also are designed to further communication and help the student reveal the underlying source of his problem. Part of nondirective behavior is active listening, or listening for the real message. For example, if a child says "I hate this school," the teacher's nondirective response, such as "You're not happy with school," simply reflects

the child's feelings without imposing any judgment or opinion. Thus the child is encouraged to provide more information about the problem and the feelings it arouses. Active listening implies recognition that initial remarks should not be taken at face value. Listeners communicate their interest in the speaker and never try to direct the conversation. Nonverbal behaviors such as head nodding (acknowledgments) and open-ended questions, called door openers, such as "Would you like to sit with me and tell me more about it?" aid in active listening.

3. *Questioning.* Step 3 on the continuum involves use of "door openers" or "reopeners" and is used when the child cannot continue without assistance. These questions must never be directive, such as "What about school do you hate?" or "Why do you hate school?" because directive questions often threaten the speaker and evoke either a superficial, evasive response or a quick withdrawal from the conversation.

4. *Directive statements.* Directive statements are included in this continuum because Gordon recognized that teachers must direct student behavior on many occasions, such as when a student is in danger. Gordon called these statements "influencing attempts" to differentiate them from the types of orders, commands, threats, lectures, judgments, advice, and preaching that he believed is typical of teacher discipline. Usually, students understand the difference between directive remarks that convey disapproval or threat and directive statements that ensure their safety and well-being.

5. *Reinforcement.* The next step, reinforcement, is interesting because Gordon reiterated Rogers's disagreement with the principles of behavior modification espoused by the behavioral psychologists (see Chapter 5). He believed that teachers could choose to use two types of authority. Type 1 is desirable because it is based on wisdom and expert advice. Type 2 is undesirable because it is based on power. Gordon regarded both positive (reward) and negative (loss of reward) reinforcement as a means of expanding the teacher's Type 2 authority, designed to ensure control over students. He suggested that use of reinforcement strategies ultimately evokes negative student behavior such as physical and verbal aggression toward others, lying, tattling, cheating, and various types of submissive behavior, such as conforming without question, apple polishing, and withdrawing.

6. *Modeling.* Modeling is important in Teacher Effectiveness Training because of the emphasis on practicing desirable behavior rather than just talking about it. Standards for behavior in school should be consistent for students and faculty; otherwise, students will view teachers as hypocrites and lose respect for authority. For example, corporal punishment should not be practiced in school when students are forbidden to fight. Teachers also should model methods of conflict resolution, discussed later.

7. *Physical intervention and isolation.* These two strategies are not advocated in Teacher Effectiveness Training unless there is physical danger to students.

Problem Ownership. A unique aspect of Teacher Effectiveness Training is a method of evaluating problems to determine whether the student or teacher is most affected. Some behavior, such as incomplete work or frequent unexcused lateness, mostly affects the student. When a student owns a problem, she must solve it. Teachers cannot supply a solution, but they often try by using responses that Gordon refers to as roadblocks. Teachers may use various types of road-blocks that may appear to them to be helpful:

- Commanding or ordering: "Stop that and do this."
- Warning or threatening: "Study or you will fail."
- Moralizing or preaching: "You should know better."
- Advising or suggesting: "Get up earlier to finish your homework."
- Teaching or lecturing: "You will never learn to divide if you can't multiply."

Teachers also may use evaluative or degrading roadblocks:

- Judging or blaming: "You never get your work done."
- Name-calling or labeling: "You act like a baby."
- Interpreting or diagnosing: "You don't really want to try."

Some roadblocks are designed to make the student's problem disappear or to make the student feel better:

- Praising or agreeing: "You did some of the work correctly."
- Reassuring or consoling: "You failed this time, but you can do better on the next test."

In two other types of roadblocks, teachers question to arrive at a solution to the problem or block communication to avoid the problem:

- Probing or interrogating: "Are you getting enough rest at night?"
- Sarcasm or humor: "You're not awake enough to tackle this paper."

All of these road-blocking strategies are ineffective because they interfere with true communication. Teachers using Teacher Effectiveness Training are advised to recognize that the problem belongs to the student. The soundest strategy to help the student solve the problem is to promote communication with nondirective behavior and active listening. When teachers actively listen, they enable students to understand their problems and propose solutions. Student efforts at self-reliance help them function independently and teach them to be responsible for their behavior.

In addition to student-owned problems, there are obvious situations where a student's behavior creates a problem for the teacher. For example, a child who disrupts class in some way creates a teacher-owned problem that evokes feelings of annoyance, frustration, resentment, anger, or irritation in the teacher. Unlike student-owned problems, teacher-owned problems cannot be handled through active listening. Instead, Gordon recommends that teachers use confronting *I-messages*. I-messages inform the student that the teacher's needs are not being met and that the teacher and student must work together to find a solution. Properly constructed I-messages have three components: *behavior*, *effect*, and *feeling*. The first component, behavior, is always formulated with "when," as in "When I can't continue my instruction because of the noise in the room. . . ." This construction specifies unacceptable student behavior in a nonblaming way. "When" also conveys the idea of a specific event at a particular time, rather than a global problem. The other two points of the I-message convey the effect of the behavior, as in "When I can't continue my instruction because of noise the entire class is forced to waste time," and how the teacher feels, as in "and I am frustrated because I can't do my job and help you learn."

I-messages must be real to students if they are to recognize the ramifications of their behavior. In fulfilling their own needs (e.g., for attention or peer approval) many students lose sight of the impact of their behavior on others. When the teacher does not respond to their behavior with hostility or anger, they have the opportunity to change without losing face. There is no power struggle.

Gordon noted that occasionally students are resistant, even when I-messages are well formulated. In this situation, teachers are advised to shift gears back to an active listening mode to induce the child to communicate his feelings and make it easier for him to change. If that does not work, a strategy called *mutual problem solving* is available. There are six steps in mutual problem solving: (a) define the problem, (b) generate possible solutions, (c) evaluate each solution, (d) make a decision, (e) determine how to implement the decision, and (f) assess the success of the decision (Gordon, 1974, p. 228).

To define the problem, the teacher begins with an I-message that expresses his position and engages in active listening to elicit the student's perception of the situation. Definitions are expressed in terms of conflicting needs, not possible solutions. Solutions are proposed by both parties and written down. The students and the teacher select the best solution from their point of view and offer rationales when they cannot accept a solution. Only solutions that everyone agrees to try may be adopted. Once a solution is selected, the teacher makes sure that it is implemented. Students help define the standards for implementation and participate in evaluating success or failure.

Conflicting Values. Problem-solving strategies often fail when the problem involves a conflict of values. Individuals differ in their beliefs about a multitude of issues, such as religion, profanity, sexual behavior, and manners. On these issues, teachers should share their perspectives with students in an open-minded way without disparaging alternative perspectives. Also, teachers should make themselves available to discuss these issues if students want to do so, or teachers can model their values for students. However, teachers cannot force their values on others without encountering resistance.

Three Spheres of Relationships. Gordon has identified three spheres or types of relationships that teachers have with students: Sphere 1 is one-to-one, Sphere 2 is one-to-group, and Sphere 3 is one-to-all. In the one-to-one sphere, students get concentrated attention from the teacher. This sphere is an ideal place to build a close relationship based on trust and affection. The Rogerian techniques of active listening, door openers, and acknowledgments can be used effectively in this sphere. The one-to-group sphere occurs when a teacher interacts with a small group of four to eight students. Although students must share the teacher's attention, students benefit from the intimate contact in the small group and have a greater opportunity for self-expression. The one-to-all sphere is the least intimate and least evocative of emotional exchanges between the teacher and the students.

A Constructivist Approach. The Teacher Effectiveness Training model of behavior management coincides closely with the constructivist approach to learning. Each student is recognized as a unique individual with unique needs and varied perspectives. Every person's point of view is valued. Students should be encouraged to present their perspectives about their school experience, and their ideas should be treated with respect. As students internalize their value as human beings, their behavior becomes more socially constructive.

Peer Mediation

Peer mediation is a methodology largely based on Rogerian principles. It is designed to promote conflict resolution as an efficient means of resolving problems in school before they erupt into incidents that violate school rules and require discipline. Peer mediation is most effective in a democratic educational climate where teachers surrender absolute control of the classroom to facilitate student decision making. Although many theorists have discussed the value of peer mediation, Bodine, Crawford, and Schrumpf (1994) have provided teachers with a structured program that can be directly applied in the classroom. The essence of their approach is the training of peer mediators to aid students in settling disputes.

According to Schrumpf, Crawford, and Bodine (1997), the implementation of a peer mediation program in a school is done through careful planning that includes multiple steps. The first step is to appoint a planning team consisting of interested faculty and students to coordinate the program and gain a commitment from faculty to participate. Step 2 involves developing policy and establishing time lines for implementation. At Step 3, student peer mediators are nominated, selected, and trained. Steps 4 and 5 involve workshops and other forms of communication for school personnel, students, parents, and community to ensure that the peer mediation process is understood. Step 6 deals with the actual daily operation of the program, for example, scheduling of sessions, supervision, ongoing training, and evaluation of the program.

The training of mediators is based on a response to conflict that is part of the Rogerian perspective. Rogerian theory holds that unsuccessful handling of conflict occurs when school authorities use two types of strategies, either passive acceptance or denial of the problem (a teacher loses and student loses approach) or authoritarian pressure to suppress the problem (a teacher wins and student loses approach or vice versa). The appropriate resolution is a win–win approach in which both participants experience a level of gratification. To promote a win–win situation, the mediator must be trained to be neutral and must be able to use many of the Rogerian strategies, including active listening, restatement of feelings, and nonthreatening questioning.

The specific steps in peer mediation include (a) agreeing to mediate, (b) presenting points of view, (c) focusing on interests, (d) creating win–win options, (e) evaluating options, and (f) creating an agreement. To begin the mediation process, the peer mediator and each participant introduce themselves. The mediator reaffirms neutrality and presents group rules (e.g., all discussions are private, participants take turns speaking and may not interrupt each other, and cooperation in problem solving is expected). Participants must agree to follow the rules.

Following agreement, the mediator elicits points of view from each participant and restates (summarizes or clarifies) each position without voicing any personal opinions or attitudes. Next, the mediator uses nonthreatening questions, for example, "What do you want?" to try to find a point of agreement where interests overlap. Having gotten a clearer idea of each person's goals, the mediator uses brainstorming to elicit ideas for solutions. Participants are instructed to present any idea without judgment or discussion and to present as many ideas as possible. The mediator records each idea presented, and then the participants evaluate each option, indicating which are acceptable or which parts of options are acceptable. The mediator circles these options and questions the participants regarding fairness and workability. Finally, the mediator selects the options that are most acceptable and helps the participants agree to a plan. The agreement is put in writing and signed by the participants.

Peer mediation is an excellent means of introducing democratic principles into the classroom.

Summary

The tenets associated with the phenomenological point of view are unlike many tenets connected with alternative approaches discussed in other chapters of this text. The latter are designed to help teachers aid children in performing more effectively within the framework of the current accepted view of appropriate teacher–learner interaction, which is basically teacher dominated. Conversely, the information presented in this chapter is designed to inspire teachers to use unconventional strategies in the classroom that conform to a different, humanistic model for teacher and learner behavior that shifts responsibility for learning to the learner. Some teachers might share the values that underlie this approach and be willing to take the risks involved in functioning in an atypical manner. Others may regard this approach as unrealistic and have little interest in applying any of the related educational strategies. Still others may consider certain of the associated strategies useful with particular children in specific circumstances. Although the theorists associated with this perspective, particularly Rogers, would encourage teachers to surrender control of instruction, at least in part, to their students, even they, from their theory base, would have to agree that the approach should be used only by those who are internally motivated to use it. Its success depends in great part on the teacher's commitment and on the quality of the personal relationships between teacher and learners.

STUDY QUESTIONS _____

1. Discuss three techniques that Perls advocated to make an individual more aware of and responsible for her actions.

2. Compare and contrast the traditional approach to teaching in most schools with those advocated by Rogers.

3. What characteristics of gestalt therapy are useful in educational settings?

4. Explain the basic premises that underlie the phenomenological approach to therapy.

5. List and discuss the seven teacher behaviors that, according to Gordon, range from the least use of power to the most use of power.

6. Use Teacher Effectiveness Training principles to discuss the steps a teacher should take to deal with a student who is habitually late for class.

7. Present the steps involved in the implementation of a peer mediation program.

References

American Psychiatric Association. (1994). *Diagnostic and statistical manual of mental disorders* (4th ed.). Washington, DC: Author.

Bodine, R. J., Crawford, D., & Schrumpf, F. (1994). *Creating the peaceable school: A comprehensive training program for teaching conflict resolution.* Champaign, IL: Research Press.

Ellis, A. (1959). Requisite conditions for basic personality change. *Journal of Consulting Psychology, 23,* 538–549.

Gordon, T. (1974). *T.E.T.: Teacher Effectiveness Training.* New York: David McKay.

Gordon, T. (1976). *P.E.T.: Parent Effectiveness Training.* New York: David McKay.

Gordon, T. (1988). *Teaching children self-discipline: At home and school.* New York: Penguin Books.

Gordon, T. (1989). *Discipline that works: Promoting self-discipline in children.* New York: Penguin Books.

Levitsky, A., & Perls, F. (1970). The rules and games of gestalt therapy. In J. Fagan & I. L. Shepherd (Eds.), *Gestalt therapy now.* Palo Alto, CA: Science and Behavior Books.

Patterson, C. (1980). *Theories of counseling and psychotherapy.* New York: Harper & Row.

Perls, F. (1969). *Gestalt therapy verbatim.* Lafayette, CA: Real People Press.

Perls, F., Hefferline, R., & Goodman, P. (1965). *Gestalt therapy: Excitement and growth in personality.* New York: Julian Press.

Rogers, C. (1939). *The clinical treatment of the problem child.* Boston: Houghton Mifflin.

Rogers, C. (1951). *Client-centered therapy: Its current practice, implications and theory.* Boston: Houghton Mifflin.

Rogers, C. (1959). A theory of therapy, personality, and interpersonal relationships, as developed in the client-centered framework. In S. Koch (Ed.), *Psychology: A study of science.* New York: McGraw-Hill.

Rogers, C. (1961). *On becoming a person.* Boston: Houghton Mifflin.

Rogers, C. (1969). *Freedom to learn.* Columbus, OH: Merrill.

Schrumpf, F., Crawford, D., & Bodine, R. J. (1997). *Peer mediation: Conflict resolution in schools.* Champaign, IL: Research Press.

Wolfgang, C. H. (1999). *Solving discipline problems: Methods and models for today's teachers* (4th ed.). New York: Wiley.

CHAPTER

SOCIOLOGICAL INTERVENTIONS: ECOLOGICAL, MILIEU, SOCIAL, AND LEGAL

Sociological interventions focus primary attention on forces emanating from the society and from all aspects of the individual's environment. Although much of the terminology used to describe the sociological perspective overlaps in meaning, for the purposes of discussion four terms are presented as independent entities and designated as ecological, milieu, social, and legal.

Introduction

The term *ecology* is defined as a science concerned with the interrelationship between organisms and their environments. The underlying assumption of the ecological model as it pertains to the study of emotional and behavioral disorders (EBDs) is that, in order to understand inappropriate behavior, one must first understand the function of the ecosystem and how it affects and is affected by an individual's behavior. This type of understanding makes it possible to plan interventions that help an individual function more effectively within his environment or ecosystem. According to Cullinan, Epstein, and Lloyd (1991), a behavior disorder is not simply a function of an individual or of any specific aspect of that individual's ecosystem. Instead, it is representative of the entire ecosystem or cultural milieu. Otherwise stated, an individual's behavior reflects the degree of compatibility between the person and the parts of his social system. Each part of the social system functions independently but also interacts with every other part. Behavior reflective of emotional disorders results from conflict between interacting parts.

Apter (1982) and Kerr and Nelson (1983) have identified the critical components of an ecological orientation toward emotional disorders in children: (a) regarding the child as an integral part of a social system; (b) understanding behavior problems exhibited by a child as a lack of balance in the social system; (c) defining the "problem" as a mismatch between the child's abilities and the demands and expectations of the environment; (d) recognizing that the goal of the intervention is to make the system work; (e) accepting that modification of any part of the system can affect other parts of the system; and (f) understanding that intervention requires a multiple focus on changing the child, the environment, and the attitudes and expectations of those in the social system.

In keeping with this holistic emphasis, ecological or milieu therapy is a generic concept implying the creation of a social organization for the express purpose of providing a treatment program for people with emotional disorders. This concept for therapy is based on the premise that the social–psychological forces playing an important role in causing problems must be addressed in their treatment. These forces in the individual's ecology include variables within the school, home, and community. The structure needed to organize a treatment program and to provide the social relationships necessary is called the therapeutic milieu or the therapeutic community.

The psychological theories underlying interventions that reflect a social frame of reference closely resemble aspects of the theoretical underpinnings of the ecological approaches. Individuals are viewed as unique social beings shaped by social forces, particularly by the types of communications they receive from others. The importance of the work of Adler (1973, 1974) and Sullivan (1953) to this type of theoretical approach has been referred to earlier in this text (see Chapter 2). Implications for interventions include an emphasis on social context, social relationships, and social interests.

Interventions based on the laws of the society are also included as reflecting a sociological perspective of EBDs. From this relatively new legal point of view, each individual is perceived as a member of a democratic society entitled to protection under the laws of that society. Also, the society is protected from the deviant behavior of certain citizens. This understanding of individual rights, as they merge and conflict with the rights of others, are important considerations in developing programs to help individuals with EBDs. The work of the attorney Forrest Gathercoal (1990, 1992) is representative of this approach.

This chapter explores various therapeutic applications of ecological theory, beginning with its historic development and including discussions of the therapeutic milieu, the life space interview, crisis intervention, and specific methods for using ecological principles in typical school settings. Also included in the chapter are discussions of a behavior management program that reflects social theory, Dreikurs and Grey's (1968) model of logical consequences, and Judicious Discipline, a behavior management approach based on the laws of the society.

Ecological and Milieu Approaches: History

Schmid (1987) explained that the rudiments of the ecological model can be traced back to antiquity. For the most part, however, the development of ecological principles is a recent phenomenon. In the 18th and early 19th centuries, a humanistic social philosophy influenced the care of the mentally ill in Europe. Essentially this philosophy held that mentally ill people were susceptible to and unable to cope with ordinary environmental stresses that did not disturb well-adjusted people. Thus, disturbed people could be helped by receiving moral, humane treatment and by being taught to cope with stress-inducing environmental influences. According to Schmid, Pinel was one of the first persons to employ basic ecological principles in revolutionizing the care of asylum patients in the 1800s. The York Quakers of England built The Retreat, a therapeutic facility in which patients were treated as guests rather than as inmates (Schmid, 1987). However, this attitude of social responsibility for the emotionally disturbed faded with the advent of the medical model in the late 19th century when the two-person treatment, doctor–patient psychotherapy, emerged and became dominant.

A humanistic social philosophy was reborn in England in 1946. That year, Dr. Thomas F. Main, an army psychiatrist, coined the term *therapeutic community* in writing about residential centers created to handle the enormous numbers of World War II military personnel with emotional disorders (Main, 1946). In the therapeutic community, therapy was an ongoing social process throughout the day, not an isolated verbal exchange between patient and psychiatrist. The staff and patients interacted freely in all aspects of normal living, and the responsibility for improved behavior and better adjustment was shared equally by all. These wards were created throughout England, Scotland, and France, both in hospitals and as self-contained treatment centers, to provide psychiatric treatment and to resettle patients in the communities where they had previously failed to adjust. The techniques used to change social attitudes within the hospital community aided in changing general social attitudes in the community at large.

The concept of the therapeutic community continued to develop under the leadership of Dr. Maxwell Jones, who wrote extensively on the subject and who headed two residential programs in England. His patients not only were involved in an in-hospital community with a definite group culture but also were expected to participate in a vocational program usually outside of the hospital. Jones felt that although the work goal was difficult for the patient, it was a realistic part of therapy and added to the success of the program (Jones, 1953).

Jones also believed it was important to involve the family in the treatment process. Patients were encouraged to return home for periodic visits and were helped to deal with the problems they experienced. Family members were counseled as a prelude to the patient's eventual release. Thus, Jones created a bridge between the therapeutic hospital community and the patient's natural family setting.

Interestingly, Main and Jones differed in their thinking about the role that classical psychotherapy should play in the therapeutic community. Main found the two therapies entirely compatible. In fact, one of his reasons for establishing therapeutic communities for former military personnel was the lack of psychiatrists available after the war (Main, 1946). Jones, on the other hand, believed that traditional psychotherapy had limited value, particularly in the hospital setting. Although the psychiatrist played an active role in Jones's model, it consisted primarily of casual contacts with a patient or with groups of patients in the therapeutic community rather than the traditional individual hour-long session held once or twice a week (Jones, 1953). Although Jones was not against psychiatric intervention, he believed that social and environmental dimensions played a more important role in the rehabilitation of adults with social and emotional disorders (Jones, 1968).

In the United States, the concept of the therapeutic community received only nominal attention until the late 1950s and early 1960s. Prior to that time, only Bettelheim and Sylvester (1948) had made any substantial reference to the notion of a therapeutic milieu. They had attempted to establish a therapeutic milieu in the Orthogenic School at the University of Chicago to avoid the syndrome "psychological institutionalism," found among many children in typical hospital-like settings. According to Bettelheim, psychological institutionalism is the impoverishment of personality that results from the lack of a warm, trusting personal interaction between patient and therapist. Therefore, in Bettelheim's model of milieu therapy, unlike later models, the most important aspect of the therapeutic community was the establishment of a relationship between patient and counselor. It was less important that children with severe disorders establish themselves as members of a social community than that they form a one-to-one relationship with an understanding and flexible adult.

Further development of the therapeutic milieu concept in the European tradition occurred with the work of Fritz Redl. In 1959 he published an article entitled "The Concept of the 'Therapeutic Milieu,'" which presented 12 variables that should be included in an artificially created milieu for disturbed children in a residential setting (Redl, 1959b). (These variables are discussed later in this chapter.)

Long before his article appeared, Redl was exploring the rationale of clinically exploiting the life events of children in a residential setting. In 1946 Redl began Pioneer House, a group home for a small number of severely disturbed children. In what was called "a hygienically prepared climate," Redl and Wineman (1951) structured the entire environment to provide ego support and used the group atmosphere as a diagnostic and therapeutic tool.

Redl took note of Bettelheim's term *therapeutic milieu* in an early book on Pioneer House, *Children Who Hate* (Redl & Wineman, 1951). Whereas Bettelheim thought of the milieu only as exposure to a total environment designed specifically for treatment, Redl believed that the prepared milieu should include aspects of the child's natural environment so that the application of milieu therapy in regular school settings would be possible. Redl believed, however, that for children with severe disorders the residential treatment design is the most effective way to provide treatment.

Redl did not eliminate psychotherapy as a treatment resource in the social milieu; however, he believed that most of the children in residential treatment centers are poor candidates for classical psychiatric treatment. They are often nonverbal, and the enormous experiential gap between their natural lifestyle and the atmosphere of the psychiatrist's office creates a total lack of relevance for the child (Redl & Wineman, 1951). Therefore, the prepared environment of the therapeutic community—in which treatment can be ongoing, 24 hours a day, in the child's own life setting—is, according to Redl, a much more valid model. The most important therapeutic tool in this context is the *life space interview*, a series of strategies for using crisis situations as a basis for treatment, discussed in detail later in this chapter.

Further expansion of the ecological approach into special education occurred during the 1950s and 1960s (Hewett, 1987). In 1956 Nicholas Hobbs began a study of programs for retarded and disturbed children that marked the introduction of the ecological model into the mainstream of special education. Hobbs (1966) argued that children learned inappropriate behavior from environmental events and that effective treatment must not only identify social realities and the individual's perception of those realities but also involve strategies for adjusting the environment.

In the 1970s Morse broadened the impact of the ecological concepts involved in life space interviewing by emphasizing strategies for *crisis intervention*, to be used in typical school environments. As was true of life space interviewing, crisis intervention involved exploiting naturally occurring situations in the environment to reach children directly after an upsetting event or encounter, when their defenses are lowered (Morse, 1976b). In the 1980s advocates of the ecological model pressed harder to provide more specific methods for teachers to use in classroom situations (Hewett, 1987), and some of those methods are discussed in the ensuing sections of this chapter.

The Therapeutic Milieu

Redl (1966) pointed out that understanding what constitutes a residential treatment milieu for children with severe emotional disorders can aid in designing school and community programs for children who have less serious problems and also can help in establishing preventive programs for all children. There are many therapeutic milieu models in existence today, particularly in drug- and alcohol-treatment centers and in psychiatric hospitals. This chapter concentrates on Redl's model, however, because it deals exclusively with children and it lends itself to wide application.

Redl (1959b) included 12 variables in the therapeutic milieu. Each is discussed briefly.[1]

1. *Social structure.* The social structure must encourage responsibility and decision making. Therefore, it must be more like a democratically run summer camp than a typical medical facility with a rigid fixed-status hierarchy of social positions that places the patient at the bottom.

The social structure must resemble the child's actual world and take advantage of the natural relationships among each child and the members of her ecosystem. In an ecologically oriented treatment center, the usual hospital class system is mitigated by establishing patient governments and by holding community meetings where the patients have a great deal to say about how the community is to be run (Rossi & Filstead, 1973).

2. *Value system.* Adults must communicate their real values to the children. Children are acutely aware of the values held by the adults who deal with them and recognize when their behavior does not reflect those values.

3. *Routines, rituals, and behavioral regulations.* Redl stated that all individuals have rituals or repetitive behaviors in their life spaces. Some rituals are

---

[1] Adapted from "The Concept of a Therapeutic Milieu," by F. Redl, 1959, *American Journal of Orthopsychiatry,* 29, pp. 721–734. Copyright 1959 by the American Orthopsychiatric Association, Inc. Adapted with permission.

maladaptive and need to be discouraged; however, others can be used therapeutically to promote a sense of security and adaptation to the milieu.

4. *Impact of the group process.* Adults must be aware of the components of the group process: "over-all group atmosphere, scapegoating, mascot cultivation, subclique formation, group-psychological role suction, exposure to group-psychological intoxication, dependency on contagion clusters, leadership tensions and so forth" (Redl, 1959b, p. 723).

5. *Trait clusters.* Although the therapeutic milieu is built around a group concept, each individual reacts to other individual personalities as well as to the group. To create a useful milieu, one must consider personality traits as psychological entities. Because one child's personality can wreak havoc with another's, it is foolish to place together two children whose personalities obviously clash.

6. *Staff attitudes and feelings.* The attitudes and feelings of the staff are perhaps the most important component of the milieu. The staff—psychiatrists, psychologists, teachers, aides, medical personnel, dieticians, cooks, and so on—must be able to give emotionally, to share feelings and opinions, and to communicate with understanding and without judgment.

7. *Behavior received.* Each child is affected by behaviors and feelings from other children, as well as from the staff. The staff help the patient understand the behaviors received from others and react to them in a beneficial way.

8. *Activity structure and nature of constituent performances.* The activities a child is asked or allowed to do constitute a large part of the impact of the milieu. Exposing children to games or activities that have rules and regulations is of clinical significance.

9. *Space, equipment, time, and props.* The distribution of time and the arrangement of space and equipment are important properties of the milieu. For example, if a teacher has begun to discuss a problem with a child and the bell rings for swimming, the effort was wasted. Similarly, if a child is given an intense life space interview in a noisy gym, the effort is in vain. The child's attention will not be focused on the interview.

10. *Seepage from the world outside.* Children are exposed to outside influences through television, movies, visitors, trips, and so forth. Any of these events may influence a child's behavior.

11. *System of umpiring services and traffic regulations between environment and child.* This system takes two forms. The first involves protecting a child from a situation or from other children. The second is to interpret experiences that a child may not understand.

12. *Thermostat for the regulation of clinical resilience.* This variable refers to flexibility. The milieu must reflect the changing needs of the children.

These 12 variables describe Redl's basis for the therapeutic community in a residential setting. However, many features of the total therapeutic milieu are applicable to school settings. Redl and Wattenberg (1959) offered five guidelines designed to help teachers implement ecological principles in the classroom.

1. *Sociometric studies.* The use of a sociogram or friendship chart can be very revealing to a teacher, who may be aware of only the obvious relationships in the class. Asking questions such as "Who would you like to sit next to you?" "Which children in the class would you choose to spend the weekend with you?" or "Who would you least like to have sit with you at lunch?" can give the teacher insight into the entire social structure of the class.

2. *The group as an organism.* A class generally assumes its own distinctive personality after being together for a considerable amount of time; for example, some classes are competitive, whereas others are cooperative. Although it may be difficult to predict what personality a group will assume, indications can be drawn from the group's previous behavior. Placing a child with an emotional disorder in a class that appears to accommodate him may make a great deal of difference in the child's behavior.

3. *Cliques and subgroups.* The personality of a group is due in part to the cliques and subgroups that form within it. Cliques vary in their attitudes and behaviors. A troubled child must be placed in a receptive clique. Practical events such as carefully selecting a child's class seat, lunch hour, or reading group may enable a teacher to attach the child to a group whose influence will be beneficial or to remove the child from one that is harmful.

4. *Role concepts and expectations.* Role expectations affect the tone of the whole group as well as individual members. For example, a particular clique may think of themselves as leaders and work hard to maintain the role. Individuals also fall into certain role classifications. Redl lists five roles that can be found in most classes:

- *Leaders.* In some groups the leader remains constant, whereas in others the role is assumed by many different people. Redl described a leader as a superior group member, exceeding the other members in intelligence, scholarship, responsibility, social participation, and socioeconomic status. However, he also pointed out that not all groups will tolerate a "superior leader." In some cases a group selects an individual who is deficient in the above characteristics and who exerts a negative influence on them. When this occurs, as it does often in school situations, the teacher has to analyze the sources of the leader's power. Is she using fear tactics or blackmail? It may then be necessary for the teacher to destroy the leader's influence by direct intervention or exposure.

- *Advocates.* Some children may not be leaders but may be thought of as such because they are facile and creative talkers. They become the negotiators or lawyers for the group. The teacher, however, must realize that their influence over the group may not be very strong.

- *Clowns.* These children usually are placed in this position by the group. Their sense of humor often is leveled at themselves, and self-display tactics frequently are used to draw attention away from the group. Often, but not always, the clown is very fat or very thin and many times feels inferior in some way. Occasionally, the class clown sets himself up as a reliever of tension, which can be a positive factor for the group. The teacher needs to understand this child's motivation to help him understand his own behavior.

- *Fall guys.* In some cases the child who takes the blame for the group's mistakes is satisfied by this role because she may feel that it impresses the group. The teacher should recognize that, in most cases, this is a weak and often incompetent child who thinks of herself as a dope and therefore feels she deserves everything she gets. The teacher must take care not to place the blame where it is easily laid but to find the real source of the problem.

- *Instigators.* These children often are responsible for class problems, but they are careful to remove themselves from direct involvement. The teacher must expose these tactics so that the group, and particularly the fall guy, can disengage from the instigator. It is also necessary for this kind of child to understand what he is doing and to know that suggestions of wrongdoing are often more serious than the actual deeds.

5. *Group atmosphere and group morale.* The atmosphere and morale of a group are extremely important components of a therapeutic milieu. The teacher is the most important agent in influencing the social climate of a classroom. One way of creating a positive group morale is by lessening teacher control of classroom activities. A teacher-directed class provides few free choices to children and is less stimulating to children than an individually paced program with activities that vary. Morale also is enhanced when the teacher's role as the center of attention in the class is reduced. In a teacher-centered class, a child is dependent on teacher approval. In a learner-centered class, where problem solving is a goal, the teacher reassures rather than directs. The most important determinant of group morale is the teacher's attitude toward the children. Children are more responsive to what teachers do than to what they say. By encouraging creativity, avoiding expressing hostility, and communicating acceptance of a child even when correcting maladaptive behavior, a teacher models

constructive attitudes and behaviors that children learn to imitate and creates a positive atmosphere for learning.

Life Space Interview

Perhaps the most important component of the therapeutic milieu as Fritz Redl conceived it is the life space interview (LSI). It reflects his assumption that therapy should occur throughout a child's day, not just during sessions with a psychiatrist. Although occasionally the impact of the environment is enough therapy for a child, more often it takes a trained adult to serve as a mediator between the environment and the child. The child's experiences in the therapeutic milieu may go unnoticed if there is no interpretation of those events.

In contrast to traditional interview techniques that refer to events long since past, the LSI is based on immediate events in the child's life. A particular incident serves as the focus of the interview, which is held immediately after and in the same vicinity as the incident. Redl (1966) proposed that anyone with whom the child interacts, such as parent, nurse, teacher, or bus driver, should be trained to conduct an LSI when the child is involved in a stressful situation or displaying maladaptive behavior. Redl's methods are used today by teachers, counselors, public school administrators, and administrators of educational treatment centers (Long, Wood, & Fecser, 2001; Naslund, 1987; F. Wood, 1990).

Life space interviewing requires both the interventionist and the student to have an adequate level of cognitive and verbal skill. Heuchert (1983) believed that the interviewer must be able to (a) evaluate her own and her student's affective state, (b) influence the student to think rationally, (c) identify stimulus for change, and (d) design a plan with follow-through. M. Wood and Weller (1981) and Long et al. (2001) compiled a list of prerequisite skills a child should possess in order to participate in an LSI. These skills include (a) some degree of awareness of self, events, and other people; (b) sufficient attention span; (c) ability to comprehend content of communication and to respond to verbal stimuli; (d) sufficient memory function to store and recall basic information; (e) some degree of trust that the interviewer really cares; (f) ability to produce sufficient oral or manual language to represent the crisis event; (g) ability to describe the characteristics of self and others; (h) ability to relate personal experiences; and (i) ability to give reasons why events occur.

Although the literature shows variations in the use of the LSI, there is consistency about the interviewing process. Generally, the interview takes place shortly after a student displays some problematic behavior. The interviewer responds to the incident by engaging the student in conversation in order to identify the antecedent factors that precipitated the behavior and to assess the child's cognitive and affective condition. By posing a series of questions, the interviewer tries to guide the student to rational thinking. When necessary, the interviewer corrects the student's perceptual distortions and presents reality. Through the process, the professional maintains a nonjudgmental but influential position, and by listening carefully conveys support to reduce the emotional intensity of the incident. The interviewing process ends with the interviewer and student reaching an agreement on more appropriate conduct for similar problems that might occur in the future.

There are six types of clinical LSIs, all focusing on immediate events in the environment (Redl, 1959a). With the exception of one interview, Emotional First Aid on the Spot, the goal is to help the child make lasting changes in his perception of the world.

1. The Reality Rub interview is used when a child consistently misperceives or distorts reality. Some children may twist reality as a defensive maneuver to gain exoneration from any wrongdoing or to protect self-esteem, whereas others may simply misinterpret environmental events. For whatever reason, it is critical that the misinterpretations be pointed out and that the child be helped to see the real situation (e.g., a relationship between behavior and realistic consequences).

2. Symptom Estrangement is used with children who use the symptoms of their disturbance for their own benefit. Typically, these children behave irresponsibly to satisfy shortsighted needs and regard their behavior as justified by the circumstances. This interview attempts to help the child examine the events that lead up to the maladaptive reaction and consider more appropriate, and potentially satisfying, ways of responding. For example, a child provoked into fighting by another child's teasing may ultimately learn that discussing the situation with a teacher may be more beneficial than fighting and getting suspended from school.

3. The Massaging Numb Value Areas LSI is used to appeal to a child's value system in order to make a case against the child's behavior. By way of value sensitivity and reasoning, a child may come to realize how his behavior has actually violated personally held standards for proper conduct. For example, a child with poor impulse control may learn not to punch a younger child, if he is made cognizant of his own belief that it is inappropriate to pick on someone younger and smaller.

4. New Tool Salesmanship is used to teach new social and interpersonal skills to children through life experiences. Often, this interview is used when other approaches are not applicable or when a child's behavior continues to be self-defeating. This LSI provides the child with alternative ways to handle a given situation.

5. Manipulation of Body or Self Boundaries is used when a child is vulnerable to the exploitation of others. Certain life incidents can be used to increase the child's feelings of self-worth. For instance, a child's good performance on a test can serve as a praiseworthy incident. Both the successful experience and the exposure to the person offering praise helps expand the child's boundaries toward the development of a healthier attitude of self-worth and pride.

6. Emotional First Aid on the Spot is used to give immediate support to a child in a stressful situation without the added purpose of a long-term therapeutic goal. Support can be in the form of listening, helping the child vent her anger, providing encouragement, maintaining communication until the child is less upset, reiterating the rules or regulations that may bear on the situation in a nonjudgmental way, or mediating in fights or conflicts.

William Morse (1969) called for the use of the LSI not only when a crisis occurs but also in less emotionally charged situations with typical children who experience problems. Morse believed that many techniques for behavior management commonly used by teachers have little effect on children. He suggested that teachers use the LSI for working through problems that occur in any classroom. To assist educators, Morse (1976b) provided a worksheet on life space interviewing with seven categories of information. The interview should explore (a) the events that instigated the problem; (b) the extent to which the problem is an isolated event or an indication of a basic pattern of behavior; (c) the child's opinion about the situation and possible solutions to the problem; (d) the child's feelings about the matter; (e) whether the child has coping skills that can be used in similar situations; (f) the means to prevent the problem from reoccurring; and (g) the school rules that pertain to the situation. Throughout these steps, it is essential that the interviewer remain nonjudgmental and listen closely without communicating anger or rejection. Additionally, the interviewer must be realistic, illustrating the relationship between behavior and consequences while helping the child produce ideas for the mitigation or solution of the problem. The interviewer should not feel obliged to solve the problem.

Crisis Intervention. The concept of crisis intervention associated with LSI was expanded by Morse (1971), who emphasized its use in schools that maintain children in least restrictive settings. The use of crises as a resource for helping children had been advocated by Caplan (1963), who noted that children experiencing intense emotions such as guilt, shame, anger, fear, and anxiety are less resistant to adult assistance. The individual who helps them cope with their feelings also is able to promote growth and change. Gilliam (1993) believed that all teachers of students with EBDs should be prepared to deal with crises.

Morse (1971, 1976a) advocated the use of a crisis teacher or helping teacher in schools to perform crisis intervention. Unlike most classroom teachers, this individual is available to intervene immediately, when and where a problem occurs. Brenner (1963) also advocated the use of a crisis teacher; however, in cases where a crisis teacher is not available, Brenner stated that the school principal rather than the classroom teacher should handle crisis situations. Brenner listed 10 points that enable an individual who did not witness the event, such as a school principal, to conduct a useful interview.[2]

1. *Be polite.* Treat the child as you would the parent, listening to what she has to say and not answering your own questions.
2. *Don't tower over a little child.* Offer the child a chair, and sit down on his level. Do not put a child in a situation where he feels trapped.
3. *When you are sure of your ground, confront a child with your knowledge of her misdeed.* This tack will not work with a child who thinks everyone is against her, but it can give most children a sense of security to know where they stand.
4. *Be sparing with your use of "why."* It is better to suggest talking about what happened or, if that is not working, to suggest a solution rather than to ask a child why he thought of doing such a terrible thing.
5. *Converse about the actual situation.* Stay on the subject and listen to the child's description of the event.
6. *When a child appears overwhelmed by guilt or shame, begin by minimizing the weightiness of the problem at hand.* Suggest that the child is not the only one who has been in this situation, that a solution is possible, and that you will work together to find it.
7. *Say what you believe the child is thinking but unable to put into words.* Comments such as "You were angry, weren't you?" or "Your feelings were hurt, weren't they?" are helpful because they are said without judgment, whereas "You're sorry, aren't you?" might well be judgmental and is therefore less desirable.
8. *Be aware of the kinds of thinking demanded by the situation.* Do not expect a child to think about a solution the way an adult might. Children do not think as adults think.
9. *Help the child with plans for specific steps to improve the situation.* Some children become so frightened by what they think might happen at home that they cannot think rationally about a solution to the problem. Their anxiety

[2] Adapted from "Life Space Interview in the School Setting," by N. B. Brenner, 1963, *American Journal of Orthopsychiatry, 33,* 717–719. Copyright 1963 by the American Orthopsychiatry Association, Inc. Adapted with permission.

must be reduced, and they must feel assured that the teacher means to help before any solution can be found. In these cases, it often is best to assure the children that the problem will be handled at school.

10. *At some point in the interview, give the child an opportunity to ask you questions.* A lot of information can be gathered by listening to a child's questions. A frightened child may have blown an incident totally out of proportion, and your answers may serve to put it in perspective.

Additional Applications to School Settings

Each preceding section of this chapter contains suggestions for applying certain aspects of ecological and milieu theories to school settings. For the most part, however, these suggestions are designed to increase teacher knowledge of ecological principles and goals. The ideas of Redl, Morse, Hobbs, and others are highly informative and thought provoking but have been criticized by Hewett (1987), Gardner (1990), and others for their lack of specificity and their lack of utility in the classroom. In that context, the more current literature includes compilations of more specific strategies for teachers in planning or structuring the school environment, counseling students, and working with parents.

Structuring the School Ecology

Noting that any approach not developed beyond a theoretical stage will fade with time because it lacks proven utility, Hewett (1987) discussed the need to develop a bridge between the ecological approach and educational reality in the classroom. He proposed the concept of person–environment fit as providing more direct ecological guidelines for hands-on practices. The person–environment fit is composed of four elements: the person, the environment, the person's perception of self, and the person's perception of the environment. The teacher is advised to explicitly define each component to determine to what degree the person and the person's perceptions coincide with environmental expectations: "Lack of fit, stress, and possible maladjustment occur when environmental expectations do not fit or match up with a person's characteristics, when environmental reinforcers or punishment are not appropriate to personal characteristics, or when persons view themselves or their environments inaccurately" (Hewett, 1987 p. 63).

Evans and Evans (1987) provided guidelines for the preparation of a behavior management plan that integrates ecological variables. Using behavioral language and principles, they called for a quantitative definition of the behavior to be altered (see Chapter 5) but expanded the paradigm to include an evaluation of the setting and the degree to which the behavior differs from expectations, demands, or levels of tolerance of others. They also advocated evaluating the success of the intervention through evidence of changes in the targeted behavior, another strategy borrowed from the behavioral model.

In directing attention to environmental variables, Evans and Evans (1987) identified three groups of important variables: biophysical, physical, and psychosocial. Biophysical variables include information on health (e.g., diet, illness, fatigue), physical impairments (e.g., neurological disorder, sensory loss), and drug usage (e.g., medication, alcohol, illicit drugs). Physical variables include resources and conditions in the home and school (e.g., food, supervision, privacy, materials, physical plant), as well as in the classroom (e.g., lighting, temperature, learning climate, instructional materials, appropriateness of curriculum). Psychosocial conditions include emotional and learning impairments, intrapersonal factors (e.g., interests, values, expectations), and interpersonal factors (e.g., the effect of behavior on teachers, parents, and peers).

Hendrickson, Gable, and Shores (1987) also combined ecological and behavioral principles. They extended the applied behavior analysis paradigm (stimulus–response–consequence) to include setting events (ecological variables) that influence the impact of antecedent stimuli on behavior. The expanded paradigm is setting events–stimulus–response–consequence. These authors cautioned that educators should confine their interest to the components of the ecosystem that pertain to school, because other external variables lie outside their control. Setting events are intrapersonal or physical and social. Within the context of the classroom, intrapersonal events refer to psychological or physiological states such as emotions, hunger, illness, and drug usage. Physical–social events refer to external conditions such as classroom noise, lighting, and teaching arrangements. Both intrapersonal and physical–social events can be manipulated by the educator to enhance the effectiveness of the educational program.

Hilton (1987) provided specific guidelines and rationales for the teacher's ecological plan:

1. Plans for the child must include the nonschool environment.

2. The child should be encouraged to discuss his environment and the significant persons in his life. This information may be shared with those persons if the child grants permission.

3. A list of relevant microcommunities (e.g., Girl Scouts, athletic clubs) should be compiled. Each source listed should be surveyed to ascertain the standards for behavior, as well as the extent to which the child's behavior differs from those standards. A detailed analysis and definition of problem behavior is necessary to establish a baseline reference point, which will be used to monitor any changes in behavior.

4. Teachers should involve other professionals (psychologists, administrators, etc.) in developing plans to alter unacceptable behavior.

5. Whenever possible, parents should be involved in the planning process. The educator or another team member should meet with parents to discuss the child's behavior and to assess the home and community environments. Although parents of children with emotional disorders are often reluctant to become involved in the planning and intervention process, it is important to develop a line of communication and to try to convince parents that their cooperation will improve the child–home relationship.

6. After gathering as much relevant information as possible, teachers should design a formal plan that fosters learning, maintenance, and generalization of the appropriate behaviors. The accuracy of the information will determine the likelihood for designing a successful intervention.

7. Whenever possible, a data bank and communication system should be established to systematically monitor the child's behavior in various environments. This system requires event record keeping to collect information about the specific components that bear on the maladaptive behavior. Without the monitoring of such information, it is impossible to evaluate the appropriateness of the intervention, its effects on all environments, and whether maintenance and generalization of new skills are taking place.

Brendtro and Van Bockern (1998) called for innovative planning, emphasizing the importance of instructional programs that use positive peer groups as primary change agents. Adults must model caring relationships for students to imitate. Youth are trained to assume problem-solving roles and to provide feedback about inconsiderate behaviors to peers. Self-government of this type encourages a positive student response (Lewis & Lewis, 1989). The group teaches new strategies for responsible behavior among members (Rhodes, 1992). Another component of the positive peer culture is helping others in the community, such as older persons and needy families.

Counseling Students

Another ecological theorist, McCarney (1987), opined that students cannot become more productive in school and ultimately in society unless educators assume a more active role in directing their psychological–social development. McCarney recommended that teachers address students' problems related to home and community by devoting more classroom time to discussing values, experiences, emotions, and interests. Buscaglia (1983) recommended that the teacher-counselor model appropriate behavior for students to imitate. For example, an accepting teacher sets an emotional tone for the class that influences the children to be accepting. In an accepting environment, teachers can devote time on a daily basis to group discussions and problem solving. Towns (1991) believed that teachers should use group time to help students share feelings and develop skills dealing with personal and interpersonal experiences. Ottens and Ottens (1982) reported success using counseling strategies within the classroom and training teachers to use those strategies. Armstrong (1998) noted that much of successful instruction has little to do with lesson plans or learning materials and much to do with the spark the teacher brings to the situation.

Working with Parents

In an ecological approach, parents are involved in many components of a child's program. Their input is sought in the development of a plan, and their cooperation in the implementation of a plan is extremely valuable. Because many problems demonstrated in the classroom have their origins in the home, one application of the ecological model is to provide parents rather than children with ongoing counseling or therapy.

Recent ecological programs have focused on comprehensive systems of care for children and their families (Friesen & Wahlers, 1993). Support services have "wrapped 'round" all aspects of children's environments in an effort to address problems in the home and elsewhere outside the school (Duchnowski, Johnson, Hall, Kutash, & Friedman, 1993).

According to Putnam (1987), one means of developing a constructive relationship between the home and the school is through parent–teacher conferences. Conferences may be instigated by either parents or teachers; however, it is incumbent upon teachers to develop a conference plan to increase the probability that the outcome will be positive. Putnam advised use of the following seven-step process:

1. Identify the basic purpose for the conference.
2. Identify the subjects, areas, and topics to be addressed and the information to be shared.
3. Develop a list of questions to be asked.
4. Collect materials to share with the parents.
5. Plan for the introduction of important topics.
6. Plan a way to close the conference in a positive manner.
7. Evaluate the conference.

Social Approach

Psychological theory that reflects a sociological perspective has been proposed by a variety of theorists. Among those individuals, Rudolf Dreikurs's work is most compelling because of his extensive interest in behavior management principles. Dreikurs, a native Austrian, was an early associate of Alfred Adler, the well-known psychotherapist who first introduced many key concepts of social psychology, including *lifestyles, inferiority complex, social interest*, and *striving for superiority*. Strongly influenced by his mentor, Dreikurs adapted and expanded Adlerian principles and presented many of his views in four books: *Psychology in the Classroom* (1968), *A New Approach to Discipline: Logical Consequences* with L. Grey (1968), *Discipline Without Tears* with P. Cassel (1972), and *Maintaining Sanity in the Classroom* with B. Grunwald and F. Pepper (1982). His most significant theoretical principle centers on the notion of mistaken goals and logical consequences for misbehavior. Dreikurs believed that human beings choose to behave in inappropriate ways because they have the incorrect belief that their behavior will meet their basic need for social acceptance. These beliefs or mistaken goals include *attention getting, power seeking, revenge seeking*, and *displaying inadequacy*.

Dreikurs, Grunwald, and Pepper (1982) identified four different attention-getting behavior patterns: active–constructive, passive–constructive, active–destructive, and passive–destructive. Active–constructive children conform to adult expectations but often are excessively perfectionistic and competitive. Passive–constructive children gain attention by manipulating adults with charm or a facade of helplessness. These individuals often are excessively self-centered, vain, and dependent on others. Active–destructive children are defiant and impertinent. They provoke others to gain attention. Passive–destructive children often are identified as "lazy." They try to manipulate others into doing as they wish by sulking and complaining about the difficulty of their work. Providing any of these students with attention, either through excessive praise or criticism, increases their attention-getting behavior. However, when teachers use autocratic or overpermissive strategies to suppress attention-getting behavior, these children often engage in power seeking.

Power-seeking children feel inferior to others and compensate for their feelings by defying adults. They argue, lie, throw tantrums, and engage in other hostile behaviors because they believe that adults dislike or disapprove of them. Their goal is to force a confrontation or power struggle with adults, and that goal becomes an end in itself. Teachers are drawn into power struggles with children when they take personal umbrage and respond to students with their own hostile or repressive strategies. This circumstance always creates a no-win situation for the teacher. If students win power struggles by continuing to engage in inappropriate behavior despite the teacher's efforts, the behavioral strategy is reinforced and they will persist in provoking power struggles. If the teacher succeeds in overpowering students, their behavior worsens and they become revenge seeking.

At the revenge-seeking stage, the student's goal is to hurt others, by behaving cruelly or violently. These individuals invite punishment because it reaffirms their negative attitudes toward authority figures. Punishment does little to improve their behavior. These students receive negative input from others, and, although they behave as though they were indifferent to the opinions of others, they become increasingly convinced of their own inadequacy. They display inadequacy, the final stage in the continuum of inappropriate behavior, when they feel worthless and unloved. At this point, they become totally unmotivated and passive in the classroom. They withdraw from social interactions and are extremely difficult to reach.

Response Patterns

Dreikurs maintained that a child's specific goals can be identified in the classroom by the teacher's response to the inappropriate behavior and by the child's response to discipline (Charles, 1992). If the teacher feels annoyed, the child's goal is attention getting. If the teacher feels threatened, the child is power seeking. If the teacher feels hurt, the child is revenge seeking. If the teacher feels powerless, the student is displaying inadequacy. Similarly, if the child stops an inappropriate behavior, then repeats it on another occasion, he is attention getting. If the goal is power seeking, he will refuse to stop, or increase the behavior; and if the goal is revenge, he will become violent or hostile. Refusal to participate or cooperate indicates that he is displaying inadequacy.

Dreikurs suggested teacher responses for each mistaken goal. Attention-getting behavior should be ignored whenever possible. When it is not possible to ignore a behavior, its significance should be discussed with the child. The teacher should identify the child's need for attention and point out the erroneous thinking that underlies that need. If the behavior persists, one useful strategy is to ask the child how many times he will require attention in a given period of time and to suggest an exaggerated number. When the child misbehaves, the teacher says his name and "number one," continuing to respond in this fashion without anger or recrimination, which would provide the attention the child is seeking. Because the teacher's response is not reinforcing, children often cease the offensive behavior.

The key to blunting power-seeking behavior is to avoid engaging in a power struggle. When teachers are threatened by power seeking, they tend to respond autocratically (with power) and exacerbate the situation. If they refuse to enter a power struggle, they cannot lose and inadvertently increase the student's status, or win and push the child to revenge seeking. They can calmly acknowledge the child's power to disrupt and discuss the thinking and needs that motivate the behavior. They can respond to power seeking by asking the student if his need could be satisfied another way or by openly acknowledging that classroom activity cannot go on until the disruptive behavior ends. Each of these strategies is preferable to increasing the probability that the child will begin revenge seeking.

Revenge seekers are difficult to curb because they do not care about consequences. Teachers must attempt to confer with them frequently, to discuss the irrational ideas that motivate their behavior, and to introduce alternatives that can earn them social acceptance from others. The teacher should provide opportunities for these children to exhibit strengths and should encourage the class to respond with understanding whenever possible.

The greatest challenge lies in motivating students who display inadequacy. Often, teachers ignore these individuals to concentrate on others who are more disruptive. However, teachers should persist in encouraging them to try, should structure situations that promote their success, and should reward their effort. It is important to recognize that their behavior is driven by fear—that they are not good enough to compete with others or to meet expectations. Reiterating that they are failures, with grades, remarks, or negative attitudes, simply reinforces their convictions about their incompetence.

Logical Consequences

According to Dreikurs, undesirable discipline techniques increase inappropriate behavior. Threats, humiliation, punishment, and remarks that display discourtesy, disrespect, dislike, and disgust are examples of techniques that should be avoided. He recommended pairing "logical consequences" with both adaptive and maladaptive behavior as a component of effective discipline, and he differentiated between discipline and punishment. Punishment is assigned arbitrarily to specific students. It is designed to hurt the student and to signify the extent of the teacher's power. The logical consequences necessary for discipline must be developed cooperatively with the class and understood and accepted as fair by the students. Logical consequences must be applied consistently and to everyone because inconsistent use promotes student resistance. With this type of plan, students choose to behave in ways that earn positive or negative consequences. They, not the teacher, determine an outcome. The more logical the relationship between inappropriate behavior and consequences, the greater the probability that students will grasp the significance of misbehavior and accept discipline as just. For example, students who deface school property should clean, repair, or replace it, and a student who disturbs others should be isolated.

Gordon (1989) noted that teachers who use the logical consequences strategy must beware of failing to maintain a clear distinction between consequences and punishment. Frequent review of consequences for behavior with the students in routine group discussions may identify better (more logical) consequences for behavior and prevent students from losing sight of the relationships between behavior and consequences. The opportunity to focus student attention on positive events in the class, engage them in problem-solving strategies, review class members' responsibilities, and discuss future plans is an added benefit of routine group discussions (Dreikurs et al., 1982).

Teaching Styles

Dreikurs equates effective discipline with teachers' styles. *Autocratic* teachers attempt to demonstrate their power over students. They are repressive, intolerant of individual differences, and attempt to control behavior through threats, sarcastic remarks, and punishment. They create behavior problems. *Permissive* teachers lack the courage and ambition to provide structure and order in the classroom. They do not teach their students the relationship between behavior and consequences by establishing fair rules and consistently enforcing them. Permissive teachers also tend to use praise, which focuses on teacher feelings, rather than encouragement, which focuses on the student's efforts. For example, "I like the way you are behaving" is praise, whereas "You must feel proud of yourself for doing so well" is encouragement. Dreikurs believed that praise promotes excessive dependency on the teacher, whereas encouragement promotes self-esteem. Permissive teachers also promote behavior problems.

Democratic teachers treat students with respect, value their opinions, and encourage their participation in operating the classroom. However, behavioral limits are established and enforced, kindly but firmly. These teachers help children learn constructive ways to solve problems and meet their personal goals. Democratic teachers help students overcome behavior problems.

Teachers are encouraged to recognize the relationship between their style and student behavior and to attempt to operate democratically.

Dreikurs's Disciples

Since Dreikurs's death, a number of disciples have expanded his work. Linda Albert published *A Teacher's Guide to Cooperative Discipline: How To Manage Your Classroom and Promote Self-Esteem* in 1989. Donald Dinkmeyer and G. D.

McKay developed the *Systematic Training for Effective Parenting* (STEP) program in 1976 and with various colleagues updated the program in 1983 (Dinkmeyer, McKay, Dinkmeyer, Dinkmeyer, & McKay, 1983). In 1987 Jane Nelsen published *Positive Discipline*, and that program was expanded in 1993 (Nelsen, Lott, & Glen, 1993). Dinkmeyer integrated the concepts of student choice, need to belong, and goal satisfaction into the STEP program. In so doing, he created a user-friendly method of applying these concepts. In the cooperative discipline program, Albert presented five key steps for teacher use. She recommended that the teacher describe the misbehavior, identify the goal of the misbehavior, choose the intervention techniques to be used, choose the encouragement techniques, and plan for parent involvement. Building self-esteem is a primary goal of Albert's program and, like Dreikurs, she emphasized the need to help problematic students be part of the class through the use of democratic procedures. To assist teachers, Albert provided practical suggestions for dealing with each of Dreikurs's four types of inappropriate student behavior patterns. Techniques to curb attention-getting include minimizing the behavior (e.g., ignore, stand near, give secret signal), legitimizing the behavior (e.g., have entire class join in, teach a lesson about the behavior), doing the unexpected (e.g., turn out the lights, play music, lower voice, cease teaching), distracting the student (e.g., ask for a favor, ask a question), noticing appropriate behavior (e.g., thank the student), and moving the student to another seat.

The power and revenge seekers may be countered by exit strategies (e.g., acknowledge student power, remove audience), time-out strategies (e.g., in classroom, in office), and consequence strategies (e.g., sequence of logical consequence rules). The inadequate student can be helped by strategies to avoid failure. These include modifying instructional methods (e.g., concrete materials, self-correcting material), providing tutoring (e.g., teacher, peers), teaching positive self-talk (e.g., positive signs in the classroom), building confidence (e.g., focusing on improvement, acknowledging the difficulty of a task), focusing on past success (e.g., repeating activities that ended in success), and recognizing achievement (e.g., applause, stars, positive time-out).

Nelsen's program emphasizing positive discipline restated many of Dreikurs's basic premises but urged teachers to focus on solutions rather than logical consequences (Nelsen, 1997). Nelsen et al. (1993) also provided valuable suggestions for holding group meetings in the classroom. To focus on solutions teachers should (a) involve students in solutions; (b) focus on the future; (c) teach the relationships among opportunity, responsibility, and consequence; (d) avoid adding punishment to a consequence; and (e) plan solutions carefully. Class meetings are an essential means of reaching solutions. At class meetings mutual respect is promoted, and every student is given the opportunity to offer solutions to problems and to discuss future plans for class activities.

Legal Approach

The legal approach to behavior management is a novel application of the sociological perspective of EBD. *Judicious Discipline* (Gathercoal, 1990), a program based on the application of legal rights, is an attempt to model school rules on the democratic principles established in the U.S. Constitution and Bill of Rights. Certain goals of Judicious Discipline resemble those associated with Dreikurs's logical consequences perspective in that both emphasize the use of democratic teaching strategies. Students are served best by educators who avoid authoritarian approaches that use fear to control behavior and who, instead, respect students' rights as individuals, even when implementing consequences for inappropriate behavior. Democratic approaches to discipline promote feelings and understanding of social responsibility in that they model the types of fair behavior that students need to learn to become valuable citizens in a democracy. Individual rights are those protected by the laws of the land, particularly the First, Fourth, and Fourteenth Amendments to the Constitution. The First Amendment guarantees freedom of religion, speech, the press, peaceful assembly, and the right to redress grievances. The Fourth Amendment protects against unreasonable searches and seizures. The Fourteenth Amendment guarantees all citizens due process of law and equal protection under the law. The legal protection guaranteed by these amendments became important for children in 1969 with the case of *Tinker v. Des Moines Independent School District* (Wolfgang, 1999), in which the U.S. Supreme Court ruled that the suspension of a high school student for protesting the Vietnam War in school was an illegal violation of the right to freedom of speech. Before that ruling, schools held control over student behavior in loco parentis. After that decision, school authorities were required to consider moving away from the use of authoritarian school rules to regulate student behavior because of the possibility of litigation.

In the Judicious Discipline model, the school represents the state. Just as the state establishes laws to protect society without violating individual rights, the school must establish laws that protect the student body and each individual. An individual's rights are negated only when his behavior can be shown to violate or interfere with any one of four areas of state interest: (a) property loss or damage, (b) legitimate educational purpose, (c) health and safety, and (d) serious disruption of the educational process. Therefore, schools may enact rules that prohibit students from engaging in acts such as defacing the school facade (property damage), failing to bring a textbook to class (educational purpose), running in the halls (health and safety), and fighting in class (disruption of the educational process). When enforcing these rules, however, school authorities must grant the student due process. The essential steps in providing due process of law are that students receive adequate notice (a clear description of the rule violated) and a fair and impartial hearing (a meeting that involves all interested parties). Also, due process requires evidence (a report of the inappropriate behavior by a teacher or other witness), opportunity for defense (the time for the student to tell his side of the story), and the right to appeal (to seek a hearing with higher authorities, including a court hearing).

Establishing a discipline policy based on these constitutional rights encourages educators to consider each school rule violation on an individual basis before determining the discipline required, rather than to establish rigid policies (e.g., truancy results in detention) that are always implemented regardless of the circumstances associated with an individual case. A democratic discipline policy also illustrates the advantages of involving students in the formulation of school rules and of ensuring that the agreed-upon rules are published as school policy and disseminated to all students and parents.

Judicious Discipline is not presented as a total model of behavior management. Instead, it is designed to provide a general frame of reference for establishing a democratic classroom and adhering to the law. Teachers are encouraged to reflect on their own teaching styles and evaluate the extent of their authoritarian orientation. Wolfgang (1999) advised teachers to ask themselves questions when confronted with a discipline problem, such as "Do I need more information about the student?" "What strategies will keep the student in school?" "How will the student perceive the consequences?" and "How can I maintain the student–teacher relationship?"

The steps for implementing Judicious Discipline (McEwan, 1991) are as follows:

1. *Make a commitment.* Teacher commitment occurs when the teacher decides to change autocratic procedures used in the past. For example, various rule violations such as lateness, lack of preparation, failure to do homework, and rudeness to others are not automatically countered with an established type of punishment. They are investigated to determine the circumstances contributing to the behavior. Various consequences, logically related to the offense, are enforced depending on those circumstances. Similarly, students who break rules with behaviors such as making inappropriate noise, getting out of a seat without permission, or refusing to follow directions are conferred with privately, not publicly embarrassed by verbal reprimands. Grades are based on academic achievement exclusively. Other behaviors, such as sloppy work or behaving inappropriately in class, do not result in lower grades.

2. *Teach democratic principles*. Democratic principles are important content for classroom instruction. Through the use of questions, the teacher leads the children to discuss the rights they have in the country and in school. The teacher integrates the rights granted in the First, Fourth, and Fourteenth Amendments to the U.S. Constitution into the discussion and explains how those rights provide the basis for school discipline policy.

3. *Establish class rules*. Students help establish class rules. Once again, the teacher uses questioning to elicit opinions about rules for discipline from the students. Students may evaluate how their democratic rights are protected or violated by rules. The teacher must emphasize the limits on individual rights imposed by the need to legally protect the school society as a whole and make clear that violations of state interests—property loss or damage, legitimate educational purpose, health and safety, and serious disruption of the educational process—result in some type of discipline. All school rules jointly created by teachers and students are signed by each student, posted, placed in a student handbook, and sent home to parents.

4. *Teach group vs. individual rights*. The teacher holds frequent discussions of group and individual rights to illustrate the balance that must be maintained. Examples of behaviors are used to clarify concepts so that students understand when their behavior will be stopped by school authorities and will subject them to disciplinary action.

5. *Teach consequences*. The teacher explains the types of consequences for various behaviors that intrude on the rights of others. There should be many consequences to draw from, depending on the circumstances that surround a specific type of behavior. In some cases, more than one consequence should follow inappropriate behavior. Lists of consequences should include apologies, loss of privileges, restitution, social isolation, exclusion from activities, suspension, and expulsion, among others.

Advocates of Judicious Discipline laud the fact that it helps students acquire the skills needed to function well in a democracy. Also, student involvement in formulating disciplinary rules increases the probability that they will be less resentful of authority when they face negative consequences for their behavior. An obvious weakness of this model is that it is logistically impossible for educators to observe every step of the due process aspects in all cases where discipline is required.

STUDY QUESTIONS

1. Present five instances when logical consequences could be used in the classroom.

2. Discuss the life space interview. How can this concept be applied in school settings?

3. What concepts underlie Judicious Discipline?

4. Discuss the role of the crisis or helping teacher.

5. Trace the theoretical roots, in terms of the models presented in Chapter 2, that have contributed most to the development of the sociological intervention strategies.

References

Adler, A. (1973). *Individual psychology* (P. Rodin, Trans.). Totowa, NJ: Littlefield Adams.

Adler, A. (1974). *Social interest, a challenge to mankind* (J. Linton & R. Vaughan, Trans.). New York: Capricorn Books.

Albert, L. (1989). *A teacher's guide to cooperative discipline: How to manage your classroom and promote self-esteem.* Circle Pines, MN: American Guidance Service.

Apter, S. (1982). *Troubled children.* New York: Pergamon Press.

Armstrong, T. (1998). *Awakening genius in the classroom.* Alexandria, VA: Association for Supervision and Curriculum Development.

Bettelheim, B., & Sylvester, E. (1948). The therapeutic milieu. *American Journal of Orthopsychiatry, 148,* 121–206.

Brendtro, L. K., & Van Bockern, S. (1998). Courage for the discouraged: A psychoeducational approach to troubled and troubling children. In E. Meyen, G. Vergason, & R. J. Whelan (Eds.), *Educating students with mild disabilities* (pp. 112–140). Denver, CO: Love.

Brenner, N. B. (1963). Life space interview in the school setting. *American Journal of Orthopsychiatry, 33,* 717–719.

Buscaglia, L. (1983). *The disabled and their parents.* Thorofare, NJ: Slack.

Caplan, G. (1963). Opportunities for school psychologists in the primary prevention. *Mental Hygiene, 47,* 525–539.

Charles, C. N. (1992). *Building classroom discipline: From models to practice* (4th ed.). New York: Penguin Books.

Cullinan, D., Epstein, N., & Lloyd, J. W. (1991). Evaluation of conceptual models of behavior disorders. *Behavioral Disorders, 16,* 148–157.

Dinkmeyer, D., & McKay, G. D. (1976). *Systematic training for effective parenting* (STEP). Circle Pines, MN: American Guidance Service.

Dinkmeyer, D., Sr., McKay, G. D., Dinkmeyer, D., Jr., Dinkmeyer, J. S., & McKay, J. L. (1983). *The next step*. Circle Pines, MN: American Guidance Service.

Dreikurs, R. (1968). *Psychology in the classroom* (2nd ed.). New York: Harper & Row.

Dreikurs, R., & Cassel, P. (1972). *Discipline without tears*. New York: Hawthorne Press.

Dreikurs, R., & Grey, L. (1968). *A new approach to discipline: Logical consequences*. New York: Hawthorne Press.

Dreikurs, R., Grunwald, B., & Pepper, F. (1982). *Maintaining sanity in the classroom: Classroom management techniques* (2nd ed.). New York: Harper & Row.

Duchnowski, A. J., Johnson, N. K., Hall, K. S., Kutash, K., & Friedman, R. M. (1993). The alternatives to residential treatment study: Initial findings. *Journal of Emotional and Behavioral Disorders, 1*(1), 17–26.

Evans, S., & Evans, W. (1987). Behavior change and the ecological model. *The Pointer, 31*, 9–12.

Friesen, B. J., & Wahlers, D. (1993). Respect and real help: Family support and children's mental health. *Journal of Emotional and Behavioral Problems, 2*(4), 12–15.

Gardner, R. (1990). Life space interviewing: It can be effective, but don't . . . *Behavioral Disorders, 15*, 111–119.

Gathercoal, F. (1990). *Judicious discipline* (2nd ed.). New York: Harper & Row.

Gathercoal, F. (1992). *Judicious parenting*. San Francisco: Caddo Gap Press.

Gilliam, J. E. (1993). Crisis management for students with emotional and behavioral problems. *Intervention in School and Clinic, 28*, 224–230.

Gordon, T. (1989). *Discipline that works: Promoting self-discipline in children*. New York: Penguin Books.

Hendrickson, J., Gable, R., & Shores, R. (1987). The ecological perspective: Setting events and behavior. *The Pointer, 31*, 40–44.

Heuchert, C. (1983). Can teachers change behavior? Try interviews. *Academic Therapy, 18*, 321–328.

Hewett, F. (1987). The ecological view of disturbed children: Shadow versus substance. *The Pointer, 31*, 61–63.

Hilton, A. (1987). Using ecological strategies when working with young children. *The Pointer, 31*, 53–55.

Hobbs, N. (1966). Helping disturbed children: Psychological and ecological strategies. *American Psychologist, 21*, 1106–1115.

Jones, N. (1953). *The therapeutic community: A new treatment method in psychiatry*. New York: Basic Books.

Jones, N. (1968). *Beyond the therapeutic community*. New Haven, CT: Yale University Press.

Kerr, N., & Nelson, C. (1983). *Strategies for managing behavior problems in the classroom*. Columbus, OH: Merrill.

Lewis, W., & Lewis, B. (1989). The psychoeducational model: Cumberland House after 25 years. In R. Lyman, S. Prentaice-Dunn, & S. Gabel (Eds.), *Residential and inpatient treatment of children and adolescents* (pp. 69–75). New York: Plenum Press.

Long, N., Wood, M., & Fecser, F. (2001). *Life space crisis intervention: Talking with students in conflict* (2nd ed.). Austin, TX: PRO-ED.

Main, T. F. (1946). The hospital as a therapeutic institution. *Bulletin of the Menninger Clinic, 10*, 66–70.

McCarney, S. (1987). Intervention in the psychosocial environment. The role of counseling in ecological intervention strategies. *The Pointer, 31*, 32–38.

McEwan, B. (1991). *Practicing judicious discipline: An educator's guide to a democratic classroom*. Davis, CA: Caddo Gap Press.

Morse, W. C. (1969). Training teachers in life space interviewing. In H. Dupont (Ed.), *Educating emotionally disturbed children: Readings* (pp. 31–40). New York: Holt, Rinehart & Winston.

Morse, W. C. (1971). Crisis intervention in school mental health and special classes for the disturbed. In N. J. Long, W. C. Morse, & R. G. Newman (Eds.), *Conflict in the classroom: The education of children with problems* (pp. 111–121). Belmont, CA: Wadsworth.

Morse, W. C. (1976a). The crisis or helping teacher. In N. J. Long, W. C. Morse, & R. G. Newman (Eds.), *Conflict in the classroom: The education of emotionally disturbed children* (pp. 67–80). Belmont, CA: Wadsworth.

Morse, W. C. (1976b). Worksheet on life space interviewing for teachers. In N. J. Long, W. C. Morse, & R. G. Newman (Eds.), *Conflict in the classroom: The education of emotionally disturbed children* (pp. 122–130). Belmont, CA: Wadsworth.

Naslund, S. (1987). Life space interviewing: A psychoeducational intervention model for teaching pupil insights and measuring program effectiveness. *The Pointer, 31*, 13–15.

Nelsen, J. (1987). *Positive discipline* (2nd ed.). New York: Ballantine Books.

Nelsen, J. (1997). No more logical consequences—at least hardly ever! Focus on solutions. *Empowering People Catalog*. Winter/Spring.

Nelsen, J., Lott, L., & Glen, H. (1993). *Positive discipline in the classroom*. Rocklin, CA: Prima.

Ottens, A., & Ottens, A. (1982). Crisis intervention as a model for counseling retarded students. *The School Counselor, 29*, 200–225.

Putnam, M. (1987). Effective interventions for mildly handicapped adolescents in the home and the community. *The Pointer, 31*, 19–24.

Redl, F. (1959a). The concept of the life space interview. *American Journal of Orthopsychiatry, 29*, 1–18.

Redl, F. (1959b). The concept of the therapeutic milieu. *American Journal of Orthopsychiatry, 29*, 721–734.

Redl, F. (1966). *When we deal with children*. New York: Free Press.

Redl, F., & Wattenberg, W. W. (1959). *Mental hygiene in teaching*. New York: Harcourt, Brace & World.

Redl, F., & Wineman, D. (1951). *Children who hate*. New York: Free Press.

Rhodes, W. C. (1992). Empowering young minds. *Journal of Emotional and Behavioral Problems, 1*(2), 309–314.

Rossi, J. J., & Filstead, W. J. (1973). *The therapeutic community*. New York: Behavioral Publications.

Schmid, R. (1987). Historical perspectives of the ecological model. *The Pointer, 31*, 5–8.

Sullivan, H. (1953). *The interpersonal theory of psychiatry*. New York: Norton.

Towns, P. (1991). *Educating disturbed adolescents: Theory and practice*. New York: Grune & Stratton.

Wolfgang, C. H. (1999). *Solving discipline problems* (4th ed.). New York: Wiley.

Wood, F. (1990). When we talk with children: The life space interview. *Behavioral Disorders, 15*, 110.

Wood, M., & Weller, D. (1981). How come it's different with some children? A developmental approach to life space interviewing. *The Pointer, 25*, 61–66.

C H A P T E R

PLAY THERAPY

Christina Ager and Phyllis L. Newcomer

Introduction

Play therapy is a general term used to describe a wide variety of therapeutic techniques. An alternative to talk or traditional therapies, play therapy allows children to use their most natural medium of expression, play, to communicate and work through troubling experiences, fears, and anxieties. Therapists from every major psychological orientation—psychoanalytic, gestalt, cognitive–behavioral, developmental—have used play therapy with success to treat children with emotional and behavioral problems (Kaduson & Schaefer, 2000). Both child-centered and therapist-directed models of play therapy have been used effectively. Many of the child-centered models (also referred to as nondirective models) emerged from the work of Carl Rogers (1951) or from the psychoanalytic traditions. Therapist-directed models are often more cognitive or behavioral in orientation. Play therapy sessions can be conducted with individual children, families, or small groups. Specific play therapy interventions are also available and include release play therapy, filial play therapy, and Theraplay.

Common Characteristics

Common characteristics of play therapy across orientation and type include the recognition of play as the central work and communication medium in childhood and the use of play materials to accomplish therapeutic goals (Osterweil,

1986). In play therapy situations a variety of toys are available to children, who during their play either begin to reenact troubling situations, deal with developmental issues, or learn relational and social skills. Children often resolve conflict through repetition, imaginary play, or verbal interactions with the therapist. Positive regard and acceptance of the child and the centrality of the relationship and interactions between the therapist and child are also important components of play therapy across theoretical orientation.

Evolution of Play Therapy

All major schools of psychology use play as a therapeutic technique. During the 1940s Virginia Axline, expanding on the theories of Carl Rogers, introduced play therapy into the mainstream of psychological therapy. Axline's play therapy used a nondirective or child-centered approach based on the idea that children thrive in a relationship of unconditional positive regard conveyed by the therapist's unqualified acceptance and genuine interest in what the child is doing. Axline believed negative environmental factors depress children's self-concept and thwart their healthy striving for self-fulfillment and that their play reflects their frustration and lack of self-awareness. Rather than interpret the child's behavior or remarks, the therapist should establish a permissive environment, afford the child total acceptance (except in cases of physically dangerous or harmful activity), and by reflecting the child's feelings, permit him to develop insights about his behavior.

Other pioneers in the field of play therapy include Levy (1938), who introduced the idea of release play therapy for children exposed to violence, and Melanie Klein (Segal, 1972), who saw symbolic play as a substitute for verbalizations and as a means of revealing the child's fantasies and unconscious feelings in the manner of free association that must be interpreted by the therapist (see Psychoanalytical Model in Chapter 2). Another pioneer, Anna Freud (1947), used play to establish a positive relationship with children that eventually led to meaningful verbalizations. Unlike Klein, she believed that children's play primarily represented experiences from their daily lives rather than the free association of unconscious thoughts. From Freud's perspective, therapeutic interpretation of personality conflicts was based primarily on the child's verbalizations.

Another avenue of psychoanalytical theory used in play therapy, relationship theory, developed from the work of Otto Rank (1936). The thrust of therapy centered on the relationship established between the therapist and the child. Play is the vehicle used to establish the relationship, and the primary clinical interpretations evolve from the manner in which the child relates to the therapist. To encourage the child's expression of his true feelings, the therapeutic environment is permissive, that is, the child is permitted to do what she wishes provided the activity is not dangerous.

As time passed, relationship theory became an increasingly important component of the approaches to play therapy used by many psychoanalytically oriented therapists (Esman, 1983). However, Ginott (1961), in his seminal work applying play therapy strategies with groups, depicted a very directive relationship between the therapist and the child. He advocated the use of therapeutic limits (rather than permissiveness) as an essential means of enhancing ego development and building a trusting relationship.

Latter-day theories underlying play therapy have incorporated principles associated with behavioral and developmental psychology. Behavioral and cognitive–behavioral theorists see children's play as reflective of their maladaptive behavior patterns and irrational thinking. These therapists do not interpret play activities as representative of unconscious feelings. Instead, they apply cognitive or behavior modification strategies during children's play activities to positively reinforce adaptive behavior or use play situations to teach constructive problem solving or coping skills (see Chapters 5 and 6). They also devise game situations to provide practice in socially cooperative behaviors such as sharing and turn taking. Developmental therapists view play as indicative of early interactions with caretakers that develop the basis for future psychological adjustment. Through play therapy they attempt to help the child experience positive and nurturing interactions similar to those missed at earlier developmental stages, thereby bridging developmental gaps and allowing children to grow.

Play

Categories and Types of Play

According to Chance (1979), "Play is like love: everybody knows what it is but nobody can define it" (p. 1). Whether or not an activity is play may depend on the state of mind of the individual who performs it. For example, using a wrestling hold on another person may or may not be play. Although definitions are elusive, Bronfenbrenner (1979) attempted to describe play. He defined it as an intrinsic activity, that is, something done for its own sake rather than as a means to an end; as spontaneous and voluntary; and as involving enjoyment.

A large body of literature exists that documents various types of play engaged in by children as they mature. Lindler (1990), interested in using play as a means of assessing young children's growth and development, synthesized the literature on the topic. Drawing largely from the work of Rubin, Fein, and Vandenberg

(1983), Lindler delineated six categories of play, classified according to types of activities as (a) exploratory or sensorimotor, (b) relational, (c) constructive, (d) dramatic, (e) games-with-rules, and (f) rough-and-tumble.

Exploratory play is "an activity which is done simply for the enjoyment of the physical sensation it creates" (p. 3). Lindler (1990) indicated that repetitive motor movements, such as banging a spoon on a table or filling and emptying a sand bucket, are exploratory play. *Relational play* involves using an object or toy as it was meant to be used (Fenson, Kagan, Kearsley, & Zelazo, 1976). A child who runs a toy car on its wheels or who puts the receiver of the toy phone to her ear is demonstrating relational play. *Constructive play* involves using objects to build or create something, as when a child builds a fence with blocks.

Dramatic (or *symbolic*) *play* (Chance, 1979; Piaget, 1962) occurs when a child pretends—to be superman, to be the mommy, to drive a car. *Games-with-rules* indicate an ability to accept procedures and limits. The children may make up the rules or may conform to rules established previously. A game of cards or hide-and-seek typifies this type of play. *Rough-and-tumble play* is characterized by high levels of activity that is both boisterous and physical, and often social. Playful wrestling is an example.

Other common categories of children's developmental play patterns include solitary, parallel, and cooperative play. Solitary play involves a single child playing alone. The play of children ages 3 and under often is parallel, without social interaction. Children may sit side by side independently engaged in their own play activities. Even their speech is usually an independent monologue related to their own play rather than a shared dialogue. Children ages 4 through 11 engage in few solitary or parallel play activities. Instead, they initiate cooperative activities as play becomes a medium for socialized interaction. They tend to share toys; show affection through hugs and pats; yield to one another's demands or suggestions; offer and ask for approval, help, or sympathy; and generally increase their dependence on one another as they decrease their dependence on adults.

As children mature, they become more assertive and aggressive. Conflicts erupt suddenly but are usually of short duration. The children continue to play cooperatively, even in rough-and-tumble play, but are more concerned with rules. Their play brings them enjoyment as they experiment freely, show imagination, and create new learning experiences. They discuss their activities enthusiastically, accept restrictions without resentment, and use their toys carefully.

Play also may be viewed in terms of the functions it performs for children. O'Connor (1991) synthesized literature that pertains to biological, intrapersonal, interpersonal, and sociocultural functions. Regarding biological functions, play is one means by which children develop basic sensory and motor skills, expend energy, and experience kinesthetic stimulation. All of these experiences help children develop a sense of themselves in relationship to their physical environment.

Play may also involve three types of intrapersonal functions. It provides children with something to do that occupies their minds; it helps them gain mastery of situations that they encounter in their exploration of the environment; and it permits them to act out fantasy or symbolically enact events they have not experienced in real life.

Two interpersonal functions are served by play. Play helps children separate from the primary caretaker and form interpersonal bonds with peers, and it teaches them a variety of social skills. Sociocultural functions are learned through games that reflect society's values and include learning rules of fairness, sharing, cooperation, and competition.

Psychoanalytic and gestalt-oriented play therapists are primarily interested in children's symbolic or dramatic play, because it involves fantasy that lends itself to interpretation. Piaget's work (1962) provided much of the scientific basis for symbolic play. He viewed play as a component of cognitive development and noted that symbolic play develops at age 4 and persists until approximately age 7. In symbolic play, children project their symbolic schema onto new objects and relive reality by repetitive behavior. Symbolic play is preceded by a stage Piaget labeled practice play, occurring when children are preverbal, in the sensorimotor stage of development, and reoccurring when children attempt new activities. In practice play, children engage in activities because they enjoy them (e.g., shaking a rattle). Symbolic play is followed by games-with-rules play, characterized by an exact imitation of reality, which persists from age 7 until age 10.

More recent research (Field, DeStefano, & Koewler, 1982) replicated Piaget's age progression data, noting fantasy play sequences that focus on objects initially, then progress to persons, and that increasingly involve the ability to plan play and to verbalize these plans. Young children's fantasies involve supernatural beings such as monsters, ghosts, and witches, whereas preadolescent fantasy is concerned with real aspects of their lives.

Although the apparent developmental sequence of play activities is important because it provides normative guidelines useful for evaluating children, Krall (1989) and Bloch and Pellegrini (1989) reported research suggesting that a variety of environmental factors influence this development. Fantasy play is affected by culture, socioeconomic class, gender, types of toys provided, length of play session, and childhood experience. Therefore, although the therapist can identify gross deviations from typical patterns of play associated with various chronological ages, as when dealing with an autistic child, the validity of the interpretation of play depends on the intense, prolonged interaction between therapist and child.

Play of Children with Social and Emotional Problems

Lindler (1990) presented broad characteristics of the play of children with social and emotional disorders. She noted deficits in (a) the structure of play, (b) the content of play, (c) awareness of self and others, (d) sense of humor, and (e) awareness of social conventions.

The structure of the dramatic play of many children with emotional or behavioral problems is marked by illogical thought processes and fragmented ideas. For example, the name and identity of a doll may be changed repeatedly and rapidly, and the actions associated with the doll may change with its identity and therefore lack continuity. This may be indicative of the rapidly changing personalities and behaviors of the adults surrounding the child or the way the child feels about herself. Also, the child may display an inability to sequence events temporally, that is, an understanding of past, present, and future.

The content of the play of children with emotional and behavioral problems often shows a preoccupation with power or control issues, fears, dependency, or loss. Anger or aggressive themes often dominate, and spontaneity may be lacking. In addition, some children are unable to emerge from fantasy because they cannot separate fantasy from reality.

Many children with emotional and behavioral problems do not evaluate the effects of their behavior on others and have difficulty incorporating other individuals into shared play. They may have extremely low frustration tolerance and poor impulse control, throwing tantrums or acting out in other ways with little or no apparent provocation. Difficulty following rules, winning or losing in a healthy way, and cooperating with others is often in evidence.

Humor is an important indicator of psychological health. The humor of children with emotional and behavioral problems often is bizarre. For example, they find humor in situations that are not seen as humorous by others, as when a well-liked toy breaks. They may also see no humor in events that other children find humorous.

Many children with emotional problems either are unaware of social conventions or choose to disregard them. In their play they are reluctant to postpone their need to gratify their impulses immediately; therefore, they interact inappropriately with others. For example, they may not wait their turn or follow the rules of a game. Often they appear unconcerned about the effect of their behavior in shaping the attitudes and opinions of others. They may be rude or sullen, failing to greet other children or to respond to remarks addressed to them, yet become upset when other children respond in kind.

Other indications of disturbed patterns of play involve levels of inhibition. Overinhibited children are extremely wary of play situations. They tend to be passive observers rather than active participants. Toys are treated like rare jewels. The child is afraid to touch them and when he does use them is concerned excessively about breaking them. Play activities lack spontaneity and bring little joy. Undue concern may be expressed about getting dirty and cleaning up any mess.

In addition to their general passivity and timidity in play situations, overinhibited children tend to rely greatly on adult support. They solicit suggestions for play activities from adults, seek permission for each act they plan to undertake, and try to gain favor from adults by doing what they believe will please them. They are not assertive in group situations, nor do they show appropriate aggression when challenged. They rarely offer social reinforcement to others. In fact, they tend to depreciate the activities of their peers by ridiculing their efforts and products.

On the other hand, children with too few inhibitions see no need to restrict impulse-gratifying behaviors. Their notion of interacting with others is to exploit or dominate. Because they are too assertive and excessively aggressive, they become furious if others resist following their suggestions and respond either by disrupting group activities by taking toys, knocking down buildings, scribbling on drawings, or engaging in physical or verbal abuse. Underinhibited children typically resent authority and resist behavioral limits. Their preferred toys are usually weapons, and their symbolic play generally involves aggressive behavior. They often deliberately break toys or disrupt games.

Evidence of severe emotional pathology such as psychosis also is evidenced in play activity. Children with psychosis may engage in a variety of bizarre behaviors. They are often impervious to the existence of other children and unresponsive to all attempts at social interaction. Even their faces are devoid of expression as they sit passively in one position or engage in some type of self-stimulating behavior, such as body rocking or hand waving. Toys are used inappropriately, often repetitiously, as when a block is banged repeatedly on the floor. Disruption of familiar routines and established patterns, such as the rearrangement of furniture or toys, is resisted with tantrums.

In short, children's play patterns often reveal the state of their mental health and reflect their perceptions of the world around them. Anger may be reflected in aggressive play or fantasy play focused around aggressive incidents. Sadness and withdrawal may preclude play or result in solitary play activities such as drawing. Children whose development has been stunted due to the trauma of abuse or neglect may play in ways developmentally more appropriate for younger children. Children with social skills deficits and anger control issues have trouble playing games with rules or maintaining equilibrium during rough-and-tumble play. In addition, the ability to play spontaneously and joyously requires a sense of security and safety often absent in those children with emotional and behavioral difficulties.

Conducting Play Therapy

Children Who Benefit from Play Therapy

A wide range of children have benefited from play therapy. Play therapy is usually employed with children between the ages of 3 and 12 who are having adjustment problems. A large number of case reports have documented success with children suffering from posttraumatic stress disorder due to violence and abuse (Kaduson & Schaefer, 2000; Webb, 1991), natural disasters, plane crashes, and war (Webb, 1991); children experiencing loss through death (Oaklander, 2000); children experiencing repeated foster placements or divorce (Trebling, 2000); and children suffering from fears and phobias (Knell, 2000). Effective play therapy has also targeted children living in chemically dependent families or families with other medical and health issues (VanFleet, 2000; Webb, 1991); children in Head Start programs (Johnson, Brulin, Winek, Krepps, & Wiley, 1999); children with attention-deficit/hyperactivity disorder (Kaduson & Schaefer, 2000), learning disabilities (Guerney, 1979), and social skills deficits (Schaefer, Jacobsen, & Ghahramanlou, 2000); and students exhibiting disruptive behaviors (McNeil, Bahl, & Herschell, 2000) or at risk for such (Post, 1999).

Predictors of Play Therapy Outcomes

LeBlanc and Ritchie (1999) conducted a meta-analysis of play therapy outcomes from 42 experimental studies to determine both the effectiveness of play therapy as an intervention and the variables that contribute to effective play therapy treatment. They found that the two characteristics of highly effective play therapy with children were parent involvement in the play therapy and duration of therapy. Parent involvement (such as in filial play therapy or Theraplay, a family model of play therapy) significantly increased the effectiveness of play therapy in alleviating presenting problems and maintaining adjustment over long-term follow-up. For duration of therapy, these authors found the efficacy of play therapy increased up to 30 to 35 sessions, after which benefits declined. This decline may be due to the intransigent nature of problems so severe as to not respond to therapy, which would be consistent with results examining the effects of therapy for children in general.

Variables found not to contribute to the success of play therapy included the nature of the presenting problem, whether therapy was conducted in a group or individually, and the age or gender of the children who were clients.

General Issues

Play therapists have identified a number of procedures that increase the effectiveness of play therapy (Ginott, 1961; Krall, 1989; Patterson, 1980). First, secure as much pertinent information about the child's problems from parents or caregivers as possible. The goal is not only to understand how the child typically behaves but also to develop some awareness of the parents' attitude toward the child and a sense of the home situation. Second, at the initial meeting with a child entering therapy, alert the child to the purpose of the interaction. Discuss the situation in terms of a problem that is making someone unhappy and emphasize that the goal of therapy is to help the child. This step is essential even when family members indicate that the matter has been explained to the child. Third, discuss the confidentiality of the meetings with parents and children. Children should understand that their revelations will not be discussed with their parents.

Other universally important issues concern the play area, toys and materials, setting limits, and involving the child's family in the therapeutic process. These require more extensive discussion. Specific models for family-based play therapy also are presented later in this chapter.

Play Therapy Areas. Most play therapy approaches require a room of comfortable size and a safe environment in which the child cannot get injured. A well-stocked playroom with toys and arts and crafts materials is often recommended. For approaches that require observation or training, playrooms with separate observation rooms complete with two-way mirrors are often recommended. If this is not possible, separating out the play area of the room and the observation area using furniture or a rug will suffice. In family-oriented play therapy approaches, such as filial play therapy, it is recommended that the number and types of toys reflect what is available in the home. In Theraplay, a developmental approach using caregivers as cotherapists, a blanket or sheet is placed on the floor of the room to denote the play therapy area, and symbolic and fantasy toys are not employed. In general, a safe, comfortable room with sufficient materials to engage children is all that is required.

Toys and Materials. Toys and materials used in play therapy sessions can be divided into five major categories: family-related and nurturance toys, aggression-related toys, expressive and construction toys, games, and other multiuse toys (see Table 10.1).

TABLE 10.1
Toys for Play Therapy

Category	Examples
Family-related and nurturance toys	Doll family, doll house/furniture, stuffed animals, puppets, dress-up clothes, dishes, kitchen set, baby doll, baby bottles
Aggression-related toys	Plastic soldiers, dinosaurs, guns, foam aggression bats, bop bag, dart guns, rubber knives
Expressive and construction toys	Clay or Play-Doh, small or large blocks, crayons or markers and paper, watercolors, sandbox and tools, construction toys, magic wand, child-made books
Games	The UnGame; Talking, Feeling, Doing Game; The Angry Monster Game; The Self-Control Game
Other multiuse toys	Cars, trucks, community vehicles, play money, doctor's kit, books

In general, most play therapy approaches recommend having a wide range of toys, including items from each of the areas shown in Table 10.1. However, certain approaches rely more heavily on some types of toys than others. For example, gestalt play therapy emphasizes the use of creative or expressive toys to tap into the child's inner self, whereas Theraplay completely avoids the use of fantasy toys. Cognitive–behavioral models rely heavily on child-made stories and books and games or activities designed to teach specific social skills or coping mechanisms. A list of catalogs and phone numbers for play therapy materials are included at the end of the chapter.

Setting Limits. The setting of limits in play therapy evokes a degree of controversy among practitioners. According to Ginott (1961), variations in techniques regarding behavioral limits may reflect different therapeutic definitions of permissiveness. Some therapists, particularly phenomenologists (see Chapter 2), define permissiveness to mean acceptance of all behavior as it appears in therapy. Others define permissiveness as acceptance of all "symbolic" behavior, such as feelings, thoughts, dreams, and wishes, as opposed to direct acting-out behaviors. Therapists adopting the symbolic behavior approach set more rigorous limits on children's overt actions. For example, they might not permit swearing, screaming, water throwing, and other such activities. They would permit and presumably encourage symbolic expressions of hostile feelings, such as puppetry that depicted matricide, patricide, or mass mayhem.

Developmental and behavioral therapists generally do not accept the notion of a permissive environment as essential to a child's growth in therapy;

rather, they view the setting of limits as essential to growth. Although the degree of therapist control in the play situation may vary, individuals with these orientations usually establish and enforce relatively firm behavioral limits.

In addition, one of the goals of approaches that include parents as therapists or cotherapists is often to help parents learn to set appropriate limits. In these cases, limit setting is an important component of therapy and a skill parents or caregivers learn to acquire through the therapeutic process.

To some extent, however, the behavioral limits set by play therapists do not necessarily reflect their theoretical orientations or their interpretation of permissiveness, but rather indicate their unique sensitivities about the behaviors they are willing to tolerate. The therapist who feels that it is inappropriate for children to swear in therapy may not be able to function properly unless he limits swearing. Another therapist may have no difficulty permitting swearing but may need to draw the line at other behaviors. Obviously, the therapist is not a machine. His particular value system must influence the manner in which play therapy is implemented.

Regardless of the factors that determine the setting of therapeutic limits, all therapists agree on several issues. *First,* the necessary limits should be established immediately and enforced consistently. For example, the therapist who cannot abide swearing must limit it immediately. *Second,* limits should be delineated clearly so that there is no confusion over acceptable and unacceptable behavior. For instance, if punching the therapist is unacceptable, so is slapping. *Third,* the establishment of limits should be done in as nonpunitive a manner as possible. The child may be told in a calm, firm manner that does not convey anger that she must stop jumping on the furniture. The therapist might say, "I know you want to jump on the furniture, but it is against the rules." If the child persists, she should be taken out of the playroom until willing to return without jumping on the furniture. At no time should the therapist voice anger with the child. *Fourth,* the child's disappointment or frustration when behavior is limited should be recognized and accepted by the therapist. The therapist should say, "I know you are angry because you can't jump on the furniture, but that is the rule." The therapist must never personalize the child's anger by responding as though her behavior is a personal insult. Children with emotional and behavioral challenges are expected to test limits. If the therapist responds to these events with calm enforcement of the limits without projecting anger or annoyance, the child will eventually learn that, although she is not permitted to engage in certain behaviors, she is still held in high regard by the therapist.

Parental Involvement. The importance of involving parents in the therapeutic process was recognized by Anna Freud in the 1940s and has been documented recently by LeBlanc and Ritchie (1999), who found significant increases in play therapy results when parents were used as therapists, such as in filial play therapy. Use of the parent as therapist demonstrates an understanding that emotional and behavioral problems of children are often relational or interpersonal in nature. However, if a parent is responsible for the trauma that led to the need for therapy, such as sexual or physical abuse or abandonment, initial therapeutic treatment for the parent and the child will be required before the parent can be engaged as a therapeutic agent. In some cases, parents or caregivers are never able to function as play therapists for their children.

Krall (1989) advocated collateral but separate treatment of parents, beginning with a focus on the child's problems but moving to the personal issues affecting the adults. On occasion, when parents and children show little improvement over time in their relationships, Krall holds joint sessions to foster better communication. She also brings the parents and children together when a particularly serious issue in their relationship emerges or when a child has made excellent progress that is not recognized by the parents.

O'Connor (1991) recognized different types of collateral work with parents, including educational sessions, sessions where the parents are trained as therapists for the child, joint or family sessions with the child, and separate sessions with parents that parallel the sessions held with the child. In the educational sessions, the therapist gives information to the parents to assist them in understanding the child. In sessions to train parents to act as therapists (a behavioral or developmental approach), parents are given specific strategies to use at home. Family sessions are useful to explore interactions occurring in the home, denoting roles that affect the child's behavior, and separate sessions are useful when interactive sessions are counterproductive.

However the sessions are structured, O'Connor (1991) recommended meeting with parents on a regular basis, usually seeing them briefly (20 minutes) before the child's play session. When their problems are not so severe as to make them uncooperative, O'Conner advocates a problem-solving approach. The parents operationally define the child's major problem, brainstorm possible solutions, evaluate the solutions for practicality, choose the one to implement, implement and evaluate effectiveness, and if effective, begin the process again with another problem.

In another approach, conjoint family therapy, both parent and child interact with the therapist as clients throughout every session, while the therapist focuses on helping them establish a more constructive interpersonal relationship. Miller (1982) advocated involving the entire family, including other children, in the therapeutic process—a method he calls crossover therapy. This type of approach is particularly helpful when families have serious communication problems.

Two specific play therapy interventions using parents or caregivers as therapists are filial play therapy and Theraplay. Both are discussed in more depth later in the chapter.

Individual or Group Therapy

Individual play therapy involves one child and the therapist and uses the relationship between the therapist and the child to provide the mechanism whereby children can express themselves freely and feel safe enough to take the risks required for therapeutic work to be accomplished. Children who have suffered emotional trauma because of a catastrophe such as a death, accident, or fire respond best to individual therapy. Usually their anxiety is generated by one particular event and can be resolved most efficiently if symbolic play is focused on a reenactment of this event. Some children who have been victimized by sexual or physical abuse also benefit from the security and anonymity of individual therapy. Children who are grieving a parent's death may also feel more able to express their sadness in individual sessions. In these cases the presence of other children only interferes with the child's progress.

Children whose presenting problems are characterized by an inability to get along with peers or develop appropriate peer relationships may benefit from group approaches to play therapy. Individual therapy prior to inclusion in a play group may be required if the child's skills are so poor that they require intense instruction or prompting that may prove embarrassing in a group. Generally, group approaches to play therapy recommend small groups of three to six children and one or two therapists.

Group-oriented play therapy has been used successfully with young children who have been sexually abused (Gallo-Lopez, 2000) and with children with social skills deficits (Schaefer et al., 2000) and as part of a teen parenting program to facilitate parent–child attachment. In addition, filial play therapy has been effectively conducted in small groups providing parents with a learning and support network.

Group Membership and Composition

Prior to inclusion in a play therapy group, each child should be individually assessed for appropriateness for the group. Examining the child's developmental history, conducting a clinical interview, and observing the child in a play situation are all necessary components of the assessment.

Ginott (1961) and Gallo-Lopez (2000) cautioned against using group-oriented play approaches with children who demonstrate (a) intense sibling rivalries, (b) sociopathic behaviors, (c) accelerated or deviant sex drives,

(d) tendencies to steal, (e) extreme hostility and aggression, and (f) gross stress reaction. It is recommended that children who engage in self-injurious behavior receive individual therapy in addition to group play therapy so that their safety can be effectively monitored.

Children who are extremely hostile toward their siblings tend to displace their feelings onto the other children in the group. If the atmosphere in the group is permissive, they may actually harm others. Such children respond more favorably to individual play sessions. Once they have gained control over their hostility, they can be integrated into a play group.

Children diagnosed with sociopathy lack concern about others and interact with them for purposes of exploitation. They are incapable of introspection and are without feelings of guilt or responsibility for wrongdoing. They detest authority and refuse to abide by rules. In group situations they prey on others and disrupt their activities. They are unable to benefit from therapeutic techniques. Neither indirect reflection of their feelings nor direct interpretation of their behavior is effective. They are poor risks for individual therapy also, because they cannot relate to the therapist.

Children with accelerated or deviant sex drives are generally better assigned to individual therapy because they might frighten other children or involve them in their activities. Similarly, children who steal should be excluded from group situations because they might steal from the other children or teach them to steal. This general guideline does not extend to children who steal only at home. These children are often either bidding for affection or seeking revenge on parents. Such stealing usually does not transfer to the group situation.

Highly aggressive children whose behavior appears to stem from deep-rooted hostility cannot benefit from group sessions. They require forceful restraints on their behavior to prevent them from injuring others. Such restraint cannot be applied in the group session without destroying the permissive environment and proving detrimental to the other children.

In addition to presenting criteria for selection or rejection of candidates for group play therapy, Ginott (1961) offered another series of guidelines to aid the practitioner in deciding which children to group together.

First, groups should consist of children with various types of symptoms so that each individual can identify with different types of persons. For instance, a passive, withdrawn child is aided by her observations of an active, acting-out child. A dependent, fearful individual gains courage from observing the behavior of stronger, more independent children.

A second guideline is an absence of ridicule within the group. The group should not be composed so that one child is the butt of barbs from more assertive peers. For instance, a fat child who has been ridiculed for obesity should not be included in a group of dominant, thin children. A group with other obese members, or with mild, unassertive children, would be more beneficial.

Ginott's third guideline deals with group tension level. Effective therapy occurs when the interaction of the group members produces a moderate level of tension. Some groups fail to generate enough tension, whereas others generate too much. For example, a group composed solely of aggressive children would be fraught with encounters, creating too much tension, whereas a group of withdrawn children would lack tension-generating encounters.

Ginott's fourth guideline recommends that the therapist avoid grouping friends and siblings. According to Ginott, therapy should promote new attitudes and relationships, and the intrusion of friends or siblings in the group blocks this type of new learning.

The fifth guideline concerns eliminating wrong heroes. Care must be taken to ensure that antisocial children do not dominate the group. The inclusion of delinquent children in a group of neurotic or immature youngsters who are not antisocial should be avoided.

Guideline 6 concerns neutralizers. A neutralizer is a child who is not greatly disturbed and who controls her overt behavior. The neutralizer is expected to influence less controlled children by example and by comments that illustrate socially acceptable behaviors.

Guidelines 7 and 8 concern group size and the age of group members. Ginott recommends no more than 5 children per group and as few as 3 if the therapist lacks experience. A generally accepted practice is that the number of children in a group should not exceed the age of the youngest child in the group. For example, if the youngest child is 4 years old, the group should have no more than 4 members. Chronological age of the group members generally should not differ by more than 12 months. However, socially immature children or youngsters with mental retardation who are rejected by their chronological peers might fit comfortably into groups of younger children. As a general rule, preschool children are at the optimal age for play therapy techniques, and the procedure loses effectiveness with children beyond the age of 10.

The ninth guideline concerns open and closed groups. Open groups accept new members periodically and integrate them into the existing group. Closed groups exclude new members once the group is operating. According to Ginott, open groups are more practical and economical because children regularly drop from therapy and must be replaced. Obviously, the new group member must be chosen carefully to avoid upsetting the other children. Whenever possible, it is beneficial to prepare the group for the departure of one member and the entrance of another child several weeks in advance.

Ginott's final guideline concerns mixed-sex groups. In accord with the Freudian notion of a period of latency in children's sexual development, this guideline recommends like-sex groups for children of school age who are in that period of sexual development. Preschool children of both sexes may be grouped together, however, since they have not entered the latency period. As stated previously, Ginott's criteria for group composition are highly subjective. By no means are they uniformly accepted, even by therapists who use psychoanalytic methodology.

Treatment Model for Group Play Therapy

Group play therapy models can be both structured and nondirective, with some therapists combining both types of activities. Generally, when both structured and nondirective methods are mixed, structured activities are followed by periods of nondirected play. This combination of approaches allows themes established by the therapist to be elaborated on and explored by the children during nondirective time. The roles of the therapist in group models of play therapy include planning and setting up the activities, providing modeling and feedback, intervening when necessary, and interpreting children's behaviors and affect. Numerous structured activities have been successfully employed in group play therapy, such as group games, cooperative activities, and reading and discussing books with therapeutic themes.

Theoretical Approaches to Play Therapy

As stated earlier, every major psychological approach has developed models for play therapy consistent with its orientation. An exhaustive presentation of the orientation and techniques used by each psychological approach is beyond the scope of this book. A brief distillation of each approach's major characteristics follows.

Cognitive–Behavioral Play Therapy

Two primary goals of cognitive–behavioral play therapy are to identify and modify maladaptive thoughts associated with children's symptoms and to teach children skills needed to successfully negotiate their environment. Successful cognitive–behavioral play therapy allows children to address issues of control, gain mastery over behaviors and skills, and to act responsibly toward themselves and others.

Designed for children ages 3 to 10, cognitive–behavioral play therapy (CBPT) has been used successfully to treat fears and phobias (Knell, 2000), selective mutism, encopresis, and divorce-related and abuse-related disorders (Knell, 1993; Knell & Moore, 1990; Knell & Ruma, 1996). Cognitive–behavioral play therapy allows children to take an active role in changing their thoughts and behaviors, thereby empowering them to feel capable of dealing with additional challenges.

Cognitive–behavioral play therapy is a directive and goal-oriented approach that organizes around four stages of therapy: introductory, assessment, middle, and termination. During the introductory stage the therapist orients the child to the play environment and the therapy process, preparing the child for what will take place. Assessment involves determining the specifics about the presenting problem and the situations in which it may emerge and developing a treatment plan. During the middle stage the treatment plan is implemented, and therapy focuses on modifying internal verbalizations, increasing the child's self-control and skill levels, and developing more adaptive responses to target stimuli. During this stage specific behavioral interventions may be employed, such as systematic desensitization, social skills instruction, emotive imagery, contingency management, positive reinforcement, shaping, stimulus fading, extinction, modeling, practice, and feedback. Cognitive interventions used in CBPT include countering irrational beliefs, positive self-statements, self-control training, and bibliotherapy (Knell, 2000). Also built into the middle stage of treatment is generalization and relapse prevention to allow children to use their new responses across various settings, people, and time. Finally, during the termination phase, the child and the family are prepared for and experience the phasing out of treatment.

Various strategies are employed. For example, the therapist might invite the target child and a small group of socially skilled peers to play Trouble or Candy Land. A social skills game such as The Self-Control Game or the Talking Feeling Doing Game (Gardner, 1998) might be used in small-group therapy. Dealing with feelings might be approached using a story such as *The Giving Tree* (Silverstein, 1986) or stories about children who have similar problems such as alcohol abuse or violence in the home. The Angry Monster Game might be used to help children deal with fears. Building a bridge out of newspaper or creating arts and crafts projects can also form the structure during which the child's feelings, thoughts, and beliefs are assessed, discussed, and worked with using the intervention strategies mentioned earlier, such as social skills instruction, emotive imagery, modeling, or practicing positive self-statements.

Knell (1993) used playing with toys and systematic desensitization to treat the phobia of a 5-year-old boy who was terrified of being in any closed space after being accidentally locked in a bathroom by his younger sister. Emotive imagery was used by Cornwall, Spence, and Schotte (1997) to effectively treat clinically significant darkness phobia in 7- to 10-year-olds.

Like other forms of play therapy, the sessions provide a safe environment for children to express their fears, anxieties, and ways of thinking. Although strategies are planned and structured prior to the session, the therapist must still be able to use spontaneous information brought to the session by the child. In all play therapy the therapist–child relationship is critical and the therapist must be capable of responding to and altering plans to meet the needs of the child at any given time. As in all play therapy, activities and games must be developmentally appropriate for children to gain greatest benefit from therapy.

Gestalt Play Therapy

Gestalt play therapy emerges out of the work of Perls (1969). Gestalt therapy focuses attention on the holistic integrative functioning of the total individual, the primacy of relationships, issues of contact and resistance, developing a strong sense of self, and focusing on the awareness and experience of behavior rather than on the behavior itself. Gestalt play therapy is designed to help the child become more aware of who she is and what she feels, needs, and wants. The goal for older children and adolescents is to become aware of unsatisfactory ways of being and to begin to make conscious choices that will better serve them.

Gestalt play therapy is also therapist directed, often using creative and expressive toys as projective techniques to strengthen the child's inner self. However, because it is relationship based, the ability of the therapist to see clearly and respond effectively to the child is essential to success. Play techniques most often employed include drawing, painting, making collages, using clay, puppet play, music, storytelling and books, drama, fantasy, imagery, and sensory/body/dance experiences. The therapist uses these techniques to focus the child on the problem and to help the child deal effectively with assimilating the problematic experiences into a healthy and capable sense of self.

Using these projective techniques, children can express deep feelings in nonthreatening, even fun ways. As the child feels safe within the therapist–child relationship, the therapist can address the feelings and issues disclosed in the child's drawings, dramatic play, and stories. Although goals and plans for progress are an integral part of gestalt therapy, expectations concerning the child's behavior or the session itself are severely cautioned against. Sensitivity to the child is primary, and so the therapist must be highly observant, noting connection and withdrawal or resistance by the look in a child's eyes, her lack of energy, and her bodily responses. Resistance is a healthy reaction, and time for the child to withdraw must be respected. The therapist's job is to remain fully connected to the child despite the child's inability to connect at any particular time.

Like other forms of play therapy, labeling feelings and normalizing reactions to disturbing events or feelings is an important component of gestalt play therapy. The therapist helps children own their feelings, accept them, work through them, and assimilate them into an integrated sense of self.

Oaklander (2000) cautioned that therapists must be mindful of the child's developmental level, capabilities, responsiveness, and levels of resistance. Her comments about development resound for all therapy with children. According to Oaklander, children can deal with issues only at their current level, and at each level of development, issues may reemerge and need to be dealt with in greater depth. Also, new issues may emerge. Therefore, termination may be temporary, and it may be healthier to view therapy for some children, as well as some adults, as intermittent and ongoing.

Nondirective or Child-Centered Play Therapy

Emerging from the phenomenological school, nondirective strategies and techniques were originally associated with the work of Carl Rogers and have been found useful by a variety of play therapists (Axline, 1947; Hobbs, 1955; Mader, 2000; Webb, 1991). As noted in Chapter 8, nondirective therapy is designed to minimize the therapist's control over the events in the therapy session. A child is viewed as a rational being, motivated toward self-actualization. To overcome problems and fulfill potential, she must be permitted to engage in activities that reflect her needs or desires. Thus, the therapist's role is not to instruct, direct, counsel, censure, shape, praise, reward, or interpret the child's behavior or remarks. It is to respond to the child's direction by reflecting her feelings and by helping her become aware of the significance of her behaviors. Axline advises the nondirective therapist to

- establish rapport and communicate an attitude of acceptance to the child;
- set and maintain a permissive atmosphere;
- recognize and reflect the child's feelings;
- permit the child, at his own pace, to reach solutions to problems; and
- set behavioral limits that do not violate the permissive atmosphere.

The first step, establishing rapport with the child, underlies the therapeutic relationship. The therapist must depict herself as a nonthreatening, nonpunitive person primarily concerned with the child's interests and desires. This attitude is conveyed to some extent by pleasant remarks and a smiling countenance. However, real rapport depends on the therapist's ability to convince the child that he is important and valued and to avoid establishing a superior adult–inferior child relationship, which is common elsewhere. Children, particularly those experiencing emotional problems, are very adept at testing the sincerity of an accepting attitude and often probe to unearth underlying authoritarian attitudes. For example, a child initially might refuse to talk to the therapist and cry for his mother. The therapist must not attempt to force the child to behave differently by urging, teasing, arguing or coercing. The therapist should *not* say, "There's nothing to cry about," "Don't cry honey, I won't hurt you," "Big boys don't cry," "Stop crying and I'll give you a surprise," "Are you a mommy's boy?" "Play with these toys, you'll like them." All of these responses, no matter how kindly meant, ignore the child's feelings about the events. Instead, the therapist must accept the child's attitude and respond only to the feelings being conveyed. She should say, "You are upset and would like your mother." This statement deals with the child's reality and informs the child that the therapeutic situation is special and is unlike most situations in which the child must interact with adults. In the therapeutic situation the child's feelings and desires are given as much consideration as those of the adults present.

In an instance such as the one just described, it might be necessary for the child's mother initially to accompany him. When he becomes absorbed in some of the play material and is less fearful, the mother can leave. It is far more important that the child's attitude toward the therapy be shaped properly than it is that the therapist's plan for a private opening session remain unaltered.

Acceptance of the child is a continuation of the attitude conveyed while establishing rapport. Acceptance is conveyed by avoiding either direct or implied criticism of the child. For example, if the child smears paint on his clothes, the therapist neither tells the child directly that it was wrong to do so nor implies criticism by telling him that a lovely shirt has been spoiled. If the child remarks that he hates his brother, the therapist does not challenge or question the remark (e.g., "Why do you hate your brother?"). Similarly, if a child spends all his time scribbling on paper with a black crayon, the therapist does not suggest that he draw pictures, use crayons of varied colors, or engage in more interesting activities. The child's behavior reflects what he feels like doing just as his remarks denote the feelings he is prepared to share. When prepared to try an alternative activity or expand his comments, he will.

Acceptance does not imply approval of a child's activity. In fact, approval, even the mildest compliment, might have adverse effects. For example, the child who paints a pretty picture might, if complimented, spend an excessive amount of time painting pictures to win more of the therapist's approval. The goal of play therapy is not to have the child do as the therapist wishes. It is to have the child express what he thinks and feels.

Step 2, establishing a permissive environment, means that children are permitted, within reason, to do as they wish in the playroom. Permissiveness is communicated verbally by telling each child that he may play with whatever toy he chooses and nonverbally by not interfering when the child tests the sincerity of the verbal statement. In some cases children are unresponsive and unwilling to play with any of the toys. The therapist must avoid insisting that the child do something. If the child sits quietly, the therapist should sit quietly as well. In other cases children deliberately engage in the behaviors that usually draw adult criticism, such as spilling water or making noise. In a permissive environment the therapist permits much behavior of this type, drawing the line when the child's activity is judged to be dangerous, abusive, or destructive. For example, the child who chooses to jump up and down while screaming may not be interrupted by the therapist, but the child who begins banging his head against the wall, destroying toys, abusing other children, or punching the therapist is stopped.

An extension of a permissive environment is one devoid of probing questions. The child must be permitted to bring forth important information after he has developed a feeling of trust in the therapist. To establish this level of interaction, the therapist must avoid prematurely imposing thoughts and ideas on the child. For example, the child who begins smashing the mother doll against the floor is not queried as to his reasons by questions such as "Do you feel angry with the mother doll?" Such questions are intrusions into the child's private world. When the child is prepared to share the emotions underlying this behavior, he will offer reasons for the actions.

Step 3, the ability to recognize and reflect feeling, is another extension of the permissive interaction between the child and the therapist. The play therapist is alert to the child's utterances and play activities for a significant remark or behavior. Significant activities are those that appear to pertain to the child's problem. For example, a child may spend a long period of time pouring water from one bucket to another—an activity that is probably nonsignificant. Finally, he dumps a bucket of water over the head of the mother doll and says, "This mother doll is mean." The actions and remarks are significant representations of his feelings, and the therapist must react to them by reflecting back the child's behavior or remarks. When the child says, "This mother doll is mean," the therapist follows with "You think the mother doll is mean," not

"You think that your mother is mean." Thus, the therapist recognizes the child's feelings without attempting to elicit an admission the child may not be able to make or accept.

Step 4 is a keystone of nondirective therapy, confidence that an individual has the ability to solve his own problems. A child can be trusted to broach sensitive subjects when ready to deal with them emotionally.

Step 5, dealing with behavioral limits, as noted earlier, evokes some controversy among play therapists regardless of theoretical orientation. Some phenomenologically oriented therapists hold that children learn through observing limits. However, Axline advocates establishing only those limits necessary for safety.

On the whole, child-centered therapists are interested in using techniques that reveal the dynamics that underlie behavior; however, unlike the psychoanalytically oriented practitioners, they focus on indications of self-confidence, levels of self-awareness, and sensitivity to experiences.

Psychoanalytic Play Therapy

The most important technique in the psychoanalytic arsenal is interpretation of the unconscious dynamics represented in children's play activity and verbal comments. A therapist interprets a child's behavior by explaining what it means. He may discuss defenses being used by the child (e.g., denial of a problem) or comment on the anger conveyed in certain activities (smashing a toy). The goal of interpretation is to release unconscious thoughts and feelings, that is, make them part of the child's consciousness so that they might eventually be altered.

Dodds (1987) noted that psychoanalytically oriented therapists are more concerned with interpretation than are therapists who profess other theoretical orientations. They observe play activities to evaluate object relations, types of defenses, sexual and aggressive drives, and psychosocial development.

Krall (1989), a psychoanalytically oriented therapist, believed that interpretation of children's play is necessary for diagnosis and is part of the ongoing therapeutic process. She also felt that there is basic agreement among practitioners with different psychological orientations regarding the components involved in interpreting play, although their interest in interpretation and methods of interpretation may vary. Drawing on the research of Howe and Silvern (1981), Pellegrini (1982), Sjolund (1981), and Udwin and Yule (1982), she directed attention to the following components of play: structural, developmental, content, materials, and process.

Structural components pertain to the child's use of space and the organization of the play. Children's play may appear closed and rigid or open and fluid.

Structures may be used as boundaries or boundaries may be absent. A child's choices, considered in light of the level of chaos in the home, indicates preferred defense strategies (e.g., closed in or acting out).

Developmental level is suggested by the child's ability to perceive and organize play objects, fine and large motor coordination, ability to develop coherent fantasy, and language usage. Ongoing patterns of play are considered with respect to general development.

The *content* of play often reveals the type of conflict the child is experiencing. A particular preoccupation with an event or object may reveal its importance, as when a child repeatedly chastises a specific doll figure. The implications of preoccupation hold greater significance when the child appears anxious or defensive while engaging in the play.

The choice of play *materials* and the sequence of the choice are both important elements in interpretation. From a psychoanalytic framework, toys are classified as representing specific functions. *Family* toys are dolls, dollhouses, people puppets, and soldiers. *Dependency* toys are stuffed animals and puppet animals, whereas *aggression* toys are guns and aggressive animals. *Expressive* toys are paints, paper and crayons; *sensory* toys are clay and Play-Doh; *motor* toys are balls and ringtoss; *representational* toys are cars, boats, planes, and trucks; and *structured* toys are building blocks and puzzles.

The child's preferred category of toys and the extent of his preoccupation with that category are noted. For example, highly aggressive children may choose aggressive toys, motor toys, and representational toys that are used aggressively. Children preoccupied with family relationships may consistently choose family toys.

Also noted are shifts in sequence as play progresses. Perhaps the child chooses objects, then animals, then people, or switches from relatively innocuous toys to those that express conflict. Continuity in play also is important, because discontinuity suggests an interplay of conflict expression alternating with anxiety and defensiveness.

The *process* of the play refers to the ongoing behavior of the child in the play therapy environment; the tension and anxiety consistently evoked by certain toys; the amount of affect expressed; and the relationship of the child to the therapist as an object. The last point is particularly important, because the child may view the therapist as a source of affection, support, and approval or as a frustrator, to be ignored or avoided.

Object relationships are extremely significant in current forms of psychodynamic therapy, because the client is viewed as transferring feelings associated with important people in his life to the therapist. As Krall (1989) stated, "The therapist offers himself/herself as a self object to whom the child can relate or organize him/herself around. It is the nature of the relationship set up that often offers the first clues to the developmental level, that is, the level of object relations, and the nature of the child's pathology" (p. 39). She explained that the child's words and actions constitute communication, but the therapeutic understanding is established by the relationship between therapist and child. To promote that relationship, the therapist establishes a permissive environment with little structure and no limits beyond the stipulation that the child may not hurt himself or the therapist.

The implications of the psychoanalytic concern with transference of feeling can be seen in the emphasis on the child–therapist relationship as a primary reflection of the goals of therapy. For children with autism the goal is to help them develop a symbiotic relationship with the therapist. With children diagnosed with borderline personality disorder, the goal is to establish a relationship that reassures them by reducing their fear of separation and abandonment. The goal for children with character problems is to enable them to act out issues with the therapist, thereby eliminating the need to act them out elsewhere. For example, children with control and oppositional issues would initially act in a controlling and oppositional manner, whereas children with deprivation and loss issues would begin the process acting out of neediness and lack of trust. Finally, the goal for children with neuroses is to use the therapeutic relationship to increase their awareness of unconscious conflicts and to help them use their verbal facility to discuss their feelings.

Developmental Play Therapy

The goals of developmental play therapy are to fill in the developmental gaps that are missing for children because of trauma and abuse, lack of care and nurturance, or ineffective parenting, thus allowing the child to move on to more age-appropriate developmental stages. As they mature, children need to learn developmental lessons, including soothing, causality, memory, coping, guilt, avoidance, and mourning. Developmental play therapy uses developmentally appropriate toys, games, and rituals to allow children to bridge developmental lags.

Jernberg (1979) described a very active role for the developmental therapist. She must diagnose deficiencies and promote remedial activities in each of the four categories that represent caretaker–child interactions: structuring, challenging, intruding, and nurturing.

Structuring activities create boundaries for the child and provide him with a sense of security. Included are activities that protect the child from danger, such as removing sharp objects from the environment or restricting play areas. As children mature, rules are the principal means for structuring their lives. Peers also provide greater structure. Caretakers who structure too much (many strict rules and harsh consequences) or too little (no consistent rules) create children who are either overdependent or who rebel against structure.

Challenging activities stimulate the child to improve his capacities. Depending on age, children may be encouraged to walk without holding on, feed themselves, dress themselves, learn to read, or engage in complex social relationships. Challenging may be overdone by pressuring children to perform tasks that are beyond their ability and frustrate them.

Intruding activities are used to interrupt children's activities when they need to be interrupted. The motor activity of an overstimulated child is intruded on to prevent him from being hurt. Similarly, a friendly shoving match between two adolescents is intruded on just as it begins to evoke anger. Intrusions are harmful when they are used to satisfy the caretaker's needs rather than to help the child.

Nurturing activities provide for the child's physical and emotional needs, for example, soothing, hugging, cooking special foods, providing protective clothing. Lack of nurturance causes children to withdraw from interaction with others or to exploit others in order to have their own needs met. Theraplay is a very specific play therapy intervention designed to provide missed nurturing for children.

Other examples of developmental play therapy include the use of toy guns to express the grief and abandonment resulting from a parent's murder, the preparation of monster poison to kill the man who raped a child's mother, and a ritualized play funeral (Shelby, 2000). Blameberry Pie is an intervention for adolescents who have survived sexual assault or rape and believe that the attack is their fault (Shelby, 2000). The therapist brings to the session a large pie tin and several smaller ones. Labeling the largest tin "Who is responsible for raping you," the therapist asks the client to write the reasons they feel responsible for the victimization on different pie wedges of colored construction paper and place them in the tin. The teenager may write, "Because I was drinking," or "Because I got in the car with him." After a complete list has been generated and placed in the pie tin, the therapist and client review the pieces of pie.

> "No wonder you feel so awful," the therapist might respond. "Look at all of those reasons in there; but this is supposed to be a pie about the rape. Let's see if the reasons all fit into this pie. Let's take one of these." The therapist or teenager selects one of the items inside the pie. "This says, 'Because I trusted him.' OK, so you trusted him. You wish you hadn't trusted someone who hurt you. That belongs in a different pie, not in a pie about who is responsible for raping you. Let's make a trust pie for that." The therapist asks the adolescent to place the paper in a smaller pie dish and label it "trust." The therapist and client select another item from the large pie tin,

discuss it, and label a different smaller pie tin (drinking, accepted a ride). (Shelby, 2000, p. 96)

After all of the pie slices have been discussed and the who is responsible for the rape pie is empty, they can discuss how the teen might be responsible for trusting, or taking a ride, or drinking but is not responsible for the rape.

Shelby also discusses "ageocentrism," a response to the "clinician's illusion" and therapists' distrust of short-term therapy. Shelby has found short-term play therapy with children to be very helpful. The "Clinician's Illusion" was coined by Cohen and Cohen (1984) to describe therapists' beliefs that most clients receive long-term treatment, when in fact short-term treatment is more the norm, with the mean number of sessions ranging from five to eight. In her theory of ageocentrism, Shelby states that adults and children live in different time scales and that it is inappropriate for adults to impose their time scale onto the children's therapy. A small amount of time from an adult's perspective may be a rather large proportion of a child's life. For example, a 2-month course of therapy for a 6-year-old is proportional to a 1-year course of treatment for a 36-year-old. She implores therapists to stop complaining about the amount of time they have to bring about change and to reframe the significance of time spent in the therapeutic process.

Shelby also offers an interesting developmental chart that may lend insight into developmental play therapy (Shelby, 2000, p. 72).

Specific Play Therapy Interventions

Some approaches to play therapy do not emanate from a specific theoretical perspective. Instead, they draw from various bodies of theory, often for a specific purpose. For example, *release play therapy* combines psychoanalytic and cognitive–behavioral models and was developed for use with children suffering from posttraumatic stress disorder. *Filial play therapy* combines family therapy, parent training, and play therapy. A primary goal of filial play therapy is to teach parents effective parenting skills. *Theraplay* combines developmental- and behavioral-based models of play therapy.

Release Play Therapy

Release play therapy is an example of an individual play therapy approach often used with children whose social and emotional problems are due to trauma such as abuse, neglect, and disasters. Release play therapy has been widely used in the last decade with excellent results (Kaduson & Schaefer,

2000). Schaefer (1994) and others contend that children are more inclined than adults to develop posttraumatic stress disorder after violent incidents. Individual play therapy for children exposed to violence is partly based on release play therapy. Release play therapy allows children to assimilate the traumatic experiences into their own schema through reenacting the trauma repeatedly and over time.

VanFleet, Lilly, and Kaduson (1999) discuss the primary role of *abreaction* in release play therapy with child victims of trauma. Abreaction refers to the inner drive of humans to re-create their experiences so that they may be assimilated. Abreaction often occurs naturally for children and adolescents who have not experienced trauma. Extremely frightening events, however, can repress a child's natural ability to abreact and therefore to successfully process the situation and progress developmentally. These authors suggest assessing five factors to determine a child's sate of abreaction and possible need for release play therapy: (a) the strength of the stimulus, (b) the intensity and duration of the fears resulting from the trauma, (c) the summation of events (repetition, simultaneous traumatic events), (d) the sensitivity of the child, and (e) whether prior experience might intensify the child's response.

The therapist's role is to assemble appropriate play materials, set the stage, and facilitate the child's play by asking the child repeatedly to "show me" what happened. Sigmund Freud (1920) noted that children repeat during play those things that have made a great impression on them and that by doing so they abreact the strength of these impressions and make themselves masters of the situation.

Because children are most often passive victims of traumatic episodes, they need to reenact them in an active way that allows them to confront the event and utilize coping strategies to resolve symptoms caused by the trauma. Miniature toys resembling persons, animals, and objects (e.g., guns, cars, buildings) associated with the actual traumatic event are used in release play. Following the Oklahoma City bombing, therapists who worked with families reported a high incidence of children playing out bombs exploding and rescue efforts in an attempt to assimilate and resolve the trauma (VanFleet et al., 1999). Additionally, children exposed to or victimized by knives might use toy knives or knives they make from clay or pointed objects to repeat the stabbing and possibly conquer the attacker.

The therapist also facilitates emotional health by using interpretation to label the emotion or affect displayed, first by the play figures, then by "kids like you," and finally by the child herself. Using the child's play metaphors is an effective way to initially introduce the ideas of how the child may be feeling, for example, "I wonder if the squirrel puppet was scared when all that screaming was going on?" The therapist can then extrapolate to "some kids would be scared around all that screaming," and finally address the child directly: "Did you ever feel really frightened when all that screaming was going on?"

Additional techniques can be used to address feelings directly, such as pairing colors with emotions (red is for anger, purple is for fear) and having children color pictures of themselves or their heart. A second technique reported by VanFleet and others (1999) is to have children blow up balloons, "filling them metaphorically with various feelings." The child and the therapist can then jump on the balloons to pop them and "make the fear and anger go away."

Filial Play Therapy

Early in the 1960s, Drs. Bernard and Louise Guerney developed filial play therapy, which combines family therapy and play therapy. In filial play therapy, therapists train and supervise parents or other primary caregivers, who then conduct play sessions with their children. Traditional child-centered play therapy focuses on building the therapeutic relationship between the professional and the child. Filial approaches to play therapy are designed to foster a therapeutic relationship between the parents and the child by teaching parents to observe themselves and their child, to use reflective listening, to allow the child self-direction, and to effectively set limits for the child.

In situations where a child is exposed to violence or trauma, parents often feel helpless or guilty about being unable to protect their child from the event. These feelings can lead to increased levels of parental stress and consequently decreased abilities to deal effectively with their child. Sometimes the entire family is traumatized (Figley, 1989). Research indicates that filial play therapy benefits families in two ways: It allows children to express their feelings where parents can hear them and helps parents to combat feelings of inadequacy by contributing actively to the child's therapy. If the parents are the perpetrators of the violence or abuse, other forms of therapy will be required prior to using filial play therapy as a reunification tool.

Goals of filial play therapy include alleviating presenting problems, improving parent–child relationships, improving parents' ability to support and raise their children, and strengthening family systems. Child–family problems that have been effectively addressed using filial play therapy include aggression, anxiety, abuse or neglect, adoption, foster care, divorce, relationship issues, trauma, chronic health problems, substance abuse, depression, and attention problems. Filial play therapy resulted in the greatest gains of all play and nonplay forms of therapy (LeBlanc, 1998; LeBlanc & Ritchie, 1999).

Research has reported specific benefits, including low dropout rates, improvement in parenting skills, increases in parent empathy toward and acceptance of their children, decreases in parental stress levels, and decreases in reports of problem behaviors (Lobaugh, 1992; Lobaugh & Landreth, 1998). Parents learn generalization skills effficiently (Johnson, 1995), and improvements in both parent behavior and child adaptation have been maintained over a 3- to 5-year follow-up (Johnson et al., 1999). Filial play therapy sessions can be done with individual families or in group play sessions and have been used with at-risk children and Head Start children as a preventive measure as well as with children already presenting problems.

Filial play therapy playrooms should be modestly equipped so that parents can provide a similar setting during home sessions. Room layout for filial play training or supervision sessions should include both a play area and an observation area.

Theraplay

Theraplay is a short-term play therapy intervention designed to facilitate better relationships between parents or guardians and their children using attachment-based play. Theraplay involves parents first as observers and then as cotherapists. Based on interpersonal theories of human development, object relations theory, and attachment theory (Booth & Lindaman, 2000), Theraplay parallels the playful engagement of parents with their infants and toddlers. Anecdotal and case study reports (Jernberg & Booth, 1999) as well as empirical data (Bernt, 1990; Morgan, 1989; Munns, Jenkins, & Berger, 1997) have provided evidence for the effectiveness of this approach.

Theraplay has been used with adopted children, children experiencing multiple foster placements, failure-to-thrive infants, and biological parents and children who have not successfully bonded or for whom abuse or neglect has negatively affected attachment. Secure attachment to a primary caregiver allows a child to develop a healthy self-image, self-confidence, the abilities to trust and deal with stressful situations, and the capacity to form healthy relationships. To develop secure attachment with children with behavioral and emotional challenges stemming from adoption, foster placement, abuse, or neglect, Theraplay provides the structure to reenact a healthy parent–infant relationship. The therapy is designed to overcome the distrust of children who have lost their first caregiver. Caregivers are often reluctant to engage with older children the way they would with infants. Theraplay provides a mechanism to foster and encourage attachment-based activities with these parent–child dyads.

Activities are viewed through the lens of four dimensions: structure, engagement, nurture, and challenge. *Structure* provides a sense of safety and security and promotes trust and confidence through predictability and dependability. *Engagement* through surprise, stimulation, and engagement sends children the message that they are fun to be with and the world is an interesting and exciting place. *Nurture* includes comforting, caretaking, affectionate, and soothing behaviors that convey to children that they are lovable and that their parent can be counted on to respond to their needs. Finally, the dimension of *challenge* is provided by presenting the child with situations that require the right amount of growth so that children learn that they can grow, become independent, and successfully take on challenges now and in the future.

According to Booth and Lindaman (2000), the following characteristics of Theraplay lead to effective treatment outcomes:

1. Intervention begins immediately.
2. Treatment is direct, active, and positive.
3. Caregivers are included in therapy.
4. A working alliance is established from the beginning.
5. Homework assignments are used.
6. Success is expected.
7. Strengths of the parent–child relationship are built upon.
8. Treatment is goal oriented, structured, and focused.
9. A time limit is established at the beginning of therapy.

The first sessions are conducted by the therapist with the parent observing. After three to five sessions, parents are brought in for the second half of the session to act as cotherapists. Special care is taken to aid the parents entering the therapy session through the use of activities designed to make the child feel special or foster closeness, such as wrapping the child up like a package for the parent to open or hiding the child under a blanket for the parent to find.

The play space for Theraplay sessions is very simple and defined by a sheet or blanket placed on the floor. No symbolic or fantasy toys are used. Pillows, blankets, food, cotton balls, lotion, or beanbag chairs set the stage for attachment activities. Each session is divided into entry activities, checkup activities, playful activities, and calming, soothing, and nurturing activities. Entry activities may include piggyback rides, hopping or jumping with the child, and so forth, and are designed to bring the child into the session in a way that is fun and engaging. Next, checkup activities focus special attention on the child and may include counting the child's freckles, touching, putting lotion or powder on the child, and attending to any hurts the child may have. Playful activities are designed to deal with specific issues presented by individual children and caregivers and parallel the play of young children. Finally, the last third of each therapy session is devoted to calming, soothing, and nurturing the child, including holding, rocking, and feeding activities.

According to O'Connor (1991), the Theraplay treatment process has six phases: introduction, exploration, tentative acceptance, negative reaction, growing and trusting, and termination. The *introduction phase* involves the creation and discussion of rules. The *exploration phase* is the time the child spends getting familiar with the therapist, for example, discussing favorite foods, television shows, hobbies. During the phase of *tentative acceptance*, the child appears to enjoy the interaction with the therapist and subtly attempts to control the sessions. However, in the ensuing phase of *negative reaction*, the child resists the relationship as it threatens to become too intimate and directs extreme anger at the therapist, usually through aggressive, acting-out behavior. In this important phase, the therapist must structure the acting-out behavior with as much nurturance as possible. As the child learns to accept this structure, the *growing and trusting phase* of therapy begins. When the relationship between the therapist and child consists primarily of positive interactions, significant others are introduced into the sessions to help the child generalize her newly learned interactive skills. The last phase, *termination*, involves emphasizing the extent of change in the child, warning her in advance of the approaching end of the sessions, and finally celebrating the end of therapy with a party.

Educational Applications

Many play therapy techniques may be applied in educational settings by mental health professionals such as counselors, social workers, and psychologists, and by classroom teachers. Mental health personnel will be interested in helping children resolve personal problems interfering with effective school adjustment. They may use clinical strategies, including interpreting children's play in a permissive environment, and may meet with parents as well. Although teachers are not trained therapists and should avoid doing counseling about severe behavior problems, there are numerous opportunities within the classroom environment to use play as a therapeutic agent. Even though not trained to make clinical interpretations of children's play, teachers can use play activities to help children learn more adaptive behaviors such as communication skills, problem-solving skills, social conventions, and appropriate social behaviors (e.g., nonaggressive methods of resolving conflict). Play also provides an opportunity to observe and get to know students in situations that differ substantially from typical classroom activities. Providing students with developmentally appropriate toys and games and observing their play patterns, choice of toys, and contextual play themes may inform the teacher about issues and concerns the child is having. In addition, by providing developmentally appropriate play materials, teachers can encourage normal development and socialization.

Play is a natural means of improving children's communication skills. Children whose inability to communicate is due to linguistic limitations may be exposed to games and activities that require them to understand and use language. For example, a game such as Simon Says requires them to listen to and act on directions, and doll play can involve speaking for the dolls.

Children whose poor communication skills are a function of disordered affect, with characteristics such as shy or withdrawn behavior, might be included in small-group play sessions with a confident, outgoing child. The confident child serves as a model for the shy child, and the shy child can be prompted to engage in game-related social activities, like taking turns and talking about the game. Later, the child is able to engage in non-game-related social interactions. Small-group play sessions provide less intimidating settings for learning social behaviors. They are also devoid of the pressures for achievement.

Problem-solving behavior is a component of many games. Board games such as Monopoly provide opportunities to stop action and have children consider behavioral options before deciding on a strategy, such as making a purchase or building a house. Games such as Trouble require a strategy to avoid being sent home by an opponent. Also, teachers can create games or activities that present children with problems to be solved. For example, a game exploring social behaviors could define a problematic circumstance (e.g., how to tell someone you have lost a borrowed toy) and award various numbers of points for socially acceptable solutions. Children can also dress up and role-play scenarios about social problems (see Chapter 11).

Play activities involving more than one participant function successfully only if the individuals are able to use socially appropriate behaviors, including social conventions, when relating to one another. Therefore, these activities provide excellent opportunities to teach children to wait their turn, share, win and lose gracefully, help others, cooperate toward a common goal, and so forth.

Use of books with feelings themes such as fear, worry, shame, and anger can be very beneficial. Teachers should discuss an emotion with the children prior to reading the story, prompt them with questions during the story, listen to the students' stories, and provide a follow-up activity such as keeping a feelings log, drawing pictures of feelings, or making a collage representing a feeling. It is often easier for children to express troubling emotions through the characters in a book or through puppetry or dolls. Games like Trouble can also be used as vehicles to talk about characteristics such as courtesy (welcoming another student to the game) and generosity (allowing another player an extra turn).

Teaching social and behavioral skills through group construction or arts and crafts projects can also be very effective. The shared goals of the project and the fun materials (blocks, clay, newspaper, papier-mâché, paints) encourage learning through play. Directing a small group of students to build bridges out of rolled-up newspapers requires students to plan cooperatively, negotiate, execute the plan, and cooperate in building the bridge. Teams whose bridges can hold a dictionary for 2 minutes are considered winners.

Songs can also be used to teach social skills to students who have trouble controlling anger and impulsiveness during game situations. Two songs specifically, "You Can't Always Get What You Want" (M. Jagger & K. Richards, 1969) and "Sweet Seasons" (C. King, 1973), have been used to teach students important messages in a fun way. "Sweet Seasons" contains the line "Sometimes you win, sometimes you lose," which has proved very effective in calming students who are angry about losing and in allowing others in the class to prompt a student starting to become angry and disruptive to remain calm and enjoy the game.

Occasionally, teachers of students with emotional and behavioral problems need to relate to a given child in private, and play provides a useful format in this circumstance. For example, the teacher may have trouble relating to a very active or aggressive child in the classroom. By scheduling that child for play sessions with the teacher, both the teacher and the child are given the opportunity to relate in a relaxed situation, establish rapport, and enjoy each other's company.

Teachers interested in proceeding with play activities would benefit from observing certain guidelines. First, play sessions should be structured according to school standards for behavior. Although many play therapists recommend a permissive environment, the teacher will achieve greater success by adopting a more directive, conservative position in setting behavioral limits. Setting limits that coincide with acceptable school standards will also ensure that the teacher does not alienate key players on the mental health team, such as administrators and counselors, who may be disturbed by children being allowed to engage in behaviors not considered acceptable.

Second, children who cannot observe behavioral limits should be excluded from participation in teacher-conducted play sessions. These children may harm other children and disrupt activities.

Third, teachers should treat play therapy sessions as part of the instructional program. For students with emotional and behavioral issues, the lessons learned during games and other play activities address needs central to the students' learning. Teachers should make the goals of the play sessions—affective growth and development—clear to students, parents, and administrators. Just as they teach addition to students who have not mastered it, teaching improved social skills to children who require additional instruction helps to clarify the role of play in classes for students with behavioral difficulties.

Fourth, teachers should use minimal resources to establish the play therapy sessions. Axline's idea of adapting a corner of the classroom as the play area is well founded. The fewer demands the teacher makes for resources, the more likely she is to be permitted to undertake the program.

Fifth, the teacher should provide opportunities for every child in the class to be part of play sessions at some time during the school year. The teacher may create subgroups within the class who engage in creative play activities such as puppet shows or art projects, as a matter of course, once a week during the school year. In these sessions, the teacher's goal is to provide children opportunities for cooperative group efforts rather than to help specific children overcome problems. The general use of play therapy sessions not only pleases and benefits the children but also prevents the activities from becoming associated exclusively with problem children.

Sixth, play materials and opportunities should be geared to the chronological age of the class. Play therapy is particularly useful with young primary-school-age children who have not obtained the level of cognitive, linguistic, or emotional development necessary to benefit from discussion sessions. These children are quite comfortable using toys, and their play illustrates their typical manner of interacting with others. If they can be helped to modify their play behaviors, their social interactions may improve and they may benefit from a wider network of friendships.

Play therapy for more mature children must employ techniques such as drawing, story writing, drama, and puppetry that are appropriate for their level of interest. These areas are discussed at greater length later Chapters 11 and 12. Older children will also benefit from table games and games with rules that require team building and cooperation.

Learning is fun. Teachers who employ toys and games in the learning process, observe their students carefully, and engage honestly and sincerely with them about important issues of feelings and actions will do much to enhance their students' personal growth and educational success.

Sources for Play Therapy Tools

Chaselle, Inc., New England School Supply, Springfield MA 01101; 800/628-8608

Childcraft, Inc., Edison, NJ 08818; 800/631-5657

Childswork/Childsplay, Philadelphia, PA 19123; 800/962-1141

Constructive Playthings, Grandview, MO 64030; 800/225-6124

Learn & Play, Mahwah, NJ 07498; 800/247-6106

Ther-a-Play Products, Glen Ellen, CA 95442; 800/333-5979

Toys for Psychotherapy with Children, Greeley, CA 95442; 800/542-9723

Toys to Grow On, Long Beach, CA 90801; 800/542-8338

STUDY QUESTIONS

1. Describe three types of play that are often used in play therapy.

2. Discuss boundary setting in play therapy.

3. Discuss five guidelines for play therapy groups.

4. Compare and contrast the cognitive–behavioral and the psycho-analytic models of play therapy.

5. What are the basic assumptions behind developmental play therapy?

6. Describe some uses of play therapy with children suffering from posttraumatic stress disorder.

References

Axline, V. (1947). *Play therapy.* Boston: Houghton Mifflin.

Bernt, C. (1990). *Theraplay as intervention for failure-to-thrive infants and their parents.* Unpublished doctoral dissertation, Chicago School of Professional Psychology.

Bloch, M., & Pellegrini, A. (1989). *The ecological context of children's play.* Norwood, NJ: Ablex.

Booth, P. B., & Lindaman, S. (2000). Therapy for enhancing attachment in adopted children. In H. G. Kaduson & C. E. Schaefer (Eds.), *Short-term play therapy for children* (pp. 194–227). New York: Guilford Press.

Bronfenbrenner, U. (1979). Foreword. In P. Chance, *Learning through play* (pp. 1–3). New York: Gardner Press.

Chance, P. (1979). *Learning through play.* New York: Gardner Press.

Childswork/Childsplay. (1992a). *Angry monster machine game.* Plainview, NY: Author.

Childswork/Childsplay. (1992b). *Self-control game.* Plainview, NY: Author.

Cohen, P., & Cohen, J. (1984). The clinician's illusion. *Archives of General Psychiatry, 41,* 1178–1182.

Cornwall, E., Spence, S. H., & Schotte, D. (1997). The effectiveness of emotive imagery in the treatment of darkness phobia in children. *Behaviour Change, 13,* 223–229.

Dodds, J. (1987). *A child psychotherapy primer.* New York: Human Sciences Press.

Esman, E. (1983). Psychoanalytic play therapy. In C. E. Schaefer & K. J. O'Connor (Eds.), *Handbook of play therapy* (pp. 264–277). New York: Basic Books.

Fenson, L., Kagan, J., Kearsley, R., & Zelazo, P. (1976). The developmental progression of manipulative play in the first two years. *Child Development, 47,* 232–236.

Field, T., DeStefano, L., & Koewler, J. (1982). Fantasy play of toddlers and preschoolers. *Developmental Psychology, 18,* 503–508.

Figley, C. R. (1989). *Helping traumatized families.* San Francisco: Jossey-Bass.

Freud, A. (1947). *The psychoanalytic treatment of children.* London: Imago.

Freud, S. (1920). Beyond the pleasure principle. In J. Strachey (Ed.), *The standard edition of the complete psychological work of Sigmund Freud* (Vol. 18, pp. 29–42). London: Hogarth Press.

Gallo-Lopez, L. (2000). A creative play therapy approach to the group treatment of young sexually abused children. In H. G. Kaduson & C. E. Schaefer (Eds.), *Short-term play therapy for children* (pp. 269–295). New York: Guilford Press.

Gardner, R. A. (1998). *The talking, feeling, and doing game.* Plainview, NY: Childswork/Childsplay LLC and Creative Therapeutics, Inc.

Ginott, H. (1961). *Group psychotherapy with children.* New York: McGraw-Hill.

Guerney, L. F. (1979, Fall). Play therapy with learning disabled children. *Journal of Clinical Child Psychology,* pp. 242–244.

Hobbs, N. (1955). Client-centered psychotherapy. In J. L. McCary (Ed.), *Six approaches to psychotherapy.* New York: Dryden Press.

Howe, P., & Silvern, E. (1981). Behavioral observation of children during play therapy: Preliminary development of a research instrument. *Journal of Personality Assessment, 45,* 168–183.

Jagger, M., & Richards, K. (1969). *You can't always get what you want.* [Recorded by the Rolling Stones]. On *Let it bleed.* [Record]. New York: Abkco.

Jernberg, A. (1979). *Theraplay.* San Francisco: Jossey-Bass.

Jernberg, A. M., & Booth, P. B. (1999). *Theraplay: Helping parents and children build better relationships through attachment-based play* (2nd ed.). San Francisco: Jossey-Bass.

Johnson, L. (1995). Final therapy: A bridge between individual child therapy and family therapy. *Journal of Family Psychotherapy, 6*(3), 55–70.

Johnson, L., Brulin, R., Winek, F., Krepps, F., & Wiley, K. P. (1999). The use of child-centered play therapy & filial therapy with Head Start families: A brief report. *Journal of Marital & Family Therapy, 25*(2), 169–176.

Kaduson, H. G., & Schaefer, C. (2000). *Short-term play therapy for children.* New York: Guilford Press.

King, C. (1971). Sweet seasons. On *Music* [Record]. New York: Sony/Columbia.

Knell, S. M. (1993). To show & not tell: Cognitive-behavioral play therapy in the treatment of elective mutism. In T. Kottman & C. Schaefer (Eds.), *Play therapy in action: A casebook for practitioners* (pp. 169–208). Northvale, NJ: Aronson.

Knell, S. M. (2000). Cognitive-behavioral play therapy for childhood fears and phobias. In H. G. Kaduson & C. E. Schaefer (Eds.), *Short-term play therapy for children* (pp. 3–27). New York: Guilford Press.

Knell, S. M., & Moore, D. J. (1990). Cognitive-behavioral play therapy in the treatment of encopresis. *Journal of Clinical Child Psychology, 19,* 55–60.

Knell, S. M., & Ruma, C. D. (1996). Play therapy with a sexually abused child. In M. A. Reinecke, F. M. Dattilio, & A. Freeman (Eds.), *Cognitive therapy with children and adolescents: A casebook for clinical practice* (pp. 367–393). New York: Guilford Press.

Krall, V. (1989). *A play therapy primer.* New York: Human Sciences Press.

LeBlanc, M. (1998). *A meta-analysis of play therapy outcomes.* Unpublished doctoral dissertation, University of Toledo, Toledo, OH.

LeBlanc, M., & Ritchie, M. (1999). Predictors of play therapy outcomes. *International Journal of Play Therapy, 8*(2), 19–34.

Levy, D. M. (1938). Release therapy in young children. *Psychiatry, 1*, 387–390.

Lindler, T. (1990). *Transdisciplinary play-based assessment*. Baltimore: Brookes.

Lobaugh, F., & Landreth, G. (1998). Filial therapy with incarcerated fathers: Effects on parental acceptance of child, parental stress, and child adjustment. *Journal of Counseling and Development, 76*(2), 157–165.

Lobaugh, F. A. (1992). *Filial therapy with incarcerated parents*. Unpublished doctoral dissertation, University of North Texas, Denton.

Mader, C. (2000). Child-centered play therapy with disruptive school students. In H. G. Kaduson & C. E. Schaefer (Eds.), *Short-term play therapy for children* (pp. 53–68). New York: Guilford Press.

McNeil, C. B., Bahl, A., & Herschell, A. D. (2000). Involving and empowering parents in short-term play therapy for disruptive children. In H. G. Kaduson & C. E. Schaefer (Eds.), *Short-term play therapy for children* (pp. 228–255). New York: Guilford Press.

Miller, W. (1982). Cross-over therapy with children and adolescents. Topeka State Hospital Collected Papers, KS.

Morgan, C. E. (1989). *Theraplay: An evaluation of the effect of short-term structured play on self-confidence, self-esteem, trust, and self-control*. Unpublished research, The York Centre for Children, Youth and Families, Richmond Hill, Ontario, Canada.

Munns, E., Jenkins, D., & Berger, L. (1997). *Theraplay and the reduction of aggression*. Unpublished research, Blue Hills Child and Family Services, Aurora, Ontario, Canada.

Oaklander, V. (2000). Short-term gestalt play therapy for grieving children. In H. G. Kaduson & C. E. Schaefer (Eds.), *Short-term play therapy for children* (pp. 28–52). New York: Guilford Press.

O'Connor, K. (1991). *The play therapy primer*. New York: Wiley.

Osterweil, Z. (1986). Time-limited play therapy: Rationale & techniques. *School Psychology International, 7*, 224–230.

Patterson, C. (1980). *Theories of counseling and psychotherapy*. New York: Harper & Row.

Pellegrini, A. (1982). Interpreting children's play. *Journal of Children in Contemporary Society, 14*, 47–58.

Perls, F. (1969). *Gestalt therapy verbatim*. Lafeyette, CA: Real People Press.

Piaget, J. (1962). *Play, dreams, and imitation in childhood*. New York: Norton.

Post, P. (1999). Impact of child-centered play therapy on the self-esteem, locus of control, and anxiety of at-risk 4th, 5th, & 6th grade students. *International Journal of Play Therapy, 8*(2), 1–18.

Rank, O. (1936). *Will therapy*. New York: Knopf.

Rogers, C. (1951). *Client-centered therapy*. Boston: Houghton Mifflin.

Rubin, K., Fein, G., & Vandenberg, B. (1983). Play. In E. M. Hetherington (Ed.), *Handbook of child psychology: Socialization, personality, and social development* (pp. 693–774). New York: Wiley.

Schaefer, C. E. (1994). Play therapy for psychic trauma in children. In K. J. O'Connor & C. E. Schaefer (Eds.), *Handbook of play therapy* (Vol. 2). New York: Wiley.

Schaefer, C. E., Jacobsen, H. E., & Ghahramanlou, M. (2000). Play group therapy for social skills deficits in children. In H. G. Kaduson & C. E. Schaefer (Eds.), *Short-term play therapy for children* (pp. 296–344). New York: Guilford Press.

Segal, H. (1972). Melanie Klein's technique of child analysis. In B. Wolman (Ed.), *Handbook of child psychoanalysis*. New York: Van Nostrand Reinhold.

Shelby, J. S. (2000). Brief therapy with traumatized children: A development perspective. In H. G. Kaduson & C. E. Schaefer (Eds.), *Short-term play therapy for children* (pp. 69–104). New York: Guilford Press.

Silverstein, S. (1986). *The giving tree*. New York: HarperCollins.

Sjolund, M. (1981). Play-diagnosis and therapy in Sweden: The Erica method. *Journal of Clinical Psychology, 37*, 322–325.

Trebling, J. A. (2000). Short-term solution-oriented play therapy for children of divorced parents. In H. G. Kaduson & C. E. Schaefer (Eds.), *Short-term play therapy for children* (pp. 144–174). New York: Guilford Press.

Udwin, O., & Yule, W. (1982). Validation data on Lowe and Costello's Symbolic Play Test. *Child Care, Health and Development, 8*, 361–366.

VanFleet, R. (2000). Short-term play therapy for families with chronic illness. In H. G. Kaduson & C. E. Schaefer (Eds.), *Short-term play therapy for children* (pp. 175–193). New York: Guilford Press.

VanFleet, R., Lilly, J. P., & Kaduson, H. (1999). Play therapy for children exposed to violence: Individual, family, and community interventions. *International Journal of Play Therapy, 8*(1), 27–42.

Webb, N. B. (1991). *Play therapy with children in crisis—A casebook for practitioners*. New York: Guilford Press.

DRAMA INTERVENTIONS

Drama as a therapeutic intervention is a group approach to therapy that integrates both verbal and nonverbal interactions. It is based on the premise that individuals gain greater understanding of society and the forces influencing their behavior if they act out significant scenes from their lives.

Psychodrama and Sociodrama

One avenue of theory and clinical practice having a significant impact on the use of drama as a therapeutic intervention is represented in the work of Jacob L. Moreno, a Vienna-born psychiatrist. Moreno, who began his clinical study of personality disorders in the early 1900s, developed a form of psychotherapy that thrust patients into representative interactions with persons whom they perceived to be contributing to their problems. Moreno's theories were, in part, a reaction against Freudian principles. He was disenchanted with the Freudian emphasis on the patient's history. He believed that persons with various emotional and behavior disorders must deal in the present (or "the here and now") with emotionally charged situations. He also objected to the relatively pessimistic Freudian view of human beings as "puppets" directed by instinctual and unconscious forces. Although Moreno, like Freud, developed a dynamic, tension-reduction theory of personality, he integrated concepts common to the humanistic and existential frames of reference. He perceived human beings as basically good, capable of striving for and achieving self-improvement. He noted that whatever the causes of personal problems, people must ultimately assume responsibility for their own behavior.

According to Moreno, personality maladjustment and emotional disorders frequently result from the pressures of integrating self with the world at large. Problem solution depends on the reduction of inner tension through the development of new insights about behavior. Such insights can evolve only when individuals are encouraged to demonstrate attitudes, beliefs, and perceptions as though they are the leading character in a play. They must act out their thoughts and feelings, as they would in real-life situations.

Moreno coined the terms *psychodrama* and *sociodrama* to describe his therapeutic approaches. Psychodrama and sociodrama are similar techniques. The therapist or director encourages participants to act out or role-play significant events. The differences between psychodrama and sociodrama lie in their purposes. In the former, the emphasis is on helping each individual in the group resolve personal problems. Consequently, the drama and the parts played by all participants focus on one individual at a time, who is designated the protagonist. Other group members, characterized as auxiliary egos, assume important roles in the drama. Still other members of the group serve as a participating audience. Sociodrama deals with broad sociological problems, such as racial or ethnic stereotypes. Various group members play important representative roles. Actors become group symbols.

The ideas introduced by Moreno when he developed psychodrama have been applied extensively. In addition to use by psychiatrists with psychologically disordered adults, they have been used to treat alcoholics, kindergarten and nursery school children, drug addicts, and delinquents. The father of gestalt therapy, Fritz Perls (1969), made extensive use of Moreno's role-playing strategies (called "monodrama," because Perls used no auxiliary egos). Even approaches as far removed philosophically from Moreno's theories as behavioral and cognitive therapies incorporate many of his strategies into their treatment procedures, for example, modeling, role playing, and rehearsal (although he is rarely given credit for introducing these techniques). Because of their importance in many uses of drama as therapy, Moreno's ideas are discussed in detail.

Principles of Psychodrama

Moreno (1964, 1973) identified six key concepts as components of psychodrama: (a) spontaneity, (b) situation, (c) encounter, (d) tele, (e) catharsis, and (f) insight. *Spontaneity* is the force behind creativity, the spark generated by psychological health. Persons with emotional and behavioral disorders typically lack spontaneity; they react to their environment with rigid, preconceived responses. Individuals must be encouraged to abandon static response patterns and to demonstrate less-inhibited actions. The psychodrama provides the opportunity for spontaneous behaviors.

In psychodrama, the *situation* may encompass any part of the disturbed person's life. Barriers of time and space are removed; thus, past and future events are portrayed as present occurrences. Actors may assume the roles of persons not currently in the protagonist's physical life space. In this way, unresolved conflicts, such as those experienced with parents or siblings, may be re-created by the protagonist. Fears of future events may also be dramatized. The emphasis on bringing all possible problems into the present is predicated on the belief that a person's perceptions of reality are a critical determinant of mental health. An old problem, such as a traumatic relationship with a parent, cannot remain buried. It must be acted out as though it was presently occurring, because it is still important to the protagonist. Such interactions often take the form of an encounter.

The *encounter* occurs when the protagonist in the psychodrama confronts herself and important people in her life. The confrontation is always in the present, although it may depict past or future events. The protagonist is forced to face other people's views of her even though they may contradict her self-perceptions. She must also examine her thoughts and emotions toward others.

Tele is a state that emerges from the encounter. It refers to the exchange of empathy and understanding between the persons involved in the psychodrama. *Catharsis* is an emotional release that occurs after a psychodramatic session. This cleansing discharge of emotion is due to the spontaneous action involved in the drama. Catharsis produces *insight,* a sudden awareness or understanding not previously experienced by the individual. When the protagonist experiences insight, she suddenly "sees" or "perceives" the situation in a new light.

Two additional key theoretical premises underlying psychodrama are the concepts of *action* and *the here and now.* Moreno believed that the passive positions assumed by clients in psychoanalysis were constricting and encouraged trivial verbal rumination. Acting out events encouraged openness and helped people expand their awareness. Similarly, experiencing events in the here and now causes individuals to feel the emotions related to significant situations rather than simply talk about them—a passive, intellectual exercise that rarely generates spontaneous awareness or insight. Enacting past or future events as though they were presently occurring promotes reality-based learning that is far more valuable than verbally rehashing past events or repressed feelings.

Components of Psychodrama and Sociodrama

Psychodrama and sociodrama always involve a specific cast of participants, including the therapist as director, the actors, and the audience. In addition, these productions follow a specific sequenced format: the warm-up, conducted by the therapist to involve the group; the actual drama, involving a series of dramatic techniques to stimulate the action; and a concluding session.

The Therapist's Role

According to Moreno (1964), the therapist, or director of the drama, is also a producer, a therapeutic agent, and an analytical observer. As the producer, she organizes the drama, using warm-up strategies that are essential to engaging the group in the event. She also supervises the ongoing flow of action, using her knowledge of therapeutic techniques and strategies to maintain continuity. After the drama, the therapist provides closure by encouraging the group to react to what has occurred.

Just as the procedures and techniques associated with psychodrama and sociodrama are used spontaneously as they are needed in the drama, the therapist's role is not prescribed but varies with the group and purpose of the drama, ranging from directive to nondirective. The therapist can be extremely directive, taking sole responsibility for the choice of topics, choosing the protagonists (especially in psychodrama) and other participants, preparing the auxiliary egos (other actors in the drama) with the precise structure of their roles, and so forth, without any input from group members. She might assume such a high level of control if the group consisted of extremely inexperienced, withdrawn, passive, or depressed individuals who were reluctant to participate freely.

Conversely, the therapist can be highly nondirective, encouraging the group to identify topics for drama, select the protagonists and other actors, contribute spontaneously to the techniques used in the flow of action, and make concluding remarks. A group of essentially healthy individuals attempting to grow psychologically and having previous experience with drama activities would be comfortable with the nondirective role of the therapist. A nondirective format is more likely to be used in sociodrama after the group gains experience enacting drama.

Actors and Audience

The actors in psychodrama always include a protagonist—either self-nominated or chosen by the therapist or the group—to provide the substance of the drama. Aspects of this individual's life, past, present, or future, are enacted to help him solve personal conflicts. The protagonist is aided by the participation of other actors, called auxiliary egos, who stand in for him or interact with him in the drama. Auxiliary egos usually are group members who appear particularly suited to enact a specific situation. For example, in a dramatic event involving the expression of resentment between the protagonist and his superior at work, the auxiliary ego might be an individual who can identify with the superior. Occasionally, auxiliary egos are selected because their typical behavior is directly opposite the type of behavior required in the drama, as when a shy woman is asked to play the part of an outspoken individual. When the demands of a particular role call for more extensive therapeutic intuition, a counselor or mental health professional is used as an auxiliary ego. Blatner (1973) listed the specific functions of auxiliary egos. These include doubling, or standing in, for the protagonist and playing a variety of roles that affect the protagonist. Such roles might include a significant other person in the protagonist's life, a general person unknown to the protagonist (e.g., a teacher or a judge), a fantasized figure (e.g., an idealized mother), an inanimate object (e.g., a car), or an abstract concept or collective stereotype (e.g., society or parents).

A protagonist is not always specified in sociodrama, which is aimed at exploring group themes rather than focusing on individual problems. When a protagonist is selected, it is not to present events from her own life but to represent a typical role associated with others. For example, an individual might enact the role of a homeless person. Similarly, in sociodrama other group members participate but usually not as auxiliary egos. They play alternative roles representing other forces in the social drama, such as that of a policeman confronting the homeless person.

In both psychodrama and sociodrama, the nonacting group members, or audience, are participants. They learn from the drama and participate in follow-up techniques after it ends, sharing their reactions to or interpretations of events and suggesting ways to apply them in their own lives.

Warm-Up

The warm-up is an important component of drama therapy in which the director sets the stage for the drama by fostering communication among the participants and establishing goals for the session. In psychodrama the director attempts to help the protagonist and the auxiliary egos prepare for the upcoming action. Just as the director's role throughout drama therapy varies from directive to nondirective with the type and purpose of the group, warm-up methods vary. They may be broadly categorized as nondirective, semidirective, and directive. All methods encourage spontaneous input from group members as they discuss the forthcoming drama. They also involve discussion of the purpose of the group, the methods used, the duration of sessions, and the responsibilities of each participant.

In a nondirective warm-up most of the responsibility for structuring the drama, including selecting the topic and choosing the actors, is assumed by the group. The discussion may begin with an open-ended assessment of group concerns or opinions. The director makes only the most general remarks, usually to stimulate group reaction and discussion. In the semidirective method the director has a particular drama topic in mind and calls it to the group's attention. She may also suggest that a certain protagonist be selected. The director remains responsive to the group's opinion, however, and alters the drama plan according to its wishes.

In a directive warm-up the director usually has selected a topic, a protagonist, and the auxiliary egos. The warm-up session may be used to share these plans with the group and to discuss individual roles in the drama. In some instances the director may use the warm-up to question the protagonist in the manner of a psychiatric interview. This will acquaint the group with the nature of the problem forming the basis of the drama and suggest the types of roles to be played.

On some occasions, roles are played by the therapist or by therapeutic aides, usually when the protagonist requires interaction with an individual who thoroughly understands the dynamics of a particular relationship. Actors are selected on the basis of their psychological needs, not their physical appearance. Thus, a tall, young male may play the role of a small, elderly woman, or vice versa.

To promote group interaction, the director may use exercises such as forming dyads among the group members by asking each participant to select another member to become acquainted with and introduce to the group. Certain nonverbal exercises can be undertaken by the dyads, such as communicating with hand gestures or taking blind walks (one person leads another who is blindfolded).

According to Blatner (1973), the director may bring the group closer to the actual drama by staging improvisations or minidramas. In these, members are encouraged to enact melodramatic roles, such as the villain harassing the fair maiden. Myths and fairy tales also can be enacted, or individuals can be asked to role-play familiar situations, such as attempting to talk a policeman out of giving a traffic ticket. Another approach is guided imagery, in which group members are asked to fantasize about a certain theme, such as a journey through a forest or a ride on a magic carpet.

Dramatic Techniques

When the director believes the group is warmed up and ready, the drama begins. The director focuses on controlling the flow of the drama by using techniques that increase or decrease emotional intensity, isolate or illustrate key issues that emerge, draw actors further into the drama, and protect the protagonist from generating excessive emotion. Moreno (1964) and his disciples have generated many techniques to ensure spontaneity in the drama. The most popular include role reversal, soliloquy, double, mirror, behind-the-back, high chair, empty chair, magic shop, and the ideal other.

In *role reversal* the protagonist exchanges roles with an auxiliary ego. For instance, a child may take the role of his father while the auxiliary ego takes the child's role. Through role reversal, the protagonist learns to appreciate another person's perspective or feelings in a situation. He also has the opportunity to see himself as others see him. In sociodrama, an individual representing Hispanic Americans may reverse roles with a person representing European Americans to enable each participant to gain increased awareness of the other's point of view.

Soliloquy is used to help the protagonist clarify his feelings when he may be unable to project them adequately in the drama or when his level of emotional involvement is too intense. He is instructed to make a spontaneous speech directly to the audience that expresses his innermost feelings and thoughts. This monologue may be an outburst of anger or just a pronouncement of general feelings. Soliloquy helps the protagonist pull back from stressful dramatic situations and gain increased understanding of his reactions to events unfolding in the drama. In psychodrama this type of learning is considered essential for catharsis and development of insight. In sociodrama it is a means of increasing the group's understanding of problems experienced by others, as when an actor representing the homeless expresses his feelings at having nowhere to turn.

Double is a technique used when the protagonist is overwhelmed by the other actors or is having difficulty expressing his feelings. Another group member, an auxiliary ego, stands with the protagonist in a psychodrama and shares his identity. In sociodrama the double may add to the range of behavior displayed by the principal actor. When used to resolve personal problems, the double may remain silent and provide moral support for the protagonist, or he may be the protagonist's alter ego and act and speak as he perceives the protagonist would. When the protagonist believes that the double's statements are accurate reflections of his feelings, he repeats them. When they are not accurate, he corrects the double by saying "no." If the double cannot approximate the protagonist's feelings, another individual may attempt the role. Strategies used by the double include dramatizing feelings, verbalizing nonverbal communications, physicalizing words and gestures, questioning the self, contradicting feelings, defending against feelings, and observing the self (Blatner, 1973).

In doubling, feelings are dramatized to maximize emotional content of an attitude. Remarks such as "I'm annoyed" may be doubled as "I'm furious." The double verbalizes nonverbal communications by remarks such as "Get away from me," used when the protagonist steps back to avoid physical contact with another actor. Physicalizing words and gestures involves nonverbal expansions of the protagonist's acts or remarks. For example, the double may shove another actor advancing too close to the protagonist. When the double feels the protagonist is not saying what he really believes, the double may try to draw the protagonist's attention to that fact, voicing contradicting feelings with a remark such as "Maybe I really don't believe this." Similarly, when the double perceives that the protagonist is using a typical defense mechanism such as displacement, he may draw attention to this defense against feelings by directing the remark "You're to blame" at another participating actor. The double also may focus awareness on the protagonist's general behavior by remarks such as "I'm really nervous."

The *mirror* technique also requires that an auxiliary ego assume the role of the protagonist. In this case, however, the protagonist joins the audience and watches the drama. The mirror technique allows the protagonist to see his behavior from another person's point of view. This is most useful when the protagonist cannot understand the impact of his behavior on others. Occasionally, the auxiliary ego is instructed to distort the protagonist's behavior, deliberately exaggerating characteristics to make them more obvious to the protagonist and to involve him more actively in the drama. The exaggeration provokes the protagonist to reenter the drama to show the way he really behaves. In sociodrama the role played by one representative actor can be expanded on or altered by another actor whose perspective increases the group's understanding of the problem.

The *behind-the-back* technique also exposes the protagonist to the views of others to increase awareness about his behavior. With this technique, however, the drama stops and the protagonist sits on a chair with his back to the audience. The director and audience discuss the protagonist, literally behind his back, speaking freely about their perceptions of the protagonist's behavior. In sociodrama, audience participation is more extensive than it is in psychodrama, and members of the group are encouraged to freely state their perceptions of behaviors associated with the key roles in the drama.

For protagonists who have difficulty asserting themselves or coping with threatening situations or for situations in social drama when a group is typically devalued in society, the *high chair* technique is used. A chair is elevated so that the protagonist is higher than anyone else on the stage. Presumably, the added height conveys a feeling of superiority and power to the protagonist, which in turn enables him to deal more effectively with persons who may dominate him.

The *empty chair* technique provides an opportunity for inadequate or unassertive persons to ventilate their feelings. The protagonist is directed to imagine his antagonist seated in an empty chair and to interact with him. Theoretically, the absence of an actual person reduces the protagonist's fears and inhibitions. He is able to give a more fluid expression of feelings. This technique is also employed to permit the protagonist to demonstrate his ideas about how key people regard him. The protagonist may reverse roles with the phantom person and interact with an imaginary self. In other words, the protagonist becomes the antagonist in the empty chair and interacts with a phantom of himself.

Two additional techniques used in psychodrama are the *magic shop* and the *ideal other*. The magic shop is a method for generating thoughts about life goals and is useful when the protagonist is ambivalent about what he wants in life. An auxiliary ego plays a storekeeper in a magic shop that sells wishes (e.g., courage, wealth, success) in return for a valued personal characteristic. The protagonist is offered anything he wants, but he must pay with something he has. The resulting dilemma forces the protagonist to reconsider aspirations and desires in light of current assets and decide what is really important. This strategy to clarify values also is useful in social drama.

The ideal other is used to reduce tension at the end of the drama. The protagonist lists the ideal characteristics of an important person in his life space. An actor assumes the role of the other person and behaves in the ideal manner suggested by the protagonist. Presumably, the protagonist enjoys experiencing a relationship that is free of strife or conflict.

These are a few of the procedures used in psychodrama and in sociodrama. In both dramatic approaches, the object is to stimulate the members of the group to recognize and respect feelings in themselves and others that affect their personal welfare and the welfare of society. The drama is designed to benefit all participants—not only the protagonist but also the actors and the audience. All group members are charged by the director with the responsibility of reflecting on the behavior displayed in the drama and are involved in the closing discussion held when the drama has ended.

The Closing Discussion

The closing discussion provides the opportunity for all group members to react to the drama. The group members are invited to help the protagonist learn from his experience by sharing incidents from their own lives that may be similar to those demonstrated in the drama. The director facilitates this sharing experience, seeking feedback designed to be supportive to the protagonist. She begins by questioning the group about their experiences and continues throughout the discussion to help them apply the dramatic events to their own lives. Consequently, all members of the group benefit from the events depicted in the drama.

Creative Drama

The development of therapeutic techniques associated with psychodrama and sociodrama during the 20th century has been paralleled by the evolution of similar dramatic strategies associated with progressive education in the form of the creative drama movement. Creative drama is a teaching technique whereby students enact various types of experiences as part of their educational process. Students may explore personal issues, social issues, or curriculum-related topics such as literature and social studies. Like psychodrama and sociodrama, creative drama is focused on the process of the drama and the experiences of the participants, not on a dramatic product such as a play. Although creative drama is not defined as therapeutic per se, it is presented as a means of helping children understand themselves, clarify their social values, and solve personal problems (Cornett, 1999). Therefore, many goals associated with the use of creative drama for educational purposes closely parallel the goals relating to the educational uses of psychodrama and sociodrama.

The creative drama movement was originated by Winifred Ward in the early 1920s when she began a program based on storytelling in the Evanston, Illinois, public schools. Creative drama became a recognized field of study in 1930. The term *creative drama* is common in the United States; similar attempts to use drama for educational purposes in other countries are known as improvisation, role playing, process drama, and educational drama. Cornett (1999), a current advocate of the benefits of creative drama, provided information pertaining to its usefulness and its basic elements (pp. 228–230), which is summarized here.

Uses of Creative Drama

- *Drama prepares individuals to cope with life's problems.* Students gain understanding by rehearsing roles that they play throughout their lives.

- *Drama involves students in creative problem solving and decision making.* Students are encouraged to act out problems in imaginative ways, and those experiences prepare them to seek their own solutions when confronted with difficult problems and decisions.

- *Drama develops verbal and nonverbal communication.* Playing dramatic roles involves communication with others through body language and spoken language.

- *Drama can enhance psychological well-being.* Dramatic roles permit a safe release of emotions and introduce constructive ways of expressing emotion.

- *Drama encourages empathetic sensitivity to other people's perspectives.* Role players learn how others feel in situations by "walking in their shoes."

- *Drama encourages cooperation and the development of social skills.* Students learn to cooperate by working together in dramatic roles and by gaining information pertaining to important social issues.

- *Drama increases ability to concentrate and comprehend.* The physical, intellectual, and emotional involvement of students in dramatic roles results in greater awareness and understanding of pertinent topics.

- *Drama promotes the understanding of moral issues and the development of values.* Values and beliefs evolve from experiences gleaned from dramatic roles.

- *Drama enables others to assess student progress through observation.* Students can reveal their understanding of a topic in dramatic dialogue.

- *Drama is fun.* Students benefit from an enjoyable learning activity.

- *Drama leads to aesthetic development.* Through dramatic techniques, students learn multiple creative methods of self-expression.

- *Drama enhances all learning.* Almost any topic can be explored through the use of drama.

Basic Elements of Creative Drama

Drama resembles literature in that both are means of expressing aspects of life. Just as students are taught the components of literature so that they can read and write more effectively, they can be taught the elements of drama. These elements include dramatic process, dramatic structure, and dramatic skills.

Dramatic process pertains to any level of involvement in drama, ranging from the simplest of pantomimes to the complex enactment of personal conflicts. Students are led from simple dramatic expressions to more complex enactions as their experience and comfort level increase.

Dramatic structure includes the elements that create drama—conflict, characters, plot, setting, and mood. *Conflict* can exist between two individuals, within an individual, between an individual and cultural rules or institutions, or between an individual and nature. *Characters* are the persons involved in conflict, including the protagonist and those who affect the protagonist. Characters are defined by and interact through their dialogue (what they say) and pantomime (how they move). *Plot* refers to the events produced by the conflict; it always has a beginning, middle, and ending. *Setting* is the time and place of the events. *Mood* is created by the behavior of the characters, the type of setting, and the pace of the drama.

Dramatic skills are learned by students as they create drama. These include use of the body (gestures, facial expressions, pantomime), verbal expression (volume, rate, tone, pitch, pause, stress, inflection, improvisation), focus (following directions, concentration), imagination (spontaneous expression, introduction of unique ideas), evaluation (taking suggestions, giving feedback, modifying behavior), social skills (cooperating with others), and audience etiquette (attending and responding with courtesy).

Educational Applications

Teachers who want to use drama in an educational setting should consider five strategies. First, introduce the concept of creative drama to the students and lead them through the stages of activities that will culminate in dramatic performance. Second, clarify the goals or purposes of each drama to be enacted. Third, plan each step for implementing specific dramas in the classroom, providing details about topic, warm-up, actor selection, role structure, and dramatic strategies. Fourth, consider the techniques to be employed to maintain the dramatic action. Fifth, select the location for the drama.

Dramatic Sequence

Creative drama is a natural outgrowth of the dramatic play engaged in by young children as they explore their worlds. As children mature, their dramatic play grows into creative drama as it increases in scope, becomes more structured, and involves innovative story lines. In educational settings, the teacher's task is to help the children feel comfortable displaying their creative spirit in the classroom. To guide teachers in accomplishing this task, McCaslin (1996) provided a graduated sequence of activities that help children enact drama. The activities begin with exercises that stimulate imagination and progress by steps to movement and rhythm exercises, pantomime, improvisation, and role playing.

The initial step, exercises that stimulate imagination, reflects the fact that imagination provides the foundation for drama. A simple exercise is to have the children walk around the room while imagining that they are walking through water, on ice, through hot sand, and so forth.

Most children participate willingly in the next step, rhythmic movement. A simple exercise is to have them march to a drumbeat. A more involved activity requires the children to perform rhythmic movements imitating various animals, such as horses, chickens, mice, frogs, cats, rabbits, snakes, monkeys, kangaroos, seagulls, pigeons, and cranes. A complex group activity is the "Old Person's Dance." To perform the dance, the class is divided into two lines facing each other. In time to music, the child at the head of a line does a movement or dance step, which the child across from her imitates and adds one step or movement to. Each person in turn imitates previous steps and adds one additional step.

Pantomime, the next dramatic activity, is particularly useful with older children and adults. It is best learned by the group before individuals attempt it. Children may perform pantomimes that develop concentration (watching a funny movie) and exercise the senses, such as seeing (finding a dropped coin), hearing (listening to a thunderstorm), smelling (unpleasant and pleasant odors), tasting (taking bitter medicine), and touching (picking up a hot potato). They also may perform an activity such as taking a bath or making a cake, or they may pantomime various moods or feelings in a variety of situations. After the children become comfortable with simple pantomime, they can progress to characterizations, such as playing firefighters struggling to rescue a trapped puppy from a burning house or portraying characters in a courtroom where a trial is taking place.

Pantomime leads quite naturally to improvisations and role playing as children add verbalizations and movements to their character development. Improvisation and role playing can vary in complexity and be appropriate for children of all ages. Scenarios may include problem resolutions, character studies, unfinished stories, and social issues, all designed to generate discussions by the class.

Goals of Drama in Education

Drama may be used in school settings to serve a variety of purposes, including the following:

- Exploring individual concerns or problems
- Conducting general affective educational programs
- Exploring common problems associated with childhood and adolescence
- Teaching social skills and coping behaviors

- Exploring social and cultural issues
- Facilitating learning
- Developing communication skills
- Conducting role training
- Developing group camaraderie
- Providing recreation

The use of drama to explore individual concerns or problems may be done in schools, but the dramatic strategies must be used judiciously. Teachers would be ill advised to use many of the dramatic procedures associated with psychodrama to explore the depth of feeling experienced by children and adolescents with serious disorders, for example, psychosis or severe depression. As noted, psychodrama, a complicated therapeutic approach, is designed to focus on one individual's personality disorder and to generate intense emotion in the protagonist. Teachers, even those trained to work with emotionally disturbed children, are not equipped to use drama for this purpose. Such treatment is the province of trained professionals, such as clinical psychologists or psychiatrists, who understand the dynamics of personality.

In circumstances where a child with a less serious disorder is willing to explore a personal problem, teachers may use any of a variety of dramatic techniques to facilitate expressions of feeling. When dramas of this type are performed, Allen and Krebs (1979) recommended that the individual exhibiting the problem (primary person) not be directly involved in the drama. She should remain a member of the audience to maintain the degree of objectivity necessary to see and understand the manner in which her behavior might contribute to her problem and be disturbing to others. However, Blatner (1973) recommended more traditional applications of drama strategies involving the protagonist. For example, the teacher may use role reversal or mirror techniques to help a physically aggressive but verbally noncommunicative child learn how his behaviors are viewed by others. Presumably, the opportunity to act out situations that often culminate in physical aggression will increase the child's ability to understand feelings that he may be unable to articulate. Specific examples of the applications of dramatic techniques with children are provided later in this chapter.

A second purpose for drama in the schools, as a component of an affective education program to teach children about feelings or emotions, conceivably could be an integral part of the teacher's instructional program. Many teachers are aware that their educational responsibility to students involves instruction in both affective and cognitive realms. However, their instructional program often pertains exclusively to cognitive areas, usually because they lack the methods to explore the affective domain. Through the use of drama, a teacher may help children learn about emotions and their effects on behavior. For example, the teacher may choose to have the class enact a drama about fear. They might explore themes such as fear of the dark, fear of animals, fear of school, and so forth. Discussions surrounding the drama should convey the fact that fear is a common emotion experienced by all people. The children could learn that fears can be overcome more easily when they are shared with others.

Helping children overcome common problems is another goal of educational drama. Most children and adolescents encounter many stumbling blocks on the road to adulthood. For example, most young children must cope with the feelings associated with the birth of siblings. Dating and its related social pressures constitute a problem for most adolescents. The availability of harmful drugs and the peer pressure to use them is another problematic area for young people. The stressful emotions associated with these experiences might be explored through drama strategies. The opportunity for the group members to act out these types of situations and to share their feelings should reduce the threat of the real-life experiences.

A fourth goal is to teach social skills and coping behaviors. Teachers may use selected aspects of drama, such as role playing, modeling, and strategy rehearsal, to help children who display maladaptive behaviors in school to learn new coping skills or practice more adaptive responses in specific situations. The children included in this group are those who, for the most part, are in control of their behavior but experience difficulty in particular situations. For example, they might have stormy interpersonal relationships or conflicts with authority figures.

A fifth goal, exploring social and cultural issues, is directly related to Moreno's sociodrama. It involves raising the group consciousness to the point where members understand the extent to which prevailing social and cultural mores shape their attitudes on such critical issues as gender, class, race, and ethnicity. In essence, the teacher has the students "walk in other people's shoes." For example, the teacher may wish to demonstrate the impact of social pressures on a particular minority group by casting various children in the roles of minority persons and having them experience the frustrations of discrimination in dramatic situations.

Sixth, drama can be used to facilitate learning. Allen and Krebs (1979) developed an innovative drama format for involving students in the learning process. They recommend organizing students into triads, then categorizing various types of subject matter into three components, each to be represented by a student. For example, government structure is executive, legislative, and judicial; direct objects may be taught by forming a subject, verb, and object;

and in a biology lesson one student (the player) is a cell, another (the producer) is any system that affects a cell (e.g., the circulatory system), and the third (the director) controls the player but not the producer. The director chooses a goal to accomplish and creates a situation that has a beginning, a middle, and an end. For example, the cell can be hemoglobin carrying lymphocytes to fight disease. The producer can assume any biological role to frustrate or facilitate the cell. The students, who have been familiarized with the vocabulary before enacting the drama, speak as the component they represent. For example, a student might say "I need more oxygen." Interaction continues through each step necessary to reach the goal, with director and producer matching wits as if playing a game of chess. When the director's goal is met, the students switch roles.

Drama can also be used in the classroom to increase children's communication facility. Children may use only gestures to communicate or may practice interpreting meaning conveyed by another person's body language. Also, children with limited use of language can be cast in roles with doubles who are more fluent. They can repeat the double's remarks while engaging in appropriate actions. As their competence increases, they may take small roles independently. Their interest in drama helps them remain motivated to use language.

Role training, an eighth use of drama in schools, is an accepted behavioral practice. Practical events in students' lives that have important implications, such as participating in an interview for employment, are practiced through role playing.

Developing group camaraderie is a goal with a great deal of practical value. Drama provides the teacher with an excellent method for shaping the class into a cohesive unit. As each individual member of the class is given the opportunity to help plan and act in a drama that is a class project, a sense of group identity is developed. Each child feels like a member of a unit and, as such, is likely to experience increased feelings of personal well being. A cooperative rather than a competitive spirit is promoted within the class. With this in mind, the teacher might choose to use drama to break the ice at the beginning of a new school year, or to integrate a new child into an established class.

A tenth goal of drama, recreation, is more important than it may at first appear. It is not uncommon throughout the course of a long school year for both teachers and their students to become less interested in school activities. As motivation decreases, so does productivity, and there is usually a corresponding increase in class-management problems. At such times the class requires recreational activities that are designed to reduce tension and raise spirits. Drama is an excellent technique for such a purpose because it provides the participants with an emotional outlet. The children create and enact a drama for the sheer fun of it. The teacher may choose to participate as an actor and to permit various members of the class to act as the director.

An additional benefit of this use of drama is to familiarize the children with the technique. Experience of this sort prepares them to participate in dramatic situations that may be directed toward more serious goals, such as teaching social values or exploring personal problems.

Steps in Implementing Drama in the Classroom

The steps for using drama in the classroom begin with the teacher's selection of one of the ten goals just discussed. Once the goal is established, the teacher must decide on the degree of control she will maintain over the components of the drama, including warm-up, cast selection, role structure, and topic selection. Then, using warm-up and improvisation strategies designed to help the children feel comfortable enacting drama, the teacher must interest and involve the children in the process. When the children are ready to participate, the drama is enacted, and the teacher must facilitate its flow by using appropriate dramatic techniques. Finally, the learning experience is summarized.

Implications of Goals. A teacher's goal for drama in the classroom should reflect her level of comfort and familiarity with the techniques. A good beginning for an inexperienced person might be role training that simulates life situations. For younger children, recreational enactments of fairy tales are enjoyable and nonthreatening (however, the children should make up the dialogue instead of performing prepared scripts). As the teacher and the children feel more comfortable with drama, the goals can be expanded and include topics that more directly affect personal growth and increased awareness.

The goal of the program, as well as the sophistication of the group relative to performing drama will influence the teacher's decisions regarding the extent to which he will structure or control aspects of the drama, including warm-up strategies, topic selection, cast selection, and role structure. Generally, the more specific the goal and the more inexperienced the group, the more control the teacher assumes for the drama.

If the drama is to be used as a form of affective instruction, the teacher may choose a general topic area and permit the group to develop the specific plans. For instance, the teacher might suggest a drama that deals with the subject of tolerance. A nondirective warm-up permits the group to develop the idea and to depict tolerance through actual situations. The choice of actors is also a group decision, and there is little preperformance role structure provided by the teacher.

On the other hand, a teacher might wish to use drama to deal with a conflict between two classmates. In this instance, the teacher introduces the topic of interest—the types of conflicts that develop among people—and includes the type of behavior occurring in the classroom. Because attention is focused on two children in particular, the teacher, and not the group, chooses to cast them in the important roles. However, their behavior is never identified publicly as providing the topic for the drama, and they are not playing themselves; they are representing a class of people who use the objectionable behavior. The teacher may brief them on the types of parts they are to play because she wants to ensure that certain behaviors are demonstrated. The dramatic arrangement is highly structured or directive, so the teacher uses the warm-up primarily to generate class interest.

Involving the Class: Warm-up, Pantomime, and Improvisation. The successful application of drama in the classroom is greatly influenced by the teacher's sensitivity to the group's attitudes and feelings about a topic, their experience with drama, and their enthusiasm for engaging in drama. Thus the teacher's previous use of the sequence of dramatic activities that are less demanding than role playing and his introduction of preperformance activities such as the warm-up are as critical as the actual management of the drama.

Children can prepare for role-playing drama by loosening up with rhythmic movements and performing simple pantomimes or improvisations. Cornett (1999) presented a variety of effective strategies. These include finger plays, such as those included in "The Itsy-Bitsy Spider"; sound and action stories, in which children echo lines or mime motions as the teacher narrates; voice change, in which students say lines as a character in a drama might say them; noiseless sounds, in which they pantomime sounds without making noise (laugh, scream, sneeze); and pass and pretend, in which they pass around an ordinary object and use it in a creative way or pantomime using it.

Cornett (1999) also recommended pantomime strategies. Among them are *invisible objects*, in which a student pretends to take an item from a basket and with pantomime shows its shape, size, texture, weight, temperature, and uses. With *mirror*, two children face each other. One child, the mirror, attempts to match the facial movements and body posture assumed by the other. In *the imaginary place* children create a setting such as a store and mime stocking it with appropriate items. The audience guesses what items the actors are miming. To perform the *tableau*, pairs or small groups of children depict a scene and freeze action at a particular place. Students may speak their thoughts at that moment. Finally, to perform a *narrative pantomime*, students mime as the teacher reads a story.

Other components of an effective warm-up are a thorough discussion of a topic for the drama by all class members. The teacher must take care to elicit opinions from reluctant speakers and to involve youngsters who otherwise might not participate. Although the teacher may be interested in a highly specific topic (bickering between children), he should introduce the topic in general terms (people's inability to get along) and permit the children to explore specific aspects through discussion. Their discussion serves to clarify their views and increases their level of understanding. A full discussion is so important that the teacher may wish to allot more than one warm-up session for its accomplishment.

When attempting to involve certain children in roles, the teacher must carefully elicit their cooperation. Obviously, a child who is reluctant to play a role cannot be forced or coerced into doing so. Because the drama is intended to instruct all group members, not just the actors, its impact is not lost on children who are not ready to become active participants. Actual role-playing involvement of many children may be accomplished only after extensive warm-up efforts, or, in many instances, only after the group has had the opportunity to practice by performing improvisation exercises.

As is true of all levels of drama, improvisations can range in difficulty from simple to complex. Cornett (1999) suggested a variety of relatively simple techniques, involving verbal improvisations. In sound-effect stories, students add vocal sound effects to stories read by the teacher. In say-it-your-way sentences, students say sentences as the characters in a role would say them.

Emotional conversation, in which two characters converse and then freeze as the audience talks about their emotions, and car wash, in which students form two facing lines and make positive remarks to peers who pass between them, are examples of a more complex level of improvisation. Even more complex are improvised scenes that require students to act out short scenes that they have planned. Each scene features conflict and involves a beginning, a middle, and an end.

Kohl (1988), who had extensive experience engaging young people in drama, also offered a variety of suggestions to facilitate improvisation. Children may be given a theme or situation and asked to act it out as they wish. Usually, initial efforts at improvisation involve only movement; voice is added later. One strategy Kohl recommended to elicit improvised movement is the use of charged themes involving common but difficult emotions. The following are examples of this strategy:

- You are standing in front of the door to a strange house with no idea of how you arrived there or what waits inside. Express in your face and body how you feel as you reach for the doorknob and slowly open the door.

- You have fallen asleep and awakened to find yourself on a strange planet. You hear footsteps approaching. What do you do?

- You have escaped from prison and are being chased. What do you do?

- You are walking under a full moon. Your skin and hair feels odd and you are being transformed into a werewolf. Act out the transformation.

Kohl (1988) also encouraged children to play persons other than themselves. He found children to be much more adept than adults at showing full ranges of emotion through words and gestures and to be more facile at assuming roles of vastly different characters. However, when children are shy, defensive, or reluctant to participate, he advocated walking as the best means of beginning improvisation. Kohl began by asking for a volunteer to walk across the room. If none was forthcoming, Kohl demonstrated his typical walk. Then he instructed the class to think of walking in a particular environment for a specific purpose (because walking is not usually a random activity), a mental exercise that enabled them to forget that an audience was watching. The next step was to ask the children to perform typical walking exercises: Walk as if you are being followed, walk through a snowstorm, strut to attract attention, walk when you do not want to reach your destination, walk like a baby who is just learning, walk up a mountain when you're 125 years old, walk home with a bad report card.

Children also enjoy improvisation activities that are extended to falling (e.g., being tripped, stumbling, fainting, dying). Kohl (1988) instructed the children to think about how they feel before, during, and after falling.

Voice is added after the children are comfortable with movement. For example, they might scream while falling or yell during a ball game. Props such as a telephone, mirror, or street sign might be used to encourage use of voice. The children might be asked to use the phone to gossip with a friend, tell someone bad news, complain to the school principal, or talk to a date while a sibling is listening on an extension. Using a mirror, they might have a conversation about school with the face (playing both roles) or pretend the person is trapped in the mirror and wants to get out. The street sign can set a scene of waiting for someone who does not arrive, meeting a spy, or meeting a lost stranger who does not speak English.

When moving from improvisation to more complex role playing, Kohl (1988) recommended that students list themes that interest them. Both the elementary-level and secondary-level students he worked with identified issues related to friendship and personal loss, as well as many other significant social and personal issues. He provided examples of scenarios related to friendship.

- Two people feel that they have never had a real friend, that they ruin their potential friendships, and that they really want a friend. They meet by chance. What do they do?

- Two of three people are best friends. The third person is jealous of their relationship and wants to be included. The two friends are talking and the third person enters. What happens?

- Two best friends are talking. One person has just been insulted because she has a physical disability. The friend is trying to support her and cheer her up.

Kohl also provided scenarios pertaining to personal loss.

- You just found out you are moving and leaving your friends. What do you say to them?

- Your father was killed in an automobile accident. What do you say to your brother and sister?

- An assassin is ready to kill you. Talk about your fear of dying.

- You have AIDS and must tell your close friends. What do you say?

Kohl (1988) engaged the students in theme development by organizing them into small groups, asking them to develop improvisations around a theme, and having them perform for the other groups. Typical themes include running away from home, jealousy over wealth, snobbery, a sinking ship, a fire, a robbery, and the outbreak of war. He noted that children are able to express a wide variety of emotions but resist showing affection unless it is real. To help them express affection, he advocated using themes involving real-life situations, such as consoling a younger sister when she falls and injures herself or rescuing a drowning kitten and asking parents for permission to keep it.

Improvisation, like all elements of educational drama, is dependent on role spontaneity. Even when children progress to the enactment of more complex dramatic themes, they must be encouraged to react sincerely in the role. Creative or educational drama differs from drama, in the usual sense of the term, in that the participants are acting out their feelings and thoughts, not reciting lines prepared by another person. This difference is essential to the use of drama as a therapeutic tool, because only the spontaneous portrayal of feelings generates new insights into behavior. Thus, the teacher may suggest a general type of role and give the actor certain dimensions of the characterization. The teacher should interfere with the ongoing action only when an actor is incapable of portraying a role because of inhibition, defensiveness, or embarrassment, and the flow of the drama is impeded. The problem of maintaining productive action in the drama requires the use of dramatic techniques.

Dramatic Techniques. Once children are able to improvise on themes and are comfortable using movement and voice to enact specific scenarios, the teacher is in a position to introduce many of the dramatic techniques associated with psychodrama and sociodrama and have the children include them in their role playing. The best way to familiarize children with these techniques is to include them in the improvisation exercises. Most of the following examples illustrating the use of dramatic techniques extend the examples of improvisation provided in the previous section.

The *soliloquy* technique is introduced by stopping the actor in midrole and asking her to tell the audience how she really feels about the events being depicted. For example, a child enacting a scene in which she is being transformed into a werewolf describes how she feels about the transformation. Initially, she may be aided by questions, asked by the teacher and the audience, such as "Are you scared?" "Will you enjoy killing people?" "Is it fun to frighten others?" Ultimately, children learn to identify the implications of their roles and to speak more freely about them.

Role reversal is used to help children take other perspectives and may be taught in any improvisation exercise involving more than one actor. For example, a child playing one of two good friends may be asked to change roles with the isolated child who is attempting to integrate himself into the friendship. Similarly, children can be asked to *double* for an actor. For instance, a child playing the role of persuading reluctant parents to permit her to keep a rescued kitten, can be joined by another child who assumes the same role; or the *mirror* technique can be used, with the initial actor being asked to join the audience while another child steps into the role.

The *behind-the-back* technique helps the audience freely reveal their feelings and attitudes about a dramatized scene and is particularly useful with older children and adolescents. The actor depicting the scene where he tells his friends he has AIDS may be asked to turn his back to the audience while they say how they really feel about this information.

When children depict sad or upsetting events in their drama, the *high chair* technique is useful. For example, the child insulted because of her physical disability may be asked to sit in the high chair and tell others how she can deal with those who reject her.

The techniques of *empty chair*, *magic shop*, and *ideal other* all lend themselves directly to improvisation. For example, the empty chair might hold a monster, fairy godmother, person from outer space, and so forth, to whom the child reacts. The magic shop provides any variety of tempting items that the child may select, such as dust that makes people and objects disappear or wings that enable him to fly. In the ideal-other scenario, the actor interacts with people who behave exactly as she wants them to when she relates to them in daily encounters.

Once children learn to use these strategies, they can apply them in more complex roles that are designed to help them recognize their true feelings about issues, resolve personal problems, clarify their values, and develop a higher sense of social responsibility. For the most part, this type of educational drama parallels sociodrama.

Sociodrama in Schools. One of the most important uses of drama in schools involves increasing children's awareness of social problems. The following examples illustrate the utilization of educational drama for this purpose.

The treatment-at-a-distance technique is used when a protagonist or individual representative of a specific class of people is not on the scene. It is particularly useful in schools that mainstream children with disabilities. Because many children with disabilities experience social rejection from classmates who are not similarly disabled, a drama held either in advance of the disabled child's enrollment or on a day when the child is absent may make the classmates more aware of that individual's feelings and cause them to behave in a friendlier fashion. The teacher may instruct a child who is likely to be particularly rejecting of a child with disabilities to be the representative actor, and set a scene in which the individual walks up to a group of classmates at lunch on his first day in class. He would like to join them. Two other actors are asked to role-play an accepting and a rejecting individual, respectively, and the audience is asked to participate in a behind-the-back interruption to give their opinions or ask questions of any of the three actors. The director may use doubles, the mirror technique, or role reversal to involve additional children in the action and to increase their level of awareness.

A similar technique is called representative protagonist. This technique does not require that a specific protagonist be associated directly with the group. The protagonist is representative of a minority subgroup within the society. For example, the director may want to depict the treatment of Native Americans by white settlers. The roles of the Native Americans may represent actual historical figures, such as Geronimo or Chief Joseph, or they may be symbolic of all Native Americans. In such an enactment, the director must remain aware that the drama is not designed to depict past history, as might be done in a children's play about the life of Geronimo. The dramatic action must occur spontaneously, in the here and now. To increase children's understanding about the implications of treatment given to a particular minority within the society, the children must feel the way members of that minority group feel.

Possibly the most useful technique to demonstrate important social issues is role reversal. Racial, sexual, and ethnic biases may be explored by having the children assume a variety of alternate roles. For instance, an African American child might play a European American child, or a boy might play a girl. The success of this type of drama is extremely dependent on the director's skill. Although the director must control the progress of the drama, she must be very careful not to force opinions on the actors that they do not share. For example, in a drama depicting sexual bias, the children must be permitted to express their true feelings. The director must avoid interfering with and censuring these expressions. The goal of drama therapy is to induce a spontaneous production of feelings, opinions, and attitudes. If the director suppresses remarks that run contrary to her own ideas about a particular issue, spontaneity is impaired. The drama becomes a social farce—the recitation of lines that are generally perceived as being what should be said. With the demise of spontaneity and the inhibition of true feelings, the opportunity for communication, catharsis, and insight that might lead to a genuine change in attitude is destroyed.

As has been suggested, other techniques may be used for the purpose of demonstrating important social issues. For instance, in a situation similar to the discussion regarding sexual bias, the teacher might want to use the mirror or double techniques to assist the children in understanding the importance of equality for the sexes. One drama might generate a variety of ideas for succeeding dramas. The teacher may decide to use educational drama on a regular basis, as part of the instructional curriculum.

Concluding Session. The concluding session is important because it gives the director the opportunity to involve the audience in the experience. The format for this session depends on the goals of the drama. If it is recreational, the children might be asked to give their opinions of the drama, discussing characters they liked or disliked; changes they would make in the drama, such as alternative endings; and so forth. If the goal involves academic learning, the director might question the class to elicit the extent to which they appear to have absorbed the points emphasized in the drama. If the goal centered on increasing awareness of self or others, the director may ask the audience how they felt about the events enacted or how the experience affected their lives. The emphasis during this type of discussion should remain on the children's feelings about what has transpired. The director should attempt to involve all the children in the concluding session, phrasing as many questions as necessary to elicit responses from the more reticent class members.

Physical Arrangements. From a practical point of view, an important advantage of drama is that it makes optimal use of imagination. The group or class members need only pretend that they are in a certain place, and, for the purposes of the drama, it becomes reality. The only necessity for staging a drama is enough space to rearrange furniture. Any room where chairs can be arranged in a semicircle to provide room for a makeshift stage at the front of the class is adequate for drama therapy. In most cases the children's regular classroom should serve nicely.

In rare instances, the teacher might decide to hold a drama in a private room or office. She might want to settle an issue that involves a subgroup of children from the class and may see no purpose in revealing the matter to the entire group. Obviously, the aims of the drama should determine where it is held.

The time necessary to stage a drama will vary depending on the teacher's aims and the children's experience and maturity. Less mature children may have difficulty sustaining the flow of action for periods longer than half an hour. When working with such children, the director must avoid attempting to depict too many important points in one dramatic session. Older or more experienced children may be perfectly capable of sustaining interest and action for an hour or more. This is particularly true when they are exploring relatively complex issues. Ideally, the course of the drama should make clear the best time to terminate it. When the group's attention wanders, the action in the drama stagnates, or the basic issues of the drama have been thoroughly explored, the time for the concluding discussion is at hand.

Benefits of Educational Drama

Advocates of drama in schools (Collins, 1997; Cornett, 1999; Kohl, 1988; McCaslin, 1996) have made several points regarding its advantages. First, it places the responsibility for growth and resolution of problems on the shoulders of the individual involved. Although people, particularly those who face a dilemma, often seek direction from an authoritative source, growth and development occur when an individual thinks for himself. Personality and related behavior changes when a person evaluates himself as objectively as possible, critically but not harshly, and takes responsibility for his conduct. The intellectual and emotional breakthroughs that often occur in drama can result in lasting changes.

Second, drama interventions place emphasis on the development of social consciousness. Individual growth is intrinsically related to the development of a philosophy of life. Such a philosophy incorporates the individual's attitudes and convictions toward others and recognizes the notion of the individual's responsibility to the group. Third, drama interventions emphasize the individual's future. This technique is designed to help the individual leave behind the concerns or cares of the past so that he might move creatively into new activities.

The fourth and most practical benefit of this approach is its efficiency. Dramatic techniques can quickly bring an individual to the point of examining underlying emotions and patterns of thought.

Most important, drama has obvious appeal for most children because they enjoy play acting. They tend to lose inhibitions more quickly than adults, and they bring a great deal of spontaneity to the dramatic situation. Therefore, provided they observe the cautions discussed in the next section, teachers who enjoy using these procedures and believe they will benefit their students can create a novel and enjoyable learning experience for children.

Cautions

Although the proper application of drama in the classroom has the potential to provide a range of benefits to the children that include fun as well as learning, outcomes depend on the teacher's scrupulous observation of certain guidelines.

First, the dramatic situations must be devoid of criticism. The teacher and the class members may make suggestions regarding certain roles, and they may offer comments about the course of the drama. However, demeaning or accusatory remarks are strictly prohibited.

Second, the children who participate in drama must do so voluntarily. Drama in schools is designed to promote affective growth. For the drama to be effective, the children must be motivated to learn or improve. Children who are apprehensive, embarrassed, or defensive are not in a position to learn efficiently. They should not be teased or coerced into active role playing. They will learn far more as members of the audience.

Third, the use of confrontation in the course of the drama must be regulated carefully. Unless a great deal of preparatory work has been done, a child should not be cast in a drama that will confront him directly with personal problems. An adolescent should be cast only when she has agreed in advance to act out the problematic situations. When confrontational drama is used, the teacher must ensure that the individual completely understands the events that will occur and is prepared to have other group members speak frankly about her behavior. Even under these circumstances, the teacher must establish clear limits about the type and tone of permissible confronting remarks.

For the most part, confronting remarks should pertain to behavior rather than to general character traits. The tone of the remarks must reflect constructive interest in helping to solve a problem rather than disgust or displeasure with the individual. For example, "You argue a lot with people" may be offered as a statement of an opinion, not as a harsh accusation.

Young people require a great deal of practice if they are to understand these distinctions. Direct confrontation should never be staged until these limits are understood by the participants.

Alternative Dramatic Techniques

The applications of drama in school settings discussed thus far have pertained exclusively to the physical enactment of drama by the children. There are certain advantages to conducting drama on that scale. It exploits children's natural predilections to act out their feelings. Thus, it is relatively unique in school settings where physical demonstrations of emotion are usually restricted. Also, the children's active involvement in the drama usually ensures their interest and attention. In some instances, however, the teacher might wish to employ dramatic techniques without resorting to active drama. Two such techniques are puppetry and storytelling.

Puppetry

Puppetry, a familiar method of entertaining children, for many years has been used as a method of helping them resolve problems. Insecure children who may fear active drama often participate willingly in puppet drama (McCaslin, 1996).

At times, a drama enacted by puppets is controlled by the puppeteer (the teacher). It is designed to illustrate the threats and fears that may be disturbing the children. Strict adherence to reality is unusual. Fantasy is incorporated readily into the script and is accepted easily by the children. A puppet may be killed in one scene and resurrected in the next. Puppets may levitate out of harm's way, cast magical spells, and leap tall buildings in a single bound. The combined use of realistic and fantasy characters is deliberate. It emphasizes the make-believe aspect of the drama while enabling the child to identify with a hero.

Throughout a puppet drama, the children are encouraged to interact with the puppets. The puppets address questions to the members of the audience, ask the children for advice or assistance, make remarks that draw the audience's attention to an event, and so forth. Usually, the children become closely involved with the puppet drama, and their behavior may be observed for clues about their feelings and attitudes. For instance, the type of life situation that they find upsetting or their feelings toward authority figures might be conveyed in their reactions to the puppets.

Teachers may use puppetry for any of the goals associated with actual drama. Many of the same dramatic techniques and formats also may be used. Children may be asked to enact specific scenes with puppets (e.g., role-play discussing the death of a parent with two sibling puppets). Through the puppet, a child may deliver a soliloquy in the middle of a scene to discuss his feelings about an episode. The teacher may choose a nondirective format or a highly structured one and may initiate a drama that explores social values, interpersonal relationships, or typical problems experienced by many children.

A nondirective use of puppetry is most useful when children have experience enacting drama with puppets. The children understand that they are not simply playing with the puppets. They take primary responsibility for the drama (i.e., choosing the topic, roles, and persons to act as puppeteers), and even make the needed puppets (Forte, 1985). The actual parts are created spontaneously by the children as they enact the drama. The teacher has two major responsibilities: the warm-up and the sum-up.

In the warm-up the teacher suggests the idea of staging a puppet drama to the students and arouses their interest. If they are enthusiastic, the teacher can offer them supportive suggestions as they discuss the project, such as possible topics, roles, or puppeteers. The teacher also can suggest that the group establish certain rules to provide structure for the drama, such as time limits, to ensure that the entire performance can be presented; action limits, to ensure that all group members have an opportunity to participate; and behavioral limits, to prohibit disruptive behaviors. Although the group should be permitted to make the ultimate decision about these issues, the warm-up period is the teacher's best opportunity to ensure that the puppet drama has the structure necessary to make it a constructive learning experience. The age of the children and their experience with puppet drama will determine the amount of suggestion and structure that a teacher must offer.

During the puppet show, the teacher becomes a member of the audience. He sets an example for active audience participation by responding enthusiastically to the action, verbally interacting with the puppets, and so forth.

After the puppet drama, the teacher leads the group in the sum-up. The group is encouraged to discuss what they have seen. The teacher's purpose during this session is to emphasize and clarify the affective messages conveyed in the drama. Questions such as "How did the hero feel?" "What caused the problem?" or "What would you have done to help?" stimulate the group to recognize and discuss affective lessons they otherwise might overlook.

The teacher who is reluctant to create puppetry drama might wish to order commercial affective teaching materials, such as Developing Understanding of Self and Others (Dinkmeyer & Dinkmeyer, 1982). The star performer of

Developing Understanding is a dolphin puppet that may be used in role-playing activities and as a leader of group discussions.

The use of puppetry in the schools has advantages. First, puppets are regarded by parents and administrators as innocuous, pleasure-evoking toys that belong in school. The teacher should encounter little resistance to staging puppet dramas in the classroom. Second, puppets are easily acquired. Because they consist only of a head and a material costume, they can be constructed by the children or purchased inexpensively. Cornett (1999) presented a variety of good ideas for making puppets out of common objects such as paper cups, clothespins, socks, paper bags, sticks, and gloves. Third, puppet shows require little space. A simple stage consisting of a square wooden frame and a curtain, set on a table, is all that is necessary to conduct puppet shows. Fourth, children love puppets. For the most part, they enter into puppet drama without self-consciousness or inhibition. Fifth, the portrayal of feelings indirectly, through puppets, rather than by direct acting, ensures that no individual will be embarrassed or upset by dramatic action that probes too deeply into sensitive areas.

Storytelling

Storytelling is regarded by many as the foundation of drama (Collins, 1997). Telling stories in dramatic fashion is far more intimate than simply reading stories aloud. Stories present living examples of problem solving, cultural differences, bonds between people, imagination, and old-fashioned fun. They evoke emotions, stimulate thought, and appeal to most people's better natures. Cornett (1999) offers suggestions to teachers to enhance the impact of storytelling. She recommends involving the audience by asking for ideas about the story, appealing to the children's curiosity, and having the children provide sound effects or pantomime the acts of the story characters.

Storytelling, as a form of drama, involves more than the simple recitation of a previously learned tale. One ideal for using storytelling is to have the children create an original story that they will tell to the group. For example, the children might be requested to create a story about a Native American woman who moves from her reservation to take a job in a large city. The story must include the characters' feelings, as well as their activities and experiences.

A storytelling project may be implemented in many ways. One means of implementation is to divide the class into small groups of three to five children and ask them to create stories about a particular theme. The teacher's role is to confer with each group as the stories are being developed. The teacher must encourage the children to cast themselves in the place of the story characters and to explore how they would feel and act in such a situation. During this period, the teacher's manner must be positive and supportive. Suggestions for story development may be offered, but the children's efforts are never criticized.

The actual storytelling may be done by one or all members of a group. The children may dramatize various roles in the story and present it like a play, or they may tell the story without role playing. After the story has been presented, the teacher helps the children restate the message it conveyed, explores the relationships between the characters' actions and feelings, and leads the group in forming generalizations from the story theme that relate to the development of social values.

A variation of storytelling technique involves the open-ended story. The teacher tells a story that incorporates issues about social or personal values, or perhaps depicts social or emotional problems, but leaves it unfinished. The teacher may provide several alternatives for ending the story and ask the children to select one or ask the children to develop an ending. For example, the teacher may create a story that presents a child in conflict with her parents and instruct the children to decide how the story character may best deal with the situation.

Story endings may be developed by each child, then discussed by the entire class, or they may be developed and debated by the class as a whole. The teacher's purpose for using the technique is to elicit alternative views of the ending and to stimulate class discussion about the implications of each alternative ending.

Empirical Verification

As has been noted, creative drama in education is seen by its advocates as a marvelous means to help children learn social values, solve personal problems, develop coping skills, and increase academic knowledge. Clinical impressions notwithstanding, it is heartening to note a representative body of research that attests to the effectiveness of drama for many of these purposes. The educational use of drama has been found to increase social interaction between typical students and students with special needs (Miller, Rynders, & Schleien, 1993); improve behavior, attitudes, and achievement (Gourgey, Bousseau, & Delgado, 1985); elevate reading comprehension skills (Dupont, 1992); increase narrative writing ability (Moore & Caldwell, 1993); and enhance overall language skills (Wagner, 1988).

✎ Study Questions _____

1. Discuss the philosophic principles that underlie psychodrama.

2. Discuss the dramatic techniques associated with creative drama. Then indicate how those techniques can be used by the teacher in a classroom situation.

3. Cite the advantages and potential dangers associated with the use of drama in schools.

4. Think of five different topics that could be introduced to your class or any group of children by using puppets.

5. Give six examples of themes for improvisation exercises. Three should involve only movement, and three should involve movement and voice.

6. Discuss two distinct types of dramatic warm-ups.

7. List the goals of drama interventions.

References

Allen, R., & Krebs, N. (1979). *Psychotheatrics: The new art of self-transformation.* New York: Garland STPM Press.

Blatner, H. (1973). *Acting in: Practical applications of psychodramatic methods.* New York: Springer.

Collins, R. (1997). Storytelling: Water from another time. *Drama Theatre Teacher, 5*(2), 6.

Cornett, C. E. (1999). *The arts as meaning makers: Integrating literature and the arts throughout the curriculum.* Upper Saddle River, NJ: Merrill.

Dinkmeyer, D., & Dinkmeyer, D. (1982). *Developing understanding of self and others.* Circle Pines, MN: American Guidance Service.

Dupont, S. (1992). The effectiveness of creative drama as an instructional strategy to enhance reading comprehension skill of fifth-grade remedial readers. *Reading Research and Instruction, 31*(3), 41–52.

Forte, I. (1985). *Puppets.* Nashville, TN: Incentive Publications.

Gourgey, A., Bousseau, J., & Delgado, J. (1985). The impact of improvisational dramatics programs on student attitudes and achievement. *Children's Theatre Review, 34*(3), 9–14.

Kohl, H. (1988). *Making theatre: Developing plays with young people.* New York: Teachers and Writers Collaborative.

McCaslin, N. (1996). *Creative drama in the classroom and beyond* (6th ed.). White Plains, NY: Longman.

Miller, H., Rynders, J., & Schleien, S. (1993). Drama: A medium to enhance social interaction between students with and without mental retardation. *Mental Retardation, 31*(4), 228–233.

Moore, B., & Caldwell, H. (1993). Drama and drawing for narrative writing in primary grades. *Journal of Educational Research, 8*(2), 100–110.

Moreno, J. L. (1964). *Psychodrama* (Vols. 1–2). Beacon, NY: Beacon House.

Moreno, J. L. (1973). Introduction. In H. Blatner (Ed.), *Acting in: Practical applications of psychodramatic methods* (pp. 1–2). New York: Springer.

Perls, F. (1969). *Gestalt therapy verbatim*. Lafayette, CA: Real People Press.

Wagner, B. J. (1988). A review of empirical research in drama and language. *Language Arts, 65*(1), 46–55.

CHAPTER

ART, MUSIC, AND DANCE THERAPY

Art, music, and dance are forms of activity therapy useful with individuals and, more commonly, with groups. They are regarded by some as independent non-verbal formats for helping individuals achieve psychological growth. Others view them as adjunctive to verbal forms of psychotherapy, that is, as techniques to reveal unconscious thoughts, promote relaxation, or enhance relationships. Although a certain mystical reverence for the healing effects of the arts has existed since primitive times, artistic expression was not recognized and widely used as a specific method for helping individuals with emotional and behavioral disorders until the latter half of the 20th century. In the period immediately following World War II, the arts served as types of occupational and recreational therapies for injured, hospitalized veterans. Currently, each artistic form has grown far beyond its original purpose and has become an independent (although interrelated) field of study.

Activity therapies share several therapeutic advantages. First, because they involve nonverbal communication, they are particularly useful with young children whose limited cognitive and linguistic competence prevents participation in verbal therapy. They also are useful for reaching persons who are socially withdrawn, psychotic, or autistic.

A second advantage is that the symbolic expression occurring in the arts may precipitate verbal expression. For example, Naumburg (1966) pointed out that the visual art form often stimulates verbal communication when the child attempts to explain or describe his production.

A third advantage is that participation in activities related to art, music, and dance provide opportunities for individuals to experience success and gain self-confidence. This aspect is important not only for individuals who are nonverbal or who have serious handicaps but also for the multitude of individuals—including children who experience achievement and behavioral difficulties in school—who perceive themselves as failures and have low self-esteem.

That artistic activities are not used exclusively with individuals suffering emotional and behavioral disorders but rather are typical forms of play experienced at some level by everyone gives rise to another advantage: The ordinary nature of these experiences makes them relatively nonthreatening and enhances their therapeutic value.

A fifth advantage pertains to the development of interpersonal relationships. Group projects such as painting a wall mural, playing an orchestral piece, or learning a new dance help children work together cooperatively. In addition to developing interpersonal skills, artistic activities provide a socially acceptable opportunity for the free expression of feelings, a sixth advantage. Many individuals with emotional and behavioral disorders, particularly those children who are overinhibited, need opportunities to express emotion without fear of violating social norms.

Similarly, a seventh advantage is that activity therapies are both stimulating and relaxing. Thus, these techniques may be used to calm children who are overexcited, excessively anxious, highly volatile, or hyperactive and to stimulate children who are poorly motivated, withdrawn, passive, or depressed. An eighth and final common advantage is that art, music, and dance activities help individuals develop cognitively, perceptually, and motorically.

Art as a Therapeutic Intervention

Definitions of art therapy vary greatly depending on the extent to which it is viewed as a principal or an adjunctive form of therapy. Some individuals, particularly those who see art as an aid to psychoanalysis, regard art therapy as a "non-verbal technique for releasing, through symbolic imagery, the unconscious, repressed emotions" (Naumburg, 1973, p. vii). Others focus on the art in art therapy as a creative process with an inherent healing quality characteristic of all types of creativity (Kramer, 1977). More recently, the American Art Therapy Association (Levick, 1983) referred to art therapy as an opportunity for nonverbal expression and communication and distinguished between two major approaches, both of which imply that the creative process of art is a means of reconciling emotional conflicts and fostering self-awareness. One involves art as a vehicle for psychotherapy in which the product is used to help individuals understand themselves. The other equates art therapy with art education and associates teaching with therapy. Therapeutic instruction encourages self-expression, communication, and growth. The art product is less important than the creative process, although both reflect aspects of personality.

Historically, the use of art as a therapeutic tool has its roots in psychoanalytic theory. Freud (1963) cited the advantage of visual art as an expression of inner experience. The field was given impetus as an independent profession by two central figures, Margaret Naumburg and Edith Kramer (Ulman, 1977). Naumburg first became aware of the importance of children's drawings in the therapeutic process when she worked as a director and art teacher in a school she founded in 1915. In the early 1940s she conducted research into the use of spontaneous art and free association in psychoanalytic therapy with children having behavior problems. She noted that art provided a more direct expression for dreams, fantasies, and fears than verbal exchanges provided. Later, she used her psychoanalytically oriented approach to help adults with schizophrenia and established the first art therapy training program at New York University in 1958 (Naumburg, 1966).

Kramer also took an early psychoanalytical perspective, although, unlike Naumburg, she focused her attention on art itself as therapeutic and minimized verbal interpretations of art. She worked as an art teacher and therapist with boys who had emotional disorders at the Wiltwyck School in the 1950s and presented her perspective of art therapy in her first book, *Art as Therapy with Children* (1971). In that text, Kramer noted that art therapy has mirrored psychoanalysis in its progressive development from early emphasis directed exclusively toward the interpretation of unconscious forces to a later emphasis on ego functions.

As Kramer suggested, spontaneous artistic expression initially was used as a projective technique, that is, as a reflection of an individual's psychic conflicts and desires, much as dreams were interpreted as being representative of such forces. The art therapist was primarily a psychotherapist, and the techniques usually were practiced in clinics or hospital settings with persons suffering from severe emotional disorders. Art expression was viewed as a more natural way to describe what so often occurred pictorially, and, therefore, as an important tool for psychoanalysis.

Changes in the characteristics of art therapy began to appear after World War II. During that period, art was used therapeutically in hospitals with wounded veterans as a component of recreational or occupational therapy. In the most basic sense, art activities provided physically and mentally traumatized patients with something to do. However, in some instances, the classical use of art to unlock the unconscious components of personality was retained.

Today a large segment of art therapy retains neo-Freudian components in its theoretical orientation. Naumburg (1966) wrote about releasing unconscious conflicts, fantasies, and dreams through artistic expression. Similarly, Kramer (1971, 1973) wrote that art therapy provided support for the ego and described the artist as one who has resolved the classic psychoanalytic conflict between the demands of the id and those of the superego. The Freudian concept of sublimation—the transformation of socially unacceptable impulses into socially acceptable artistic products—remains a key premise for much of art therapy.

However, despite the strong association with psychoanalytic theory, various other perspectives have affected art therapy (Junge, 1994). These include an increased emphasis on cognitive development and art (Silver, 1978, 1990); art as a reflection of imagery and visual expression (Lusebrink, 1990); a psycho-cybernetic model of art therapy that emphasizes the importance of purposeful, information-processing behaviors (Nucho, 1987); the influence of existential theory and the human potential movement (Betersky, 1987; Wadeson, 1980, 1987); and the metaphysical, healing power of art (McNiff, 1992). Consequently, the current practice of art therapy departs from the traditional psychoanalytic approach in many respects. It frequently focuses on present situations and feelings rather than on past conflicts. Also, the art therapist often uses nondirective techniques, acting only to facilitate the child's production. Contrary to typical psychoanalytic methods, the child rather than the therapist makes all interpretations of the artistic product. In addition, among many art therapists, greater emphasis is placed on creating the artistic products than on their therapeutic value. Finally, art is used to directly influence learning, including aspects of the academic curriculum. Although there remains variability among practitioners regarding the relative importance of art versus therapy, Ulman (1977) remarked that anything that is called art therapy must genuinely partake of both art and therapy.

Another significant change pertains to the uses of art therapy. Originally developed for use in psychiatric settings, art therapy is now conducted in nursing homes, clinics, and educational settings (Wadeson, 1980). Family art therapy has been developed (Kwiatkowska, 1978). Also, in addition to using art therapy with handicapped learners such as children with mental retardation, learning disabilities, or emotional disorders, educators are applying the techniques with typical learners. In many settings, the line between enlightened art instruction and art therapy has grown less clear, as the goal of both endeavors is on growth through personal expression. As is true of other types of therapy discussed in this chapter, the techniques used in art therapy may be altered to meet the needs of particular groups in varied settings. However, using art therapy with typical and atypical children in educational settings is dependent on some degree of knowledge of children's ability to draw.

Children's Visual Art Ability

An extensive body of research provides evidence of the characteristics of children's performance in visual arts. Eisner (1972) and Cornett (1999) have summarized the research:

1. The characteristics of children's art change with chronological age. Art becomes more complex, detailed, and cohesive as children mature. Also they can produce more complex shapes.

2. Children exaggerate the aspects of the artwork that are most meaningful to them.

3. Drawing often is used to express ideas, whereas painting expresses emotion.

4. Form, color, and composition are related to personality.

5. Children in different cultures create similar visual forms.

6. School-age children draw the human figure most often.

7. Young children do not consult a model or still life when they draw.

8. Drawing skills tend to arrest at adolescence, and spontaneous drawing often ceases.

9. Children in preschool and primary school tend to focus on form and ignore the larger context.

10. No significant gender difference in visual art ability has been found.

11. Children prefer art forms that are visually similar to the level they can produce.

12. Children's artistic skill improves with instruction.

According to Selfe (1983), who briefly discussed the theoretical approaches explaining children's ability to draw, four major schools of thought are discussed in the literature: developmental, empirical, holistic, and emotive. The most widely accepted theory holds that drawing ability develops as children mature and is influenced by general cognitive development. Gardner (1993) has suggested that artistic skills grow in waves and involve multiple areas of intelligence as they increase.

In a review of early investigations of children's ability to draw, Harris (1963) considered Luquet's (1927) work most important. Luquet depicted three stages of development: preschematic, schematic, and visual realism. The preschematic stage occurs between 2 and 5 years of age. The child scribbles and makes crude attempts to draw forms that depict objects in his experience. He is unable to position the forms, coordinate lines, or synthesize elements in the drawing. The schematic stage or stage of "intellectual realism" occurs between the ages of 5 and 10. The child draws his concept of an object with all of its components but does not consider the fixed viewpoint. The visual or photographic realism stage occurs after age 10 and is characterized by relatively true-to-life drawings of visual scenes from a fixed viewpoint. The progressive development of drawing competence in children is not debated. Debate is provoked by the assumption that this ability corresponds with general cognitive development. (Goodenough's [1923] Draw-a-Man test of intellectual ability is based on this theoretical perspective of children's drawings.) Theories emphasizing cognitive development generally view the developmental process as largely innate. Selfe (1983) discussed the work of Helga Eng (1952) and Jean Piaget (1971) in this context. Eng believed that the development of drawing ability parallels other aspects of cognitive development, including thoughts and concepts as revealed by language. She observed that children aged about 4 to 9 draw from memory; they do not look at models even when they are provided. What they draw depends on what they have drawn—their mental image of the object. Piaget maintained that perception depends on conception; that is, the child cannot perceive the characteristics of perspective or proportion in objects until he has the mental concepts they pertain to. The child's conception of an object is more important than the representation in the environment or external world.

Brookes (1996) expanded on the cognitive perspective. She differentiated between symbolic and realistic drawing. Symbolic or natural drawing is a form of nonverbal communication that progresses with age in predictable fashion. Children create symbols to depict subjects, such as stick-figure images of family. At age 8 or 9, children mature beyond this stage and want to draw realistically. However, realistic drawing requires instruction, much as learning to read or write requires instruction. Without proper training, many children stop drawing.

Several different perspectives dispute the cognitive theories. The empiricist or behavioral point of view (Freeman, 1980) maintains that developmental sequence of drawing skills is totally dependent on opportunity to learn. Children's representations change with exposure to the task and practice solving the problems inherent in the task. The holistic perspective (Arnheim, 1970, 1989) differentiates between imitation (copying the visual appearance of a two-dimensional object) and representation (free drawing three-dimensional subjects). Arnheim concluded that young children readily produce two-dimensional copies. When they produce representational drawings, they are not making inept attempts to render realistic images; they are accurately depicting their visual experiences with the object or subject being drawn. For example, children draw both the inside and outside of a house in a picture because they conceptualize or visualize a house in that manner. That visualization is their realistic perception, which they faithfully render. Arnheim cautioned against premature attempts to influence children's intuitive productions.

Finally, the emotive theories (Koppitz, 1968) insist that children's drawings reflect a total response to the environment, particularly their feelings and emotions, not simply cognitive growth or learning opportunity. This premise strongly influences the psychoanalytical approach to interpreting children's artwork.

Anomalous Drawings

Selfe (1983) explained the representational drawings of children with mental handicaps or emotional disorders. To provide guidelines for understanding normal representational drawing and for making comparisons between normal and anomalous efforts, Selfe reported the results of research into the components of drawing that are necessary to produce photographic realism. These components include proportion, dimensions, size scaling, and occlusion.

- *Proportion.* When drawing the human figure, children up to 10 years of age do not draw photographically realistic proportions. Generally, the size of the head is overestimated in relationship to the body. At ages 5 and 6, the head is larger than the trunk, and it shrinks with age.

- *Dimensions.* Children of 5 and 6 years usually portray three-dimensional objects in flat canonical representations. At 7 to 8 years, about one quarter of typical children add elevations of three-dimensional objects, and by 9 to 10 years, more than a third still depict only flat elevations.

- *Size Scaling.* All children show some understanding of size scaling, although there is an age-related trend toward accuracy. At 5 to 6 years, children usually underestimate accurate size; and although performance improves, by 9 to 10 years some typical children still are unable to scale accurately.

- *Occlusion.* The ability to perceive the relationships between surfaces, including hidden lines (occlusion), does not appear until after 7 years of age and develops with age. Accurate rendering depends on the complexity of the object being drawn. Asymmetrical, unfamiliar, and complex objects are extremely difficult, and children separate forms depicted as overlapping.

Selfe's research with children with serious impairments, such as autism and mental retardation, showed that despite indications of severe cognitive limitations, they tended to produce amazingly high levels of photographic realism in their representations compared with those of typical children of similar ages. Thus, they appeared to be able to observe the subject to be drawn from a fixed viewpoint, unlike their nondisabled peers, who produced their own unique schema of the subject. Selfe questioned the generally accepted notion that the ability to produce photographic realism in drawings is a function of general cognitive development. She agreed with Arnheim's (1970) holistic perspective regarding the development of drawing competence and concluded that the remarkable ability to represent photographic realism often shown by children with severe cognitive and neurological disabilities is due to cognitive limitations—an inability to conceptualize the subjects that are drawn and a reliance on imitation.

Art and Emotional Disturbance

According to experts in the field of art therapy, drawings produced by individuals suffering from serious types of emotional disorders vary greatly; however, certain prevalent themes and characteristics are associated with specific disorders. Wadeson (1980) noted that much of the evidence of prevailing themes is associated with art produced by persons diagnosed with schizophrenia. An example of this type of literature focuses on change in content and style over the course of illness, as in the series of cats drawn by the artist Louis Wain during his illness. The cat drawings progressed from realistic to fanciful to completely abstract.

Wadeson (1980) also reported that the content and style of psychotic art provide some indication of specific pathological conditions. Individuals with schizophrenia often produce highly symbolic drawings (e.g., a female emerging from a fertilized ovum reaching toward a phallic-skull representing nuclear holocaust). In some cases, body parts are distorted and facial expressions are bizarre or stiff. Also, geometric patterns are often used, and writing or labeling is integrated into the drawing. Often pictures are fragmented, although they may be highly detailed and overelaborated. Unusual colors or a single color may be used. Spatial organization may be disturbed.

In contrast, individuals with depression often produce art that features scenes of death, torture, suicide, grief, and mourning. Frequently, few ideas are represented and figures are immobile. Somber or dark colors are frequently used, and products generally lack detail and appear incomplete (e.g., a stem with several unelaborated leaves done without color).

Individuals who experience bipolar manic-depressive states tend to generate art that is more colorful and more complete. Often the content involves sexual symbols and euphoric themes. Form and detail are neglected in favor of wild color and bold strokes that suggest motion and excitement.

Wadeson (1980), who emphasized the variability of the art produced by persons with psychosis, despite the patterns noted above, does not believe similar representative characteristics can be associated with less severe psychological disorders. In these cases, interpretation of art generally reflects a psychoanalytic orientation; the product represents aspects of the individual's unconscious needs. For example, a highly fearful, dependent individual asked to draw his dreams might produce a legless, disembodied person reaching toward a larger, solid individual.

Kramer (1971) supported this psychoanalytic perspective, noting that children with emotional disorders use art to defend the ego. Often they persist in repetitive drawings (e.g., the same squared head of a monster) that reassure them. They might identify with the repeated image as a source of protection or use it as a focal point for their fear. They will progress from this pattern only when they feel sufficiently secure and confident to do so.

Another variation of repetitive patterns in art to defend the ego is reflected when children with psychoses cover the paper with one color. So strong is their need for uniformity that, when given trays with different-color paints, they mix them together to produce one color. Kramer believed the sameness is comforting to these children.

These types of useful repetitive productions are contrasted with the non-creative, stereotyped art (reproductions of saccharine themes, as in greeting card decorations) that is often taught in classrooms and that provides no outlet for children's emotions. They also differ from the stereotyped art produced by children with mental retardation or brain damage, as well as the repetitive work of children who attempt to recapture former successes. In these instances, the spontaneous improvisation reflecting true art is absent.

Another dynamic interpretation (Kramer, 1971; Naumburg, 1966) involves the relationship between art and aggression. At the most basic level, art may serve as an outlet for pent-up anger. For example, children frustrated by excessive parental restrictions may need to smear paint on the paper for a time before they can engage in more structured activities. Other children, fearing their own aggressive feelings, draw fierce subjects (e.g., a snarling tiger) and cage or trap them. Still others identify with the aggressor, producing a fierce subject (father dragon) and a smaller version of the subject (baby dragon). These artistic releases are beneficial, allowing asocial ideas and feelings to be expressed without fear of reprisal.

Kramer believes that children's art becomes constricted and empty when conformity is emphasized and creativity is repressed. Therefore, well-behaved children who are overcontrolled may generate empty, lifeless compositions. Some emotionally troubled children who resist authority may create more interesting, dynamic art than their conforming classmates. However, in other cases their productions may be equally sterile, depending on the forces influencing their behavior.

Role of the Art Therapist

Just as there are differences in defining art therapy, opinions differ regarding the therapist's role. A critical issue pertains to the amount of weight that should be assigned to behaving as a psychotherapist as opposed to acting as an artist and teacher. This divergence of opinion can be traced to the positions adopted by the two central figures in the field of art therapy, Naumburg and Kramer.

Naumburg's (1966) work reflected her belief that the art therapist should be well trained in psychoanalytical principles. The art therapist's primary function is to use artistic expression as a projective technique—to uncover unconscious forces in the personality. The therapist need not have artistic talent but should have a sympathetic interest in the creative arts. Clearly, Naumburg's position is closely aligned to the traditional conceptualizations of the art therapist's role.

In contrast, Kramer conceived of the art therapist as a well-balanced combination of artist, teacher, and therapist. She wrote of the art therapist (1973, p. 5): "He is no psychotherapist, and it is not his function to interpret deep unconscious content to his students." She added, "The basic aim of the art therapist is to make available to disturbed persons the pleasures and satisfaction which creative work can give, and by his insight and therapeutic skill to make such experiences meaningful and valuable to the total personality" (pp. 5–6).

Kramer recognized the need for the art therapist to have an understanding of therapeutic value of art. She agreed that it is unlikely that the products of art therapy can be considered art. However, whereas Naumburg considered creativity as secondary to the development of symbolic communication through the arts, Kramer stressed that the creative work is of primary importance. She believed that the creative process is healing and that the quality of the creative work can serve as a measure of therapeutic success. Kramer's emphasis on art as a creative force makes her work an appropriate resource, not only for art therapists but also for all teachers who view art as an effective way to reach and motivate students.

Ulman (1977) pointed out that although Naumburg and Kramer presented what seem to be opposing points of view, in actual practice the conflict is not absolute. Indeed, they agreed on the two basic principles that define the role of the art therapist. One of the principles is "The art therapist must exhibit total acceptance of creative works that constitute a sincere effort." The art therapist must make no aesthetic judgment on the quality or simplicity of the product. This acceptance conveys respect for each child's individuality, and creates a noncompetitive atmosphere for the art therapy session. The second principle is "The art therapist must carefully consider how much direction to provide." In some cases a nondirective environment is preferable. The child may be permitted to choose the place, time, and frequency of the therapy. She also has a free choice of both the medium to use and the subject matter. Most important, the child interprets the product. The therapist plays a supportive role, giving assistance when necessary, eliciting the child's interpretations with open-ended questions, and offering encouragement. In other cases the therapist may need to stimulate the child's interest by presenting ideas and offering opinions.

Liebmann (1986) added to these principles by developing guidelines to help art therapy participants interpret their efforts. The simplest strategy is to ask each person to talk about his work, without comments from others. Extending that strategy, after the individual's remarks, others may ask questions or offer comments. Another strategy is to have participants review their pictures done over a period of time to identify any recurring patterns or themes and to discuss their impressions. Finally, Liebmann suggested use of a gestalt technique: asking the person to be the painting, that is, to talk about it as if he were it. For example, the child who painted the caged tiger would be asked to be the tiger and talk about how he feels.

Liebmann also discussed the therapist's role in forming and conducting group art therapy. She noted that groups may be structured or unstructured. Unstructured groups meet together to create art but work independently on personal projects. Structured groups meet to share a common task. Some groups combine both approaches. In some cases structure may involve one simple rule that places almost no restrictions on the participants, such as "Draw anything you like." Greater structure is provided when a theme is stipulated, as in "Draw a picture of a person." Even greater structure is used in "Draw your family." Liebmann and many current advocates of the therapeutic use of art (Wachowiak & Clements, 1996) believe that the use of structured techniques is important because people often have difficulty beginning an art project. Also, structure often reduces anxiety (particularly among children with emotional disorders), and sharing a theme not only encourages social interactions but also unites the group.

The final point regarding the therapist's role is made by every principal contributor to the field: Not every individual can benefit from therapeutic art activities, and some must be excluded from the group. Persons who are persistently uncooperative and disruptive may respond better to other types of therapeutic activity. Also, Kramer (1971) described children who cannot progress beyond precursory activities with the materials, such as smearing and scribbling, that do not lead to the creation of symbolic configurations. Additionally, some children simply spill, splash, or pound the materials, behaviors that lead to loss of control. Although Kramer urged initial tolerance, children operating at this level might best be involved with art techniques as individuals rather than as group members.

Techniques

The techniques of therapeutic art are those that stimulate artistic production. In the simplest sense, these involve giving children access to art materials and watching them create. However, for the majority of children, who require more structure, certain techniques have been developed to stimulate participation. With the exception of the scribble technique provided by Kramer (1971), all of the following procedures are adapted from Cornett (1999), Denny (1977), Liebmann (1986), and Wachowiak and Clements (1996) and are designed for use by general education classroom teachers. Other than the motivational activities and warm-up, they are listed here under the trait they are purported to develop in the artists.

Motivational Activities and Warm-Up. The goal of the warm-up is to direct the students' thinking toward the creative art project. The teacher introduces the art activity and, with careful questioning, elicits the students' ideas about it. For example, the teacher might show the students several objects and ask how they might be arranged, what might make the objects nice to look at, what might happen if the objects were turned or moved, or how increased light might change the appearance of the objects.

Wachowiak and Clements (1996) suggested motivational activities that include planning field trips to expose students to an art topic. For example, students can be helped to directly perceive patterns and objects in nature (e.g., the variations in flowers and trees) or still-life arrangements through guided observation that focuses on the subtleties of the topic. Then teachers may present visual material about the topic, discuss the topic, or use poems, music, and stories to represent the topic. In addition, children can be led to recall experiences (e.g., a sporting event) through questioning (describe the players, the stadium, the people watching) until they feel comfortable to begin the art project.

Additional warm-up techniques include the following:

- *Elements of shape.* Students are given 1 minute to identify all the circles, curved lines, straight lines, or angles in the room.
- *Brainstorming.* Students are asked to think about a work of art. For example, how they might change a painting, how a painting might look if a specific part were removed, or how to combine two paintings.
- *Collections.* Students collect items to use in art projects (e.g., dried flowers, leaves, stones, bottles, or buttons).

Trait-Developing Activities

Exploration: Encourages spontaneous expression

- *Scribble technique.* The individual first "draws" in the air; then she draws those movements on paper while keeping her eyes closed. Next the child looks at the scribble from all sides until she sees a form to elaborate on to produce a drawing.
- *Blob and wet paper technique.* The individual allows ink, paint, or watercolors to flow naturally on the paper. She may fold the paper to make blots. She then develops the design created.
- *Media exploration.* The individual is given free choice of media to experiment with. She may choose to work in a single medium such as clay or use mixed media such as crayons and paint. Artistic products are stimulated by the type of material chosen.
- *Color exploration.* The individual is encouraged to select the colors she likes most or least and to work with them in free composition. Colors may be chosen to represent moods or the world around the individual.
- *Mirror image.* The individual is given a line drawing and asked to draw the mirror image.

Rapport Building: Encourages interaction among participants

- *Conversational drawing.* Partners sit across from each other and take turns adding lines, shapes, colors, and so on to a single drawing. When the drawing is completed, the partners discuss their product.
- *Cooperative group painting.* A group member produces a painting that is elaborated on by other group members. For example, if the individual paints a picture of a person, group members might

improve the work by adding detail. The group discusses all changes that are made in the picture.

- *Painting with an observer.* One child paints and the partner comments on the painting by saying anything that enters her mind. The painter responds to the commentary.

- *Group sculptures or collages.* The group jointly produces a sculpture or collage.

Expression of Inner Feelings: Encourages understanding of feelings

- *Problems and feelings.* The individual paints her present mood or a recent or recurring problem.

- *Dreams and fantasies.* The individual paints dreams and fantasies, especially those that are repeated. She may depict entire dreams or just the parts that interest or trouble her the most.

- *Affective words.* The individual paints in response to words that relate to psychological states, such as love, hate, beauty, freedom. She may also express contrasting word pairs, such as strength–weakness.

- *Three wishes.* The individual depicts her wishes. These are discussed, particularly their realistic and unrealistic aspects.

- *Music and poetry.* The individual may paint in response to either musical or poetic stimulation or respond to completed paintings by creating music or poetry.

- *Lifeline.* The person draws her life as a journey or road map, including events encountered along the way.

- *Past, present, and future.* The person draws images of her past, present, or future. Time may be varied, as in 10 years ago, last year, 10 years from now, next year, or at particular ages.

- *Important memories.* A person draws a memory that is important in some way. It can be happy, sad, or both.

Self-Perception: Encourages awareness of body image and personal needs

- *Self-portraits.* The individual may depict himself realistically or abstractly in any medium, including pastels, paint, clay, or collage.

- *Phenomenal, ideal, and real self-portraits.* The individual is instructed first to draw any person he wishes to draw. Next, he is requested to draw himself as he would like to look and, finally, to draw himself as he really is.

- *Immediate states.* The individual selects one or more of the following phrases to paint: "I am," "I feel," "I have," and "I do." Discussions of creations may follow.

- *Metaphorical portraits.* The person draws himself as some type of object. The choice can be left open or can be structured as to type of object—an animal, tree, building, or so on.

- *Advertisements.* The person draws or paints an advertisement for himself. He may depict a store displaying personal qualities. Others in the group may be invited to add to the advertisement.

- *Aspects of self.* The person makes a map with himself at the center and arranges different aspects affecting his life around him at various distances.

- *Good and bad self.* The individual depicts his good side and bad side by making masks for each self, putting faces on both sides of a paper bag, or painting positive and negative aspects.

Interpersonal Relations: Encourages awareness of others

- *Portraits of group members.* Group members draw one another. The group discusses the drawings.

- *Portraits by combined effort.* One member of a group creates a self-portrait. Each group member adds something to the portrait to make it more like the subject. When the drawing is finished, the subject may ask the others about their contributions. He may also change the portrait to fit his self-perception.

- *Pair portraits technique.* Group members choose partners. Each member draws a self-portrait and a picture of his partner.

- *Group mural.* The group works cooperatively on a large surface, such as brown wrapping paper, a wall, or a sidewalk. The subject matter may be determined prior to the course of painting.

- *Draw your family.* The individual may draw his family or the family he wishes to have. The individual need not include himself in the drawing.

- *Friendship series.* The person draws friends in the past or present or the qualities of friends.

Environmental Relations: Encourages awareness of one's relationship to the environment

- *House–Tree–Person.* The individual relates a human figure to the common environmental features of tree and house in a single drawing or painting.

- *Elements picture series.* The individual may paint the elements of air, earth, fire, and water in rapid sequence. Discussions following completion center on the artist's feelings toward the natural forces of the environment.

- *Collage and assemblage.* The individual creates a product with a combination of two- and three-dimensional material (e.g., magazine pictures, fabric, wood, or any other natural objects). He pastes or glues them together to portray any theme of interest.

- *Personal landscape.* The person draws or paints a landscape that he relates to, either favorably or unfavorably. He might add himself to the painting.

Guided Imagery: Encourages group members to draw on their imaginations and visualize feelings and sensations evoked during fantasy experiences

- *Magic carpet ride.* The group is instructed to think about this type of imaginative journey and to draw symbols of the feelings and sensations it evokes (e.g., floating off the ground, soaring high, feeling sunshine).

- *Secret cave.* The group visualizes a secret cave in a specific setting. They try to smell the flowers, hear the brook nearby, feel the coolness inside and the warmth outside, and so forth. They draw their feelings and sensations.

- *Magic shop.* This fantasy involves visiting an intriguing old shop, exploring the wares, touching the appealing goods, and experiencing their magic. Related images are drawn.

Links to Other Expressive Arts

In addition to the specific techniques presented above, Liebmann (1986) encouraged art therapists and teachers to link art projects with other expressive forms such as movement, music, poetry, and drama. Movement might be integrated by having the group members act out emotions and then paint them or move like the sea and paint the sea. Dance, another form of movement, is involved by having the group members dance together and then paint the feelings evoked.

Music may be used to evoke feeling that is painted once or painted on various occasions and compared with previous efforts. Similarly, poetry can serve as a stimulus for painting the scenes or events described.

Drama and dramatic readings also may serve as stimuli for drawings or paintings, and themes evoked by artwork may be expanded and acted out. Puppets may be created and used in storytelling or drama.

Educational Applications

In recent years, there has been an increasing interest in therapeutic art as an educational technique. Recent surveys of students' opinions have revealed that they rate art as more interesting and enjoyable than other areas of the curriculum (Wachowiak & Clements, 1996). Advocates of art education believe that it contributes to academic excellence, personal growth, social growth and change, and cognitive development. Art can unite children from diverse cultural backgrounds and develop a sense of community. Although there are relatively few art therapy programs in the schools, progressive art educators and classroom teachers have the opportunity to integrate selected techniques into programs that are useful with persons who have emotional and behavioral disorders and with typical learners. Considerations include selecting candidates for the program; determining physical arrangements, such as place, time, and materials; and most important, establishing the appropriate role for the teacher in an educational setting.

Candidates. According to art education advocates, art activities are appropriate for most persons of all ages. Kramer (1971) pointed out that it is most useful when children have the capacity to produce original artistic products, and she set the optimal age range from 3 to 13 years. Children within this age range have learned to distinguish between art and play, an important distinction because art makes greater demands than play. Children at this level of development understand what is expected of them and are willing to attempt artistic tasks voluntarily.

Kramer, as well as other experts, has also noted that although art therapy traditionally has been used with children who have serious emotional disorders, the use of therapeutic art activities in schools need not be limited to those individuals. Although art is used by personnel trained in art therapy to make contact with children whose severe handicaps permit them few, if any, alternative avenues of communication, it also may be used by teachers without specific training in art therapy to help children whose emotional problems are mild or moderate, or with typical children and adolescents. In the latter circumstance, techniques can be applied with entire groups or classes.

Physical Arrangements. The freedom of choice given the client in classical art therapy is not usually possible in the classroom. The teacher's program must conform to realistic limitations in space, time, and materials. The teacher probably will not have a special room available for art therapy but will need to find space within the classroom. Although this type of arrangement might appear to be less than ideal, it actually has several advantages. The teacher can permit some children to engage in art activities while she helps others perform other tasks. It is also convenient for the children, who can work on their art projects during their free time, as well as for the teacher, who need not transport students, materials, and other equipment from one room to another.

Most experts recommend that a specific classroom area be maintained exclusively for art activities. If desks, chairs, and materials remain in place, the children have easy access to them. Also, art activities can be quite messy, and attempting to conduct them in an area used simultaneously for other activities usually creates problems.

Running water and a sink are important components of any type of art program. When they are not available in the classroom, the teacher must improvise. Plastic dishpans or metal tubs may be filled with water and kept in the art area. Pitchers or lipped cups should be provided to distribute water needed to mix paints or wet clay. Piles of paper towels and newspapers should be readily available. Selected places should be set aside to dry and store pictures.

Having established where to conduct art therapy techniques, the teacher must consider appropriate time lines for the sessions. Generally, sessions lasting approximately 1 hour are recommended. This amount of time is usually sufficient for children to set up, create, and clean up. As to the frequency of the sessions, Kramer (1971) suggested that two scheduled sessions per week are adequate for most children. However, children who are difficult to reach through other media but who participate enthusiastically in art projects may be permitted to spend additional time in such activities.

The most often used art materials are those that are simple, familiar, and easily manipulated. The three basic media often recommended because of their simplicity and multiple uses are paint, clay, and crayonlike materials. All three are readily available in most schools. Tempera or poster paint is preferred to oils and watercolors because it is colorful; easy to use, control, and mix; quick to dry; and can be applied to wet or dry clay. Both oils and watercolors require greater skill to use. Although watercolors are available in convenient containers and dry quickly, they are difficult to control while painting. Oils are easier to apply but are very slow to dry. Paint can be applied to a variety of surfaces, including paper, wood, canvas, fabric, paper plates, and rocks (if white glue is added to the paint). Clay has the advantage of being the most directly manipulable of the art materials. Children inhibited by a paintbrush or a crayon often find clay to be a suitable alternative. Also, it is easier to handle and manage than paint. The crayonlike materials recommended include crayons, chalk, pastels, and charcoal. Crayons should be used with young children and with older children who are still in the stages of primitive or line drawing. They provide rich colors that are easily controlled. Chalks, pastels, and charcoal are recommended for older children and adolescents who are able to control them in the shading and blending of color.

In more elaborate settings with more experienced students, recommendations for materials include melted crayons for encaustic paintings, tiles for mosaics, waxes and dyes for batiks, plaster for carving sculpture, and glazes for ceramics (Wachowiak & Clements, 1996).

Other materials needed are brushes of different sizes; items that are surfaces for paint, including different sizes and types of paper and a large roll of brown wrapping paper; oil-cloth pads; sponges; cups or cans for water; popsicle sticks for stirring paint; and cardboard tubes to roll out clay. Each child should have his own set of materials. Individual equipment is especially important when working with children who might become extremely upset if desired materials are missing or misplaced. Each individual kit should contain two or three brushes, a set of crayonlike materials, a container for water, and a tray for mixing colors. Kramer (1971) suggested using muffin tins for mixing paint; Pine (1977) opted for the less expensive bendable ice-cube trays.

There are several kinds of materials that are not recommended for use in schools. Fingerpaints, long considered a basic tool of classic art therapy because they permit direct expression of inner feelings, are regarded as inappropriate material in the classroom, where the primary goal is a creative production. Commercially produced products such as coloring books and paint-by-number kits should never be used, because they do not involve a creative process. According to Kramer (1977, p. 109), "The greatest objection against coloring books is their bad taste, saccharine sweetness, and insipid content"; and painting by numbers is "possibly the most destructive of all pseudo-arts" (p. 108). She suggests that if the situation calls for busywork rather than creative activity, crafts such as weaving or embroidery are preferable. (Art therapists differentiate between art and craft: Art is a creative activity culminating in an original product, whereas craft involves transforming raw material into something useful.)

The final component of the physical arrangements necessary to conduct art therapy within the classroom is the establishment of a highly structured set of rules for the use and maintenance of the art area. Before involving the children in creative art projects, the teacher must consult with them to specify precisely what behaviors are appropriate in the art area and the circumstances under which the area may be used (when, for how long, and for what reasons). They also must reach agreement about where objects are stored, and the children must assume responsibility for various chores. It is important that the children do not become overstimulated by the art materials and behave chaotically. Even when clear rules are provided, the teacher may find that certain children simply cannot use art techniques constructively and must be excluded from the activity.

The Teacher's Role. The usefulness of therapeutic art techniques in classroom situations depends on the teacher's ability to follow certain practical operational guidelines that conform to a realistic set of goals.

The first guideline is that the teacher become familiar with the basic elements of art—line, shape, value, color, space, texture, and pattern (Wachowiak & Clements, 1996). *Lines,* as conveyed in the line drawing, are the structural foundation of graphic composition and pictorial design. Lines differ; they may go in various directions, be patterned or unpatterned, flowing or static, bold or delicate, dynamic or hesitant. Objects in nature such as veins in leaves, feathers, flower petals, and veined rocks can be used to demonstrate the variety of lines.

Shape can be created by merging lines in definitive ways (e.g., square, round, oval, or triangular) or by amorphous images (e.g., color washes or charcoal smudges). Shapes represented by natural objects such as nuts, fruits, leaves, and eggs illustrate the variations and subtle differences that make artistic renditions interesting. In painting, shapes of objects and figures are positive shapes, and the area around them is negative space.

Value is a continuum of the light-to-dark aspects of visual art. Every color (hue) has a value, defined as shade (dark) or tint (light). Contrasting values (lighter colors next to darker colors) create dramatic compositions.

Color consists of hue (e.g., blue), value, and intensity (saturation or brightness–dullness). Wachowiak and Clements (1996) advised teachers to help students handle the overwhelming challenge of color by limiting the number of colors used, limiting the color intensity by dulling or mixing the color with its complementary hue (e.g., red and green), and stressing the importance of value by varying the shades of colors. Many well-known works of art provide examples of masterful use of value and color.

Space is defined either as the negative area (area surrounding shapes and forms) between two positive objects (area occupied by shapes or forms) or as space-in-depth. In painting, the illusion of space-in-depth is achieved by vertical placement of figures or objects, distinct details in foreground and understated details in background, diminished size with distance, bright colors in foreground and dull colors in background, and receding objects higher on the picture.

Texture and *pattern* are secondary elements that make the composition more interesting. Textures can be rough, smooth, jagged, or bumpy. Patterns are repetitions of elements in any number of ways (e.g., a leopard's spots).

The teacher using art techniques in the classroom need not be a gifted artist. She need only have sufficient information to interest the children in artistic expression and guide their creative efforts.

The second guideline is that the teacher should focus on the creative process. The goal is to help the children express themselves through art, not to have them produce a masterpiece. Therefore, each child's honest, creative effort should be valued and used as an avenue for increasing self-esteem and building a positive, trusting relationship. The art produced by each child should represent his feelings and ideas. Producing artwork that conforms to restrictive teacher specifications does not provide a child with the opportunity to respond creatively to the activity. When a child lacks imagination and stares at a blank paper without attempting to participate, the teacher should stimulate him with suggestions of materials and topics. Materials with inherent structure such as fabric and clay are particularly useful. When a child who originally was interested and active in art sessions becomes unmotivated, the teacher should encourage him to try alternative materials. Kramer (1971) suggested that a child under 10 should concentrate on the basic media: paint, clay, and crayonlike materials. Children approaching adolescence (ages 11–13) need a broader choice of materials to avoid boredom. Finally, certain children with handicaps require direction toward particular types of materials. Both Kramer (1971) and Pine (1977) recommended clay and other touchable materials for children identified as hyperactive, brain-injured, or blind or visually impaired. Pine also suggested that children with schizophrenia not be required to make too many decisions. The teacher should have them decide only what to make and should select their materials.

The third guideline incorporates two major strategies of therapeutic art. The teacher's main strategy (Naumburg, 1973) is to convince the children that their feelings, thoughts, and experiences are worthwhile material for artistic expression. The children must understand that perfect duplication of existing material does not constitute creative art. The second strategy is to help the children set realistic goals. They must learn to accept technical limitations and must be brought to realize that no mistakes in art are irreparable.

The teacher's goals for the therapeutic art program are more general than the program guidelines, but no less important. The first goal is to *foster individual growth*. Basically, all children benefit from additional outlets for their emotions, particularly when they feel free of the fear of failure or criticism. The second goal is to *promote interpersonal and group relationships*. Group art sessions help children learn to encourage and understand one another. The optimal group size to promote positive interrelationships varies with the children involved. It can consist of as few as 2 or as many as 10. The critical variable is that the teacher maintain a noncompetitive atmosphere. Pine (1977) suggested that the teacher remind the members of the group that they draw differently from one another, not necessarily better or worse. The third goal of art therapy is to *establish communication* through the creative process. A good means of achieving this goal is to exhibit each child's work. Themal (1977, p. 105) wrote, "Exhibition, besides giving the children a feeling of accomplishment, meets another need, perhaps the greatest need of all . . . to communicate."

Therapeutic Music

Traditional music therapy is a newer discipline than art therapy and lacks its psychoanalytical roots. However, there is some similarity in the historical development of these activity approaches, with both music and art used as therapeutic activities by occupational and recreational therapists in post–World War II years. Now, music therapy has come to be recognized as a unique therapeutic method and is used extensively in psychiatric hospitals and in programs for children with handicaps. It also has expanded its influence in education and currently is used with all types of students to improve their educational experiences and promote learning.

Gaston (1968) traced the history of music therapy through three stages of development over 35 years. In the first stage, music was regarded as an almost magical healing agent, and the therapist's role was minimized. This period was followed by one that featured a zealous regard for the therapist's role and deemphasized the musical element. Finally, in the third stage, the emphases of the first two stages were balanced so that the elements of music and therapy were considered mutually supportive ingredients in the music therapy process. Since the delineation of these three stages, music therapy has undergone further changes that constitute a fourth stage of development. In the 1970s, music was represented as a methodology to promote behavioral change. Michel (1976) noted that therapeutic music must seek to accomplish specific treatment goals by changing behavior from undesirable to desirable and that each treatment must be individualized. More recently, members of the medical community, such as Gaynor (1994), have reported that music has repeatedly demonstrated the power to reduce stress and help people overcome both physical and emotional disorders.

The devotees of music therapy cite its specific advantages (Cornett, 1999):

• *Music provides a universal means of communication.* It can be adapted for use with persons of various ages, backgrounds, and intellectual and emotional levels. It can provide a full continuum of self-expression, from simple rhythm to complex harmony. It can be a passive listening activity or an active participation activity. It can be used with individuals or groups.

• *Music encourages the development of a variety of healthy personality traits.* Among these are self-subordination and the acceptance of responsibility. The individual must learn to delay gratification of personal whims and to play a role that often involves coordinating activities with others in a cooperative manner. Other healthy traits are learned because music is a structured activity that encourages discipline and self-directed behavior. It also is a creative process whereby the individual has the opportunity to add his personal stamp on the musical activity.

• *Music is a nonthreatening way for children to develop a sense of achievement, which enhances self-esteem.* Children take pride in creating music and view the music as a representative facet of their world. Children who may have difficulty succeeding at other school-related activities may be successful making music.

• *Music connects the affective, cognitive, and psychomotor domains of development.* Music activity changes the brain by activating areas in both hemispheres and stimulating whole-brain involvement. Music creates positive moods and constructive thinking.

• *Music is a valuable avenue for learning.* Learning songs and music also involves learning language, speech, rhyming, rhythm, and many other abilities. Learning music requires critical listening, attending, and concentration. A review of research into students' responses to musical experiences in school showed significant gains in critical thinking, cognitive skills, and language abilities, as well as improvement in self-concept and social skills (Trusty & Oliva, 1994).

Other benefits of music are that it is entertaining, universally understood, and appreciated at some level by almost all people. At the very least, it provides a useful icebreaker and therefore can be used in conjunction with other types of therapeutic interventions, such as behavioral therapy and reality therapy. Because music bonds people, it is a useful tool in establishing a trusting relationship between child and therapist or teacher. Group singing promotes group spirit. Shared experiences that provide a sense of accomplishment promote relationships (Page, 1995).

Human Responses to Music

More than one famous person (e.g., Oliver Wendell Holmes, Nietzsche, and Goethe) has commented on the importance of music to the human spirit (Cornett, 1999). Each culture throughout recorded time has produced different music to fulfill needs of expression and communication. Thus, music is essential to human beings, a vehicle for releasing emotion and stating ideas.

There is evidence that music affects the functioning of the central nervous system. In early research, Pribram (1964) found a relationship between familiar and novel sound and patterns of electric activity in the brain. Extreme repetition of the familiar led to neural inhibition and drowsiness. Novelty produced alert responses; however, excessive novelty (without familiar patterns) resulted in a return to the inactive, inattentive state. Apparently, music is received with interest and alertness when there is a familiar theme and a number of variations on that theme. Also, entrainment (the tendency for two rhythms to synchronize with each other) is a neurological response that occurs when brain rhythms imitate external rhythms (Armstrong, 1994; Page, 1995).

Other investigations have supported the conclusion that human response to music is innate. Observational studies of infants conducted by Krumhansl and Jusczyk (1990) revealed patterns of attention to natural music segments of Mozart minuets as opposed to unnatural segments (pauses inserted in the middle of phrases). Gardner (1983) documented evidence that infants imitate pitch, volume, melodic contour, and rhythm of their mothers' songs.

According to Priestley (1984), rhythm is the essence of music. Unlike melody, harmony, and counterpoint, which have existed for less than a thousand years, rhythm has existed for millions of years. Research shows that people tend to ignore or avoid music that has no rhythmic order. Also, they respond differently when exposed to rhythmic and nonrhythmic music with respect to galvanic skin response, pupillary dilatation, electromyograms, and picture drawing. All soothing lullabies have monotonously regular rhythm. Rhythm encourages people to act together, cheer, dance, march, chant, and so forth.

Kramer (1971) noted that, among the activity therapies, music is least related to general development. Typical children with musical talent acquire specific musical skills, and their performances reveal very little about maturational levels in other areas or their emotional states. Similarly, atypical children with impaired development may show excellent competence in music. Indeed, if they are unable to relate to people, they may direct great energy to achievement in music and surpass in ability peers whose development is unimpaired.

All experts in this area agree that music fulfills the human need for aesthetic expression and is therefore a physiological component of well-being.

Most people are gratified by music, whether they hear it or engage in noncompetitive achievement (Cornett, 1999).

Elements That Define Music

The level of children's response to music is determined to some degree by their ability to understand the key components of music. According to Cornett (1999), these elements include rhythm, beat and accent, tempo, meter, syncopation, melody, pitch, timbre, dynamics, texture, harmony, form, and ostinato.

Rhythm refers to an ordered, recurrent alternation in the forward movement of sound in music. In songs, words often correspond to the rhythm of the music. Rhythm is composed of accent and beat, meter, tempo, and syncopation. *Beat* refers to pulsation of sound, whereas *accent* is the placement of the strongest emphasis (as in one, two, *three*). *Meter* is the arrangement or basic pattern of sound in rhythm (as in triple meter), and *tempo* refers to the speed of the music. *Syncopation* occurs when the regular meter in music is displaced or made uneven, usually by stressing the weak beat.

Melody is an agreeable progression of sounds in a recognizable pattern that comprises the tune. Melody includes *pitch*, the high or low tones in the pattern, and may be based on major or minor scales. Melodies in a Western scale of music usually involve octaves or the eight notes between any pitched notes (e.g., C at one pitch and C one octave higher).

Timbre is the unique quality given to sound by its overtones or resonance. Different timbres can be created by striking a stick against different surfaces. *Dynamics* refers to the volume (i.e., relative loudness or softness of a sound) and provides emotion to the music. *Texture* is increasing the complexity of the music by layering or combining voices or instruments. *Harmony* involves the blending of sounds or two or more pitches simultaneously (e.g., chords). *Form* refers to the structure or pattern (the order of repetition, as in ABA or ternary form, and ABACA or rondo form) of music. Form encompasses musical styles such as classical or jazz. *Ostinato* involves repeating melodic content persistently at the same pitch throughout the composition.

Music and Children with Special Needs

Alvin (1976) and Streeter (1980) noted that music is unique in that children with handicaps respond much as normal children respond. Most children experience pleasure, some react negatively, but almost none are indifferent. Their positive responses may be *physical*, the instinctive reaction to rhythm; *sensuous*, similar to the feel of certain material or the odor of certain fragrances; *intellectual*, a desire to know or remember what is heard; or *emotional*, a recognition of aroused feelings that is crucial to music sensibility. Music, therefore, is an avenue to reach children who cannot be reached by other means.

Drawing on years of research and clinical involvement with typical and atypical children, Alvin (1976), a leader in the development of music as an independent approach to therapy, formulated and validated numerous premises pertaining to children's respective responses to music. She found that among the individuals without handicaps, those who were older and more sophisticated reacted more negatively than their younger peers to music with harmonic dissonance. The younger children were too immature to react to the dissonance, responding instead to the rhythm. However, children with psychoses or other serious emotional disorders tended to react like the older group without handicaps and rejected dissonant music. Also, most children were sensitive to melodic intervals of music, enjoying the continuity of musical lines, as well as the deviant intervals between notes. All of the children, even those with serious handicaps, were sensitive to speed, pitch, and intensity and based their listening preferences on those qualities. Like children without disorders, children with psychoses, cerebral palsy, and anxiety disorders were affected by sequences of sounds. The pentatonic scale (a scale with five tones, the fourth and seventh tones being omitted) was sedating, as was music played in a low register and music played at low volumes. Elevating register and volume had an exciting effect. Rhythmical or dance music provoked an urge to move or dance. Although children enjoy rhythm, a repetitive, percussive element was highly stimulating and often had detrimental effects, particularly when children were tired, tense, or highly anxious.

As a rule, all of the children were aware that music made them feel happy, although the emotionally stable individuals were more conscious of the impact and better able to express their feelings. Rigid and unimaginative children preferred music accompanied by stories, whereas more musically sensitive individuals were sustained by the music alone. Many of the more intelligent children were so moved by the music that they created lovely essays and poetry that described it. Children with handicaps were aided in this type of effort when the music had an imaginative title. Other intelligent children reacted to aspects of the performance other than the music, such as the instruments involved. When this type of reaction was accompanied by sensitivity to the music, it was often an indication of interest in performing.

Alvin (1976) believed that music contributes to the general growth of children with handicaps, as an emotional outlet, means of socialization, agent of sensory development, and mental stimulus. Satisfying emotional experiences are brought about by creative musical activities suitable to the child's handicap and level of maturity. These may include singing or playing an instrument in rudimentary fashion, processes that help the child use language and increase motor and kinesthetic abilities. They also include listening activities that increase ability to attend and evoke feelings. Children involved in these activities are able to identify with the music, absorbing ideas and showing feeling not often encountered previously. They develop a sense of security that may have been absent. They also absorb the form and structure of the music, characteristics they reveal when they attempt to make up tunes.

Alvin also equated (a) the progression in music from playing with an instrument and using one's voice in unstructured ways to playing on an instrument and singing coherently to (b) the progression from play to work. This process involves delaying immediate gratification and accepting the responsibility to move toward a goal—an important aspect of growth for children with handicaps. Achievement leads to self-confidence and greater self-respect.

Alvin worked primarily with young children but gave some attention to adolescents. She recognized the dramatic change in musical preferences that accompanies adolescence, concluding that adolescents with and without handicaps become preoccupied with pop music because it is an important emotional outlet and a basis for group identification. She believed that the repetitive aspects of the music adolescents prefer and their insatiable need to hear it indicate that their musical preferences make them feel more secure. Also, adolescents need hero worship, and the pop music singer fulfills this need. The infantile text of pop songs expresses the adolescent's immature feelings. Alvin has concluded that it is better to accept the musical choices made by adolescents while attempting to interest them in more mature types of music, such as jazz.

Role of the Therapist

Unlike the art therapist, the music therapist is not bound closely to psychoanalytic theory. Instead, the therapist is a generalist who uses music to change individual behaviors. In the role of generalist, the music therapist is expected to remain flexible, that is, to identify each child's specific needs and, through *improvisation*, to spontaneously alter the therapeutic program to meet those needs. Thus, improvisation is basic to the therapist's role when working with individuals or groups.

Nordoff and Robbins (1970, 1977, 1983) provided descriptions of their use of improvisation with young children who suffered from psychoses. They searched out a region of contact with each child by improvising rhythms and melodies in therapy. For example, each time a specific child entered the room, the therapist played a simple, rhythmic series of notes that became the child's signature song. Also, as children toyed with instruments—strumming, banging, or pounding them haphazardly—the therapist attempted to accompany the random sounds to create a pattern or melody. The goal was to reach or communicate with the child musically, to help him attend to the music as more than noise. As the child's response changed, so did his musical stimulation. The therapist might begin to sing words to the signature song and to gently encourage the child to sing as well. All attempts at involvement should be indirect, as direct approaches are usually met with resistance or further withdrawal from reality. Nordoff and Robbins believe that live music is best for providing many opportunities to improvise; however, when dealing with autistic or autistic-like children who refuse human contact, tape recorders or transistors can be useful.

For group work with children who have less serious impairments, the therapist is advised not to plan musical activities on an organized basis. A variety of activities should be undertaken, such as singing, listening, playing, dancing, and storytelling. Each activity should be short, and the therapist should be alert to the children's preferences. Also, the therapist should vary the types of music, including both stimulating and sedating examples. The therapist also must remain aware of the children's changing moods, because they tire or bore quickly with activities that they initially found appealing. Most individuals associated with the therapeutic use of music agree that their goal is not to produce good musicians. In certain cases, this result may occur incidentally; however, the ultimate goal is to help children improve their attitudes, behaviors, and skills so that they might function better in society. Priestley (1984) and Cornett (1999) listed more specific goals. They may be categorized as general, personal, social, and musical.

General Goals

1. To promote emotional health and development
2. To provide emotional release
3. To provide physiological release

Personal Goals

1. To build self-confidence and self-esteem
2. To increase attention span
3. To help accept personal limits
4. To provide acceptable ways of expressing feelings

Social Goals

1. To develop social awareness
2. To stimulate communication
3. To foster satisfactory interpersonal relationships
4. To increase range and flexibility of behavior in social interactions

Musical Goals

1. To introduce the beauty and joy of music
2. To provide a release for creative self-expression
3. To channel latent musical abilities
4. To offer an opportunity to display skills and accomplishments

Techniques

Priestley (1984) believed that all children can be reached by music if the presentation of techniques is appropriate. Music offers a variety of techniques that may be used with individuals or with groups.

Individual Therapeutic Techniques. As noted, individual music therapy is most often used with children who have severe emotional disorders and pervasive developmental disabilities (e.g., autism and schizophrenia). Many of these musical interventions take place in hospital or clinical settings. Usually these sessions begin with improvisations. The therapist plays an instrument, usually the piano, seeking to evoke a musical response from the patient. The patient's response might be vocal or instrumental. If instruments are involved, drums or cymbals are the usual choices in initial sessions. If the child responds, the therapist attempts to accompany the musical effort. The goal is to use the music to heighten the child's contact with reality and to provide a method of communication for children who either have not developed or have lost the ability to express themselves verbally. Other individual therapy techniques are essentially adaptations of group therapy procedures.

Group Therapeutic Techniques. In recent years, group application of music therapy techniques has gained popularity. Group therapy involves three basic techniques: listening, singing, and playing.

1. *Listening.* Listening is the most passive of the group techniques and is often the precursor to involvement in singing or playing. At the most elementary level, the therapist simply plays music or recordings of music while the group listens. More active listening is stimulated by the use of several activities:

- *Telling a story to music.* The children are encouraged to listen to the music, then to make up a story to fit the music. They may tell the story orally, write it down, or draw a picture depicting it. Alvin (1976) suggested giving a title to the musical piece to stimulate the listener's imagination.

- *Expressing feeling to music.* The children are instructed to listen, then to tell how music makes them feel. They may show their feelings in nonverbal ways such as dance, painting, or poetry.

- *Using music as a source of subject matter.* The musical pieces are used to promote intelligent discussion. Topics such as the period or type of music represented, the composer's life, or the instruments used in the recording might be discussed.

- *Comparing types of music.* Children are asked to compare a variety of musical pieces on an emotional level (e.g., which makes them happiest, saddest, most excited, and least excited) and to consider their relative appropriateness in certain situations (e.g., which helps them get up in the morning, which would their mother like best, and so forth).

2. *Singing.* Singing, although a verbal technique, can provide a form of communication that is less threatening than speech. Group singing also provides a social foundation for the development of interpersonal relations. Nordoff and Robbins (1983) recommended that songs used in music therapy relate to the children's personal experiences. Alvin (1976) recommended that the songs relate to concrete situations and enjoyable experiences. Generally, the songs used in music therapy fall into four categories: happy songs, which express various uplifting feelings in a stimulating manner; purposeful songs, which express a set of actions; thoughtful songs, which express material of a meditative nature; and lyrical songs, which express feelings of tenderness and wonder.

A technique often used to open a singing session with young children is a greeting or name song. For example, the children's names can be sung, as in "Hello Sally, Hello Sally, How Are You?" to the tune of "Frere Jacques." Other songs that enhance communication, develop awareness, and promote basic academic learning may involve spelling common words, counting, identifying colors, or singing the days of the week or months of the year.

3. *Playing.* Playing music has the advantages of involving the children in the live production of music, teaching them new skills, and being completely nonverbal. Nordoff and Robbins (1983) categorized the best instruments for playing in music therapy as those that are sturdy and attractive, produce a good sound, and have a variety of uses. For young children or older children who have no experience with complex instruments, they recommended the use of simple rhythm instruments such as resonator bells, drums, tambourines, rattles, shakers, maracas, bells, triangles, xylophones, and tone blocks. The therapist gives each child an instrument, demonstrates its use, and leads the group, usually by playing a recording of a rhythmic composition.

Music-playing activities for older children might involve more complex instruments, such as guitar, banjo, ukulele, and autoharp. The recorder is an excellent alternative for use with groups because it is inexpensive and relatively easy to play. According to Alvin (1976), the flute is one of the best instruments to promote communication in the classroom with groups of children with emotional and behavioral disorders. The flute's range of expression can be soothing or lively, and it can be rhythmical without being percussive. Although it has a varied repertoire of music, it does not evoke overexcited, hyperactive behavior. Similarly, Alvin recommended the guitar for withdrawn individuals because stringed instruments that are plucked are more stimulating to children.

Obviously, the therapist using these instruments must have expertise as a musician. Also, the children must evidence a great interest in musical activities and be capable of learning to play such instruments. Under these circumstances, the children can be taught simple songs and can play together as a group after very little practice.

Educational Applications

As early as 1976, Michel predicted that the field of music therapy would transform from its institutionally based beginnings and become an important force in health-related services and educational programs. Similarly, the role of the music therapist would evolve from a clinical specialist to that of a music resource person within the schools. The accuracy of Michel's predictions is supported by the current status of music as a source of therapy in educational settings. Although music specialists are not always readily available in schools, there is a growing awareness that music is a valuable asset for teachers of all types of children, and particularly for children with special needs. Music can be integrated into any teacher's instructional program. To use music techniques successfully, the teacher must plan a program by considering which students should participate, what physical arrangements (such as space, time, and materials) are necessary, what goals must be set, and what music activities will best meet those goals.

Candidates. The vast majority of people, regardless of age, appreciate music and are capable of responding when they hear it. Most children demonstrate musical sensibility; that is, they experience a pleasurable reaction to musical sounds. Some children also have musical aptitude, the talent to perform music well. Children who have both may achieve high levels of musical ability. Others, who have either sensibility or aptitude, are responsive to music geared to their competence and preferences. Children who have neither are negative or indifferent to music, but they are rarely encountered. When they are encountered, they should be excluded from the program.

The key to helping children benefit from music is to interest them in the program by using techniques appropriate for their age and particular needs. For example, adolescents are not enthralled by juvenile songs. Also, involving a class of children with emotional and behavioral disorders in a music program may take longer to achieve than interesting a group of typical learners. As is true of art techniques, the teacher must enthusiastically present innovative strategies that encourage creativity if the children are to make an enthusiastic response.

Physical Arrangements. The essential physical component for a music program is space. Most classroom sessions will involve groups and will require a relatively large amount of space. However, unlike an art area, a music area need not remain static. It can be established when needed simply by rearranging the portable elements of the classroom. The single exception to this rule recommended by most experts is the establishment of a permanent listening corner. This small section of the classroom should be kept available for the children, who may wish to spend free time listening to music, may require music as a calming influence, or may choose to listen to music as an earned reinforcement or reward.

Music activities are generally easy to schedule as part of the school day. Unlike art, they require little time for setup and cleanup. Nordoff and Robbins (1983) suggested a time range of 20 to 60 minutes per session, depending on the age and interests of the children and the complexity of the instruments they are using.

The materials used in a classroom program probably will be readily available to the teacher. In addition to the teacher's own materials, school-based resources are the music teacher, the library, equipment for playing and recording music, and occasionally musical instruments. For a program of listening activities, the teacher will require a compact disc or tape player, accompanying headphones (if available), and musical recordings that vary in type, including popular music, jazz, classical, country, and music associated with other cultures. As has been noted, music may be sedating or stimulating in varying degrees, and examples of all types should be included in the program. Stimulating music tends to increase physical activity and reduce mental activity, has a fast tempo, detached (staccato) lines, complex and dissonant harmonies, and abrupt dynamic changes. In contrast, sedating music tends to reduce physical activity and increase contemplation, has a slow tempo, smooth (legato) lines, simple harmonies, and little dynamic change. The teacher can refer to the following sources as examples of publications that aid in the selection of pieces: *Making Music with the Young Handicapped Child* (Streeter, 1980), *World of Music: An Introduction to the Music of the World's People* (Tilton, 1992),

Teaching Kids To Sing (Phillips, 1992), *Listen to the Music* (Eakle, 1992), and *Music Fundamentals, Methods, and Materials for the Elementary Classroom Teacher* (Rozmajzi & Boyer-White, 1996).

Singing activities require only a selection of songs and, if desired, a musical instrument for accompaniment. Songbooks typically used with children in regular education are suitable for use with children who have special needs. Two sources of useful material are *Sing and Shine On! A Teacher's Guide to Multicultural Song Leading* (Page, 1995) and *The Music Teacher's Almanac: Ready-To-Use Music Activities for Every Month of the Year* (Mitchell, 1992). These sources are useful primarily with young children. Materials for adolescents should include a variety of classical, popular, and folk music that may be sung chorally or as solo pieces. A useful source is *Working with the Adolescent Voice* (Cooksey, 1992).

The choice of accompaniment for singing activities depends on the teacher's ability to play a musical instrument. If he cannot play, accompaniment can be vocal. If the teacher is not confident about his singing ability, the accompaniment can be produced with recordings.

Teaching Goals and Activities. It would be inappropriate for teachers to consider using music strategies as an avenue to practice psychotherapy. The role of teacher belies such emphasis. Goals for the therapeutic use of music in the school must be consistent with functions of a teacher. The techniques and methods associated with the music program must be integrated into the total education program and be consistent with the interests of the class. The following goals are suggested:

- *To produce a relaxing atmosphere.* Often children, particularly those with emotional problems, become overstimulated by classroom events. In these situations the teacher may use recorded music to calm the group.

- *To provide an opportunity to be successful.* Some children who may perform poorly academically or socially have the inherent aptitude to excel at vocal or instrumental musical activities. The opportunity to develop and display their talent can be an important avenue to increasing self-esteem.

- *To reinforce or reward children.* Musical activities can serve as a reward for improved behavior, completion of work, and so on.

- *To provide an expressive outlet.* Musical activities, such as those associated with singing or playing in a rhythm band, are good ways to "blow off steam." Often, permitting children who have learning and behavioral problems to ventilate in this socially acceptable way helps prevent displays of undesirable behavior.

- *To encourage social interactions.* All children, but particularly those with learning and behavioral problems, benefit from opportunities to work cooperatively with one another. Music is an excellent resource to encourage such activity.

- *To connect music to curricular areas.* Music can be woven into all aspects of the curriculum, including science, social studies, reading, language arts, and mathematics.

To meet any of these educational goals, teachers should orient the children to the program by using energizers or warm-ups as a first step, introducing basic musical concepts as a second step, and integrating music into the curriculum as a third step. Cornett (1999) provided examples of activities for each step of the program.

1. **Energizing and Warm-Up Activities**

   - *Clap phrases.* The students clap the rhythms to well-known songs.

   - *Echo rhythms.* The teacher claps a series of rhythms and is imitated by the class.

   - *Musical memories.* Students are told to close their eyes and imagine sounds described by the teacher (e.g., birds singing, gentle rainfall, bells tolling, clocks striking).

   - *Rhythm mirror.* The group forms a circle with one child in the middle. The middle child claps a rhythm that the other children copy. The middle child changes places with another child, who then leads the group.

   - *Balloon movement.* The children wave balloons in time to classical music.

   - *Word choirs.* Students form a choir line and are given a general topic (e.g., joy). When pointed to by the teacher, each child sings a word related to the topic (e.g., *fun*). As the teacher points to each child on a random basis, each child sings his or her word.

2. **Basic Musical Concepts**

   - *Hum melodies.* The teacher hums the first line of a song familiar to the children. She adds lines until the children guess the song, then everyone sings it. Also, a child can be designated to do the humming.

- *Cumulative melodies.* Each child selects a well-known song to hum. The first child begins humming her song, then the second child begins his song, and so on until each child is humming different music at the same time. This overlapping of melodies is counterpoint.

- *Kazoo melodies.* The teacher plays a song on the kazoo that the children imitate on their kazoos.

- *Environmental sounds.* The teacher tapes familiar sounds in the environment. The children must classify them according to pitch—high, middle, or low.

- *Guess who.* The children close their eyes. A child tapped on the shoulder by the teacher sings one word. The other children guess who has sung. The uniqueness of each singing voice is illustrated.

- *Name the instrument.* Children close their eyes and guess which instrument is being played. The unique sounds of each instrument are illustrated.

- *Dynamic volume.* The teacher has the children sing loudly or softly in response to hand signals.

- *Sound effects textured story.* The teacher reads a story. The children provide vocal or instrumental sound effects on cue. For example, children say moo or click sticks when the word *cow* is mentioned.

- *Commons and rounds.* The students learn harmony by singing with a tape of rounds, then singing without the tape. Movements associated with each line help them remember their parts.

- *Spoken rounds and ostinato.* One group of children recites a poem, while the other recites an ostinato (repeats something over and over).

- *Music concentration.* The teacher draws various notes on the board while the children repeat the names of the symbols. The children close their eyes as the teacher erases symbols; then the children try to name the erased symbols.

- *Instrument rummy.* The teacher replaces the face cards of a 52-card deck with sets of strings, brass, woodwinds, and percussion instruments. The object is to acquire 4 cards in each set. Players are dealt 5 cards. At each turn, the player draws 1 card and either discards face up or keeps it. The winner has the most instrumental sets when the end of the deck is reached.

3. Music and Curriculum

Science

- *Science songs.* Students study an aspect of science, then write words about the lesson to familiar tunes.

- *Body parts rap.* Students rap the bones in the body.

- *Musical seasons stories.* The students mime events associated with a season as the teacher plays appropriate seasonal music.

Social Studies

- *States and capitals chant.* Students chant names in time to a drumbeat.

- *Multicultural storybook.* Students collect songs from different cultures. Each small group may work on a different culture, and the class shares results.

- *Music current events.* Students find clippings of events related to music.

- *History time line.* The teacher plays music from various musical periods. The students study the periods and prepare posters depicting aspects of life in each period (e.g., clothing or architecture).

- *History through music.* The teacher plays songs associated with historical events (e.g., sailing ships, wars, slavery).

Reading and Language Arts

- *Write out songs.* The students write the words to familiar songs, then create their own verses.

- *Musician expert.* The students select a musician, do research, and write a paper or a story about the musician's life and work.

- *Student interviews.* The students interview a guest musician, then write a newspaper story about that individual.

- *Music and stories.* The students listen to music, then write stories about it.

- *Songwriting.* Students compose songs.

- *Music dictionary.* Students create a dictionary of music terms, concepts, composers, instruments, and so forth.

- *Compare and contrast.* Students compare versions of the same song.

Mathematics

- *Number lyrics.* The students sing familiar songs but replace the lyrics with numbers (e.g., odd numbers or multiplication tables).

- *Counting songs.* Students sing songs involving counting (e.g., "One Potato, Two Potato").

- *Number water music.* The teacher fills ten 10-inch glasses with 1 inch to 10 inches of water (an inch added to each glass) and numbers the glasses from 1 to 10. The students tap out number sequences and listen for pitches.

Therapeutic Dance

History and Background

Dance therapy is defined as "the specific use of dance movements as a means of nonverbal communication, emotional release of hostile and tender feelings, physical relaxation and increased self-awareness" (Toombs, 1968, p. 2). Dance is traditionally associated with music, and dance therapy often is considered a component of music therapy. In some cases, dance is a simple extension of an elaborate music therapy program; in others, however, dance is far more important and complex than the music. Like music, dance is an essential component of the human experience. It is present is some form in all cultures and is believed to extend to the time of primitive peoples, who used it to express their awe of the unknown (Toombs, 1968). Historically, dances have been used by various peoples, including native Americans, as religious events—persuading the gods to bring rain, vanquish enemies, produce game for food, and so forth. Over time, its mystical influence diminished; however, it continued to be regarded as a superb form of self-expression and an outlet for emotions.

As an activity therapy, dance has advocates who regard it as a fundamental resource for reaching individuals with serious disorders who, because of their extensive pathology, are rarely involved constructively in verbally based therapy. Many schools of therapeutic thought, including the psychoanalytic, gestalt, existential, and phenomenological approaches, as well as psychodrama (Bernstein, 1979), integrate dance into their therapeutic activities with persons who are more intact. In these instances, dance is believed to help individuals release unconscious feelings, to take them beyond their typical patterns of intellectualizing, and to provide them with a cathartic outlet. Chace (1975), the foremost innovator in the development of dance therapy as a specific discipline, believed that the movements in dance permit an individual to express psychic states that are more primitive than language. Currently, dance is used extensively with adult and child populations.

Dance and Development

The capacity to dance, which is dependent on motor development, is related to the maturation of the brain. Some theorists such as Piaget (1977) view spatial perception and motor development as innate components of general cognitive development. An alternative explanation suggests that movements represented by dance, as well as music and visual art, are innately governed but constitute distinct forms of intelligence (Gardner, 1983). Bodily–kinesthetic intelligence, as represented in dance, appears early in development. Children respond to rhythm with body movements even before they walk. Later, young children intuitively move in distinct dance patterns, spinning, twirling, and so forth, when they hear music. With maturation, they obtain greater motor control and perform any variety of expressive dance movements. In early stages these patterns of movement (usually to music) are similar across cultures (Bjorklund, 1990). As children grow and are exposed to the dances specific to their particular culture, their patterns of movement in dance become culturally relative. Children's attitudes toward dance and their willingness to engage in dance activities are influenced by cultural mores and their specific experiences.

Dance and Disabilities

Unlike music, dance is a relatively accurate indicator of impairment or disability. A great body of research attests to the bodily–kinesthetic impairment associated with mental retardation, cerebral palsy, brain dysfunction, and severe disorders such as psychosis and autism. Movements have been described as clumsy, jerky, awkward, slow, and generally lacking in coordination.

Similarly, dance and other forms of movement provide clear reflections of typical individuals' emotional states. A person's manner of movement reveals much about the individual's comfort with his or her body, self-confidence, level of inhibition, ability to interact with others, and enjoyment of expressive, nonverbal activities. Highly inhibited, self-conscious individuals may avoid dance or may participate only to the extent of repeating stereotyped steps without regard for rhythm. Rigidity of posture and restricted movements signal discomfort and repressed emotion. Many overcontrolled children who perform well in academic areas reveal their loss of spontaneity and developing inability to express emotion by their inhibited response to dance. Conversely, other children unable to achieve in academic areas may retain their freedom of expression and excel at dance.

Espenak (1981) documented that certain moods or attitudes are expressed through characteristic postures used in dance: (a) dejected attitude—slumped shoulders, head on chest, fumbling steps, (b) retiring attitude—inward-drawn shoulders, head lowered, (c) heightened tension—shoulders lifted to ears, head in neck, elbows tense, hands nervous, and (d) aggressive attitude—strutting chest, swagger, accent on heels. Extending her research, Espenak developed a battery of six movement diagnostic tests that measure emotional states: confidence, balance, kinesthetic awareness, coordination, attention span, and anxiety.

Dance Formats and Techniques

Dance therapy for seriously disordered persons is designed to interpret an individual's movements as representative of emotions and to establish a means of communication. Usually, little or no consideration is given to the beauty or grace of dance movements, and rehearsed dance patterns are not involved. According to Chace (1975), the most appropriate format in dance therapy for persons with severe impairments (psychosis, autism, brain damage) involves creative dance. Because its form is flexible and its technique is based on natural functional movements of the body, it is the most adaptable form of dance, useful to meet the specific needs of a variety of individuals suffering diverse disabilities. In creative dance, spontaneous movements expressing individual feelings are encouraged, even in group approaches.

Drawing on her vast clinical experience as a dance therapist, Chace developed an extensive body of techniques for implementing creative dance therapy with individuals suffering severe, chronic disabilities. She recommended admitting everyone to a dance group formed as a circle. No one is forced to participate; individuals may choose to simply watch or leave. Although the goal is to promote group dance and the ensuing social interactions, each individual initially receives the therapist's personal attention. After selecting music to influence mood (happy, carefree, invigorating, sedating) and encouraging an individual to dance, the therapist plays an accepting, supporting role, responding to the person's movements, however unusual or bizarre they may be. The therapist may perform movements that are qualitatively similar to those of the individual (although not mimicking) or may attempt to express a positive emotion of safety or welcome. Sometimes the behavior of the group member determines the therapist's choice of movements. The therapist might approach a very passive, fearful individual with both palms upward, moving backward and forward to elicit hand clapping. The therapist might meet an aggressive person with movement suggesting submission. Persons having a particularly difficult day might require slow, repetitive movements. The therapist performs these initial one-to-one contacts by moving quickly from one person to another, seeming to make the contacts occur simultaneously. Gradually, the individual group members become comfortable enough to engage in group activity with the therapist as the catalyst.

Chace believed that the circle formation was a helpful means of involving the entire group in the dance. Various individuals are able to assume the leader's role and spontaneously improvise movements that others might follow. The circle also enables the therapist to invite physical contact with group members through gestures and movements. However, actual touch always is initiated by the individual. Basically, the therapist's role is to create an atmosphere of free expression through nondirective activity that avoids predetermined structure.

Chace (1975) also described dance therapy programs for persons with less severe psychological disorders. For these individuals, she believed that dancing should be conducted as it is in the community. Dance classes might be established to teach new, interesting dances and encourage social interactions similar to those encountered in typical society. These classes might be integrated with other forms of activity, such as art, drama, and music.

Dance therapy developed specifically for children has followed the same patterns as that initiated for adults. Essentially, the form and techniques have depended on type and degree of disability and program goals. Relatively loosely structured strategies, such as creative dance, are used to make contact with children whose serious disabilities limit their use of language (Leventhal, 1980). More structured forms of dance, such as the circling used in ring-around-the-rosy and snake line dances, also have been used to encourage interactions among children with serious disorders.

The increased application of dance techniques with children who suffer mild disorders, or who have no disorders, over the years since the inception of dance as a therapeutic intervention has resulted in the extension of strategies to include more stylized forms of dance used in ordinary social situations. The goals of these programs have been to help children and adolescents feel more secure about their physical selves and develop useful social skills. Although this progressive extension of the use of dance has increased the applicability of dance in education, some advocates remain convinced that creative, interpretive dancing is the principal tool for unlocking the emotions of children and revealing emotional and behavioral problems. Espenak (1981) recommended weekly creative dance classes as a means of providing children an outlet for self-expression, believing that dance activities enabled participants to establish missing kinesthetic awareness and experience corresponding emotions.

Role of the Therapist

In traditional creative dance therapy, the therapist assumes a nondirective role, acting not like a dance instructor but as a facilitator of each individual's participation in the dance. The steps in this process begin with the creation of a warm, friendly environment that signifies acceptance and safety to the participants. Music is a component of the environment, particularly rhythmic music that invites dance. Both the music and the style of dance must be suited to the needs of the participants; therefore, the therapist attempts to become familiar with the background and particular problems of each potential member of the dance group. This knowledge, however, must be accompanied by sensitivity to the affect presented by each person who enters the dance room and reacts to the circumstances.

As the use of dance therapy has spread, the therapist's role has varied with the format of the dance group, the types of individuals involved, and the goals of the therapy. Therapists attempting to involve seriously impaired, nonverbal clients in creative dancing usually demonstrate aspects of dance, such as swaying, and invite each client to participate by gestures, facial expressions, and body postures. However, because the goal is not to have people model or imitate the therapist but to encourage them to move in accordance with their feelings, the therapist attempts to minimize her role as soon as group members begin to respond.

In other circumstances, when the goal is to promote social interactions through dance, and particularly when more highly structured dance formats are being used, the therapist may model or demonstrate steps for participants to imitate. Even in these cases, however, the nondirective therapist seeks the participants' input regarding the format. All potential group members, including individuals suffering from psychoses, choose whether and how they will participate. Children who do not have serious disabilities might be presented with a variety of dance options to choose from, or might be involved in different types of dance throughout multiple sessions. Regardless of the format, it is essential that the therapist not attempt to dominate during the dancing unless the participants request specific demonstrations. Also, the therapist should be accepting of each individual's efforts. The emphasis is on participation rather than excellent performance.

In addition to varying dance formats with circumstances, therapists use a variety of strategies to involve individuals in the therapeutic activities. The choices depend on the developmental and emotional status of the participants. Groups of young, uninhibited individuals or persons accustomed to dancing may be stimulated to participate in a therapeutic dance program by relatively brief discussions. When individuals are defensive about dance, they can be made more comfortable through the use of a graduated progression of movements that proceeds from physical activities such as aerobics done to music, to aerobic activities that include dance steps, to dance. Although some persons may never progress beyond the level of physical exercise, their activity still provides a desirable means of tension reduction.

Educational Applications

Dance, like art and music, is an important component of an integrated, creative arts curriculum for use in education. Advocates of a creative arts curriculum have pointed out that often the use of dance in schools has been limited to infrequent social gatherings in middle schools or high schools for the entire student body or members of a specific grade. Although events of this type may be enjoyable for the socially able, they are unlikely to increase the intellectual, physical, social, and emotional well-being of much of the student body. Dance activities designed to facilitate students' growth and development must be carefully designed and implemented regularly. The goals of including dance as an area of study for all children are similar to those associated with other types of activity therapy. They include the following:

- Increasing sensitivity and cooperation
- Improving self-discipline
- Developing self-concept and confidence
- Providing opportunities for problem solving
- Providing a means of communication
- Providing cultural understanding
- Enhancing social skills
- Releasing tension and channeling aggression

Formats for the use of dance in education vary greatly, ranging from unstructured creative dance to highly structured forms of social dance. The specific program used should meet the needs of the potential participants. To ensure positive student outcomes, Cornett (1999) recommended that all educational dance programs be based on the Seven National Standards for Dance, published by the Music Educators National Conference in 1994. These standards require students to be able to do the following:

1. Identify movement elements in dance
2. Understand choreography

3. Use dance to create meaning
4. Use creative thinking skills in dance
5. Understand the influence of dance in various cultures
6. Connect dance with healthy living
7. Connect dance with other disciplines

Candidates for Dance Programs. Most school-age children are capable of participating in and enjoying some form of dance, and most would benefit from the activity. The motor coordination and body control associated with dancing is beneficial to children's physical and emotional development. Younger children are likely to be enthusiastic about the opportunity to engage in physical activities and are usually less inhibited than preadolescent children and adolescents. The older individuals are more likely to participate if the music is particularly appealing and if the dance format interests them. Usually they are initially resistant to unstructured, interpretive dance.

Dance is a particularly useful activity with students who have emotional disorders. It provides them with a physical outlet for tension and aggression, gives them the opportunity to perform well in a nonacademic area, and establishes the basis for positive relationships with their peers. However, when used with this population, care must be taken to provide structured behavioral rules for participation. Also, student interest in dance must often be stimulated. Attempts to show the relationship between athletic prowess and dance are particularly useful motivators for reluctant participants.

Children with severe disorders may be exposed to programs of creative expressive dance to establish communication or to more structured approaches to dance to encourage social interactions such as hand holding, touching, and marching shoulder to shoulder. These programs might also integrate components of music therapy to encourage verbalization through singing simple songs.

Participation in dance programs of all types should be voluntary. Therefore, disinterested children probably will self-exclude. However, any child who consistently violates the group rules should be excluded from the program.

Physical Arrangements. Space is the most significant consideration associated with a dance program. A large room specifically allocated for music and dance is most desirable. If that is not available, the gymnasium or the stage area of an auditorium may be used. If there are no resources outside the classroom, space within the classroom might be made available for dance activities involving small numbers of children (2 to 4), while the nondancing class members engage in related activities, such as singing or drawing how the music or dance makes them feel.

Records or live music may be used to stimulate the dance. The music selected should relate to the type of dance and the purpose of the activity, as discussed in the music therapy section of this chapter.

The Teacher's Role. The teacher who wants to use dance techniques in the classroom must understand the concept of movement, must be familiar with the basic elements of dance and creative movement, and must be aware of the relationship of pantomime and imagery to dance. Bodily movement is necessary for dance, but even synchronized, gymnastic movements to music (such as step aerobics) is not dance. Movement becomes dance (creative movement) when it communicates the will and spirit of the performer in an original kinesthetic expression of feelings. Pantomime is not dance because it usually involves imitation, not creative movement. Appropriate instruction by the teacher is necessary to evoke dance rather than imitation. For example, the direction "Move like a horse" tends to evoke imitation, whereas the question "What kind of movements might a horse make?" is more likely to evoke creative movement. Imagery is necessary to dance but must be evoked after exploration of the aspects of movement, lest it lead to pantomime. Cornett (1999) recommended using similes and metaphors to stimulate the imagination of movement. For example, ask the child to move as if she were as fluid as a flowing river.

Basic Elements. The basic elements of dance include body, energy, space, and time (Cornett, 1999). *Body* includes body parts, body shapes, and body actions. Body parts and the way an individual folds or shapes his body are always used in communication. People wave a hand to greet and hunch their shoulders to shrink themselves when depressed. Body actions may be stationary (nonlocomotor, e.g., stretching, falling, shaking, and bending) or locomotor (e.g., running, walking, skipping, hopping, jumping, and sliding). *Energy* refers to the force the dancer expends and includes attack (smooth or sharp), weight (heavy or light), tension (tight or loose), and flow (sudden or sustained). *Space* is the area the body uses and includes directions, size, destination, and pathways (direct or indirect). *Time* includes rhythm, speed or tempo, emphasis (light or strong), duration, and phrases (patterns of movement).

Implementation of Dance Techniques. To successfully implement a dance program, the teacher need not be an expert dancer and need not demonstrate dances. Creative, innovative dance does not require expertise at dance, and more stylized, structured dances can be demonstrated by an experienced guest. A teacher who is aware of the concepts of dance discussed in the previous section can use the same sound techniques to teach dance as are used to teach other aspects of the basic curriculum.

Dance is introduced most effectively into the curriculum when the students are taught why it is important. This type of discussion should be open-ended. The students' ideas should be elicited, and the role of dance in various cultures should be explored. The teacher's questions should encourage diverse responses.

Students also need to be made aware that the purpose of an educational dance program is the dance process, not the product. Learning to be a good dancer is not the goal of the program. Dance is a vehicle to heighten understanding of the curriculum and increase understanding of self and others. The teacher can clarify the purpose of the program by having the children use movements to reinforce all learning and to illustrate points they wish to make verbally. Joyce (1994) noted that this type of dance need not be accompanied by music. However, when music is used, Cornett (1999) recommended that it be instrumental, promote dancing, have different tempos, involve a variety of instruments, often be classical, and include folk music from different countries.

To implement the dance program, Cornett (1999) recommended that the teacher use warm-ups and energizers to prepare the students for future dance activities, then teach the basic elements, and finally integrate dance into the curriculum. She provided examples of activities for each of these purposes, some of which are presented here.

Energizers and Warm-ups

- *No words.* The teacher uses motions, rather than speech, to give the students directions. Students communicate the same way with a partner. The students must tell with movements, rather than showing their partners what to do. After the exercise, the role of movements in communication should be discussed.

- *Stretches to music.* The teacher directs the students to do simple stretching exercises, such as reaching up overhead and to the floor with knees bent; repeating to each side; doing head and shoulder rolls, forward and backward; slow windmills; ankle rotations, forward and backward; and shoulder shrugs. Slow, nonrhythmic music can accompany these movements.

- *"Simon Says" with dance elements.* Play "Simon Says" with dance elements—body, energy, space, and time. For example, have the children move as though their bodies were circles, weighed a million pounds, were flying in different directions, and were driven by different beats.

- *Freeze.* The teacher plays music while the children move in a variety of ways. When the teacher stops the music, the children must freeze in position. When the music begins, the children must move in the frozen shape.

- *Five-shape concentration.* The teacher connects the numbers one to five with five body shapes. The children rehearse performing each shape in response to each number the teacher calls in sequence. Then, as the teacher calls numbers quickly and randomly, the children must shift from shape to shape.

- *Movement chain.* The children stand in two lines. When the teacher signals, the children at the beginning of each line begin a movement that is repeated by every child in line. When all of the children have performed the movement, the two children who began go to the end of the line and two new children begin the process with a new movement. This exercise continues until all of the children have had the opportunity to innovate a movement.

- *Back-to-back dancing.* Pairs of children lean back-to-back and begin dancing to music. They must try to stay together as the music increases gradually from slow to fast tempo.

Basic Dance Elements

- *Movement words card sort.* The teacher asks the children to call out ways to move and writes them on cards. The students then sort the cards into locomotor or nonlocomotor (stationary) categories.

- *Shake it up.* When signaled, students shake or move a body part. They freeze when told to, then describe their body shapes. The process continues with different movements and different positions.

- *Adopt a dance.* The children form pairs. Each student gives a unique interpretation to a dance step or movement. When signaled, the partners adopt each other's dance step. New pairs are formed and the process continues.

- *Pass-it-on moves.* The children form a circle. In time to music, one child starts a dance step or movement that the other children imitate in sequence. Then the person to the right of the initial child performs a step, and so on.

- *Video response.* The children watch a movie that involves dance. They are instructed to note the dance elements and how they communicate an idea or feeling.
- *Balancing moves.* The students stand on spots and perform particular movements while balancing a book on their heads.
- *Statues.* The students assume a shape and, when signaled, change to another shape, until they have learned three shapes. These three shapes are performed at different speeds as a statue dance.

Dance and Curriculum

Science
- *Tool dance.* The students explore movements associated with various tools, such as shovels, axes, hoes, and saws. Then they discuss the types of movements involved.
- *Science insect dances.* Each student chooses an insect to explore through movement. The movements should relate to eating, running, flying, and so forth.
- *Bird flight.* Groups of students select different types of birds, research their patterns of flight, then create dances that depict their flight. They must pay attention to changes in formation, speed and level of flight, and body parts.
- *Weather dance.* The students freeze in shapes that depict various types of weather, such as rain, snow, and sunshine. Shapes are changed as the teacher announces weather changes.

Social Studies
- *Work movements.* The students brainstorm different types of work, such as sawing, chopping, sweeping, washing, and hoeing. Each individual creates a work dance using real or imagined props associated with a specific task. Music can be added. The dance should have a beginning, middle, and end.
- *Dance a historical event.* The students brainstorm movements that would have been part of a historical event, such as storming the Alamo. They dance the movements in slow motion, changing rhythm and space.
- *Holiday and season dances.* The children brainstorm movements that might occur at a holiday event, such as trimming a tree at

Christmas or having a turkey dinner at Thanksgiving. They dance in turn, each child adding different movements.

- *Multicultural folktale dance.* The children discuss events in a folktale, such as the legend of Johnny Appleseed, and dance the movements associated with the legend.

Reading and Language Arts

- *Syllables.* The teacher says multisyllabic words and has the children change the basic elements of dance (body part or shape, energy, space, and time) as each syllable is said. For example, the word *refrigerator* has five syllables, so students assume five body shapes, at five tempos, and so forth.

- *Compare and contrast.* The students use jumping to show contrasts between word pairs, such as heavy–light, tall–short, and smooth–rough. They also should compare ways of performing the same move, such as ways of walking.

- *Word walls and webs.* Students look for action and movement words in their reading materials. These words are listed on paper hung on the wall, then used to stimulate movement.

- *Parts of speech.* The students list words that are specific parts of speech and create dance movements for the words.

Math

- *Geometric shapes.* The students walk around, then, when the teacher calls out a shape (e.g., square), freeze in that shape. This exercise also may be done with letters of the alphabet.

- *Telling time.* The teacher makes a large clock on the floor with masking tape. Children take turns standing in the middle of the clock and attempting to stretch their arms to match times supplied by the teacher.

- *Twos and threes.* To teach number groups, the teacher calls out a movement and a pattern, such as jump in twos, with a pause after two jumps. The dance can involve different movements and patterns.

- *Math dance.* The students choreograph a dance using instructions in math terms. For example, take three hops forward, take one step back, pause for three counts, hop once to the right, hop once to the left, and take two steps back.

Conclusion

The thrust of this chapter has been to provide suggestions for the use of art, music, and dance in the classroom. The intent is not to promote these techniques as substitutes for comprehensive therapeutic interventions for children with emotional and behavioral disorders. These strategies to promote creativity simply increase a teacher's ability to facilitate learning, expedite the social and emotional growth of some children, and reach others who might otherwise remain unreachable.

STUDY QUESTIONS

1. Discuss the predominant theory that underlies art therapy.

2. Plan an art, music, or dance project adapted for regular students within the classroom.

3. Develop an integrated educational plan for children with mild emotional and behavioral disorders that combines art, music, or dance techniques with either behavioral or cognitive interventions.

4. List 10 art techniques you might employ to stimulate children's drawing. Specify the trait that you think the techniques develop.

5. Develop an integrated music and dance program for children with autism.

References

Alvin, J. (1976). *Music for the handicapped child*. London: Oxford University Press.

Armstrong, T. (1994). *Multiple intelligence in the classroom*. New York: Penguin Books.

Arnheim, R. (1970). *Visual thinking*. London: Faber & Faber.

Arnheim, R. (1989). *Thoughts on art education*. Los Angeles: Getty Center for Education in the Arts.

Bernstein, P. (1979). *Eight theoretical approaches in dance movement therapy*. Dubuque, IA: Kendall/Hunt.

Betersky, M. (1987). Phenomenology of therapeutic art expression and art therapy. In J. A. Rubin (Ed.), *Approaches to art therapy* (pp. 117–139). New York: Wiley.

Bjorklund, D. (1990). *Children's strategies: Contemporary views of cognitive development*. Hillsdale, NJ: Erlbaum.

Brookes, M. (1996). *Drawing with children*. New York: Putnam.

Chace, M. (1975). *Marion Chace: Her papers*. Columbia, MD: American Dance Therapy Association.

Cooksey, J. M. (1992). *Working with the adolescent voice*. St. Louis, MO: Concordia.

Cornett, C. E. (1999). *The arts as meaning makers*. Upper Saddle River, NJ: Prentice Hall.

Denny, J. (1977). Techniques for individual and group art therapy. In E. Ulman and P. Dachinger (Eds.), *Art therapy in theory and practice* (pp. 48–69). New York: Schocken Books.

Eakle, K. (1992). *Listen to the music! Listening guide for 42 musical selections*. Richmond, British Columbia, Canada: Breerwood.

Eisner, E. (1972). *Educating the artistic vision*. New York: Macmillan.

Eng, H. (1952). *The psychology of children's drawings*. London: Routledge & Kegan Paul.

Espenak, L. (1981). *Dance therapy: Theory and applications*. Springfield, IL: Thomas.

Freeman, N. (1980). *Strategies of representation in young children*. London: Academic Press.

Freud, S. (1963). New introductory lectures on psychoanalysis. In J. Strachey (Ed.), *Dreams* (pp. 21–59). London: Hogarth Press.

Gardner, H. (1983). *Frames of mind: The theory of multiple intelligences*. New York: Basic Books.

Gardner, H. (1993). *Creating minds*. New York: Basic Books.

Gaston, E. (1968). Man and music. In E. T. Gaston (Ed.), *Music in therapy* (pp. 12–21). New York: Macmillan.

Gaynor, M. L. (1994). *Sounds of healing*. New York: Random House.

Goodenough, F. (1923). *Children's drawings as a measure of intellectual maturity*. New York: Harcourt, Brace and World.

Harris, D. (1963). *Children's drawings as measures of intellectual maturity*. New York: Harcourt, Brace and World.

Joyce, M. (1994). *First step in teaching creative dance to children* (3rd ed.). Mountain View, CA: Mayfield.

Junge, M. B. (1994). *A history of art therapy in the United States*. Mundelein, IL: American Art Therapy Association.

Koppitz, E. (1968). *Psychological evaluation of children's human figure drawing*. New York: Grune & Stratton.

Kramer, E. (1971). *Art as therapy with children*. New York: Shocken Books.

Kramer, E. (1973). *Art therapy in a children's community*. Springfield, IL: Thomas.

Kramer, E. (1977). Art and craft. In E. Ulman and P. Dachinger (Eds.), *Art therapy in theory and practice* (pp. 204–229). New York: Schocken Books.

Krurnhansl, C., & Jusczyk, P. (1990). Infants' perception of phrase structure in music. *Psychological Science, 1*, 70–73.

Kwiatkowska, H. (1978). *Family therapy and evaluation through art*. Springfield, IL: Thomas.

Leventhal, M. (1980). *Movement and growth: Dance therapy for the special child*. New York: New York University Press.

Levick, M. (1983). *They could not talk and so they drew*. Springfield, IL: Thomas.

Liebmann, M. (1986). *Art therapy for groups*. London: Croom Helm.

Luquet, G. (1927). *Les dessins d'un enfant [The drawings of a child]*. Paris: Alcan.

Lusebrink, J. B. (1990). *Imagery and visual expression in therapy*. New York: Plenum Press.

McNiff, S. (1992). *Art as medicine: Creating a therapy*. New York: Random House.

Michel, D. (1976). *Music therapy: An introduction to therapy and special education through music*. Springfield, IL: Thomas.

Mitchell, L. (1992). *The music teacher's almanac: Ready-to-use music activities for every month of the year*. West Nyack, NY: Parker.

Music Educators National Conference. (1994). *National standards for arts education*. Reston, VA: Author.

Naumburg, M. (1966). *Dynamically oriented art therapy: Its principles and practices*. New York: Grune & Stratton.

Naumburg, M. (1973). *An introduction to art therapy: Studies of the "free" art expression of behavior problem children and adolescents as a means of diagnosis and therapy*. New York: Teachers College Press.

Nordoff, P., & Robbins, C. (1970). *Therapy in music for handicapped children*. London: Gollancz.

Nordoff, P., & Robbins, C. (1977). *Creative music therapy: Individualized treatment for the handicapped child*. New York: John Day.

Nordoff, P., & Robbins, C. (1983). *Music therapy in special education*. St. Louis, MO: MMB Music.

Nucho, A. O. (1987). *The psychocybernetic model of art therapy*. Springfield, IL: Thomas.

Page, N. (1995). *Sing and shine on! A teacher's guide to multicultural song leading*. Portsmouth, NH: Heinemann.

Phillips, K. H. (1992). *Teaching kids to sing*. New York: Schirmer Books.

Piaget, J. (1971). *Mental imagery in the child*. London: Routledge & Kegan Paul.

Piaget, J. (1977). *The development of thought: Equilibration of cognitive structures*. New York: Viking Press.

Pine, S. (1977). Fostering growth through art education, art therapy, and art in psychotherapy. In E. Ulman & P. Dachinger (Eds.), *Art therapy in theory and practice* (pp. 70–101). New York: Schocken Books.

Pribram, K. (1964). Neurological notes on the art of educating. In E. R. Hilgard (Ed.), *Theories of learning and instruction* (pp. 319–331). Chicago: National Society for the Study of Education.

Priestley, M. (1984). *Music therapy in action*. St. Louis, MO: MMB Music.

Rozmajzi, M., & Boyer-White, R. (1996). *Music fundamentals, methods, and materials for the elementary classroom teacher*. White Plains, NY: Longman.

Selfe, L. (1983). *Normal and anomalous representational drawing ability in children*. London: Academic Press.

Silver, R. A. (1978). *Developing cognitive and creative skills through art*. Baltimore: University Park Press.

Silver, R. A. (1990). *Silver drawing test of cognitive skills and adjustment*. Mamaroneck, NY: Ablin Press.

Streeter, E. (1980). *Making music with the young handicapped child*. London: Music Therapy Publications.

Themal, J. (1977). Children's work as art. In E. Ulman & P. Dachinger (Eds.), *Art therapy in theory and practice* (pp. 102–132). New York: Schocken Books.

Tilton, J. T. (Ed.). (1992). *World of music: An introduction to the music of the world's peoples* (2nd ed.). New York: Schirmer Books.

Toombs, M. (1968). Dance therapy. In E. T. Gaston (Ed.), *Music in therapy*. New York: Macmillan.

Trusty, J., & Oliva, G. (1994). The effects of arts and music education on students' self-concept. *Update: Applications of Research in Music Education, 13*(1), 23–28.

Ulman, E. (1977). Art therapy: Problems of definition. In E. Ulman & P. Dachinger (Eds.), *Art therapy in theory and practice* (pp. 133–161). New York: Schocken Books.

Wachowiak, F., & Clements, R. (1996). *Emphasis art: A qualitative art program for elementary and middle schools* (6th ed.). New York: Longman.

Wadeson, H. (1980). *Art psychotherapy*. New York: Wiley.

Wadeson, H. (1987). An eclectic approach to art therapy. In J. A. Rubin (Ed.), *Approaches to art therapy* (pp. 140–162). New York: Wiley.

A P P E N D I X

UNDERLYING RATIONALE
AND BASIC CONCEPTS
OF BEHAVIORAL PSYCHOLOGY

(Note: *The concepts discussed in this appendix are fundamental to under-*
standing behavioral theory. There are many additional terms pertaining more
directly to the practical applications of that theory, and those are introduced in
Chapter 5, "Behavioral Therapy." Also, all references for this appendix are
incorporated into those for Chapter 5.)

The basic rationale of the behavioral approach is that all behavior, normal and
abnormal, is learned according to the same principles and that all behavior can
be modified or altered according to those principles. This emphasis on learning
illustrates the importance of environmental factors in shaping behavior and
suggests that alterations or adjustments of components in the environment will
cause alterations in behavior. Thus, the behavioral approach places primary
emphasis on the *manipulation of environmental events* to provide the individual
with learning experiences that promote adaptive behavior.

Behavioral theorists have formulated three major sets of principles to
explain how behavior is learned: classical or respondent conditioning, instrumental or operant conditioning, and observation learning or modeling.

Classical Conditioning

First illustrated by Ivan Pavlov (1848–1939), classical conditioning demonstrates how stimuli come to evoke reflex responses. These responses, termed
respondents, are involuntary or autonomic, that is, they appear to be outside the
individual's control or sphere of learning. For example, responses such as pupil
constriction to the stimulus of light or a startle reaction to a loud noise stimulus appear to occur without conscious effort. The light and sound are termed
unconditioned stimuli, and the responses they trigger are *unconditioned responses*.
When an unconditioned stimulus is paired frequently with a neutral stimulus,

that is, one that does not elicit a reflex response, the neutral stimulus (now referred to as a *conditioned stimulus*) eventually will elicit the respondent behavior (now termed a *conditioned response*). For example, if a neutral stimulus such as a white rabbit were presented to a child, and the introduction of the rabbit was followed by a loud noise (unconditioned stimulus) that evoked a startle reaction (unconditioned response), eventually the presentation of the rabbit would evoke the startle reaction. In effect, the child's response is dependent on the *arrangement of preceding stimuli*. With this type of experiment, Watson and Rayner (1920) conditioned an 11-month-old boy, Albert, to fear a white rat and appeared to prove that fears can be acquired through classical conditioning.

Operant Conditioning

A term introduced by Skinner (1953), *operant conditioning* refers to behavior that is not reflexive. Operants are responses performed because of the consequences that follow them. For instance, a child who utters "mama" and receives a great deal of parental attention will be likely to utter "mama" again. The consequences of the behavior were such that the probability of the response reoccurring was increased. In operant conditioning, the events that follow behavior usually are termed *reinforcements*.

(Note: *The traditional distinctions between operant and classical conditioning as presented here are becoming somewhat blurred. Current behavioral research demonstrates that the differentiation between voluntary and involuntary responses is no longer a valid indicator of two distinct types of conditioning paradigms. Responses such as heart rate, blood pressure, galvanic skin responses, and so on, which were once considered involuntary, have been shown to be changeable through operant conditioning.*

Also, in applied situations, it is often impossible to distinguish between respondent and operant behaviors. A child may demonstrate fear at the sight of a rabbit as a function of the association of the animal with a loud noise (respondent behavior) or may exhibit fear because parents react with increased attention (operant behavior). Finally, operant behaviors, which are usually conceived of as being influenced by events that follow the response, may also be controlled by preceding stimuli. If a response has been reinforced in a given environmental situation, certain cues from that situation will increase the probability that the response will occur again. Thus, the child who utters "mama" because of the affectionate hug that follows the response is likely to utter "mama" at the sight of the mother entering the room. The response is in no way involuntary; therefore, it cannot be construed as a classical response. Despite the theoretical overlap of these two conditioning paradigms, the behavioral literature often represents them as separate entities. This necessitated discussing them as such in this text.)

Observational Learning

Observational learning or modeling involves learning that is not dependent on performance. Simply stated, behaviors are learned through observation of a model who demonstrates those behaviors. The learner acquires the response cognitively (Bandura, 1977). Once learned, or internalized, the response may or may not be performed, depending on environmental circumstances. The consequences of performing the response is one circumstance. Bandura (1965) demonstrated that children who watched an adult demonstrate aggressive behavior, such as striking a doll, performed aggressive behavior when the model either had been rewarded or ignored. They were less likely to behave aggressively when the adult had been punished. Badura subsequently proved that all the children had learned the aggressive behavior by showing that they all behaved aggressively when given an incentive for aggressive behavior.

The characteristics of the models is another circumstance affecting performance. Greater imitation usually occurs when models are high in prestige, status, or expertise, and when they are similar in appearance, race, and socioeconomic status to the learner. According to Bandura (1969), modeling encompasses both classical and operant responses and affects both the development of new responses and the frequency of performing previously learned responses.

Reinforcement. Reinforcement constitutes the basis of operant conditioning. It involves the contingency of behavior—it always increases the frequency of a response. There are two types of reinforcement: positive and negative. *Positive reinforcement* is an event following behavior that increases the frequency of that behavior. In the example used previously, when the frequency of the child's uttering "mama" was increased by parental attention, the attention was positive reinforcement. A positive reinforcer is not necessarily a reward, although the two terms are often used as synonyms, and rewards often do act as positive reinforcers. The difference lies in the effect on behavior. A positive reinforcer must increase the frequency of the response it follows. Rewards, although appreciated by the recipient, often do not do so. For example, an individual rewarded for saving a drowning child may never demonstrate that behavior again. Also, an event that may appear subjectively to be unrewarding, such as criticism, may act as a positive reinforcer to the individual who, when criticized for a behavior, repeats it. In contrast, an event that subjectively appears to be rewarding, such as praise, may cause diminished responding in a child who is suspicious of praise. Therefore, in this instance, praise is not a positive reinforcer.

Generally, positive reinforcers are categorized in two ways: as *primary* or *unconditioned* reinforcers or as *secondary* or *conditioned* reinforcers. Primary reinforcers are unlearned, natural events that diminish drive states. For example, food and water are automatically reinforcing to an individual who is thirsty and hungry. Their reinforcing value does not depend on previous learning. Of course, because primary reinforcers are associated with internal drive states, their reinforcing value alters as those drive states change. Thus, food is not a good reinforcer if an individual is not hungry.

Secondary reinforcers are events such as praise, money, tokens, grades, and so on that are not automatically reinforcing but whose reinforcement potential is learned. Originally, these reinforcers are neutral in value, but they acquire reinforcing properties because they have been paired with primary reinforcers or previously conditioned secondary reinforcers. For example, money becomes a reinforcer because it has been paired with a primary reinforcer such as food or an alternative secondary reinforcer such as a toy. Similarly, tokens may become secondary reinforcers if they are paired with a conditioned secondary reinforcer such as money or a primary reinforcer such as food.

Money serves to illustrate another category of reinforcers, referred to as *generalized conditioned reinforcers*. These are particularly effective in altering behavior because they have been paired with a wide variety of reinforcing events. For example, money may have been paired with items and events such as food, fun, relaxation, comfort, warmth, and status—all useful reinforcers. The reinforcing value of money is greater than any of these independent items, because it may be exchanged for any of them. Thus, the strength of generalized conditioned reinforcers is derived from the value of the reinforcers with which they have been associated. Obviously, tokens are another example of generalized reinforcers. They may be used to secure a variety of alternative or backup reinforcers.

The types of reinforcement discussed thus far all have been stimuli presented after a response. An alternative and distinct reinforcement category involves reinforcing a response with another response. The Premack (1965) principle states that "of any pair of responses or activities in which an individual engages, the most probable one will reinforce the less probable one." In other words, if the opportunity to perform a high-probability response is made contingent on performance of a low-probability response, the frequency of the low-probability response will increase. Thus, if eating chocolate cake (a high-probability response) were made contingent on finishing homework, the frequency of homework-completing behavior would increase. In applying this principle, one must ensure that a high-probability behavior is a preferred behavior and not simply one that occurs frequently. Taking out the trash might have a high frequency of occurrence but probably is not a preferred behavior. Therefore, it would not serve as a reinforcer for finishing homework.

Negative reinforcement involves an aversive stimulus whose removal increases the probability of occurrence of the response it follows. For example, visiting a dentist is reinforced by the discontinuation of pain. A more contrived example might involve the presentation of a loud, unpleasant noise that is discontinued when the desired response is performed. Obviously, a negative reinforcer must be presented to an individual before the response so that it can be removed when the response occurs.

Often, negative reinforcement is confused with punishment. The difference lies in the fact that negative reinforcement always increases the probability of response occurrence, whereas punishment decreases it. In applied situations this distinction is often lost, and, in fact, many behaviorists refer to punishing stimuli as negative reinforcers, and others wisely avoid confusion by using the term *negative contingency* to include punishment and negative reinforcement. However, the distinction is useful because it shows how discontinuation of an unpleasant circumstance can reinforce behavior (and also provides a rationale for the old joke about the man who kept banging his head against the wall because it felt so good when he stopped).

As is true of positive reinforcement, there are primary and secondary negative reinforcers. Stimuli that are automatically aversive, such as shock or pain, are primary reinforcers. The aversive quality of secondary reinforcers is learned through association with primary reinforcers. For example, a parent's raised hand, associated previously with pain, may increase a child's attention to work.

Punishment is defined as "a reduction of the future probability of a specific response as a result of the immediate delivery of a stimulus for that response" (Azrin & Holz, 1966, p. 381). The key words in the definition are *reduction, future,* and *immediate.*

As was noted previously, a *reduction* or decrease in the response distinguishes punishment from negative reinforcement. In a more practical vein, the notion of behavior reduction distinguishes the behavioral concept of punishment from the popular conception. For instance, it is commonly and subjectively assumed that a spanking is punishment. However, from the behavioral perspective, if the response that has elicited the spanking does not diminish, then the aversive stimulus, spanking, is not punishment. In fact, it might be reinforcing, as when a spanked child continues to exhibit a certain maladaptive behavior to secure adult attention. Similarly, a criminal is said to be punished for crime by imprisonment. If the aversive stimulus, imprisonment, does not lead to a decrease in criminal activity, it does not fit the behavioral definition of punishment.

The word *future* is important because it distinguishes between the immediate cessation of behavior while an aversive stimulus such as spanking is administered and the long-term frequency of occurrence of the behavior. Azrin and Holz (1966) hold that response reduction during punishment is not a sufficient outcome and that punishment as an effective contingency requires future reduction in the frequency of a response.

According to Azrin and Holz (1966), the *immediate* delivery of the aversive stimulus is of critical importance in determining the effectiveness of punishment. Delays between the maladaptive response and punishment should be avoided. Other determinants of effectiveness that they have discovered are that punishment should be as intense as possible, continuous, and introduced at maximum strength rather than gradually. Also, extended periods of punishment should be avoided, motivation to emit the punished response should be reduced, and alternative reinforced responses should be available.

Craighead, Kazdin, and Mahoney (1976) elaborated further on the use of punishment. They stated that each occurrence of a maladaptive response should be punished, responses incompatible with the punished response should be reinforced, and a description of the punishment contingency should be given whenever possible. They also distinguished between two types of punishment, punishment by application and punishment by removal.

Punishment by application occurs when an aversive stimulus is applied after a response. Examples might be spanking, scolding, getting a traffic ticket, or a self-induced contingency such as illness caused by overeating. *Punishment by removal* involves the discontinuation of a positive reinforcer after a response. Examples are loss of permission to watch television because of poor grades, loss of dessert because of refusal to eat other food, or loss of tokens earned previously.

Despite what appears to be current evidence that punishment, when used correctly, is a valuable therapeutic device, it remains a touchy issue, evoking much disagreement among behavioral therapists. For example, the possibility of negative side effects remains as a detriment to its use in applied situations. Craighead and others (1976) listed as possible side effects increased emotional responding, avoidance of the punishing agent, and imitation of the use of punishment. They conclude that the use of extinction is often preferable, except in situations where the behavior is so dangerous to the child that it must be decreased quickly, such as head banging or fire setting.

Extinction. Extinction refers to the decrease in response strength that follows cessation of reinforcement. A behavior that has increased in frequency because of positive reinforcement will decrease when that reinforcement is withheld.

Thus, a child whose tantrums have been reinforced by parental attention will cease the behavior when the attention is not given.

Craighead and others (1976) pointed out that the term *extinction* is often used as a synonym for reduction of behavior brought about by a variety of interventions, such as punishment. In fact, the term applies only to the reduction of a previously established bond between a response and its consequences. Its practical applications generally involve ignoring a response that had previously been reinforced, usually by attention, such as when a teacher ignores a child who calls out and answers without raising his hand, after the teacher had previously recognized him and reinforced that behavior. Often, extinction results in a temporary increase in response rate before the subsequent decrease, as when the child calls out more consistently when ignored before discontinuing the behavior.

Spontaneous Recovery. After a response has been extinguished and a rest period has occurred, the reintroduction of the conditioned stimulus will cause the response to reappear. For instance, a dog that was originally trained to come when a whistle sounds but has undergone extinction and no longer answers a whistle will, after a period of time, once again respond to the whistle.

Spontaneous recovery also refers to increases in behavior that occur after cessation of punishment. Thus, a behavior, such as calling out in class, that has been controlled through either withdrawal of privileges or application of aversive stimuli may increase if the punishment is suspended.

Reacquisition. After spontaneous recovery, the conditioned response can be returned to maximum strength faster than the rate demonstrated during the initial training. It also reextinguishes faster when the reinforcement is withdrawn.

Stimulus Control. A response may be reinforced when it is associated with certain stimuli and may not be reinforced in the presence of other stimuli. When it is reinforced consistently, the eliciting stimulus signals that reinforcement is coming and is termed *discriminative stimulus*. Therefore, the probability of a response occurring can be arranged through stimulus control, that is, presenting or removing the discriminative stimulus.

Higher Order Conditioning. Higher order conditioning involves pairing a formerly neutral stimulus (light) that has become a conditioned stimulus after association with an unconditioned stimulus (food) with a second neutral stimulus (tone). The second stimulus, tone, becomes a conditioned stimulus exclusively through association with light. It is never associated with the unconditioned stimulus.

Habit-Family Hierarchy. Any given stimulus may be attached to a variety of possible responses, each having different habit strength. Habit strength refers to the probability that the response will occur. The greater the habit strength, the more likely the response will appear first, that is, before those with lesser habit strength. If the response is not appropriate, in that it is either punished or not reinforced, its strength declines. If habit strength drops below that of the second response in the hierarchy, then the second response will occur. For example, if a child's highest habit strength response to the teacher's stimulus "Clean up your desk" is to make paper airplanes out of wastepaper, that response will be demonstrated. Teacher nonreinforcement may drop the strength of that response and raise a more adaptive response to the top of her hierarchy.

Drive. Drive pertains to motivational forces that interact with habit strength to produce reaction potential. Reaction potential is simply the probability that the individual will perform a response.

Inhibition. Inhibition refers to the internal forces that mitigate against the repetition of a response. Hull (1943) hypothesized that inhibiting forces related to fatigue build up and interfere with response performance. These inhibiting factors explain the distinction between massed and spaced practice in motor learning. Spaced practice, with rest periods between trials, is significantly more effective than massed practice, with no rest periods for learning motor tasks. Presumably, inhibition reduces learning when practice is massed and has no effect when practice is spaced.

Reinforcement Schedules. Reinforcement schedules are the arrangements used to control the contingencies of behavior. The simplest schedule, *continuous reinforcement*, requires that the response be reinforced each time it occurs. A schedule involving reinforcement of a response on an intermittent rather than a consistent basis is called *intermittent reinforcement*. Research has demonstrated that continuous reinforcement is more effective in eliciting a higher rate of the desired responses during the initial period of learning; however, intermittent reinforcement is more efficient for response maintenance. Also, when intermittent reinforcement is used, the conditioned response is far more resistant to extinction once reinforcement is discontinued.

Schedules for intermittent reinforcement can be arranged according to the number of responses, a *ratio schedule*, or on the basis of the time interval between reinforcements, an *interval schedule*. In other words, a ratio schedule involves reinforcement following a given number of responses, whereas an interval schedule requires that the responses be reinforced after a specified period of time has elapsed.

With both ratio and interval schedules, the delivery of reinforcers can be unvarying, or *fixed*, or they can be *variable*. Therefore, four basic reinforcement schedules may be used: fixed ratio, variable ratio, fixed interval, and variable interval.

With a *fixed-ratio schedule*, reinforcement is delivered after a certain previously established number of responses. For example, a child might be reinforced after every fourth demonstration of the desired response. The reinforcement schedule is fixed-ratio: 4. A *variable-ratio schedule* also involves reinforcement after a previously established number of responses; however, the number of responses required for reinforcement is based on an average. Therefore, if an average of 4 responses was required over eight trials, the number of responses per trial might be 1, 4, 2, 7, 5, 6, 3, 4, which average 4 responses per trial. Thus, the child on a reinforcement schedule of variable-ratio: 4 would, over the course of eight trials, be required to demonstrate the same number of responses to earn reinforcement as his peer on a fixed-ratio: 4 schedule. However, he would not be aware of the number of responses required for reinforcement, as is usually the case with a fixed-ratio schedule.

The unpredictability of the response schedule is one benefit to using variable-ratio schedules. They typically result in a consistent rate of response because the subject never knows when reinforcement will occur. In contrast, fixed schedules produce inconsistent response rates. Responses occur rapidly until reinforcement, then drop off for periods of time. The length of time during which the desired response is not performed is directly related to the largeness of the ratio necessary for reinforcement. Larger ratios produce longer pauses.

With a *fixed-interval schedule*, an unvarying time period is established and the first response to occur after that interval passes is reinforced. Thus, if the schedule were fixed-interval: 5, and the 5 referred to minutes, the first response after each 5-minute period elapsed is reinforced. Subsequent responses during that interval are not reinforced. A *variable-interval schedule*, like the variable-ratio schedule, is computed on an average. If the schedule were variable-interval: 5 over 10 trials, the time intervals in minutes necessary for reinforcement might be 4, 9, 3, 7, 8, 2, 6, 5, 2, 4, which average to 5.

As is the case with ratio schedules, fixed-interval schedules lead to inconsistent rates of responding. Pauses occur after reinforcement; however, in this case they are extended until the end of the interval, when the individual anticipates reinforcement. Once again, the variable scheduling prevents this type of anticipation and results in more consistent performance and a higher rate of response.

A comparison of the two types of scheduling reveals that ratio scheduling usually produces a higher response rate. Obviously, an increased number of responses means more frequent reinforcement, whereas with interval schedules the number of responses has no bearing on reinforcement.

The establishment of a comprehensive program of reinforcement might begin with continuous reinforcement. Once the level of performance reaches a satisfactory rate, an intermittent reinforcement schedule that slowly and progressively establishes longer time intervals between reinforcers might be used. Ultimately, the reinforcement would be discontinued and, because of the strength of the intermittent scheduling, the desired response would continue to occur, that is, it would be highly resistant to extinction.

Shaping. Shaping involves breaking down a response into a series of sequenced steps and reinforcing each successive step until the terminal response is demonstrated. It is a useful procedure in instances where a desired behavior is not in the subject's repertoire and therefore cannot be reinforced. For example, a mute child who lacks the ability to say *boy* cannot be reinforced for that behavior. The verbal behavior must be shaped through reinforcement of successive approximations until *boy* is produced and, from that point on, can be reinforced whenever it occurs. Successive approximations are the sequenced steps that lead the child closer to the production of the word *boy*. He might begin by imitating the sound /b/, then the sound /o/, and so on, in as many steps as necessary until the word is produced. Similarly, shaping is necessary to evoke the performance of tasks that are too complex for the child to produce in toto. For example, the high jump is dependent on the mastery of sequenced lower order motor behaviors. In shaping behavior, each new step is introduced only after the preceding step has been firmly established and is displayed with high frequency. As learning occurs, the criterion for reinforcement is altered slightly so that the next response more closely resembles the final goal.

Chaining. A chain is a sequence of two or more behaviors. Generally, the successive responses in a chain are part of the individual's behavioral repertoire. The ordering or chaining of these behaviors culminates in a particular complex behavior. Direct reinforcement occurs when the final response in a chain is performed. Earlier behaviors in the sequence are maintained or reinforced by discriminative stimuli, that is, events that signal reinforcement for a particular response. An example of chaining can be seen in the behavior of a violinist who performs a difficult concert and is reinforced by critical acclaim, public applause, and a high salary. The chain of behaviors that culminated in the performance might have been initiated by an agreement with an agent to give a concert. Responses that followed might have included selection of music, preparation of the violin, and practicing the music. (Obviously, each of these steps could be reduced into smaller segments, but these should illustrate the point.) The ultimate response, the concert, which precedes direct reinforcement, acts as a discriminative stimulus; that is, it signals that reinforcement is coming. It also becomes a reinforcer in its own right for the previous link, practicing the music. In turn, practicing acts as a reinforcer for preparing the violin, and that behavior is a reinforcer for selecting the music. In other words, the chaining procedure is a sequence of backward reinforcement, with the last directly reinforced response precipitating the reinforcing properties of all preceding responses. In plain language, one might say, "You can't earn the reinforcement if you don't give the concert, you can't give the concert if you don't practice, you can't practice if the instrument isn't ready, and you can't play the instrument if you have no music."

Prompts. Prompts are auxiliary stimuli or events such as verbal directions, gestures, or cues that help bring about a response. They are antecedent events in that they precede the response. If the prompt is used frequently to help produce a response, and the response is reinforced, it will eventually act as a discriminative stimulus and signal that reinforcement will follow the response. Usually, prompts are faded or dropped from the antecedent stimuli as the desired response is more firmly established. For example, the teacher says, "One and one are /tt/." The prompt /tt/ eventually is eliminated.

References

Azrin, N., & Holz, W. (1966). Punishment. In W. Honig (Ed.), *Operant behaviors: Areas of research and application* (pp. 380–447). New York: Appleton-Century-Crofts.

Bandura, A. (1965). Influence of models' reinforcement contingencies on the acquisition of imitative responses. *Journal of Personality and Social Psychology, 1*, 589–595.

Bandura, A. (1969). *Principles of behavior modification.* New York: Holt, Rinehart & Winston.

Bandura, A. (1977). *Social learning theory.* Englewood Cliffs, NJ: Prentice Hall.

Craighead, W., Kazdin, A., & Mahoney, M. (1976). *Behavior modification.* Boston: Houghton Mifflin.

Hull, C. (1943). *Principles of behavior.* New York: Appleton-Century-Crofts.

Premack, D. (1965). Reinforcement theory. In D. Levin (Ed.), *Nebraska symposium on motivation* (pp. 123–180). Lincoln: University of Nebraska.

Skinner, B. F. (1953). *Science and human behavior.* New York: Macmillan.

Watson, J. B., & Rayner, R. (1920). Conditioned emotional reaction. *Journal of Experimental Psychiatry, 3*, 1–14.

ABOUT THE AUTHOR

In addition to this textbook, **Phyllis Newcomer** is the author of numerous journal articles pertaining to the field of special education. She also has worked with several co-authors to develop eight well-known educational tests, including the *Test of Language Development–Primary*, the *Test of Language Development–Intermediate*, and the *Diagnostic Achievement Battery*. Newcomer's extensive career in special education includes stints as a teacher of children with emotional and behavioral disorders, school psychologist, director of special services, and professor of special education. Most of her academic career was spent at Beaver College (now Arcadia University) in Pennsylvania. While there she served as chairperson of the Education Department, and for many years was editor of the *Learning Disability Quarterly*. In August 2001 Newcomer retired from her academic position and currently divides her time between residences in Santa Fe, New Mexico, and Austin, Texas, where she continues her professional work.

AUTHOR INDEX

SUBJECT INDEX